COMPARATIVE POLITICS

COMPARATIVE POLITICS

CLASSIC AND CONTEMPORARY READINGS

J. Tyler Dickovick and Jonathan Eastwood, eds.

WASHINGTON AND LEE UNIVERSITY

NEW YORK   OXFORD

OXFORD UNIVERSITY PRESS

Oxford University Press is a department of the University of Oxford.
It furthers the University's objective of excellence in research,
scholarship, and education by publishing worldwide.

Oxford   New York
Auckland   Cape Town   Dar es Salaam   Hong Kong   Karachi
Kuala Lumpur   Madrid   Melbourne   Mexico City   Nairobi
New Delhi   Shanghai   Taipei   Toronto

With offices in
Argentina   Austria   Brazil   Chile   Czech Republic   France   Greece
Guatemala   Hungary   Italy   Japan   Poland   Portugal   Singapore
South Korea   Switzerland   Thailand   Turkey   Ukraine   Vietnam

For titles covered by Section 112 of the US Higher Education
Opportunity Act, please visit www.oup.com/us/he for the
latest information about pricing and alternate formats.

Published by Oxford University Press
198 Madison Avenue, New York, New York 10016
http://www.oup.com

Library of Congress Cataloging-in-Publication Data
Names: Dickovick, James Tyler, 1973- editor. | Eastwood, Jonathan, editor.
Title: Comparative politics : classic and contemporary readings / Tyler
    Dickovick and Jonathan Eastwood, eds.
Description: Oxford ; New York : Oxford University Press, [2017]
Identifiers: LCCN 2015043122 | ISBN 9780199730957 (pbk.)
Subjects: LCSH: Comparative government.
Classification: LCC JF51 .C61517 2017 | DDC 320.3--dc23 LC record available
    at http://lccn.loc.gov/2015043122

Printing number: 9 8 7 6 5 4 3 2 1

Printed in the United States of America
on acid-free paper

CONTENTS

ACKNOWLEDGMENTS

The authors are grateful to the editorial, design, and marketing staff at Oxford University Press. We particularly appreciate the efforts of Jennifer Carpenter, Tony Mathias, Simon Benjamin, Michele Laseau, Brianna Provenzano, and Matt Rohal, among others including, Roxanne Klaas, the production manager of the project.

We owe a debt of gratitude, as well, to the following people, who reviewed the manuscript in its development and who gave generously of their time and expertise:

Lisa Baldez, Dartmouth College

Mark A. Cichock, University of Texas at Arlington

William Crowther, UNC Greensboro

Julie A. George, Queens College, City University of New York

Natalie A. Kistner, James Madison University

Eric Langenbacher, Georgetown University

Ricardo Rene Laremont, SUNY Binghamton

Claire M. Metelits, Washington State University

Boyka Stefanova, University of Texas at San Antonio

The book would not have been the same without the assistance and insight from these outstanding scholars and teachers. Meanwhile, any errors you may find in the book remain our own. We welcome your feedback and thank you for your support.

INTRODUCTION

This volume brings together major articles and book chapters from the field of comparative politics. It comprises both "classic" pieces—including many influential works from the 20th century—and more recent contributions that have synthesized and significantly advanced research in the field. We have selected pieces for this book that do several things. First and most important, the selections represent major theoretical schools of thought for addressing major research questions in comparative politics. (Some of these schools of thought are discussed later.) Although it is not possible to cover the spectrum of the field with only a few texts, we believe this set of readings gives a clear sense of how thinkers differ in understanding the causes of major events in world politics. Second, these influential pieces have shaped the way political scientists understand the world. They provide readers with entry points into the field and are not just summaries of work. Third, we have edited the readings to make them accessible to the educated reader approaching comparative politics for the first time. These readings will require effort, but we believe that with some dedication, college and university students should be able to comprehend and comment meaningfully on them. The key purpose of the volume you are now reading is to allow you as students to sink your teeth a bit more deeply into theoretical work in comparative politics.

We designed the book to be read in conjunction with our *Comparative Politics: Integrating Theories, Methods, and Cases* (Oxford University Press, 2016), although it can also function as a stand-alone volume of major readings. We wrote *Comparative Politics* to teach the basics of this field by exploring the development of theories, the deduction of hypotheses from theories, and the testing of hypotheses against evidence. In that textbook, the core goal is for students to learn how to *analyze politics comparatively* rather than just learn a bunch of facts established by researchers or opinions based on authority. Each chapter begins with an overview of the key concepts needed to analyze the theme in question. It then makes use of typologies to help set up causal questions. Finally, it examines major theories that aim to answer the most important "why" question in the area of research under discussion. For example, Chapter 3 of the text begins by walking readers through the concept of the modern state and some of its key features, like bureaucracy, impersonality, and sovereignty. It then details the types of functions that the modern state tends to perform. Next, it considers a core theoretical question in this area of political science: why did modern states emerge? The textbook considers a range of theories to address each of these questions. Throughout the chapter, reference is made to country case studies that illustrate the concepts and causal arguments. This basic format—moving from concepts to major theories and linking them to empirical evidence—is replicated for the major issues in comparative politics.

In *Comparative Politics: Integrating Theories, Methods, and Cases,* students encounter theories in "Insights" boxes that offer brief summaries of a classic work. Here students can read excerpts of such works and others like them. In many cases, the selections here correspond to the works mentioned in the Insights boxes from the textbook. In some cases, however, we have added alternative readings that we thought would be more meaningful or accessible to undergraduate readers.

THEORIES IN COMPARATIVE POLITICS

We argue that in its essence comparative politics is a distinctive and useful method for answering "why" questions in a scientific way. In this selection of readings, we approach the major why questions with direct attention to the role of theories in comparative politics. A theory is a general answer to a persistent why question or range of why questions. For example, one important question in comparative politics asks why some regimes are more democratic than others (or, conversely, why some regimes are more authoritarian than others). A theory is not a mere hunch or guess that an analyst has, but the product of social scientists' joint efforts to answer this question through the application of the scientific method. We do not call ideas a theory until they have evidence behind them and are well developed. Usually students (or professional researchers for that matter) do not just make up brand-new, completely unprecedented theories in response to questions. Rather, most often, we read the existing literature, study theories that others have developed, consider the success and difficulties those theories have encountered, and modify them accordingly, evaluating them, ultimately, by testing their implications against evidence. Occasionally, of course, people come up with grand new, or "revolutionary," theoretical innovations (Kuhn, 1962), but this is not the norm, and it is not usually the optimal strategy for a beginning student in the field of comparative politics.

Scholars in comparative politics use a wide range of types of evidence when assessing explanatory theories. What unites all of them is that this evidence is *empirical,* which, roughly speaking, means that it is gathered systematically through observation of the world. For some purposes, this means quantitative measures of economic performance or population characteristics (e.g., a country's gross domestic product or its basic demographic composition). For others, it means observations gathered through experimental methods. For still others, it means surveys in which people are asked questions and researchers then search for patterns in the responses. Other methods of evidence gathering include field observation, which sometimes involves living in distinct communities and writing about the basic social patterns observed there. Finally, some scholars use historical and documentary evidence. For example, scholars studying historical processes in comparative politics sometimes do archival research, reading old letters, official documents, newspapers, and other texts for clues that allow them to assess the relevant theories. The key point here is that to do comparative social *science* we must actually test our theories using the most relevant and reliable data we can find.

You might think that we could just look at the evidence and it would show us the proper theory, but it is not that simple. First, theories are not just summaries of observations. We cannot, for example, simply list all of the qualities we see in democratic and authoritarian regimes and call this a theory. Rather, theories go *beyond* simple observations to make general causal claims that answer why questions (and sometimes "how" questions) about the observable world. We use observations to see whether and how well theories fit with the evidence we have. On the basis of this research, we draw *causal inferences* about what factors or variables cause the outcomes we observe (King et al., 1994; Morgan and Winship, 2007). For instance, we might wonder why some countries, such as Egypt, saw their authoritarian regimes collapse in the "Arab Spring" in 2011. Three different theories to explain this occurrence might focus on factors such as (1) economic changes in the society at large, (2) decisions by major political actors or groups, and (3) the international spread of democratic ideas and norms. These theories need not be mutually exclusive, but can be combined to create a broad explanation. Close examination of the case study, as well as close consideration of what each of these major theories implies, would allow us to determine how much support there is for certain theoretical perspectives.

Most of the theories in this book—and, indeed, in contemporary comparative politics—try to tackle fairly specific and concrete problems rather than attempting to settle the biggest and most general questions of social and political thought. For example, we want to know why some countries are more democratic than others or why revolutions happen in some cases and not others.[1]

Nonetheless, even practical theories rest on often unspoken assumptions about how the world works, and it is important for us to be attentive to them. These assumptions should be tested, but we cannot test them all at once. For example, as we shall see, some theories (which we refer to below as "rationalist" theories) begin with the assumption that the best way to look at any political situation is by treating *individuals* as the key actors, identifying their interests and preferences, and formally modeling their decision-making processes, assuming at least some limited rationality on their part. If we take such an approach, we can then try to answer why questions on the bases of these assumptions. Our model of their decision making can then be tested on the basis of its fit with actual behavior. But note that this is a far cry from testing whether each of these *assumptions*— individuals as key actors, their preferences and interests as causally important, their

---

1. This is what the sociologist Robert K. Merton once called "theories of the middle range" (Merton, 1967 [1949]).

rationality as a driver of outcomes—is correct. Indeed, as we shall see in a moment, not all researchers share in precisely these assumptions. When we make assumptions, we try to do so provisionally and skeptically, to be clear about what assumptions we are making and why, and to avoid being dogmatic about them.

In may be helpful to have an overview of the clusters of assumptions that scholars draw on in doing comparative politics. One way to think about this is by categorizing theories in terms of basic assumptions they make to answer fundamental questions about political action:

• WHO, OR WHAT, ARE THE KEY "ACTORS" OR "UNITS" IN POLITICAL SOCIETY?

Possible answers include individuals, social classes, organizations (like the state, or political parties, or social movement organizations), institutions (like property rights or the system of divided government), cultural constellations (like shared attitudes about political participation), ideas being transmitted through social networks, or networks themselves, among many other possibilities. Note that some theories might assume that only one sort of actor is involved (e.g., just individual people), whereas other theories might be open to multiple types of actors (e.g., individual people but also organizations that might have their own collective interests, like political parties or the state). We may think of politics as operating on multiple levels: perhaps individuals make decisions that matter, but their environments matter too. Some, called "methodological individualists," argue that social science theories always need to pitch their ultimate accounts at the level of the choices and behavior of individual people (e.g., Elster, 2007; Hedström and Bearman, 2009; Schelling, 2006). Others argue that social-level processes have "emergent" properties (e.g., Gintis, 2009; Greenfeld, 2013), meaning characteristics that cannot be analyzed solely in terms of individual behavior. For still others, broad, impersonal social forces are the key drivers of political life, and individuals matter little if at all.

• WHAT, IN GENERAL, CAUSE THEIR ACTION/BEHAVIOR?

Possible answers include objective interests and rational calculations of individuals; their subjective preferences; their irrational tendencies and passions; norms and other institutions; embeddedness in certain networks; membership in certain groups or classes; and economic and geographic conditions. One line of thinking tends to assume that people make choices to maximize their utility and that utility is easy to assess or "objective." Another related line of inquiry assumes that people wish to maximize their utility, but that they do so as established by their preferences, which may vary in relation to personal or cultural factors. A third tends to see individual-spanning phenomena like norms as driving behavior. For example, consider the decision to vote. I may vote because it is in my interest to do so (although in large elections this is almost never true, if we mean that our vote will bring about our preferred result). I may vote because voting is of value to me, although I know my vote will not influence the outcome. Or I may vote simply because not doing so in my community would be unacceptable; here one could argue that the community norm is the cause, not my choice. The astute reader might look for affinities between these examples and assumptions about actors mentioned previously. Remember that theories can assume one set of causes as paramount or can admit that two or more play a role.

• HOW *FREE* ARE ACTORS TO ACT?

Possible answers include that individual agents make independent choices; individuals act in groups collectively; individuals respond to incentives formed by political and economic institutions; individuals act (often unconsciously) in accordance with or in response to social and cultural norms; and social factors such as economic structure or social networks shape events, not individuals. Different theoretical traditions in comparative politics emphasize greater and lesser degrees of social determination versus independent action by individual actors. (We will not get into the thorny and perennial philosophical debate about free will, although this relates to it.) Some assume that if you have clear answers with regard to the first two questions mentioned (who are the key actors and what causes their action?), you could make good predictions about what will happen. Others assume greater levels of indeterminacy. One end of the spectrum is that actors can be "agents." This means that they can make their own choices, and it implies that they could choose to not pursue their interests or preferences or that they could reject culturally and institutionally encoded norms and so forth. At the other end of the spectrum, actors exercise little power; rather, social structures, such as the economy or cultural norms, shape behavior and strongly condition how people act. (The argument about where theories should be located on this spectrum is sometimes called the "structure-agency" debate.) Different answers to these questions link to contrasting ideas about what explanation is and about what makes a good explanation. If you assume that people everywhere tend to act the same way if they face the same circumstances, then you probably think that if we just know enough about the actors in question and their environment, we could make lawlike generalizations about them. This is sometimes considered "deterministic." If you assume that social situations are too complex and or exhibit too much indeterminacy for lawlike theories to grasp, then you probably think that most social-scientific explanation is "probabilistic" and cannot account for everyone's actions, since individuals and groups can always choose to defy the behavioral tendencies that we observe. It is worth noting that much of contemporary social science takes the second view and treats social scientific explanations as probabilistic (e.g., Lieberson and Lynn, 2002). Many of the selections in this book will not make explicit their positions on these issues, but we think that if you try to ask these questions of each theory, you will likely understand each theory better and think more critically about it.

As you might guess, responses to these key questions tend to "cluster" into several distinct patterns of responses. In other words, certain sets of assumptions often go together in the background to theories of comparative politics. In the following set of descriptions, we simplify groups of theories somewhat, but we think that you will nevertheless find it helpful. Remember, however, that not all theories fall neatly into one of these groups, and many theories share assumptions from different clusters.

(1) THE RATIONALIST APPROACH

Perhaps the most influential underlying set of assumptions in contemporary political science is what we call the rationalist approach. This includes the assumptions that (a) individuals are the most important actors (and perhaps the only actors) in politics; (b) individuals' preferences typically align with their objectively discernible interests, which are often economic in character; (c) these preferences provide us with clues as to the motives for their behavior; and (d) individuals are mostly rational meaning that they select the best way to pursue their preferences and that their preferences are consistent. One of the major tools often used in the rationalist approach is game theory, which involves the modeling of the strategic situations faced by key actors. Examples of the rationalist approach (or works that have an affinity with this approach) found in this book include those by Kuran, Laitin, and Gill.

(2) THE MATERIALIST APPROACH

This approach shares some of the assumptions of the rationalist approach, but differs in key respects. It shares with rationalism the notion that key actors in politics pursue their interests (especially their economic interests). However, this approach tends to emphasize group actors and organizations. The most important example of such theories historically has been the emphasis on classes, or groups of people linked by their economic status. In its classic form, articulated by Karl Marx, the materialist theory sees politics as the product of the struggle between contending classes.[2] More recent versions of the materialist approach sometimes emphasize organizational actors other than classes, such as the state, militaries, or social movements based on shared identities (such as ethnicity or gender). Inequalities and conflict lie at the root of this approach. Examples of works drawing (at least in part and in sometimes different ways) on this set of assumptions include the excerpts by Lipset and Skocpol.

(3) THE CULTURALIST APPROACH

This approach begins by emphasizing that human beings are cultural, with a focus on the shared meanings of social and political life (e.g., Geertz, 1973). From this point of view, groups and individuals define the ultimate goals and values of politics in starkly different terms and not just according to their individual or class interests. Culturalist approaches often differ from the rationalist or materialist approaches presented previously in arguing that people around the world do not all fundamentally think or act in similar ways. Indeed, in some cases, from this point of view, values might even be arbitrary. The central claim of this approach is that values, beliefs, and/or norms are the main drivers of political behavior. Thus, different institutional arrangements are best understood as reflections of the values, purposes, and customs of the individuals in their midst. Human beings "construct" politics through their actions in the world. Examples of works drawing on this set of assumptions include the excerpts by Weber, Huntington, and Fukuyama.

---

2. To be clear, not all of the "materialist" theories are linked to "Marxist" thought: one can be a "materialist" and be procapitalism, for example.

(4) INSTITUTIONAL APPROACHES TO POLITICS

Widespread in contemporary theories of comparative politics is the idea that institutions are critically important to understanding differences between cases: indeed, "institutionalism" in its many forms is so widespread that we treat it as a fourth perspective here, although it shares assumptions with the three perspectives noted previously. There is some disagreement about what an institution is. The core idea is that an institution is a persistent, patterned way of doing things, what Douglass North (1990) famously called the "rules of the game" in any given area of social life. Institutions, therefore, structure people's behavior. They can do so through inculcating norms in individuals, through providing models for action, and by sanctioning and coercing certain types of conduct. Note that when you use the word "institution" in ordinary speech, you probably use it as a synonym for "organization," but social scientists draw a distinction between these terms. An organization is concrete, like the particular university where you are taking this course or a particular business corporation. An institution exists at a higher level of abstraction (Searle, 2010). Thus, "the university" is an institution, whereas Oxford University or The Ohio State University is an organization: Ohio State and Oxford take the forms they do because both reflect the institution "the university." In other words, organizations reflect institutional models. Examples of institutionalist approaches in this book include readings by Mahoney and Villegas; Acemoglu and Robinson; Meyer and his collaborators; and numerous others.

Scholars have emphasized that there are several kinds of "institutionalism" (Campbell, 2004; Hall and Taylor, 1996). They overlap on some key issues, but differ on others. We can think of these different kinds of institutionalism as linked to the other theoretical clusters noted previously. Some approaches to institutionalism are related to the rationalist approach and tend to view institutions as more or less stable arrangements produced by the interactions of individuals. Some approaches are linked to the "materialist" approach, emphasizing the group economic interests served by particular institutional configurations and explaining the persistence of institutions as being caused by those underlying interests. Some approaches are "cultural," emphasizing the symbolic character of institutions. From this point of view, institutions owe more to the meanings actors attach to them than to the rational calculation of interests or the struggle between groups for power and other resources.

This might seem fairly abstract, so let us turn to an example. Consider the three types of institutionalism, informed by rationalism, materialism, and culturalism, respectively. How would each of these explain the persistence of the constitutional model of government found in the United States?

The rationalist approach would explain American constitutionalism as a basically stable equilibrium that holds because no relevant actors can unilaterally make themselves better off by behaving outside of the constitutionally enshrined framework. In other words, from this point of view, legal institutions (and institutions in general) are crafted because they are the best way for the actors who make them to pursue their chosen ends, given the actions selected by everyone else involved. These decisions are made by multiple actors given each other's preferences and position, access to resources, knowledge of each other's likely course of action, and so forth.

Sometimes this leads to "bad equilibria": situations in which individuals cannot unilaterally make themselves better off through changing their strategy, but in which most or all *could* be better off if they could coordinate a collective change in strategy. Some would describe authoritarian polities and societies struggling with development problems as stuck in bad equilibria (e.g., Graham, 2009). For example, if a country has high corruption, many individuals might have to engage in corrupt practices to get by, although they might all be better off if they could simultaneously agree to desist. In contrast, many would consider constitutional democracies "good equilibria." This set of institutional arrangements has allowed for relative political freedoms, a growth-oriented economy, and democratic governance. The rationalist explanation assumes, in essence, that most people think that they are better off with this system than with some other one or at least that this is the best institutional environment they can reasonably expect to get. This approach seems to imply that, all else being equal, institutional environments will converge on a common model, the most efficient one. Of course, "special interests" can try to thwart institutional development for their own benefit, yielding inefficient institutions. And in authoritarian political contexts, power is often exerted to maintain bad equilibria. A good deal of scholarship has focused on the question of how polities move from such to more "inclusive" (Acemoglu and Robinson, 2012) or "open" (North et al., 2009) institutions, sometimes holding up the United States (and Great Britain before it) as an example.

The materialist approach to institutions (sometimes called "historical institutionalism") might explain American constitutionalism by arguing, in contrast, that it persists because it serves the interests of powerful elites. Some versions of this approach would stress the role of economic elites, arguing that the constitution itself was created at a particular "critical juncture" in which wealthy white men (the "founding fathers") were predominant. For this reason, for example, the constitution allowed slavery to continue and even treated slaves as three-fifths of a person for the purpose of allocating state-level representation in the national government. According to scholars of this persuasion, when constitutional protections and guarantees have been extended, this has been because of the contentious action of oppressed groups (like nonlandowning men in the early 19th century and later African Americans, women, and others). In short, this perspective views institutional arrangements as fundamentally shaped by the exercise of power as contesting groups pursue their interests. The key question for such theories is not which set of institutional arrangements is most efficient, but who are the most powerful actors who can shape institutions for their benefit.

The culturalist approach to institutions (sometimes called "sociological institutionalism" or, within sociology, "new institutionalism") explains American constitutionalism by linking it to key aspects of how the American polity was symbolically constructed. For example, this approach might argue that American culture prizes individualism and personal freedoms or that the idea of constitutionalism itself is a cultural model or template that has spread across the world, changing the political game in most polities (Meyer et al., 1997;

Law and Veersteeg, 2011). As a result, from this point of view, American institutions protecting individual rights and freedoms reflect American cultural preferences and tendencies. Another version of this approach might attempt to locate the tradition of political and social thought that influenced the design of major political institutions in the political–cultural tradition that preceded it historically, seeing the revolution as an extension of intellectual and political debates from the European Renaissance and, especially, 17th-century England (Pocock, 2003 [1975]). Institutional change, from this point of view, follows from cultural change more generally and institutions are best thought of as a form of culture.

As our brief discussion of different kinds of institutionalism illustrates, different clusters of assumptions overlap with and cross-pollinate each other (Campbell, 2004). Individual theorists often draw on assumptions from different clusters in sophisticated ways. We group them here in the simplified way that we do for the sake of clarity. As we have noted, it is difficult to simultaneously test this whole set of assumptions. Rather, the relative utility of these perspectives is typically judged by the practical theorizing they facilitate.

A NOTE ON READING THIS BOOK

We invite you to think about the pros and cons of the assumptions mentioned here and to keep them in mind as you read the excerpts in this book. For each selected reading, think about what is being said (and what is left unsaid) about the basic questions discussed in this introduction.

- *What theories does the author seem to work with, or what "cluster(s)" (if any) might they associate with?*
- *What assumptions does the author make?*
- *Who (or what) are the actors?*
- *What kinds of factors does the analyst think could cause their behavior?*
- *How free are the actors to act: that is, how "deterministic" are the explanations offered? What does the author say about what it would take to show that one explanation is better than another?*

We expect you will find that the basic clusters of differences we identified here are often reflected in the range of theoretical positions used to explain specific outcomes in comparative politics.

The organization of this volume follows that established in *Comparative Politics: Integrating Theories, Methods, and Cases.* It begins with two chapters that deal with comparative political analysis more generally. The first chapter includes readings that focus on what makes a good research question and what makes for good concepts in comparative politics. The second chapter gets students thinking about how theories are tested, moving from a classic piece in the philosophy of science to more recent work by political scientists about the nuts and bolts of case comparisons and why we use them. The rest of the book is then organized around different theoretical questions and themes, including the modern state (Chapter 3); political economy (Chapter 4); the nature and causes of economic development (Chapter 5); democracy and democratization (Chapter 6); democratic breakdown, authoritarianism, and authoritarian persistence (Chapter 7); constitutions and constitutional design (Chapter 8); legislatures (Chapter 9); executives (Chapter 10); political parties and interest groups (Chapter 11); revolutions and related forms of contention (Chapter 12); national identities (Chapter 13); gender, race, and ethnicity (Chapter 14); ideology and religion (Chapter 15); and the nexus between comparative politics and international relations (Chapter 16). In each chapter, plural theoretical perspectives are represented.

Let us quickly recap. We have encouraged you to think about the theoretical assumptions made by the different authors included in this volume and to be particularly attentive to the actors they identify, what they think causally impacts behavior, how much "agency" actors have, and what makes a good explanation. In closing this introduction, we encourage students to do one more thing beyond what we have already recommended. Comparative politics depends on theory, but it is not just the elaboration of theoretical claims. As will be made clearer in the next two chapters, comparative politics aspires to be a scientific enterprise that aims to deduce hypotheses from theories and put those hypotheses to the empirical test. This text emphasizes debates about major theoretical claims in comparative politics, but we encourage students to remain attentive to methods: keep your eye on what the authors here say about how they did (and how we should) accomplish the important task of learning and knowing what we can about the world.

Please note that the readings included in this book have been excerpted. As is customary in volumes of this sort, some sections of the certain texts were excised in the process. For a full consideration of their authors' arguments in all of their detail, please see the original works.

All readings are used by permission.

WORKS CITED AND FURTHER READING

Acemoglu, Daron, and James Robinson. 2012. *Why Nations Fail: The Origins of Power, Prosperity, and Poverty.* New York: Crown.

Campbell, John L. 2004. *Institutional Change and Globalization.* Princeton, NJ: Princeton University Press.

Elster, Jon. 2007. *Explaining Social Behavior: More Nuts and Bolts for the Social Sciences.* New York: Cambridge University Press.

Geertz, Clifford. 1973. *The Interpretation of Cultures.* New York: Basic Books.

Gintis, Herbert. 2009. *The Bounds of Reason: Game Theory and the Unification of the Behavioral Sciences.* Princeton, NJ: Princeton University Press.

Graham, Carol. 2009. *Happiness around the World: The Paradox of Happy Peasants and Miserable Millionaires.* New York: Oxford University Press.

Greenfeld, Liah. 2013. *Mind, Modernity, Madness: The Impact of Culture on Human Experience.* Cambridge, MA: Harvard University Press.

Hall, Peter A., and Rosemary Taylor. 1996. "Political Science and the Three New Institutionalisms," *Political Studies* 44(5): 936–957.

Hedström, Peter, and Peter Bearman. 2009. "What Is Analytical Sociology All About? An Introductory Essay," in P. Hedström and P. Bearman, eds., *Oxford Handbook of Analytical Sociology*, pp. 3–24. New York: Oxford University Press.

Law, David S., and Mila Versteeg. 2011. "The Evolution and Ideology of Global Constitutionalism," *California Law Review* 99(5): 1163–1258.

Lieberson, Stanley and Freda B. Lynn. 2002. "Barking up the Wrong Branch: Scientific Alternatives to the Current Model of Sociological Science," *Annual Review of Sociology* 28: 1–19.

King, Gary, Robert O. Keohane, and Sidney Verba. 1994. *Designing Social Inquiry: Scientific Inference in Qualitative Research*. Princeton, NJ: Princeton University Press.

Kuhn, Thomas. 1962. *The Structure of Scientific Revolutions*. Chicago: University of Chicago Press.

Merton, Robert K. 1967 [1949]. *On Theoretical Sociology: Five Essays, Old and New*. New York: Free Press.

Meyer, John W., John Boli, George Thomas, and Francisco Ramírez. 1997. "World Society and the Nation-State," *American Journal of Sociology*, 103 (1): 144–181.

Morgan, Stephen L., and Christopher Winship. 2007. *Counterfactuals and Causal Inference: Methods and Principles for Social Research*. New York: Cambridge University Press.

North, Douglass C. 1990. *Institutions, Institutional Change, and Economic Performance*. New York: Cambridge University Press.

North, Douglass C., John Joseph Wallis, and Barry R. Weingast. 2009. *Violence and Social Orders: A Conceptual Framework for Interpreting Recorded Human History*. New York: Cambridge University Press.

Pocock, J. G. A. 2003 [1975]. *The Machiavellian Moment: Florentine Political Thought and the Atlantic Republican Tradition*. Princeton, NJ: Princeton University Press.

Schelling, Thomas C. 2006 [1978]. *Micromotives and Macrobehavior*. New York: Norton.

Searle, John. 2010. *Making the Social World: The Structure of Human Civilization*. New York: Oxford University Press.

1

QUESTIONS, CONCEPTS, AND COMPARATIVE POLITICAL ANALYSIS

Section 1 of this book, composed of two chapters, takes a wide-angle view of comparative politics. Before we can get into debating theories of why states take the forms that they do, why some countries vary in terms of economic development, or why social and political revolutions sometimes happen but often do not, we must think about how to make comparisons. The introductory essay for this book introduced some major theories of comparative social science. Here we begin to think about the basic steps involved in formulating, clarifying, and testing theories.

Comparative politics seeks to answer important questions about the real world. To answer such questions, we must ask them as well. This often involves starting with a hunch or point of curiosity. We might call this "preanalytic": there is something on our mind that we have some vague ideas about, but we have not yet analyzed them or thought about them systematically. Perhaps you have noted a seeming relationship between two variables in the world and want to know more about it. For example, countries located in tropical versus temperate regions may be more or less likely to be authoritarian. The curiosity we feel about this question is important, and our analysis will be better if we do not lose sight of it. However, in most cases, before answering our questions we must think hard about them and identify the key concepts we will be working with, revising and clarifying our questions in the process. In the example above, we would need to think more about what we mean by "tropical" and "temperate," how we might want to draw the dividing lines between these categories as we "measure" them, and so forth. Even more important, we would want to think more fully about what we mean by "authoritarian" and figure out how we are going to measure authoritarianism (i.e., determine whether a given regime is authoritarian or even try to say *how* authoritarian it is). Many of these basics of approaching research questions are referred to in the readings in Chapter 1 of this section.

The second chapter in this section (Chapter 2) focuses on what we do once we have good questions. Its readings cover the basic logic of hypothesis testing and consider contrasting views on the nature of comparative analysis. As you will see, scholars in comparative politics have a range of opinions about what can and cannot be accomplished through case studies and small-N comparisons (i.e., research designs in which we compare a small number of cases after giving them in-depth treatment).

CHAPTER 1

THE COMPARATIVE APPROACH: AN INTRODUCTION

This opening chapter introduces two big themes in comparative political analysis: the importance of asking good questions and of using good concepts. Although it may seem obvious that we need good questions and concepts, achieving this is more difficult than you might expect.

Good questions have several key characteristics. First, they are interesting. Reasonable people can disagree, however, about what is and what is not interesting. One way to measure this is by trying to figure out whether a question matters for anyone beyond yourself. Second, good questions that matter usually capture your curiosity (and, hopefully, that of other people) *and* might produce knowledge that could make a difference in people's lives, at least indirectly. For example, asking why societies tend to democratize in waves (Huntington, 1991; Markoff, 1996); or why some societies vary so much in ensuring representation of women (Krook, 2010); or why intergroup violence happens in some places but not others (Varshney, 2002) are examples of political science questions that most people would recognize as both intellectually interesting and producing useful knowledge (if we can answer them!). Note that all of these are "why" questions that demand *explanations* as answers. These explanations often are tested using different types of empirical evidence, a process discussed in Chapter 2. This does not mean that we never have good questions in comparative social science that ask "how" or "what" (which demand *descriptions* as answers) but that the best questions are usually why questions. Third, good questions should also be answerable through *hypothesis testing*. In other words, we must be able to think theoretically about possible answers, develop hypotheses on the basis of these possible answers, and then test our hypotheses against some set of data. Finally, good questions must be novel, not in the sense that nobody has ever asked them before, but rather in that they have not yet satisfactorily been answered.

Coming up with good concepts might be even more difficult. Scholars commonly recognize that good concepts should be clear, coherent, and useful (for a more extensive list of the qualities of good concepts, see Gerring, 1999). That is, they should make sense and be logically consistent, and they should allow us to capture the kinds of interesting variation we need to ask and answer our why questions. One thing that introductory students in the social sciences often do not initially understand is that concepts may be different in the social sciences than in fields like physics or biology. That is, many concepts in the physical sciences may be "natural kinds," meaning that they reflect underlying differences in nature. For example, hydrogen and helium are different because they have a different number of electrons. Much of what we study in comparative politics and its cognate fields, however, is not like this. For example, the line between a democracy and an authoritarian dictatorship (as discussed in Chapters 6 and 7) is not clearly given in nature. This does not mean that there is no difference between democracy and authoritarianism, but that we need to make our own conceptual choices about the precise lines we are going to draw between them. This matters because the choices we make about the concepts we are going to use have ripple effects throughout our research. Different concepts produce different answers. Indeed, clarifying concepts may force us to go back and rethink our original questions. On the one hand, this can be an advantage, because we can use concepts that are closely tailored to the questions we ask in our individual studies. On the other hand, it produces potential problems: some scholars feel that a degree of conceptual standardization is necessary if we are going to build knowledge over time. In other words, to accumulate an understanding of what causes important outcomes such as "democracy," political scientists may need to agree (at least roughly) on what we mean by "democracy" in the first place!

In the readings in this chapter, we have two discussions of questions (asking and answering them) and one of concepts. The first reading, by Jared Diamond, introduces a good why question and shows why this particular question matters. As you read it, try to figure out what makes this a good question. The second reading, by Daron Acemoglu and James Robinson, starts with a similar question and focuses on thinking theoretically about different possible answers to that question and using the comparative method to try to answer it. The third reading, by David Collier and Steven Levitsky, looks at some of the difficulties that arise when we try to conceptualize something like "democracy": at first glance, it seems obvious what we mean by this term, but on reflection, we realize that democracy is a complex notion in need of clear conceptualization. The same is true, of course, of other major concepts in comparative politics, such as authoritarianism, development, nationalism, or revolution.

WORKS CITED

Gerring, John. 1999. "What Makes a Concept Good? A Criterial Framework for Understanding Concept Formation in the Social Sciences," *Polity* 31(3): 357–393.

Huntington, Samuel. 1991. *The Third Wave: Democratization in the Late 20th Century.* Norman: University of Oklahoma Press.

Krook, Mona Lena. 2010. *Quotas for Women in Politics: Gender and Candidate Selection Reform Worldwide.* New York: Oxford University Press.

Markoff, John. 1996. *Waves of Democracy: Social Movements and Political Change.* Thousand Oaks, CA: Pine Forge Press.

Varshney, Ashutosh. 2002. *Ethnic Conflict and Civic Life: Hindus and Muslims in India.* New Haven, CT: Yale University Press.

JARED DIAMOND

1.1 GUNS, GERMS, AND STEEL
The Fates of Human Societies

The brief excerpt from Jared Diamond included here is from his 1997 book, *Guns, Germs, and Steel: The Fates of Human Societies*. In the excerpt, Diamond describes the central question of the book. A friend from the Pacific island of Papua New Guinea asked him to explain why American and European visitors were so much better off in material terms than the island population. This seemingly simple question is actually extraordinarily complex and difficult to answer. For our purposes, the point is the question itself. Comparative political analysts try to ask big, important questions. One reason we do so is curiosity. Another is that the answers have implications for things that we value, like redressing inequalities, reducing poverty, or encouraging democracy. Many individual research projects and papers ask smaller, more manageable, questions, but our broader research is often guided by more overarching questions of the sort that Diamond and his friend ask here. What is a big question about comparative politics or the social world that captures your imagination?

PROLOGUE

YALI'S QUESTION

We all know that history has proceeded very differently for peoples from different parts of the globe. In the 13,000 years since the end of the last Ice Age, some parts of the world developed literate industrial societies with metal tools, other parts developed only nonliterate farming societies, and still others retained societies of hunter–gatherers with stone tools. Those historical inequalities have cast long shadows on the modern world, because the literate societies with metal tools have conquered or exterminated the other societies. While those differences constitute the most basic fact of world history, the reasons for them remain uncertain and controversial. This puzzling question of their origins was posed to me 25 years ago in a simple, personal form.

In July 1972 I was walking along a beach on the tropical island of New Guinea, where as a biologist I study bird evolution. I had already heard about a remarkable local politician named Yali, who was touring the district then. By chance, Yali and I were walking in the same direction on that day, and he overtook me. We walked together for an hour, talking during the whole time.

Yali radiated charisma and energy. His eyes flashed in a mesmerizing way. He talked confidently about himself, but he also asked lots of probing questions and listened intently. Our conversation began with a subject then on every New Guinean's mind—the rapid pace of political developments. Papua New Guinea, as Yali's nation is now called, was at that time still administered by Australia as a mandate of the United Nations, but independence was in the air. Yali explained to me his role in getting local people to prepare for self-government.

After a while, Yali turned the conversation and began to quiz me. He had never been outside New Guinea and had not been educated beyond high

Diamond, Jared. 1997. *Guns, Germs, and Steel: The Fates of Human Societies*. New York: W.W. Norton.

school, but his curiosity was insatiable. First, he wanted to know about my work on New Guinea birds (including how much I got paid for it). I explained to him how different groups of birds had colonized New Guinea over the course of millions of years. He then asked how the ancestors of his own people had reached New Guinea over the last tens of thousands of years, and how white Europeans had colonized New Guinea within the last 200 years.

The conversation remained friendly, even though the tension between the two societies that Yali and I represented was familiar to both of us. Two centuries ago, all New Guineans were still "living in the Stone Age." That is, they still used stone tools similar to those superseded in Europe by metal tools thousands of years ago, and they dwelt in villages not organized under any centralized political authority. Whites had arrived, imposed centralized government, and brought material goods whose value New Guineans instantly recognized, ranging from steel axes, matches, and medicines to clothing, soft drinks, and umbrellas. In New Guinea all these goods were referred to collectively as "cargo."

Many of the white colonialists openly despised New Guineans as "primitive." Even the least able of New Guinea's white "masters," as they were still called in 1972, enjoyed a far higher standard of living than New Guineans, higher even than charismatic politicians like Yali. Yet Yali had quizzed lots of whites as he was then quizzing me, and I had quizzed lots of New Guineans. He and I both knew perfectly well that New Guineans are on the average at least as smart as Europeans. All those things must have been on Yali's mind when, with yet another penetrating glance of his flashing eyes, he asked me, "Why is it that you white people developed so much cargo and brought it to New Guinea, but we black people had little cargo of our own?"

It was a simple question that went to the heart of life as Yali experienced it. Yes, there still is a huge difference between the lifestyle of the average New Guinean and that of the average European or American. Comparable differences separate the lifestyles of other peoples of the world as well. Those huge disparities must have potent causes that one might think would be obvious.

Yet Yali's apparently simple question is a difficult one to answer. I didn't have an answer then. Professional historians still disagree about the solution; most are no longer even asking the question. In the years since Yali and I had that conversation, I have studied and written about other aspects of human evolution, history, and language. This book, written twenty-five years later, attempts to answer Yali.

Although Yali's question concerned only the contrasting life-styles of New Guineans and of European whites, it can be extended to a larger set of contrasts within the modern world. Peoples of Eurasian origin, especially those still living in Europe and eastern Asia, plus those transplanted to North America, dominate the modern world in wealth and power. Other peoples, including most Africans, have thrown off European colonial domination but remain far behind in wealth and power. Still other peoples, such as the aboriginal inhabitants of Australia, the Americas, and southernmost Africa, are no longer even masters of their own lands but have been decimated, subjugated, and in some cases even exterminated by European colonialists.

Thus, questions about inequality in the modern world can be reformulated as follows. Why did wealth and power become distributed as they now are, rather than in some other way? For instance, why weren't Native Americans, Africans, and Aboriginal Australians the ones who decimated, subjugated, or exterminated Europeans and Asians?

We can easily push this question back one step. As of the year A.D. 1500, when Europe's worldwide colonial expansion was just beginning, peoples on different continents already differed greatly in technology and political organization. Much of Europe, Asia, and North Africa was the site of metal-equipped states or empires, some of them on the threshold of industrialization. Two Native American peoples, the Aztecs and the Incas, ruled over empires with stone tools. Parts of sub-Saharan Africa were divided among small states or chiefdoms with iron tools. Most other peoples—including all those of Australia and New Guinea, many Pacific islands, much of the Americas, and small parts of sub-Saharan Africa—lived as farming tribes or even still as hunter–gatherer bands using stone tools.

Of course, those technological and political differences as of A.D. 1500 were the immediate cause of the modern world's inequalities. Empires with steel weapons were able to conquer or exterminate tribes with weapons of stone and wood. How, though, did the world get to be the way it was in A.D. 1500?

Once again, we can easily push this question back one step further, by drawing on written histories and archaeological discoveries. Until the end of the last Ice Age, around 11,000 B.C., all peoples on all continents were still hunter–gatherers. Different rates of development on different continents, from 11,000 B.C. to A.D. 1500, were what led to the technological and political inequalities of A.D. 1500. While Aboriginal Australians and many Native Americans remained hunter–gatherers, most of Eurasia and much of the Americas and sub-Saharan Africa gradually developed agriculture, herding, metallurgy, and complex political organization. Parts of Eurasia, and one area of the Americas, independently developed writing as well. However, each of these new developments appeared earlier in Eurasia than elsewhere. For instance, the mass production of bronze tools, which was just beginning in the South American Andes in the centuries before A.D. 1500, was already established in parts of Eurasia over 4,000 years earlier. The stone technology of the Tasmanians, when first encountered by European explorers in A.D. 1642, was simpler than that prevalent in parts of Upper Paleolithic Europe tens of thousands of years earlier.

Thus, we can finally rephrase the question about the modern world's inequalities as follows: why did human development proceed at such different rates on different continents? Those disparate rates constitute history's broadest pattern and my book's subject.

While this book is thus ultimately about history and prehistory, its subject is not of just academic interest but also of overwhelming practical and political importance. The history of interactions among disparate peoples is what shaped the modern world through conquest, epidemics, and genocide. Those collisions created reverberations that have still not died down after many centuries, and that are actively continuing in some of the world's most troubled areas today.

For example, much of Africa is still struggling with its legacies from recent colonialism. In other regions—including much of Central America, Mexico, Peru, New Caledonia, the former Soviet Union, and parts of Indonesia—civil unrest or guerrilla warfare pits still-numerous indigenous populations against governments dominated by descendants of invading conquerors. Many other indigenous populations—such as native Hawaiians, Aboriginal Australians, native Siberians, and Indians in the United States, Canada, Brazil, Argentina, and Chile—became so reduced in numbers by genocide and disease that they are now greatly outnumbered by the descendants of invaders. Although thus incapable of mounting a civil war, they are nevertheless increasingly asserting their rights.

In addition to these current political and economic reverberations of past collisions among peoples, there are current linguistic reverberations—especially the impending disappearance of most of the modern world's 6,000 surviving languages, becoming replaced by English, Chinese, Russian, and a few other languages whose numbers of speakers have increased enormously in recent centuries. All these problems of the modern world result from the different historical trajectories implicit in Yali's question.

DARON ACEMOGLU AND JAMES ROBINSON

1.2 WHY NATIONS FAIL

The Origins of Power, Prosperity, and Poverty

In this excerpt from their book, *Why Nations Fail*, Daron Acemoglu and James Robinson introduce their strategy of using the comparative method to answer a big "why" question. Their question is similar to that of Jared Diamond, introduced in the previous reading: why are some countries so much richer than others? In the excerpt that follows, you will see them consider several major theories of comparative economic development. Their own theory emphasizes institutions. Indeed, they suspect that "inclusive economic and political institutions" foster growth, whereas "extractive" institutions keep countries poor. This is not simply a speculative idea, but rather hypotheses they aim to test by logically comparing cases and seeing whether this theory explains the observed patterns better than competing explanations. How do they do this?

SO CLOSE AND YET SO DIFFERENT

THE ECONOMICS OF THE RIO GRANDE

The city of Nogales is cut in half by a fence. If you stand by it and look north, you'll see Nogales, Arizona, located in Santa Cruz County. The income of the average household there is about $30,000 a year. Most teenagers are in school, and the majority of the adults are high school graduates. Despite all the arguments people make about how deficient the U.S. health care system is, the population is relatively healthy, with high life expectancy by global standards. Many of the residents are above age sixty-five and have access to Medicare. It's just one of the many services the government provides that most take for granted, such as electricity, telephones, a sewage system, public health, a road network linking them to other cities in the area and to the rest of the United States, and, last but not least, law and order. The people of Nogales, Arizona, can go about their daily activities without fear for life or safety and not constantly afraid of theft, expropriation, or other things that might jeopardize their investments in their businesses and houses.

Equally important, the residents of Nogales, Arizona, take it for granted that, with all its inefficiency and occasional corruption, the government is their agent. They can vote to replace their mayor, congressmen, and senators; they vote in the presidential elections that determine who will lead their country. Democracy is second nature to them.

Life south of the fence, just a few feet away, is rather different. While the residents of Nogales, Sonora, live in a relatively prosperous part of Mexico, the income of the average household there is about one-third that in Nogales, Arizona. Most adults in Nogales, Sonora, do not have a high school degree, and many teenagers are not in school. Mothers have to worry about high rates of infant mortality. Poor public health conditions mean it's no surprise that the residents of Nogales, Sonora, do not live as long as their northern neighbors. They also don't have access to many public amenities. Roads are in bad condition south of the fence. Law and order is in worse condition. Crime is high, and opening a business is a risky activity. Not only do you risk robbery, but getting all the permissions and greasing all the palms just to open is no easy endeavor.

Acemoglu, Daron and James Robinson. 2012. *Why Nations Fail*. New York: Crown Business.

Residents of Nogales, Sonora, live with politicians' corruption and ineptitude every day.

In contrast to their northern neighbors, democracy is a very recent experience for them. Until the political reforms of 2000, Nogales, Sonora, just like the rest of Mexico, was under the corrupt control of the Institutional Revolutionary Party, or Partido Revolucionario Institucional (PRI).

How could the two halves of what is essentially the same city be so different? There is no difference in geography, climate, or the types of diseases prevalent in the area, since germs do not face any restrictions crossing back and forth between the United States and Mexico. Of course, health conditions are very different, but this has nothing to do with the disease environment; it is because the people south of the border live with inferior sanitary conditions and lack decent health care.

But perhaps the residents are very different. Could it be that the residents of Nogales, Arizona, are grandchildren of migrants from Europe, while those in the south are descendants of Aztecs? Not so. The backgrounds of people on both sides of the border are quite similar. After Mexico became independent from Spain in 1821, the area around "Los dos Nogales" was part of the Mexican state of Vieja California and remained so even after the Mexican–American War of 1846–1848. Indeed, it was only after the Gadsden Purchase of 1853 that the U.S. border was extended into this area. It was Lieutenant N. Michler who, while surveying the border, noted the presence of the "pretty little valley of Los Nogales." Here, on either side of the border, the two cities rose up. The inhabitants of Nogales, Arizona, and Nogales, Sonora, share ancestors, enjoy the same food and the same music, and, we would hazard to say, have the same "culture."

Of course, there is a very simple and obvious explanation for the differences between the two halves of Nogales that you've probably long since guessed: the very border that defines the two halves. Nogales, Arizona, is in the United States. Its inhabitants have access to the economic institutions of the United States, which enable them to choose their occupations freely, acquire schooling and skills, and encourage their employers to invest in the best technology, which leads to higher wages for them. They also have access

to political institutions that allow them to take part in the democratic process, to elect their representatives, and replace them if they misbehave. In consequence, politicians provide the basic services (ranging from public health to roads to law and order) that the citizens demand. Those of Nogales, Sonora, are not so lucky. They live in a different world shaped by different institutions. These different institutions create very disparate incentives for the inhabitants of the two Nogaleses and for the entrepreneurs and businesses willing to invest there. These incentives created by the different institutions of the Nogaleses and the countries in which they are situated are the main reason for the differences in economic prosperity on the two sides of the border.

Why are the institutions of the United States so much more conducive to economic success than those of Mexico or, for that matter, the rest of Latin America? The answer to this question lies in the way the different societies formed during the early colonial period. An institutional divergence took place then, with implications lasting into the present day. To understand this divergence we must begin right at the foundation of the colonies in North and Latin America.

TOWARD A THEORY OF WORLD INEQUALITY

We live in an unequal world. The differences among nations are similar to those between the two parts of Nogales, just on a larger scale. In rich countries, individuals are healthier, live longer, and are much better educated. They also have access to a range of amenities and options in life, from vacations to career paths, that people in poor countries can only dream of. People in rich countries also drive on roads without potholes, and enjoy toilets, electricity, and running water in their houses. They also typically have governments that do not arbitrarily arrest or harass them; on the contrary, the governments provide services, including education, health care, roads, and law and order. Notable, too, is the fact that the citizens vote in elections and have some voice in the political direction their countries take.

The great differences in world inequality are evident to everyone, even to those in poor countries, though many lack access to television or the Internet.

It is the perception and reality of these differences that drive people to cross the Rio Grande or the Mediterranean Sea illegally to have the chance to experience rich-country living standards and opportunities. This inequality doesn't just have consequences for the lives of individual people in poor countries; it also causes grievances and resentment, with huge political consequences in the United States and elsewhere. Understanding why these differences exist and what causes them is our focus in this book. Developing such an understanding is not just an end in itself, but also a first step toward generating better ideas about how to improve the lives of billions who still live in poverty.

The disparities on the two sides of the fence in Nogales are just the tip of the iceberg. As in the rest of northern Mexico, which benefits from trade with the United States, even if not all of it is legal, the residents of Nogales are more prosperous than other Mexicans, whose average annual household income is around $5,000. This greater relative prosperity of Nogales, Sonora, comes from maquiladora manufacturing plants centered in industrial parks, the first of which was started by Richard Campbell, Jr., a California basket manufacturer. The first tenant was Coin-Art, a musical instrument company owned by Richard Bosse, owner of the Artley flute and saxophone company in Nogales, Arizona. Coin-Art was followed by Memorex (computer wiring); Avent (hospital clothing); Grant (sunglasses); Chamberlain (a manufacturer of garage door openers for Sears); and Samsonite (suitcases). Significantly, all are U.S.-based businesses and businessmen, using U.S. capital and know-how. The greater prosperity of Nogales, Sonora, relative to the rest of Mexico, therefore, comes from outside.

The differences between the United States and Mexico are in turn small compared with those across the entire globe. The average citizen of the United States is seven times as prosperous as the average Mexican and more than ten times as the resident of Peru or Central America. She is about twenty times as prosperous as the average inhabitant of sub-Saharan Africa, and almost forty times as those living in the poorest African countries such as Mali, Ethiopia, and Sierra Leone. And it's not just the United States. There is a small but growing group of rich countries—mostly in Europe and

North America, joined by Australia, Japan, New Zealand, Singapore, South Korea, and Taiwan—whose citizens enjoy very different lives from those of the inhabitants of the rest of the globe.

The reason that Nogales, Arizona, is much richer than Nogales, Sonora, is simple; it is because of the very different institutions on the two sides of the border, which create very different incentives for the inhabitants of Nogales, Arizona, versus Nogales, Sonora. The United States is also far richer today than either Mexico or Peru because of the way its institutions, both economic and political, shape the incentives of businesses, individuals, and politicians. Each society functions with a set of economic and political rules created and enforced by the state and the citizens collectively. Economic institutions shape economic incentives: the incentives to become educated, to save and invest, to innovate and adopt new technologies, and so on. It is the political process that determines what economic institutions people live under, and it is the political institutions that determine how this process works. For example, it is the political institutions of a nation that determine the ability of citizens to control politicians and influence how they behave. This in turn determines whether politicians are agents of the citizens, albeit imperfect, or are able to abuse the power entrusted to them, or that they have usurped, to amass their own fortunes and to pursue their own agendas, ones detrimental to those of the citizens. Political institutions include but are not limited to written constitutions and to whether the society is a democracy. They include the power and capacity of the state to regulate and govern society. It is also necessary to consider more broadly the factors that determine how political power is distributed in society, particularly the ability of different groups to act collectively to pursue their objectives or to stop other people from pursuing theirs.

As institutions influence behavior and incentives in real life, they forge the success or failure of nations. Individual talent matters at every level of society, but even that needs an institutional framework to transform it into a positive force. Bill Gates, like other legendary figures in the information technology industry (such as Paul Allen, Steve Ballmer, Steve Jobs, Larry Page, Sergey Brin, and Jeff Bezos), had immense talent and ambition. But he ultimately responded to incentives. The schooling system in the United States enabled Gates and others like him to acquire a unique set of skills to complement their talents. The economic institutions in the United States enabled these men to start companies with ease, without facing insurmountable barriers. Those institutions also made the financing of their projects feasible. The U.S. labor markets enabled them to hire qualified personnel, and the relatively competitive market environment enabled them to expand their companies and market their products. These entrepreneurs were confident from the beginning that their dream projects could be implemented: they trusted the institutions and the rule of law that these generated and they did not worry about the security of their property rights. Finally, the political institutions ensured stability and continuity. For one thing, they made sure that there was no risk of a dictator taking power and changing the rules of the game, expropriating their wealth, imprisoning them, or threatening their lives and livelihoods. They also made sure that no particular interest in society could warp the government in an economically disastrous direction, because political power was both limited and distributed sufficiently broadly that a set of economic institutions that created the incentives for prosperity could emerge.

This book will show that while economic institutions are critical for determining whether a country is poor or prosperous, it is politics and political institutions that determine what economic institutions a country has. Ultimately the good economic institutions of the United States resulted from the political institutions that gradually emerged after 1619. Our theory for world inequality shows how political and economic institutions interact in causing poverty or prosperity, and how different parts of the world ended up with such different sets of institutions.

Our brief review of the history of the Americas begins to give a sense of the forces that shape political and economic institutions. Different patterns of institutions today are deeply rooted in the past because once society gets organized in a particular way, this tends to persist. We'll show that this fact comes from the way that political and economic institutions interact.

This persistence and the forces that create it also explain why it is so difficult to remove world inequality and to make poor countries prosperous. Though institutions are the key to the differences between the two Nogaleses and between Mexico and the United States, that doesn't mean there will be a consensus in Mexico to change institutions. There is no necessity for a society to develop or adopt the institutions that are best for economic growth or the welfare of its citizen, because other institutions may be even better for those who control politics and political institutions. The powerful and the rest of society will often disagree about which set of institutions should remain in place and which ones should be changed. Carlos Slim would not have been happy to see his political connections disappear and the entry barriers protecting his business fizzle—no matter that the entry of new businesses would enrich millions of Mexicans. Because there is no such consensus, what rules society ends up with is determined by politics: who has power and how this power can be exercised. Carlos Slim has the power to get what he wants. Bill Gates's power is far more limited. That's why our theory is about not just economics but also politics. It is about the effects of institutions on the success and failure of nations—thus the economics of poverty and prosperity; it is also about how institutions are determined and change over time, and how they fail to change even when they create poverty and misery for millions—thus the politics of poverty and prosperity.

DAVID COLLIER AND STEVEN LEVITSKY*

1.3 DEMOCRACY WITH ADJECTIVES

Conceptual Innovation in Comparative Research

In this piece Collier and Levitsky consider the surprisingly difficult issue of conceptualizing democracy. But the piece is about more than the conceptualization of democracy as such: in the end, it is really about conceptualization itself. They discuss at length Giovanni Sartori's famous "ladder of generality" or "ladder of abstraction." In essence, Sartori argued that concepts can be more or less specific: we can make them more or less specific by adding "attributes" or additional criteria. For example, a general definition of democracy might say that it involves regular, free elections. We can make the concept more specific by adding that those elections include broad citizen participation, nondiscriminatory access to the polls, multiple parties, and a free press. For certain kinds of questions—for example, if we are trying to determine whether the United Kingdom became "more democratic" in the 18th century—adding specificity might make our task harder. But for other sorts of questions—for example, if we want to compare the extent to which different 21st-century Latin American polities are democratic—a more specific and restrictive concept will be more useful, among other reasons because it will allow us to create "subtypes." Take note of how Collier and Levitsky also discuss a number of other strategies for getting concepts right, and they emphasize the critical importance of thinking, speaking, and writing clearly about our concepts.

The recent global wave of democratization has presented scholars with the challenge of dealing conceptually with a great diversity of postauthoritarian regimes. Although the new national political regimes in Latin America, Africa, Asia, and the former communist world share important attributes of democracy, many of them differ profoundly both from each other and from the democracies in advanced industrial countries. Indeed, many are not considered fully democratic.

This article argues that scholars respond to this challenge by pursuing two potentially contradictory goals. On the one hand, researchers attempt to increase *analytic differentiation* in order to capture the diverse forms of democracy that have emerged. On the other hand, scholars are concerned with *conceptual validity*.

Specifically, they seek to avoid the problem of conceptual stretching that arises when the concept of democracy is applied to cases for which, by relevant scholarly standards, it is not appropriate.[1] The result has been a proliferation of alternative conceptual forms, including a surprising number of subtypes involving democracy "with adjectives."[2] Examples from among the hundreds of subtypes that have appeared include "authoritarian democracy," "neopatrimonial democracy," "military-dominated democracy," and "protodemocracy."

This proliferation has occurred despite the efforts by leading analysts to standardize usage of the term democracy on the basis of procedural definitions in the tradition of Joseph Schumpeter and Robert A. Dahl.[3] In important respects this standardization has been successful. Yet as democratization has continued

Collier, David, & Steven Levitsky. 1997. "Democracy with Adjectives: Conceptual Innovation in Comparative Research," *World Politics* 49(3): 430–451.

and attention has focused on an increasingly diverse set of cases, the proliferation of subtypes and other conceptual innovations has continued. Hence, given the risk of growing conceptual confusion, the earlier effort to standardize usage must now be supplemented by assessing the structure of meaning that underlies these diverse forms of the concept.

This article initiates this assessment, focusing on qualitative categories[4] employed in the study of recent cases of democratization at the level of national political regimes, with particular attention to work on Latin America.[5] Our goal is twofold: to make more comprehensible the complex structure of the alternative strategies of conceptual innovation that have emerged and to examine the trade-offs among these strategies. We begin with Sartori's well-known strategies of moving up and down a ladder of generality—strategies aimed at avoiding conceptual stretching and increasing differentiation, respectively. Because this approach cannot be used to pursue both goals at once, we find that scholars have often turned to other strategies: creating "diminished" subtypes of democracy, "precising" the definition of democracy by adding defining attributes, and shifting the overarching concept with which democracy is associated (for example, from democratic *regime* to democratic *state*).

More broadly, the analysis seeks to encourage scholars to be more careful in their definition and use of concepts. The subtypes and other conceptual forms examined here are, after all, generally critical components of the main substantive arguments presented by these researchers, often advancing the author's overall characterization of the case or cases in question. These are the "data containers" that convey the most salient facts about the regimes under discussion.[6] If one is to describe the new regimes adequately, these data containers must be employed in a clear and appropriate manner.

Improved description, in turn, is essential for assessing the *causes* and *consequences* of democracy, which is a central goal of this literature. Many studies have treated democracy as an outcome to be explained, including major works of comparative-historical analysis and old and new studies of "social requisites."[7] Other analyses have looked at the impact of democracy and of specific types of democracy on economic growth, income distribution, economic liberalization and adjustment, and international conflict.[8] In these studies, the results of causal assessment can be strongly influenced by the meaning of democracy employed by the author.[9] We hope that the present discussion can serve as a step toward a greater consistency and clarity of meaning that will provide a more adequate basis for assessing causal relationships.

It merits emphasis that these strategies of conceptual innovation are by no means unique to qualitative research on recent democratization. They are found in many conceptual domains, both in the social sciences and beyond.[10] A further goal of this article is therefore to advance the broader understanding of how qualitative researchers deal with these basic issues of analytic differentiation and conceptual validity.

I. DEFINITIONS OF DEMOCRACY IN RESEARCH ON RECENT DEMOCRATIZATION

In his famous analysis of "essentially contested concepts," the philosopher W. B. Gallie argues that democracy is *the* appraisive political concept *par excellence*."[11] Correspondingly, one finds endless disputes over appropriate meaning and definition. However, the goal of Gallie's analysis is not simply to underscore the importance of such disputes, but to show that a recognition of the contested status of a given concept opens the possibility of understanding each meaning within its own framework. With reference to democracy, he argues that "politics being the art of the possible, democratic targets will be raised or lowered as circumstances alter," and he insists that these alternative standards should be taken seriously on their own terms.[12]

In this spirit, we focus on the procedural definitions that have been most widely employed in research on recent democratization at the level of national political regimes. These definitions refer to democratic *procedures*, rather than to substantive policies or other outcomes that might be viewed as democratic. These definitions are also "minimal," in that they deliberately focus on the smallest possible number of attributes that are still seen as producing a viable standard for democracy; not surprisingly, there is disagreement about which attributes are needed for the definition to be viable. For example, most of these scholars differentiate what they view as the more specifically political features of the regime from characteristics of the society and economy, on the grounds that the latter are more appropriately analyzed as potential causes or consequences of democracy, rather than as features of democracy itself.[13]

Within this framework, we focus on a "procedural minimum" definition that presumes fully contested elections with full suffrage and the absence of massive fraud, combined with effective guarantees of civil liberties, including freedom of speech, assembly, and association.[14] However, there is by no means consensus on a single definition. Some scholars, for example, have created an *"expanded procedural minimum"* definition by adding the criterion that elected governments must have effective power to govern—which, as we will see below, is a crucial issue in some countries.

II. SARTORI'S STRATEGIES

We first consider Sartori's strategies for achieving differentiation and avoiding conceptual stretching. Sartori builds on a basic insight about the organization of concepts: a significant aspect of the relationship between the meaning of concepts and the range of cases to which they apply can be understood in terms of a "ladder of generality."[15] This ladder is based on a pattern of inverse variation between the number of defining attributes and number of cases. Thus, concepts with *fewer* defining attributes commonly apply to *more* cases and are therefore higher on the ladder of generality, whereas concepts with *more* defining attributes apply to *fewer* cases and hence are lower on the ladder.

DIFFERENTIATION

One of Sartori's goals is to show how conceptual differentiation can be increased by moving *down* the ladder of generality to concepts that have more defining attributes and fit a narrower range of cases. These concepts provide the more fine-grained distinctions that for some purposes are invaluable to the researcher.[16] This move down the ladder is often accomplished through the creation of what we will call "classical" subtypes of democracy.[17] Classical subtypes are understood as *full* instances of the root definition[18]

of democracy in relation to which they are formed, at the same time that they are differentiated vis-à-vis other classical subtypes of this concept. Thus, "parliamentary democracy," "multiparty democracy," and "federal democracy" are all considered *definitely* democratic (by whatever standard the author is using), at the same time that each is considered a particular *type* of democracy (see Figure 1.1). In research on recent cases of democratization, the use of classical subtypes to achieve differentiation is found, for example, in the important debate on the consequences of parliamentary, as opposed to presidential, democracy.[19]

Moving down the ladder of generality provides useful differentiation, and the subtypes just noted play an important role in the recent literature. Yet subtypes formed in this manner may leave the analyst vulnerable to conceptual stretching, because they presume the cases under discussion are definitely democracies. If the particular case being studied is less than fully democratic, then the use of these subtypes as a tool of conceptual differentiation may not be appropriate. Analysts therefore seek concepts that distinguish among different *degrees* of democracy, in addition to distinguishing among different *types* of democracy. Because classical subtypes of democracy only contribute to the second of these two goals, they have not been the most common means of conceptual differentiation in studies of recent democratization.

AVOIDING CONCEPTUAL STRETCHING

Sartori's proposal for avoiding conceptual stretching is to move *up* the ladder of generality to concepts that have fewer defining attributes and correspondingly fit a broader range of cases.[20] In the present context, this involves concepts located *above* democracy on the ladder of generality. Scholars commonly view democracy as a specific type in relation to the overarching concept of regime. Hence, if they have misgivings as to whether a particular case is really a *democratic* regime, they can move up the ladder and simply call it a regime.

However, because shifting to a concept as general as regime entails a great loss of conceptual differentiation, scholars have typically moved to an intermediate level (Figure 1.1)—adding adjectives to the term regime and thereby generating classical subtypes to differentiate specific *types* of regime. The resulting subtypes remain

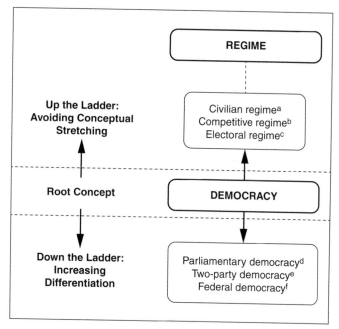

FIGURE 1.1 The Ladder of Generality: Increasing Differentiation versus Avoiding Conceptual Stretching

Source: [a]John A. Booth, "Framework for Analysis," in John A. Booth and Mitchell A. Seligson, eds., *Elections and Democracy in Central America* (Chapel Hill: University of North Carolina Press, 1989), 26. [b]Ruth Berins Collier and David Collier, *Shaping the Political Arena: Critical Junctures, the Labor Movement, and Regime Dynamics in Latin America* (Princeton: Princeton University Press, 1991), 354. [c]James Petras and Fernando Ignacio Leiva, *Democracy and Poverty in Chile: The Limits to Electoral Politics* (Boulder, Colo.: Westview Press, 1994), 89. [d]Juan J. Linz. "Presidential or Parliamentary Democracy: Does It Make a Difference?" in Juan J. Linz and Arturo Valenzuela, eds., *The Failure of Presidential Democracy* (Baltimore: Johns Hopkins University Press, 1994), 3. [e]Mark J. Gasiorowski, "The Political Regimes Project," *Studies in Comparative International Development* 25 (Spring 1990), 113. [f]Raymond Duncan Gastil, "The Comparative Survey of Freedom: Experiences and Suggestions," *Studies in Comparative International Development* 25 (Spring 1990), 35.

more general than the concept of democracy, in that they encompass not only democracies but also some *non*-democracies. Examples include "civilian regime," "competitive regime," and "electoral regime." Although scholars thus achieve some conceptual differentiation in relation to regime, they do not specifically commit themselves to the idea that the case under discussion is a democracy. A similar pattern is followed when scholars use a synonym for regime, as in "civilian rule" and "competitive polity."[21]

Although climbing the ladder of generality helps to avoid conceptual stretching, it has an important drawback. Because these subtypes remain *more general* than the concept of democracy, this approach leads to a loss

of conceptual differentiation. Thus, taken together, Sartori's two strategies can advance one or the other of these goals, but not both at once. As a consequence, many scholars have turned to other strategies.

III. DIMINISHED SUBTYPES

An alternative strategy of conceptual innovation, that of creating "diminished" subtypes,[22] can contribute both to achieving differentiation and to avoiding conceptual stretching. It is a strategy widely used in the literature on recent democratization. Two points are crucial for understanding diminished subtypes. First, in contrast to the classical subtypes discussed above, diminished subtypes are *not* full instances of the root definition of "democracy" employed by the author who presents the subtype. For example, "limited-suffrage democracy" and "tutelary democracy" are understood as less than complete instances of democracy because they lack one or more of its defining attributes.[23] Consequently, in using these subtypes the analyst makes a more modest claim about the extent of democratization and is therefore less vulnerable to conceptual stretching.

The second point concerns differentiation. Because diminished subtypes represent an incomplete form of democracy, they might be seen as having *fewer* defining attributes, with the consequence that they would be *higher* on the ladder of generality and would therefore provide less, rather than more, differentiation. However, the distinctive feature of diminished subtypes is that they generally identify specific attributes of democracy that are *missing*, thereby establishing the diminished character of the subtype, at the same time that they identify other attributes of democracy that are *present*. Because they specify missing attributes, they also increase differentiation, and the

diminished subtype in fact refers to a *different* set of cases than does the root definition of democracy.

The inclusion and exclusion of cases that occurs with a diminished subtype, as opposed to moving up or down the ladder of generality, can be illustrated with the examples of contemporary Britain, the United States, and Guatemala (Figure 1.2). Britain and the United States, but probably *not* Guatemala (at least up through the mid-1990s), would be seen as democratic in terms of the procedural minimum definition. If we climb the ladder of generality, we find that the broader concept of "electoral regime"[24] encompasses all three cases. Lower down on the ladder the classical subtype "parliamentary democracy" would include one of the two democracies, that is, Britain. By contrast, the diminished subtype "illiberal democracy" would include only Guatemala, the case that specifically did *not* fit the root definition of democracy.[25]

Diminished subtypes, then, are a useful means to avoid conceptual stretching in cases that are less than fully democratic. They also provide differentiation by creating new analytic categories. Various scholars

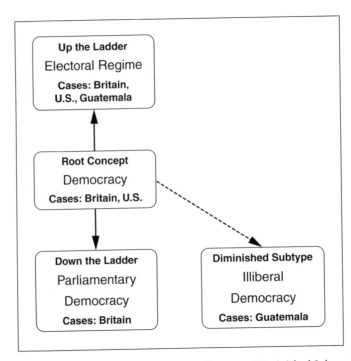

FIGURE 1.2   Inclusion and Exclusion of Cases: Ladder of Generality versus Diminished Subtypes

have pointed to the need to move beyond a dichotomous conceptualization of authoritarianism and democracy and recognize the "hybrid" or "mixed" character of many postauthoritarian regimes.[26] Figure 1.3 suggests that this recognition has indeed occurred, and on a rather large scale.

For countries that are less than fully democratic, however, the question arises as to whether it would be better to avoid identifying them as subtypes of democracy, for example, in cases of gross violations of civil liberties and/or severe restrictions on electoral competition. An example of such questioning is Bruce Bagley's rejection of the numerous diminished subtypes of democracy that have been applied to the National Front period in Colombia (1958–74); these include "restricted," "controlled," "limited," "oligarchical," "elitist," and "elitist-pluralist" democracy. Bagley instead characterizes Colombia as a subtype of authoritarianism: as an "inclusionary authoritarian regime."[27] Other scholars have addressed this issue by climbing the ladder of generality to labels such as "civilian," "competitive," or "electoral" regime, which are found in the upper part of Figure 1.1. A third option is to use dismissive subtypes like those noted above, such as "facade democracy," in which the adjective essentially cancels the democratic character of the subtype. Scholars should be self-conscious about the analytic and normative implications of choosing to form subtypes in relation to democracy, as opposed to some other concept.

IV. PRECISING THE DEFINITION OF DEMOCRACY

Another strategy of conceptual innovation focuses on the definition of democracy itself and is concerned with "precising" the definition by adding defining attributes.[28] As the concept is extended to new settings, researchers may confront a particular case that is classified as a democracy on the basis of a commonly accepted definition yet is not seen as fully democratic in light of a larger shared understanding of the concept. This mismatch between the case and the formal definition may lead analysts to make explicit one or more criteria that are implicitly understood to be part of the overall meaning, but that are not included in the

definition. The result is a new definition intended to change the way a particular case is classified. Although this procedure of precising the definition could be seen as raising the standard for democracy, it can also be understood as adapting the definition to a new context. This innovation increases conceptual differentiation, by adding a further criterion for establishing the cutoff between democracy and nondemocracy. The strategy may thereby also avoid conceptual stretching because it does not apply the label "democracy" to cases that, in light of this new criterion, the analyst sees as incompletely democratic. Although the use of this strategy may arise from a concern with adapting the concept of democracy to fit a particular context, the modified definition should not be understood as being relevant only to that context. Indeed, the modified definition can also provide new insight into other cases for which the significance of the new defining attributes had not previously been fully appreciated.

One example of precising the definition is the emergence of the standard of an expanded procedural minimum, noted above. In several Central American countries, as well as in South American cases such as Chile and Paraguay, one legacy of authoritarian rule has been the persistence of "reserved domains" of military power over which elected governments have little or no authority.[29] Hence, despite free or relatively free elections, civilian governments in these countries are seen by some analysts as lacking effective power to govern. In light of these authoritarian legacies, and often in response to claims that because these countries have held free elections they are "democratic," some scholars have modified the procedural minimum definition of democracy by specifying as an explicit criterion that the elected government must to a reasonable degree have effective power to rule. With this revised definition, countries such as Chile, El Salvador, and Paraguay have been excluded by some scholars from the set of cases classified as democracies, even though they held relatively free elections.[30] These scholars have thus adapted the definition to explicitly include an attribute that is often taken for granted in studies of advanced industrial democracies but that is absent in these Latin American cases.

This revised definition has received substantial acceptance, although there certainly has not been full agreement on the treatment of specific cases. For example, in analyzing Chile in the post-1990 period, Rhoda Rabkin takes exception to the usage adopted by scholars who introduced the expanded procedural minimum definition. She argues that the problem of civilian control of the military does not represent a sufficient challenge to the democratically elected government to qualify Chile as a "borderline" democracy.[31]

Precising the definition can thus usefully serve both to introduce finer differentiation and to avoid conceptual stretching, and the associated debates have raised essential issues about the meaning that scholars wish to attach to the term "democracy." Yet caution is in order. Among the alternative strategies of conceptual innovation examined in this article, precising in a sense introduces the most drastic change: it modifies the definition of democracy itself. If an innovation based on precising is widely accepted, it has the important effect of changing the definitional point of departure with reference to which all of the other strategies are pursued, in effect unsettling the "semantic field" in which these scholars are working.[32] By contrast, the introduction of a new subtype does not affect the semantic field in the same way. In a literature in which conceptual confusion is a recurring problem, the analytic gains from precising the definition must be weighted against the cost of unsettling the semantic field.

Hence, it is important that scholars avoid "definitional gerrymandering,"[33] in the sense of introducing a new definition every time they encounter a somewhat anomalous case. However, the contrast between the first example (adding the criterion of effective power to govern) and the third example (adding horizontal accountability) shows that scholars may in fact impose constructive limits on precising. In the first example, the inability of elected governments to exercise effective power was seen as invalidating their democratic character. By contrast, in the third example, involving heavy-handed assertions of power by the president, a crucial point is that these presidents *are* elected leaders. Hence, it might be argued that it is appropriate to treat these regimes as meeting a minimal standard for democracy and to avoid precising—as long as (1) they maintain presidential elections and a general respect for civil liberties and the legislature and (2) opposition parties are not banned or dissolved (as occurred in Peru in 1992).

Finally, the initiative of precising can raise the issue of bringing back into the definition of democracy attributes that scholars previously had explicitly decided to exclude. An example is the concern with social relationships in the Tocquevillean approach. These authors could be seen as remaining within a procedural framework, in the sense that they argue that political participation becomes less meaningful in the context of extreme social inequality. However, this conceptual innovation reintroduces features of social relations in a way that nonetheless represents a major shift from earlier recommendations about which attributes should be included in definitions of democracy.

V. SHIFTING THE OVERARCHING CONCEPT

Yet another strategy of conceptual innovation is to shift the overarching concept, in relation to which democracy is seen as a specific instance—that is, as a classical subtype. Thus, although scholars most commonly view democracy as a subtype of the overarching concept "regime" (and the procedural criteria for democracy discussed above would routinely be understood as applying to the regime), some recent literature has understood democracy as a subtype in relation to other overarching concepts, as in "democratic government" and "democratic state." Hence, when a given country is labeled "democratic," the meaning can vary according to the overarching concept to which the term is attached.

To summarize, the strategy of shifting among alternative overarching concepts can serve to introduce finer differentiation by creating an additional analytic category. When the strategy is used to lower the standard for declaring a case to be a democracy, it can also help avoid stretching the concept of a democratic regime. When the strategy is used to raise the standard it is not relevant to the problem of conceptual stretching, because it is not concerned with avoiding what might be seen as the mistake of calling a given case a democratic regime. Rather, it provides *additional* information about cases that are accepted as having democratic regimes.

VI. CONCLUDING OBSERVATIONS

We have examined strategies of conceptual innovation used by analysts of recent democratization as they seek to meet a twofold challenge: increasing analytic differentiation in order to adequately characterize the diverse regimes that have emerged in recent years and maintaining conceptual validity by avoiding conceptual stretching. Our goal has been both to make more comprehensible the complex structure of these strategies and to evaluate the strengths and weaknesses of the strategies. Even when these scholars proceed intuitively, rather than self-consciously, they tend to operate within this structure, which, as noted above, is by no means unique to research on recent democratization.[34] Yet, in the interest of conceptual

and analytic clarity, it is far more desirable for them to proceed self-consciously, with a full awareness of the trade-offs among the different strategies.

Figure 1.3 provides an overview of this analytic structure. Conceptual innovation has occurred at the three levels of the root concept of democracy itself, the subtypes, and the overarching concept. We observed that Sartori's strategies of (1) moving down the ladder of generality to classical subtypes of democracy and (2) moving up the ladder to classical subtypes of regime can usefully serve either to increase differentiation or to avoid conceptual stretching, but they cannot do both simultaneously. These two goals can be achieved simultaneously, however, by (3) creating diminished subtypes, (4) precising the

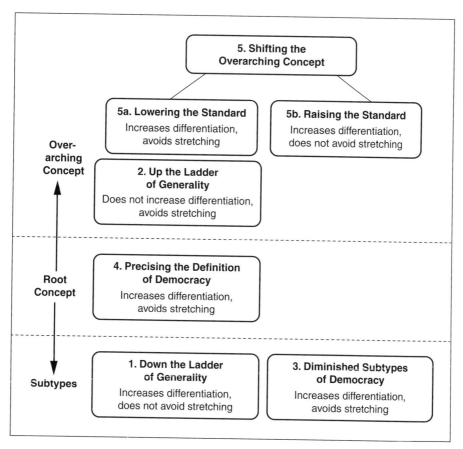

FIGURE 1.3 Evaluating the Conceptual Innovations: Contribution to Increasing Differentiation and Avoiding Conceptual Stretching

definition of democracy by adding defining attributes, and (5a) shifting the overarching concept as a means of lowering the standard. By contrast (5b), shifting the overarching concept to raise the standard for democracy does not serve to avoid conceptual stretching vis-à-vis the concept of a democratic regime, but it does introduce new differentiation.

We have also underscored issues that are distinctive to particular strategies. Diminished subtypes are useful for characterizing hybrid regimes, but they raise the issue of whether these regimes should in fact be treated as subtypes of democracy, rather than subtypes of authoritarianism or some other concept. The strategy of precising the definition is subject to the perennial problem of scholarly disputes over definitions of democracy, as well as to the problem of imposing limits on definitional gerrymandering. Although the strategy of shifting the overarching concept with the goal of raising the standard is not relevant to the problem of conceptual stretching, it does allow scholars to introduce new analytic issues without abandoning a procedural definition of democracy and of regime.

Finally, these strategies share two common problems. First, given the complex structure of these strategies, the potential for confusion and miscommunication is considerable. It is imperative that scholars clearly define and explicate the conception of democracy they are using so as to situate themselves unambiguously in relation to this structure.

Second, this literature faces a major dilemma in the proliferation of concepts and terms, many of which mean approximately the same thing. The consequence, once again, can be growing scholarly confusion. Although new terms are created in part because scholars are pursuing these goals of differentiation and avoiding conceptual stretching, they may also be introduced with the goal of developing compelling labels that vividly draw attention to novel forms of democracy.[35] In the literature on national political regimes over the past three decades, important analytic innovations have periodically been introduced in conjunction with the creation and/or systematization of concepts and concept labels that vividly capture important constellations of phenomena: for example, "authoritarianism," "polyarchy,"

"bureaucratic authoritarianism," "corporatism," and "consociational democracy."[36] Correspondingly, the invention of additional concepts that play this same role is an important goal in the ongoing study of regimes. However, if research on democratization degenerates into a competition to see who can come up with the next famous concept, the comparative study of regimes will be in serious trouble.

Hence, we propose another major objective of concept usage, one that introduces a further trade-off vis-à-vis the two goals of achieving differentiation and avoiding conceptual stretching. In addition to pursuing these goals, scholars should aim for parsimony and avoid excessive proliferation of new terms and concepts. Otherwise, the advantages that derive from the conceptual refinements discussed in this article will be overridden by the resulting conceptual confusion.

NOTES

*   We acknowledge the valuable suggestions of Ruth Berins Collier, Larry Diamond, Andrew Gould, Peter Houtzager, Marcus Kurtz, Terry Karl, David Laitin, George Lakoff, Arend Lijphart, James Mahoney, Scott Mainwaring, Carol Medlin, Gerardo Munck, Guillermo O'Donnell, Michael Pretes, Philippe Schmitter, Laura Stoker, Mark Turner, Samuel Valenzuela, and participants in the Berkeley Working Group on Comparative Method. Steve Levitsky's participation in this research was supported by a National Science Foundation Graduate Fellowship, and David Collier's work on this project at the Center for Advanced Study in the Behavioral Sciences was supported by National Science Foundation Grant no. SBR-9022192.

1. Giovanni Sartori, "Concept Misformation in Comparative Politics," *American Political Science Review* 64 (December 1970); and David Collier and James E. Mahon, Jr., "Conceptual 'Stretching' Revisited: Adapting Categories in Comparative Analysis," *American Political Science Review* 87 (December 1993).

2. A parallel expression, "democracy without adjectives," appeared in debates in Latin America among observers concerned with the persistence

of incomplete and qualified forms of democracy. See, for instance, Enrique Krauze, *Por una democracia sin adjetivos* (Mexico City: Joaquín Mortiz/Planeta, 1986).

3. Schumpeter, *Capitalism, Socialism and Democracy* (New York: Harper, 1947); and Dahl, *Polyarchy: Participation and Opposition* (New Haven: Yale University Press, 1971).

4. Along with the qualitative categories that are the focus of this discussion, valuable quantitative indicators have been developed for comparing recent cases of democratization. Ultimately, it will be productive to bring together insights about the strategies of conceptual innovation employed in these alternative approaches. However, an essential prior step, which is our present concern, is to learn more about the conceptual innovations introduced by scholars who employ qualitative categories.

5. We are thus not primarily concerned with the literature on advanced industrial democracies, although this literature is an important point of reference in the studies we are examining. In a few places, we have included recent studies of countries that are not actually part of the current episode of democratization, but whose relatively new democracies are a point of comparison in the studies under review, for example, Colombia. We also include a few references to other historical cases that have been used in recent scholarship as important points of analytic contrast.

6. Sartori (fn. 1), 1039.

7. Barrington Moore, Jr., *Social Origins of Dictatorship and Democracy: Lord and Peasant in the Making of the Modern World* (Boston: Beacon Press, 1966); Gregory M. Luebbert, *Liberalism, Fascism, or Social Democracy: Social Classes and the Political Origins of Regimes in Interwar Europe* (New York: Oxford University Press, 1991); Dietrich Rueschemeyer, Evelyne Huber Stephens, and John D. Stephens, *Capitalist Development and Democracy* (Chicago: University of Chicago Press, 1992); Seymour Martin Lipset, "Some Social Requisites of Democracy: Economic Development and Political Legitimacy," *American Political Science Review* 53 (March 1959); and

idem, "The Social Requisites of Democracy Revisited," *American Sociological Review* 59 (February 1994); John B. Londregan and Keith T. Poole, "Does High Income Promote Democracy?" *World Politics* 49 (October 1996); and Adam Przeworski and Fernando Limongi, "Modernization: Theories and Facts," *World Politics* 49 (January 1997).

8. Adam Przeworski and Fernando Limongi, "Political Regimes and Economic Growth," *Journal of Economic Perspectives* 7 (Summer 1993); Kenneth A. Bollen and Robert W. Jackman, "Political Democracy and the Size Distribution of Income," *American Sociological Review* 50 (August 1985); Larry Sirowy and Alex Inkeles, "The Effects of Democracy on Economic Growth and Inequality: A Review," *Studies in Comparative International Development* 25 (Spring 1990); Karen L. Remmer, "The Politics of Economic Stabilization: IMF Standby Programs in Latin America, 1954–1984," *Comparative Politics* 19 (October 1986); Barbara Stallings and Robert Kaufman, eds., *Debt and Democracy in Latin America* (Boulder, Colo.: Westview Press, 1989); Bruce Russett, *Grasping the Democratic Peace: Principles for a Post–Cold War World* (Princeton: Princeton University Press, 1993); Michael E. Brown, Sean M. Lynn-Jones, and Steven E. Miller, eds., *Debating the Democratic Peace: An International Security Reader* (Cambridge: MIT Press, 1996); Alfred Stepan and Cindy Skach, "Constitutional Frameworks and Democratic Consolidation: Parliamentarianism versus Presidentialism," *World Politics* 46 (October 1993); Juan J. Linz and Arturo Valenzuela, eds., *The Failure of Presidential Democracy* (Baltimore: Johns Hopkins University Press, 1994); and Guillermo O'Donnell, "Delegative Democracy," *Journal of Democracy* 5 (January 1994).

9. See, for example, Kenneth A. Bollen and Robert W. Jackman, "Democracy, Stability, and Dichotomies," *American Sociological Review* 54 (August 1989), 613–16; and Russett (fn. 8), 15–16.

10. For an analysis that focuses on some of these same strategies with reference to another social science concept, see David Collier, "Trajectory of

a Concept: 'Corporatism' in the Study of Latin American Politics," in Peter H. Smith, ed., *Latin America in Comparative Perspective: New Approaches to Method and Analysis* (Boulder, Colo.: Westview Press, 1995). For discussions by linguists and cognitive scientists of the intuitive structure that underlies these strategies, see D. A. Cruse, *Lexical Semantics* (Cambridge: Cambridge University Press, 1986), chap. 6; George Lakoff, *Women, Fire, and Dangerous Things: What Categories Reveal about the Mind* (Chicago: University of Chicago Press, 1987), chaps. 2, 6; and John R. Taylor, *Linguistic Categorization: Prototypes in Linguistic Theory*, 2d ed. (Oxford: Oxford University Press, 1989), chaps. 2–3.

11. W. B. Gallie, "Essentially Contested Concepts," *Proceedings of the Aristotelian Society* 56 (London: Harrison and Sons, 1956), 184; emphasis in original.

12. Ibid., quote at 186; see also pp. 178, 189, 190, 193.

13. For discussions of procedural definitions, see Guillermo O'Donnell and Philippe C. Schmitter, *Transitions from Authoritarian Rule: Tentative Conclusions about Uncertain Democracies* (Baltimore: Johns Hopkins University Press, 1986), chap. 2; Samuel P. Huntington, "The Modest Meaning of Democracy," in Robert A. Pastor, ed., *Democracy in the Americas: Stopping the Pendulum* (New York: Holmes and Meier, 1989); Schumpeter (fn. 3); and Dahl (fn. 3). On minimal definitions, see Giuseppe Di Palma, *To Craft Democracies: An Essay on Democratic Transitions* (Berkeley: University of California Press, 1990), 28; and Samuel P. Huntington, *The Third Wave: Democratization in the Late Twentieth Century* (Norman: University of Oklahoma Press, 1991), 9. On treating characteristics of the society and economy as a cause or consequence of democracy, see Juan J. Linz, "Totalitarian and Authoritarian Regimes," in Fred I. Greenstein and Nelson W. Polsby, eds., *Handbook of Political Science*, vol. 3 (Reading, Mass.: Addison–Wesley, 1975), 182; and Terry Lynn Karl, "Dilemmas of Democratization in Latin America," *Comparative Politics* 23 (October 1990), 2.

14. O'Donnell and Schmitter (fn. 13), 8; Larry Diamond, Juan J. Linz, and Seymour Martin Lipset, "Preface," in Diamond, Linz, and Lipset, eds., *Democracy in Developing Countries: Latin America* (Boulder, Colo.: Rienner, 1989), xvi; Di Palma (fn. 13), 16. See also Juan J. Linz, *The Breakdown of Democratic Regimes: Crisis, Breakdown, and Reequilibration* (Baltimore: Johns Hopkins University Press, 1978), 5.

15. Sartori (fn. 1), 1040, actually refers to a ladder of "abstraction." However, because the term *abstract* is often understood in contrast to *concrete*, this label can be confusing. We therefore find that "ladder of generality" expresses the intended meaning more clearly.

16. Sartori (fn. 1), 1041.

17. We refer to these as classical subtypes because they fit within the "classical" understanding of categorization discussed by such authors as Lakoff (fn. 10), 9 and passim; and Taylor (fn. 10), chap. 2.

18. In referring to the root definition, we do not imply that it is the "correct" definition of the relevant concept (in this case, of democracy). It is simply the definition that, for a particular author, is the point of departure in forming the subtype. We will occasionally use the expression "root concept" to refer to the concept (again, in the present context, democracy) that is the point of departure for the various conceptual innovations analyzed here.

19. Linz and Valenzuela (fn. 8); Stepan and Skach (fn. 8); and Giovanni Sartori, *Comparative Constitutional Engineering: An Inquiry into Structures, Incentives, and Outcomes* (New York: New York University Press, 1994).

20. Sartori (fn. 1), 1041.

21. See, respectively, Richard Wilson, "Continued Counterinsurgency: Civilian Rule in Guatemala," in Barry Gills, Joel Rocamora, and Richard Wilson, eds., *Low Intensity Democracy: Political Power in the New World Order* (London: Pluto Press, 1993); and Terry Lynn Karl, "Democracy by Design: The Christian Democratic Party in El Salvador," in Giuseppe Di Palma and Laurence Whitehead, eds., *The Central American Impasse* (London: Croom Helm, 1986).

22. The idea of diminished subtypes builds on the discussion of radial concepts in Collier and Mahon (fn. 1), 850–52. See also Lakoff (fn. 10), chap. 6.

23. Because they are less than complete instances, it might be objected that they are not really "subtypes" of democracy at all. Drawing on a term from cognitive linguistics, one can refer to them as conceptual "blends" that are derived in part from the concept of democracy. However, to avoid referring repeatedly to "subtypes and blends," it seems simpler in the discussion below to call them subtypes. See Gilles Fauconnier and Mark Turner, "Conceptual Projection and Middle Spaces," Report no. 9401, Department of Cognitive Science (San Diego: University of California, San Diego, 1994).

24. This subtype is understood to have the meaning explained above in the discussion of Figure 1.1.

25. Regarding illiberal democracy, see Figure 1.3. Two further points about diminished subtypes should be underscored. First, if scholars fail to identify the root definition of democracy in relation to which they form subtypes, it is difficult to determine whether a given subtype is classical or diminished. Second, the fact that a subtype refers to what might be understood as a "problematic" feature of democracy does not necessarily mean that it is a diminished subtype. For example, O'Donnell's concept of "delegative democracy," which refers to cases with weak horizontal accountability among the branches of government, in fact meets his minimum definition of democracy, given that he does not include horizontal accountability in the definition. See O'Donnell (fn. 8), 56. Hence, in his usage, delegative democracy is a classical subtype. For a discussion of subtypes that refer to "problematic" democracies, see a longer version of the present analysis in David Collier and Steven Levitsky, "Democracy 'with Adjectives': Conceptual Innovation in Comparative Research," Working Paper no. 230 (Notre Dame, Ind.: The Kellogg Institute, University of Notre Dame, 1996), 20–26. The above characterization of delegative democracy as a classical subtype should be understood as correcting the assessment of this subtype presented in Collier (fn. 10), 147–48.

26. James M. Malloy, "The Politics of Transition in Latin America," in James M. Malloy and Mitchell A. Seligson, eds., *Authoritarians and Democrats: Regime Transition in Latin America* (Pittsburgh: University of Pittsburgh Press, 1987), 256–57; Catherine M. Conaghan and Rosario Espinal, "Unlikely Transitions to Uncertain Regimes? Democracy without Compromise in the Dominican Republic and Ecuador," *Journal of Latin American Studies* 22 (October 1990), 555; Jonathan Hartlyn, "Crisis-Ridden Elections (Again) in the Dominican Republic: Neopatrimonialism, Presidentialism, and Weak Electoral Oversight," *Journal of Interamerican Studies and World Affairs* 36 (Winter 1994), 93–96; Terry Lynn Karl, "The Hybrid Regimes of Central America," *Journal of Democracy* 6 (Summer 1995); and Francisco Weffort, *Qual democracia?* (São Paulo: Companhia das Letras, 1992), 89–90.

27. Bagley, "Colombia: National Front and Economic Development," in Robert Wesson, ed., *Politics, Policies, and Economic Development in Latin America* (Stanford, Calif: Hoover Institution Press, 1984), 125–27.

28. See Giovanni Sartori, "Guidelines for Concept Analysis," in Sartori, ed., *Social Science Concepts: A Systematic Analysis* (Beverly Hills, Calif.: Sage Publications, 1984), 81; and Irving M. Copi and Carl Cohen, *Introduction to Logic,* 9th ed. (New York: Macmillan, 1994), 173–75. In *Social Science Concepts* (p. 42), Sartori also uses this as a verb, as in "to precise" a definition.

29. J. Samuel Valenzuela, "Democratic Consolidation in Post-Transitional Settings: Notion, Process, and Facilitating Conditions," in Scott Mainwaring, Guillermo O'Donnell, and J. Samuel Valenzuela, eds., *Issues in Democratic Consolidation: The New South American Democracies in Comparative Perspective* (Notre Dame, Ind.: University of Notre Dame Press, 1992), 70.

30. Karl (fn. 13), 2; Valenzuela (fn. 29); and Brian Loveman, "'Protected Democracies' and Military Guardianship: Political Transitions in Latin

America, 1979–1993," *Journal of Interamerican Studies and World Affairs* 36 (Summer 1994). See also Humberto Rubin, "One Step Away from Democracy" *Journal of Democracy* 1 (Fall 1990).

31. Rhoda Rabkin, "The Aylwin Government and 'Tutelary' Democracy: A Concept in Search of a Case?" *Journal of Interamerican Studies and World Affairs* 34 (Winter 1992–93), 165.

32. On the problem of unsettling the semantic field, see Sartori (fn. 28), 51–54.

33. Jennifer Whiting, personal communication, suggested this term.

34. See again references in note 10.

35. For a reminder of how important vivid labels can be, one need only look at the impressive evolution of game theory, with its codification of different patterns of political interaction designated by such labels as "prisoners' dilemma,"

"chicken," "stag hunt," "slippery slope," and "battle of the sexes."

36. Juan J. Linz, "An Authoritarian Regime: Spain," in Erik Allardt and Yrjö Littunen, eds., *Cleavages, Ideologies and Party Systems: Contributions to Comparative Political Sociology*, Transactions of the Westermarck Society, vol. 10 (Helsinki: Academic Bookstore, 1964); Dahl (fn. 3); Guillermo O'Donnell, *Modernization and Bureaucratic-Authoritarianism: Studies in South American Politics*, Institute of International Studies, Politics of Modernization Series no. 9 (Berkeley: University of California, 1973); Philippe C. Schmitter, "Still the Century of Corporatism?" *Review of Politics* 36 (January 1974); and Arend Lijphart, *Democracy in Plural Societies: A Comparative Exploration* (New Haven: Yale University Press, 1977).

CHAPTER 2

THEORIES, HYPOTHESES, AND EVIDENCE

In Chapter 1, we read about asking and answering good questions, as well as constructing and using good concepts. Those are often considered the fundamental building blocks of comparative political analysis. But how does comparative politics use the scientific method to answer its questions? This second chapter includes readings that cast light on this question.

The readings move from the more general to the more specific. We begin with a classic work by the philosopher Karl Popper on the logic of hypothesis testing (or what he calls the method of "conjectures and refutations"). If Popper is right, these arguments apply to hypothesis testing in general across the sciences, including social science. We then turn to a contemporary classic by three social scientists (Gary King, Robert Keohane, and Sidney Verba), *Designing Social Inquiry*, which makes a distinctive argument about a common logic across different types of social science analysis. If they are right, both mathematically oriented researchers that use many cases and qualitatively oriented researchers with their in-depth studies of one case or several cases are doing something logically similar when they try to test their hypotheses: they are using empirical evidence to draw "causal inferences." This is followed by a recent piece on comparative-historical analysis (by James Mahoney and Celso Villegas), one that gets close to the heart of the main type of comparative political analysis, about which you will read in later sections of this book.

Paying attention to the logic of using comparisons to test hypotheses is important. Indeed, this is what this discipline is all about. Comparative politics, above all, is a method. The readings in this chapter should be useful to you independent of the sorts of comparative political science questions you want to understand. In other words, they are equally relevant to questions about economic development, about democracy, about nationalism, or about institutional design, among many other topics we might study.

2.1 OBJECTIVE KNOWLEDGE
An Evolutionary Approach

In this excerpt, the philosopher of science Karl Popper provides a concise articulation of his highly influential conception of how science progresses. Many people think that science advances by testing hypotheses and proving them correct. According to Popper, this is naive. Although we can never be sure that our theories and hypotheses are true, we can try our best to prove them *wrong*. If we are unable to prove them wrong despite our best efforts, we can draw the conclusion that they are *probably* true: the notion that science achieves absolute certainty is a myth. Although Popper discusses *all* sciences, as you read, consider how this excerpt applies to comparative politics in particular.

I have so often described what I regard as the self-correcting method by which science proceeds that I can be very brief here: *The method of science is the method of bold conjectures and ingenious and severe attempts to refute them.*

A bold conjecture is a theory with a great content—greater at any rate than the theory which, we are hoping, will be superseded by it.

That our conjectures should be bold follows immediately from what I have said about the aim of science and the approach to truth: boldness, or great content, is linked with great truth content; for this reason, falsity content can at first be ignored.

But an increase in truth content is in itself not sufficient to *guarantee* an increase in verisimilitude; since increase in content is a purely logical affair, and since increase in truth content goes with increase in content, the only field left for scientific debate—and especially to empirical tests—is whether or not the falsity content has also increased. Thus our competitive search for verisimilitude turns, especially from the empirical point of view, into a competitive comparison of falsity contents (a fact which some people regard as a paradox). It seems as if it holds in science also that (as Winston Churchill once put it) wars are never won but always lost.

We can never make absolutely certain that our theory is not lost. All we can do is to search for the falsity content of our best theory. We do so by trying to refute our theory; that is, by trying to test it severely in the light of all our objective knowledge and all our ingenuity. It is, of course, always possible that the theory may be false even if it passes all these tests; this is allowed for by our search for verisimilitude. *But if it passes all these tests then we may have good reason to conjecture that our theory, which as we know has a greater truth content than its predecessor, may have no greater falsity content. And if we fail to refute the new theory, especially in fields in which its predecessor has been refuted, then we can claim this as one of the objective reasons for the conjecture that the new theory is a better approximation to truth than the old theory.*

CRITICAL DISCUSSION, RATIONAL PREFERENCE, AND THE PROBLEM OF THE ANALYTICITY OF OUR CHOICES AND PREDICTIONS

Seen in this way, the testing of scientific theories is part of their critical discussion; or, as we may say, it is part of their rational discussion, for in this context

Popper, Karl. 1972. *Objective Knowledge: An Evolutionary Approach.* Oxford: Clarendon Press

I know no better synonym for "rational" than "critical." The critical discussion can never establish sufficient reason to claim that a theory is true; it can never "justify" our claim to knowledge. But the critical discussion can, if we are lucky, establish sufficient reasons for the following claim:

"This theory seems at present, in the light of a thorough critical discussion and of severe and ingenious testing, by far the *best* (the strongest, the best tested); and so it seems the one nearest to truth among the competing theories."

To put it in a nutshell: we can never rationally justify a theory—that is, a claim to know its truth—but we can, if we are lucky, rationally justify a preference for one theory out of a set of competing theories, for the time being; that is, with respect to the present state of the discussion. And our justification, though not a claim that the theory is true, can be the claim that there is every indication at this stage of the discussion that the theory is *a better approximation to the truth* than any competing theory so far proposed.

Let us now consider two competing hypotheses h_1 and h_2. Let us abbreviate by d_t some description of the state of the discussion of these hypotheses at the time t, including of course the discussion of relevant experimental and other observational results. Let us denote by

(1) $c(h_1, d_t) < c(h_2, d_t)$

the statement that the *degree of corroboration* of h_1 in the light of the discussion d_t is inferior to that of h_2. And let us ask what kind of assertion (1) is.

In actual fact (1) will be a somewhat uncertain assertion, if for no other reason than that $c(h_1, d_t)$ changes with the time t, and *can* change as fast as thought. In many cases, the truth or falsity of (1) will be just a matter of opinion.

But let us assume "ideal" circumstances. Let us assume a prolonged discussion which has led to stable results, and especially to agreement on all the evidential components, and let us assume that there is no change of opinion with t for some considerable period.

Under such circumstances we can see that, while the evidential elements of d_t are of course empirical, the statement (1) can be, provided d_t is sufficiently explicit, *logical* or (unless you dislike the term) "*analytic*."

This is particularly clear if $c(h_1, d_t)$ should be negative, because the agreement of the discussion at time t is that the evidence refutes h_1, while $c(h_2, d_t)$ is positive, because the evidence supports h_2. Example: take h_1 to be Kepler's theory, and h_2 to be Einstein's theory. Kepler's theory may be agreed at time t to be refuted (because of the Newtonian perturbations), and Einstein's theory may be agreed at time t to be supported by the evidence. If d_t is sufficiently explicit to entail all this, then

(1) $c(h_1, d_t) < c(h_2, d_t)$

amounts to the statement that some unspecified negative number is smaller than some unspecified positive number, and this is the kind of statement which may be described as "logical" or "analytic."

Of course, there will be other cases; for example, if "d_t" is merely a name like "the state of the discussion on 12 May 1910." But just as one would say that the result of the comparison of two known magnitudes was analytic, so we can say that the result of the comparison of two degrees of corroboration, if sufficiently well known, will be analytic.

But only if the result of the comparison is sufficiently well known can it be said to be the basis of a rational preference; that is, only if (1) holds can we say that h_2 is rationally preferable to h_1.

Let us see further what will happen if h_2 in the sense explained is *rationally preferable* to h_1: we shall base our theoretical predictions as well as the practical decisions which make use of them upon h_2 rather than upon h_1.

All this seems to me straightforward and rather trivial. But it has been criticized for the following reasons.

If (1) is analytic, then the decision to prefer h_2 to h_1 is also analytic, and therefore *no new synthetic predictions* can come out of the preference for h_2 over h_1.

I am not quite certain, but the following seems to me to sum up the criticism which was first advanced by Professor Salmon against my theory of corroboration: either all the steps described are analytic—then there can be no synthetic scientific predictions; or there are synthetic scientific predictions—then some steps cannot be analytic, but must be genuinely synthetic or ampliative, and therefore inductive.

I shall try to show that the argument is invalid as a criticism of my views, h_2 is, as is generally admitted, synthetic, and *all* (non-tautological) *predictions* are derived from h_2 rather than from the inequality (1). This is enough to answer the criticism. The question why we prefer h_2 over h_1 is to be answered by reference to d_t, which, if sufficiently specific, is also non-analytic.

The motives which led to our choice of h_2 cannot alter the synthetic character of h_2. The motives—in contrast to ordinary psychological motives—are *rationally justifiable preferences*. This is why logic and analytic propositions play a role in them. If you like, you can call the motives "analytic." But these analytic *motives for choosing* h_2 never make h_2 *true*, to say nothing of "analytic"; they are at best logically inconclusive reasons for *conjecturing* that it is the most truthlike of the hypotheses competing at the time t.

SCIENCE: THE GROWTH OF KNOWLEDGE THROUGH CRITICISM AND INVENTIVENESS

I see in science one of the greatest creations of the human mind. It is a step comparable to the emergence of a descriptive and argumentative language, or to the invention of writing. It is a step at which our explanatory myths become open to conscious and consistent criticism and at which we are challenged to invent new myths. (It is comparable to the conjectural step in the early days of the genesis of life when types of mutability became an object of evolution through elimination.)

Long before criticism there was growth of knowledge—of knowledge incorporated in the genetic code. Language allows the creation and mutation of explanatory myths, and this is further helped by written language. But it is only science which replaces the elimination of error in the violent struggle for life by non-violent rational criticism.

GARY KING, ROBERT KEOHANE, AND SIDNEY VERBA

2.2 DESIGNING SOCIAL INQUIRY
Scientific Inference in Qualitative Research

The following is an excerpt from an important book on the theory and methodology of social science by Gary King, Robert Keohane, and Sidney Verba. The book, which has been a staple of the training of graduate students in political science and related fields since the 1990s, is often referred to as KKV (after the last names of the three authors). The book is famous for its central argument that quantitative (that is, statistical) and qualitative (that is, descriptive/narrative) approaches, rather than being two completely different ways to do social science, are actually based on a single logic: "causal inference." They believe that although social science indeed tries to answer "why" questions as discussed in the previous section, causes as such are not *directly* observable. For example, a candidate may give a certain reason in deciding to run for office, but we cannot really get inside her head to observe whether that is the true cause behind her decision (nor can we even be sure that she really knows all the causes of her action). This presents challenges for causal inference. At the level of large-scale social processes, we see something similar: for example, economic development is correlated with democracy. We can see this using statistics. However, we cannot directly see whether one is causing the other through these same statistics. Instead, we must try to think of ways of drawing inferences about causality. For example, perhaps we think that economic development causes democracy because it creates a middle class, as a number of scholars have argued: we can search for data that would allow us to see whether the growth of a middle class tends to "mediate" between development and democratization. Do you think that KKV privileges the logic of quantitative research at the expense of qualitative methods?

THE *SCIENCE* IN SOCIAL SCIENCE

INTRODUCTION

Two Styles of Research, One Logic of Inference

Our main goal is to connect the traditions of what are conventionally denoted "quantitative" and "qualitative" research by applying a unified logic of inference to both. The two traditions appear quite different; indeed they sometimes seem to be at war. Our view is that these differences are mainly ones of style and specific technique. The same underlying logic provides the framework for each research approach. This logic tends to be explicated and formalized clearly in discussions of quantitative research methods. But the same logic of inference underlies the best qualitative research, and all qualitative and quantitative researchers would benefit by more explicit attention to this logic in the course of designing research.

The *styles* of quantitative and qualitative research are very different. Quantitative research uses numbers and statistical methods. It tends to be based on numerical measurements of specific aspects of phenomena; it abstracts from particular instances to seek general description or to test causal hypotheses; it seeks measurements and analyses that are easily replicable by other researchers.

King, Gary, Robert Keohane, and Sidney Verba. 1994. *Designing Social Inquiry: Scientific Inference in Qualitative Research.* Princeton: Princeton University Press.

Qualitative research, in contrast, covers a wide range of approaches, but by definition, none of these approaches relies on numerical measurements. Such work has tended to focus on one or a small number of cases, to use intensive interviews or depth analysis of historical materials, to be discursive in method, and to be concerned with a rounded or comprehensive account of some event or unit. Even though they have a small number of cases, qualitative researchers generally unearth enormous amounts of information from their studies. Sometimes this kind of work in the social sciences is linked with area or case studies where the focus is on a particular event, decision, institution, location, issue, or piece of legislation. As is also the case with quantitative research, the instance is often important in its own right: a major change in a nation, an election, a major decision, or a world crisis. Why did the East German regime collapse so suddenly in 1989? More generally, why did almost all the communist regimes of Eastern Europe collapse in 1989? Sometimes, but certainly not always, the event may be chosen as an exemplar of a particular type of event, such as a political revolution or the decision of a particular community to reject a waste disposal site. Sometimes this kind of work is linked to area studies where the focus is on the history and culture of a particular part of the world. The particular place or event is analyzed closely and in full detail.

A major purpose of this book is to show that the differences between the quantitative and qualitative traditions are only stylistic and are methodologically and substantively unimportant. All good research can be understood—indeed, is best understood—to derive from the same underlying logic of inference. Both quantitative and qualitative research can be systematic and scientific. Historical research can be analytical, seeking to evaluate alternative explanations through a process of valid causal inference. History, or historical sociology, is not incompatible with social science (Skocpol 1984: 374–86).

Breaking down these barriers requires that we begin by questioning the very concept of "qualitative" research. We have used the term in our title to signal our subject matter, not to imply that "qualitative" research is fundamentally different from "quantitative" research, except in style.

Most research does not fit clearly into one category or the other. The best often combines features of each. In the same research project, some data may be collected that is amenable to statistical analysis, while other equally significant information is not. Patterns and trends in social, political, or economic behavior are more readily subjected to quantitative analysis than is the flow of ideas among people or the difference made by exceptional individual leadership. If we are to understand the rapidly changing social world, we will need to include information that cannot be easily quantified as well as that which can. Furthermore, all social science requires comparison, which entails judgments of which phenomena are "more" or "less" alike in degree (i.e., quantitative differences) or in kind (i.e., qualitative differences).

Defining Scientific Research in the Social Sciences

Our definition of "scientific research" is an ideal to which any actual quantitative or qualitative research, even the most careful, is only an approximation. Yet, we need a definition of good research, for which we use the word "scientific" as our descriptor.[1] This word comes with many connotations that are unwarranted or inappropriate or downright incendiary for some qualitative researchers. Hence, we provide an explicit definition here. As should be clear, we do not regard quantitative research to be any more scientific than qualitative research. Good research, that is, scientific research, can be quantitative or qualitative in style. In design, however, scientific research has the following four characteristics:

1. **The goal is inference.** Scientific research is designed to make descriptive or explanatory *inferences* on the basis of empirical information about the world. Careful descriptions of specific phenomena are often indispensable to scientific research, but the accumulation of facts alone is not sufficient. Facts can be collected (by qualitative or quantitative researchers) more or less systematically, and the former is obviously better than the latter, but our particular definition of science requires the additional step of attempting to infer beyond the immediate data to something broader that is not directly observed. That

something may involve *descriptive inference*—using observations from the world to learn about other unobserved facts. Or that something may involve *causal inference*—learning about causal effects from the data observed. The domain of inference can be restricted in space and time—voting behavior in American elections since 1960, social movements in Eastern Europe since 1989—or it can be extensive—human behavior since the invention of agriculture. In either case, the key distinguishing mark of scientific research is the goal of making inferences that go beyond the particular observations collected.

2. **The procedures are public.** Scientific research uses explicit, codified, and *public* methods to generate and analyze data whose reliability can therefore be assessed. Much social research in the qualitative style follows fewer precise rules of research procedure or of inference. As Robert K. Merton ([1949] 1968:71–72) put it, "The sociological analysis of qualitative data often resides in a private world of penetrating but unfathomable insights and ineffable understandings. . . . [However,] science . . . is public, not private." Merton's statement is not true of all qualitative researchers (and it is unfortunately still true of some quantitative analysts), but many proceed as if they had no method—sometimes as if the use of explicit methods would diminish their creativity. Nevertheless they cannot help but use some method. Somehow they observe phenomena, ask questions, infer information about the world from these observations, and make inferences about cause and effect. If the method and logic of a researcher's observations and inferences are left implicit, the scholarly community has no way of judging the validity of what was done. We cannot evaluate the principles of selection that were used to record observations, the ways in which observations were processed, and the logic by which conclusions were drawn. We cannot learn from their methods or replicate their results. Such research is not a *public* act. Whether or not it makes good reading, it is not a contribution to social science.

All methods—whether explicit or not—have limitations. The advantage of explicitness is that those limitations can be understood and, if possible, addressed. In addition, the methods can be taught and shared. This process allows research results to be compared across separate researchers and research projects, studies to be replicated, and scholars to learn.

3. **The conclusions are uncertain.** By definition, inference is an imperfect process. Its goal is to use quantitative or qualitative data to learn about the world that produced them. Reaching perfectly certain conclusions from uncertain data is obviously impossible. Indeed, uncertainty is a central aspect of all research and all knowledge about the world. Without a reasonable estimate of uncertainty, a description of the real world or an inference about a causal effect in the real world is uninterpretable. A researcher who fails to face the issue of uncertainty directly is either asserting that he or she knows everything perfectly or that he or she has no idea how certain or uncertain the results are. Either way, inferences without uncertainty estimates are not science as we define it.

4. **The content is the method.** Finally, scientific research adheres to a set of rules of inference on which its validity depends. Explicating the most important rules is a major task of this book.[2] The content of "science" is primarily the methods and rules, not the subject matter, since we can use these methods to study virtually anything. This point was recognized over a century ago when Karl Pearson (1892: 16) explained that "the field of science is unlimited; its material is endless; every group of natural phenomena, every phase of social life, every stage of past or present development is material for science. The unity of all science consists alone in its method, not in its material."

These four features of science have a further implication: science at its best is a *social enterprise*. Every researcher or team of researchers labors under limitations of knowledge and insight, and mistakes are unavoidable, yet such errors will likely be pointed out by others. Understanding the social character of science can be liberating since it means that our work need not be beyond criticism to make an important contribution—whether to the description of a problem or its conceptualization, to theory or to the evaluation of theory. As long as our work explicitly addresses (or attempts to redirect) the concerns of the community of scholars and uses public methods to arrive at inferences that are consistent with rules of science and the information at our disposal, it is likely to make a contribution. And the contribution of even a minor article is greater than that of the "great work" that stays forever in a desk drawer or within the confines of a computer.

MAJOR COMPONENTS OF RESEARCH DESIGN

Social science research at its best is a creative process of insight and discovery taking place within a well-established structure of scientific inquiry. The first-rate social scientist does not regard a research design as a blueprint for a mechanical process of data-gathering and evaluation. To the contrary, the scholar must have the flexibility of mind to overturn old ways of looking at the world, to ask new questions, to revise research designs appropriately, and then to collect more data of a different type than originally intended. However, if the researcher's findings are to be valid and accepted by scholars in this field, all these revisions and reconsiderations must take place according to explicit procedures consistent with the rules of inference. A dynamic process of inquiry occurs within a stable structure of rules.

Social scientists often begin research with a considered design, collect some data, and draw conclusions. But this process is rarely a smooth one and is not always best done in this order: conclusions rarely follow easily from a research design and data collected in accordance with it. Once an investigator has collected data as provided by a research design, he or she will often find an imperfect fit among the main research questions, the theory and the data at hand. At this stage, researchers often become discouraged. They mistakenly believe that other social scientists find close, immediate fits between data and research. This perception is due to the fact that investigators often take down the scaffolding after putting up their intellectual buildings, leaving little trace of the agony and uncertainty of construction. Thus the process of inquiry seems more mechanical and cut-and-dried than it actually is.

Some of our advice is directed toward researchers who are trying to make connections between theory and data. At times, they can design more appropriate data-collection procedures in order to evaluate a theory better; at other times, they can use the data they have and recast a theoretical question (or even pose an entirely different question that was not originally foreseen) to produce a more important research project. The research, if it adheres to rules of inference, will still be scientific and produce reliable inferences about the world.

Wherever possible, researchers should also improve their research designs before conducting any field research. However, data has a way of disciplining thought. It is extremely common to find that the best research design falls apart when the very first observations are collected—it is not that the theory is wrong but that the data are not suited to answering the questions originally posed. Understanding from the outset what can and what cannot be done at this later stage can help the researcher anticipate at least some of the problems when first designing the research.

Improving Theory

A social science theory is a reasoned and precise speculation about the answer to a research question, including a statement about why the proposed answer is correct. Theories usually imply several more specific descriptive or causal hypotheses. A theory must be consistent with prior evidence about a research question. "A theory that ignores existing evidence is an oxymoron. If we had the equivalent of 'truth in advertising' legislation, such an oxymoron should not be called a theory" (Lieberson 1992:4; see also Woods and Walton 1982).

The development of a theory is often presented as the first step of research. It sometimes comes first in practice, but it need not. In fact, we cannot develop a theory without knowledge of prior work on the subject and the collection of some data, since even the research question would be unknown. Nevertheless, despite whatever amount of data has already been collected, there are some general ways to evaluate and improve the usefulness of a theory. We briefly introduce each of these here but save a more detailed discussion for later chapters.

First, choose theories that could be wrong. Indeed, vastly more is learned from theories that *are* wrong than from theories that are stated so broadly that they could not be wrong even in principle.[3] We need to be able to give a direct answer to the question: What evidence would convince us that we are wrong?[4] If there is no answer to this question, then we do not have a theory.

Second, to make sure a theory is falsifiable, choose one that is capable of generating as many *observable implications* as possible. This choice will allow more tests of the theory with more data and a greater variety of data, will put the theory at risk of being falsified more times, and will make it possible to collect data so as to build strong evidence for the theory.

Third, in designing theories, be as concrete as possible. Vaguely stated theories and hypotheses serve no purpose but to obfuscate. Theories that are stated precisely and make specific predictions can be shown more easily to be wrong and are therefore better.

Moreover, if we are wrong, we need not stop writing after admitting defeat. We may add a section to our article or a chapter to our book about future empirical research and current theoretical speculation. In this context, we have considerably more freedom. We may suggest additional conditions that might be plausibly attached to our theory, if we believe they might solve the problem, propose a modification of another existing theory or propose a range of entirely different theories. In this situation, we cannot conclude anything with a great deal of certainty (except perhaps that the theory we stated at the outset is wrong), but we do have the luxury of inventing new research designs or data-collection projects that could be used to decide whether our speculations are correct. These can be very valuable, especially in suggesting areas where future researchers can look.

Thinking Like a Social Scientist: Skepticism and Rival Hypotheses

The uncertainty of causal inferences means that good social scientists do not easily accept them. When told A causes B, someone who "thinks like a social scientist" asks whether that connection is a true causal one. It is easy to ask such questions about the research of others, but it is more important to ask them about our own research. There are many reasons why we might be skeptical of a causal account, plausible though it may sound at first glance. We read in the newspaper that the Japanese eat less red meat and have fewer heart attacks than Americans. This observation alone is interesting. In addition, the explanation—too much steak leads to the high rate of heart disease in the United States—is plausible. The skeptical social scientist asks about the accuracy of the data (how do we know about eating habits? what sample was used? are heart attacks classified similarly in Japan and the United States so that we are comparing similar phenomena?). Assuming that the data are accurate, what else might explain the effects: Are there other variables (other dietary differences, genetic features, life-style characteristics) that might explain the result? Might we have inadvertently reversed cause and effect? It is hard to imagine how not having a heart attack might cause one to eat less red meat but it is possible. Perhaps people lose their appetite for hamburgers and steak late in life. If this were the case, those who did not have a heart attack (for whatever reason) would live longer and eat less meat. This fact would produce the same relationship that led the researchers to conclude that meat was the culprit in heart attacks.

It is not our purpose to call such medical studies into question. Rather we wish merely to illustrate how social scientists approach the issue of causal inference: with skepticism and a concern for alternative explanations that may have been overlooked. Causal inference thus becomes a *process* whereby each conclusion becomes the occasion for further research to refine and test it. Through successive approximations we try to come closer and closer to accurate causal inference.

NOTES

1. We reject the concept, or at least the word, "quasi-experiment." Either a research design involves investigator control over the observations and values of the key causal variables (in which case it is an experiment) or it does not (in which case it is nonexperimental research). Both

experimental and nonexperimental research have their advantages and drawbacks: one is not better in all research situations than the other.

2. Although we do cover the vast majority of the important rules of scientific inference, they are not complete. Indeed, most philosophers agree that a complete, exhaustive inductive logic is impossible, even in principle.

3. This is the principle of falsifiability (Popper 1968). It is an issue on which there are varied positions in the philosophy of science. However, very few of them disagree with the principle that theories should be stated clearly enough so that they could be wrong.

4. This is probably the most commonly asked question at job interviews in our department and many others.

REFERENCES

Lieberson, Stanley. 1992. "Einstein, Renoir, and Greeley: Some Thoughts about Evidence in Sociology." *American Sociological Review* 56 (February): 1–15.

Merton, Robert K. [1949] 1968. *Social Theory and Social Structure.* Reprint. New York: Free Press.

Pearson, Karl. 1892. *The Grammar of Science.* London: J. M. Dent and Sons, Ltd.

Popper, Karl R. 1968. *The Logic of Scientific Discovery.* New York: Harper and Row.

Skocpol, Theda. 1984. "Emerging Agendas and Recurrent Strategies in Historical Sociology." In Theda Skocpol, ed. *Vision and Method in Historical Sociology.* New York: Cambridge University Press.

Woods, John, and Douglas Walton. 1982. *Argument: The Logic of the Fallacies.* New York: McGraw-Hill Ryerson Ltd.

JAMES MAHONEY AND CELSO M. VILLEGAS

2.3 HISTORICAL ENQUIRY
AND COMPARATIVE POLITICS

Whereas the previous piece (by King, Keohane, and Verba) provides a general overview of the idea of causal inference and how it might be operative in social science, Mahoney and Villegas delve into the more specific issues involved in comparative-historical analysis. This type of analysis—which is foundational in comparative politics—is based on the recognition that social and political phenomena are processes that unfold in time. As such, we cannot just study them "in the present," but must take the greater historical context into consideration. To be clear, this means that *most* questions of comparative politics are historical. This seems obvious in some cases (for example, how and why did the Bourbon and Pombaline Reforms in 18th-century Latin America impact subsequent political developments differently in the various colonies?), but it is equally true of more "contemporary cases" (for example, why are some current Latin American regimes more left leaning than others?). Mahoney and Villegas describe current trends in historically oriented comparative politics and highlight the differences between "within-case" and "cross-case" analysis, as well as different ways of explaining difference over time. Be particularly attentive to their discussion of the important concept of "path dependence."

Historical enquiry has always been central to the field of comparative politics. Scholars from Alexis de Tocqueville and Max Weber to Gabriel Almond and Seymour Martin Lipset to Theda Skocpol and Margaret Levi have explained political dynamics by comparing the historical trajectories of two or more cases. In doing so, they have suggested that the roots of major political outcomes often rest most fundamentally with causal processes found well in the past. Moreover, they have maintained that to elucidate these causal processes one must look closely at the unfolding of events over substantial periods of time.

Comparative analysts who engage in historical enquiry have explored topics almost as varied as those that characterize contemporary political science. And they have developed explanations that cross the full gamut of theoretical orientations in the field. One cannot therefore delimit historical analysis by subject matter or theoretical orientation. Nevertheless, comparativists who practice historical analysis do employ a distinctive approach to asking and answering questions. Most basically, these analysts ask questions about the causes of major outcomes in particular cases. The goal of their analyses then becomes explaining adequately the specific historical outcomes in each and every case that falls within their argument's scope (Mahoney and Rueschemeyer 2003). By adopting this approach, historical researchers differ from cross-national statistical analysts, who are concerned with generalizing about average causal effects for large populations and who do not ordinarily seek to explain specific outcomes in particular cases. Whereas a cross-national statistical analyst might ask about the average causal effect of development on democracy for a large population of cases, a historical researcher will ask about the causal factors that make possible or combine to produce democracy in

Mahoney, James and Celso Villegas. 2007. "Historical Enquiry and Comparative Politics," in Carles Boix and Susan Stokes, eds., *Oxford Handbook of Comparative Politics*, pp. 73–89. New York: Oxford University Press.

one or more particular cases (Mahoney and Goertz 2006). Or, to cite actual research, historical analysts ask about the causes of contrasting state-regime complexes in specific early modern European cases (Downing 1992; Ertman 1997; Tilly 1990); the factors that wrought different kinds of welfare states in the advanced capitalist countries (Esping-Andersen 1990; Hicks 1999; Huber and Stephens 2001); the origins of social revolution in certain types of historical and contemporary countries (Foran 2005; Goldstone 1991; Skocpol 1979); and the sources of democracy and dictatorship in regions such as Central America (Mahoney 2001; Paige 1997; Yashar 1997). In each of these research areas, the goal of analysis is to explain specific outcomes of interest in the particular sets of cases under investigation.[1]

This orientation to asking and answering questions is associated with at least three other methodological traits which also help us to recognize historical research as a singular approach within comparative politics. First, historical analysts employ their own distinctive tools of causal analysis. Some of these tools involve techniques for analyzing necessary and/or sufficient causes, whereas others entail procedures for assessing hypotheses through within-case analysis. Both kinds of techniques contrast in major ways with statistical methods (Brady and Collier 2004; George and Bennett 2005; Mahoney 2004; Mahoney and Goertz 2006). Second, historical analysts are centrally concerned with the temporal dimensions of political explanation. To account for the occurrence of specific outcomes, they attribute great causal weight to the duration, pace, and timing of events (Pierson 2004; Thelen 2003). Finally, historical researchers develop a deep understanding of their major cases and establish a strong background in the relevant historiography. This kind of case expertise is essential for the successful explanation of particular outcomes in specific cases, and it is achieved through the mastery of secondary and/or primary source material (Skocpol 1984; Ragin 1987). Here we explore each of these three traits in turn.

1 METHODS OF CAUSAL ANALYSIS

1.1 CROSS-CASE ANALYSIS

Early discussions of cross-case analysis and hypothesis testing in historical research usually focused on Mill's methods of agreement and difference (e.g., Skocpol

and Somers 1980) and Przeworski and Teune's (1970) most similar and most different research designs. In more recent periods, however, the methodology of necessary and sufficient conditions, Boolean algebra, and fuzzy-set logic have superseded earlier formulations (e.g., Goertz and Starr 2003; Ragin 1987, 2000).

Mill's methods of agreement and difference are tools for eliminating necessary and sufficient causes (see Dion 1998; George and Bennett 2005; Mahoney 1999). The method of agreement is used to eliminate potential *necessary* causes, whereas the method of difference is used to eliminate potential *sufficient* causes. The methods usually operate deterministically, such that a single deviation from a hypothesized pattern of necessary or sufficient causation is enough to conclude that a given factor is not (by itself) necessary or sufficient for the outcome of interest. While this deterministic approach is controversial,[2] methodologists agree that it is essential to the ability of the methods of agreement and difference to systematically eliminate rival hypotheses when only a small number of cases are selected.

Methods designed to test necessary and/or sufficient causes need not be deterministic, however. One can easily evaluate causes that are necessary or sufficient at some quantitative benchmark, such as necessary or sufficient 90 percent of the time (e.g., Braumoeller and Goertz 2000; Dion 1998; Ragin 2000). And if a modest number of cases is selected (e.g., N = 15), scholars can achieve standard levels of statistical confidence for their findings. Likewise, there is no reason why one needs to use dichotomous variables when testing hypotheses about necessary or sufficient causation. For example, necessary causation can mean that the absence of a particular range of values on a continuously coded independent variable will always (or usually) be associated with the absence of a particular range of values on a continuously coded dependent variable.

In comparative politics, a widely used method of cross-case analysis is typological theory (George and Bennett 2005). With this technique, one treats the dimensions of a typology as independent variables; different values on the dimensions reflect alternative values on independent variables. The categories or "types" in the cells of the typology represent the values on the dependent variable. The dimensions of the typology are thus hypothesized to be jointly (not individually) sufficient for particular values on the dependent variable. There are numerous examples of works in comparative politics that implicitly or explicitly employ this kind of typological theory— Downing's (1992) study of political regimes in Europe, Goodwin's (2001) work on revolutions, and Jones-Luong's (2002) analysis of party and electoral system dynamics, for example.

Other methods evaluate necessary and sufficient causes with more formal techniques. Perhaps the best known of these is Boolean algebra (Ragin 1987), which is used to test whether combinations of dichotomous variables are jointly sufficient for an outcome. Because several different combinations of factors may each be causally sufficient, this method allows for multiple paths to the same outcome, or what is sometimes called equifinality. More recently, Ragin (2000) has introduced fuzzy-set analysis to assess continuously coded variables within a probabilistic Boolean framework. Dozens of comparative studies have now used Ragin's techniques for testing hypotheses about necessary and sufficient causes (see the citations at www.compasss.org/).

To conclude, cross-case analysis usually involves the assessment of hypotheses about necessary and/or sufficient causation, and a whole class of methodologies exists for testing these kinds of hypotheses. By contrast, as multiple methodologists (both qualitative and quantitative) have pointed out, mainstream statistical techniques are not designed for the analysis of necessary and sufficient causes (Braumoeller 2003; Goertz and Starr 2003; but see Clark, Gilligan, and Golder 2006).

1.2 WITHIN-CASE ANALYSIS

Writings on within-case analysis have a distinguished pedigree in the field of qualitative methods (e.g., Barton and Lazarsfeld 1969; Campbell 1975; George and McKeown 1985). In recent years, there has been considerable effort to formally codify the specific procedures entailed in different modes of within-case analysis (e.g., George and Bennett 2005; Brady and Collier 2004; Mahoney 1999). We briefly discuss some of these procedures.

First, some historical researchers use insights from within their cases to locate the intervening mechanisms linking a hypothesized explanatory variable to an outcome. These scholars follow methodological writings that suggest that causal analysis not only involves establishing an association between explanatory variables and an outcome variable, but also entails identifying the intervening mechanisms that link explanatory variables with the outcome variable (Hedstrom and Swedberg 1998; Goldthorpe 2000). Intervening mechanisms are the processes through which an explanatory variable produces a causal effect. The effort to infer causality through the identification of mechanisms can be called "process tracing" (George and McKeown 1985; George and Bennett 2005) and the data thereby generated are "causal-process observations" (Brady and Collier 2004).

Process tracing is often used to help analysts who work with a small number of cases avoid mistaking a spurious correlation for a causal association. Specifically, mechanisms that clearly link a presumed explanatory variable and outcome variable increase one's confidence in the hypothesis. For example, Skocpol's (1979, 170–1) work on the origins of social revolutions employs process tracing to reject the hypothesis that ideologically motivated vanguard movements caused social revolutions. Although ideologically motivated vanguard movements were active in her three cases of social revolution, she contends that they were not responsible for triggering widespread revolts against landlords and states. Rather, the movements were marginal to the central political processes that characterized social revolutions in France, Russia, and China, appearing on the scene only to take advantage of situations they did not create.

Other scholars use process tracing not to eliminate causal factors but to support their own explanations. For example, Collier and Collier (1991) identify mechanisms linking different types of labor incorporation periods with different types of party systems. In their analysis of Colombia and Uruguay, Collier and Collier systematically identify the processes and events through which the incorporation pattern of "electoral mobilization by a traditional party" led to the party system outcome of "electoral stability and social conflict." These processes included: a period in which the party that oversaw incorporation briefly maintained power, the gradual emergence of conservative opposition, a period of intense political polarization, a military coup, and, finally, the creation of party system marked by stable electoral politics and social conflict. Each of these events acts as a mechanism linking labor incorporation with a particular party system outcome. Indeed, although any work can potentially benefit from process tracing, it is an especially important tool for those studies such as Collier and Collier's in which explanatory and outcome variables are separated by long periods of time.

A given hypothesis might suggest specific features of a case besides the main outcome that should be present if the central hypothesis is correct. These features need not be intervening variables. Thus, some historical researchers use within-case analysis not to identify intervening mechanisms, but to evaluate whether certain hypothesized features are in fact present. This is how Marx (1998) proceeds in his comparative study of racial orders in the United States, South Africa, and Brazil. He asserts that where whites were divided, as in the US and South Africa following the Civil War and Boer War, white unity and nationalist loyalty were forged through the construction of systems of racial domination that systematically excluded blacks. Where no major intra-white cleavage developed, as in Brazil, whites did not have to achieve unity through exclusion and thus a much higher degree of racial harmony could develop.

Marx supports this argument using within-case evidence that confirms implicit and explicit predictions about other things that should be true if this argument is valid. For instance, Marx suggests that, if intra-white conflict really is decisive, efforts to enhance black status should produce increased white conflict along the North–South fault line in the US and between British and Afrikaners in South Africa. By contrast, progressive racial reforms should not generate similar intra-white divisions in Brazil. Likewise, if intra-white divisions really are the key, then Marx suggests that we should see evidence that more progressive white factions view political stability as more important than racial equality. His historical narrative then backs up these propositions. Overall, he suggests that it is highly unlikely that these auxiliary facts are accidental; rather, he contends that they are symptoms of a valid main thesis.

2 METHODS OF TEMPORAL ANALYSIS

Historical enquiry in comparative politics is sensitive to temporal processes. Researchers often understand cases as spatial units within which one observes patterns of temporally ordered events, such as sequences, cycles, and abrupt changes. While statistical researchers will sometimes develop hypotheses that consider temporal dimensions, the focus of historical researchers on specific outcomes in particular cases calls central attention to temporality. At the level of particular cases, issues of timing and sequencing often seem paramount in a way that may not be true when one wishes to generalize about averages for large populations using available quantitative data. Hence, when a historical researcher hypothesizes that "X is causally related to Y," it is quite likely that variable X is defined in part by temporal dimensions, such as its duration or its location in time vis-à-vis other variables. In this sense, "history matters" to comparative-historical researchers in part because temporally defined concepts are key variables of analysis. We can examine here three temporal concepts that historical researchers use frequently: path dependence, duration, and conjuncture.

2.1 PATH DEPENDENCE

The concept of path dependence is associated with the effort of researchers to understand the repercussions of early events on subsequent and possibly historically distant outcomes. A quite significant literature in economics, political science, and sociology now exists to codify the various tools of analysis used to study path-dependent sequences (Arthur 1994; David 1985; Goldstone 1998; North 1990; Pierson 2000, 2004; Mahoney 2000; see also Clemens and Cook 1999; Collier and Collier 1991; Thelen 2003). For our purposes, two examples illustrate the breadth of the use of this concept.

Goldstone (1998, 2007) argues that the industrial revolution in England was the result of a path-dependent process. He contends that "there was nothing necessary or inevitable" about England's breakthrough to modern industrialism (1998, 275). Rather, the outcome was a product of a number of small events that happened to come together in eighteenth-century

England. Perhaps most importantly, the industrial revolution depended on the advent of Thomas Newcomen's first steam engine in 1712—it made possible the subsequent creation of more efficient steam engines that dramatically improved the extraction of coal. Efficient coal extraction reduced the price of coal. In turn:

> Cheap coal made possible cheaper iron and steel. Cheap coal plus cheap iron made possible the construction of railways and ships built of iron, fueled by coal, and powered by engines producing steam. Railways and ships made possible mass national and international distribution of metal tools, textiles, and other products that could be more cheaply made with steam-powered metal-reinforced machinery. (1998, 275)

Thus, the sequence of events leading to the industrial revolution ultimately depended on the advent of the first steam engine. Yet, Newcomen did not pursue his invention in order to spur an industrial revolution. Instead, he was trying to devise a means to pump water from deep-shaft coal mines: the steam engine removed water by turning it into vapor. It was necessary to remove water from the mine shafts because the surface coal of the mines had been exhausted, which had led the miners to dig deeper, which had caused the mines to fill with water. And of course the surface coal of the mines was exhausted in the first place because England was exceptionally dependent on coal for heating. Going even further back, as Goldstone does, England was dependent on coal (rather than wood) because of its limited forest area, its cold climate, and its geology, which featured thick seams of coal near the sea.

Orren's (1991) study of *Belated Feudalism* offers a different kind of example of path dependence, one in which path dependence involves the stable reproduction of a particular outcome. Orren calls attention to the remarkable persistence of status-based labor legislation in the United States. From its inception until well into the twentieth century, the United States legally defined all able-bodied individuals without independent wealth as workers who could be subject to criminal charges for not selling their labor in the marketplace. This "law of master and servant" was originally established in feudal England, but it managed to

carry over into the United States, and it then persisted for more than 150 years despite the supposed liberal orientation of American culture.

To explain this specific outcome, Orren emphasizes the key role of American courts in upholding the law. In her view, judges enforced the law because they believed it was legitimate, even though it increasingly clashed with American mores and norms. Specifically, "the judges believed that what was as stake was no less than the moral order of things," and hence upheld the law (Orren 1991, 114). Orren emphasizes that American judges did not follow precedent simply because of personal gain (1991, 90). Likewise, she contends that judges did not simply support legislation on behalf of the interests of economic elites, even though the employment legislation clearly benefited employers (1991, 91). Rather, she argues "that the law of labor relations was on its own historical track, and that it carried protection of business interests along for the ride" (1991, 112).

In both examples of path dependence, Goldstone and Orren identify "critical junctures" where events early in the process have lasting effects, even after those initial causes have disappeared. Scholars using the critical juncture concept emphasize how such events are contingent—that is, they are unpredictable by theory or perhaps truly random (Mahoney 2000; David 1985)—and focus on how these events, at that time, were hardly an indication of the path to follow. The invention of the Newcomen steam engine in England affecting the industrial revolution is a case in point: Newcomen did not intend to begin an industrial revolution, nor was his machine heralded at that time as the harbinger of the tremendous transformation to come, yet it spurred a series of events that led England down an unrepeatable path towards industrialization.

Other scholars have focused on important political choices during critical juncture periods whose institutional implications were unforeseen, but would have significant results in the future. Collier and Collier's (1991) study of labor incorporation provides the iconic example of critical junctures—the means by which political elites managed the introduction of labor into the political sphere had lasting, long-term effects on party dynamics far removed from the initial decision to forcibly exclude labor or incorporate it through populist, traditional, or radical parties. Certainly political elites in Chile and Brazil did not assume that through their repression of labor in the 1930s they would precipitate the political conditions for military coups in 1973 and 1964, respectively.

Goldstone's argument in particular shows how path dependence may involve reaction–counterreaction dynamics, such that an initial event triggers a reaction and thereby logically leads to another quite different event, which triggers its own reaction, and so on, until a particular outcome of interest is reached. Mahoney uses the phrase "reactive sequence" to characterize these "chains of temporally ordered and causally connected events" (2000, 526). The narrative mode of analysis used in historical analysis generally describes sequences characterized by tight causal linkages that are nearly uninterruptible, such that A leads to B, which leads to C, which leads to D, and so on until one arrives at Z, or the logical termination point of the sequence.

By contrast, Orren's argument focuses on a kind of path-dependent sequence in which a particular outcome happens to occur at a critical juncture, and then this outcome is subject to self-reproducing mechanisms, causing it to repeatedly exist across time, even long after its original purposes have ceased. Scholars use the label "self-reproducing" to describe these sequences in which a given outcome is stably reinforced over time (Thelen 2003; Pierson 2004; Mahoney 2000). Self-reproducing sequences are also the norm in work on increasing returns, which models processes in which each step in a particular direction induces further movement in that same direction (Arthur 1994, 1989; Pierson 2000).

In some cases, however, self-reproduction and lock-in capture only part of a path-dependent process; scholars may look to ideas such as institutional layering and conversion to explain why and how certain aspects of institutions persist and why some aspects change. According to Thelen, "institutional survival is often strongly laced with elements of institutional *transformation* to bring institutions in line with changing social, political, and economic conditions" (2003, 211, emphasis in the original). Through institutional layering, actors choose not to remake existing institutional configurations, but instead add new components that bring the institution in alignment with their needs. For example, the Bill of Rights and subsequent amendments to the US constitution altered pre-existing arrangements while leaving the core the same. In addition, institutions initially set up to foster a certain social or political arrangement are often "converted" to suit other purposes. Orren's analysis of the law of master and servant is a good example of this: while the law in its English form fostered feudal ties between landlord and serf, as American judges reinterpreted it, the law was converted to support free labor policy.

2.2 DURATION AND CONJUNCTURAL ANALYSIS

Historical researchers also evoke duration as a key temporal variable by exploring the causes of the length of a given process for a particular outcome (Aminzade 1992, 459). According to Mickey and Pierson, "attending to duration can both help scholars more clearly specify the mechanisms by which independent variables affect outcomes of interest, and can help generate new causal accounts" (2004, 7). Some duration arguments refer to repeated processes over a long time period. For example, Huber and Stephens's (2001) work on welfare states in advanced industrial countries highlights the importance of "electoral success over *an extended period of time*" to the maintenance of long-lasting welfare state institutions (Pierson 2004, 85, emphasis in the original). Other duration arguments explore the importance of slow-moving processes that may take years to unfold. For instance, Tilly's (1990) analysis of state making is centrally concerned with explaining the pace at which modern states were formed in Europe across perhaps centuries of time.

The fact that many sequences of events have a typical or normal duration allows one to speak of processes that are "too short" or "too long" or "just right" (Mickey and Pierson 2004, 15). Compressed processes often lead to significantly different outcomes because they entail a particularly rapid sequence of events. Karl notes that oil booms spur compressed processes of economic and social development. "The restraint inherent in more limited revenues . . . is abruptly removed, both psychologically and in reality" (1997, 66). As a result:

> Policymakers, once torn between their preoccupations with diversity and equity, now think they can do both. The military demands modernized weapons and improved living conditions; capitalists seek credits and subsidies; the middle class calls for increased social spending, labor for higher wages, and the unemployed for the creation of new jobs. (Karl 1997, 65)

Bureaucracies expand uncontrollably and "ultimately contribute to growing budget and trade deficits and foreign debt" (1997, 65). For Karl, oil booms accelerate processes that eventually overwhelm states and produce economic busts.

Historical researchers also often develop hypotheses about the intersection of various causal processes (see Aminzade 1992; Pierson 2004; Zuckerman 1997). If and when two or more processes meet in time and/or space can have a large impact on subsequent outcomes. Conjunctural analysis considers specifically the intersection point of two or more separately determined sequences, or as Pierson puts it, "the linking of discrete elements or dimensions of politics in the passage of time" (2004, 55).

In his classic work *Modernization and Bureaucratic-Authoritarianism*, O'Donnell (1979) notes certain social conditions that gradually came into being and then remained as "constants" throughout subsequent Argentine history. Each such condition worked to "load the dice more and more against an effectively working political system" (1979, 118). By the 1960s, three historical constants came together: political traditions and social processes for national unification, international economic integration, and political mobilization (O'Donnell 1979, 119–31). The conjuncture or coming together of these processes served to limit the political choices available to actors in a way that would not have been true if the sequences did not intersect at this particular time. Ultimately, the conjuncture had the effect of stimulating a determined effort by established sectors "to close any significant political access to a politically activated urban popular sector" (O'Donnell 1979,

131). In turn, this outcome set the stage for the emergence of harsh bureaucratic–authoritarian regimes.

REFERENCES

AMINZADE, R. 1992. Historical sociology and time. *Sociological Methods and Research*, 20: 456–80.

ARTHUR, W. B. 1989. Competing technologies and lock-in by historical events. *Economic Journal*, 99: 116–31.

ARTHUR, W. B. 1994. *Increasing Returns and Path Dependence in the Economy*. Ann Arbor: University of Michigan Press.

BARTON, A. H., and LAZARSFELD, P. 1969. Some functions of qualitative analysis in social research. Pp. 163–205 in *Issues in Participant Observation*, ed. G. J. McCall and J. L. Simmons. Reading, Mass.: Addison-Wesley.

BRADY, H. E., and COLLIER, D. eds. 2004. *Rethinking Social Inquiry: Diverse Tools, Shared Standards*. Lanham, Md.: Rowman & Littlefield.

BRAUMOELLER, B. F. 2003. Causal complexity and the study of politics. *Political Analysis*, 11 (3): 209–33.

BRAUMOELLER, B. F., and GOERTZ, G. 2000. The methodology of necessary conditions. *American Journal of Political Science*, 44 (4): 844–58.

CAMPBELL, D. T. 1975. "Degrees of freedom" and the case study. *Comparative Political Studies*, 8: 178–93.

CLARK, W. R., GILLIGAN, M. J., and GOLDER, M. 2006. A simple multivariate test for a symmetric hypotheses. *Political Analysis*, 14: 311–31.

CLEMENS, E. S., and COOK, J. M. 1999. Politics and institutionalism. *Annual Review of Sociology*, 25: 441–66.

COLLIER, R. B., and COLLIER, D. 1991. *Shaping the Political Arena: Critical Junctures, the Labor Movement, and Regime Dynamics in Latin America*. Princeton: Princeton University Press.

DAVID, P. A. 1985. Clio and the economics of QWERTY. *American Economic Review*, 75: 332–7.

DION, D. 1998. Evidence and inference in the comparative case study. *Comparative Politics*, 30 (2): 127–45.

DOWNING, B. M. 1992. *The Military Revolution and Political Change: Origins of Democracy and Autocracy in Early Modern Europe.* Princeton: Princeton University Press.

ERTMAN, T. 1997. *Birth of the Leviathan: Building States and Regimes in Medieval and Early Modern Europe.* Cambridge: Cambridge University Press.

ESPING-ANDERSEN, G. 1990. *Three Worlds of Welfare Capitalism.* Cambridge: Polity.

FORAN, J. 2005. *Taking Power: On the Origins of Third World Revolutions.* Cambridge: Cambridge University Press.

GEORGE, A. L., and BENNETT, A. 2005. *Case Studies and Theory Development in the Social Sciences.* Cambridge, Mass.: MIT Press.

GEORGE, A. L., and McKEOWN, T. J. 1985. Case studies and theories of organizational decision making. *Advances in Information Processing in Organizations,* 2: 21–58.

GOERTZ, G., and STARR, H. eds. 2003. *Necessary Conditions: Theory, Methodology, and Applications.* Lanham, Md.: Rowman and Littlefield.

GOLDSTONE, J. A. 1991. *Revolution and Rebellion in the Early Modern World.* Berkeley and Los Angeles: University of California Press.

GOLDSTONE, J. A. 1998. The problem of the "early modern" world. *Journal of Economic and Social History of the Orient,* 41: 249–84.

GOLDSTONE, J. A. 2007. *The Happy Chance: The Rise of the West in Global Context, 1500–1800.* Cambridge, Mass.: Harvard University Press.

GOLDTHORPE, J. H. 1997. Current issues in comparative macrosociology: a debate on methodological issues. *Comparative Social Research,* 16: 1–26.

GOLDTHORPE, J. H. 2000. Causation, statistics, and sociology. Pp. 137–60 in *On Sociology: Numbers, Narratives, and the Integration of Research and Theory,* ed. J. H. Goldthorpe. Oxford: Oxford University Press.

GOODWIN, J. 2001. *No Other Way Out: States and Revolutionary Movements, 1945–1991.* New York: Cambridge University Press.

HEDSTROM, P., and SWEDBERG, R. eds. 1998. *Social Mechanisms: An Analytical Approach to Social Theory.* New York: Cambridge University Press.

HICKS, A. 1999. *Social Democracy and Welfare Capitalism.* Ithaca, NY: Cornell University Press.

HUBER, E., and STEPHENS, J. D. 2001. *Development and Crisis of the Welfare State: Parties and Politics in Global Markets.* Chicago: University of Chicago Press.

JONES-LUONG, P. 2002. *Institutional Change and Political Continuity in Post-Soviet Central Asia: Power Perception, and Pacts.* Cambridge: Cambridge University Press.

KARL, T. L. 1997. *The Paradox of Plenty: Oil Booms and Petro States.* Berkeley and Los Angeles: University of California Press.

LIEBERSON, S. 1991. Small N's and big conclusions: an examination of the reasoning in comparative studies based on a small number of cases. *Social Forces,* 70: 307–20.

MAHONEY, J. 1999. Nominal, ordinal, and narrative appraisal in macrocausal analysis. *American Journal of Sociology,* 103 (4): 1154–96.

MAHONEY, J. 2000. Path dependence in historical sociology. *Theory and Society,* 29: 507–48.

MAHONEY, J. 2001. *The Legacies of Liberalism: Path Dependence and Political Regimes in Central America.* Baltimore: Johns Hopkins University Press.

MAHONEY, J. 2004. Comparative-historical methodology. *Annual Review of Sociology,* 30: 81–10i.

MAHONEY, J. and GOERTZ, G. 2006. A tale of two cultures: contrasting quantitative and qualitative research. *Political Analysis,* forthcoming.

MAHONEY, J. and RUESCHEMEYER, D. 2003. Comparative historical analysis: achievements and agendas. pp. 3-38 in *Comparative Historical Analysis in the Social Sciences,* ed. J. Mahoney and D. Rueschemeyer. Cambridge: Cambridge University Press.

MARX, A. W. 1998. *Making Race and Nation: A Comparison of South Africa, the United States, and Brazil.* Cambridge: Cambridge University Press.

MICKEY, R. W., and PIERSON, P. 2004. As long as it takes: duration and the explanation of political outcomes. Paper presented at the Workshop on Comparative Politics, Yale University.

NORTH, D. C. 1990. *Institutions, institutional Change and Economic Performance.* Cambridge: Cambridge University Press.

O'DONNELL, G. 1979. *Modernization and Bureaucratic-Authoritarianism*. Berkeley: Institute of International Studies.

ORREN, K. 1991. *Belated Feudalism: Labor, the Law, and Liberal Development in the United States*. Cambridge: Cambridge University Press.

PAIGE, J. M. 1997. *Coffee and Power: Revolution and the Rise of Democracy in Central America*. Cambridge, Mass.: Harvard University Press.

PIERSON, P. 2000. Increasing returns, path dependence, and the study of politics. *American Political Science Review*, 94: 251–67.

PIERSON, P. 2004. *Politics in Time: History, Institutions, and Social Analysis*. Princeton: Princeton University Press.

PRZEWORKSI, A., and TEUNE, H. 1970. *The Logic of Comparative Social Inquiry*. New York: Wiley.

RAGIN, C. C. 1987. *The Comparative Method: Moving beyond Qualitative and Quantitative Strategies*. Berkeley and Los Angeles: University of California Press.

RAGIN, C. C. 2000. *Fuzzy-Set Social Science*. Chicago: University of Chicago Press.

SKOCPOL, T. 1979. *States and Social Revolutions: A Comparative Analysis of France, Russia, and China*. Cambridge: Cambridge University Press.

SKOCPOL, T., ed. 1984. *Vision and Method in Historical Sociology*. New York: Cambridge University Press.

SKOCPOL, T., and SOMERS, M. 1980. The uses of comparative history in macrosocial inquiry. *Comparative Studies in Society and History*, 22: 174–97.

THELEN, K. 2003. How institutions evolve: insights from comparative historical analysis. pp. 208–40 in *Comparative Historical Analysis in the Social Sciences*, ed. J. Mahoney and D. Rueschemeyer. Cambridge: Cambridge University Press.

TILLY, C. 1990. *Coercion, Capital, and European States, AD 990–1990*. Cambridge: B. Blackwell.

YASHAR, D. J. 1997. *Demanding Democracy: Reform and Reaction in Costa Rica and Guatemala, 1870s–1950s*. Stanford, Calif.: Stanford University Press.

ZUCKERMAN, A. S. 1997. Reformulating explanatory standards and advancing theory in comparative politics. Pp. 277–310 in *Comparative Politics: Rationality, Culture, and Structure*, ed. M. I. Lichbach and A. S. Zuckerman. Cambridge: Cambridge University Press.

NOTES

* James Mahoney's work on this project is supported by the National Science Foundation under Grant No. 0093754. We thank Carles Boix and Susan Stokes for helpful comments on a previous draft.

1. It bears emphasis that historical researchers often generalize their explanations across all cases that fall within their theory scope. However, the scope of their theory—defined as a domain in which assumptions of causal homogeneity are valid—is usually restricted to a small to medium number of cases. For a discussion, see Mahoney and Rueschemeyer (2003, 7–10); Mahoney and Goertz (2006).

2. Statistical methodologists usually assume that determinism is wholly inappropriate for the social sciences (e.g., Lieberson 1991; Goldthorpe 1997). Some qualitative methodologists share this view. However, determinism can be justified on the grounds that, when one is *not* generalizing from a sample to large population, but rather explaining particular cases, it is meaningless to say that a cause exerts a probabilistic effect. For any particular case, a cause either exerts a given effect or it does not.

2

THE STATE, DEVELOPMENT, DEMOCRACY, AND AUTHORITARIANISM

Section 2 moves from the more abstract issues discussed in the introduction and the previous section to a set of issues that many consider the "bread and butter" of comparative politics. In the readings in these units, you will find less discussion about what a theory is, how one formulates a good concept, or the logic of comparison. Instead, you will see some analysts' efforts to ask an important question, generate a theory or set of hypotheses about that question, and begin testing their ideas with evidence. At the same time, the issues discussed in Section I of the book remain relevant, and we encourage you to think about what you read in Section II (and subsequent sections) in light of what you learned there. For example, it would be legitimate for you to ask of any given reading whether the key concepts are clearly and usefully formulated or whether the comparative method is being used properly in the ways outlined in Section I. Likewise, you might consider "reading back" to Section I. Perhaps a reading in Section II will show you something that is potentially problematic about Popper's "conjecture and refutation" model or that King, Keohane, and Verba have too narrow a conception of the uses of qualitative comparison.

The big questions in Section II focus on issues like the rise of the modern state (Chapter 3), the political economy of advanced economies (Chapter 4), the nature and explanation of economic development in lower-income countries (Chapter 5), and the differences between democratic and authoritarian regimes (Chapters 6 and 7, respectively). In each chapter, the emphasis is on causal arguments to address questions such as why the modern state emerged, why countries have different economic performance, and why countries have different regime types. Most of the theories and arguments discussed here are pitched at a "macro" level, meaning that they make sweeping comparisons as they aim to generalize about processes that affect entire societies and even global issues.

CHAPTER 3

THE STATE

Many people consider the state the fundamental actor in modern politics. This is because the state is the basic unit for much of contemporary political action. Think about all of the things that states do. Even libertarians, who favor minimizing state action, want states to provide for the common defense (no small matter in the 21st century); maintain basic infrastructure, such as roads, bridges, and airports; and protect core rights like property and the enforcement of legitimate contracts (which means a judicial system for arbitrating disputes and an executive for enforcing laws). Virtually every modern state aims to do much more than this, participating in education, health care, the provision of various kinds of social insurance, and support for research and technological development. States vary in their ability to perform the tasks they set for themselves—we can locate them on a continuum that ranges from state weakness to state strength—and also in which tasks they and their citizens define as fundamental (despite a lot of overlap).

Comparative politics asks many questions about states. Perhaps the most fundamental explanatory question is "Why did modern states emerge?" This most consequential of political organizations has not been around forever, and given how important it is in modern politics, the question of its origins is important. Another related question is "Why did the organizational form of the modern state spread or 'diffuse' so completely over the past several centuries?" Yet another is "Why do states share some common features and differ notably in other respects?" As we will see, this is often asked about features of the welfare state, as noted by Esping-Andersen in the next chapter.

This chapter includes two readings that provide examples of theoretical answers to some of these questions. First is a reading from Max Weber, one of the founders of both sociology and contemporary political science. Here Weber (1946) famously argues that what makes a state different from other ways of organizing politics is that it exclusively exercises the "legitimate use of force." As you read it, pay special attention to what he means by "legitimacy," and to the brief discussion of the different ways that such legitimacy can be established.

The second reading is from Robert Bates on the conflictual origins of states. This is a contemporary iteration of an old theory, perhaps the most influential theory of state formation, going back at least to Thomas Hobbes (2010 [1651]; for loosely related arguments emphasizing conflict as fundamental to state-building see Tilly, 1992; Centeno, 2002; Herbst, 2000; and North et al., 2009) and even earlier.

In reading Weber and Bates on the modern state, consider where they agree and also have some differences. Namely, both emphasize violence and force in their understanding of what the state is, but Bates argues that the modern state emerged mainly as an outcome of violence, whereas Weber also introduces more "cultural" factors in his discussion of different forms of legitimation from one place to another. How much such or factors beyond simply violence drive the formation of states?

WORKS CITED

Centeno, Miguel Angel. 2002. *Blood and Debt: War and the Nation-State in Latin America.* University Park: Pennsylvania State University Press.

Herbst, Jeffrey. 2000. *States and Power in Africa: Comparative Lessons in Authority and Control.* Princeton, NJ: Princeton University Press.

Hobbes, Thomas. 2010 [1651]. *Leviathan, Or the Matter, Forme, and Power of a Common-Wealth Ecclesiasticall and Civil* (Ian Shapiro, ed.). New Haven, CT: Yale University Press.

North, Douglass C., John Joseph Wallis, and Barry R. Weingast. 2009. *Violence and Social Orders: A Conceptual Framework for Interpreting Recorded Human History.* New York: Cambridge University Press.

Tilly, Charles. 1992. *Coercion, Capital, and European States, AD 990-1992.* Oxford: Blackwell.

Weber, Max. 1958, "Politics as a Vocation," in H. H. Gerth and C. Wright Mills, eds. *From Max Weber: Essays in Sociology.* Oxford: Oxford University Press.

MAX WEBER

3.1 POLITICS AS A VOCATION

This reading is from one of the most important founding scholars in the modern social sciences. In it, Max Weber offers what has probably been the most influential definition of the state in political science. As you read it, be attentive not only to the substance of the definition, but also to his definitional strategy. What does Weber seem to think makes a good definition? How does he define the field of politics? Furthermore, why does he not choose to describe all of the incidental features of states, focusing instead on a couple of characteristics he considers "definitive"? And why does he emphasize the "monopoly on the legitimate use of force" along with the "territorial" aspects of states? Likewise, be attentive to his discussion of three "ideal types" of legitimacy. What does he mean by "legitimacy"? Is he offering a judgment about which governments are, and which are not, legitimate? Does he think we can neatly separate different political systems into "traditional," "charismatic," and "legal-rational" ("domination" through "legality") types? Although this passage is short, it is best read closely and slowly.

POLITICS AS A VOCATION

This lecture, which I give at your request, will necessarily disappoint you in a number of ways. You will naturally expect me to take a position on actual problems of the day. But that will be the case only in a purely formal way and toward the end, when I shall raise certain questions concerning the significance of political action in the whole way of life. In today's lecture, all questions that refer to what policy and what content one should give one's political activity must be eliminated. For such questions have nothing to do with the general question of what politics as a vocation means and what it can mean. Now to our subject matter.

What do we understand by politics? The concept is extremely broad and comprises any kind of *independent* leadership in action. One speaks of the currency policy of the banks, of the discounting policy of the Reichsbank, of the strike policy of a trade union; one may speak of the educational policy of a municipality

or a township, of the policy of the president of a voluntary association, and, finally, even of the policy of a prudent wife who seeks to guide her husband. To-night, our reflections are, of course, not based upon such a broad concept. We wish to understand by politics only the leadership, or the influencing of the leadership, of a *political* association, hence today, of a *state*.

But what is a "political" association from the sociological point of view? What is a "state"? Sociologically, the state cannot be defined in terms of its ends. There is scarcely any task that some political association has not taken in hand, and there is no task that one could say has always been exclusive and peculiar to those associations which are designated as political ones: today the state, or historically, those associations which have been the predecessors of the

"Politik als Beruf," *Gesammelte Politische Schriften* (Muenchen, 1921), pp. 396–450. Originally a speech at Munich University, 1918, published in 1919 by Duncker & Humblodt, Munich.

Weber, Max. 1946. "Politics as a Vocation," trans. and ed., H.H. Gerth and C. Wright Mills, *From Max Weber*. New York: Oxford University Press.

modern state. Ultimately, one can define the modern state sociologically only in terms of the specific *means* peculiar to it, as to every political association, namely, the use of physical force.

"Every state is founded on force," said Trotsky at Brest-Litovsk. That is indeed right. If no social institutions existed which knew the use of violence, then the concept of "state" would be eliminated, and a condition would emerge that could be designated as "anarchy," in the specific sense of this word. Of course, force is certainly not the normal or the only means of the state—nobody says that—but force is a means specific to the state. Today the relation between the state and violence is an especially intimate one. In the past, the most varied institutions—beginning with the sib—have known the use of physical force as quite normal. Today, however, we have to say that a state is a human community that (successfully) claims the *monopoly of the legitimate use of physical force* within a given territory. Note that "territory" is one of the characteristics of the state. Specifically, at the present time, the right to use physical force is ascribed to other institutions or to individuals only to the extent to which the state permits it. The state is considered the sole source of the "right" to use violence. Hence, "politics" for us means striving to share power or striving to influence the distribution of power, either among states or among groups within a state.

This corresponds essentially to ordinary usage. When a question is said to be a "political" question, when a cabinet minister or an official is said to be a "political" official, or when a decision is said to be "politically" determined, what is always meant is that interests in the distribution, maintenance, or transfer of power are decisive for answering the questions and determining the decision or the official's sphere of activity. He who is active in politics strives for power either as a means in serving other aims, ideal or egoistic, or as "power for power's sake," that is, in order to enjoy the prestige-feeling that power gives.

Like the political institutions historically preceding it, the state is a relation of men dominating men, a relation supported by means of legitimate (i.e., considered to be legitimate) violence. If the state is to exist, the dominated must obey the authority claimed by the powers that be. When and why do men obey? Upon what inner justifications and upon what external means does this domination rest?

To begin with, in principle, there are three inner justifications, hence basic *legitimations* of domination.

First, the authority of the "eternal yesterday," i.e. of the mores sanctified through the unimaginably ancient recognition and habitual orientation to conform. This is "traditional" domination exercised by the patriarch and the patrimonial prince of yore.

There is the authority of the extraordinary and personal *gift of grace* (charisma), the absolutely personal devotion and personal confidence in revelation, heroism, or other qualities of individual leadership. This is "charismatic" domination, as exercised by the prophet or—in the field of politics—by the elected war lord, the plebiscitarian ruler, the great demagogue, or the political party leader.

Finally, there is domination by virtue of "legality," by virtue of the belief in the validity of legal statute and functional "competence" based on rationally created *rules*. In this case, obedience is expected in discharging statutory obligations. This is domination as exercised by the modern "servant of the state" and by all those bearers of power who in this respect resemble him.

It is understood that, in reality, obedience is determined by highly robust motives of fear and hope—fear of the vengeance of magical powers or of the power-holder, hope for reward in this world or in the beyond—and besides all this, by interests of the most varied sort. Of this we shall speak presently. However, in asking for the "legitimations" of this obedience, one meets with these three "pure" types: "traditional," "charismatic," and "legal."

ROBERT H. BATES

3.2 PROSPERITY AND VIOLENCE
The Political Economy of Development

In this excerpt from Robert Bates's short and accessible book, *Prosperity and Violence*, we find a brief account of European state formation. This argument is a variation on what is sometimes called the "bellicist theory" of the state, which emphasizes that modern states are created out of the violent struggle between different social actors. Highly functional modern states are those that truly establish the Weberian monopoly on force, implementing rule of law. Weaker states are more likely to behave in a "predatory" manner, which for Bates and other political scientists means serving as agents for private interests: in other words, some groups can capture the state and use it to benefit themselves, persecuting their enemies and funneling "rents" to themselves and their cronies. As you read this, consider whether this theory about predatory behavior has relevance for contemporary politics and, if so, where and under what conditions.

THE FORMATION OF STATES

In sixteenth-century England, when the monarch surveyed the political landscape, she saw Bedford in the southwest, Pembroke in Wales, Arundel in Sussex, Norfolk in East Anglia, Derby in the northwest, and Northumberland in the northeast. By the seventeenth century, each magnate and his family had been defeated or seduced by the center. Possessing greater revenues, the monarchy mobilized greater force. And by channeling wealth through politics, the monarch was able to transform the behavior of rural kin groups; when their standing came to depend less upon "territorial power than upon influence in London" (Stone 1965, 257), the heads of such groups invested less in rural domination and more in playing the game of court politics.

The economic transformation of the countryside thus inspired a quest for new ways of structuring political life. In response to the demands for peace, monarchs transformed the local order, demilitarizing kinship, co-opting elites, and incorporating local communities into a system that terminated, rather than exacerbated, conflict. In addition, monarchs innovated new ways of tapping the private wealth of their citizens. Among the most significant was the creation of parliaments—fora in which they could trade concessions in public policies for the payment of public revenues.

The magnitude of the monarch's concessions depended, of course, on the bargaining power of the taxpayer. When the monarch taxed land, he had little need to make concessions; being immobile, land could be seized and returned only after accounts had been settled. But when goods were "mobile," in the phrasing of the time, then the monarch needed to engender a willingness to pay, for such property could be moved and hidden and taxes thereby evaded. As commerce replaced farming and the economy became monetized, private citizens found it still easier to elude the tax collector. And parliaments then became even more important, as monarchs trimmed their political programs the better to fit the preferences of private citizens, whom they wanted to contribute to the costs of their wars. By thus surrendering a portion of

Bates, Robert H. 2001. *Prosperity and Violence: The Political Economy of Development.* New York: W.W. Norton.

their sovereign powers to the people's representatives, kings augmented their military might.

Wars imparted sharp shocks to the economy, however; the magnitude of those shocks increased with the sophistication of military technologies. Monarchs therefore could not rely on taxes alone; they could not hope to wring from their economies the resources necessary to pay the full costs of a war. What they could not raise through taxation, they needed to borrow.

When governments borrowed, the loans were of much greater magnitude than those sought by private borrowers. The debts incurred by merchants were short term, often merely covering a particular transaction. By contrast, the debts of government were of long duration, at least those of military campaigns, and sometimes those of protracted conflicts. In addition, loans to commerce could be made at low risk: lenders could seize the goods of a debtor. But loans to governments were made at greater risk: monarchs, being sovereign, could renege on their obligation to repay.

To increase the willingness of those with capital to lend, governments therefore sought ways to offer security to their creditors. They allowed bankers to become "tax farmers," collectors of customs or the managers of conquered lands; title to the taxes and incomes provided security for their loans to the treasury. Alternatively, monarchs granted monopolies to their creditors: assured of high profits from monopolies created by the government, chartered companies and licensed purveyors were willing to run the risks of lending. Such measures only went part way toward addressing the concerns of investors, however; for just as monarchs could renege on their debts, so too might they abrogate such agreements. The costs of borrowing therefore remained high, because creditors demanded compensation for lending large amounts for long durations to governments that could renege with impunity.

Insofar as the European governments "solved" the problem of financing public debt, they did so by building upon the institutions that they had forged to levy taxes, that is their parliaments. Seventeenth-century England offers the most compelling example. As had the Habsburgs before them, the French

coveted the wealth of the lowlands; the Dutch therefore feared the renewal of war. Surveying the polity that lay across the Channel, the Dutch spied both opportunity and danger. They found the wealth of the English economy attractive. But they were disturbed by the danger posed by the polity, and, in particular, by the Stuarts, the ruling lineage, who possessed religious preferences and financial needs that rendered them susceptible to pressures from France. Building a fleet that rivaled the Spanish Armada in size, Dutch invaders joined English opponents to Stuart rule, drove the Stuarts from the throne, and replaced them with their own ruling lineage, the House of Orange. The House of Orange had long since learned how to finance, raise, and equip a disciplined army. The Dutch polity consisted of a federation of urban-based assemblies. The most efficient way to mobilize revenues, its ruling family had learned, was to bargain for them in parliaments.

To address the concerns of creditors, William of Orange therefore acknowledged the sovereignty of England's Parliament, which meant, in this context, two specific things. The first was parliamentary control over policy. The second was parliamentary control over public finances, which implied control over taxation and the financing of the public debt. In effect, those who controlled the wealth of the nation would now finance only those ventures for which they were willing to pay. By thus limiting his power, the monarch reduced the risks faced by lenders and so lowered the costs of borrowing. As canny in devising political solutions to financial problems as they were in fighting wars, the Dutch transformed English political institutions in ways that gave political assurances to investors and augmented the flow of capital to the state and revenues to its military.

The need to secure finances from citizens in order to pay for wars therefore produced a characteristic structure of political institutions in early modern times: parliamentary government.

In historical Europe, then, states emerged from war. Governments pursued policies that promoted the growth of the economy and the rise of parliamentary institutions not because they wanted to but because they had to, the better to secure the resources with which to fight. In what was to become the advanced industrial world, as states developed, coercion therefore did not disappear. States fought abroad. Neither did they forswear the use of force at home; rather, they altered the purposes for which force was employed. To a greater degree than before, they employed it to terminate feuds and secure property rights; to promote the creation of wealth rather than to plunder it; and to exchange policy concessions for public revenues from private citizens. As states developed, then, coercion served new purposes. It provided the political foundations for development.

WORKS CITED

Stone, Lawrence. 1965. *The Crisis of the Aristocracy, 1558–1641.* Oxford: Clarendon Press.

CHAPTER 4

POLITICAL ECONOMY

The previous chapter dealt with the question of emergence of the modern state: what is the state, and why did states form? In this chapter, we begin to see how the various topics of comparative politics feed into one another. We focus in this chapter on the political economy, or roughly speaking, how politics affects economic outcomes and vice versa. Of course, probably the main political actor that affects the political economy is the state itself. In particular, major questions and debates in comparative politics have examined whether a big and strong state is beneficial or harmful for economic growth and development. (You might think that "big and strong" sounds positive, but long-standing arguments have held that such states can tend to be overbearing, intrusive, and sometimes dictatorial, which is not necessarily a recipe for economic growth and success.) In considering political economy, we ask two related questions in this chapter, both of which consider the role of the state as an important feature. First, what causes economic growth and performance, and in particular what role does the state play in promoting or hindering economic outcomes? A second question is, why do some states become much larger and more active than others? That is, why do some countries have very large states while others have relatively more limited states?

The first reading is by Milton Friedman, a Nobel Prize-winning economist and advocate of the view that economic growth is caused primarily by the extent to which a country's economy is based on the free market. A corollary of Friedman's view is that government intervention is the primary hindrance to economic success. This theory is prevalent in the United States, among other countries, given the perception that the U.S. is a relatively free-market, small-state type of economy. (The extent to which the U.S. has a relatively small state is actually referenced in the next reading in this chapter, and whether the country always has been free-market historically is a deeper question we cannot address fully here.) In short, Friedman favors a quite limited role for the state in the economy. We do not offer a direct counterpoint to this argument here, though we do so in the next chapter where we introduce an argument about state quality and its importance for economic development, especially in developing economies.

Our second reading, by Gøsta Esping-Andersen, takes on the question of why states differ in form or structure, in this case focusing on different types of "welfare states." There are many theories about why some states are more generous in their social benefits than others (say Scandinavia having relatively generous states compared to several Anglophone countries), and also about why they go about providing social assistance in different ways; Esping-Andersen's is one of the best known arguments. In thinking about Friedman and Esping-Andersen together, consider the possible advantages and disadvantages of robust states. Do you think that limited state intervention is better for certain outcomes in political economy, and that more robust state intervention is better for others? Consider an outcome such as economic growth along with other outcomes such as poverty, inequality, and economic competitiveness.

MILTON FRIEDMAN

4.1 USING THE MARKET FOR SOCIAL DEVELOPMENT

Milton Friedman was one of the leading proponents of free market economics in the 20th century. In this piece, he highlights the advantages of policy reforms that move toward free, private markets. From a starting point where government has a major role in an economy, he considers the alternatives of partial versus total privatization and of gradual versus rapid decontrol; Friedman comes down on the side of total and rapid reduction of the government's role in the economy, arguing that this will best spur economic performance. Friedman is also cognizant of some of the impediments to his preferred policies and discusses how political obstacles tend to support the status quo, even when this is not optimal for the economy. As you read this, consider how arguments like Friedman's fit into the major policy debates about the government's role in the economy of your home country.

INTRODUCTION

An episode during an earlier visit to China impressed me strongly with the wide gulf of understanding that separates people immersed in different economic institutions. That gulf makes it extremely important to stress over and over basic principles and ideas that all of us simply take for granted with respect to the system to which we are accustomed. The episode in question occurred when my wife and I had lunch with a deputy minister of one of the government departments who was shortly going to the United States to observe the American economy. Our host wanted help from us on whom to see.

His first question in that connection was, "Who in the United States is in charge of materials distribution?" That question took my wife and me aback. I doubt that any resident of the United States, however unsophisticated about economics, would even think of asking such a question. Yet it was entirely natural for a citizen of a command economy to ask such a question. He is accustomed to a situation in which somebody decides who gets what from whom, whether that be who gets what materials from whom or who gets what wages from whom.

My initial answer was to suggest that he visit the floor of the Chicago Mercantile Exchange where commodities such as wheat, cotton, silver, and gold are traded. This answer understandably baffled our host, so I went on to elaborate on the fact that there was no single person—or even committee of persons—"in charge of materials distribution." There are a Department of Commerce and a Department of the Interior that are concerned with materials production and distribution in a wholly different way. But they do not determine who gets how much of what. They collect information, examine the situation in various industries, evaluate legislation, and so on. Legislation (for example, tax and foreign trade laws) certainly affects the course of materials prices and distribution, but no single person or political body is "in charge of materials distribution" in the sense in which there is or has been such a person or political body in China or the Soviet Union. In consequence, I was forced to answer in terms that my host found

Friedman, Milton. 1989 "Using the Market for Social Development," *Cato Journal* 8(3): 567–579.

extremely difficult to comprehend. Needless to say, that is not a criticism of him. Given his background, it is almost inconceivable that he could have understood how the market can distribute a variety of materials among millions of different people for thousands of uses untouched, as an ad might say, by political hands.

The miracle of the market is precisely that out of the chaos of people screaming at one another, making arcane signals with their hands, and fighting on the floor of the Chicago Mercantile Exchange, somehow or other the corner store always seems to have enough bread, the bakery always seems to have enough flour, and the miller always seems to have enough wheat. That is the miracle of the way the market coordinates the activities of millions of people, and does so in a wholly impersonal way through prices that, if left completely free, do not involve any corruption, bribes, special influence, or need for political mechanisms.

Let me now turn more directly to the topic at hand. In some ways, referring to "the market" puts the discussion on the wrong basis. The market is not a cow to be milked; neither is it a sure-fire cure for all ills. In literal terms, the market is simply a meeting of people at a specified place and time for the purpose of making deals. Needless to say, "meeting" and "place" are often euphemisms; they do not involve physical getting together. As of the moment, there is a market in foreign exchange that encompasses the world. People get together through satellites, telephones, and other means. Moreover, the deals made in or through a market are not restricted to those involving money, purchases, or sales. Scientists who cooperate with one another in advancing their discipline, whether it be physics, chemistry, economics, or astronomy, are effectively making deals with one another. Their market is a set of interrelated journals, conferences, and so on.

The market is a mechanism that may be mobilized for any number of purposes. Depending on the way it is used, the market may contribute to social and economic development or it may inhibit such development. Using or not using the market is not the crucial distinction. Every society, whether communist, socialist, social democratic, or capitalist, uses the market. Rather, the crucial distinction is private property or no private property. Who are the participants

in the market and on whose behalf are they operating? Are the participants government bureaucrats who are operating on behalf of something called the state? Or are they individuals operating directly or indirectly on their own behalf?

That is why, in an earlier paper delivered in China, I advocated the widest possible use not of the market but of "free private markets" (Friedman [1980] 1982). The words "free" and "private" are even more important than the word "market." The wider use of the market that is sweeping the world is better described as "privatization"—transferring government-owned enterprises to private hands and thereby giving greater scope to the invisible hand of which Adam Smith wrote. In 1987 alone, over $90 billion of assets and enterprises were privatized by governments around the world.

In this paper I propose to discuss some of the problems that arise when a society tries to replace a command economy with the invisible hand of the market. Those problems are not restricted to societies that have tried to use command as their basic economic mechanism, such as China and the Soviet Union. The same problems arise in Western economies, such as the United States, Great Britain, and Germany, in which command elements have become more extensive over time and in which there are attempts to reverse that process. Privatizing government-owned enterprises in the West, such as the postal service in the United States and railroads and utilities in other countries, raises problems that are identical with those that arise in replacing command and government ownership by voluntary cooperation and private ownership in China and the Soviet Union. In consequence, China can learn a great deal by studying the experience of privatization in Western countries. At the moment, the most extensive experience of that kind is doubtless in Great Britain. Much has been written about the British experience, and it provides many instructive examples about correct and incorrect ways to privatize.[1]

I shall organize my discussion under three headings: partial versus total decontrol (or deregulation or privatization); gradual versus immediate decontrol; and overcoming political obstacles or, in more technical economic terms, short-circuiting rent seeking. Although the same issues arise whatever the domain in which command is replaced by voluntary cooperation—whether economic, political, or social—I shall restrict my comments to the economic domain. A concluding section discusses the general problem of the tyranny of the status quo.

PARTIAL VERSUS TOTAL DECONTROL

Introducing a greater role for private market mechanisms in one sector of an economy may be partially or completely frustrated by the limited scope of the change. Consider what has been regarded as a major move toward wider use of the market, namely creation of the European common market and the attempt to achieve free trade among the common market countries. It has now been nearly 40 years since the Schuman plan for a coal and steel community was adopted, yet no observer will dispute that free trade within the common market is still an ideal rather than a reality. The latest bit of evidence is the recent agreement to *really* eliminate all barriers by 1992. Had the initial common market agreement been successful, that elimination would have been achieved many years ago. What was the problem? Why is there no real United States of Europe? In my view, the answer is that decontrol was adopted even in principle only for goods and services but not for money. The separate countries retained full authority over their national moneys. More important, they refused to adopt a system of freely floating exchange rates—that is, the free exchange of one currency for another at whatever rates of exchange were voluntarily agreed to in free private markets. The refusal to let the private market determine the rates of exchange among currencies was a fatal weakness.

I first reached that conclusion in the fall of 1950 when I spent a few months as a consultant in Paris to the then Marshall Plan agency. My assignment was to assess the likely consequences of the proposed coal and steel community. I concluded that free trade within a common market could not be achieved unless currencies as well as goods and services were freed from government control. That analysis was the basis for my article on "The Case for Flexible Exchange Rates" published in 1953. As I stated in that article (p. 157):

A system of flexible or floating exchange rates—exchange rates freely determined in an open market

primarily by private dealings and, like other market prices, varying from day to day—[is] absolutely essential for the fulfillment of our basic economic objective: the achievement and maintenance of a free and prosperous world community engaging in unrestricted multilateral trade. . . . Liberalization of trade, avoidance of allocations and other direct controls, both internal and external, harmonization of internal monetary and fiscal policies—all these problems take on a different cast and become far easier to solve in a world of flexible exchange rates and its corollary, free convertibility of currencies.

Experience during the 35 years since that article was published has, I believe, provided much additional evidence for the validity of this proposition.

Currently, China is faced with precisely the same problem. But my purpose in discussing it here is not to present again the case for a system of freely floating exchange rates but rather to give a striking illustration of how limiting decontrol or privatization to one area, while not extending it to closely related areas, can largely frustrate the basic objective.

A second example is from the United States. Although nominally private, U.S. airlines were subject to extensive government control with respect to the prices they could charge and the markets they could serve. Deregulation of the airlines in 1978 has enhanced competition, resulted in widespread and substantial reductions in prices, and increased the range of services. In consequence, there has been a major expansion in the volume of air traffic. However, while U.S. airlines were deregulated or, as I would prefer to put it, privatized, airports were not. They remain government-owned and operated.[2] Private enterprise has had no difficulty in producing all the planes the airlines find it profitable to use, and private airlines have had no difficulty in finding pilots or attendants. On the other hand, planes are often delayed because facilities or provisions for landing them at government-run airports are inadequate, at great inconvenience to passengers. Naturally, the government responds by trying to blame the private airlines: It has started requiring them to report delays in meeting their scheduled arrival times and publishing summary reports on the on-time performance of several airlines. Repeated proposals have been made that—even if government retained the ownership and operation of the airports—rights to gates, both with respect to number of gates and to the times at which they are to be used, should be auctioned off. Unfortunately, the opposition of airlines, which have vested interests in the gates and times assigned to them by government agencies, has prevented the adoption of even such incomplete reforms. Of course, a far better solution would be to privatize the airports.

A third example is privatizing some areas of manufacturing while keeping the production or pricing of the raw materials under government control. The failure of the prices of the raw materials to conform to their market value means that private operation, however efficient privately, may be socially wasteful. Let me illustrate with an extreme example that I came across in India many years ago. It had to do with the manufacture of bicycles in a small community in the Punjab. The government of India controlled the production of steel and rationed the output to users, rather than auctioning off the steel produced at whatever prices the market would yield. As a result, the producers of bicycles could not get the amount of steel they were willing to buy at the officially set price of steel. However, there was a private market in finished or semifinished steel products. The bicycle manufacturers supplemented their government ration of steel by buying semifinished steel products and melting them down—hardly an efficient way to convert iron ore and coal into bicycles.

Let me cite some obvious examples for China. Introduction of a considerable element of privatization in agriculture has produced a remarkable increase in agricultural output and productivity—the most dramatic manifestation of China's success in widening the use of the private market. But it is clear that the very success has created a real problem. The overwhelming majority of the Chinese population is employed in agriculture. Even a relatively small improvement in agricultural productivity means the release from agriculture of workers who can now be more usefully employed in industry. Yet, the bulk of industry remains in the command economy; it has not been privatized, deregulated, or fully subjected to the competitive market process.

There has been a real attempt to change the way government-owned enterprises operate in China.

The people in charge have been told to use market mechanisms, and an attempt has been made to provide incentives for them to do so. However, as long as industrial enterprises are government-owned, there are severe limits to the ability of politically sensitive managers (bureaucrats) to respond effectively to market pressures. The most serious limitation is on flexibility, that is, on the willingness or ability of managers in state-owned enterprises to be venturesome, to undertake risky projects that are likely to fail but have a real, if small, chance of spectacular success. Again, the problem is universal. Every study of the United States or Great Britain demonstrates that small enterprises—not the mega-corporations that are household names—are responsible for most of the new jobs. In China, the opportunity for such private enterprises is narrowly limited.

A much wider privatization of economic activity would greatly reduce the difficulty of absorbing the workers released from agriculture. That is precisely what happened in the United States and in the rest of the world during the 19th and 20th centuries. The fraction of the American population employed in agriculture in the early 19th century was over 90 percent—not far from the fraction currently employed in China—but it is now 2 or 3 percent. True, the transition in the West took much longer and proceeded at a more gradual pace than either should be or can be hoped for in China. Nonetheless, if the command sector of the economy had been as extensive in the United States then as it is now, let alone as extensive in China, the transition would never have occurred to anything like the same extent. The experience of Russia over the past 70 years is persuasive evidence. The way to expedite the transition in China is to proceed with privatization as rapidly and on as wide a scale as possible. Private enterprises would then spring up all over the place to absorb the working force.

A second example for China is similar to the problem I described for the common market: the difference between the extent of freedom in the production and distribution of goods and services and in the production and distribution of money. The substantial freeing of many prices, particularly those of agricultural and similar goods, has not been accompanied by the privatization of the banking system. As

I understand it, the Chinese government indirectly determines what happens to the money supply through the credits it grants state enterprises. One result has been a rapid increase in the quantity of money and, not surprisingly, rapid upward pressure on prices, so that inflation, both open and repressed, has reared its ugly head.

It is much easier to point out the problems raised by partial use of the market than it is to draw any explicit implications for policy. It is easy to say that the best thing to do is to go all the way. However, in many really interesting and important cases, it is simply not politically feasible to do so. It would be clearly helpful in such cases to have some maxims that would suggest a way to draw the boundaries. However, it is not easy to do so in the abstract. I suspect that the only possible way to proceed is to analyze each case separately in light of the general economic principles embodied in price and monetary theory.

GRADUALISM VERSUS SHOCK TREATMENT

When should reform be gradual, and when is radical and immediate change appropriate? One alternative is illustrated by the tale of the tortoise and the hare, when the "slow but steady" tortoise reaches the finish line ahead of the much speedier but more erratic hare. The other is illustrated by the maxim, there is no sense in cutting a dog's tail off by inches. This is one of the most difficult problems encountered in widening the scope of the market. Let me illustrate with foreign trade. Suppose a country that has had high levels of tariffs decides to move to a free trade position. The case for moving gradually is clear. Capital has been invested in ways that will no longer represent an effective use of private resources under the new conditions. Much of that capital is in the form of machinery, buildings, human skills, and the like. Is it not clearly both more equitable and more efficient to reduce the tariffs gradually? That would give the owners of specialized resources the opportunity to withdraw their capital gradually and thus would reduce the costs imposed on them by the change.

The case for eliminating the tariff in one fell swoop, that is, for shock treatment, is more subtle, yet at the level of economic efficiency, compelling. Insofar as it is economically efficient to use the specialized resources in the absence of a tariff, they will be used. If any return over marginal cost can be obtained by continuing to use the specialized human and other resources, it is better to get that return than to get nothing. The burden would be imposed on the owners of the specialized resources immediately, but technical disinvestment would proceed only as rapidly as the specialized labor and other resources could be employed more productively elsewhere. On the other hand, gradual reduction in the tariff makes it privately profitable to continue using the specialized resources at a higher level than is socially efficient, thereby imposing unnecessary costs on the community.

The possibly valid arguments for gradualism are not technical and economic but equitable and political, and neither of these is clear-cut. The individuals who invested in the protected industries did so with the full knowledge that the authorities that imposed the tariffs could eliminate them. The existence of such a possibility kept down the amount of capital invested in the industry and permitted the owners of such capital to earn a higher return than otherwise. Why is it now equitable for consumers to bear part of the owners' costs of adjustment? Politically, gradualism encourages the protected industries to spend resources to reverse the decision.

The analysis is complicated even further by considering the activities that will tend to expand under the new circumstances, that is, the industries that will replace the former so-called protected industries. Here, too, issues about efficiency, equity, and politics require attention.

Ending an ongoing inflation raises similar problems. Eliminating inflation in one fell swoop, if not anticipated long in advance, may cause widespread capital losses. Long-term contracts entered into with one expectation about the likely rate of inflation may now suddenly be rendered inappropriate. The case on equity grounds for a gradual transition is far stronger for moderate degrees of inflation than for tariffs. The effects of both the prior inflation and its unanticipated ending are more pervasive and affect more people who have not only been harmed rather than benefited by the prior inflation but would be harmed again by its abrupt end. Reducing inflation gradually eases the transition and reduces the cost of achieving noninflationary growth.

However, much depends on the height of the inflation. If inflation is extremely high—at annual rates in triple digits—the situation is very different. Almost all participants in the market will have adjusted their arrangements so that any longstanding commitments are fully indexed. Abrupt disinflation will impose few costs because financial and other institutions have been adapted to radical changes in the rate of inflation. Indeed, such adaptations represent a major cost of high and erratic inflation. Gradual elimination is sometimes not even feasible because there is not time enough—the dog will be dead before its extra long tail can be cut off by inches.

Direct controls over prices—whether general or specific, for example, on rents or exchange rates—are almost always best ended at once. Margaret Thatcher properly ended exchange rate controls in Britain overnight and completely. Gradual adjustment only prolongs the harm done by controls and provides unjustified benefits to "insiders." The shortages and queues and other distortions produced by trying to hold prices below their market level would continue though they might get shorter, and additional problems arise because gradualism encourages speculation about reversal and encourages opponents to seek reversal. A similar proposition holds for attempts to keep prices above market levels—as is so amply demonstrated by the agricultural policies of the United States, Japan, and the common market.

OVERCOMING POLITICAL OBSTACLES

This subject has already inevitably intruded into the preceding section. The general issue here is how to overcome political obstacles to widening the market. The danger is not alone that these obstacles will frustrate the attempt to free the market but equally that overcoming political obstacles will destroy the advantages of freeing the market. The challenge is to find ways to overcome obstacles that do not have those effects. The experience of the West with privatization is particularly helpful in this connection. Perhaps the most extensive body of experience and the experience that has been most widely analyzed is the British experience with privatization, and I strongly recommend to our Chinese friends seeking to widen the market that they examine the evidence of privatization in Britain.

A simple case from the United States that illustrates the problem is privatizing the post office. The U.S. Postal Service has a monopoly in first-class mail because of the private express statutes, which make it a crime for individuals to offer common-carrier first-class service. Various attempts to do so have only succeeded in prosecution, which has ended the attempts. Privatization has been creeping in at the margin, first in the form of alternate parcel service. The United Parcel Service, a strictly private enterprise, and other parcel delivery companies have taken over the bulk of the Postal Service's prior business. In addition, private messenger services have developed, of which the best known is Federal Express, which has been so successful that numerous competitors have emerged. Developments that technological advances would have encouraged no matter how postal service was organized have doubtless been speeded up. Examples are electronic mail via computers and telephones, and facsimile service, again over telephones. These examples illustrate the ingenuity of private markets in exploiting the opportunities offered by the inefficiency of government enterprises.

Repeated attempts have been made to seek the repeal of the private express statutes so that private individuals and enterprises could compete with the U.S. Postal Service. However, such attempts always bring violent protests from the postal employee unions, from the executives of the Postal Service, and from rural communities that feel they would be deprived of postal service. On the other hand, few people have a strong and concentrated interest leading them to favor repealing the private express statutes. Entrepreneurs who might in fact enter the business if it were open to private entry do not know in advance that they would do so. Hundreds of thousands of people who would doubtless obtain employment in a privately developed postal system do not have the slightest idea that they would do so.

I recall a personal experience. I urged a congressman who believed as strongly as I did that it would be desirable to repeal the private express statutes to introduce a bill to that effect. He said, "You and I know the powerful groups who will testify and lobby against such a bill. Can you give me a list of people who will be equally willing to testify and work in favor of such a bill? People who will have some influence on Congress? People with a strong personal interest other than academic economists?" I admitted that I could not do so and he never introduced the bill. Vested interests have been built up in the postal monopoly. Few vested interests have been built up in opposing the postal monopoly, though there are some. That situation may be changing as corporations such as Federal Express and United Parcel Service begin to see the possibilities open to them.

One way to overcome the opposition to privatization, widely used in Britain, is, as described by Robert Poole (1988, p. 25),

> to identify potential opponents and cut them in on the deal, generally by means of stock ownership. Two specific applications of the principle are employee stock ownership and popular capitalism. . . .
>
> The opportunity to become shareholders can dramatically change the incentives of unionized civil servants, as illustrated in the case of British Telecom. Union officials denounced the planned privatization of Telecom, telling their members not to purchase the shares which were being offered to them at a discount. Yet in the end, sensing the chance to make money, some 96 percent of the workforce bought shares.

Poole also uses British Telecom to illustrate the second technique, popular capitalism: "To encourage telephone customers to buy shares, they were offered vouchers granting them a discount on their phone bills if they held their shares for at least six months. And to prevent institutions and large firms from buying up the lion's share, initial purchases were limited to 800 shares per buyer."

A pitfall to be avoided in adopting such expedients is to sweeten the deal by converting a government monopoly into a private monopoly—which may be an improvement but falls far short of the desirable outcome. The U.S. Postal Service illustrates that pitfall as well as the fallacy that mimicking the form of private enterprise can achieve the substance. It was established as a

supposedly independent government corporation that would not be subject to direct political influence and that would operate on market principles. That has hardly been the outcome, and understandably so. It remained a monopoly and never developed a strong private interest in efficiency.

My own favorite form of privatization is not to sell shares of stock at all but to give government-owned enterprises to the citizens. Who, I ask opponents, owns the government enterprises? The answer invariably is, "The public." Well, then, why not make that into a reality rather than a rhetorical flourish? Set up a private corporation and give each citizen one or one hundred shares in it. Let them be free to buy or sell the shares. The shares would soon come into the hands of entrepreneurs who would either maintain the enterprise, for example, the postal system, as a single entity if it was most profitable to do so or break it up into a number of entities if that seemed most profitable. I know only one major case in which this procedure was followed, namely in British Columbia (see Ohashi and Roth 1980, part 1). Unfortunately, the collapse of energy prices made this venture less than an outstanding success. Nonetheless, it is well worth studying.

A final example illustrates the point in another way. The Russians have permitted small private plots in agriculture. Those private plots are estimated to occupy about 3 percent of the arable land in the Soviet Union, and roughly one-third of all domestic food products in the Soviet Union are sold as coming from those private plots. I have chosen my words carefully. I did not say that one-third were "produced on those private plots," because in my opinion that would not be correct. Much of the food sold as coming from the private plots has indeed been produced on them, but I strongly suspect that much has also been diverted from collective farms.

For decades, it has been clear to the rulers of the Soviet Union that they could increase the domestic output of agriculture substantially by increasing the size and role of the private plots. Why have they not done so? Surely not because of ignorance. The answer clearly is that privatization would tend to establish independent centers of power that would reduce the political power of the bureaucracy. The rulers regarded the political price they would have to pay as higher than the economic reward. As of the moment, largely I suspect under the influence of the extraordinary success of such a policy in China, President Gorbachev is talking about a considerable expansion in private plots. It is by no means clear whether he will succeed.

TYRANNY OF THE STATUS QUO

The problems of overcoming vested interests, of frustrating rent seeking, apply to almost every attempt to change government policy, whether the change involves privatization, or eliminating military bases, or reducing subsidies, or anything else. The resulting "Tyranny of the Status Quo," as my wife and I entitled a recent book (Friedman and Friedman 1984) discussing a range of such cases in the United States, is the major reason that political mechanisms are so much less effective than free-market mechanisms in encouraging dynamic change, and in producing growth and economic prosperity.

Few simple maxims exist for overcoming the tyranny of the status quo. But there is one that ties in closely with the earlier discussion of gradual versus abrupt change. If a government activity is to be privatized or eliminated, by all means do so completely. Do not compromise by partial privatization or partial reduction. That simply leaves a core of determined opponents who will work diligently and often successfully to reverse the change. The Reagan administration repeatedly attempted, for example, to privatize Amtrak (the railroad passenger service) and to eliminate the Legal Services Corporation. In each case, it settled for a reduction in budget, achieving a fairly transitory victory. On the other hand, the complete abolition of the Civil Aeronautics Board gives far greater hope that airline deregulation is here to stay.

In conclusion, there are better and worse ways to privatize a command economy, but there is no magic formula for shifting painlessly from a command to a voluntary exchange economy. Nonetheless, the potential rewards are so great that, if the shift can be achieved, transitional costs will pale into insignificance. It is a tribute to the current leaders of China that they recognize that the potential gains dwarf the transitional costs and that they are engaged in a serious effort to make the transition. The Chinese people would be the main but by no means the only beneficiaries of the success of this effort. All the peoples of the world would benefit. Peace and widely shared prosperity are the ultimate prizes of the worldwide use of voluntary cooperation as the major means of organizing economic activity.

NOTES

1. An excellent source for Britain and other countries is Hanke (1987).
2. In Britain, however, the British Airports Authority, which controls some airports, has been privatized.

REFERENCES

Friedman, Milton. "The Case for Flexible Exchange Rates." In Friedman, *Essays in Positive Economics*, pp. 157–203. Chicago: University of Chicago Press, 1953. Reprinted in *The Essence of Friedman*, pp. 461–98. Edited by Kurt R. Leube. Stanford, California: Hoover Institution Press, 1987.

Friedman, Milton. "How to Use Market Mechanisms in Connection with Central Planning." Lecture no. 4, presented in Beijing on 30 September 1980 and in Shanghai on 4 October 1980 under the auspices of the Chinese Academy of Social Sciences. Translated into Chinese and published in *On Inflation: Four Lectures in China*, pp. 50–67. Beijing: Chinese Social Sciences Publishing House, 1982.

Friedman, Milton, and Friedman, Rose D. *Tyranny of the Status Quo*. New York: Harcourt Brace Jovanovich, 1984.

Hanke, Steve H., ed. *Privatization and Development*. San Francisco: Institute for Contemporary Studies Press, 1987.

Ohashi, T. M., and Roth, T. P. *Privatization: Theory & Practice*. Vancouver, B.C., Canada: The Fraser Institute, 1980.

Poole, Robert W., Jr. "Stocks Populi, A Privatization Strategy." *Policy Review*, no. 46 (Fall 1988): 24–29.

GØSTA ESPING-ANDERSEN

4.2 THE THREE WORLDS OF WELFARE CAPITALISM

The following is an excerpt from Gøsta Esping-Andersen's *The Three Worlds of Welfare Capitalism.* The book is most famous for the typology of welfare states that Esping-Andersen constructs. They differ not only in their levels of generosity but also in the very ways in which the provision of basic services is structured. For example, some welfare states ensure that basic citizen needs are met through directly providing services. Others rely, in part, on regulating private companies such that they provide some benefits. Some programs are universal, benefiting all citizens (like Social Security in the United States). Others are targeted at particular constituencies. The three main forms of welfare state identified by Esping-Andersen are the corporatist, liberal, and social democratic varieties. Other scholars have attempted to modify or add to this typology. Esping-Andersen also offers an explanation for why welfare states take these different forms, briefly described in this selection. You can consider how comparative analysis might be used to evaluate this explanation.

WELFARE-STATE REGIMES

As we survey international variations in social rights and welfare-state stratification, we will find qualitatively different arrangements between state, market, and the family. The welfare-state variations we find are therefore not linearly distributed, but clustered by regime-types.

In one cluster we find the "liberal" welfare state, in which means-tested assistance, modest universal transfers, or modest social-insurance plans predominate. Benefits cater mainly to a clientele of low-income, usually working-class, state dependents. In this model, the progress of social reform has been severely circumscribed by traditional, liberal work-ethic norms: it is one where the limits of welfare equal the marginal propensity to opt for welfare instead of work. Entitlement rules are therefore strict and often associated with stigma; benefits are typically modest. In turn, the state encourages the market, either passively—by guaranteeing only a minimum—or actively—by subsidizing private welfare schemes.

The consequence is that this type of regime minimizes de-commodification-effects, effectively contains the realm of social rights, and erects an order of stratification that is a blend of a relative equality of poverty among state-welfare recipients, market-differentiated welfare among the majorities, and a class-political dualism between the two. The archetypical examples of this model are the United States, Canada and Australia.

A second regime-type clusters nations such as Austria, France, Germany, and Italy. Here, the historical corporatist-statist legacy was upgraded to cater to the new "post-industrial" class structure. In these conservative and strongly "corporatist" welfare states, the liberal obsession with market efficiency and commodification was never preeminent and, as such, the granting of social rights was hardly ever a seriously contested issue. What predominated was the preservation of status differentials; rights, therefore, were attached to class and status. This corporatism was subsumed under a state edifice perfectly ready to displace the market as a provider of welfare; hence,

Esping-Andersen, Gøsta. 1990. *The Three Worlds of Welfare Capitalism.* Princeton: Princeton University Press.

private insurance and occupational fringe benefits play a truly marginal role. On the other hand, the state's emphasis on upholding status differences means that its redistributive impact is negligible.

But the corporatist regimes are also typically shaped by the Church, and hence strongly committed to the preservation of traditional family-hood. Social insurance typically excludes non-working wives, and family benefits encourage motherhood. Day care, and similar family services, are conspicuously under-developed; the principle of "subsidiarity" serves to emphasize that the state will only interfere when the family's capacity to service its members is exhausted.

The third, and clearly smallest, regime-cluster is composed of those countries in which the principles of universalism and de-commodification of social rights were extended also to the new middle classes. We may call it the "social democratic" regime-type since, in these nations, social democracy was clearly the dominant force behind social reform. Rather than tolerate a dualism between state and market, between working class and middle class, the social democrats pursued a welfare state that would pro-mote an equality of the highest standards, not an equality of minimal needs as was pursued elsewhere. This implied, first, that services and benefits be up-graded to levels commensurate with even the most discriminating tastes of the new middle classes; and, second, that equality be furnished by guaranteeing workers full participation in the quality of rights en-joyed by the better-off.

This formula translates into a mix of highly de-commodifying and universalistic programs that, nonetheless, are tailored to differentiated expectations. Thus, manual workers come to enjoy rights identical to those of salaried white-collar employees or civil servants; all strata are incorporated under one univer-sal insurance system, yet benefits are graduated ac-cording to accustomed earnings. This model crowds out the market, and consequently constructs an essen-tially universal solidarity in favor of the welfare state. All benefit; all are dependent; and all will presumably feel obliged to pay.

The social democratic regime's policy of emanci-pation addresses both the market and the traditional family. In contrast to the corporatist-subsidiarity model, the principle is not to wait until the family's capacity to aid is exhausted, but to preemptively socialize the costs of family-hood. The ideal is not to maximize dependence on the family, but capacities for individual independence. In this sense, the model is a peculiar fusion of liberalism and socialism. The result is a welfare state that grants transfers directly to children, and takes direct responsibility of caring for children, the aged, and the helpless. It is, accordingly, committed to a heavy social-service burden, not only to service family needs but also to allow women to choose work rather than the household.

Perhaps the most salient characteristic of the social democratic regime is its fusion of welfare and work. It is at once genuinely committed to a full-employment guarantee, and entirely dependent on its attainment. On the one side, the right to work has equal status to the right of income protection. On the other side, the enormous costs of maintaining a soli-daristic, universalistic, and de-commodifying wel-fare system means that it must minimize social problems and maximize revenue income. This is ob-viously best done with most people working, and the fewest possible living off of social transfers.

Neither of the two alternative regime-types es-pouse full employment as an integral part of their welfare-state commitment. In the conservative tradi-tion, of course, women are discouraged from work-ing; in the liberal ideal, concerns of gender matter less than the sanctity of the market.

We show that welfare states cluster, but we must recognize that there is no single pure case. The Scan-dinavian countries may be predominantly social democratic, but they are not free of crucial liberal ele-ments. Neither are the liberal regimes pure types. The American social-security system is redistributive, compulsory, and far from actuarial. At least in its early formulation, the New Deal was as social demo-cratic as was contemporary Scandinavian social democracy. And European conservative regimes have incorporated both liberal and social democratic im-pulses. Over the decades, they have become less cor-porativist and less authoritarian.

Notwithstanding the lack of purity, if our essen-tial criteria for defining welfare states have to do with the quality of social rights, social stratification, and the relationship between state, market, and family, the world is obviously composed of distinct regime-clusters. Comparing welfare states on scales of more or less or, indeed, of better or worse, will yield highly misleading results.

THE CAUSES OF WELFARE-STATE REGIMES

If welfare states cluster into three distinct regime-types, we face a substantially more complex task of identifying the causes of welfare-state differences. What is the explanatory power of industrialization, economic growth, capitalism, or working-class political power in accounting for regime-types? A first superficial answer would be: very little. The nations we study are all more or less similar with regard to all but the variable of working-class mobilization. And we find very powerful labor movements and parties in each of the three clusters.

A theory of welfare-state developments must clearly reconsider its causal assumptions if it wishes to explain clusters. The hope of finding one single powerful causal force must be abandoned; the task is to identify salient interaction-effects. Based on the preceding arguments, three factors in particular should be of importance: the nature of class mobilization (especially of the working class); class–political coalition structures; and the historical legacy of regime institutionalization.

There is absolutely no compelling reason to believe that workers will automatically and naturally forge a socialist class identity; nor is it plausible that their mobilization will look especially Swedish. The actual historical formation of working-class collectivities will diverge, and so also will their aims, ideology, and political capacities. Fundamental differences appear both in trade-unionism and party development. Unions may be sectional or in pursuit of more universal objectives; they may be denominational or secular; and they may be ideological or devoted to business-unionism. Whichever they are, it will decisively affect the articulation of political demands, class cohesion, and the scope for labor-party action. It is clear that a working-class mobilization thesis must pay attention to union structure.

The structure of trade-unionism may or may not be reflected in labor-party formation. But under what conditions are we likely to expect certain welfare-state outcomes from specific party configurations? There are many factors that conspire to make it virtually impossible to assume that any labor, or left-wing, party will ever be capable, single-handedly, of structuring a welfare state. Denominational or other divisions aside, it will be only under extraordinary historical circumstances that a labor party alone will command a parliamentary majority long enough to impose its will. The traditional working class has hardly ever constituted an electoral majority. It follows that a theory of class mobilization must look beyond the major leftist parties. It is a historical fact that welfare-state construction has depended on political coalition-building. The structure of class coalitions is much more decisive than are the power resources of any single class.

The emergence of alternative class coalitions is, in part, determined by class formation. In the earlier phases of industrialization, the rural classes usually constituted the largest single group in the electorate. If social democrats wanted political majorities, it was here that they were forced to look for allies. One of history's many paradoxes is that the rural classes were decisive for the future of socialism. Where the rural economy was dominated by small, capital-intensive family farmers, the potential for an alliance was greater than where it rested on large pools of cheap labor. And where farmers were politically articulate and well-organized (as in Scandinavia), the capacity to negotiate political deals was vastly superior.

The role of the farmers in coalition formation and hence in welfare-state development is clear. In the Nordic countries, the necessary conditions obtained for a broad red–green alliance for a full-employment welfare state in return for farm-price subsidies. This was especially true in Norway and Sweden, where farming was highly precarious and dependent on state aid. In the United States, the New Deal was premised on a similar coalition (forged by the Democratic Party), but with the important difference that the labor-intensive South blocked a truly universalistic social security system and opposed further welfare-state developments. In contrast, the rural economy of continental Europe was very inhospitable to red–green coalitions. Often, as in Germany and Italy, much of agriculture was labor-intensive; hence the unions and left-wing parties were seen as a threat. In addition, the conservative forces on the continent had succeeded in incorporating farmers into "reactionary" alliances, helping to consolidate the political isolation of labor.

Political dominance was, until after World War II, largely a question of rural class politics. The construction of welfare states in this period was, therefore, dictated by whichever force captured the farmers. The absence of a red–green alliance does not necessarily imply that no welfare-state reforms were possible. On the contrary, it implies which political force came to dominate their design. Great Britain is an exception to this general rule, because the political significance of the rural classes eroded before the turn of the century. In this way, Britain's coalition-logic showed at an early date the dilemma that faced most other nations later; namely, that the rising white-collar strata constitute the linchpin for political majorities. The consolidation of welfare states after World War II came to depend fundamentally on the political alliances of the new middle classes. For social democracy, the challenge was to synthesize working-class and white-collar demands without sacrificing the commitment to solidarity.

Since the new middle classes have, historically, enjoyed a relatively privileged position in the market, they have also been quite successful in meeting their welfare demands outside the state, or, as civil servants, by privileged state welfare. Their employment security has traditionally been such that full employment has been a peripheral concern. Finally, any program for drastic income-equalization is likely to be met with great hostility among a middle-class clientele. On these grounds, it would appear that the rise of the new middle classes would abort the social democratic project and strengthen a liberal welfare-state formula.

The political leanings of the new middle classes have, indeed, been decisive for welfare-state consolidation. Their role in shaping the three welfare-state regimes described earlier is clear. The Scandinavian model relied almost entirely on social democracy's capacity to incorporate them into a new kind of welfare state: one that provided benefits tailored to the tastes and expectations of the middle classes, but nonetheless retained universalism of rights. Indeed, by expanding social services and public employment, the welfare state participated directly in manufacturing a middle class instrumentally devoted to social democracy.

In contrast, the Anglo-Saxon nations retained the residual welfare-state model precisely because the new middle classes were not wooed from the market to the state. In class terms, the consequence is dualism. The welfare state caters essentially to the working class and the poor. Private insurance and occupational fringe benefits cater to the middle classes. Given the electoral importance of the latter, it is quite logical that further extensions of welfare-state activities are resisted.

The third, continental European, welfare-state regime has also been patterned by the new middle classes, but in a different way. The cause is historical. Developed by conservative political forces, these regimes institutionalized a middle-class loyalty to the preservation of both occupationally segregated social-insurance programs and, ultimately, to the political forces that brought them into being. Adenauer's great pension-reform in 1957 was explicitly designed to resurrect middle-class loyalties.

CONCLUSION

We have here presented an alternative to a simple class-mobilization theory of welfare-state development. It is motivated by the analytical necessity of shifting from a linear to an interactive approach with regard to both welfare states and their causes. If we wish to study welfare states, we must begin with a set of criteria that define their role in society. This role is certainly not to spend or tax; nor is it necessarily that of creating equality. We have presented a framework for comparing welfare states that takes into consideration the principles for which the historical actors have willingly united and struggled. When we focus on the principles embedded in welfare states, we discover distinct regime-clusters, not merely variations of "more" or "less" around a common denominator.

The historical forces behind the regime differences are interactive. They involve, first, the pattern of working-class political formation and, second, political coalition-building in the transition from a rural economy to a middle-class society. The question of political coalition-formation is decisive. Third, past reforms have contributed decisively to the institution-alization of class preferences and political behavior. In the corporatist regimes, hierarchical status-distinctive social insurance cemented middle-class loyalty to a peculiar type of welfare state. In liberal regimes, the middle classes became institutionally wedded to the market. And in Scandinavia, the fortunes of social de-mocracy over the past decades were closely tied to the establishment of a middle-class welfare state that ben-efits both its traditional working-class clientele and the new white-collar strata. The Scandinavian social democrats were able to achieve this in part because the private welfare market was relatively undeveloped and in part because they were capable of building a welfare state with features of sufficient luxury to sat-isfy the wants of a more discriminating public. This also explains the extraordinarily high cost of Scandi-navian welfare states.

But a theory that seeks to explain welfare-state growth should also be able to understand its re-trenchment or decline. It is generally believed that welfare-state backlash movements, tax revolts, and roll-backs are ignited when social expenditure bur-dens become too heavy. Paradoxically, the opposite is true. Anti-welfare-state sentiments over the past decade have generally been weakest where welfare spending has been heaviest, and vice versa. Why?

The risks of welfare-state backlash depend not on spending, but on the class character of welfare states. Middle-class welfare states, be they social democratic (as in Scandinavia) or corporatist (as in Germany), forge middle-class loyalties. In contrast, the liberal, residualist welfare states found in the United States, Canada and, increasingly, Britain, depend on the loyalties of a numerically weak, and often politically residual, social stratum. In this sense, the class coali-tions in which the three welfare-state regime-types were founded, explain not only their past evolution but also their future prospects.

CHAPTER 5

DEVELOPMENT

One of the most basic questions in comparative politics is why some countries have become wealthy, whereas others remain low income. Another way of saying this is that many comparativists are interested in the determinants of economic and social development in different countries, along with the quality of economic performance. We want to understand the politics behind why some countries have performed well and others poorly, in part because of intellectual curiosity, but also in large part so we can help improve policies to better peoples' lives around the world.

Of course, *development* can be defined in many ways. Some scholars choose to focus on the overall growth of an economy, as measured by such indicators as the gross domestic product per person (or GDP per capita). Others may focus on other indicators, such as inequality, poverty, life expectancy, or literacy rates. Scholars may choose to focus on the development opportunities for certain groups, such as women, children, or ethnic or racial minorities. Still others focus on environmental sustainability, quality of life, or "happiness." These can all be valid ways of measuring development (as long as an analyst is clear and consistent about which measure one is using). Although development can be examined in many ways, economic growth in particular is seen as a key correlate of many other aspects of development.

In this chapter, we use two selections to examine this question of the causes of development, with an emphasis on why economic growth happens. It should be noted at the outset (and is true for the remaining chapters in the book) that this selection of two readings cannot cover all the important theories of development. In fact, one of the leading theories of why development happens was actually introduced in the previous chapter, where a selection by Milton Friedman represented the argument that free markets and limited roles for states are the best way to run economies; that argument is equally present in debates about developed and developing countries alike. Similarly, selections in Chapter 1 of this book by Diamond and Acemoglu and Robinson (which were used at that point to illustrate how scholars ask research questions) also offer leading theories about the effects on development of geography and certain institutions, respectively.

The two selections here complement those previous readings. The first is by Atul Kohli, who examines the process of "state-directed" development. Kohli notes that there is a long-standing debate about whether development is best driven by markets or by state action. He adds a new element to the debate by discussing the types of states and conditions under which states can work together with private capital to promote growth. This can be thought of short-hand as the *quality* of state action mattering more for development than just the *quantity* of state action. The second piece is by Francis Fukuyama, from his book *Trust*. Fukuyama explains the growth of modern economies as a result of the existence of trust as a key cultural attribute. Fukuyama helps illustrate how we can use cultural theories to explain development without falling into noxious arguments about the "unsuitability" of certain groups for achieving progress.

As noted above, the readings here focus primarily on the causes of economic growth. However, as also noted, the study of development is about many other outcomes as well. Are the explanations offered in the selected readings equally applicable to these other indicators of development?

ATUL KOHLI

5.1 STATE-DIRECTED DEVELOPMENT

Political Power and Industrialization in the Global Periphery

Kohli examines the role that states play in building modern, industrial economies. In his argument, economic development is the consequence of effective states, whereas economic stagnation occurs when states are ineffective. The cause of success is not the amount of state intervention in an economy, but the quality of the state that does the intervening. Kohli distinguishes among several types of states. One supports capitalist development (cohesive-capitalist states, as was found in South Korea and at times in Brazil). At the other end of the spectrum, neopatrimonial states (as found in Nigeria) are characterized by economic failure and a lack of coherent efforts to build industrial economies. In between are fragmented-multiclass states (as found in India and at other times in Brazil), which produce some "middling" performance. Note that the power and capacity of states is shaped in large part by historical developments in the different countries, including colonialism. Do you think that this focus on history means that individual political actors or policies do not matter?

STATES AND INDUSTRIALIZATION IN THE GLOBAL PERIPHERY

Legitimate states that govern effectively and dynamic industrial economics are widely regarded today as the defining characteristics of a modern national state. Ever since Western countries developed such political economies a few centuries back, those left behind have sought to catch up. Among late developers, countries such as Japan and Russia avoided being colonialized by consolidating their respective states and adopting alternative strategies of industrialization, with varying results. The search for development among later late-industrializers of Asia, Africa, and Latin America intensified mainly after the Second World War, when numerous activist states emerged as sovereign. It is clear from the vantage point of the end of the twentieth century that state-led development efforts have been more successful in some parts of the global periphery than in others. This book looks at the role states have played in fostering different rates and patterns of economic development especially via deliberate industrialization.

States in most peripheral countries of Asia, Africa, and Latin Americans are important, active economic actors, engaged in varying patterns of state intervention. In some developing countries the state's economic role has come to be associated with both rapid industrial transformation and enhanced equity. In other cases, by contrast, governments and bureaucrats have pilfered the economic resources of their own societies, failing to stimulate economic growth and facilitating transfer of wealth into the hands of unproductive elites. In yet other cases, state intervention is associated with mixed outcomes: States have helped to solve some important economic problems, while ignoring other problems and creating new ones.

This study undertakes a comparative analysis of the state as an economic actor in developing countries. Why have some of these states been more

Kohli, Atul. 2004. *State-Directed Development: Political Power and Industrialization in the Global Periphery.* Cambridge: Cambridge University Press.

successful at facilitating industrialization than others? This question really has two components: What features distinguish state intervention in the more successful cases from intervention in the less successful cases? and How does one explain varying state capacities to choose and implement economic decisions? The first question of patterns of state intervention focuses both on the state's policy choices and on its relationship with such key economic actors as business and labor. By contrast, the second question, concerning state capacities, looks to the institutional character of the state itself, an identity often assumed well before the political elite initiated deliberate industrialization. This book then is about patterns of state construction and patterns of state intervention aimed at promoting industrialization.

It is mainly an inductive study that seeks a general understanding of the state as an economic actor in developing countries via detailed analyses of four major developing countries of the twentieth century: South Korea, Brazil, India, and Nigeria (see Table 5.1 and Figure 5.1.). These cases provide a range of variation in state capacities to pursue economic transformation, from a fairly effective, growth-promoting state in South Korea to a rather ineffective and corrupt Nigerian state, with Brazil and India providing mixed cases. What helps to explain these variations? Indeed, this is a key puzzle in late-late-development.

The main argument of the book, drawn from comparative historical analysis of these four countries, is that the creation of effective states within the developing world has generally preceded the emergence of industrializing economies. This is because state intervention in support of investor profits has proved to be a precondition for industry to emerge and flourish among late-late-developers. Patterns of state authority, including how the politics of the state are organized and how state power is used, have decisively influenced the economic context within which private economic decisions are made. They are thus important, nay, critical, for understanding varying rates and patterns of industrialization. Patterns of state authority, in turn, often exhibit long-term continuities. Colonialism in the first half of the twentieth century, especially, was defining of the state institutions that emerged in developing countries, and that in turn molded their economies in the second half of the century.

The political economy debate on why some parts of the developing world have had faster-growing economies than others polarized in the last two decades of the twentieth century around a more neoliberal, promarket position, on the one hand, and a statist argument, on the other hand. The promarket position emerged nearly hegemonic, especially among some economists and development policy practitioners.[1] For its part, the statist argument, often articulated by interdisciplinary scholars of development, provided a cogent scholarly dissent.[2] This book hopes to advance this debate further yet by developing the existing

TABLE 5.1 SOME RELEVANT INDICATORS OF KOREA, BRAZIL, INDIA, AND NIGERIA

	Korea	Brazil	India	Nigeria
GDP per capita (Current PPP $)	15,074	7,446	2,388	859
Population (millions)	47	170	1016	127
Annual % growth in GDP per capita, 1950–2000	5.2	2.8	2.3	0.9
Gini coefficient	32 (1998)	61 (1998)	38 (1997)	51 (1997)
National poverty head count (population %)	N/A	17 (1990)	29 (2000)	34 (1993)
Adult illiteracy (% of population aged 15 and above)	2	13	43	36
Government expenditure (% of GDP, 1995)	14.6	18.6	14.2	Not known
Public investment (% of gross domestic investment, 1998)	27	19	30	Not known
Contribution of state-owned enterprises (% of GDP, 1990)	10	7	13	Not known

Source: World Bank. World Development Indicators. Data for 2000 unless otherwise noted.

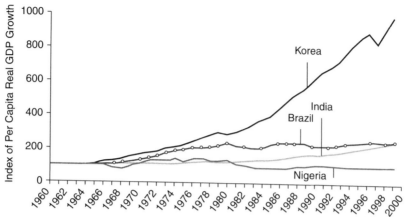

FIGURE 5.1   Pattern of Per Capita GDP Growth: Korea, Brazil, India, and Nigeria, 1960–2000.
Note: The data are taken from the World Bank's World Development Indicators. For the purposes of illustration, the data were transformed such that the 1960 GDP per capita of each country is represented as an index of 100. I would like to thank Evan Lieberman and Maya Tudor for their assistance with this figure.

statist position, though not by adopting an aggressive antimarket position. On the contrary, one of the themes of this study is that state intervention in rapid industrializers was often characterized by market-reinforcing behavior, understood in the sense of supporting profitability for private investors—and not as strengthening competitiveness or openness or, even less, as a state's self-limiting proclivity. The state versus market mind-set thus is simply not very helpful for understanding how the interaction of states and markets has served to produce a range of economic outcomes.

THE ARGUMENT

Industrialization involves social change. While its narrow outcome is an increase in industrial production from existing or new factories, a broader set of societal changes have also generally accompanied, if not preceded, industrial development. [These include a situation of political stability, the availability of experienced entrepreneurs and of a capable urban work force and mobilizable capital, the emergence of a market for industrial goods, and the presence of a growing body of technical knowledge. It is not surprising that among the earliest, "spontaneous" industrializers, such as England, the process occurred slowly, over centuries, and was "caused" not by any single development but by the merging of several

streams of underlying changes]. It was Gerschenkron who first argued persuasively that follower countries within Europe did not reproduce England's "spontaneous" model. Instead, he held, they needed a more organized initiative from banks or states to help to generate "a movement on a broad front" to help industry to take off by mobilizing capital, creating a work force, and facilitating technology transfer.[3] What was true for late-developers within Europe or Japan was, of course, doubly true for late-late-industrializers of the developing world. Since the mid-twentieth century, states have sought to promote industry in most countries of Asia, Africa, and Latin America. What is also clear from the vantage point of the end of the century, however, is that this half-century of effort has seen considerably more success in some parts of the developing world than in others. Explaining these divergent pathways is the main task of this book.

Based on detailed comparative analysis of four countries that vary from success to failure, I argue that the way state power is organized and used has decisively influenced rates and patterns of industrialization in the global periphery.

State Types

Referring to ideal types, I identify three historical patterns of how state authority is organized and used in the developing world, neopatrimonial states, cohesive-capitalist states, and fragmented-multiclass states. Although these labels are less than fully satisfactory, they are better than most others in use. In any case, the focus ought to be more on the patterns described by the categories than on the labels themselves.

In addition to centralized and coercive control over a territory, a defining characteristic of all modern states is a well-established public arena that is both normatively and organizationally distinguishable from private interests and pursuits. Unfortunately, for a variety of historical reasons, this distinction between the public and the private realms was never well established in a number of developing country states, especially African states. As a result, a number of distorted states emerged with weakly centralized and barely legitimate authority structures, personalistic leaders unconstrained by norms or institutions, and bureaucracies of poor quality. These states are labeled here as neopatrimonial because, despite the façade of a modern state, public officeholders tend to treat public resources as their personal patrimony. These are therefore not really modern, rational-legal states. Whether organized as a nominal democracy or as a dictatorship, state-led development under the auspices of neopatrimonial states has often resulted in disaster, mainly because both public goals and capacities to pursue specific tasks in these settings have repeatedly been undermined by personal and narrow group interests. Of the cases analyzed in this study, Nigeria best exemplifies this ideal-typical tendency.

Cohesive-capitalist and fragmented-multiclass states are two of the other ideal-typical states to be found in the contemporary developing world. The more effective modern rational-legal states in the developing world tend to vary mainly along two dimensions: cohesion of state authority and the state's class commitments. Cohesion of authority is manifest at both the intraelite and the elite-mass levels, and variations in patterns of authority demarcate the more cohesive states from the more fragmented ones. Developing country states may also be narrowly committed to working with capitalists or may rest their power and goals on a more multiclass base.[4]

The cohesive-capitalist states, sometimes called developmental states, are situated opposite neopatrimonial states on the political effectiveness continuum.[5] These states are characterized by cohesive politics, that is, by centralized and purposive authority structures that often penetrate deep into the society. For a variety of historical reasons these states have tended to equate rapid economic growth with national security and thus defined it as a priority. In their pursuit of rapid growth, cohesive-capitalist states have carved out a number of identifiable links with society's major economic groups and devised efficacious political instruments. Especially notable among the social links is a close alliance with producer or capitalist groups. An important corollary of this political arrangement is a tight control over labor. The main political instrument of these states is, of course, a competent bureaucracy. Since a narrow elite alliance between the state and capital is difficult to hold together, politics within these units has often been repressive and authoritarian, with leaders often using ideological mobilization (e.g., nationalism and/or anticommunism) to win acceptance in the society. Cohesive-capitalist states in developing countries, such as in South Korea under Park Chung Hee and in Brazil during both Estado Novo and the military dictatorship, thus share some organizational and class characteristics with fascist states of interwar Europe and Japan.[6] (Obviously, however, these states do not draw explicit comparisons with discredited fascism, and they tend to shy away from the politics of mass mobilization and ethnic cleansing.) For better or for worse, these states have also proved to be the most successful agents of deliberate state-led industrialization in peripheral countries.

In between the two extremes of political effectiveness defined by neopatrimonial states on the one end and cohesive-capitalist states on the other lie fragmented-multiclass states. Unlike neopatrimonial states, fragmented-multiclass states are real modern states. They command authority, and a public arena within them is often well enough established that leaders are held accountable for poor public policies and performance. Unlike in cohesive-capitalist states, however, public authority in these states tends to be more fragmented and to rest on a broader class alliance—meaning that these states are not in a position to define their goals as narrowly or to pursue them as effectively as are cohesive-capitalist states. Leaders of fragmented-multiclass states thus need to worry more about political support than do leaders of other types of developing country states. For example, they must typically pursue several goals simultaneously, as they seek to satisfy multiple constituencies. Industrialization and economic growth may be an important state goal, but it is only one among others: agricultural development, economic redistribution, welfare provision, and maintaining national sovereignty. Policy formulation and implementation, moreover, is often politicized, either because of intraelite conflicts or because state authority does not penetrate deep enough down in the society to incorporate and control the lower classes. When confronted by mobilized opposition, fragmented-multiclass states typically become obsessed with issues of legitimacy and often find themselves promising more than they can deliver. While not all fragmented-multiclass states are necessarily democracies, all developing country democracies with plebiscitarian politics and weak institutions constitute a special subset of fragmented-multiclass states. The cases of India and Brazil in several periods exemplify this type of state. Attempting to pursue a complex state-led agenda with limited state capacities, then, fragmented-multiclass states tend to be middling performers on numerous dimensions, including the promotion of industrialization and growth.

Neopatrimonial states and the two more modern, rational-legal types of states, namely, cohesive-capitalist and fragmented-multiclass states, are ideal types of developing country states and are not found in a pure form in any of the countries discussed below. Instead, countries in specific periods exhibit more of one tendency than another. When comparing and analyzing state types empirically, one generally needs to focus on some such state characteristics as leadership goals, degree of centralization of public authority, downward penetration of public authority, political organization of the mobilized political society, scope of state intervention in economy, and quality of the economic bureaucracy. It may be easy in an abstract fashion to suggest, as I have, that cohesive-capitalist states are characterized by the top leadership equating rapid economic growth with national security, a highly centralized and penetrating public authority, state-controlled political society (though in close alliance with capitalist groups), and a highly interventionist state, with a good quality economic bureaucracy. Neopatrimonial and fragmented-multiclass states have been similarly characterized in their pure form. Real historical records of actual countries, however, seldom reveal state types in their ideal-typical form; states instead tend more toward one set of characteristics than another, opening the way for more complex analyses.

State Types and Patterns of Industrialization

If authority structures in the developing world can be variously categorized as neopatrimonial, cohesive-capitalist, and fragmented-multiclass states, the first relevant question for this study concerns how these states influence economic outcomes. The nearly exclusive focus in the literature on appropriate policy choices is incomplete, even misleading. Policy choices matter, of course, but these choices must be explained. More important, the impact of the same policy applied in two different settings may vary because of the contextual differences, some of the more obvious being varying global conditions and different initial conditions of an economy. The import of these issues will become clear in due course, but now the contextual difference that deserves emphasis—because it is significant and generalizable across cases—concerns the varying political and institutional conditions in which economic policies are chosen and pursued.

More specifically, identifying variations in how states are organized and in the institutionalized relationship of the state to the private sector is key to understanding the relative effectiveness of state intervention in the economy. In the cases examined in this study, this relationship varies along a continuum stretching from considerable convergence in goals to mutual hostility between the state and the private sector. I argue that, other things being equal, the setting that has proved to be most conducive (i.e., serves as a necessary but not a sufficient condition) to rapid industrial growth in the developing world is one in which the state's near-exclusive commitment to high growth coincided with the profit-maximizing needs of private entrepreneurs. The narrow ruling coalition in these cases was a marriage of repression and profits, aimed at economic growth in the name of the nation. Cohesive-capitalist states have generally created such political economies. Turning their countries into state-guided corporations of sorts, they have tended to be the fastest growers in the developing world.

Growth-oriented cohesive-capitalist states pursued their commitment to high growth by developing trade and industry with well-designed, consistent, and thoroughly implemented state intervention. Specific policy measures varied but were generally aimed at easing supply-and-demand constraints faced by private entrepreneurs. Some of these interventions were direct, and others, indirect. On the supply side, for example, we find that cohesive-capitalist states helped to facilitate the availability of capital, labor, technology, and even entrepreneurship. Thus supply of capital was boosted at times by superior tax collection and public investment, at other times by using publicly controlled banks to direct credit to preferred private firms and sectors, and at yet other times by allowing inflation to shift resources from both agriculture and urban labor to private industrialists. Repression was also a key component in enabling private investors to have a ready supply of cheap, "flexible," and disciplined labor. Examples of less-direct interventions on the supply side include promotion of technology by investing in education and research and development and/or by bargaining with foreign firms to enable technology transfer.

On the demand side, too, cohesive-capitalist states have pursued a variety of policies to promote their growth commitment. These have included expansionist monetary and fiscal policies, and tariffs and exchange-rate policies aimed at boosting domestic demand. And when domestic demand was not sufficient, these states have just as readily adopted newer policies that shift the incentives in favor of export promotion or, more likely, that help to promote production for both domestic and foreign consumption.

There was thus significant variation in the specific policy measures undertaken by cohesive-capitalist states. Only some policies, such as labor discipline, necessitated a repressive state. But what most policies adopted by cohesive-capitalist states reflected instead was a single-minded and unyielding political commitment to growth, combined with a political realization that maximizing production requires assuring the profitability of efficient producers but not of inefficient ones. Sometimes this required getting prices right, but just as often it required "price distortions," such as undervaluing exchange rates, subsidizing exports, and holding wages back behind productivity gains. The central issue concerned the state's goals and capacities, expressed in the institutionalized relationship between the state and the private sector. Cohesive-capitalist states in successful industrializers have thus been pragmatically—and often ruthlessly—procapitalist, much more than they have been purely and ideologically promarket. Among the cases in this study, South Korea under Park Chung Hee and Brazil during Estado Novo and under military rule most clearly fit this political economy model.

Perfect coincidence between the goals of the state and those of private elites has been rare in the developing world, depending as it does on the difficult-to-acquire political precondition of cohesive state power and a narrow alliance between the state and the capital-owning elites. Instead, many ruling elites governed states with fragmented political institutions and defined the public good more broadly. The elites pursued (or, at least, debated) several crucial goals simultaneously: economic growth, redistribution, legitimacy, and national sovereignty. Policy intervention in these fragmented-multiclass states was aimed not only at promoting growth but also at enhancing legitimacy and short-term welfare provision.

Mixed political goals of fragmented-multiclass states had several consequences for choosing and pursuing development policies. First, ruling elites were less focused in these cases on assessing state intervention strictly from the vantage point of growth consequences. Diffuse goals, in turn, enabled various groups and individuals to capture state resources for short-term, consumption-oriented benefits. Second, the relationship of the state to the private sector in such contexts was considerably more complex than in cohesive-capitalist states, sometimes cooperative but just as often conflictual. And third, both policy making and implementation were more politicized, diluting their unidirectional effectiveness.

Fragmented-multiclass states are thus actually more "normal" than the other two ideal-typical cases being discussed here. But because the choice of economic strategy and of policy tools in these cases reflected the logic of both growth and politics, the institutional setting of fragmented-multiclass states was seldom conducive to achieving hypergrowth in industry. The case of India supports such a general contention, as do the cases of Brazil and South Korea in select periods.

Let us consider specific examples of the political economy dynamics of fragmented-multiclass states. Fragmented-multiclass states were neither more nor less interventionist than cohesive-capitalist states, but they were generally less effective at alleviating the supply-and-demand constraints faced by their investors. Again, for example, when it came to mobilizing capital in many fragmented-multiclass states, tax-collecting capacities were limited, public-spending priorities included numerous goals other than growth promotion, attempts to direct credit easily evolved into cronyism, and inflation as a tool of resource transfer could readily become a liability for political leaders concerned about their legitimacy. Periodic hostility on the part of the state elite toward private investors made the latter, both domestic and foreign, reluctant to invest. Repression of labor was also not a ready alternative in fragmented-multiclass states, thus making it difficult for investors to mobilize a cheap and docile labor force.

On the demand side, monetary and fiscal policies seldom reflected consistent growth commitment but fluctuated instead with political cycles characterized by greater or lesser legitimacy. And finally, tariff and exchange-rate policies adopted to protect the national economy, and thus to promote demand for indigenous goods, often created powerful interest groups. As these groups were difficult to dislodge, fragmented-multiclass states found themselves more rigidly committed to a particular development path. In sum, fragmented-multiclass states, like cohesive-capitalist states, sought to promote industrialization, but they did so less effectively because their goals were more plural and their political capacities less developed. In other words, varying patterns of state authority decisively influenced developmental trajectories.

According to this line of argument, the worst setting for industrialization on the periphery was the states that had no clear public goals and whose leaders reduced the state to an arena for personal aggrandizement. These neopatrimonial states have unfortunately constituted a significant subset of the developing world. State intervention in these cases has often been motivated either by the need to build short-term political support via patronage or by personal greed—or sometimes by both. The relationship of the state and the private sector in such contexts has just as often been mutually corrupt: Political instability, inconsistent policies, and pilfering of public resources for personal and sectional gains have all hurt state-led efforts to promote industry and growth. The case of Nigeria provides a striking instance of such a development path, though elements of the same are also evident elsewhere.

We will see that neopatrimonial states, like cohesive-capitalist and fragmented-multiclass states, have also intervened heavily in their economies but with disastrous results. Neopatrimonial states have often emerged in societies with weak private sectors, but instead of strengthening the private sector, these states have appropriated scarce economic resources and diverted them everywhere but toward productive investment. Inconsistent economic policies, failure to support indigenous capitalists, poor-quality but activist labor, and political instability have all reinforced the existing weakness of the national private sector in manufacturing and industry.

Given this profound weakness of domestic capitalism, neopatrimonial states have sought to undertake economic activities directly or invited foreign goods and producers to fill the vacuum. Given the states' nondevelopmental proclivities and organizational weakness, efforts to produce goods in the public sector have generally failed. The remaining alternative of importing goods or attracting foreign investment makes sense only if there are alternative sources of income and demand. For a country such as

Nigeria, oil exports provided a ready source of income and demand, which was met by foreign goods and producers; this is less true for other neopatrimonial states. Commodity booms, however, seldom last forever. The political incapacity to anticipate such cycles, plan for them, and cut back on imports and public expenditures when circumstances so demand further aggravate the tragedies of commodity-dependent neopatrimonial states. Given such state weakness, the question remains, is there a way out of these repetitive cycles of developmental disasters in neopatrimonial states?

Patterns of State Construction

If goals and capacities of the state, especially as they are expressed in the institutionalized relationship of the state and the private sector, are important for understanding relative effectiveness of state intervention, the next logical, though historically prior question, concerns the origins of this variation itself. Why have some states succeeded in harnessing the energies of their private sectors to facilitate rapid industrialization, whereas others have created a mutually corrupt relationship, leading to waste and stagnation? Or, more specifically, why have some parts of the developing world ended up with cohesive-capitalist states, others with neopatrimonial states, and yet others, probably the majority, with fragmented-multiclass states? This question forces the analysis to take a more historical turn.

The first general observation concerning the roots of different state types is that states acquired some of their core characteristics well before they became activist states, ready to pursue deliberate industrialization. While this is demonstrated throughout this book via historical analysis, two theoretical observations as to why this should be so are offered here. First, institutions are social patterns that gel only over time; and once gelled, they often endure beyond the forces that brought them into being. Breakdowns and discontinuities in institutions are not uncommon, but these are often dramatic, requiring explanation. What also requires explanation is how institutions are established. By contrast, continuity is in the nature of institutions, as patterns that endure through a variety of underlying mechanisms such as

internal order and shared norms, boundaries vis-à-vis the broader social context, socialization of new members, and support from the society in which they function.

What is true for societal institutions in general—and this is the second theoretical observation—is even more true for state institutions. States centralize coercion, and both state formation and basic changes in the state's authority structure often involve the use of significant organized power, if not organized coercion. Organizing power and coercion, however, are never easy. Not only do such efforts face opposition from existing centers of power with a vested interest in continuity, but they are also plagued by numerous problems such as mobilizing resources, accessing technology, and overcoming obstacles of collective action. Those responsible for constructing states must therefore possess a clear preponderance of power to impress their institutional design on national societies. Institutions of a modern state in the developing world have thus often originated by acts of coercion imposed by external powers, and, once founded, their basic patterns have just as often continued well beyond the intentions and interest of the founders.

Basic state forms in the developing world emerge and change mainly via a series of infrequent big bangs. Of course, it will become clear in due course that incremental changes, via the development of either new social classes or such new political forces as parties, are also very much part of an ongoing process of how the character of a state changes. Basic changes, however, by which I mean, say, the transformation of a neopatrimonial state into a cohesive-capitalist state or even into a fragmented-multiclass state, tend to be rare because such changes require decisive political intervention. Variations in the state's basic authority structures in the developing world can thus be seen as a product of three sets of competing influences capable of such decisive political intervention: colonialism, nationalist movements, and coercive politics of national armed forces.

The impact of colonialism on state formation was especially significant because most developing country states are the product of colonialism, and their respective forms were molded decisively by this encounter with more advanced political economies. Once established, core institutional characteristics acquired during colonial rule have also proved difficult to alter. Anticolonial nationalist movements were one potential organized force capable of altering the basic state forms inherited from colonialism. With only a few notable exceptions, however, such as India or the more revolutionary nationalists, such as in China or Vietnam, anticolonial nationalist movements in much of Asia and Africa were too superficial and/or fragmented to alter the inherited state forms decisively. More forceful actions to reorder the nature of state authority were taken instead by organized armed forces. But even armed intervention was rarely decisive in altering a state's developmental goals and capacities—either because the armed forces were internally divided or because they lacked civilian collaborators.

The significance of colonialism in constructing alternative state types thus looms large in this study. The study of the impact of colonialism on developing countries has often focused on economic matters. As important as this is, the relative neglect of political analysis has been unfortunate for colonialism was first and foremost an act of political control, which led well-organized states with dynamic economies to establish supremacy over a variety of disorganized, poor peoples of Asia and Africa.[7] Economic exploitation was very much a part of colonialism, as was racial subjugation and humiliation. All this was possible by means of direct political control, however varied the structures and processes of establishing that control. This variation occurred because the realities on the ground differed, in part because different colonizers brought different ideologies of rule with them and in part because the urgency, motive, and capacities of colonizers differed across place and time. The cumulative impact was that colonialism in some parts of the developing world laid the foundation for what would eventually emerge as cohesive-capitalist states, in other parts, as neopatrimonial states, and in yet other parts, as fragmented-multiclass states. Specific historical experiences of at least the two more extreme cases of Korea and Nigeria, briefly illustrated here, can help to clarify this general observation.

South Korea's cohesive-capitalist state, for example, originated during Japanese colonial rule, which differed in important respects from the colonialism of the European powers. As late developers, the Japanese made extensive use of state power for their own economic development, and they used the same state power to pry open and transform Korea within a relatively short period of time. The Japanese colonial impact was thus intense, brutal, and deeply architectonic. Three patterns of what eventually became South Korea's cohesive-capitalist, growth-promoting state originated in this period: A relatively corrupt and ineffective agrarian bureaucracy was transformed into a highly authoritarian and penetrating political organization; the state established close and working production-oriented alliances with the dominant classes; and a well-developed system of state control of the lower classes was created. Over time, as one would expect, these structures were battered by numerous new forces and some significant changes ensued. Nevertheless, the core state-class characteristics endured, eventually providing South Korea with a framework for the evolution of a high-growth political economy.

By contrast, British colonialism in Nigeria created a highly distorted state that readily evolved into a neopatrimonial and ineffective set of political organizations. Britain ruled Nigeria on the cheap, expending as little energy as possible. Within the shell of a modern colonial state and cloaked in the ideology of indirect rule, the British essentially utilized various "traditional" rulers to impose order. At its core, colonialism in Nigeria thus reinforced a pattern of patrimonial and personalistic rule that failed to centralize authority, to develop an effective civil service, and relatedly, to develop even such minimal political capacities as the ability to collect direct taxes. The public realm that came into being was barely demarcated from private and sectional interests in terms of both culture and organization. After the Second World War, when the colonial state's access to resources grew and the state became more and more involved in the economy, these distorted beginnings were further accentuated, as the state became further enmeshed in particularistic and personalistic networks. The political elite of sovereign Nigeria were never able to overcome the original deficiencies of state construction. They simply went from crisis to crisis, both controlling and wasting the society scarce developmental resources.

Power for Development

Power is the currency that states use to achieve their desired ends. Power may be more or less legitimate, and it may be used positively as an incentive or negatively as punishment or threat of punishment. The fact that some states have been more successful than others at propelling industrialization suggests that successful states possessed a greater degree of power to define and pursue their goals.

A full understanding of why some states are more efficacious than others at facilitating industrial transformation has to be centered around a concept of power as a societal resource that varies in quantity and can thus grow or decline. Efficacious states simply have more power at their disposal than less efficacious ones: Cohesive-capitalist states thus command a lot more power to define and pursue their goals than neopatrimonial states, with fragmented-multiclass states falling somewhere in between along the continuum. Key determinants of this variation in state power for development are organizational characteristics of state institutions, on the one hand, and the manner in which states craft their relations with social classes, especially producer classes, on the other hand.

Some states are simply more purposive and better organized than others. Some states also choose to work closely with their dominant classes, whereas others, facing a variety of pressures, maintain some distance. Maximum power to propel industrialization is generated when purposive, well-organized states work closely with producing classes. Under these circumstances—the circumstances of cohesive-capitalist states—coercive, organizational, mobilizational, and economic powers of a society are aggregated and can help to propel economic change. If one thinks of the process of industrialization as a chariot, one can imagine states and entrepreneurs as two horses that may pull it. The chariot will move rapidly if both horses are strong and if both pull in the same direction. When the two horses do not pull in the same direction—as is often the case in fragmented-multiclass states, where states and entrepreneurs sometimes work together, but just as often do not—society's power resources will be dissipated, and the chariot of industrialization will not move as rapidly and smoothly. And when both horses are feeble—the case of poorly formed neopatrimonial states with weak private sectors—power to propel economic change will be lacking and the economic chariot may not move very far at all.

To sum up, this is a study that probes the role of the state as an economic actor in select developing countries by analyzing both the patterns of state construction and the patterns of state intervention aimed at promoting industrialization and economic growth. The central question throughout is how one can best understand the degree to which a state is developmentally effective. Since the states under consideration often acquired some of their core characteristics in the first half of the twentieth century, the time period under consideration for each country is generally the century as whole. However, it is also important to note at the outset that this is not study of the more "neoliberal" phase of development that many countries entered toward the end of the twentieth century. The analysis of each case thus concludes around the time period when these states embraced a more market-oriented development strategy. While the empirical accounts are aimed at developing general themes—themes that are introduced briefly above and that are discussed further in the conclusion—they are also meant to stand alone, providing a fairly full analytical story of individual countries within a coherent, comparative framework. The challenge of striking an appropriate balance between the generalizing frame of social science and the more specific individual histories is a perennial one. It will be up to the readers to decide how well that challenge has been met here, both in terms of getting individual country stories "right" and, more important, in terms of developing a persuasive general argument.

NOTES

1. See, for example, Anne Krueger, "The Political Economy of the Rent Seeking Society," *American Economic Review* 64 (1974): 291–303; Deepak Lal, *The Poverty of "Development" Economics*, Hobart Paperback no. 16 (London: Institute of Economic Affairs, 1983); and World Bank, *Development Report* (New York: Oxford University Press, 1991).

2. Among others, see Robert Wade, *Governing the Market: Economic Theory and the Role of Government in East Asian Industrialization* (Princeton, N.J.: Princeton University Press, 1990); Alice Amsden, *Asia's Next Giant: South Korea and Late Industrialization* (New York: Oxford University Press, 1989); and Peter Evans, *Embedded Autonomy: State and Industrial Transformation* (Princeton, N.J.: Princeton University Press, 1995).

3. See Alexander Gerschenkron, *Economic Backwardness in Historical Perspective* (Cambridge: Harvard University Press, 1962), esp. chap. 1.

4. Careful readers may wonder whether such other combinations as cohesive-multiclass and fragmented-capitalist are also possible. The short answer is yes, but generally not in the developing world. A well-organized social democracy, such as Sweden, may illustrate the cohesive-multiclass category, and the United States may be a good example of a fragmented-capitalist state. A fuller discussion of these state types is beyond the scope of this study, though some such issues are discussed in due course, especially in the conclusion.

5. It will become clear in due course, especially in the section on Korea, why I prefer the concept of cohesive-capitalist states over "developmental states." Suffice it to note here that the idea that developmental states facilitate development strikes me as too obvious for both analytical and normative comfort. A label such as cohesive-capitalist states (in an earlier draft, I had used the term "neofascist states") instead both captures better a state's independent political characteristics—by which I mean the ideology, organization, and the underlying class alliances—and cautions observers to take note of the costs incurred by the type of "development" these states promote.

6. Generalizing about "fascist-style regimes" during the interwar years, Claudio Segre notes that "within wide national variations, fascist states had certain characteristics and aspirations in common. In their political systems, they created police states, one party systems led by a charismatic dictator. Their economic systems aimed to develop some form of national socialism. The government was to play an active role in controlling the economy, but unlike Marxian socialism, the state was not to take over the means of production. Fascist socialism was directed at the interests of the nation. . . . Fascism also aspired to some form of the corporatist state. . . . Fascist regimes mobilized and disciplined societies to transform themselves far more rapidly than would have been the case under a laissez-faire system." See his entry on "fascism" in *The Oxford Companion to Politics of the World* (New York: Oxford University Press, 2001), 274–76.

7. See, for example, D. K. Fieldhouse. *Colonialism, 1870–1945: An Introduction* (New York: St. Martin's Press, 1981).

FRANCIS FUKUYAMA

5.2 TRUST

The Social Virtues and the Creation of Prosperity

Fukuyama's piece sets up a comparative distinction between countries that have deep reservoirs of trust and those that do not. According to this piece, "a nation's well-being, as well as its ability to compete, is conditioned by a single, pervasive cultural characteristic: the level of trust inherent in the society." Fukuyama notes examples of high trust in private companies in three of the world's largest and most successful economies of the 20th century: Germany, Japan, and the United States. He contrasts this with vignettes from places such as southern Italy and the inner-city United States, where trust is lacking and economies suffer. Fukuyama links the idea of trust to notions of "social capital" and the art of association, arguing that strong linkages between people and within groups is important for maintaining vibrant economies. Can you think of ways that the economic policies noted by Friedman, the types of state welfare provision discussed by Esping-Andersen (both from the previous chapter), and the historical institutions highlighted by Kohli (in the other reading in this chapter) would affect social trust? And vice versa?

ON THE HUMAN SITUATION
AT THE END OF HISTORY

As we approach the twenty-first century, a remarkable convergence of political and economic institutions has taken place around the world. Earlier in this century, deep ideological cleavages divided the world's societies. Monarchy, fascism, liberal democracy, and communism were bitter competitors for political supremacy, while different countries chose the divergent economic paths of protectionism, corporatism, the free market, and socialist centralized planning. Today virtually all advanced countries have adopted, or are trying to adopt, liberal democratic political institutions, and a great number have simultaneously moved in the direction of market-oriented economies and integration into the global capitalist division of labor.

As I have argued elsewhere, this movement constitutes an "end of history," in the Marxist-Hegelian sense of History as a broad evolution of human societies advancing toward a final goal.[1] As modern technology unfolds, it shapes national economies in a coherent fashion, interlocking them in a vast global economy. The increasing complexity and information intensity of modern life at the same time renders centralized economic planning extremely difficult. The enormous prosperity created by technology-driven capitalism, in turn, serves as an incubator for a liberal regime of universal and equal rights, in which the struggle for recognition of human dignity culminates. While many countries have had trouble creating the institutions of democracy and free markets, and others, especially in parts of the former communist world, have slid backward into fascism or anarchy, the world's advanced countries have no alternative model of political and economic organization other than democratic capitalism to which they can aspire.

This convergence of institutions around the model of democratic capitalism, however, has not meant an end to society's challenges. Within a given

Fukuyama, Francis. 1995. *Trust: The Social Virtues and the Creation of Prosperity*. New York: Free Press.

institutional framework, societies can be richer or poorer, or have more or less satisfying social and spiritual lives. But a corollary to the convergence of institutions at the "end of history" is the widespread acknowledgment that in postindustrial societies, further improvements cannot be achieved through ambitious social engineering. We no longer have realistic hopes that we can create a "great society" through large government programs. The Clinton administration's difficulties in promoting health care reform in 1994 indicated that Americans remained skeptical about the workability of large-scale government management of an important sector of their economy. In Europe, almost no one argues that the continent's major concerns today, such as a high continuing rate of unemployment or immigration, can be fixed through expansion of the welfare state. If anything, the reform agenda consists of cutting back the welfare state to make European industry more competitive on a global basis. Even Keynesian deficit spending, once widely used by industrial democracies after the Great Depression to manage the business cycle, is today regarded by most economists as self-defeating in the long run. These days, the highest ambition of most governments in their macro-economic policy is to do no harm, by ensuring a stable money supply and controlling large budget deficits.

Today, having abandoned the promise of social engineering, virtually all serious observers understand that liberal political and economic institutions depend on a healthy and dynamic civil society for their vitality.[2] "Civil society"—a complex welter of intermediate institutions, including businesses, voluntary associations, educational institutions, clubs, unions, media, charities, and churches—builds, in turn, on the family, the primary instrument by which people are socialized into their culture and given the skills that allow them to live in broader society and through which the values and knowledge of that society are transmitted across the generations.

A strong and stable family structure and durable social institutions cannot be legislated into existence the way a government can create a central bank or an army. A thriving civil society depends on a people's habits, customs, and ethics—attributes that can be shaped only indirectly through conscious political action and must otherwise be nourished through an increased awareness and respect for culture.

Beyond the boundaries of specific nations, this heightened significance of culture extends into the realms of the global economy and international order. Indeed, one of the ironies of the convergence of larger institutions since the end of the cold war is that people around the world are now even more conscious of the cultural differences that separate them. For example, over the past decade, Americans have become much more aware of the fact that Japan, an erstwhile member of the "free world" during the cold war, practices both democracy and capitalism according to a different set of cultural norms than does the United States. These differences have led to considerable friction at times, as when the members of a Japanese business network known as a *keiretsu* buy from one another rather than from a foreign company that might offer better price or quality. For their part, many Asians are troubled by certain aspects of American culture, such as its litigiousness and the readiness of Americans to insist upon their individual rights at the expense of the greater good. Increasingly, Asians point to superior aspects of their own cultural inheritance, such as deference to authority, emphasis on education, and family values, as sources of social vitality.[3]

The increasing salience of culture in the global order is such that Samuel Huntington has argued that the world is moving into a period of "civilizational clash," in which the primary identification of people will not be ideological, as during the cold war, but cultural.[4] Accordingly, conflict is likely to arise not among fascism, socialism, and democracy but among the world's major cultural groups: Western, Islamic, Confucian, Japanese, Hindu, and so on.

Huntington is clearly correct that cultural differences will loom larger from now on and that all societies will have to pay more attention to culture as they deal not only with internal problems but with the outside world. Where Huntington's argument is less convincing, however, is that cultural differences will necessarily be the source of conflict. On the contrary, the rivalry arising from the interaction of different cultures can frequently lead to creative change, and there are numerous cases of such cultural cross-stimulation. Japan's confrontation with Western culture after the arrival of Commodore Perry's "black ships" in 1853 paved the way for the Meiji Restoration and Japan's subsequent industrialization. In the past generation, techniques like lean manufacturing—the process of eliminating buffers from the manufacturing process to facilitate feedback from the factory floor—have made their way from Japan to the United States, to the latter's benefit. Whether the confrontation of cultures leads to conflict or to adaptation and progress, it is now vitally important to develop a deeper understanding of what makes these cultures distinctive and functional, since the issues surrounding international competition, political and economic, increasingly will be cast in cultural terms.

Perhaps the most crucial area of modern life in which culture exercises a direct influence on domestic well-being and international order is the economy. Although economic activity is inextricably linked with social and political life, there is a mistaken tendency, encouraged by contemporary economic discourse, to regard the economy as a facet of life with its own laws, separate from the rest of society. Seen this way, the economy is a realm in which individuals come together only to satisfy their selfish needs and desires before retreating back into their "real" social lives. But in any modern society, the economy constitutes one of the most fundamental and dynamic arenas of human sociability. There is scarcely any form of economic activity, from running a dry-cleaning business to fabricating large-scale integrated circuits, that does not require the social collaboration of human beings. And while people work in organizations to satisfy their individual needs, the workplace also draws people out of their private lives and connects them to a wider social world. That connectedness is not just a means to the end of earning a paycheck but an important end of human life itself. For just as people are selfish, a side of the human personality craves being part of larger communities. Human beings feel an acute sense of unease—what Emile Durkheim labeled *anomie*—in the absence of norms and rules binding them to others, an unease that the modern workplace serves to moderate and overcome.[5]

The satisfaction we derive from being connected to others in the workplace grows out of a fundamental human desire for recognition. As I argued in *The End of History and the Last Man*, every human being seeks to have his or her dignity recognized (i.e., evaluated at its proper worth) by other human beings. Indeed, this drive is so deep and fundamental that it is one of the chief motors of the entire human historical process. In earlier periods, this desire for recognition played itself out in the military arena as kings and princes fought bloody battles with one another for primacy. In modern times, this struggle for recognition has shifted from the military to the economic realm, where it has the socially beneficial effect of creating rather than destroying wealth. Beyond subsistence levels, economic activity is frequently undertaken for the sake of recognition rather than merely as a means of satisfying natural material needs.[6] The latter are, as Adam Smith pointed out, few in number and relatively easily satisfied. Work and money are much more important as sources of identity, status, and dignity, whether one has created a multinational media empire or been promoted to foreman. This kind of recognition cannot be achieved by individuals; it can come about only in a social context.

Thus, economic activity represents a crucial part of social life and is knit together by a wide variety of norms, rules, moral obligations, and other habits that together shape the society. As this book will show, one of the most important lessons we can learn from an examination of economic life is that a nation's well-being, as well as its ability to compete, is conditioned by a single, pervasive cultural characteristic: the level of trust inherent in the society.

Consider the following vignettes from twentieth-century economic life:

- During the oil crisis of the early 1970s, two automakers on opposite sides of the world, Mazda and Daimler-Benz (maker of Mercedes-Benz luxury cars), were both hit with declining sales and the prospect of bankruptcy. In both cases, they were bailed out by a coalition of companies with which they had traditionally done business, led by a large bank: Sumitomo Trust, in the instances of Mazda, and the Deutsche Bank, in the case of Daimler. In both cases, immediate profitability was sacrificed for the sake of saving the institution—in the German case, to prevent it from being bought out by a group of Arab investors.

- The recession of 1983–1984 that ravaged America's industrial heartland also hit the Nucor Corporation very hard. Nucor had just entered the steel-making business by building mini-mills using a new German continuous-casting technology. Its mills were built in places like Crawfordsville, Indiana, outside the traditional rust belt, and were operated by nonunionized workers, many of them former farmers. To deal with the drop in revenues, Nucor put its employees—from the CEO to the lowliest maintenance worker—on a two- or three-day workweek, with a corresponding cut in pay. No workers were fired, however, and when the economy and the company recovered, it enjoyed a tremendous esprit de corps that contributed to its becoming a major force in the American steel industry.[7]

- In the Toyota Motor Company's Takaoka assembly plant, any of the thousands of assembly line workers who work there can bring the entire plant to a halt by pulling on a cord at his or her workstation. They seldom do. By contrast, workers at the great Ford auto plants like Highland Park or River Rouge—plants that virtually defined the nature of modern industrial production for three generations—were never trusted with this kind of power. Today, Ford workers, having adopted Japanese techniques, are trusted with similar powers, and have greater control over their workplace and machines.

- In Germany, shop foremen on the floor of a typical factory know how to do the jobs of those who work under them and frequently take their place if the need arises. The foreman can move workers from one job to another and evaluates them based on face-to-face dealings. There is great flexibility in promotion: a blue-collar worker can obtain credentials as an engineer by attending an extensive in-company training program rather than going to a university.

The common thread that runs through these four apparently unrelated vignettes is that in each case, economic actors supported one another because they believed that they formed a community based on mutual trust. The banks and suppliers that engineered the Mazda and Daimler-Benz rescues felt an obligation to support these auto companies because the latter had supported them in the past and would do so again in the future. In the German case, moreover, there was a nationalistic feeling that such an important trademark German name as Mercedes-Benz should not fall into non-German hands. Workers at Nucor were willing to accept severe cuts in their weekly pay because they believed that the managers who devised the pay cut plan were hurting as well and were committed to not laying them off. The workers at the Toyota plant were given immense power to stop the entire assembly line because management trusted them not to abuse that power, and they repaid this trust by using that power responsibly to improve the line's overall productivity. Finally, the workplace in Germany is flexible and egalitarian because workers trust their managers and fellow workers to a higher degree than in other European countries.

The community in each of these cases was a cultural one, formed not on the basis of explicit rules and regulations but out of a set of ethical habits and reciprocal moral obligations internalized by each of the community's members. These rules or habits gave members of the community grounds for trusting one another. Decisions to support the community were not based on narrow economic self-interest. The Nucor management could have decided to award themselves bonuses while laying off workers, as many other American corporations did at the time, and Sumitomo Trust and Deutsche Bank could perhaps have maximized their profits by selling off their failing assets. Solidarity within the economic community in question may have had beneficial consequences over the long run for the bottom line; certainly Nucor's workers were motivated to give their company an extra measure of effort once the recession was over, as was the German foreman whose company helped him to become an engineer. But the reason that these economic actors behaved as they did was not necessarily because they had calculated these economic consequences in advance; rather, solidarity within their economic community had become an end in itself. Each was motivated, in other words, by something broader than individual self-interest. As we will see, in all successful economic societies these communities are united by trust.

By contrast, consider situations in which the absence of trust has led to poor economic performance and its attendant social implications:

- In a small town in southern Italy during the 1950s, Edward Banfield noted that the wealthy citizens were unwilling to come together to found either a school or hospital, which the town needed badly, or to build a factory, despite an abundance of capital and labor, because they believed it was the obligation of the state to undertake such activities.
- In contrast to German practice, the French shop foreman's relations with his or her workers are regulated by a thicket of rules established by a ministry in Paris. This comes about because the French tend not to trust superiors to make honest personal evaluations of their workers. The formal rules prevent the foreman from moving workers from one job to another, inhibiting development of a sense of workplace solidarity and making very difficult the introduction of innovations like the Japanese lean manufacturing system.
- Small businesses in American inner cities are seldom owned by African-Americans; they tend to be controlled by other ethnic groups, like the Jews earlier in this century and Koreans today. One reason is an absence of strong community and mutual trust among the contemporary African-American "underclass." Korean businesses are organized around stable families and benefit from rotating credit associations within the broader ethnic community; inner-city African-American families are weak and credit associations virtually nonexistent.

These three cases reveal the absence of a proclivity for community that inhibits people from exploiting economic opportunities that are available to them. The problem is one of a deficit of what the sociologist James Coleman has called "social capital": the ability of people to work together for common purposes in groups and organizations.[8] The concept of human capital, widely used and understood among economists, starts from the premise that capital today is embodied less in land, factories, tools, and machines than, increasingly, in the knowledge and skills of human beings.[9] Coleman argued that in addition to skills and knowledge, a distinct portion of human capital has to do with people's ability to associate with each other, that is critical not only to economic life but to virtually every other aspect of social existence as well. The ability to associate depends, in turn, on the degree to which communities share norms and values and are able to subordinate individual interests to those of larger groups. Out of such shared values comes trust, and trust, as we will see, has a large and measurable economic value.

With regard to the ability to form spontaneous communities such as those detailed above, the United States has had more in common with Japan and Germany than any of these three has with Chinese societies like Hong Kong and Taiwan, on the one hand, and Italy and France on the other. The United States, like Japan and Germany, has historically been a high-trust, group-oriented society, despite the fact that Americans believe themselves to be rugged individualists.

But the United States has been changing rather dramatically over the past couple of generations with respect to its art of association. In many ways, American society is becoming as individualistic as Americans have always believed it was: the inherent tendency of rights-based liberalism to expand and multiply those rights against the authority of virtually all existing communities has been pushed toward its logical conclusion. The decline of trust and sociability in the United States is also evident in any number of changes in American society: the rise of violent crime and civil litigation; the breakdown of family structure; the decline of a wide range of intermediate social structures like neighborhoods, churches, unions, clubs, and charities; and the general sense among Americans of a lack of shared values and community with those around them.

This decline of sociability has important implications for American democracy, perhaps even more so than for the economy. Already the United States pays significantly more than other industrialized countries for police protection and keeps more than 1 percent of its total population in prison. The United States also pays substantially more than does Europe or Japan to its lawyers, so that its citizens can sue one another. Both of these costs, which amount to a measurable percentage of gross domestic product annually, constitute a direct tax imposed by the breakdown of trust in the society. In the future, the economic effects may be more far-reaching; the ability of Americans to start and work within a wide variety of new organizations may begin to deteriorate as its very diversity lowers trust and creates new barriers to cooperation. In addition to its physical capital, the United States has been living off a fund of social capital. Just as its savings rate has been too low to replace physical plant and infrastructure adequately, so its replenishment of social capital has lagged in recent decades. The accumulation of social capital, however, is a complicated and in many ways mysterious cultural process. While governments can enact policies that have the effect of depleting social capital, they have great difficulties understanding how to build it up again.

The liberal democracy that emerges at the end of history is therefore not entirely "modern." If the institutions of democracy and capitalism are to work properly, they must coexist with certain premodern cultural habits that ensure their proper functioning. Law, contract, and economic rationality provide a necessary but not sufficient basis for both the stability and prosperity of postindustrial societies; they must as well be leavened with reciprocity, moral obligation, duty toward community, and trust, which are based in habit rather than rational calculation. The latter are not anachronisms in a modern society but rather the sine qua non of the latter's success.

NOTES

1. See Francis Fukuyama, *The End of History and the Last Man* (New York: Free Press, 1992).
2. For an excellent discussion of the origins of civil society and its relationship to democracy, see Ernest Gellner, *Conditions and Liberty: Civil Society and Its Rivals* (London: Hamish Hamilton, 1994).
3. For a more detailed discussion of this point, see Francis Fukuyama, "The Primacy of Culture," *Journal of Democracy* 6 (1995): 7–14.
4. Samuel P. Huntington, "The Clash of Civilizations?" *Foreign Affairs* 72 (1994): 22–49.
5. According to Durkheim, "Society is not alone in its interest in the formation of special groups to regulate their own activity, developing within them what otherwise would become anarchic; but the individual, on his part, finds joy in it, for anarchy is painful to him. He also suffers from pain and disorder produced whenever interindividual relations are not submitted to some regulatory influence." *The Division of Labor in Society* (New York: Macmillan, 1933), p. 15.
6. See Fukuyama (1992), particularly chap. 21, "The Thymotic Origins of Work."
7. For a readable account of Nucor's rise as a steel company, see Richard Preston, *American Steel* (New York: Avon Books, 1991).
8. James S. Coleman, "Social Capital in the Creation of Human Capital," *American Journal of Sociology* 94 (1988): S95–Sl20. See also Robert D. Putnam, "The Prosperous Community: Social Capital and Public Life," *American Prospect* 13 (1993): 35–42; and Putnam, "Bowling Alone," *Journal of Democracy* 6 (1995): 65–78. According to Putnam, the first use of the term *social capital* was by Jane Jacobs, in *The Death and Life of Great American Cities* (New York: Random House, 1961), p. 138.
9. Gary S. Becker, *Human Capital: A Theoretical and Empirical Analysis*, 2d ed. (New York: National Bureau of Economic Research, 1975).

CHAPTER 6

DEMOCRACY AND DEMOCRATIZATION

Democracy is one of the most fundamental, albeit complex, concepts in comparative politics. First, it describes how some countries are organized politically. That is, some countries can be considered democratic and others not. This is an important distinction for describing similarities and differences between countries. Most scholars and citizens alike would agree that living in a democracy means a quite different political life than one finds in an authoritarian regime.

Beyond this descriptive use as a concept, democracy is also an idea that many observers really care about: democracy is seen as a goal, since many people would like to see their society become more "democratic." Even if many observers realize that democracy does not always bring other good things (like economic success and social justice), it often does mean political participation and inclusion for the many and not just the few. The normative or moral appeal of democracy is not our emphasis here, but it does heighten our academic interest in this concept.

Through the readings, ask yourself what democracy means and why it happens. This chapter uses a selection of well-known pieces that seek to address these questions. In terms of defining the concept, democracy is often linked to notions of greater participation in public life for the citizenry at large. Most obviously for many observers, this links to the idea of holding elections that are reasonably free and fair, in which multiple candidates and parties can compete. However, as Philippe Schmitter and Terry Lynn Karl note in their article, democracy also requires civil liberties and rights for citizens beyond election time. The idea of democracy as it is conceptualized here can be called a "procedural" definition because it focuses on the minimum standards and procedures (such as voting and the expression of rights) that allow a country to meet the threshold of being considered a democracy. However, there are competing definitions of democracy offered by other scholars that take a more "substantive" focus, emphasizing that the extent of democracy should be measured by a society's achievements in areas such as civic participation or reductions in inequalities.

Defining democracy has been a central debate in comparative politics and explaining why democracy happens has been another. This question about the causes of democracy is fundamental in political life. Given the importance of this question, several major theories have arisen to explain it. A leading theory comes under the rubric of "modernization." It holds that social and economic changes in a society (such as economic development) lead to changes in the political structure of a country. Other theories would focus on other factors: changes in the norms, values, and ideas of important political actors, or the role other countries play in promoting democracy or the role of specific individuals and groups (say, Mahatma Gandhi and his followers in India) in the democratization process.

Our second selection reflects a modernization perspective. Seymour Martin Lipset in 1959 wrote one of the definitive statements linking economic and social modernization to democratization. The piece excerpted here has helped shape the debate on democratization ever since. In considering Lipset, ask yourself if you could think of cases (namely different countries around the world) that don't fit with the predictions of this model. What characteristics would you be looking for in a country that you might use to critique Lipset's article? (Hint: you will be looking for cases that on the variable "regime type" and on the variable "level of modernization" don't match Lipset's prediction.) If you identify such a country, can you think of other variables that might be affecting the regime type that you observe?

PHILIPPE C. SCHMITTER AND TERRY LYNN KARL

6.1 WHAT DEMOCRACY IS . . . AND IS NOT

Schmitter and Karl have written an important piece about the concept of democracy. They begin by defining some of the key characteristics of democracy, building particularly on the idea of "polyarchy" (roughly speaking, "rule by the many") forwarded by Robert Dahl. The authors also add a couple of additional features to Dahl's classic definition. One of the most important themes in this selection is the idea that democracy is about much more than just having free and fair elections. Although the political rights surrounding elections are important, so too are the many civil rights and civil liberties that make possible the full participation of nearly all citizens in civic life. Schmitter and Karl then proceed to discuss what democracy is not. In particular, they argue that democracy should not be measured in substantive terms by whatever other good things it provides. For them, democracy is a set of procedures and rules, not a recipe for the good life in all areas of the economy and society. Is this a satisfying definition of democracy or would you argue for a more "substantive" definition?

WHAT DEMOCRACY IS

Let us begin by broadly defining democracy and the generic *concepts* that distinguish it as a unique system for organizing relations between rulers and the ruled. We will then briefly review *procedures*, the rules and arrangements that are needed if democracy is to endure. Finally, we will discuss two operative *principles* that make democracy work. They are not expressly included among the generic concepts or formal procedures, but the prospect for democracy is grim if their underlying conditioning effects are not present.

One of the major themes of this essay is that democracy does not consist of a single unique set of institutions. There are many types of democracy, and their diverse practices produce a similarly varied set of effects. The specific form democracy takes is contingent upon a country's socioeconomic conditions as well as its entrenched state structures and policy practices.

Modern political democracy is a system of governance in which rulers are held accountable for their actions in the public realm by citizens, acting indirectly through the competition and cooperation of their elected representatives.[1]

A *regime or system of governance* is an ensemble of patterns that determines the methods of access to the principal public offices; the characteristics of the actors admitted to or excluded from such access; the strategies that actors may use to gain access; and the rules that are followed in the making of publicly binding decisions. To work properly, the ensemble must be institutionalized—that is to say, the various patterns must be habitually known, practiced, and accepted by most, if not all, actors. Increasingly, the preferred mechanism of institutionalization is a written body of laws undergirded by a written constitution, though many enduring political norms can have an informal, prudential, or traditional basis.[2]

For the sake of economy and comparison, these forms, characteristics, and rules are usually bundled together and given a generic label. Democratic is one; others are autocratic, authoritarian, despotic, dictatorial, tyrannical, totalitarian, absolutist, traditional, monarchic, oligarchic, plutocratic, aristocratic, and

Schmitter, Philippe C., and Terry Lynn Karl. 1991. "What Democracy Is . . . and Is Not," *Journal of Democracy* 2(3): 75–88.

sultanistic.[3] Each of these regime forms may in turn be broken down into subtypes.

Like all regimes, democracies depend upon the presence of *rulers*, persons who occupy specialized authority roles and can give legitimate commands to others. What distinguishes democratic rulers from nondemocratic ones are the norms that condition how the former come to power and the practices that hold them accountable for their actions.

The *public realm* encompasses the making of collective norms and choices that are binding on the society and backed by state coercion. Its content can vary a great deal across democracies, depending upon preexisting distinctions between the public and the private, state and society, legitimate coercion and voluntary exchange, and collective needs and individual preferences. The liberal conception of democracy advocates circumscribing the public realm as narrowly as possible, while the socialist or social-democratic approach would extend that realm through regulation, subsidization, and, in some cases, collective ownership of property. Neither is intrinsically more democratic than the other—just *differently* democratic. This implies that measures aimed at "developing the private sector" are no more democratic than those aimed at "developing the public sector." Both, if carried to extremes, could undermine the practice of democracy, the former by destroying the basis for satisfying collective needs and exercising legitimate authority; the latter by destroying the basis for satisfying individual preferences and controlling illegitimate government actions. Differences of opinion over the optimal mix of the two provide much of the substantive content of political conflict within established democracies.

Citizens are the most distinctive element in democracies. All regimes have rulers and a public realm, but only to the extent that they are democratic do they have citizens. Historically, severe restrictions on citizenship were imposed in most emerging or partial democracies according to criteria of age, gender, class, race, literacy, property ownership, tax-paying status, and so on. Only a small part of the total population was eligible to vote or run for office. Only restricted social categories were allowed to form, join, or support political associations. After

protracted struggle—in some cases involving violent domestic upheaval or international war—most of these restrictions were lifted. Today, the criteria for inclusion are fairly standard. All native-born adults are eligible, although somewhat higher age limits may still be imposed upon candidates for certain offices. Unlike the early American and European democracies of the nineteenth century, none of the recent democracies in southern Europe, Latin America, Asia, or Eastern Europe has even attempted to impose formal restrictions on the franchise or eligibility to office. When it comes to informal restrictions on the effective exercise of citizenship rights, however, the story can be quite different. This explains the central importance (discussed below) of procedures.

Competition has not always been considered an essential defining condition of democracy. "Classic" democracies presumed decision making based on direct participation leading to consensus. The assembled citizenry was expected to agree on a common course of action after listening to the alternatives and weighing their respective merits and demerits. A tradition of hostility to "faction" and "particular interests" persists in democratic thought, but at least since *The Federalist Papers* it has become widely accepted that competition among factions is a necessary evil in democracies that operate on a more-than-local scale. Since, as James Madison argued, "the latent causes of faction are sown into the nature of man," and the possible remedies for "the mischief of faction" are worse than the disease, the best course is to recognize them and to attempt to control their effects.[4] Yet while democrats may agree on the inevitability of factions, they tend to disagree about the best forms and rules for governing factional competition. Indeed, differences over the preferred modes and boundaries of competition contribute most to distinguishing one subtype of democracy from another.

The most popular definition of democracy equates it with regular *elections*, fairly conducted and honestly counted. Some even consider the mere fact of elections—even ones from which specific parties or candidates are excluded, or in which substantial portions of the population cannot freely participate—as a sufficient condition for the existence of democracy.

This fallacy has been called "electoralism" or "the faith that merely holding elections will channel political action into peaceful contests among elites and accord public legitimacy to the winners"—no matter how they are conducted or what else constrains those who win them.[5] However central to democracy, elections occur intermittently and only allow citizens to choose between the highly aggregated alternatives offered by political parties, which can, especially in the early stages of a democratic transition, proliferate in a bewildering variety. During the intervals between elections, citizens can seek to influence public policy through a wide variety of other intermediaries: interest associations, social movements, locality groupings, clientelistic arrangements, and so forth. *Modern democracy, in other words, offers a variety of competitive processes and channels for the expression of interests and values—associational as well as partisan, functional as well as territorial, collective as well as individual. All are integral to its practice.*

Another commonly accepted image of democracy identifies it with *majority rule.* Any governing body that makes decisions by combining the votes of more than half of those eligible and present is said to be democratic, whether that majority emerges within an electorate, a parliament, a committee, a city council, or a party caucus. For exceptional purposes (e.g., amending the constitution or expelling a member), "qualified majorities" of more than 50 percent may be required, but few would deny that democracy must involve some means of aggregating the equal preferences of individuals.

A problem arises, however, when *numbers* meet *intensities.* What happens when a properly assembled majority (especially a stable, self-perpetuating one) regularly makes decisions that harm some minority (especially a threatened cultural or ethnic group)? In these circumstances, successful democracies tend to qualify the central principle of majority rule in order to protect minority rights. Such qualifications can take the form of constitutional provisions that place certain matters beyond the reach of majorities (bills of rights); requirements for concurrent majorities in several different constituencies (confederalism); guarantees securing the autonomy of local or regional governments against the demands of the

central authority (federalism); grand coalition governments that incorporate all parties (consociationalism); or the negotiation of social pacts between major social groups like business and labor (neocorporatism). The most common and effective way of protecting minorities, however, lies in the everyday operation of interest associations and social movements. These reflect (some would say, amplify) the different intensities of preference that exist in the population and bring them to bear on democratically elected decision makers. Another way of putting this intrinsic tension between numbers and intensities would be to say that "in modern democracies, votes may be counted, but influences alone are weighted."

Cooperation has always been a central feature of democracy. Actors must voluntarily make collective decisions binding on the polity as a whole. They must cooperate in order to compete. They must be capable of acting collectively through parties, associations, and movements in order to select candidates, articulate preferences, petition authorities, and influence policies.

But democracy's freedoms should also encourage citizens to deliberate among themselves, to discover their common needs, and to resolve their differences without relying on some supreme central authority. Classical democracy emphasized these qualities, and they are by no means extinct, despite repeated efforts by contemporary theorists to stress the analogy with behavior in the economic marketplace and to reduce all of democracy's operations to competitive interest maximization. Alexis de Tocqueville best described the importance of independent groups for democracy in his *Democracy in America*, a work which remains a major source of inspiration for all those who persist in viewing democracy as something more than a struggle for election and re-election among competing candidates.[6]

In contemporary political discourse, this phenomenon of cooperation and deliberation via autonomous group activity goes under the rubric of "civil society." The diverse units of social identity and interest, by remaining independent of the state (and perhaps even of parties), not only can restrain the arbitrary actions of rulers, but can also contribute to forming better citizens who are more aware of the preferences of others, more self-confident in their actions, and more civic-minded in their willingness to sacrifice for the common good. At its best, civil society provides an intermediate layer of governance between the individual and the state that is capable of resolving conflicts and controlling the behavior of members without public coercion. Rather than overloading decision makers with increased demands and making the system ungovernable,[7] a viable civil society can mitigate conflicts and improve the quality of citizenship—without relying exclusively on the privatism of the marketplace.

Representatives—whether directly or indirectly elected—do most of the real work in modern democracies. Most are professional politicians who orient their careers around the desire to fill key offices. It is doubtful that any democracy could survive without such people. The central question, therefore, is not whether or not there will be a political elite or even a professional political class, but how these representatives are chosen and then held accountable for their actions.

As noted above, there are many channels of representation in modern democracy. The electoral one, based on territorial constituencies, is the most visible and public. It culminates in a parliament or a presidency that is periodically accountable to the citizenry as a whole. Yet the sheer growth of government (in large part as a byproduct of popular demand) has increased the number, variety, and power of agencies charged with making public decisions and not subject to elections. Around these agencies there has developed a vast apparatus of specialized representation based largely on functional interests, not territorial constituencies. These interest associations, and not political parties, have become the primary expression of civil society in most stable democracies, supplemented by the more sporadic interventions of social movements.

PROCEDURES THAT MAKE DEMOCRACY POSSIBLE

The defining components of democracy are necessarily abstract, and may give rise to a considerable variety of institutions and subtypes of democracy. For democracy to thrive, however, specific procedural norms must be followed and civic rights must be respected. Any polity that fails to impose such restrictions upon itself, that fails to follow the "rule of law" with regard to its own procedures, should not be considered democratic. These procedures alone do not define democracy, but their presence is indispensable to its persistence. In essence, they are necessary but not sufficient conditions for its existence.

Robert Dahl has offered the most generally accepted listing of what he terms the "procedural minimal" conditions that must be present for modern political democracy (or as he puts it, "polyarchy") to exist:

1. Control over government decisions about policy is constitutionally vested in elected officials.
2. Elected officials are chosen in frequent and fairly conducted elections in which coercion is comparatively uncommon.
3. Practically all adults have the right to vote in the election of officials.
4. Practically all adults have the right to run for elective offices in the government. . . .
5. Citizens have a right to express themselves without the danger of severe punishment on political matters broadly defined. . . .
6. Citizens have a right to seek out alternative sources of information. Moreover, alternative sources of information exist and are protected by law.
7. . . . Citizens also have the right to form relatively independent associations or organizations, including independent political parties and interest groups.[8]

These seven conditions seem to capture the essence of procedural democracy for many theorists, but we propose to add two others. The first might be thought of as a further refinement of item (1), while the second might be called an implicit prior condition to all seven of the above.

8. Popularly elected officials must be able to exercise their constitutional powers without being subjected to overriding (albeit informal) opposition from unelected officials. Democracy is in

jeopardy if military officers, entrenched civil servants, or state managers retain the capacity to act independently of elected civilians or even veto decisions made by the people's representatives. Without this additional caveat, the militarized polities of contemporary Central America, where civilian control over the military does not exist, might be classified by many scholars as democracies, just as they have been (with the exception of Sandinista Nicaragua) by U.S. policy makers. The caveat thus guards against what we earlier called "electoralism"—the tendency to focus on the holding of elections while ignoring other political realities.

9. The polity must be self-governing; it must be able to act independently of constraints imposed by some other overarching political system. Dahl and other contemporary democratic theorists probably took this condition for granted since they referred to formally sovereign nation-states. However, with the development of blocs, alliances, spheres of influence, and a variety of "neocolonial" arrangements, the question of autonomy has been a salient one. Is a system really democratic if its elected officials are unable to make binding decisions without the approval of actors outside their territorial domain? This is significant even if the outsiders are themselves democratically constituted and if the insiders are relatively free to alter or even end the encompassing arrangement (as in Puerto Rico), but it becomes especially critical if neither condition obtains (as in the Baltic states).

HOW DEMOCRACIES DIFFER

Several concepts have been deliberately excluded from our generic definition of democracy, despite the fact that they have been frequently associated with it in both everyday practice and scholarly work. They are, nevertheless, especially important when it comes to distinguishing subtypes of democracy. Since no single set of actual institutions, practices, or values embodies democracy, polities moving away from authoritarian rule can mix different components to produce different democracies. It is important to recognize that these do not define points along a single continuum of improving performance, but a matrix of potential combinations that are *differently* democratic.

1. *Consensus*: All citizens may not agree on the substantive goals of political action or on the role of the state (although if they did, it would certainly make governing democracies much easier).
2. *Participation*: All citizens may not take an active and equal part in politics, although it must be legally possible for them to do so.
3. *Access*: Rulers may not weigh equally the preferences of all who come before them, although citizenship implies that individuals and groups should have an equal opportunity to express their preferences if they choose to do so.
4. *Responsiveness*: Rulers may not always follow the course of action preferred by the citizenry. But when they deviate from such a policy, say on grounds of "reason of state" or "overriding national interest," they must ultimately be held accountable for their actions through regular and fair processes.
5. *Majority rule*: Positions may not be allocated or rules may not be decided solely on the basis of assembling the most votes, although deviations from this principle usually must be explicitly defended and previously approved.
6. *Parliamentary sovereignty*: The legislature may not be the only body that can make rules or even the one with final authority in deciding which laws are binding, although where executive, judicial, or other public bodies make that ultimate choice, they too must be accountable for their actions.
7. *Party government*: Rulers may not be nominated, promoted, and disciplined in their activities by well-organized and programmatically coherent political parties, although where they are not, it may prove more difficult to form an effective government.
8. *Pluralism*: The political process may not be based on a multiplicity of overlapping, voluntaristic, and autonomous private groups. However, where there are monopolies of representation, hierarchies of association, and obligatory

memberships, it is likely that the interests involved will be more closely linked to the state and the separation between the public and private spheres of action will be much less distinct.

9. *Federalism*: The territorial division of authority may not involve multiple levels and local autonomies, least of all ones enshrined in a constitutional document, although some dispersal of power across territorial and/or functional units is characteristic of all democracies.

10. *Presidentialism*: The chief executive officer may not be a single person and he or she may not be directly elected by the citizenry as a whole, although some concentration of authority is present in all democracies, even if it is exercised collectively and only held indirectly accountable to the electorate.

11. *Checks and Balances*: It is not necessary that the different branches of government be systematically pitted against one another, although governments by assembly, by executive concentration, by judicial command, or even by dictatorial fiat (as in time of war) must be ultimately accountable to the citizenry as a whole.

While each of the above has been named as an essential component of democracy, they should instead be seen either as indicators of this or that type of democracy, or else as useful standards for evaluating the performance of particular regimes. To include them as part of the generic definition of democracy itself would be to mistake the American polity for the universal model of democratic governance. Indeed, the parliamentary, consociational, unitary, corporatist, and concentrated arrangements of continental Europe may have some unique virtues for guiding polities through the uncertain transition from autocratic to democratic rule.[9]

WHAT DEMOCRACY IS NOT

We have attempted to convey the general meaning of modern democracy without identifying it with some particular set of rules and institutions or restricting it to some specific culture or level of development. We have also argued that it cannot be reduced to the regular holding of elections or equated with a particular notion of the role of the state, but we have not said much more about what democracy is not or about what democracy may not be capable of producing.

There is an understandable temptation to load too many expectations on this concept and to imagine that by attaining democracy, a society will have resolved all of its political, social, economic, administrative, and cultural problems. Unfortunately, "all good things do not necessarily go together."

First, democracies are not necessarily more efficient economically than other forms of government. Their rates of aggregate growth, savings, and investment may be no better than those of nondemocracies. This is especially likely during the transition, when propertied groups and administrative elites may respond to real or imagined threats to the "rights" they enjoyed under authoritarian rule by initiating capital flight, disinvestment, or sabotage. In time, depending upon the type of democracy, benevolent long-term effects upon income distribution, aggregate demand, education, productivity, and creativity may eventually combine to improve economic and social performance, but it is certainly too much to expect that these improvements will occur immediately— much less that they will be defining characteristics of democratization.

Second, democracies are not necessarily more efficient administratively. Their capacity to make decisions may even be slower than that of the regimes they replace, if only because more actors must be consulted. The costs of getting things done may be higher, if only because "payoffs" have to be made to a wider and more resourceful set of clients (although one should never underestimate the degree of corruption to be found within autocracies). Popular satisfaction with the new democratic government's performance may not even seem greater, if only because necessary compromises often please no one completely and because the losers are free to complain.

Third, democracies are not likely to appear more orderly, consensual, stable, or governable than the autocracies they replace. This is partly a byproduct of democratic freedom of expression, but it is also a reflection of the likelihood of continuing disagreement over new rules and institutions. These products of imposition or compromise are often initially quite ambiguous in nature and uncertain in effect until actors have learned how to use them. What is more, they come in the aftermath of serious struggles motivated by high ideals. Groups and individuals with recently acquired autonomy will test certain rules, protest against the actions of certain institutions, and insist on renegotiating their part of the bargain. Thus the presence of antisystem parties should be neither surprising nor seen as a failure of democratic consolidation. What counts is whether such parties are willing, however reluctantly, to play by the general rules of bounded uncertainty and contingent consent.

Governability is a challenge for all regimes, not just democratic ones. Given the political exhaustion and loss of legitimacy that have befallen autocracies from sultanistic Paraguay to totalitarian Albania, it may seem that only democracies can now be expected to govern effectively and legitimately. Experience has shown, however, that democracies too can lose the ability to govern. Mass publics can become disenchanted with their performance. Even more threatening is the temptation for leaders to fiddle with procedures and ultimately undermine the principles of contingent consent and bounded uncertainty. Perhaps the most critical moment comes once the politicians begin to settle into the more predictable roles and relations of a consolidated democracy. Many will find their expectations frustrated; some will discover that the new rules of competition put them at a disadvantage; a few may even feel that their vital interests are threatened by popular majorities.

Finally, democracies will have more open societies and polities than the autocracies they replace, but not necessarily more open economies. Many of today's most successful and well-established democracies have historically resorted to protectionism and closed borders, and have relied extensively upon public institutions to promote economic development. While the long-term compatibility between democracy and capitalism does not seem to be in doubt, despite their continuous tension, it is not clear whether the promotion of such liberal economic goals as the right of individuals to own property and retain profits, the clearing function of markets, the private settlement of disputes, the freedom to produce without government regulation, or the privatization of state-owned enterprises necessarily furthers the consolidation of democracy. After all, democracies do need to levy taxes and regulate certain transactions, especially where private monopolies and oligopolies exist. Citizens or their representatives may decide that it is desirable to protect the rights of collectivities from encroachment by individuals, especially propertied ones, and they may choose to set aside certain forms of property for public or cooperative ownership. In short, notions of economic liberty that are currently put forward in neoliberal economic models are not synonymous with political freedom—and may even impede it.

Democratization will not necessarily bring in its wake economic growth, social peace, administrative efficiency, political harmony, free markets, or "the end of ideology." Least of all will it bring about "the end of history." No doubt some of these qualities could make the consolidation of democracy easier, but they are neither prerequisites for it nor immediate products of it. Instead, what we should be hoping for is the emergence of political institutions that can peacefully compete to form governments and influence public policy, that can channel social and economic conflicts through regular procedures, and that have sufficient linkages to civil society to represent their constituencies and commit them to collective courses of action. Some types of democracies, especially in developing countries, have been unable to fulfill this promise, perhaps due to the circumstances of their transition from authoritarian rule.[10] The democratic wager is that such a regime, once established, will not only persist by reproducing itself within its initial confining conditions, but will eventually expand beyond them.[11] Unlike authoritarian regimes, democracies have the capacity to modify their rules and institutions consensually in response to changing circumstances. They may not immediately produce all the goods mentioned above, but they stand a better chance of eventually doing so than do autocracies.

NOTES

1. The definition most commonly used by American social scientists is that of Joseph Schumpeter: "that institutional arrangement for arriving at political decisions in which individuals acquire the power to decide by means of a competitive struggle for the people's vote." *Capitalism, Socialism and Democracy* (London: George Allen and Unwin, 1943), 269. We accept certain aspects of the classical procedural approach to modem democracy, but differ primarily in our emphasis on the accountability of rulers to citizens and the relevance of mechanisms of competition other than elections.

2. Not only do some countries practice a stable form of democracy without a formal constitution (e.g., Great Britain and Israel), but even more countries have constitutions and legal codes that offer no guarantee of reliable practice. On paper, Stalin's 1936 constitution for the USSR was a virtual model of democratic rights and entitlements.

3. For the most valiant attempt to make some sense out of this thicket of distinctions, see Juan Linz, "Totalitarian and Authoritarian Regimes" in *Handbook of Political Science*, eds. Fred I. Greenstein and Nelson W. Polsby (Reading, Mass.: Addison Wesley, 1975), 175–411.

4. "Publius" (Alexander Hamilton, John Jay, and James Madison), *The Federalist Papers* (New York: Anchor Books, 1961). The quote is from Number 10.

5. See Terry Karl, "Imposing Consent? Electoralism versus Democratization in El Salvador," in *Elections and Democratization in Latin America, 1980–1985*, eds. Paul Drake and Eduardo Silva (San Diego: Center for Iberian and Latin American Studies, Center for US/Mexican Studies, University of California, San Diego, 1986), 9–36.

6. Alexis de Tocqueville, *Democracy in America*, 2 vols. (New York: Vintage Books, 1945).

7. This fear of overloaded government and the imminent collapse of democracy is well reflected in the work of Samuel P. Huntington during the 1970s. See especially Michel Crozier, Samuel P. Huntington, and Joji Watanuki, *The Crisis of Democracy* (New York: New York University Press, 1975). For Huntington's (revised) thoughts about the prospects for democracy, see his "Will More Countries Become Democratic?," *Political Science Quarterly* 99 (Summer 1984): 193–218.

8. Robert Dahl, *Dilemmas of Pluralist Democracy* (New Haven: Yale University Press, 1982), 11.

9. See Juan Linz, "The Perils of Presidentialism," *Journal of Democracy* 1 (Winter 1990): 51–69, and the ensuing discussion by Donald Horowitz, Seymour Martin Lipset, and Juan Linz in *Journal of Democracy* 1 (Fall 1990): 73–91.

10. Terry Lynn Karl, "Dilemmas of Democratization in Latin America," *Comparative Politics* 23 (October 1990): 1–23.

11. Otto Kirchheimer, "Confining Conditions and Revolutionary Breakthroughs," *American Political Science Review* 59 (1965): 964–974.

SEYMOUR MARTIN LIPSET

6.2 SOME SOCIAL REQUISITES OF DEMOCRACY
Economic Development and Political Legitimacy[1]

Lipset's piece is a major statement on the role that economic modernization plays in making democracy more likely. Lipset focuses particularly on four factors—income, level of industrialization, education, and urbanization—and argues that democracy becomes more likely as these increase. In other words, there is a positive correlation between modernization and democracy, as shown by several tables in this excerpt. Two items in Lipset's article further help to illustrate important points about how social scientists reach conclusions. The first appears early in the article, where Lipset has a passage on how "deviant cases" can be used to improve theories about why things happen (such as why countries are democratic or not). Another important piece is the distinction between correlation and causation. Lipset spends much of the article on correlations, but pay close attention to the end of this excerpt, where his causal argument takes shape. Finally, consider whether you have any critiques of Lipset's evidence and his theory. Is there anything about the way he groups countries that is problematic? Might there be other theories or causal factors that could explain why some of these countries are democracies and others are not?

I. INTRODUCTION

A sociological analysis of any pattern of behavior, whether referring to a small or a large social system, must result in specific hypotheses, empirically testable statements. Thus, in dealing with democracy, one must be able to point to a set of conditions that have actually existed in a number of countries, and say: democracy has emerged out of these conditions, and has become stabilized because of certain supporting institutions and values, as well as because of its own internal self-maintaining processes. The conditions listed must be ones which differentiate most democratic states from most others.

A recent discussion by a group of political theorists on the "cultural prerequisites to a successfully functioning democracy" points up the difference between the approach of the political sociologist and the political philosopher to a comparable problem.[2]

A considerable portion of this symposium is devoted to a debate concerning the contribution of religion, particularly Christian ethics, toward democratic attitudes. The principal author, Ernest Griffith, sees a necessary connection between the Judeo-Christian heritage and attitudes which sustain democratic institutions; the other participants stress the political and economic conditions which may provide the basis for a consensus on basic values which does not depend on religion; and they point to the depression, poverty, and social disorganization which resulted in fascism in Italy and Germany, in spite of strongly religious populations and traditions. What is most striking about this discussion is its lack of a perspective which assumes that theoretical propositions must be subject to test by a systematic comparison of *all* available cases, and which treats a deviant case properly as one case out of many. In this symposium, on the contrary,

Lipset, Seymour Martin. 1959. "Some Social Requisites of Democracy: Economic Development and Political Legitimacy" *American Political Science Review* 53(1): 69–105.

deviant cases which do not fit a given proposition are cited to demonstrate that there are *no* social conditions which are regularly associated with a given complex political system. So the conflicts among political philosophers about the necessary conditions underlying given political systems often lead to a triumphant demonstration that a given situation clearly violates the thesis of one's opponent, much as if the existence of some wealthy socialists, or poor conservatives, demonstrated that economic factors were not an important determinant of political preference.

The advantage of an attempt such as is presented here, which seeks to dissect the conditions of democracy into several interrelated variables, is that deviant cases fall into proper perspective. The statistical preponderance of evidence supporting the relationship of a variable such as education to democracy indicates that the existence of deviant cases (such as Germany, which succumbed to dictatorship in spite of an advanced educational system) cannot be the sole basis for rejecting the hypothesis. A deviant case, considered within a context which marshals the evidence on all relevant cases, often may actually strengthen the basic hypothesis if an intensive study of it reveals the special conditions which prevented the usual relationship from appearing.[3] Thus, electoral research indicates that a large proportion of the more economically well-to-do leftists are underprivileged along other dimensions of social status, such as ethnic or religious position.

Controversy in this area stems not only from variations in methodology, but also from use of different definitions. Clearly in order to discuss democracy, or any other phenomenon, it is first necessary to define it. For the purposes of this paper, democracy (in a complex society) is defined as a political system which supplies regular constitutional opportunities for changing the governing officials. It is a social mechanism for the resolution of the problem of societal decision-making among conflicting interest groups which permits the largest possible part of the population to influence these decisions through their ability to choose among alternative contenders for political office.

Comparative generalizations dealing with complex social systems must necessarily deal rather summarily with particular historical features of any one society within the scope of the investigation. In order to test these generalizations bearing on the differences between countries which rank high or low in possession of the attributes associated with democracy, it is necessary to establish some empirical measures of the type of political system. Individual deviations from a particular aspect of democracy are not too important, as long as the definitions unambiguously cover the great majority of nations which are located as democratic or undemocratic. The precise dividing line between "more democratic" and "less democratic" is also not a basic problem, since presumably democracy is *not* a quality of a social system which either does or does not exist, but is rather a complex of characteristics which may be ranked in many different ways. For this reason it was decided to divide the countries under consideration into two groups, rather than to attempt to rank them from highest to lowest. Ranking *individual* countries from the most to the least democratic is much more difficult than splitting the countries into two classes, "more" or "less" democratic, although even here borderline cases such as Mexico pose problems.

Efforts to classify all countries raise a number of problems. Most countries which lack an enduring tradition of political democracy lie in the traditionally underdeveloped sections of the world. It is possible that Max Weber was right when he suggested that modern democracy in its clearest forms can only occur under the unique conditions of capitalist industrialization.[4] Some of the complications introduced by the sharp variations in political practices in different parts of the earth can be reduced by dealing with differences among countries within political culture areas. The two best areas for such internal comparison are Latin America as one, and Europe and the English-speaking countries as the other. More limited comparisons may be made among the Asian states, and among the Arab countries.

The main criteria used in this paper to locate European democracies are the uninterrupted continuation of political democracy since World War I, *and* the absence over the past 25 years of a major political movement opposed to the democratic "rules of the game."[5] The somewhat less stringent criterion employed for Latin America is whether a given country has had a history of more or less free elections for most of the post–World War I period. Where in Europe we look for stable democracies, in South America we look for countries which have not had fairly constant dictatorial rule (see Table 6.1). No detailed analysis of the political history of either Europe or Latin America has been made with an eye toward more specific criteria of differentiation; at this point in the examination of the requisites of democracy, election results are sufficient to locate the European countries, and the judgments of experts and impressionistic assessments based on fairly well-known facts of political history will suffice for Latin America.[6]

II. ECONOMIC DEVELOPMENT AND DEMOCRACY

Perhaps the most widespread generalization linking political systems to other aspects of society has been that democracy is related to the state of economic development. Concretely, this means that the more well-to-do a nation, the greater the chances that it will sustain democracy. From Aristotle down to the present, men have argued that only in a wealthy society in which relatively few citizens lived in real poverty could a situation exist in which the mass of the population could intelligently participate in politics and could develop the self-restraint necessary to avoid succumbing to the appeals of irresponsible demagogues. A society divided between a large impoverished mass and a small favored elite would result either in oligarchy (dictatorial rule of the small upper stratum) or in tyranny (popularly based dictatorship). And these two political forms can be given modern labels: tyranny's modern face is Communism or Peronism; oligarchy appears today in the form of traditionalist dictatorships such as we find in parts of Latin America, Thailand, Spain or Portugal.

TABLE 6.1 CLASSIFICATION OF EUROPEAN, ENGLISH-SPEAKING, AND LATIN AMERICAN NATIONS BY DEGREE OF STABLE DEMOCRACY

European and English-Speaking Nations		Latin American Nations	
Stable Democracies	Unstable Democracies and Dictatorships	Democracies and Unstable Dictatorships	Stable Dictatorships
Australia	Austria	Argentina	Bolivia
Belgium	Bulgaria	Brazil	Cuba
Canada	Czechoslovakia	Chile	Dominican Republic
Denmark	Finland	Colombia	Ecuador
Ireland	France	Costa Rica	El Salvador
Luxemburg	Germany (West)	Mexico	Guatemala
Netherlands	Greece	Uruguay	Haiti
New Zealand	Hungary		Honduras
Norway	Iceland		Nicaragua
Sweden	Italy		Panama
Switzerland	Poland		Paraguay
United Kingdom	Portugal		Peru
United States	Rumania		Venezuela
	Spain		
	Yugoslavia		

As a means of concretely testing this hypothesis, various indices of economic development—wealth, industrialization, urbanization and education—have been defined, and averages (means) have been computed for the countries which have been classified as more or less democratic in the Anglo-Saxon world and Europe and Latin America.

In each case, the average wealth, degree of industrialization and urbanization, and level of education is much higher for the more democratic countries, as the data presented in Table 6.2 indicate. If we had combined Latin America and Europe in one table, the differences would have been greater.[7]

TABLE 6.2 A COMPARISON OF EUROPEAN, ENGLISH-SPEAKING, AND LATIN AMERICAN COUNTRIES, DIVIDED INTO TWO GROUPS, "MORE DEMOCRATIC" AND "LESS DEMOCRATIC," BY INDICES OF WEALTH, INDUSTRIALIZATION, EDUCATION, AND URBANIZATION[1]

A. Indices of Wealth					
Means	Per Capita Income[2] in $	Thousands of Persons per Doctor[3]	Persons per Motor Vehicle[4]	Telephones per 1,000 Persons[5]	Radios per 1,000 Persons[6]	Newspaper Copies per 1,000 Persons[7]
European and English-speaking Stable Democracies	695	.86	17	205	350	341
European and English-speaking Unstable Democracies and Dictatorships	308	1.4	143	58	160	167
Latin American Democracies and Unstable Dictatorships	171	2.1	99	25	85	102
Latin American Stable Dictatorships	119	4.4	274	10	43	43
Ranges						
European Stable Democracies	420–1,453	.7–1.2	3–62	43–400	160–995	242–570
European Dictatorships	128–482	.6–4	10–538	7–196	42–307	46–390
Latin American Democracies	112–346	.8–3.3	31–174	12–58	38–148	51–233
Latin American Stable Dictatorships	40–331	1.0–10.8	38–428	1–24	4–154	4–111

B. Indices of Industrialization		
Means	Percentage of Males in Agriculture[8]	Per Capita Energy Consumed[9]
European Stable Democracies	21	3.6
European Dictatorships	41	1.4
Latin American Democracies	52	.6
Latin American Stable Dictatorships	67	.25

Ranges		
European Stable Democracies	6–46	1.4–7.8
European Dictatorships	16–60	.27–3.2
Latin American Democracies	30–63	.30–0.9
Latin American Stable Dictatorships	46–87	.02–1.27

C. Indices of Education

Means	Percentage Literate[10]	Primary Education Enrollment per 1,000 Persons[11]	Post-Primary Enrollment per 1,000 Persons[12]	Higher Education Enrollment per 1,000 Persons[13]
European Stable Democracies	96	134	44	4.2
European Dictatorships	85	121	22	3.5
Latin American Democracies	74	101	13	2.0
Latin American Dictatorships	46	72	8	1.3
Ranges				
European Stable Democracies	95–100	96–179	19–83	1.7–17.83
European Dictatorships	55–98	61–165	8–37	1.6–6.1
Latin American Democracies	48–87	75–137	7–27	.7–4.6
Latin American Dictatorships	11–76	11–149	3–24	.2–3.1

D. Indices of Urbanization

Means	Percent in Cities over 20,000[14]	Percent in Cities over 100,000[15]	Percent in Metropolitan Areas[16]
European Stable Democracies	43	28	38
European Dictatorships	24	16	23
Latin American Democracies	28	22	26
Latin American Stable Dictatorships	17	12	15
Ranges			
European Stable Democracies	28–54	17–51	22–56
European Dictatorships	12–44	6–33	7–49
Latin American Democracies	11–48	13–37	17–44
Latin American Stable Dictatorships	5–36	4–22	7–26

[1] A large part of this table has been compiled from data furnished by International Urban Research, University of California, Berkeley, California.
[2] United Nations, Statistical Office, *National and Per Capita Income in Seventy Countries*, 1949, Statistical Papers, Series E, No. 1, New York, 1950, pp. 14–16.
[3] United Nations, *A Preliminary Report on the World Social Situation, 1952*, Table 11, pp. 46–8.
[4] United Nations, *Statistical Yearbook, 1956*, Table 139, pp. 333–338.
[5] *Ibid.*, Table 149, p. 387.

(continued)

[6] *Ibid.*, Table 189, p. 641. The population bases for these figures are for different years than those used in reporting the numbers of telephones and radios, but for purposes of group comparisons, the differences are not important.

[7] United Nations, *A Preliminary Report . . . , op. cit.*, Appendix B, pp. 86–89.

[8] United Nations, *Demographic Yearbook, 1956*, Table 12, pp. 350–370.

[9] United Nations, *Statistical Yearbook, 1956, op. cit.*, Table 127, pp. 308–310. Figures refer to commercially produced energy, in equivalent numbers of metric tons of coal.

[10] United Nations, *A Preliminary Report . . . , op. cit.*, Appendix A, pp. 79–86. A number of countries are listed as more than 95 percent literate.

[11] *Ibid.*, pp. 86–100. Figure's refer to persons enrolled at the earlier year of the primary range, per 1,000 total population, for years ranging from 1946 to 1950. The first primary year varies from five to eight in various countries. The less developed countries have more persons in that age range per 1,000 population than the more developed countries, but this biases the figures presented in the direction of increasing the percentage of the total population in school for the less developed countries, although fewer of the children in that age group attend school. The bias from this source thus reinforces the positive relationship between education and democracy.

[12] *Ibid.*, pp. 86–100.

[13] UNESCO, *World Survey of Education*, Paris, 1955. Figures are the enrollment in higher education per 1,000 population. The years to which the figures apply vary between 1949 and 1952, and the definition of higher education varies for different countries.

[14] Obtained from International Urban Research, University of California, Berkeley, California.

[15] *Ibid.*

[16] *Ibid.*

The main indices of *wealth* used here are per capita income, number of persons per motor vehicle and per physician, and the number of radios, telephones, and newspapers per thousand persons. The differences are striking on every score, as Table 6.2 indicates in detail. In the more democratic European countries, there are 17 persons per motor vehicle compared to 143 for the less democratic countries. In the less dictatorial Latin American countries there are 99 persons per motor vehicle, as against 274 for the more dictatorial ones.[8] Income differences for the groups are also sharp, dropping from an average per capita income of $695 for the more democratic countries of Europe to $308 for the less democratic ones; the corresponding difference for Latin America is from $171 to $119. The ranges are equally consistent, with the lowest per capita income in each group falling in the "less democratic" category, and the highest in the "more democratic" one.

Industrialization—indices of wealth are clearly related to this, of course—is measured by the percentage of employed males in agriculture, and the per capita commercially produced "energy" being used in the country, measured in terms of tons of coal per person per year. Both of these indices show equally consistent results. The average percentage of employed males working in agriculture and related occupations was 21 in the "more democratic" European countries, and 41 in the "less democratic," 52 in the "less dictatorial" Latin American countries, and 67 in the "more dictatorial." The differences in per capita energy employed in the country are equally large.

The degree of *urbanization* is also related to the existence of democracy.[9] Three different indices of urbanization are available from data compiled by International Urban Research (Berkeley, California), the percentage of the population in places of 20,000 and over, the percentage in communities of 100,000 and over, and also the percentage residing in standard metropolitan areas. On all three of these indices of urbanization, the more democratic countries score higher than the less democratic, for both of the political culture areas under investigation.

Many have suggested that the better educated the population of a country, the better the chances for democracy, and the comparative data available support this proposition. The "more democratic" countries of Europe are almost entirely literate: the lowest has a rate of 96 percent, while the "less democratic" nations have an average literacy rate of 85 percent. In Latin America, the difference is between an average rate of 74 percent for the "less dictatorial" countries and 46 percent for the "more dictatorial."[10] The educational enrollment per thousand total population at three different levels, primary, post-primary, and higher educational, is equally consistently related to the degree of democracy. The tremendous disparity is shown by the extreme cases of Haiti and the United States. Haiti has fewer children (11 per thousand) attending school in the primary grades than the United States has attending colleges (almost 18 per thousand).

The relationship between education and democracy is worth more extensive treatment since an entire philosophy of democratic government has seen in increased education the spread of the basic requirement of democracy.[11] As Bryce wrote with special reference to Latin America, "education, if it does not make men good citizens, makes it at least easier for them to become so."[12] Education presumably broadens men's outlooks, enables them to understand the need for norms of tolerance, restrains them from adhering to extremist and monistic doctrines, and increases their capacity to make rational electoral choices.

The evidence bearing on the contribution of education to democracy is even more direct and strong in connection with individual behavior *within* countries, than it is in cross-national correlations. Data gathered by public opinion research agencies which have questioned people in different countries with regard to their belief in various democratic norms of tolerance for opposition, to their attitudes toward ethnic or racial minorities, and with regard to their belief in multi-party as against one-party systems have found that *the most important single factor differentiating those giving democratic responses from others has been education.* The higher one's education, the more likely one is to believe in democratic values and support democratic practices.[13] All the relevant studies indicate that education is far more significant than income or occupation.

These findings should lead us to anticipate a far higher correlation between national levels of education and political practice than in fact we do find. Germany and France have been among the best educated nations of Europe, but this by itself clearly did not stabilize their democracies. It may be, however, that education has served to inhibit other antidemocratic forces. Post-Nazi data from Germany indicate clearly that higher education is linked to rejection of strong-man and one-party government.[14]

If we cannot say that a "high" level of education is a sufficient condition for democracy, the available evidence does suggest that it comes close to being a necessary condition in the modern world. Thus if we turn to Latin America, where widespread illiteracy still exists in many countries, we find that of all the nations in which more than half the population is illiterate, only one, Brazil, can be included in the "more democratic" group.

There is some evidence from other economically impoverished culture areas that literacy is related to democracy. The one member of the Arab League which has maintained democratic institutions since World War II, Lebanon, is by far the best educated (over 80 percent literacy) of the Arab countries. In the rest of Asia east of the Arab world, only two states, the Philippines and Japan, have maintained democratic regimes without the presence of large antidemocratic parties since 1945. And these two countries, although lower than any European state in per capita income, are among the world's leaders in educational attainment. The Philippines actually ranks second to the United States in its proportion of people attending high school and university, while Japan has a higher level of educational attainment than any European state.[15]

Although the various indices have been presented separately, it seems clear that the factors of industrialization, urbanization, wealth, and education, are so closely interrelated as to form one common factor.[16] And the factors subsumed under economic development carry with it the political correlate of democracy.[17]

A number of processes underlie these correlations, observed in many areas of the world, in addition to the effect, already discussed, of a high level of education and literacy in creating or sustaining belief in democratic norms. Perhaps most important is the relationship between modernization and the form of the "class struggle." For the lower strata, economic development, which means increased income, greater economic security, and higher education, permit those in this status to develop longer time perspectives and more complex and gradualist views of politics. A belief in secular reformist gradualism can only be the ideology of a relatively well-to-do lower class.[18] Increased wealth and education also serve democracy by increasing the extent to which the lower strata are exposed to cross pressures which will reduce the intensity of their commitment to given ideologies and make them less receptive to supporting extremist ones. The operation of this process will be discussed in more detail in the second part of the paper, but essentially it functions through enlarging their involvement in an integrated national culture as distinct from an isolated lower class one, and hence increasing their exposure to middle-class values. Marx argued that the proletariat were a revolutionary force because they have nothing to lose but their chains and can win the whole world. But Tocqueville in analyzing the reasons why the lower strata in America supported the system paraphrased and transposed Marx before Marx ever made this analysis, by pointing out that "only those who have nothing to lose ever revolt."[19]

Increased wealth is not only related causally to the development of democracy by changing the social conditions of the workers, but it also affects the political role of the middle class through changing the shape of the stratification structure so that it shifts from an elongated pyramid, with a large lower-class base, to a diamond with a growing middle-class. A large middle class plays a mitigating role in moderating conflict since it is able to reward moderate and democratic parties and penalize extremist groups.

National income is also related to the political values and style of the upper class. The poorer a country, and the lower the absolute standard of living of the lower classes, the greater the pressure on the upper strata to treat the lower classes as beyond the pale of human society, as vulgar, as innately inferior, as a lower caste. The sharp difference in the style of living between those at the top and those at the bottom makes this psychologically necessary. Consequently, the upper strata also tend to regard political rights for the lower strata, particularly the right to share in power, as essentially absurd and immoral. The upper strata not only resist democracy themselves, but their often arrogant political behavior serves to intensify extremist reactions on the part of the lower classes.

The general income level of a nation will also affect its receptivity to democratic political tolerance norms. The values which imply that it does not matter greatly which side rules, that error can be tolerated even in the governing party can best develop where (a) the government has little power to affect the crucial life chances of most powerful groups, or (b) there is enough wealth in the country so that it actually does not make too much difference if some redistribution does take place. If loss of office is seen as meaning serious loss for major power groups, then they will be readier to resort to more drastic measures in seeking to retain or secure office. The wealth level will also affect the extent to which given countries can develop "universalistic" norms among its civil servants and politicians (selection based on competence; performance without favoritism). The poorer the country, the greater the emphasis which is placed on nepotism, *i.e.*, support of kin and friends. The weakness of the universalistic norms reduces the opportunity to develop efficient bureaucracy, a condition for a modern democratic state.[20]

Less directly linked but seemingly still associated with greater wealth is the presence of intermediary organizations and institutions which can act as sources of countervailing power, and recruiters of participants in the political process in the manner discussed by Tocqueville and other exponents of what has come to be known as the theory of the "mass society."[21] They have argued that a society without a multitude of organizations relatively independent of the central state power has a high dictatorial as well as a revolutionary potential. Such organizations serve a number of functions necessary to democracy: they are a source of countervailing power, inhibiting the state or any single major source of private power from dominating all political resources; they are a source of new opinions; they can be the means of communicating ideas, particularly opposition ideas, to a large section of the citizenry; they serve to train men in the skills of politics; and they help increase the level of interest and participation in politics. Although there are no reliable data which bear on the relationship between national patterns of voluntary organizations and national political systems, evidence from studies of individual behavior within a number of different countries demonstrates that, independently of other factors, men who belong to associations are more likely to hold democratic opinions on questions concerning tolerance and party systems, and are more likely to participate in the political process—to be active or to vote. Since we also know that, within countries, the more well-to-do and the better educated one is, the more likely he is to belong to voluntary organizations, it seems likely that the propensity to form such groups is a function of level of income and opportunities for leisure within given nations.[22]

It is obvious that democracy and the conditions related to stable democracy discussed here are essentially located in the countries of northwest Europe and their English-speaking offspring in America and Australasia. It has been argued by Max Weber among others that the factors making for democracy in this area are a historically unique concatenation of elements, part of the complex which also produced capitalism in this area. The basic argument runs that capitalist economic development (facilitated and most developed in Protestant areas) created the burgher class whose existence was both a catalyst and a necessary condition for democracy. The emphasis within Protestantism on individual responsibility furthered the emergence of democratic values. The greater initial strength of the middle classes in these countries resulted in an alignment between burghers and throne, an alignment which preserved the monarchy, and thus facilitated the legitimation of democracy among the conservative strata. Thus we have an interrelated cluster of economic development, Protestantism, monarchy, gradual political change, legitimacy and democracy.[23] Men may argue as to whether any aspect of this cluster is primary, but the cluster of factors and forces hangs together.

NOTES

1. This paper was written as one aspect of a comparative analysis of political behavior in western democracies which is supported by grants from the Behavioral Sciences Division of the Ford Foundation and the Committee on Comparative Politics of the Social Science Research Council. Assistance from Robert Alford and Amitai Etzioni is gratefully acknowledged. It was originally presented at the September 1958 meetings of the American Political Science Association in St. Louis, Missouri.

2. Ernest S. Griffith, John Plamenatz, and J. Roland Pennock, "Cultural Prerequisites to a Successfully Functioning Democracy: A Symposium," this REVIEW, Vol. 50 (1956), pp. 101–137.

3. A detailed example of how a deviant case and analysis advances theory may be found S. M. Lipset, M. Trow, and J. Coleman, *Union Democracy*, (Glencoe: The Free Press, 1956). This book is a study of the political process inside the International Typographical Union, which has a long-term two-party system with free elections and frequent turnover in office, and is thus the clearest exception to Robert Michels' "iron law of oligarchy." The research, however, was not intended as a report on this union, but rather as the best means available to test and amplify Michels' "law." The study could only have been made through a systematic effort to establish a basic theory and derive hypotheses. The best way to add to knowledge about the internal government of voluntary associations seemed to be to study the most deviant case. In the process of examining the particular historical and structural conditions sustaining the two-party system in the ITU, the general theory was clarified.

4. See Max Weber, "Zur Lage der burgerlichen Demokratie in Russland," *Archiv für Sozialwissenschaft und Sozialpolitik*, Vol. 22 (1906), pp. 346 ff.

5. The latter requirement means that no totalitarian movement, either Fascist or Communist, received 20 percent of the vote during this time. Actually all the European nations falling on the democratic side of the continuum had totalitarian movements which secured less than seven percent of the vote.

6. The historian Arthur P. Whitaker, for example, has summarized the judgments of experts on Latin America to be that "the countries which have approximated most closely to the democratic ideal have been . . . Argentina, Brazil, Chile, Colombia, Costa Rica, and Uruguay." See "The Pathology of Democracy in Latin America: A Historian's Point of View," this REVIEW, Vol. 44 (1950), pp. 101–118. To this group I have added Mexico. Mexico has allowed freedom of the press, of assembly and of organization, to opposition parties, although there is good evidence that it does not allow them the opportunity to win elections, since ballots are counted by the incumbents. The existence of opposition groups,

contested elections, and adjustments among the various factions of the governing *Partido Revolucionario Institucional* does introduce a considerable element of popular influence in the system. The interesting effort of Russell Fitzgibbon to secure a "statistical evaluation of Latin American democracy" based on the opinion of various experts is not useful for the purposes of this paper. The judges were asked not only to rank countries as democratic on the basis of purely political criteria, but also to consider the "standard of living" and "educational level." These latter factors may be conditions for democracy, but they are not an aspect of democracy as such. See Russell H. Fitzgibbon, "A Statistical Evaluation of Latin American Democracy," *Western Political Quarterly*, Vol. 9 (1956), pp. 607–619.

7. Lyle W. Shannon has correlated indices of economic development with whether a country is self-governing or not, and his conclusions are substantially the same. Since Shannon does not give details on the countries categorized as self-governing and non-self-governing, there is no direct measure of the relation between "democratic" and "self-governing" countries. All the countries examined in this paper, however, were chosen on the assumption that a characterization as "democratic" is meaningless for a non-self-governing country, and therefore, presumably, all of them, whether democratic or dictatorial, would fall within Shannon's "self-governing" category. Shannon shows that underdevelopment is related to lack of, self-government; my data indicate that once self-government is attained, development is still related to the character of the political system. See Shannon (ed.), *Underdeveloped Areas* (New York: Harper, 1957), and also his article, "Is Level of Government Related to Capacity for Self-Government?" *American Journal of Economics and Sociology*, Vol. 17 (1958) pp. 367–382. In the latter paper, Shannon constructs a composite index of development, using some of the same indices, such as inhabitants per physician, and derived from the same United Nations sources, as appear in the tables to follow. Shannon's work did not come to my attention until after this paper was prepared, so that the two papers can be considered as separate tests of comparable hypotheses.

8. It must be remembered that these figures are means, compiled from census figures for the various countries. The data vary widely in accuracy, and there is no way of measuring the validity of compound calculated figures such as those presented here. The consistent direction of all these differences, and their large magnitude, is the main indication of validity.

9. Urbanization has often been linked to democracy by political theorists. Harold J. Laski asserted that "organized democracy is the product of urban life," and that it was natural therefore that it should have "made its first effective appearance" in the Greek city states, limited as was their definition of "citizen." See his article "Democracy" in the *Encyclopedia of the Social Sciences* (New York: Macmillan, 1937), Vol. V, pp. 76–85. Max Weber held that the city, as a certain type of political community, is a peculiarly Western phenomenon, and traced the emergence of the notion of "citizenship" from social developments closely related to urbanization. For a partial statement of his point of view, see the chapter on "Citizenship," in *General Economic History* (Glencoe: The Free Press, 1950), pp. 315–338. It is significant to note that before 1933 the Nazi electoral strength was greatest in small communities and rural areas. Berlin, the only German city of over two million, never gave the Nazis over 25 percent of the vote in a free election. The modal Nazi, like the modal French Poujadist or Italian neo-Fascist today, was a self-employed resident of a small town or rural district. Though the communists, as a workers' party, are strongest in the working-class neighborhoods of large cities within countries, they have great electoral strength only in the less urbanized European nations, e.g., Greece, Finland, France, Italy.

10. The pattern indicated by a comparison of the averages for each group of countries is sustained by the ranges (the high and low extremes) for each index. Most of the ranges overlap, that is,

some countries which are in the low category with regard to politics are higher on any given index than some which are high on the scale of democracy. It is noteworthy that in both Europe and Latin America, the nations which are lowest on any of the indices presented in the table are also in the "less democratic" category. Conversely, almost all countries which rank at the top of any of the indices are in the "more democratic" class.

11. See John Dewey, *Democracy and Education* (New York, 1916).

12. Quoted in Arthur P. Whitaker, *op. cit.*, p. 112; see also Karl Mannheim, *Freedom, Power and Democratic Planning* (New York, 1950).

13. See C. H. Smith, "Liberalism and Level of Information," *Journal of Educational Psychology*, Vol. 39 (1948), pp. 65–82; Martin A. Trow, *Right Wing Radicalism and Political Intolerance*, Ph.D. dissertation, Columbia University, 1957, p. 17; Samuel Stouffer, *Communism, Conformity and Civil Liberties* (New York, 1955), pp. 138–9; K. Kido and M. Suyi, "Report on Social Stratification and Mobility in Tokyo, . . . Mobility in Tokyo, III: The Structure of Social Consciousness," *Japanese Sociological Review* (January 1954), pp. 74–100.

14. Dewey has suggested that the character of the educational system will influence its effect on democracy, and this may shed some light on the sources of instability in Germany. The purpose of German education, according to Dewey, writing in 1916, was "disciplinary training rather than . . . personal development." The main aim was to produce "absorption of the aims and meaning of existing institutions," and "thoroughgoing subordination" to them. This point raises issues which cannot be entered into here, but indicates the complex character of the relationship between democracy and closely related factors, such as education. See Dewey, *Democracy and Education, op. cit.*, pp. 108–110. It suggests caution, too, in drawing optimistic inferences about the prospects of democratic developments in Russia, based on the great expansion of education now taking place there.

15. Ceylon, which shares with the Philippines and Japan the distinction of being the only democratic countries in South and Far Asia in which the Communists are unimportant electorally, also shares with them the distinction of being the only countries in this area in which a *majority* of the population is literate. It should be noted, however, that Ceylon does have a fairly large Trotskyist party, now the official opposition; and while its educational level is high for Asia, it is much lower than either Japan or the Philippines.

16. A factor analysis carried out by Leo Schnore, based on data from 75 countries, demonstrates this. (To be published).

17. This statement is a "statistical" statement, which necessarily means that there will be many exceptions to the correlation. Thus we know that poorer people are more likely to vote for the Democratic or Labor parties in the U.S and England. The fact that a large minority of the lower strata vote for the more conservative party in these countries does not challenge the proposition that stratification position is the main determinant of party choice, given the multivariate causal process involved in the behavior of people or nations. Clearly social science will never be able to account for (predict) all behavior.

18. See S. M. Lipset, "Socialism—East and West—Left and Right," *Confluence*, Vol. 7 (Summer 1958), pp. 173–192.

19. Alexis de Tocqueville, *Democracy in America*, Vol. I (New York: Alfred A. Knopf, Vintage edition, 1945), p. 258.

20. For a discussion of this problem in a new state, see David Apter, *The Gold Coast in Transition* (Princeton University Press, 1955), esp. chapters 9 and 13. Apter shows the importance of efficient bureaucracy, and the acceptance of bureaucratic values and behavior patterns, for the existence of a democratic political order.

21. See Emil Lederer, *The State of the Masses* (New York, 1940); Hannah Arendt, *Origins of Totalitarianism* (New York, 1950); Max Horkheimer, *Eclipse of Reason* (New York, 1947); Karl Mannheim, *Man and Society in an Age of Reconstruction* (New

York, 1940); Philip Selznick, *The Organizational Weapon* (New York, 1952); José Ortega y Gasset, *The Revolt of the Masses* (New York, 1932).

22. See Edward Banfield, *The Moral Basis of a Backward Society* (Glencoe: The Free Press, 1958), for an excellent description of the way in which abysmal poverty serves to reduce community organization in southern Italy. The data which do exist from polling surveys conducted in the United States, Germany, France, Great Britain, and Sweden show that somewhere between 40 and 50 percent of the adults in these countries belong to voluntary associations, without lower rates of membership for the less stable democracies, France and Germany, than among the more stable ones, the United States, Great Britain, and Sweden. These results seemingly challenge the general proposition, although no definite conclusion can be made, since most of the studies employed non-comparable categories. This point bears further research in many countries. For the data on these countries see the following studies: for France, Arnold Rose, *Theory and Method in the Social Sciences* (Minneapolis: University of Minnesota Press, 1954), p. 74; and O. R. Gallagher, "Voluntary Associations in France," *Social Forces*, Vol. 36 (Dec. 1957), pp. 154–156; for Germany, Erich Reigrotski, *Soziale Verflechtungen in der Bundesrepublik* (Tubingen: J. C. B. Mohr, 1956), p. 164; for the U. S., Charles R. Wright and Herbert H. Hyman, "Voluntary Association Memberships of American Adults: Evidence from National Sample Surveys," *American Sociological Review*, Vol. 23 (June 1958), p. 287, and J. C. Scott, Jr., "Membership and Participation in Voluntary Associations," *id.*, Vol. 22 (1957), pp. 315–326; Herbert Maccoby, "The Differential Political Activity of Participants in a Voluntary Association," *id.*, Vol. 23 (1958), pp. 524–533; for Great Britain see Mass Observation, *Puzzled People* (London: Victor Gollanz, 1947), p. 119; and Thomas Bottomore, "Social Stratification in Voluntary Organizations," in David Glass, ed., *Social Mobility in Britain* (Glencoe: The Free Press, 1954), p. 354; for Sweden see Gunnar Heckscher, "Pluralist Democracy: The Swedish Experience," *Social Research*, Vol. 15 (December 1948), pp. 417–461.

23. In introducing historical events as part of the analysis of factors *external* to the political system, which are part of the causal nexus in which democracy is involved, I am following in good sociological and even functionalist tradition. As Radcliffe-Brown has well put it, ". . . one 'explanation' of a social system will be its history, where we know it—the detailed account of how it came to be, what it is and where it is. Another 'explanation' of the same system is obtained by showing . . . that it is a special exemplification of laws of social psychology or social functioning. The two kinds of explanation do not conflict but supplement one another." A. R. Radcliffe-Brown, "On the Concept of Function in Social Science," *American Anthropologist*, New Series, Vol. 37 (1935), p. 401; see also Max Weber, *The Methodology of the Social Sciences* (Glencoe: The Free Press, 1949), pp. 164–188, for a detailed discussion of the role of historical analysis in sociological research.

CHAPTER 7

AUTHORITARIAN REGIMES AND DEMOCRATIC BREAKDOWN

Roughly half of the world's 7 billion people live in countries that are not full democracies, according to the watchdog group Freedom House. Although the past two decades have seen many countries become more democratic, authoritarian regimes are still common across much of the world, especially in Africa and Asia; they also exist in Latin America and parts of Europe. Some people would argue that even mostly democratic regimes sometimes retain some authoritarian elements. As is the case with democracy, political scientists want to be able to answer conceptual and causal questions about authoritarianism: we want to understand what authoritarian regimes are and why they come about and persist.

One of the most important features of the study of authoritarianism is the diversity of different types of authoritarian (or nondemocratic) regimes. Scholars of authoritarian regimes thus regularly begin their studies with descriptions (or often typologies) of what their regimes are. Authoritarianism can be found in many forms. It can range from modest infringements on liberties that keep a country from being fully democratic on the one hand to the genocidal totalitarianism of Nazi Germany on the other. There are many hybrids of democracy and authoritarianism and many regimes that are stuck somewhere between the two ends of the spectrum.

We first include a selection from two scholars (Steven Levitsky and Lucan Way) who have worked to help conceptualize and define the deceptively thin dividing line between authoritarianism and democracy. As the authors note, countries are not always on their way to full democracy: authoritarianism can be a stable equilibrium. In fact, even most authoritarian regimes today hold regular elections and attempt to portray these as free and fair (even when they are not).

There are many possible causes of authoritarianism. We cannot enumerate or provide examples of all the possibilities here, but will highlight two related schools of thought. First are social and historical-institutional arguments, as seen in the work by Barrington Moore here. The origins of authoritarianism are found in the arrangements and interactions that make up a society and how these play out over time. Coalitions of different actors—such as social classes—can shape the history of a country through their choices and behaviors, and this will affect the type of governing regime that emerges. Arguments in this historical-institutionalist vein emphasize the power of social actors and how they shape history. A second line of argument holds that economic factors matter most; the excerpt from Acemoglu and Robinson in this chapter reflects some of these arguments. For instance, high levels of poverty and inequality (or the lack of economic modernization) may contribute to the likelihood of authoritarianism. In looking at these selections, do you find one or the other line of argument conforms best to your expectations? Does this give you insight into your own assumptions and theoretical beliefs, or into what sorts of evidence and types of arguments you find most persuasive in general?

STEVEN LEVITSKY AND LUCAN WAY

7.1 THE RISE OF COMPETITIVE AUTHORITARIANISM

This article describes "one particular type of 'hybrid' regime," which the authors call competitive authoritarianism. Levitsky and Way explain that countries with this type of regime possess formal democratic institutions (such as elections and civil liberties), but that these rights and liberties are infringed and violated to such an extent that the regime itself is more authoritarian than democratic. The authors explain how this category of regimes differs from many other types of flawed democracies, and it also differs from other types of full-blown authoritarian regimes. The article enumerates several arenas in which opposition may challenge these regimes (namely elections, the legislature, the judiciary, and the media) and discusses the political tensions and sources of instability that arise in these systems. In outlining the various paths to competitive authoritarianism, Levitsky and Way stake a claim that not all regimes should be presumed to be transitioning toward democracy. It is necessary, they argue, to explain the "emergence or persistence of nondemocratic regimes." Considering current events, can you think of countries around the world that we can understand better using the concept of competitive authoritarianism?

DEFINING COMPETITIVE AUTHORITARIANISM

This article examines one particular type of "hybrid" regime: *competitive authoritarianism.* In competitive authoritarian regimes, formal democratic institutions are widely viewed as the principal means of obtaining and exercising political authority. Incumbents violate those rules so often and to such an extent, however, that the regime fails to meet conventional minimum standards for democracy. Examples include Croatia under Franjo Tudjman, Serbia under Slobodan Milošević, Russia under Vladimir Putin, Ukraine under Leonid Kravchuk and Leonid Kuchma, Peru under Alberto Fujimori, and post-1995 Haiti, as well as Albania, Armenia, Ghana, Kenya, Malaysia, Mexico, and Zambia through much of the 1990s. Although scholars have characterized many of these regimes as partial or "diminished" forms of democracy, we agree with Juan Linz that they

may be better described as a (diminished) form of authoritarianism.[1]

Competitive authoritarianism must be distinguished from democracy on the one hand and full-scale authoritarianism on the other. Modern democratic regimes all meet four minimum criteria: 1) Executives and legislatures are chosen through elections that are open, free, and fair; 2) virtually all adults possess the right to vote; 3) political rights and civil liberties, including freedom of the press, freedom of association, and freedom to criticize the government without reprisal, are broadly protected; and 4) elected authorities possess real authority to govern, in that they are not subject to the tutelary control of military or clerical leaders.[2] Although even fully democratic regimes may at times violate one or more of these criteria, such violations are not broad or systematic enough to seriously impede democratic

Levitsky, Steven, and Lucan Way. 2002. "The Rise of Competitive Authoritarianism," *Journal of Democracy* 13(2): 51–65.

challenges to incumbent governments. In other words, they do not fundamentally alter the playing field between government and opposition.[3]

In competitive authoritarian regimes, by contrast, violations of these criteria are both frequent enough and serious enough to create an uneven playing field between government and opposition. Although elections are regularly held and are generally free of massive fraud, incumbents routinely abuse state resources, deny the opposition adequate media coverage, harass opposition candidates and their supporters, and in some cases manipulate electoral results. Journalists, opposition politicians, and other government critics may be spied on, threatened, harassed, or arrested. Members of the opposition may be jailed, exiled, or—less frequently—even assaulted or murdered. Regimes characterized by such abuses cannot be called democratic.

Competitive authoritarianism must therefore be distinguished from unstable, ineffective, or otherwise flawed types of regimes that nevertheless meet basic standards of democracy, and this includes what Guillermo O'Donnell has called "delegative democracies."[4] According to O'Donnell, delegative democracies are characterized by low levels of horizontal accountability (checks and balances) and therefore exhibit powerful, plebiscitarian, and occasionally abusive executives. Yet such regimes meet minimum standards for democracy. Delegative democracy thus applies to such cases as Argentina and Brazil in the early 1990s, but not to Peru after Fujimori's 1992 presidential self-coup.

Yet if competitive authoritarian regimes fall short of democracy, they also fall short of full-scale authoritarianism. Although incumbents in competitive authoritarian regimes may routinely manipulate formal democratic rules, they are unable to eliminate them or reduce them to a mere façade. Rather than openly violating democratic rules (for example, by banning or repressing the opposition and the media), incumbents are more likely to use bribery, co-optation, and more subtle forms of persecution, such as the use of tax authorities, compliant judiciaries, and other state agencies to "legally" harass, persecute, or extort cooperative behavior from critics. Yet even if the cards are stacked in favor of autocratic incumbents, the persistence of meaningful democratic institutions creates arenas

through which opposition forces may—and frequently do—pose significant challenges. As a result, even though democratic institutions may be badly flawed, both authoritarian incumbents and their opponents must take them seriously.

In this sense, competitive authoritarianism is distinct from what might be called "façade" electoral regimes—that is, regimes in which electoral institutions exist but yield no meaningful contestation for power (such as Egypt, Singapore, and Uzbekistan in the 1990s). Such regimes have been called "pseudodemocracies," "virtual democracies," and "electoral authoritarian" regimes. In our view, they are cases of full-scale authoritarianism.[5] The line between this type of regime and competitive authoritarianism can be hard to draw, and noncompetitive electoral institutions may one day become competitive (as occurred in Mexico). It is essential, however, to distinguish regimes in which democratic institutions offer an important channel through which the opposition may seek power from those regimes in which democratic rules simply serve as to legitimate an existing autocratic leadership.

Finally, competitive authoritarianism must be distinguished from other types of hybrid regimes. Regimes may mix authoritarian and democratic features in a variety of ways, and competitive authoritarianism should not be viewed as encompassing all of these regime forms. Other hybrid regime types include "exclusive republics"[6] (regimes with strong democratic institutions but highly restrictive citizenship laws) and "tutelary" or "guided" democracies—competitive regimes in which nondemocratic actors such as military or religious authorities wield veto power.

FOUR ARENAS OF DEMOCRATIC CONTESTATION

Due to the persistence of meaningful democratic institutions in competitive authoritarian regimes, arenas of contestation exist through which opposition forces may periodically challenge, weaken, and occasionally even defeat autocratic incumbents. Four such arenas are of particular importance: 1) the electoral arena; 2) the legislature; 3) the judiciary; and 4) the media.

1. **The electoral arena.** The first and most important arena of contestation is the electoral arena. In

authoritarian regimes, elections either do not exist or are not seriously contested. Electoral competition is eliminated either de jure, as in Cuba and China, or de facto, as in Kazakhstan and Uzbekistan. In the latter, opposition parties are routinely banned or disqualified from electoral competition, and opposition leaders are often jailed. In addition, independent or outside observers are prevented from verifying results via parallel vote counts, which creates widespread opportunities for vote stealing. As a result, opposition forces do not present a serious electoral threat to incumbents, and elections are, for all intents and purposes, noncompetitive. Thus Kazakhstani president Nursultan Nazarbayev was reelected in 1999 with 80 percent of the vote, and in Uzbekistan, President Islam Karimov was reelected in 2000 with 92 percent of the vote, (As a rule of thumb, regimes in which presidents are reelected with more than 70 percent of the vote can generally be considered noncompetitive.) In such cases, the death or violent overthrow of the president is often viewed as a more likely means of succession than his electoral defeat.

In competitive authoritarian regimes, by contrast, elections are often bitterly fought. Although the electoral process may be characterized by large-scale abuses of state power, biased media coverage, (often violent) harassment of opposition candidates and activists,[7] and an overall lack of transparency, elections are regularly held, competitive (in that major opposition parties and candidates usually participate), and generally free of massive fraud. In many cases, the presence of international observers or the existence of parallel vote-counting procedures limits the capacity of incumbents to engage in large-scale fraud. As a result, elections may generate considerable uncertainty, and autocratic incumbents must therefore take them seriously. For example, Russian president Boris Yeltsin in 1996 and Ukrainian president Leonid Kuchma in 1999 faced strong electoral challenges from former communist parties. Despite concerted efforts to use blackmail and other techniques to secure votes,[8] Kuchma won only 35 percent of the vote in the first round of the 1999 presidential elections and 56 percent in the second round. In Kenya, longtime autocrat Daniel arap Moi won reelection with bare pluralities in 1992 and 1997, and in Zimbabwe, the opposition Movement for Democratic Change nearly won the 2000 parliamentary elections.

In several cases, opposition forces have managed to defeat autocratic incumbents or their hand-picked candidates, as occurred in Nicaragua in 1990, Zambia in 1991, Malawi and Ukraine in 1994, Albania in 1997, and Ghana in 2000.

Although incumbents may manipulate election results, this often costs them dearly and can even bring them down. In Peru, for example, Fujimori was able to gain reelection in 2000 but was forced to resign amid scandal months later. Similarly, efforts by Milošević to falsify Serbian election results in 2000 led to a regime crisis and the president's removal. Regime crises resulting from electoral fraud also occurred in Mexico in 1988 and Armenia in 1996.

2. **The legislative arena.** A second arena of contestation is the legislature. In most full-scale authoritarian regimes, legislatures either do not exist or are so thoroughly controlled by the ruling party that conflict between the legislature and the executive branch is virtually unthinkable. In competitive authoritarian regimes, legislatures tend to be relatively weak, but they occasionally become focal points of opposition activity. This is particularly likely in cases in which incumbents lack strong majority parties. In both Ukraine and Russia in the 1990s, for example, presidents were faced with recalcitrant parliaments dominated by former communist and other left-wing parties. The Ukrainian parliament repeatedly blocked or watered down economic reform legislation proposed by President Kuchma, and in 2000–2001, despite Kuchma's threats to take "appropriate" measures if it did not cooperate, parliament blocked the president's effort to call a referendum aimed at reducing the powers of the legislature. Although incumbents may attempt to circumvent or even shut down the legislature (as in Peru in 1992 and Russia in 1993), such actions tend to be costly, particularly in the international arena. Thus both Fujimori and Yeltsin held new legislative elections within three years of their "self-coups," and Yeltsin continued to face opposition from the post-1993-coup parliament.

Even where incumbent executives enjoy large legislative majorities, opposition forces may use the legislature as a place for meeting and organizing and (to the extent that an independent media exists) as a public platform from which to denounce the regime.

In Peru, despite the fact that opposition parties exerted little influence over the legislative process between 1995 and 2000, anti-Fujimori legislators used congress (and media coverage of it) as a place to air their views. In Ukraine in November 2000, opposition deputy Aleksandr Moroz used parliament to accuse the president of murder and to distribute damaging tapes of the president to the press.

3. **The judicial arena.** A third arena of potential contestation is the judiciary. Governments in competitive authoritarian regimes routinely attempt to subordinate the judiciary, often via impeachment, or, more subtly, through bribery, extortion, and other mechanisms of co-optation. In Peru, for example, scores of judges—including several Supreme Court justices—were entwined in the web of patronage, corruption, and blackmail constructed by Fujimori's intelligence chief, Vladimiro Montesinos. In Russia, when the Constitutional Court declared Yeltsin's 1993 decree disbanding parliament to be unconstitutional, Yeltsin cut off the Court's phone lines and took away its guards. In some cases, governments resort to threats and violence. In Zimbabwe, after the Supreme Court ruled that occupations of white-owned farmland—part of the Mugabe government's land-redistribution policy—were illegal, independent justices received a wave of violent threats from pro-government "war veterans." Four justices, including Chief Justice Anthony Gubbay, opted for early retirement in 2001 and were replaced by justices with closer ties to the government.

Yet the combination of formal judicial independence and incomplete control by the executive can give maverick judges an opening. In Ukraine, for example, the Constitutional Court stipulated that President Kuchma's referendum to reduce the powers of the legislature was not binding. In Slovakia, the Constitutional Court prevented Vladimir Mečiar's government from denying the opposition seats in parliament in 1994, and in Serbia, the courts legitimized local opposition electoral victories in 1996. Courts have also protected media and opposition figures from state persecution. In Croatia, the courts acquitted an opposition weekly that had been charged with falsely accusing President Tudjman of being a devotee of Spain's Francisco Franco. Similarly, in Malaysia in 2001, a High Court judge released two dissidents who

had been jailed under the regime's Internal Security Act and publicly questioned the need for such a draconian law.[9]

Although competitive authoritarian governments may subsequently punish judges who rule against them, such acts against formally independent judiciaries may generate important costs in terms of domestic and international legitimacy. In Peru, for example, the pro-Fujimori congress sacked three members of the Constitutional Tribunal in 1997 after they attempted to block Fujimori's constitutionally dubious bid for a third presidential term. The move generated sharp criticism both domestically and abroad, however, and the case remained a thorn in the regime's side for the rest of the decade.

4. **The media.** Finally, the media are often a central point of contention in competitive authoritarian regimes. In most full-blown autocracies, the media are entirely state-owned, heavily censored, or systematically repressed. Leading television and radio stations are controlled by the government (or its close allies), and major independent newspapers and magazines are either prohibited by law (as in Cuba) or de facto eliminated (as in Uzbekistan and Turkmenistan). Journalists who provoke the ire of the government risk arrest, deportation, and even assassination. In competitive authoritarian regimes, by contrast, independent media outlets are not only legal but often quite influential, and journalists—though frequently threatened and periodically attacked—often emerge as important opposition figures. In Peru, for example, independent newspapers such as *La República* and *El Comercio* and weekly magazines such as *Sí* and *Caretas* operated freely throughout the 1990s. In Ukraine, newspapers such as *Zerkalo nedeli, Den,* and, more recently, *Vicherni visti* functioned as important sources of independent views on the Kuchma government.

Independent media outlets often play a critical watchdog role by investigating and exposing government malfeasance. The Peruvian media uncovered a range of government abuses, including the 1992 massacre of students at La Cantuta University and the forgery of the signatures needed for Fujimori's party to qualify for the 2000 elections. In Russia, Vladimir Gusinsky's Independent TV was an important source of criticism of the Yeltsin government, particularly with respect to its actions in Chechnya. In Zimbabwe, the *Daily News* played an important role in exposing the abuses of the Mugabe government. Media outlets may also serve as mouthpieces for opposition forces. In Serbia, the Belgrade radio station B-92 served as a key center of opposition to Milošević in the second half of the 1990s. Newspapers played an important role in supporting opposition forces in Panama and Nicaragua in the late 1980s.

Executives in competitive authoritarian regimes often actively seek to suppress the independent media, using more subtle mechanisms of repression than their counterparts in authoritarian regimes. These methods often include bribery, the selective allocation of state advertising, the manipulation of debts and taxes owed by media outlets, the fomentation of conflicts among stockholders, and restrictive press laws that facilitate the prosecution of independent and opposition journalists. In Russia, the government took advantage of Independent TV's debts to the main gas company, Gazprom, to engineer a takeover by government-friendly forces. In Peru, the Fujimori government gained de facto control over all of the country's privately owned television stations through a combination of bribery and legal shenanigans, such as the invalidation of Channel 2 owner Baruch Ivcher's citizenship. Governments also make extensive use of libel laws to harass or persecute independent newspapers "legally." In Ghana, for example, the Jerry Rawlings government used colonial-era libel statutes to imprison several newspaper editors and columnists in the 1990s, and in Croatia, the Open Society Institute reported in 1997 that major independent newspapers had been hit by more than 230 libel suits. Similarly, Armenia's government used libel suits to quiet press criticism after the country's controversial 1996 elections.[10]

Yet efforts to repress the media may be costly to incumbents in competitive authoritarian regimes. For example, when in 1996 the Tudjman government in Croatia tried to revoke the license of Radio 101, a popular independent station in the capital, the massive protests that broke out both galvanized the opposition and temporarily split the ruling party. In Ukraine in 2000, charges that President Kuchma had sought the killing of an opposition journalist led to large domestic protests and partial isolation from the West. In Peru, the persecution and exiling of Ivcher provoked substantial protest at home and became a focal point of criticism abroad.

INHERENT TENSIONS

Authoritarian governments may coexist indefinitely with meaningful democratic institutions. As long as incumbents avoid egregious (and well-publicized) rights abuses and do not cancel or openly steal elections, the contradictions inherent in competitive authoritarianism may be manageable. Using bribery, co-optation, and various forms of "legal" persecution, governments may limit opposition challenges without provoking massive protest or international repudiation.

Yet the coexistence of democratic rules and autocratic methods aimed at keeping incumbents in power creates an inherent source of instability. The presence of elections, legislatures, courts, and an independent media creates periodic opportunities for challenges by opposition forces. Such challenges create a serious dilemma for autocratic incumbents. On the one hand, repressing them is costly, largely because the challenges tend to be both formally legal and widely perceived (domestically and internationally) as legitimate. On the other hand, incumbents could lose power if they let democratic challenges run their course.[11] Periods of serious democratic contestation thus bring out the contradictions inherent in competitive authoritarianism, forcing autocratic incumbents to choose between egregiously violating democratic rules, at the cost of international isolation and domestic conflict, and allowing the challenge to proceed, at the cost of possible defeat. The result is often some kind of regime crisis, as occurred in Mexico in 1988; Nicaragua in 1990; Zambia in 1991; Russia in 1993; Armenia in 1996; Albania in 1997; Ghana, Peru, Serbia, and Ukraine in 2000; and Zambia (again) in 2001. A similar crisis appears likely to emerge in Zimbabwe surrounding the March 2002 presidential election.

In some cases, such as those of Kenya, Malaysia, Russia, and Ukraine, autocratic incumbents weathered the storm. In several of these countries, the regime cracked down and dug in deeper. In other cases, such as Nicaragua in 1990, Zambia in 1991, and Ghana and

Mexico in 2000, competitive authoritarian governments failed to crack down and lost power. In still other cases, including Peru and Serbia, autocrats attempted to crack down but, in doing so, were badly weakened and eventually fell.

But succession is not democratization. Although in many cases (Croatia, Nicaragua, Peru, Slovakia, Serbia) incumbent turnover resulted in democratic transitions, in other cases, including Albania, Zambia, Ukraine, and Belarus, newly elected leaders continued or even intensified many of the authoritarian practices of their predecessors. Hence, while the removal of autocratic elites creates an important *opportunity* for regime change and even democratization, it does not ensure such an outcome.

Although it is beyond the scope of this article to explain variations in the capacity of competitive authoritarian regimes to survive crises brought about by episodes of democratic contestation, one pattern is worth noting.[12] In regions with closer ties to the West, particularly Latin America and Central Europe, the removal of autocratic incumbents has generally resulted in democratization in the post–Cold War period. In Latin America, for example, four out of five competitive authoritarian regimes democratized after 1990 (the Dominican Republic, Mexico, Nicaragua, and Peru, but not Haiti). Similarly, during the same period four out of five competitive authoritarian regimes in Central Europe democratized (Croatia, Serbia, Slovakia, and Romania, but not Albania). By contrast, the record of competitive authoritarian regimes in Africa and the former Soviet Union is strikingly different. Among former Soviet republics, only one competitive authoritarian regime (Moldova) democratized in the 1990s.

This evidence suggests that proximity to the West may have been an important factor shaping the trajectory of competitive authoritarian regimes in the 1990s. Linkages to the West—in the form of cultural and media influence, elite networks, demonstration effects, and direct pressure from Western governments—appear to have raised the costs of authoritarian entrenchment, making the democratization of competitive authoritarian regimes more likely. Where Western linkages were weaker, or where alternative, nondemocratic hegemons (such as Russia or China) exerted substantial influence, competitive authoritarian regimes were more likely either to persist or to move in a more authoritarian direction.

PATHS TO COMPETITIVE AUTHORITARIANISM

Although competitive authoritarian regimes are not a new phenomenon (historical examples include parts of East Central Europe in the 1920s and Argentina under Perón from 1946 to 1955), they have clearly proliferated in recent years. Competitive authoritarianism emerged out of three different regime paths during the 1990s. One path was the decay of a full-blown authoritarian regime. In these cases, established authoritarian regimes were compelled—often by a combination of domestic and international pressure—either to adopt formal democratic institutions or to adhere seriously to what had previously been façade democratic institutions. Yet due to the weakness of opposition movements, transitions fell short of democracy, and incumbents proved adept at manipulating or selectively adhering to the new democratic rules, Transitions of this type occurred across much of sub-Saharan Africa, where economic crisis and international pressure compelled established autocrats to call multiparty elections, but where many transitions fell short of democratization and many autocrats retained power.

A second path to competitive authoritarianism was the collapse of an authoritarian regime, followed by the emergence of a new, competitive authoritarian regime. In these cases, weak electoral regimes emerged, more or less by default, in the wake of an authoritarian breakdown. Although the absence of democratic traditions and weak civil societies created opportunities for elected governments to rule autocratically, these governments lacked the capacity to consolidate authoritarian rule. This path was followed by such postcommunist countries as Armenia, Croatia, Romania, Russia, Serbia, and Ukraine, as well as by Haiti after 1994.

A third path to competitive authoritarianism was the decay of a democratic regime. In these cases, deep and often longstanding political and economic crises created conditions under which freely elected governments undermined democratic institutions—either via a presidential "self-coup" or through selective, incremental abuses—but lacked the will or capacity to eliminate them entirely. Examples of such transitions include Peru in the early 1990s and perhaps contemporary Venezuela.

The roots of this recent proliferation lie in the difficulties associated with consolidating both democratic *and* authoritarian regimes in the immediate post–Cold War period. Notwithstanding the global advance of democracy in the 1990s (and the democratic optimism that it inspired among scholars), in much of the world democratic regimes remained difficult to establish or sustain. A large number of transitions took place in countries with high levels of poverty, inequality, and illiteracy; weak states and civil societies; institutional instability; contested national borders; and—in parts of the former communist world—continued domination by the state of the economy, major religious institutions, and other areas of social activity.

Yet if the prospects for full-scale democratization remained bleak in much of the post–Cold War world, so too were the prospects for building and sustaining full-scale authoritarian regimes.[13] In large part, this change was a product of the post–Cold War international environment. Western liberalism's triumph and the Soviet collapse undermined the legitimacy of alternative regime models and created strong incentives for peripheral states to adopt formal democratic institutions. As Andrew Janos has argued, periods of liberal hegemony place a "web of constraints" on nondemocratic governments that seek to maintain international respectability and viability. Thus, during the brief period of liberal hegemony that followed World War I, relatively authoritarian governments in Central Europe faced strong pressure to tolerate a semifree press, regular scrutiny from opposition members of parliament, and a quasi-independent judiciary.[14] When Western liberal states are challenged by authoritarian counter-hegemonic powers, however, these "webs of constraints" tend to disappear. Counter-hegemonic powers provide alternative sources of legitimacy and military and economic assistance, thereby weakening the incentive for governing elites to maintain formal democratic institutions. Thus the emergence of Nazi Germany and Soviet Russia as regional powers contributed to the collapse of Central European hybrid regimes in the 1930s, and the strength of the Soviet Union facilitated the establishment

of Leninist dictatorships across much of the Third World during the Cold War. When Western powers face a challenger to their hegemony, they are more likely to tolerate autocracies that can present themselves as buffers against their rivals.

The 1990s marked a period of Western liberal hegemony similar to that of the 1920s but much broader in scope. International influences took many forms, including demonstration effects, conditionality (as in the case of European Union membership), direct state-to-state pressure (in the form of sanctions, behind-the-scenes diplomacy, and even direct military intervention), and the activities of emerging transnational actors and institutions. In this new context, the liberal democratic model gained unprecedented acceptance among post-communist and Third World elites. Perhaps more importantly, the absence of alternative sources of military and economic aid increased the importance of being on good terms with Western governments and institutions. Although the effect of international pressure varied considerably across regions (and even across countries), for most governments in most poorer and middle-income countries, the benefits of adopting formal democratic institutions—and the costs of maintaining overtly authoritarian ones—rose considerably in the 1990s.

Emerging and potential autocrats also confronted important domestic impediments to the consolidation of authoritarian regimes. To consolidate a fully closed regime, authoritarian elites must eliminate all major sources of contestation through the systematic repression or co-optation of potential opponents. Such action requires both elite cohesion and a minimally effective—and financially solvent—state apparatus. Resource scarcity has made it more difficult for leaders to sustain the patronage networks that previously undergirded authoritarian state structures. In addition, uncertain hierarchical control over repressive organs, while heightening the risk of civil war, has also increased the difficulty of consolidating authoritarian rule. Finally, in many postcommunist regimes the dispersal of control over different state and economic resources among different groups made it difficult for any single leader to establish complete control, resulting in a kind of pluralism by default.

A substantial number of regimes *were* able to overcome the domestic and international obstacles to authoritarian rule in the 1990s. Some benefited from pockets of permissiveness in the international system, due in large part to economic or security issues that trumped democracy promotion on Western foreign policy agendas. Others benefited from state control over revenues from valuable commodities (such as oil), which undermined the development of an autonomous civil society and gave rulers the means to co-opt potential opponents, and still others took advantage of quasi-traditional elite networks that facilitated the establishment of neopatrimonial regimes (as in Central Asia).

Yet in much of Africa, Latin America, and postcommunist Eurasia in the 1990s, emerging or potential autocrats lacked these advantages. Due to a combination of international pressure, state weakness, and elite fragmentation, many incumbents found the cost of co-opting or repressing opponents to be prohibitively high. As a result, even some highly autocratic leaders were unable to eliminate important arenas of contestation. The sources of authoritarian weakness varied across cases. In Albania and Haiti, for example, international factors were probably decisive in preventing full-scale authoritarian rule. In Africa, a contraction of resources caused by the end of Cold War sponsorship and the conditionality imposed by international financial institutions left some governments too weak to co-opt or repress even relatively feeble opposition challenges.[15] In post-Soviet countries such as Moldova, Russia, and Ukraine, the fragmentation of control over state and economic resources generated political competition even where civil society remained weak. What is common to virtually all of these cases, however, is that pluralism and democratic contestation persisted less because elites wanted them than because elites simply could not get rid of them.

In the 1990s, then, competitive authoritarian regimes were most likely to emerge where conditions were unfavorable to the consolidation of either democratic or authoritarian regimes. It must be noted, of course, that such conditions do not necessarily result in competitive authoritarianism. In some cases, including El Salvador, Mali, and Mongolia, democracy may take hold in spite of highly unfavorable conditions. In other cases, the breakdown of authoritarian rule may result in state collapse and civil war, as occurred in Liberia, Sierra Leone, and Somalia.

CONCEPTUALIZING NONDEMOCRACIES

We conclude by echoing Thomas Carothers' call to move beyond what he calls the "transition paradigm."[16] It is now clear that early hopes for democratization in much of the world were overly optimistic. Many authoritarian regimes have survived the "third wave" of democratization. In other cases, the collapse of one kind of authoritarianism yielded not democracy but a new form of nondemocratic rule. Indeed, a decade after the collapse of the Soviet Union, the majority of the world's independent states remained nondemocratic. Yet whereas an extensive literature has emerged concerning the causes and consequences of democratization, emerging types of democracy, and issues of democratic consolidation, remarkably little research has been undertaken on the emergence or persistence of nondemocratic regimes.

The post–Cold War Western liberal hegemony, global economic change, developments in media and communications technologies, and the growth of international networks aimed at promoting democracy and human rights all have contributed to reshaping the opportunities and constraints facing authoritarian elites. As a result, some forms of authoritarianism, such as totalitarianism and bureaucratic authoritarianism, have become more difficult to sustain. At the same time, however, several new (or partially new) nondemocratic regime types took on greater importance in the 1990s, including competitive authoritarianism. A range of other nondemocratic outcomes also gained in importance, including other types of hybrid regimes, postcommunist patrimonial dictatorships, and cases of sustained state collapse ("chaosocracy").[17] Research on these nondemocratic outcomes is critical to gaining a better understanding of the full (rather than hoped for) set of alternatives open to post–Cold War transitional regimes.

NOTES

The authors thank Jason Brownlee, Timothy Colton, Michael Coppedge, Keith Darden, Jorge Domínguez, Steve Hanson, Marc Morjé Howard, Rory MacFarquhar, Mitch Orenstein, Maria Popova, Andreas Schedler, Oxana Shevel, and Richard Snyder for their comments on earlier drafts of this article.

1. Juan J. Linz, *Totalitarian and Authoritarian Regimes* (Boulder, Colo.: Lynne Rienner, 2000), 34.

2. See Scott Mainwaring, Daniel Brinks, and Aníbal Pérez Linan, "Classifying Political Regimes in Latin America, 1945–1999," *Studies in Comparative International Development* 36 (Spring 2001). This definition is consistent with what Larry Diamond calls "mid-range" conceptions of democracy (Larry Diamond, *Developing Democracy*, 13–15).

3. Obviously, the exact point at which violations of civil and political rights begin to fundamentally alter the playing field is difficult to discern and will always be open to debate. However, the problem of scoring borderline cases is common to all regime conceptualizations.

4. Guillermo O'Donnell, "Delegative Democracy," *Journal of Democracy* 5 (January 1994): 55–69.

5. Larry Diamond, *Developing Democracy*, 15–16; Richard Joseph, "Africa, 1990–1997"; Jason Brownlee, "Double Edged Institutions: Electoral Authoritarianism in Egypt and Iran," paper presented at the 2001 Annual Meeting of the American Political Science Association, San Francisco, 30 August–2 September 2001.

6. Philip G. Roeder, "Varieties of Post-Soviet Authoritarian Regimes," *Past-Soviet Affairs* 10 (January–March 1994): 61–101.

7. In Kenya, government-backed death squads were responsible for large-scale violence, particularly in ethnic minority areas. See Joel Barkan and Njuguna Ng'ethe, "Kenya Tries Again," in Larry Diamond and Marc F. Plattner, eds., *Democratization in Africa* (Baltimore: Johns Hopkins University Press, 1999), 185. Substantial violence against opposition forces was also seen in Serbia and Zimbabwe in the 1990s.

8. See Keith Darden, "Blackmail as a Tool of State Domination: Ukraine Under Kuchma," *East European Constitutional Review* 10 (Spring–Summer 2001): 67–71.

9. *The Economist*, 14 July 2001, 37.

10. H. Kwasi Prempeh, "A New Jurisprudence for Africa," *Journal of Democracy* 10 (July 1999): 138; Nebojsa Bjelakovic and Sava Tatic, "Croatia: Another Year of Bleak Continuities," *Transitions-on-Line, http://archive.tol.cz/countries/croar97.html* (1997). Mikhail Diloyen, "Journalists Fall through the Legal Cracks in Armenia," *Eurasia Insight* (June 2000).

11. These dilemmas are presented in an insightful way in Andreas Schedler, "The Nested Game of Democratization by Elections," *International Political Science Review* 23 (January 2002).

12. For a more developed explanation, see Steven Levitsky and Lucan A. Way, "Competitive Authoritarianism: Hybrid Regime Change in Peru and Ukraine in Comparative Perspective," Studies in Public Policy Working Paper No. 355 (Glasgow: University of Strathclyde Center for the Study of Public Policy, 2001).

13. On obstacles to authoritarianism in the former Soviet Union, see Philip G. Roeder, "The Rejection of Authoritarianism," in Richard Anderson, M. Stephen Fish, Stephen E. Hanson, and Philip G. Roeder, *Postcommunism and the Theory of Democracy* (Princeton: Princeton University Press, 2001).

14. Andrew Janos, *East Central Europe in the Modern World: The Politics of Borderlands From Pre- to Postcommunism* (Stanford, Calif.: Stanford University Press, 2000), 97–99.

15. Michael Bratton and Nicolas van de Walle, *Democratic Experiments in Africa: Regime Transitions in Comparative Perspective* (New York: Cambridge University Press, 1997), 100.

16. Thomas Carothers, "The End of the Transition Paradigm," *Journal of Democracy* 13 (January 2002): 5–21.

17. See Richard Snyder, "Does Lootable Wealth Breed Disorder? States, Regimes, and the Political Economy of Extraction," paper presented at the 2001 Annual Meeting of the American Political Science Association, San Francisco, 30 August–2 September 2001. See also Juan J. Linz, *Totalitarian and Authoritarian Regimes*, 37.

BARRINGTON MOORE

7.2 SOCIAL ORIGINS OF DICTATORSHIP AND DEMOCRACY

Lord and Peasant in the Making of the Modern World

As its title suggests, this book is about the origins of both democracy and dictatorship. Moore assesses some of the most significant instances of authoritarian rule in the 20th century—Nazi Germany and fascist Japan and communist Russia (or the Soviet Union) and China. He argues that the origins of these dictatorships can be found in the relative powers of different major political actors. In particular, three groups matter: landowners, commercial and industrial interests (known as the bourgeoisie), and peasants. The fascist regimes in Germany and Japan emerged from a path in which historically powerful economic elites (especially landowners) prevented the commercial and industrial classes from leading economic and political modernization. This "revolution from above" was reactionary and exclusionary, culminating in fascism. In Russia and China, the urban classes were weak and the peasantry was large, which served as a recipe for communist revolution to overthrow the old regime as a pathway to the modern world. These paths to dictatorship contrast with the recipe for eventual democracy found in England, France, and the United States: a "bourgeois" revolution led by commercial interests, merchants, and the like. It was when a forceful impetus from this social class was absent that dictatorship emerged. From this comes the pithy phrase sometimes used to describe Moore's argument: "no bourgeoisie, no democracy." If you have read Section I consider whether Moore's theory has affinities with the approach to comparative analysis offered by Mahoney and Villegas.

This book endeavors to explain the varied political roles played by the landed upper classes and the peasantry in the transformation from agrarian societies (defined simply as states where a large majority of the population lives off the land) to modern industrial ones. Somewhat more specifically, it is an attempt to discover the range of historical conditions under which either or both of these rural groups have become important forces behind the emergence of Western parliamentary versions of democracy, and dictatorships of the right and the left, that is, fascist and communist regimes.

Since no problem ever comes to the student of human society out of a blue and empty sky, it is worthwhile to indicate very briefly the considerations behind this one. For some time before beginning this work in earnest more than ten years ago, I had become skeptical of the thesis that industrialism was the main cause of twentieth-century totalitarian regimes, because of the very obvious fact that Russia and China were overwhelmingly agrarian countries when the communists established themselves. For a long time before that I had been convinced that adequate theoretical comprehension of political systems had to come to terms with Asian institutions and history. Hence it seemed at least a promising strategy to investigate what political currents were set up among the classes who lived off the countryside

Moore, Barrington. 1966. *Social Origins of Dictatorship and Democracy: Lord and Peasant in the Making of the Modern World.* Boston: Beacon Press.

and to devote as much attention to Asian as to Western societies.

From this standpoint the analysis of the transformation of agrarian society in specific countries produces results at least as rewarding as larger generalizations. It is important, for example, to know how the solution of agrarian problems contributed to the establishment of parliamentary democracy in England and the failure as yet to solve very different ones constitutes a threat to democracy in India. Furthermore, for any given country one is bound to find lines of causation that do not fit easily into more general theories. Conversely too strong a devotion to theory always carries the danger that one may overemphasize facts that fit a theory beyond their importance in the history of individual countries. For these reasons the interpretation of the transformation in several countries takes up the largest part of the book.

In the effort to understand the history of a specific country a comparative perspective can lead to asking very useful and sometimes new questions. There are further advantages. Comparisons can serve as a rough negative check on accepted historical explanations. And a comparative approach may lead to new historical generalizations. In practice these features constitute a single intellectual process and make such a study more than a disparate collection of interesting cases. For example, after noticing that Indian peasants have suffered in a material way just about as much as Chinese peasants during the nineteenth and twentieth centuries without generating a massive revolutionary movement, one begins to wonder about traditional explanations of what took place in both societies and becomes alert to factors affecting peasant outbreaks in other countries, in the hope of discerning general causes. Or after learning about the disastrous consequences for democracy of a coalition between agrarian and industrial élites in nineteenth- and early twentieth-century Germany, the much discussed marriage of iron and rye—one wonders why a similar marriage between iron and cotton did not prevent the coming of the Civil War in the United States; and so one has taken a step toward specifying configurations favorable and unfavorable to the establishment of modern Western democracy. That comparative analysis is no substitute for detailed investigation of specific cases is obvious.

Generalizations that are sound resemble a large-scale map of an extended terrain, such as an airplane pilot might use in crossing a continent. Such maps are essential for certain purposes just as more detailed maps are necessary for others. No one seeking a preliminary orientation to the terrain wants to know the location of every house and footpath. Still, if one explores on foot—and at present the comparative historian does exactly that a great deal of the time—the details are what one learns first. Their meaning and relationship emerges only gradually. There can be long periods when the investigator feels lost in an underbrush of facts inhabited by specialists engaged in savage disputes about whether the underbrush is a pine forest or a tropical jungle. He is unlikely to emerge from such encounters without scratches and bruises. And if he draws a map of the area he has visited, one of the natives may well accuse him of omitting his own house and clearing, a sad event if the researcher has actually found much sustenance and refreshment there. The outcry is likely to be all the sharper if at the end of the journey the explorer tries to set down in very brief form for those who may come later the most striking things that he has seen. That is exactly what I shall try to do now, to sketch in very broad strokes the main findings in order to give the reader a preliminary map of the terrain we shall explore together.

In the range of cases examined here one may discern three main historical routes from the preindustrial to the modern world. The first of these leads through what I think deserve to be called bourgeois revolutions. Aside from the fact that this term is a red flag to many scholars because of its Marxist connotations, it has other ambiguities and disadvantages. Nevertheless, for reasons that will appear in due course I think it is a necessary designation for certain violent changes that took place in English, French, and American societies on the way to becoming modern industrial democracies and that historians connect with the Puritan Revolution (or the English Civil War as it is often called as well), the French Revolution, and the American Civil War. A key feature in such revolutions is the development of a group in society with an independent economic base, which attacks obstacles to a democratic version of capitalism that have been inherited from the past. Though a great deal of the impetus has come from trading and manufacturing classes in the cities, that is very far from the whole story. The allies this bourgeois impetus has found, the enemies it has encountered, vary sharply from case to case. The landed upper classes, our main concern at the start, were either an important part of this capitalist and democratic tide, as in England, or if they opposed it, they were swept aside in the convulsions of revolution or civil war. The same thing may be said about the peasants. Either the main thrust of their political efforts coincided with that toward capitalism and political democracy, or else it was negligible. And it was negligible either because capitalist advance destroyed peasant society or because this advance began in a new country, such as the United States, without a real peasantry.

The first and earlier route through the great revolutions and civil wars led to the combination of capitalism and Western democracy. The second route has also been capitalist, but culminated during the twentieth century in fascism. Germany and Japan are the obvious cases, though only the latter receives detailed treatment in this study for reasons given above. I shall call this the capitalist and reactionary form. It amounts to a form of revolution from above. In these countries the bourgeois impulse was much weaker. If it took a revolutionary form at all, the revolution was defeated. Afterward sections of a relatively weak commercial and industrial class relied on dissident elements in the older and still dominant ruling classes, mainly recruited from the land, to put through the political and economic changes required for a modern industrial society, under the auspices of a semi-parliamentary regime. Industrial development may proceed rapidly under such auspices. But the outcome, after a brief and unstable period of democracy, has been fascism. The third route is of course communism, as exemplified in Russia and in China. The great agrarian bureaucracies of these countries served to inhibit the commercial and later industrial impulses even more than in the preceding instances. The results were twofold. In the first place these urban classes were too weak to constitute even a junior partner in the form of modernization taken by Germany and Japan, though there were attempts in this direction. And in the absence of more than the most feeble steps toward modernization a

huge peasantry remained. This stratum, subject to new strains and stresses as the modern world encroached upon it, provided the main destructive revolutionary force that overthrew the old order and propelled these countries into the modern era under communist leadership that made the peasants its primary victims.

Finally, in India we may perceive still a fourth general pattern that accounts for the weak impulse toward modernization. In that country so far there has been neither a capitalist revolution from above or below, nor a peasant one leading to communism. Likewise the impulse toward modernization has been very weak. On the other hand, at least some of the historical prerequisites of Western democracy did put in an appearance. A parliamentary regime has existed for some time that is considerably more than mere façade. Because the impulse toward modernization has been weakest in India, this case stands somewhat apart from any theoretical scheme that it seems possible to construct for the others. At the same time it serves as a salutary check upon such generalizations. It is especially useful in trying to understand peasant revolutions, since the degree of rural misery in India where there has been no peasant revolution is about the same as in China where rebellion and revolution have been decisive in both premodern and recent times.

To sum up as concisely as possible, we seek to understand the role of the landed upper classes and the peasants in the bourgeois revolutions leading to capitalist democracy, the abortive bourgeois revolutions leading to fascism, and the peasant revolutions leading to communism. The ways in which the landed upper classes and the peasants reacted to the challenge of commercial agriculture were decisive factors in determining the political outcome. The applicability of these political labels, the elements that these movements do and do not share in different countries and at different times, will I hope become clear in the course of subsequent discussion. One point, on the other hand, is worth noticing right away. Though in each case one configuration emerges as the dominant one, it is possible to discern subordinate ones that become the dominant features in another country. Thus in England, during the latter part of the French Revolution and until after the end of the Napoleonic wars, there existed some of the elements of a reactionary configuration recognizable as a dominant feature in Germany: a coalition between the older landed élites and the rising commercial and industrial ones, directed against the lower classes in town and countryside (but able at times to attract significant lower-class support on some issues). Indeed this reactionary combination of elements turns up in some form in each society studied, including the United States. To illustrate further, royal absolutism in France shows some of the same effects on commercial life as do the great bureaucratic monarchies of tsarist Russia and Imperial China. This type of observation encourages somewhat greater confidence in the possibility that empirically based categories may transcend particular cases.

Nevertheless there remains a strong tension between the demands of doing justice to the explanation of a particular case and the search for generalizations, mainly because it is impossible to know just how important a particular problem may be until one has finished examining all of them. This tension is responsible for a certain lack of symmetry and elegance in the presentation, which I deplore but have been unable to eliminate after several rewritings. Again the parallel with the explorer of unknown lands may not be amiss: he is not called upon to build a smooth and direct highway for the next band of travellers. Should he be their guide, he is thought to acquit himself adequately if he avoids the time-consuming back-tracks and errors of his first exploration, courteously refrains from leading his companions through the worst of the underbrush, and points out the more dangerous pitfalls as he guides them warily past. If he makes a clumsy misstep and stumbles into a trap, there may even be some in the party who not only enjoy a laugh at his expense, but may also be willing to give him a hand to set him forth on his way once more. It is for such a band of companions in the search for truth that I have written this book.

DARON ACEMOGLU AND JAMES ROBINSON

7.3 ECONOMIC ORIGINS OF DICTATORSHIP AND DEMOCRACY

This book by Acemoglu and Robinson casts the origins of regime types in terms of the rational choices made by different actors in a political system. The basic distinction is between the elite rulers (who generally wield various kinds of power—political, economic, and social) and the masses. The authors make use of four cases to explore the paths to dictatorship and democracy: Great Britain, Argentina, Singapore, and South Africa. Britain was a gradual and steady transition to democracy, whereas Argentina zigzagged back and forth between democracy and authoritarianism. Singapore became emblematic of a stable authoritarianism with relatively little repression, whereas South Africa was the best example of authoritarianism that relied heavily on repression. The explanation for these differences relies on the calculations of elites faced with differing levels of economic inequality, risks of social unrest, and costs of repression. In Britain, gradual democracy came about through successive concessions to the working classes against the backdrop of increasing threats of disorder that would have increasingly posed threats to elites. In Argentina, high economic inequality created divisions that resulted in social protests, bringing down dictatorships alternating with the military reacting to topple democracies. In Singapore, greater social equality meant that the government provided economic benefits to the populace, which preempted both demands for democracy and the need for severe repression. Finally, in South Africa until the 1990s, inequality was high and the costs of repressing the populace were relatively low for many years, which resulted in a white governing elite that used violence to dominate the black majority.

In passing, note the title of this book and compare it to that of Moore's book previously; the "economic origins" title is an explicit nod to the "social origins," and the choice of that single adjective highlights the core difference between the two arguments. Which of these two "Origins of Dictatorship and Democracy" do you find more convincing?

PART ONE. QUESTIONS AND ANSWERS

PATHS OF POLITICAL DEVELOPMENT

To understand why some countries are democracies whereas others are not, it is useful to distinguish between different characteristic paths that political institutions take over time. Only some of these paths end in democracy, at least at this moment in time. These stylized paths help us to orient ourselves among the complexities of real-world comparisons, and they illustrate the main mechanisms that we believe link the economic and political structure of a society to political institutions.

There are four main paths of political development. First, there is a path that leads from nondemocracy gradually but inexorably to democracy. Once created, democracy is never threatened, and it endures and consolidates. Britain is the best example of such a path of political development. Second, there is a path

Acemoglu, Daron, and James Robinson. 2006. *Economic Origins of Dictatorship and Democracy.* New York: Cambridge University Press.

that leads to democracy but where democracy, once created, quickly collapses. Following this, the forces that led to the initial democratization reassert themselves, but then democracy collapses again and the cycle repeats itself. This path—where democracy, once created, remains unconsolidated—is best exemplified by the Argentinian experience during the twentieth century. Logically, a third path is one in which a country remains nondemocratic or democratization is much delayed. Because there are important variations in the origins of such a path, it is useful to split nondemocratic paths into two. In the first path, democracy is never created because society is relatively egalitarian and prosperous, which makes the nondemocratic political status quo stable. The system is not challenged because people are sufficiently satisfied under the existing political institutions. Singapore is the society whose political dynamics we characterize in this way. In the second of these nondemocratic paths, the opposite situation arises. Society is highly unequal and exploitative, which makes the prospect of democracy so threatening to political elites that they use all means possible, including violence and repression, to avoid it. South Africa, before the collapse of the apartheid regime, is our canonical example of such a path.

From its roots, like many colonial societies, South Africa was a society of great inequalities, both economic and political. In the twentieth century, this inheritance led to a highly undemocratic polity in which only whites were enfranchised. After the Second World War, Africans began to successfully mobilize against this political status quo, and they were able to exert increasing pressure, rendering the existing apartheid regime infeasible and threatening mass revolt. Attempts by the regime to make concessions, although leaving the system basically unaltered, failed to achieve this objective, and the apartheid regime maintained power through the use of extensive repression and violence. In 1994, the regime was forced to democratize rather than risk potentially far worse alternatives.

The Agenda

We see four very different paths of political development in these narratives. Britain exemplifies the path to consolidated democracy, without any significant

reversals in the process. Argentina illustrates the possibility of a transition to an unconsolidated democracy, which then reverts back to nondemocracy, with the process potentially repeating itself multiple times. Singapore is an example of a society in which a non-democratic regime can survive a long time with relatively minor concessions but also without significant repression. South Africa before the collapse of apartheid exemplifies a nondemocratic regime that survives by using repression. We now propose a framework to understand these various paths and develop predictions for when we expect to see one path versus another.

OUR ARGUMENT

Why did Britain, Argentina, Singapore, and South Africa follow different political paths? More generally, why are some countries democratic whereas others are ruled by dictatorships or other nondemocratic regimes? Why do many nondemocracies transition into democracy? What determines when and how this transition takes place? And, relatedly, why do some democracies, once created, become consolidated and endure whereas others, like many of those in Latin America, fall prey to coups and revert back to dictatorship?

These are central questions for political science, political economy, and social science more generally, but there are neither widely shared answers nor an accepted framework to tackle them. The aims of this book are to develop a framework for analyzing these questions, provide some tentative answers, and outline future areas for research. As part of our investigation, we first provide an analysis of the role of various political institutions in shaping policies and social choices, emphasizing how politics differs in democratic and nondemocratic regimes. To do so, we model the attitudes of various individuals and groups toward different policies and, therefore, toward the political institutions leading to these policies.

To facilitate the initial exposition of our ideas, it is useful to conceive of society as consisting of two groups—the elites and the citizens—in which the latter are more numerous. Our framework emphasizes that social choices are inherently conflictual. For example, if the elites are the relatively rich individuals—for short, the rich—they will be opposed to redistributive taxation; whereas the citizens, who will be relatively poor—for short, the poor—will be in favor of taxation that would redistribute resources to them. More generally, policies of social choices that benefit the elites will be different from those that benefit the citizens. This conflict over social choices and policies is a central theme of our approach.

Who is the majority and who is the elite? This depends to some extent on context and the complex way in which political identities form in different societies. In many cases, it is useful to think of the elite as being the relatively rich in society, as was the case in nineteenth-century Britain and Argentina. However, this is not always the case; for instance, in South Africa, the elites were the whites and, in many African countries, the elites are associated with a particular ethnic group. In other societies, such as Argentina during some periods, the elite is the military.

Our Theory of Democratization

Consider the simplest dynamic world we can imagine: there is a "today" and a "tomorrow," and the elites and the citizens care about policies both today and tomorrow. There is nothing that prevents society from adopting a different policy tomorrow from the one it chose today. Thus, it is not sufficient for the citizens to ensure policies they prefer today; they would also like similar policies to be adopted tomorrow. Suppose we are in a nondemocratic society, which generally looks after the interests of the elites. Citizens have de facto political power today, so they can obtain the policies they like, but they are unsure whether they will have the same political power tomorrow. Given that we are in a nondemocratic society, tomorrow the elites may become more powerful and assertive and the citizens may no longer have the same political power. Can they ensure the implementation of the policies they like both today and tomorrow?

This is where political institutions may be important relative to the static world described previously. Institutions, by their nature, are *durable*—that is, the institutions of today are likely to persist until tomorrow. A democratic society is not only one where there is one-person-one-vote today but also one that is expected to remain democratic at least in the near future. This durability was already implicit in our definition of political institutions as a means of allocating political power: they regulate the *future* allocation of political power. For example, democracy means that tomorrow there will be a vote to determine policies or to decide which party will rule and the whole population will participate. Non-democracy means that much of the population will be excluded from collective decision-making processes.

Imagine how that the citizens do not simply use their de facto political power today to obtain the policies they like now, but they also use their political power to change the political system from nondemocracy to democracy. If they do so, they will have effectively increased their de jure political power in the future. Instead of nondemocracy, we are now in a democratic regime where there will be voting by all. With their increased political power, the citizens are therefore more likely to secure the policies they like tomorrow as well.

We have now moved toward a richer theory of democratization: transition to democracy—or, more generally, a change in political institutions—emerges as a way of regulating the future allocation of political power. The citizens demand and perhaps obtain democracy so that they can have more political say and political power tomorrow. Returning to the beliefs of the Chartist J. R. Stephens (quoted in Briggs 1959), we can now see that he was correct in demanding universal suffrage as a means of securing the "right to a good coat . . . a good hat . . . a good roof . . . [and] a good dinner" for working men rather than directly demanding the coat, the roof, and the dinner. Those would have been only for today, whereas universal suffrage could secure them in the future as well.

Notice an important implicit element in the story: *the transitory nature of de facto political power.* The citizens are presumed to have political power today but uncertain about whether they will have similar power tomorrow. The balance between the elites and the citizens or, more generally, between various social groups is not permanent, is not set in stone, is not the same today as it will be tomorrow; it is transitory. This is reasonable in the dynamic and uncertain world in which we live. It will be even more compelling when we think of the sources of political power for the disenfranchised citizens in nondemocracy. First, let us try to understand why the transitory nature of political power matters. Suppose that the citizens have the same political power tomorrow as they have today. Why should they need political institutions to help them? If their political power is sufficient to obtain the policies they like (even to obtain the institutions they like) today, then it will be so in the future as well, and there will be no need to change the underlying political institutions. It is precisely the transitory nature of political power—that the citizens have it today and may not have it tomorrow—that creates a demand for change in political institutions. The citizens would like to lock in the political power they have today by changing political institutions—specifically, by introducing democracy and greater representation for themselves—because without the institutional changes, their power today is unlikely to persist.

So why do the citizens have political power in nondemocracy? The answer is that they have de facto rather than de jure political power. In nondemocracy, the elites monopolize de jure political power but not necessarily de facto political power. The citizens are excluded from the political system in nondemocracy, but they are nonetheless the majority and they can sometimes challenge the system, create significant social unrest and turbulence, or even pose a serious revolutionary threat. What is there to stop the majority of the population overwhelming the elite, which constitutes a minority, and taking control of society and its wealth, even if the elites have access to better guns and hired soldiers? After all, the citizens successfully occupied Paris during the Paris Commune, overthrew the existing regime in the 1917 Russian Revolution, destroyed the dictatorship of Somoza in Nicaragua in 1979, and in many other instances created significant turbulence and real attempts at revolution. However, a real threat from the citizens requires the juxtaposition of many unlikely factors: the masses need to solve the collective-action problem necessary to organize themselves,[1] they need to find the momentum to turn their organization into an effective force against the regime, and the elites—who are controlling the state apparatus—should be unable to use the military to effectively suppress the

uprising. It is, therefore, reasonable that such a challenge against the system would only be transitory: in nondemocracy, if the citizens have political power today, they most likely will not have it tomorrow.

Imagine now that there is an effective revolutionary threat from the citizens against nondemocracy. They have the political power today to get what they want and even to overthrow the system. They can use their political power to obtain "the coat, the roof, and the dinner," but why not use it to obtain more, the same things not only for today but also in the future? This is what they will get if they can force a change in political institutions. Society will make a transition to democracy and, from then on, policies will be determined by one-person-one-vote, and the citizens will have more political power, enabling them to obtain the policies they desire and the resulting coat, roof, and dinner.

In practice, however, changes in political institutions do not simply happen because the citizens demand them. Transitions to democracy typically take place when the elite controlling the existing regime extend voting rights. Why would they do so? After all, the transfer of political power to the majority typically leads to social choices that the elite doesn't like—for instance, higher taxes and greater redistribution away from it in the future, precisely the outcomes it would like to prevent. Faced with the threat of a revolution, wouldn't the elite like to try other types of concessions, even giving the citizens the policies they want, rather than give away its power? To answer this question, let us return to the period of effective revolutionary threat. Imagine that the citizens can overthrow the system and are willing to do so if they do not get some concessions, some policies that favor them and increase their incomes and welfare.

The first option for the elite is to give them what they want today: redistribute income and more generally adopt policies favorable to the majority. But, suppose that concessions today are not sufficient to dissuade the citizens from revolution. What can the elite do to prevent an imminent and, for itself, extremely costly revolution? Well, it can promise the same policies tomorrow. Not only a coat, a roof, and a dinner today but also tomorrow. Yet, these promises may not be *credible*. Changing policy in the direction preferred by the citizens is not in the immediate interest of the elite. Today, it is doing so to prevent a revolution. Tomorrow, the threat of revolution may be gone, so why should it do so again? Why should it keep its promises? No reason and, in fact, it is unlikely to do so. Hence, its promises are not necessarily credible. Noncredible promises are worth little and, unconvinced by these promises, the citizens would carry out a revolution. If it wants to save its skin, the elite has to make a credible promise to set policies that the majority prefer; in particular, it must make a credible commitment to future pro-majority policies. A credible promise means that the policy decision should not be the elite's but rather placed in the hands of groups that actually prefer such policies. Or, in other words, it has to transfer political power to the citizens. A credible promise, therefore, means that it has to change the future allocation of political power. That is precisely what a transition to democracy does: it shifts future political power away from the elite to the citizens, thereby creating *a credible commitment to future pro-majority policies*. The role that political institutions play in allocating power and leading to relatively credible commitments is the third key building block of our approach.

Why, if a revolution is attractive to the citizens, does the creation of democracy stop it? This is plausibly because revolution is costly. In revolutions, much of the wealth of a society may be destroyed, which is costly for the citizens as well as the elite. It is these costs that allow concessions or democratization by the elite to avoid revolution. In reality, it will not always be the case that democracy is sufficiently pro-majority that it avoids revolution. For example, the citizens may anticipate that, even with universal suffrage, the elite will be able to manipulate or corrupt political parties or maybe it will be able to use its control of the economy to limit the types of policies that democracy can implement. In such circumstances,

anticipating that democracy will deliver few tangible rewards, the citizens may revolt. However, to limit the scope of our analysis, we normally restrict our attention to situations where the creation of democracy avoids revolution. Historically, this seems to have been typical, and it means that we do not delve deeply into theories of revolution or into the modeling of post-revolutionary societies.

We now have our basic theory of democratization in place. In nondemocracy, the elites have de jure political power and, if they are unconstrained, they will generally choose the policies that they most prefer; for example, they may choose low taxes and no redistribution to the poor. However, nondemocracy is sometimes challenged by the citizens who may pose a revolutionary threat—when they temporarily have de facto political power. Crucially, such political power is transitory; they have it today and are unlikely to have it tomorrow. They can use this power to undertake a revolution and change the system to their benefit, creating massive losses to the elites but also significant collateral damage and social losses. The elites would like to prevent this outcome, and they can do so by making a credible commitment to future pro-majority policies. However, promises of such policies within the existing political system are often noncredible. To make them credible, they need to transfer formal political power to the majority, which is what democratization achieves.

NOTE

1. That is, individuals should be convinced to take part in revolutionary activity despite the individual costs and the collective benefits to them as a group.

WORKS CITED

Briggs, Asa (1959). *Chartist Studies*. London: Macmillan.

SECTION

3

INSTITUTIONS OF GOVERNMENT

The previous section focused on questions of the state, regime type (or democracy and authoritarianism), and economic development. Yet comparative political scientists are also interested in concrete questions about the institutions—such as branches of government and political parties of actors—that shape politics. The units in this section focus on such questions.

Most modern governments can fruitfully be studied by distinguishing between the structures of government. Virtually all modern polities base their governments on constitutions. Thus, here we cover major theories of constitutionalism and constitutional design. This includes the separation of powers between levels of government (such as national, state, and local) and how the constitution is interpreted by judiciaries; these make up Chapter 8. We then include readings that analyze legislatures and the relationship between legislatures and the electoral systems to which they are linked (Chapter 9), followed by readings that analyze executives and the implications of different institutional designs of the executive branch (Chapter 10). The section's last chapter (Chapter 11) focuses on political parties and interest groups. As such, it constitutes a bridge to Section 4 of the book, which focuses on topics in political sociology emphasizing state–society relations.

CHAPTER 8

CONSTITUTIONS AND CONSTITUTIONAL DESIGN

In contemporary politics, the ideas of constitutionalism and the constitutional order of government are foundational. Every polity in the world has a constitution that lays out its basic political structure and the division of power within the country. To be clear, not every constitution guarantees rights and justice in a country, not every well-written constitution is followed to the letter by governments, nor is every constitution written in a single document (as the particular case of the United Kingdom shows). Yet the idea of constitutionalism—of having a basic charter of foundational political laws that at least rhetorically derives from the consent or interests of the citizenry—is pervasive. Constitutions generally lay out the structure of the legislative and executive branches (as seen in Chapters 9 and 10) and make provisions regarding how groups may act collectively in their political interests (as seen in Chapter 11), but for the purposes of this chapter, we focus on two main items found in constitutions: the vertical division of power between levels of government and the possible provision for a judiciary that is responsible for interpreting the constitutionality of laws.

The first theme in this chapter concerns how representation and administration are structured across a national territory. Some polities are relatively centralized, meaning they feature a strong central government in a unified state, typically involving standardized practices in all regions of the country. Other systems are more decentralized. In more decentralized polities, relatively significant powers and resources are held by regional, local, or communal bodies. (As examples, France would traditionally be seen as quite centralized and the United States as decentralized.) Federalism is a key form of decentralization in which significant powers reside with sub-national governments, and it is the subject of an excerpt from Daniel Elazar. In this reading, Elazar defines federalism and notes its possible advantages for different polities, including those in developing countries.

The second theme in this chapter focuses on whether and under what circumstances judiciaries assess the constitutionality of actions by other branches, sometimes called "judicial review." The selection by Ran Hirschl addresses the apparent growth in the power of judiciaries in several countries around the world. As you read these excerpts, think about the potential positive and negative consequences of federalism and of strong and weak forms of judicial review. How might these elements of constitutional design affect important challenges like maintaining democracy, maximizing representation, and avoiding conflict between different social groups?

DANIEL J. ELAZAR

8.1 EXPLORING FEDERALISM

The first excerpt examines the question of the vertical division of power within a system, a treatment of federalism by Daniel Elazar. It offers a rather theoretical perspective—a readable, succinct, and reasonably comprehensive view—on what federalism is and what it is designed to achieve. Elazar characterizes federalism as combining "self-rule" with "shared rule" or balancing a diffusion of power with some necessary concentration of power. As he puts it, "[f]ederalism has to do with the need of people and polities to unite for common purposes yet remain separate to preserve their respective integrities." The presence of a federal system, for its proponents, best allows for the accommodation of diverse perspectives or even different peoples within a nation-state. While Elazar focuses on the prospective advantages of federalism in this piece, note that he (like most other scholars) does not assume that federalism will always work, and elsewhere he diagnoses the varying conditions that have allowed certain federal systems to succeed although others have failed.

1

WHY FEDERALISM?

Human, and hence scholarly, concern with politics focuses on three general themes: the pursuit of political justice to achieve political order; the search for understanding of the empirical reality of political power and its exercise; and the creation of an appropriate civic environment through civil society and civil community capable of integrating the first two themes to produce the good political life. Political science as a discipline was founded and has developed in pursuit of those three concerns. In that pursuit, political scientists have uncovered or identified certain architectonic principles, seminal ideas, and plain political truths that capture the reality of political life or some significant segment of it and relate that reality to larger principles of justice and political order and to practical yet normative civic purposes.

One of the major recurring principles of political import which informs and encompasses all three themes is federalism—an idea that defines political justice, shapes political behavior, and directs humans toward an appropriately civic synthesis of the two. Through its covenantal foundations, federalism is an idea whose importance is akin to natural law in defining justice and to natural right in delineating the origins and proper constitution of political society. Although those foundations have been somewhat eclipsed since the shift to organic and then positivistic theories of politics, which began in the mid-nineteenth century, federalism as a form of political organization has grown as a factor shaping political behavior. Now, in the crisis of transition from the modern to the postmodern epochs, the federal idea is resurfacing as a significant political force just as it did in the transition from the late medieval to the modern epoch, which took place from the sixteenth to the eighteenth centuries.[1]

Federalism is resurfacing as a political force because it serves well the principle that there are no simple majorities or minorities but that all majorities are compounded of congeries of groups, and the corollary principle of minority rights, which not only protects the possibility for minorities to preserve themselves but forces majorities to be compound rather than artificially simple. It serves those

Elazar, Daniel. 1987. *Exploring Federalism*. Tuscaloosa: University of Alabama Press.

principles by emphasizing the consensual basis of the polity and the importance of liberty in the constitution and maintenance of democratic republics. Both principles are especially important in an increasingly complex and interdependent world, where people and peoples must live together whether they like it or not and even aspire to do so democratically. Hence it is not surprising that peoples and states throughout the world are looking for federal solutions to the problems of political integration within a democratic framework.

2

WHAT IS FEDERALISM?

Federalism has to do with the need of people and polities to unite for common purposes yet remain separate to preserve their respective integrities.[2] It is rather like wanting to have one's cake and eat it too. Since that is the natural human condition, at least half the work of politics, if not 90 percent of it, is directed to somehow accommodating that logically insoluble problem. Under certain circumstances, federalism is a highly useful device for doing just that. Consequently, federal ideas and arrangements have emerged repeatedly in the course of human history as major devices to try to accommodate that condition.[3] Ours is one of those times.

Federal principles grow out of the idea that free people can freely enter into lasting yet limited political associations to achieve common ends and protect certain rights while preserving their respective integrities. As the very ambiguity of the term "federal" reveals, federalism is concerned simultaneously with the diffusion of political power in the name of liberty and its concentration on behalf of unity or energetic government. The federal idea itself rests on the principle that political and social institutions and relationships are best established through covenants, compacts, or other contractual arrangements, rather than, or in addition to, simply growing organically; in other words, that humans are able to make constitutional choices.

What Is Federalism Designed to Achieve?

Federalism is designed to achieve some degree of political integration based on a combination of self-rule and shared rule. Although its form may be used under other circumstances, it is appropriate only when and where that kind of political integration is sought. Political integration on a federal basis demands a particular set of relationships, beginning with the relationship between the two faces of politics, power and justice. On one hand, politics deals with the organization of power, in the words of Harold Laswell, with "who gets what, when, and how." Politics, however, is simultaneously concerned with the pursuit of justice—with the building and maintenance of the good polity, however defined. All political life represents some interaction of these two faces of politics, whereby the organization and distribution of power are informed by some particular conception of justice, whereas the pursuit of justice is shaped (and limited) by the realities of power.[4]

Federalism in its most limited form is usually defined as having to do with the distribution and sharing of power, but even in that limited form there is an implicit commitment to a conception of justice that holds, among other things, that a distribution of powers is necessary and desirable. On the other hand, federalism in its broadest sense is presented as a form of justice—emphasizing liberty and citizen participation in governance—but one which is inevitably linked to political reality because it must still be concerned with the distribution of powers. One of the primary attributes of federalism is that it cannot, by its very nature, abandon the concern for either power or justice but must consider both in relationship to each other, thus forcing people to consider the hard realities of political life while at the same time maintaining their aspirations for the best polity.

It is not unfair to say that one purpose of federalism is to achieve this linking of the real and the ideal—or the prosaic details of who does what and gets what on a daily basis—with the messianic aspirations for justice. This effort to require humans constantly to grapple with both the prosaic and messianic in relation to each other, never allowing the human pursuit of ideal states to bring people to ignore the hard realities of politics and never allowing people's concern for the hard reality of politics to give them an excuse for ignoring considerations of justice, can be seen as the pedagogic dimension of federalism.

Federalism's emphasis on structure *and* process, on the necessity to organize governing constitutionally in a certain way and then to live up to the constitutional demands, provides both governors and governed in federal polities with a continuing seminar in governance in which they must constantly ask the questions: Is it possible? Is it right? Is it good? Such diverse devices as the opinions of the American federal Supreme Court and the Swiss referendum process represent continuing forums for discussing the philosophy and practice of government, replete with considerations of the possible, the right, and the good from the different perspectives present in each civil society at any given time. In short, by providing a continuing stream of constitutional questions that require public attention, federalism generates a continuing referendum on first principles. The advantages of this continuing seminar for civic education are not to be minimized, and federal arrangements may be sufficiently justified for this reason alone.

With regard to both faces of politics, federalism leads to a concern with the distribution of power. *The Federalist* puts the matter as follows:

> In a single republic, all the power surrendered by the people is submitted to the administration of a single government: and the usurpations are guarded against by a division of the government into distinct and separate departments. In the compound republic of America, the power surrendered by the people is first divided between two distinct governments, and then the portion allotted to each is subdivided among distinct and separate departments. Hence a double security arises to the rights of the people. The different governments will control each other, at the same time each will be controlled by itself.[5]

Federalism tries to take people as they are—"warts and all," in Abraham Lincoln's felicitous phrase—assuming humanity to have the capacity for self-government but the weaknesses that make all human exercise of power potentially dangerous. So the first task of federalism is to harmonize human capacity with human weakness, to create institutions and processes that enable people to exercise their capacity for self-government to the maximum and even grow in that capacity. At the same time federalism

attempts to prevent the abuse of power derived from inherent deficiencies in human nature and, wherever possible, direct the results of those deficiencies to useful ends.[6]

Although there are federal theories that begin with the assumption of the goodness or unlimited perfectibility of human nature, all successful federal systems have been rooted in the recognition of man's dual capacity for virtue and vice and have sought to respond accordingly. Their success as political systems is attributable in no small measure to that realistic sense of both the limits and possibilities of man as a political animal. Hence it is from their experience that a proper understanding of the ends of federalism must be derived. Even those who see in federalism a possibility for the reconstruction of all human relationships and their reconstitution on the basis of coordinative rather than hierarchical arrangements need to see as the first end of federalism the effort to grapple with the dynamic and mixed character of humanity.

Accommodating Diversity

From the foregoing discussion, it should be possible to draw some conclusions about the uses of federalism in the Third World countries. Most immediately, federalism has proved useful in accommodating diversity. Indeed, once there is a commitment to the accommodation of diversity, federal solutions are likely to follow as a matter of course. Most of the resistance to federal solutions has come precisely from those who do not wish to accommodate diversity but to eliminate it. Perhaps enough has been said about this theme already, but it should be recalled that it has more than one dimension. That is, it is not only a question of particular rulers opposing diversity but of particular tribal, ethnic, or religious communities within the polity opposing it as well—some of whom are victims of discrimination and persecution because they are minorities but who would not behave differently if they were to acquire power.

Thus it is hard to say that Zaïre, which abandoned a proposed federal, or at least quasi-federal, arrangement upon achieving independence from Belgium—and which, as a result, was plagued by periodic efforts on the part of Katanga, now Shaba, to secede—would have become more federal had the Katangese won. When Moïse Tshombe, the original leader of the Katangese secession movement, briefly became president of all of Zaïre, he was no more friendly to diversity than were those who opposed him and ultimately had him assassinated. In short, the peoples of Zaïre, whatever their tribal, ethnic, or regional background, seem to be interested in promoting the exclusive rule of their particular group, not in finding a modus vivendi through power sharing.[7]

In Nigeria, constant efforts are required on the part of the other two major partners in the Nigerian federation plus the many minor ones to accommodate the demands of the centralistically oriented Hausa, which are not only substantively great but structurally difficult as well. The rule of the Nigerian military junta during the 1970s, whatever its other drawbacks, was, for its time, the most reasonable way of preventing Hausa dominance or secession, thereby preserving the federal structure as a means of accommodating diversity. Before returning power to the civil authorities, the junta succeeded in dividing the Hausa Northern State into a number of smaller ones as part of a general redivision of Nigeria's territory into nineteen states.

In situations in which federalism rests upon a structured elite, as in Malaysia or the United Arab Emirates, the elite has a strong commitment to maintaining the diversity it represents. Since the elites are dominant in both cases, it is difficult to analyze what would happen without them, although in both cases such diversity as exists among the population is not strictly along the lines of the federal territorial divisions. Malays representing the major force, if not the majority of all the states of Malaysia, have antipathy toward the Chinese, who form a minority everywhere. Only in Singapore do the Chinese represent a majority, which is one of the reasons why Singapore seceded from Malaysia—and was, indeed, allowed and even encouraged to do so by the other members of the federation. In the UAE, some tribal groupings cross emirate boundaries, others do not; but apparently there is not an intense problem of diversity among the population.

Pakistan, on the other hand, is a country founded ostensibly on the principle of unity—in this case, Islamic unity—that did not give appropriate recognition to ethnic differences within the Islamic whole. Consequently, each successive ruler of Pakistan has attempted to centralize power in strong-man fashion, while at the same time the population insists on the diffusion of power to accommodate the country's ethnic diversity. Federalism survives in Pakistan on paper and, to a greater or lesser extent, diffusion of power survives in practice, principally because of the weakness of the central government vis-à-vis the provincial and subprovincial groups rather than out of any desire on the part of the former to make federalism work.

The essentially abortive Philippine effort to grant some measure of autonomy to the Moros of Mindanao and other southern Philippine islands has failed to date because, despite a certain lip service to the accommodation of diversity, neither side was particularly interested in such an accommodation. President Ferdinand Marcos enjoyed a sufficient monopoly of power in the center to prevent implementation from that side, while the Moros possess sufficient power to maintain the guerrilla war they are conducting on behalf of their revolution. The result is a stalemate actively reflected in continuing military operations rather than a quasi-federal accommodation. Since it seems clear that neither side can achieve its exclusive goals, violent stalemate is likely to continue indefinitely unless an agreement along federal or quasi-federal lines is reached.

Diversity is not likely to disappear in the Third World, any more than it has in the first or second, even, in some cases, after centuries of concerted effort at national integration through homogenization. Only massacre or expulsion of minorities can change that situation. In most of the Third World countries, the number and diffusion of tribal, ethnic, religious, or linguistic groups is such that even those ugly options are not likely to bring about the desired homogeneity. Consequently, federal arrangements may be the only useful way to deal with diversity.

Strengthening Liberty

In the Third World, as elsewhere, federalism is a means for strengthening liberty. This, too, is one of the reasons that failures are more numerous than successes in that segment of the world. Very few of the

Third World regimes are interested in strengthening liberty. Their commitment to independence and nation-building does not necessarily include a commitment to freedom for the people involved. Often, to the contrary, every argument is used to justify the restriction of freedom and even the elimination of those traditional liberties that do exist, such as tribal and customary liberties, in the name of national independence and national development. In such cases, federalism—which is, almost by its very nature, a constant goad in the direction of the maintenance of liberty and a certain reminder of its importance in a polity striving toward democracy—is at best an embarrassment and at worst a real hindrance. Again, the successful examples all testify to the importance of federalism for strengthening liberty, whether in the case of India, which has clear democratic aspirations, or in the cases of Malaysia and the UAE, which at least wish to preserve the liberties of the constituent rulers.

Spreading Economic Development

The importance of federalism in spreading economic development and its benefits has been almost entirely overlooked. By and large, what has passed for national development in the Third World is not national at all, but rather concentrated in a single metropolitan area, usually that of the capital. This area not only has monopolized the infusion of new resources to the country but has managed to drain the countryside of a major share of such resources as existed there prior to independence. The resultant impoverishment of the countryside without appreciable progress in the metropolis has become a feature of Third World national economics which reflects a vicious circle. As the countryside becomes impoverished, its people migrate to the metropolis in search of opportunity or, in most cases, sheer survival. In their masses, they overwhelm the metropolis and transform it into what has come to be known as the Calcutta syndrome. The metropolis absorbs all wealth-generating capacity; people rush to the center, so that the new capacity is lost in the magnitude of the problems created. The only ones to benefit are the ruling class, whose members are able to siphon off a substantial share of the development funds for their own personal use or for their Swiss bank accounts.

Development in federal countries suffers from some of these Third World problems. But because of the existence of federalism, the new resources are inevitably spread over a number of centers. At the very least, the capital of every federated state has some claim on the national resources, and together they work to prevent the single metropolis syndrome. This means that more people have a chance to benefit from development efforts. At least, it means that some of the worst excesses of resource concentration are eliminated, and a basis for truly national development begins to emerge.

India and Nigeria are prime examples. Although Calcutta and, of late, Bombay and Lagos suffer from the worst aspects of the rural–urban migration, in both countries one does not have to live in Calcutta, Bombay, or Lagos to gain benefit from economic development. Rather, development efforts have been spread throughout the country, if not uniformly, at least in significant ways. Many people who have stayed home or migrated to less prominent centers have managed to improve their lot, if not sufficiently, at least more than their peers in more centralized states. This phenomenon deserves to be studied in detail.

It is clear that, as always, politics influences economics as well as vice versa, particularly in the contemporary world, where state intervention is once again crucial in the economic realm. The way in which politics is structured affects the economic future of every inhabitant of any particular polity. Thus although economic measures that do not differentiate between segments of the polity may suggest equality, the realities of economic resource use and development may be quite different. The politics of federalism offers a means for extending economic benefits more widely than has otherwise been the case in the Third World.

NOTES

1. For a detailed discussion of this transition, see John Kincaid and Daniel J. Elazar, eds., *The Covenant Connection: Federal Theology and the Origins of Modern Politics* (Durham, N.C.: Carolina Academic Press, 1985).

2. This chapter is an expansion and reworking of material presented in previous articles by the author, particularly "The Ends of Federalism," in Max Frenkel, ed., *Foedralismus als Partnerschaft* (Bern: Peter Lang, 1977), and "Urbanism and Federalism: Twin Revolutions of the Modern Era," *Publius* 5, no. 2 (1975): 15–40.

3. Most of the principal recent works dealing with federalism are cited below. Others of general interest include the articles "Federalism" and "Federation" in David M. Sills, ed., *International Encyclopedia of the Social Sciences* (New York: Macmillan, 1968), 6:169–78; *The Federal Polity*, special issue of *Publius* 3, no. 2 (1973); Arthur Maas, ed., *Area and Power: A Theory of Local Government* (Glencoe, Ill.: Free Press, 1959); Arthur Macmahon, ed., *Federalism: Mature and Emergent* (New York: Columbia University Press, 1955); and Stephen L. Schechter, ed., *Federalism and Community*, special issue of *Publius* 5, no. 2 (1975), especially the articles by Schechter, Duchacek, Djordevic, and Elazar.

4. See Alain Greilsammer, *Les mouvements federalistes en France* (Nice: Presses d'Europe, 1975), and Heisler, ed., *Politics in Europe*.

5. Richard Rose and his colleagues at the University of Strathclyde have been working on an appropriate theory of the United Kingdom in this vein. See Center for the Study of Public Policy publications, which can be obtained by writing the center at the university, McCance Building, 16 Richmond Street, Glasgow G1 1XQ, Scotland; also see Richard Rose and Peter Madgwick, *The Territorial Dimension in United Kingdom Politics* (London: Macmillan, 1982).

6. See the notes of James Fratto on the post–Napoleonic Netherlands in the Archives of the Center for the Study of Federalism. See also James W. Skillen, "From Covenant of Grace to Tolerant Public Pluralism: The Dutch Calvinist Contribution" (paper presented at the Center for the Study of Federalism, Workshop on Covenant and Politics, Philadelphia, February 27–29, 1980).

7. See Daniel J. Elazar, "The Compound Structure of Public Service Delivery Systems in Israel," in Vincent Ostrom and Francine Pennell Bish, eds., *Comparing Urban Service Delivery Systems* (Beverly Hills: Sage Publications, 1977), pp. 47–82.

RAN HIRSCHL

8.2 TOWARDS JURISTOCRACY
The Origins and Consequences of the New Constitutionalism

Many scholars have argued that judiciaries are important bulwarks of both individual and group rights and that strong, independent judiciaries mitigate the risk of the "tyranny of the majority." In the book *Towards Juristocracy*, Hirschl notes the growing power of judiciaries over time in interpreting constitutions. He puzzles about the degree of power conferred to political actors such as judges and high court justices (which might be called "juristocrats") who are most often unelected yet make massively consequential decisions about what can and cannot be law. In Hirschl's interpretation, the rise of juristocracy can be explained by the motives of political elites who seek to remove debates about certain controversial issues from the public sphere. These elites are more capable of preserving their own prestige and power if they can ensure that judiciaries have decision-making authority. Courts in turn protect the power of economic and political elites, defending and preserving the status quo rather than generating more justice or progressive social change. In Hirschl's view, juristocracy thus becomes a way of tempering democracy. In a sense, it puts certain issues under a "cloak" or judge's robe, rather than exposing it to the white-hot light of political fighting. Hirschl finds this juristocratic strategy to be pursued especially in countries with meaningful and powerful political divides, such as South Africa and Israel. As you read, consider whether the conventional defense of strong judiciaries as the defenders of rights or Hirschl's critique of "juristocracy" is more convincing. Could each view hold some truth? Under what conditions might "juristocracy" become especially problematic?

Over the past few years the world has witnessed an astonishingly rapid transition to what may be called *juristocracy*. Around the globe, in more than eighty countries and in several supranational entities, constitutional reform has transferred an unprecedented amount of power from representative institutions to judiciaries. The countries that have hosted this expansion of judicial power stretch from the Eastern Bloc to Canada, from Latin America to South Africa, and from Britain to Israel. Most of these countries have a recently adopted constitution or constitutional revision that contains a bill of rights and establishes some form of active judicial review. An adversarial American-style rights discourse has become a dominant form of political discourse in these countries. The belief that judicially affirmed rights are a force of social change removed from the constraints of political power has attained near-sacred status in public discussion. National high courts and supranational tribunals have become increasingly important, even crucial, political decision-making bodies. To paraphrase Alexis de Tocqueville's observation regarding the United States, there is now hardly any moral or political controversy in the world of new constitutionalism that does not sooner or later become a judicial one.[1] This global trend toward

Hirschl, Ran. 2007. *Towards Juristocracy: The Origins and Consequences of the New Constitutionalism.* Cambridge, MA: Harvard University Press.

juristocracy is arguably one of the most significant developments in late-twentieth- and early-twenty-first-century government.[2]

The emergence of this new method of pursuing political goals and managing public affairs has been accompanied and reinforced by an almost unequivocal endorsement of the notion of constitutionalism and judicial review by scholars, jurists, and activists alike. According to the generic version of this canonical view, the crowning proof of democracy in our times is the growing acceptance and enforcement of the idea that democracy is not the same thing as majority rule; that in a real democracy (namely a constitutional democracy rather than a democracy governed predominantly by the principle of parliamentary sovereignty), minorities possess legal protections in the form of a written constitution, which even a democratically elected assembly cannot change. Under this vision of democracy, a bill of rights is part of fundamental law, and judges who are removed from the pressures of partisan politics are responsible for enforcing those rights. In fact, American constitutional scholars often argue that the foundation of the United States was based on precisely this understanding of constitutional democracy. As Ronald Dworkin, perhaps the most prominent proponent of this view, observes, every member of the European Union as well as other "mature democracies" (in Dworkin's words) subscribe to the view that democracy must protect itself against the tyranny of majority rule through constitutionalization and judicial review.[3] Even countries such as Britain, New Zealand, and Israel—described fairly recently as the last bastions of Westminster-style parliamentary sovereignty—have recently embarked on a comprehensive constitutional overhaul aimed at introducing principles of constitutional supremacy into their respective political systems.

This sweeping worldwide convergence to constitutionalism, many theorists contend, stems from modern democracies' post–World War II commitment to the notion that democracy entails far more than a mere adherence to the principle of majority rule. Not least, we are often reminded, it reflects these polities' genuine commitment to entrenched, self-binding protection of basic rights and civil liberties in an attempt to safeguard vulnerable groups and individuals from the potential tyranny of political majorities. Accordingly, the seemingly undemocratic characteristics of constitutions and judicial review are often portrayed as reconcilable with majority rule or simply as necessary limits on democracy. In short, judicial empowerment through the constitutionalization of rights and the establishment of judicial review now appear to be the widely accepted conventional wisdom of contemporary constitutional thought.

The constitutionalization of rights and the corresponding establishment of judicial review are widely perceived as power-diffusing measures often associated with liberal and/or egalitarian values. As a result, studies of their political origins tend to portray their adoption as a reflection of progressive social or political change, or simply as the result of societies' or politicians' devotion to a "thick" notion of democracy and their uncritical celebration of human rights. Yet most of the assumptions regarding the power-diffusing, redistributive effects of constitutionalization, as well as the assumptions regarding its predominantly benevolent and progressive origins, remain for the most part untested and abstract.

Even critics of the view that constitutionalism is an all-out "good thing" have not paid much attention to the actual political origins or consequences of judicial empowerment through constitutionalization. Instead, these critics have been almost exclusively preoccupied with the well-rehearsed normative debate over the "countermajoritarian" nature of judicial review and the "democratic deficit" inherent in transferring important policy-making prerogatives from elected and accountable politicians, parliaments, and other majoritarian decision-making bodies to the judiciary.[4] Indeed, one can count on the fingers of one hand the works that use concrete empirical and inductive inquiry to question the democratic credentials of constitutionalism and judicial review.

Scholars of constitutional law and politics also tend toward parochialism regarding the constitutional arrangements and practices of other countries. Most existing studies on the political origins and consequences of judicial power are based on the United States' exceptional, if not downright idiosyncratic, constitutional legacy. Several important critical assessments of the 1982 constitutionalization of rights in Canada have appeared over the past decade.[5] A few other single-country studies have examined the significant political role of national high courts in advanced democracies that have adopted a variety of administrative and judicial review procedures during the postwar decade.[6] In addition, several very fine studies have assessed the utility of constitutional engineering in the former Eastern Bloc countries,[7] and a spate of scholarship concerns judicial politics in Western Europe and the EU.[8] However, with a few notable exceptions,[9] genuinely comparative studies of the origins and consequences of constitutional transformation and judicial empowerment are rare, and those that do exist often lack coherent methodology. In short, despite the fact that courts now play a key role in dealing with the most contentious social and political issues, the field of comparative judicial studies in general, and the study of the political origins and consequences of judicial empowerment in particular, remain relatively underresearched and undertheorized.

In an attempt to move beyond the abstract rhetoric and parochialism that have all too often dogged the academic debate over constitutionalism, in this book I examine the political origins and consequences of constitutional revolutions in four countries: Canada (which adopted the Canadian Charter of Rights and Freedoms in 1982); New Zealand (which enacted the New Zealand Bill of Rights Act in 1990); Israel (which adopted two new Basic Laws protecting a number of core civil liberties in 1992); and South Africa (which adopted an interim Bill of Rights in 1993, a final Bill of Rights in 1996, and a new Constitutional Court in 1995). Drawing on a systematic analysis of these four recent constitutional revolutions, I address three major questions:

1. What are the political origins of the recent constitutionalization trend? That is, to what extent is the expansion of judicial power through the constitutionalization of rights and the establishment of judicial review a reflection of a genuinely progressive revolution in a given polity? Or, conversely, is it a means by which preexisting sociopolitical struggles in that polity are carried out?

2. What is the real impact of the constitutionalization of rights and the fortification of judicial review on national high courts' interpretive attitudes toward progressive notions of distributive justice, and what are the extrajudicial effects of constitutionalization on the actual advancement of such notions?

3. What are the political consequences of judicial empowerment through constitutionalization, and what are the implications for twenty-first-century democratic government of the unprecedented judicialization of politics that proceed through the constitutionalization of rights and the establishment of judicial review?

In short, this study aims to put the political origins and consequences of constitutionalization to the test.

BEYOND THE AMERICAN EXPERIENCE

"For the past two centuries," writes critic Daniel Lazare, "the Constitution has been as central to American political culture as the New Testament was to medieval Europe. Just as Milton believed that 'all wisdom is enfolded' within the pages of the Bible, all good Americans, from the National Rifle Association to the ACLU, have believed no less of this singular document."[10] Indeed, remarkably profound symbolic and practical effects are attributed to the American Bill of Rights and judicial review by scholars, legal practitioners, and political activists. Over the past two decades, however, a number of closely reasoned and well-researched critical studies have sought to revisit the optimistic, albeit untested and abstract, court-centric consensus of the post-*Brown* generation in American constitutional law scholarship. While these studies successfully undermine the complacent view that constitutional catalogues of rights and judicial review are unequivocally positive, they draw almost exclusively on the experience of the American "rights revolution" and that country's history of judicial review. It is remarkable how rarely books and articles on American constitutional law and politics, for example, refer to constitutions and bills of rights in other countries. As George Fletcher notes, a striking feature of the American jurisprudential debate is its provinciality. The arguments are put forward as though the American legal system were the only legal system in the world.[11] Indeed, many American scholars of constitutional law and politics treat the term "constitution" as though it were a proper name rather than a concept whose nature, origins, and consequences could best be understood by examining and comparing a variety of instances of constitutionalism. American parochialism with regard to other countries' constitutional arrangements and practices is especially remarkable given the scope of the trend toward the adoption of constitutional catalogues of rights, the fortification of judicial review, and the consequent judicialization of politics that has recently swept the world. Despite an increasing number of notable exceptions, American scholarship on constitutional law and politics still tends to ignore comparable developments in other countries.

The dearth of comparative research into the origins and consequences of constitutionalization is not merely a problem in terms of aesthetics or intellectual taste; it has important methodological implications. Relatively few American constitutionalists have examined how this process has unfolded outside the United States. This means that American critics of judicial review have systematically failed to address a common observation made by proponents of judicial review, namely that there is no experimental control for the U.S. case. We know what the U.S. Supreme Court has done in the name of judicial review, but we do not know what the relevant legislatures would have done if the Supreme Court had eschewed or been deprived of this power.

The American experience of active judicial review is nearing its bicentennial. This long history makes a diachronic, quasi-experimental, prelegislation-postlegislation empirical investigation into the impact of the constitutionalization of rights and the establishment of judicial review in the United States difficult, perhaps impossible, to conduct. This is not so of countries with a relatively short experience of judicial review, where it is possible to hold other variables to manageable levels. While the extremely rich and diverse constitutional jurisprudence of the U.S. Supreme Court over the past two centuries provides us with an abundance of data pertaining to judicial interpretation and behavior, the American constitutional legacy is perhaps the least appropriate example to use in assessing the function of judicial review in the pursuit of social justice: there is no alternative domestic model against which to measure the achievements of the U.S. Constitution. Moreover, a study that concentrates solely on the singular American constitutional legacy is necessarily going to produce idiosyncratic conclusions not readily transferable to other political and legal contexts. In contrast, the fact that many countries have moved toward the constitutionalization of rights and the establishment of judicial review over the past few decades provides fertile terrain for investigating the political origins and consequences of these changes.

The recent constitutional revolutions in Canada, New Zealand, and Israel, for example, provide nearly ideal testing ground for identifying the political origins and consequences of the constitutionalization of rights and the fortification of judicial review, for several reasons. First, all three countries have undergone a major constitutional reform over the past two decades that introduced such changes; yet, unlike many former Eastern Bloc countries, for example, the dramatic constitutional changes in all three countries were not accompanied by, nor did they result from, major changes in political regime. In these countries, therefore, it is possible to disentangle the political origins of constitutionalization from other possible explanations and to distinguish the impact of judicial empowerment by looking at changes in judicial interpretation and the judicialization of politics. Second, the constitutional revolutions in Canada, New Zealand, and Israel took place in societies deeply divided along political, economic, and ethnic lines. A study of these three countries therefore allows us to assess the significance of preexisting sociopolitical struggles in the move toward judicial empowerment through constitutionalization in each polity. Third, the recent constitutional overhaul in Canada, New Zealand, and Israel marked a departure from the Westminster model of parliamentary supremacy and the established British legal tradition of judicial restraint in these countries. This has provided the Canadian Supreme Court, the New Zealand Court of Appeal, and the Israeli Supreme Court with the necessary institutional framework to become more vigilant in protecting basic rights and liberties. Indeed, these three national courts have reacted with great enthusiasm to the constitutionalization of rights and the fortification of judicial review in their respective domains by adjudicating many landmark constitutional rights cases over the past decade. Fourth, all three polities possess a strong British common law legal tradition. This common inheritance eliminates variations in legal tradition as possible explanations for differences in legal activity and judicial interpretation among the three countries. Fifth, these countries represent different models of judicial review and distinct variances in constitutional rights status while remaining within the context of an established democratic tradition. Precisely because the recent constitutional revolutions in Canada, New Zealand, and Israel have taken place in established democracies, framers of the new constitutional arrangements could not ignore the countermajoritarian tendency embedded in constitutionalism and judicial review. Persisting political traditions of parliamentary sovereignty and democratic representation had to be taken into account by those who initiated the constitutional overhaul in these countries. The result has been the development of a variety of innovative institutional mechanisms aimed at compensating for the countermajoritarian difficulty embedded in judicial review. The significance of formal institutional factors can thus be assessed while accounting for variations in legal and political outcomes of constitutionalization as experienced by all three polities.

The widely celebrated South African constitutional revolution meanwhile represents a most difficult case to scholars skeptical of the conventional views concerning the progressive driving forces behind bills of rights and the overwhelmingly positive effects of such bills. Prior to the enactment of the 1993 interim Bill of Rights (replaced by the final Bill of Rights in 1996), there was perhaps no other developed country in the postwar world in which the gap between popular will and constitutional arrangement was so wide. In addition to issues of material inequality, the notorious apartheid regime excluded over 80 percent of South Africa's population from any meaningful participation in the democratic political arena. The abolition of apartheid in early 1991, the constitutionalization of rights in 1993, the first inclusive national election in 1994, and the establishment of the Constitutional Court in 1995

together mark a dramatic shift in the formal status of the vast majority of nonwhite South Africans. Few would doubt the crucial symbolic importance of these measures to the historically disenfranchised groups in South Africa. The practical effects of South Africa's constitutional rights revolution, however, appear to be much more nuanced and ought to be examined carefully. Moreover, from a methodological standpoint, "most difficult cases" have an important merit: our confidence in a given set of hypotheses is enhanced once it has proven to hold true even in the most challenging cases. It is precisely for this reason that I have chosen to refer to the South African constitutional revolution throughout the present study and to examine some of its political origins and salient de facto consequences, along with those of Canada, New Zealand, and Israel.

To address this puzzle, I develop a new explanation of judicial empowerment through constitutionalization as a form of self-interested *hegemonic preservation*. My underlying assumptions in developing this explanation for constitutionalization and judicial empowerment are: (1) the expansion of judicial power is an integral part and an important manifestation of the concrete social, political, and economic struggles that shape a given political system and cannot be understood in isolation from them; (2) the political origins of constitutional reform cannot be studied in isolation from the political origins of constitutional stalemate and stagnation; (3) other variables being equal, prominent political, economic, and judicial actors are likely to favor the establishment of institutional structures that will benefit them the most; and (4) constitutions and judicial review hold no purse strings and have no independent enforcement power, but nonetheless limit the institutional flexibility of political decision-makers. Thus, voluntary self-limitation through the transfer of policy-making authority from majoritarian decisionmaking arenas to courts seems, prima facie, to run counter to the interests of power-holders in legislatures and executives. The most plausible explanation for voluntary, self-imposed judicial empowerment is therefore that political, economic, and legal power-holders who either initiate or refrain from blocking such reforms estimate that it serves their interests to abide by the limits imposed by increased judicial intervention in the political sphere. In other words, those who are eager to pay the price of judicial empowerment must assume that their position (absolute or relative) would be improved under a juristocracy.

Specifically, I suggest that judicial empowerment through constitutionalization is best understood as the product of a strategic interplay between three key groups: threatened political elites, who seek to preserve or enhance their political hegemony by insulating policy making in general, and their policy preferences in particular, from the vicissitudes of democratic politics while they profess support for democracy; economic elites, who view the constitutionalization of rights, especially property, mobility, and occupational rights, as a means of placing boundaries on government action and promoting a free-market, business-friendly agenda; and judicial elites and national high courts, which seek to enhance their political influence and international reputation. In other words, I argue that strategic legal innovators—political elites in association with economic and judicial elites who have compatible interests—determine the timing, extent, and nature of constitutional reforms.

While the benefits of constitutionalization for economic libertarians and judicial elites appear obvious, its appeal for hegemonic sociopolitical forces and their political representatives may at first glance look questionable. However, when their policy preferences have been, or are likely to be, increasingly challenged in majoritarian decision-making arenas, elites that possess disproportionate access to, and influence over, the legal arena may initiate a constitutional entrenchment of rights and judicial review in order to transfer power to supreme courts. Based on the courts' relatively high public reputation for professionalism and political impartiality, their record of adjudication, and the justices' ideological preferences, these elites may safely assume that their policy preferences will be less effectively contested under the new arrangement. Judicial empowerment through constitutionalization may provide an efficient institutional solution for influential groups who seek to preserve their hegemony and who, given an erosion in their popular support, may find strategic drawbacks

in adhering to majoritarian policy-making processes. More "demographically representative" political processes are, in other words, a catalyst, not an outcome, of constitutionalization. The constitutionalization of rights is therefore often not a reflection of a genuinely progressive revolution in a polity; rather, it is evidence that the rhetoric of rights and judicial review has been appropriated by threatened elites to bolster their own position in the polity. By keeping popular decision-making mechanisms at the forefront of the formal democratic political process while shifting the power to formulate and promulgate certain policies to semiautonomous professional policy-making bodies, those who possess disproportionate access to, and have a decisive influence upon, such bodies minimize the potential threat to their hegemony.

CONCLUSION: THE ROAD TO JURISTOCRACY AND THE LIMITS OF CONSTITUTIONALIZATION

The constitutional rights revolutions in Canada, New Zealand, Israel, and South Africa (as well as in numerous other countries throughout the world of new constitutionalism) are still in their formative stages. Any attempt to generalize about the impact of constitutionalization of rights on these and other countries must therefore be tentative. Yet although no definitive conclusions as to the origins and consequences of constitutionalization can be offered, I believe that some general (though admittedly speculative) lessons can be drawn from the findings presented here.

The expansion of judicial power through constitutionalization and the corresponding acceleration of the judicialization of politics in so many countries over the past few decades may shed light on an aspect of constitutional politics that is often overlooked: the political origins of constitutionalization. Although the adoption of a constitutional catalogue of rights provides the necessary institutional framework for the judicialization of politics, it is certainly not a sufficient condition for generating the high level of judicialized politics we have seen in the four countries studied here. The rise of constitutionalization and judicial review, and the corresponding transfer to the courts of questions such as the future of the Canadian confederation, national healing in the wake of apartheid, the fate of the Maori, or the meaning of a "Jewish and democratic" state could not have developed and cannot be understood in isolation from the major struggles that form the Canadian, South African, New Zealand, and Israeli political systems. To be sure, none of these problems is uniquely or intrinsically legal. It is therefore unclear at first glance why a political regime would vest extended authority in the courts to resolve them. What is more, the broadened political jurisdiction of the courts vis-à-vis the declining power of legislatures is especially perplexing since courts, even with their new powers, still do not hold independent purse strings, nor have they any means of independently enforcing their power. Yet they have been given authority to limit the institutional flexibility of political decision-makers. Judicial empowerment through constitutionalization seems, prima facie, to run counter to the interests of power-holders in legislatures and executives. How then can we explain the increasingly common transfer of power from majoritarian policy-making arenas to national high courts?

As one of those people who (as it was said of Lyndon Johnson) "seldom think of politics more than 18 hours a day," I have advanced here a strategic notion of judicial empowerment through constitutionalization as driven primarily by political interests to insulate certain policy preferences from popular pressures. At the very least, the judicialization of fundamental political questions offers a convenient refuge for politicians seeking to avoid making difficult no-win moral and political decisions. After all, when contentious political issues are treated as legal questions, the concomitant assumption is that judges and courts, rather than elected representatives in majoritarian decision-making arenas, should resolve them. A more astute examination suggests that the transfer of these and other "big questions" from the political sphere to the courts has been tacitly supported, if not actively initiated, by political actors representing hegemonic elites and established interests. Judicial empowerment through constitutionalization provides these elites and their political representatives with effective means for reducing the risks to themselves and to the institutional apparatus within which they operate. The removal of policy-making power from legislatures and executives and its investiture in courts may become attractive to political power-holders for any of several reasons: when they seek to gain public support for their contentious views by relying on national high courts' public image as professional and apolitical decision-making bodies; when they regard public disputes in majoritarian decision-making arenas as likely to put their own policy preferences at risk; or when they estimate that abiding by the limits imposed by expanded judicial power will enhance their absolute or relative position vis-à-vis rival political elements and their alternative worldviews or policy preferences.

The constitutionalization of rights and the establishment of judicial review is therefore not driven solely, or even primarily, by politicians' genuine commitment to progressive notions of social justice or to an elevated vision of universal rights. It is driven in many cases by attempts to maintain the social and political status quo and to block attempts to seriously challenge it through democratic politics. As my analysis of the political origins of the constitutional revolution in these four polities suggests, judicial empowerment through constitutionalization is more often than not the result of a strategic tripartite pact between hegemonic, yet increasingly threatened, political elites seeking to insulate their policy preferences from the vicissitudes of democratic politics; economic elites who share a commitment to free markets and a concomitant antipathy to government; and supreme courts seeking to enhance their symbolic power and institutional position.

Unlike economic and judicial elites, whose interest in constitutionalization is self-evident, political power-holders' proconstitutionalization impulse appears to be counterintuitive. However, the analysis presented here reveals that political support for constitutionalization can be productively analyzed in terms of an interest-based hegemonic preservation approach. Governing elites in divided, rule-of-law polities face a constant struggle to preserve their hegemony. Such elites are likely to advocate a delegation of power to the judiciary (a) when their hegemony is increasingly challenged in majoritarian decision-making arenas by policy preferences of peripheral groups; (b) when the judiciary in that polity enjoys a reputation for rectitude and political impartiality; and (c) when the courts in that polity are inclined to rule in accordance with hegemonic ideological and cultural propensities.

Indeed, as we have seen, national high courts seldom diverge on a long-term basis from national metanarratives and the interests of hegemonic political forces. The rare exceptions to this pattern are not likely to transform a given polity's formative metanarratives or to alter its historically rooted patterns of power inequalities. Furthermore, even occasional judicial deviations are not likely to survive in the face of a more powerful political sphere. Those who established judicial empowerment as a response to challenges to their political hegemony have succeeded in protecting their policy preferences from the vagaries of democratic politics without risking the dangers of delegation.

The hegemonic preservation thesis may help us understand judicial empowerment through constitutionalization as part of a broader trend whereby crucial policy-making functions are increasingly insulated from majoritarian control. As we have seen, the world seems to have been seized by a craze for constitutionalization and judicial review. The transformation of judicial institutions into major political actors has not been limited to the national level; at the supranational level, the European Court of Justice interprets the treaties upon which the European Union is founded and has been awarded an increasingly important status by legislators, executives, and judiciaries in the EU member-states in dealing with interstate legal and economic disputes. The European Court of Human Rights in Strasbourg, the judicial arm of the forty-one-member Council of Europe, has in effect become the final court of appeal on human-rights issues for most of Europe. The judgments of these European courts (as well as of other supranational tribunals, such as the Inter-American Court of Human Rights) carry great weight and have forced many countries to incorporate transnational legal standards into their domestic legal system. The expansion of the EU and the consequent territorial expansion of its courts not only transformed European politics, it also extended the exercise of judicial power to new or charged political settings. Present calls for the adoption of a global constitution and for the establishment of a permanent international tribunal for war crimes and human rights violations also suggest that the law and courts in general, and the constitutionalization of rights in particular, are increasingly becoming key factors in international politics.

NOTES

1. Alexis de Tocqueville, *On Democracy* (New York: Knopf, [1835] 1945), 280.
2. C. N. Tate and T. Vallinder, eds., *The Global Expansion of Judicial Power* (New York: New York University Press, 1995), 5.
3. See Ronald Dworkin, *A Bill of Rights for Britain* (London: Chatto and Windus, 1990).
4. For recent critiques of judicial review on democratic grounds, see, e.g., Mark Tushnet, *Taking the Constitution away from the Courts* (Princeton, N.J.: Princeton University Press, 1999); Jeremy Waldron, *The Dignity of Legislation* (Oxford: Oxford University Press, 1999); Waldron, "Judicial Review and the Conditions for Democracy," *Journal of Political Philosophy* 6 (1998): 335–355; James Allan, "Bills of Rights and Judicial Power— A Liberal's Quandary," *Oxford Journal of Legal Studies* 16 (1996): 337–352; Jeremy Waldron, "A Rights-Based Critique of Constitutional Rights," *Oxford Journal of Legal Studies* 13 (1993): 18–51; Ian Shapiro, *Democratic Justice* (New Haven: Yale University Press, 1999); Robert Burt, *The Constitution in Conflict* (New Haven: Yale University Press, 1992); and Amy Gutmann and Dennis Thompson, *Democracy and Disagreement* (Cambridge, Mass.: Harvard University Press, 1996). For critiques of judicial review on conservative-populist grounds, see, e.g., Robert H. Bork, *The Tempting of America: The Political Seduction of the Law* (New York: Free Press, 1990); and Bork, *Coercing Virtue: The Worldwide Rule of Judges* (Toronto: Vintage Canada, 2002).

5. Michael Mandel, *The Charter of Rights and the Legalization of Politics in Canada,* 2nd ed. (Toronto: Thompson Educational Publishing, 1994); Christopher Manfredi, *Judicial Power and the Charter* (Toronto: Oxford University Press, 2001); F. L. Morton and Rainer Knopff, *The Charter Revolution and the Court Party,* 2nd ed. (Toronto: Broadview Press, 2000); and Kent Roach, *The Supreme Court on Trial: Judicial Activism or Democratic Dialogue* (Toronto: Irwin Law, 2001).

6. See Alec Stone, *The Birth of Judicial Politics in France* (New York: Oxford University Press, 1992); Donald Kommers, *The Constitutional Jurisprudence of the Federal Republic of Germany,* 2nd ed. (Durham: Duke University Press, 1997); Mary Volcansek, *Constitutional Politics in Italy: The Constitutional Court* (New York: St. Martin's Press, 2000); and collections of predominantly single-country essays such as Tate and Vallinder's *Global Expansion of Judicial Power.*

7. Jon Elster et al., *Institutional Design in Post-Communist Societies* (Cambridge: Cambridge University Press, 1998), to name only one recent example.

8. See, e.g., publications by Karen Alter, Geoffrey Garrett, Sally Kenney, Walter Mattli, Anne-Marie Slaughter, Alec Stone Sweet, and J. H. H. Weiler, to name a few leading scholars who have published extensively in the area of European and EU public law and judicial politics.

9. See e.g. Alec Stone Sweet, *Governing with Judges: Constitutional Politics in Europe* (Oxford: Oxford University Press, 2000); William Prillaman, *The Judiciary and Democratic Decay in Latin America* (Westport, Conn.: Praeger, 2000); and Leslie Friedman Goldstein, *Constituting Federal Sovereignty: The European Union in Comparative Context* (Baltimore: Johns Hopkins University Press, 2001).

10. Daniel Lazare, "America the Undemocratic," *New Left Review* 232 (1998): 3–31, 21.

11. George Fletcher, "Comparative Law as a Subversive Discipline," *American Journal of Comparative Law* 46 (1998): 683–700, 691. For a critique of American parochialism in this regard see, e.g., Ran Hirschl, "Looking Sideways, Looking Backwards, Looking Forwards," *University of Richmond Law Review* 43 (2000): 414–441; Bruce Ackerman, "The Rise of World Constitutionalism," *Virginia Law Review* 83 (1997): 771–797; and Martin Shapiro, "Public Law and Judicial Politics," in Ada Finifter, ed., *Political Science: The State of the Discipline* (Washington, D.C.: American Political Science Association, 1993).

CHAPTER 9

LEGISLATURES AND LEGISLATIVE ELECTIONS

Comparative political analysts ask many questions about legislatures, but one main set of questions concerns how and to what extent legislatures represent constituencies. The two readings included here discuss the fundamental issue of representation at a theoretical level (see Pitkin), along with explanations of how legislators behave that are based on real empirical experiences in Latin America (see Morgenstern).

Many analysts of comparative politics bracket the question of what representation means in theory to focus on how legislatures actually operate. An important point of departure here is that elected representatives in legislatures are not simply ideal "public servants" who reflect the wishes of their constituents (if they have a "mandate") or act in their interest (if they are "independent"). Rather, many analysts assume or argue that legislators have their own interests in mind, an assumption consistent with but not exclusive to the rationalist perspective discussed in this book's introduction—such as getting reelected—and that they accordingly respond to incentives (see Mayhew, 1974). These incentives and how legislators respond are shaped by the institutions in which they operate. This means not only how the legislature itself operates (such as how representatives are elected), but also the balance of political power between the legislature and the executive, and how this is shaped by institutions such as political parties. In this vein, we consider the work of Scott Morgenstern on legislatures in Latin America, which focuses on some distinctive features of legislatures in the Latin American context.

Taken together, these readings show that legislatures are more internally complex than is seen in the simplistic vision that they represent the interest of a governing majority and pass laws that reflect the preferences of that majority. Legislators are often internally conflicted as to their role (as Pitkin's argument implies) and are simultaneously involved in political maneuvers with respect to other branches. For this reason, we can expect that the research agenda on the functioning of legislatures will continue to raise significant topics going forward. As you read these excerpts, consider whether the readings offer a view of how a legislature might operate in an "ideal world," or if legislatures and other representative bodies will inevitably have limitations.

WORKS CITED

Mayhew, David. 1974. *Congress: The Electoral Connection.* New Haven, CT: Yale University Press.

HANNAH PITKIN

9.1 THE CONCEPT OF REPRESENTATION

This excerpt looks at the issue that Pitkin calls the "mandate–independence" controversy in the issue of representation. A simple way to think about this is to think about what you would want from your elected representative. Would you want him to do whatever you prefer, or would you want him to exercise the "better judgment" that may come from experience and knowledge (even if the reasons seem unclear to you)? Would you want your congressperson or member of parliament to operate as if you have given her a "mandate" to do exactly as you wish, or would you want that representative to act with "independence"? (Keep in mind, of course, that the person elected will not always be the person you voted for or from the party you preferred, and that sometimes your elected representative may align with *someone else's* preferences, not yours.) As you may recognize, neither of these positions is the clear winner. We want representatives to exercise their judgment and be more than just automatons that reflect the polls, but we also want them to be responsive to what the constituents prefer. All this begs the question, *What is representation?* The selection from Pitkin offers perspectives that others have taken on this. What do you take from these positions and Pitkin's summary? If we assume that both the "mandate" and the "independence" perspectives have merit, where would you place yourself on this spectrum and why?

THE MANDATE–INDEPENDENCE CONTROVERSY

Representation means the making present of something which is nevertheless not literally present. What I should like to say about substantive acting for others is that the represented thing or person is present in the action rather than in the characteristics of the actor, or how he is regarded, or the formal arrangements which precede or follow the action. But this locution is far from clear, and we still have the task of specifying what kind or manner of action is required here.

The suggestion probably most familiar from the literature on representation is that the representative must do what his principal would do, must act as if the principal himself were acting.[1] This is a very tempting account because of its obvious proximity to the idea of making-the-represented-present, the idea of resemblance and reflection found in the descriptive view, and the idea of democratic consent associated with modern representative government. But on closer examination it entails problems. If we think of a representative acting not merely for a single principal but for an entire constituency; an unorganized set of people, then "Act as if your constituents were acting themselves" becomes a questionable slogan. If the contemplated action is voting, then presumably (but not obviously) it means that the representative must vote as a majority of his constituents would. But any activities other than voting are less easy to deal with. Is he really literally to deliberate as if he were several hundred thousand people? To bargain that way? To speak that way? And if not that way, then how?

The slogan is not even right for a representative acting for a single principal; even representing one man is not a matter of imitation. For example, I am attending a business conference as Jones's representative,

---

Pitkin, Hannah. 1972. *The Concept of Representation.* Berkeley: University of California Press.

chosen to act for him there because it is a financial con-ference and he has no head for figures. The time comes to make a decision. I ask myself, "What would Jones do?" But the answer is clear: he would throw up his hands in horrified defeat at the sight of all those figures, and would probably make the wrong decision. Surely it is not my obligation or role to do that for him. Imitation is not what is called for here; acting for another is not acting on the stage. But the only alternatives seem to be either that I do what Jones would want, or that I do what seems best for him, in terms of his interest.

So, again, the two familiar elements of wishes and welfare seem to be the only available choices. But these two elements form two opposed sides in a long-standing debate, undoubtedly the central classic con-troversy in the literature of political representation. The question at issue may be summarized as: Should (must) a representative do what his constituents want, and be bound by mandates or instructions from them; or should (must) he be free to act as seems best to him in pursuit of their welfare? This mandate–independence controversy has become encrusted with a number of other issues, partly related but partly irrelevant. It occurs mostly in contexts where political representa-tion is at stake; so the basic question is soon entangled with such issues as the relative priority of local versus national interest, the role of political parties, and the nature of political questions. It tends to be complicated also by the differences between representing a single principal and representing a diverse political constitu-ency. Still, the underlying conceptual problem is worth isolating and examining in its own right. What I shall argue about this conceptual dispute is, first, that the way in which it is usually formulated makes a consis-tent answer impossible; second, that the meaning of representation nevertheless supplies a consistent posi-tion about a representative's duties; and, third, that this consistent position only sets outer limits, within which there remains room for a wide range of views on how a political representative should act or what dis-tinguishes good from bad representing. A writer's posi-tion in this range of views is correlated with his conception of political life in the broadest sense: his ideas on the nature of political issues, the relative ca-pacities of rulers and ruled, the nature of man and society—in short, what we might call his metapolitics.

A number of positions have at one time or an-other been defended, between the two poles of man-date and independence. A highly restrictive mandate theorist might maintain that true representation occurs only when the representative acts on explicit instructions from his constituents, that any exercise of discretion is a deviation from this ideal. A more moderate position might be that he may exercise some discretion, but must consult his constituents before doing anything new or controversial, and then do as they wish or resign his post. A still less extreme position might be that the representative may act as he thinks his constituents would want, unless or until he receives instructions from them, and then he must obey. Very close to the indepen-dence position would be the argument that the rep-resentative must do as he thinks best, except insofar as he is bound by campaign promises or an election platform. At the other extreme is the idea of com-plete independence, that constituents have no right even to exact campaign promises; once a man is elected he must be completely free to use his own judgment.

But whatever his precise position, a theorist is likely to invoke the appropriate analogies and adver-bial expressions to defend it. A mandate theorist will see the representative as a "mere" agent, a servant, a delegate, a subordinate substitute for those who sent him. The representative, he will say, is "sent as a ser-vant," not "chosen with dictatorial powers," and so the purpose which sent him must have been the con-stituents' purpose and not his own.[2] They sent him to do something for them which they might have chosen to do for themselves, which they are perfectly capable of doing and understanding.[3] Hence the rep-resentative was sent to pursue his constituents' will and not his own. Other mandate theorists invoke the metaphors of descriptive representation, seeing the representative as a mechanical device through which his constituents act—a mirror or megaphone. As to the national interest, the mandate theorist is likely to argue that the sum of local constituencies is the nation, and the sum of constituency interests is the national interest. Besides, if each representative was not intended to act as an agent of his locality, why was he locally elected?[4]

Independence theorists, too, have appropriate analogies at their disposal; they see the representative as a free agent, a trustee, an expert who is best left alone to do his work. They thus tend to see political questions as difficult and complex, beyond the capacities of ordinary men. In any case, they argue, a constituency is not a single unit with a ready-made will or opinion on every topic; a representative cannot simply reflect what is not there to be reflected.[5] Further, if each representative were pledged to and instructed by his constituency, political compromise would become impossible. It is necessary to leave room for the crucial activities of the legislature itself—the formulating of issues, the deliberation and compromise on which decisions should be based. And, as Burke asked, what sort of a system is it "in which the determination precedes the discussion; in which one set of men deliberate, and another decides; and where those who form the conclusion are perhaps three hundred miles distant from those who hear the arguments?"[6]

Further, the independence theorist argues that the representative, although locally elected, must pursue the national interest, which will by no means emerge automatically from the sum of local constituency desires. He must be left free of instructions so that he can pursue it.[7] Moreover, to allow a representative to act only on instructions is to rob him of all dignity and thus to undermine respect for the government.[8]

These are the two sides of the controversy in primitive form. Frequently they are complicated, however, by arguments about political parties. One argument is that in the modern state the legislator is neither bound by the wishes of his constituency nor free to act in the national interest as he sees it, but that he is bound to act in accord with the program of his political party. Sometimes this view is expressed by saying he is the representative of his party.[9] A second possibility is to regard parties as a link between local wishes and national interests. The party presumably has a program on national issues; by electing the member of a certain party, the voters in each constituency express their wishes on this program. The legislator is then bound to this program because of his duty to party and his duty to his

constituents' wishes, and (presumably) because it accords with his view of the national interest (why else is he in that party?).[10] Third, it has been argued on the independence side, particularly by continental writers, that the interests of party are partial and special and not equivalent to the national interest; so the representative must be left free of party obligations to act in the national interest as he sees it.[11]

Various compromise positions have been taken. Some writers argue that both extremes are true: the representative has an obligation both to the wishes of his constituents and to the best policy as he sees it; but they do not tell us how to reconcile the two.[12] Some maintain that the representative's duty to his constituency is to plead their cause, to speak for them; but that he must then vote in accord with his own judgment.[13] Many writers have argued that time is the crucial factor; that the representative is not bound by every temporary whim or wish of his constituents, but must obey their long-range, deliberate desires. Some seem to take the curious position that a representative must ignore his constituents except just at election time, and that at election time they must remove him if they are not pleased.

What is most striking about the mandate–independence controversy is how long it has continued without coming any nearer to a solution, despite the participation of many astute thinkers. Each in turn takes a position—pro mandate or pro independence—but the dispute is never settled. The two sides seem to talk past each other; their arguments do not meet. Each seems convincing when read in isolation. Nor do the compromise solutions seem satisfactory. This state of affairs has led some commentators to reject further (as they put it) normative speculation, and to call for empirical investigation of what representatives in fact do.[14] Such investigation leads them either into a survey of historical examples, or into studies of legislative behavior and public opinion in the contemporary world.

NOTES

1. Carl J. Friedrich, "Representation and Constitutional Reform," *Western Political Quarterly,* I (June, 1948), 127: "representation, and more particularly

political representation, is associated with institutional arrangements which are intended to insure that the 'representative' participates in whatever authority he is wielding on behalf of those he represents in such a way as to permit one to say that he acted 'in their stead,' or 'as they would have acted, had they been able to participate themselves.'" James Hogan, *Election and Representation* (1945), p. 141, says: "the representative acting as if the constituent himself were present." Talleyrand-Perigord in the French National Assembly of 1789, cited in Karl Loewenstein, *Volk und Parlament* (Munich, 1922), p. 193, said that the deputy is, "l'homme que le bailliage charge de vouloir en son nom, mais de vouloir comme il voudrait lui-même, s'il pouvait se transporter au rendez-vous général." And Senator William Maclay of Pennsylvania, cited m Robert Luce, *Legislative Principles* (Boston, 1930), p. 462: "Were my constituents here, what would they do?"

2. For example, Senator Maclay cited in Luce, p. 462.

3. For example, Richard Overton, "A Remonstrance of Many Thousand Citizens" (1646), *Leveller Manifestoes of the Puritan Revolution*, ed. Don M. Wolfe (New York, 1944), p. 113.

4. See for example, Luce, *op. cit.*, p. 507; Lewis Anthony Dexter, "The Representative and His District," *Human Organization*, XVI (Spring, 1957), 3.

5. Henry J. Ford, *Representative Government* (New York, 1924), pp. 147–148. Cf. Madison's views and those of James Wilson, cited in John A. Fairlie, "The Nature of Political Representation," *American Political Science Review*, XXXIV (April, 1940), 243–244. This argument is often linked with the view that political questions are too complex and difficult for public opinion to cope with. See for example Sir Henry Maine, *Popular Government*, pp. 89–92, cited in Luce, *op. cit.*, p. 492.

6. "Speech to the Electors of Bristol" (1774), *Burke's Politics* (New York, 1949), p. 115; cf. Hogan, *op. cit.*, p. 109; T. D. Woolsey, *Political Science*, I, 296, cited in Luce, *op. cit.*, p. 479.

7. This point is often made by Burke. See also Loewenstein, *Volk und Parlament*, pp. 193–194;

James Wilford Garner, *Political Science and Government* (New York, 1928), p. 666.

8. This argument is common among the German theorists: Gerhard Leibholz, *Das Wesen der Repräsentation* (Berlin, 1929), pp. 73, 92–93, 140, 166; Hans J. Wolff, *Organschaft und juristische Person* (Berlin, 1934), pp. 54–60.

9. For instance, Howard Lee McBain, *The Living Constitution* (New York, 1948), p. 208; Anthony Downs, *An Economic Theory of Democracy* (New York, 1957), pp. 89–90; Garner, *op. cit.*, p. 665.

10. Gerhard Leibholz, *Strukturprobleme der modernen Demokratie* (Karlsruhe, 1958), pp. 75–76 *et passim*; Hans Kelsen, *Vom Wesen und Wert der Demokratie* (Tübingen, 1929), pp. 21–22. This view is linked with the modern doctrine of the mandate—the obligation of the majority party to abide by voter decisions on the issues in an election; see Cecil S. Emden, *The People and the Constitution* (Oxford, 1956).

11. Leibholz, *Das Wesen der Repräsentation*, pp. 98–101, 104, 113–114; Simon Sterne, *Representative Government* (Philadelphia, 1871), pp. 51–61.

12. For instance, Carl J. Friedrich, *Constitutional Government and Democracy* (Boston, 1950), p. 263; or William Howard Taft, *Popular Government*, p. 62, cited in Luce, *op. cit.*, p. 495.

13. For instance, Jeremy Bentham, "Constitutional Code," p. 44, cited in Samuel Bailey, *The Rationale of Political Representation* (London, 1835), p. 142. Another compromise position was suggested by Abraham Lincoln as a candidate for the Illinois legislature in 1836: "If elected, I shall consider the whole people of Sangamon my constituents, as well those that oppose as those that support me. While acting as their representative I shall be governed by their will on all subjects upon which I have the means of knowing what their will is, and upon all others I shall do what my own judgment teaches me will best advance their interests." Cited in Luce, *op. cit.*, p. 471.

14. For instance in Heinz Eulau *et al.*, "The Role of the Representative," *American Political Science Review*, LIII (September, 1959), 748; John C. Wahlke and Heinz Eulau, eds., *Legislative Behavior* (Glencoe, Ill., 1959), p. 6.

SCOTT MORGENSTERN

9.2 EXPLAINING LEGISLATIVE POLITICS IN LATIN AMERICA

In considering Morgenstern, keep in mind that legislators might behave differently in different countries. One reason for this might be the institutional structure of a given legislature, which would shape the incentives of self-interested legislators. Of course, there may be other reasons why legislatures behave differently in different places, including distinct histories, norms and values, or political divisions in a society. In looking at Latin America, Morgenstern finds marked contrasts with the U.S. Congress. As a result, he suggests that claims about legislative behavior based on the U.S. model should be treated as hypotheses that can be tested looking at other cases and that a viable comparative *theory* about legislatures should not be based on the United States alone. Among the main distinctions Morgenstern makes is the observation that Latin American legislatures tend to be "reactive," responding to initiatives from the executive branch, whereas the U.S. Congress might be more "proactive." Other distinctions include less of a focus on reelection than in the United States, in part because a time as a legislator in some Latin American countries creates chances for individuals to contest other political roles (such as being elected mayor or governor in Brazil) or seize lucrative opportunities in private life. What other distinctive features of Latin American legislatures does Morgenstern identify in this piece?

Instead of focusing on presidents, militaries, financial sector bureaucrats, or social actors, the preceding pages have placed the Argentine, Brazilian, Chilean, and Mexican legislatures at the center of democratic politics. While the authors all agree that the legislatures are potent, it is also clear that the legislatures take a less proactive role than does the U.S. Congress. In this chapter I draw on the previous chapters to argue that the legislatures take a generally reactive role, but within this role there is great variance in the way in which the legislatures assert their power and insert themselves into the policy process. I argue further that the chapters have also offered significant evidence that, as postulated in the introduction, many of the differences are explicable by institutional variation.

The country chapters are arranged to focus on substantive questions about executive–legislative relations

and the role of parties in organizing the business of the legislature. In this conclusion I return to the thematic questions raised in the introduction about the importance of reelection rates, electoral systems, partisan alignments, and constitutional powers on legislative politics. In doing so, this chapter has two primary goals. First, a main methodological strategy of this book has been to borrow from the U.S. model in deriving descriptions of key pieces of the legislative process and explanations for legislative behavior in Latin America. But, we have also shown that the assumptions embedded in models of the U.S. Congress must become variables in a comparative context. In particular, in contrast to members of the U.S. Congress, many Latin American legislators are less focused on reelection, more reliant on party leaders, and/or concerned with intrapartisan rivals at election time, not members or

Morgenstern, Scott. 2002. "Explaining Legislative Politics in Latin America", pp. 413–445 in Scott Morgenstern and Benito Nacif, eds. 2002. *Legislative Politics in Latin America*. Cambridge: Cambridge University Press.

opponents of a single majority party, and faced with distinct amalgamations of constitutional powers. This chapter, therefore, reviews the range that these variables (*qua* U.S. assumptions) take in our four countries and discusses how the book's authors used them in our collective effort to move toward a comparative explanation of legislative behavior.

The second goal is to use these explanations to move us toward a typology of legislatures, which Gary W. Cox and I then apply in the succeeding chapter to a discussion about presidential reactions in the face of distinct legislative types.[1] The starting point for this typology is the assumption that democratic assemblies insert themselves into the policy-making process in one or more of three basic ways: (1) originative: making and breaking executives, who then shoulder most of the policy-making burden; (2) proactive: initiating and passing their own legislative proposals; and (3) reactive: amending and/or vetoing executive proposals. European parliaments are the primary examples of originative/reactive assemblies. The U.S. Congress and the assemblies of the U.S. states are the primary examples of proactive/reactive assemblies.

In Latin America, legislatures typically cannot get rid of presidents they dislike and lack the resources to fashion their own legislative proposals. Thus, they are neither originative nor proactive; they are merely reactive.

Within this general category legislatures can still range greatly, from "subservient" to "recalcitrant," with "workable" and "venal" options in between. These abstract ideal-types, which are developed in this and the succeeding chapter in more detail, are not meant as descriptions of our specific cases. The defined categories, however, do give us a starting point from which to understand and analyze the Latin American legislatures and the presidential reactions to them in a comparative context.

A typology of legislatures must take into account many factors. Twenty years ago Mezey (1979) created a simple categorization based on the democratic support of the legislative institutions and the legislature's policy-making power. Among the Latin American cases that Mezey considered, only the Costa Rican and Mexican (!) legislatures gained admittance to the "more supported" category, as those in the Southern Cone were all under dictatorial rule. On the axis differentiating policy-making power, Mezey then coded the Chilean, Uruguayan, and Costa Rican legislatures as "strong," while the others in Latin America were placed in the "modest" category (above some in Africa or under Soviet rule that were considered to have little or no power). Today the legislatures of Argentina, Brazil, Chile, and Mexico (and most others in Latin America) would all fit into the "more supported" category. This book has shown that it also would be incorrect to code any of these legislatures as having only modest policy-making power. Each of the legislatures under study here clearly asserts itself and shapes the policy process. This does not necessarily require the proactive stance taken by the U.S. Congress. Although several chapters showed that the legislatures do initiate a significant number of bills, it is clear that their greatest role is in blocking unfavorable legislation or shaping outcomes by pressuring the president to change proposals or amending executive bills. My hypothesis for this chapter is that the manner in which these generally reactive legislatures play their roles is largely a function of the reelection drive, the party structure, the electoral system, and the constitution. Other factors that emerge from the chapters, including ideology, ties between the president and the parties, and the federal structure, also count, and I will therefore discuss these issues as well.

DEFINING THE LEGISLATURES' TYPES[2]

This chapter has highlighted how the reelection drive, the party and electoral system, the Constitution, and other factors influence the means and motivations of legislators, and hence the legislatures' type. Strong binds between the legislature and the president, for example, can turn a potentially proactive legislature into a passive or at best reactive institution. The legislators' reelection motivations and the electoral system are related, in that they affect how strongly legislators are tied to their constituents. Legislators must contrast these sometimes competing motivations in their efforts to build a professional institution, seek spoils for their constituents, work with other legislators in pursuit of national policy goals, or simply follow executive directives. Legislators in Mexico, Argentina, and Brazil—where there were respectively 0, 20, and 35% of legislators returning to their posts in recent elections—should be looking to grab what they can and run. As argued in other chapters, such legislators should be particularly responsive to presidents (or others) who control resources that the legislators can use to line their pockets, improve their future career prospects, or pay off their patrons. While certainly interested in the electoral benefits of the pork-barrel, legislators who envision longer legislative careers (e.g., Chile, where about 70% of the lower House members generally return to their posts and another 10–15% attempt a move to the Senate) should also be worried about policy outcomes. This concern can be electorally motivated; since elections turn on a combination of candidate qualities and policy, reelection-minded legislators should involve themselves in the policy process.[3]

It is also important to note that, even if legislators are motivated to engage themselves in the policy process, not all enjoy the institutional framework to make their efforts fruitful. Some are hamstrung by constitutions that limit, for example, significant changes to the budget. Others are cut short due to party factionalism or fragmentation (multipartism) that slows collective action.

Aside from these institutional variables, partisan ideology has a clear effect on whether a legislature will be parochial or policy-oriented. Strong ideological parties should be less venal than a diverse coalition of politicians seeking fame, fortune, and power. Again, Chilean parties are distinctive. On the center-left, the two post-dictatorship Chilean presidents have enjoyed the support of a coalition banded together for its strong opposition to Pinochet. The Chilean right, alternatively, is strongly associated with Pinochet and his regime. One of the two main rightist parties, the UDI, is intensely ideological; many of its legislators were mayors during the Pinochet regime and many were personally trained by a charismatic and rabidly anti-communist recent martyr (Jaime Guzmán). UDI party members are unlikely to bend on crucial policy issues for an extra bridge in their district. In contrast, presidents in Argentina and Brazil are neither supported nor opposed by such ideologically driven and organized parties. In neither of these countries has any single party or group of parties won the anti-authoritarian banner, and the PT in Brazil, which currently has only 11% of the legislative seats, is the only significant class-based party.[4] The Peronists in Argentina had an ideological root based on their populist history, but Menem has effectively destroyed that party's legacy.

This discussion suggests that these factors orient the legislatures into several general categories. Leaving aside the proactive U.S.-style legislature, the two extremes of our reactive cases are marked by the *subservient* legislature, which bows to presidential dictates, and the *recalcitrant* legislature that blocks most presidential advances. In the middle are legislatures that are generally *workable*, frequently assenting to presidential bills but generally requiring compromises or payoffs in exchange for the assent.

The pre-1997 Mexican legislature fit pretty squarely into the subservient category. There the presidents faced legislatures filled with progressively ambitious politicians, a large majority of whom were highly disciplined and loyal to the president. Other cases do not fit as neatly into a single category, but the tendencies are clear. The post-Pinochet Chilean presidents have faced reelection-driven legislators with greater freedom from the executive and stronger ties to their constituents. This independence is tempered, however, since the majority of these legislators have been in coalition with the president. At the same time, the Chilean legislature faces two important limitations: The majority coalition is composed of several competing parties, and it is constitutionally restrained in important ways. In sum, while some factors push the legislature toward proactivity, a number rein it in, thus yielding a generally reactive but *workable* legislature.

The Argentine and Brazilian legislatures also lie on this continuum. The Argentine Congress has been somewhat closer to the Mexican model, as the presidents have commanded progressively ambitious politicians and highly disciplined parties. But, Alfonsin, Menem, and now De la Rúa have not always enjoyed majority control in both Houses. The Argentine legislature has therefore not been subservient, but neither has it been as active as the Chilean legislature.

Finally, the Brazilian legislature is perhaps the most difficult to categorize, due to the heterogeneity of its membership. Many members do have static ambitions, but many are closely tied to state politicians and seek future jobs in state governments. The legislature is quite fractious, but some presidents have built working majorities. Others, however, have not been able to cobble together support. Further, the electoral system has helped to generate factious parties, which has favored pork payoffs to individual legislators over policy compromises among unified parties. This legislature, thus, has ranged between the *recalcitrant* and a relatively *venal* variety of a *workable* type.

By themselves these categories provide a summary of legislative politics in Latin America. They also imply something about politics more generally, as their titles insinuate interactions with the executive. This interaction is the subject of the succeeding epilogue.

CONCLUSION

In light of warnings about the dangers of presidentialism (Linz 1990), concerns with the strength of presidents vis-à-vis the legislature (Shugart and Carey 1992), and premonitions about the quality of delegated democracy (O'Donnell 1994), the role of the legislatures in consolidating democracy across Latin America has come under greater scrutiny.

In this book we have attempted to take a first step toward building an understanding of these institutions by addressing three empirical themes: executive–legislative relations, the legislative structure, and the policy-making process. These have been perennial themes in the American literature, and we thus sought to apply the theoretical framework developed for studies of the U.S. Congress to our four cases. Further, we argued that the American model was appropriate, since Argentina, Brazil, Chile, and even Mexico are consolidating, if not fully consolidated, democracies, and all employ presidential rather than parliamentary forms of government. But, we found that even the assumption about legislators' desire for reelection, which drives much of the literature on the U.S. Congress, is inapplicable generally. We thus converted this—along with assumptions implicit in the U.S. model about the electoral system, the party system, and the Constitution—into independent variables. This process of defining a set of independent variables that can capture a diverse group of cases is an important step toward defining a general comparative model of legislative politics. As we have shown, this framework is useful in building theoretical explanations of why these legislatures look and function as they do.

In their explanations, the chapters have shown that the legislatures insert themselves into the policy process in a variety of ways. But, as a result of different legislator goals, constitutional power endowments, party arrangements, and other factors, the legislatures' structure and function are quite different from the proactive U.S. Congress. Even within this generally "reactive" category, the Latin American legislatures also differ amongst themselves, filling a typology that ranges from subservient to recalcitrant. In our epilogue, Gary W. Cox and I apply this typology to a discussion of the interaction of presidents with the different legislative types. We argue that presidents are keenly aware of the majority's construction, unity, and loyalty and condition their political strategies to the expected reaction of the legislature. This political dynamic rounds out our study of legislative politics.

BIBLIOGRAPHY

Cox, Gary W. and Mathew D. McCubbins. 1993. *Legislative Leviathan: Party Government in the House.* Berkeley: University of California Press.

Cox, Gary W. and Scott Morgenstern. 2001. "Latin America's Reactive Assemblies and Proactive Presidents." *Comparative Politics* 33(2): 171–189.

Linz, Juan. 1990. "The Perils of Presidentialism." *Journal of Democracy* 1(1): 51–69.

Mezey, Michael. 1979. *Comparative Legislatures.* Durham, NC: Duke University Press.

O'Donnell, Guillermo. 1994. "Delegative Democracy." *Journal of Democracy* 5, 1: 55–69.

Shugart, Matthew and John Carey. 1992. *Presidents and Assemblies.* New York: Cambridge University Press.

NOTES

1. The succeeding discussion about legislative types comes directly from Cox and Morgenstern (2001).
2. Parts of this section were borrowed from Cox and Morgenstern (2001).
3. See Cox and McCubbins (1993).
4. There are several other small leftist parties, none of which approaches 10% of the legislature.

CHAPTER 10

EXECUTIVES

In the popular imagination, the field of politics is often associated with the idea of executives. We often think of national leaders, including heads of state (such as presidents) and heads of government (such as prime ministers), when we think of how politics works. In 2015, for example, many citizens speak of the United States' politics being defined by the "Obama administration" or of the early to mid-2000s as the "George W. Bush years," although in many ways the legislature is the branch with the greatest powers in making laws. This section presents some of the classic debates about the nature and functioning of the executive branch of government.

One major debate concerns the question of whether "presidential" or "parliamentary" systems of government yield better outcomes, especially in terms of democratic functioning and stability. Juan Linz (1990) famously argued that presidentialism is a risky institutional design, but here Scott Mainwaring and Matthew Shugart challenge this assumption. Note that they outline Linz's argument before offering their theoretical and empirical critique of his work. Another big debate concerns how to use institutional design to reduce the risks of conflict between distinct groups. This debate extends beyond an analysis of executives, but because the executive branch symbolizes and represents a good deal of power, it is especially important. Here we read a piece by Arend Lijphart, a distinguished analyst of "consociational" systems that use institutional design for power sharing in "divided societies." Finally, we read an excerpt from Robert Jackson and Carl Rosberg that considers executive power in Africa, where presidents for some time seemed to be relatively unconstrained by other institutions. They write of what is sometimes called "personalist" rule in the African context, a concept that might remind you of some of certain authoritarian regimes you read about in Chapter 7. As you go through the readings in the current chapter, think about whether there is an ideal way to structure the executive branch and whether "one-size-fits-all" solutions are feasible or should be discouraged.

WORKS CITED

Linz, Juan. 1990. "The Perils of Presidentialism." *Journal of Democracy* 1(1): 51–69.

SCOTT MAINWARING AND MATTHEW SOBERG SHUGART

10.1 JUAN LINZ, PRESIDENTIALISM, AND DEMOCRACY

A Critical Appraisal

This reading has the nice feature of offering a critical review of a major argument in the field. The argument is that made by Juan Linz, and it is an argument that might seem surprising to many Americans at first glance, although it might seem familiar to many living in other Anglophone countries (such as the United Kingdom, Canada, Australia, New Zealand, or Jamaica). There is a major distinction between *parliamentary systems*, in which heads of government are elected by members of the legislature (typically called a parliament), and *presidential systems*, in which executives are directly elected by the populace and are distinct from the legislature and have their own sets of powers. The basic line of argument provided by Linz is that parliamentary systems of government are preferable to presidential systems of government in certain fundamental ways. In particular, says Linz, parliamentarism does a better job of protecting and securing democracy than presidentialism. As Mainwaring and Shugart note, Linz offers five principal reasons for this. In this piece, the authors summarize Linz's argument and then evaluate it critically. They concur with Linz in several ways, but also raise theoretical objections and then challenge Linz on the interpretation of the empirical evidence. The piece offered here thus surveys the important debate about presidential versus parliamentary systems and provides a constructive critique of the argument. See whether you can identify the theoretical critique and the empirical critique. Reflecting on your own country's experience, does this argument make sense? Can you identify reasons or causes for why your country does or does not fit the expectations coming from Linz's theory?

Since the 1960s Juan J. Linz has been one of the world's foremost contributors to our understanding of democracy, authoritarianism, and totalitarianism. Although many of his contributions have had a significant impact, few have been as far-reaching as his essay "Presidential or Parliamentary Democracy: Does It Make a Difference?," originally written in 1985. The essay argued that presidentialism is less likely than parliamentarism to sustain stable democratic regimes. It became a classic even in unpublished form. Among both policymakers and scholars it spawned a broad debate about the merits and especially the liabilities

of presidential government. Now that the definitive version of the essay has appeared, we believe that a critical appraisal is timely. This task is especially important because Linz's arguments against presidentialism have gained widespread currency.

This article critically assesses Linz's arguments about the perils of presidentialism. Although we agree with several of Linz's criticisms of presidentialism, we disagree that presidentialism is particularly oriented towards winner-takes-all results.[1] We argue that the superior record of parliamentary systems has rested partly on where parliamentary government has been

Mainwaring, Scott, and Matthew Soberg Shugart. 1997. "Juan Linz, Presidentialism, and Democracy: A Critical Appraisal," *Comparative Politics* 29(4): 449–471.

implemented, and we claim that presidentialism has some advantages that partially offset its drawbacks. These advantages can be maximized by paying careful attention to differences among presidential systems. Other things being equal, presidentialism tends to function better where presidencies have weak legislative powers, parties are at least moderately disciplined, and party systems are not highly fragmented. Finally, we argue that switching from presidentialism to parliamentarism could exacerbate problems of governability in countries with undisciplined parties. Even if parliamentary government is more conducive to stable democracy, much rests on what kind of parliamentarism and presidentialism is implemented.[2]

By presidentialism we mean a regime in which, first, the president is always the chief executive and is elected by popular vote or, as in the U.S., by an electoral college with essentially no autonomy with respect to popular preferences and, second, the terms of office for the president and the assembly are fixed. Under pure presidentialism the president has the right to retain ministers of his or her choosing regardless of the composition of the congress.

THE PERILS OF PRESIDENTIALISM: LINZ'S ARGUMENT

Linz bases his argument about the superiority of parliamentary systems partially on the observation that few long established democracies have presidential systems. He maintains that the superior historical performance of parliamentary democracies stems from intrinsic defects of presidentialism. He analyzes several problems of presidential systems. We briefly summarize the five most important issues.

First, in presidential systems the president and assembly have competing claims to legitimacy. Both are popularly elected, and the origin and survival of each are independent from the other.[3] Since both the president and legislature "derive their power from the vote of the people in a free competition among well-defined alternatives, a conflict is always latent and sometimes likely to erupt dramatically; there is no democratic principle to resolve it."[4] Linz argues that parliamentarism obviates this problem because the executive is not independent of the assembly. If the majority of the assembly

favors a change in policy direction, it can replace the government by exercising its no confidence vote.

Second, the fixed term of the president's office introduces a rigidity that is less favorable to democracy than the flexibility offered by parliamentary systems, where governments depend on the ongoing confidence of the assembly. Presidentialism "entails a rigidity . . . that makes adjustment to changing situations extremely difficult; a leader who has lost the confidence of his own party or the parties that acquiesced [in] his election cannot be replaced."[5] By virtue of their greater ability to promote changes in the cabinet and government, parliamentary systems afford greater opportunities to resolve disputes. Such a safety valve may enhance regime stability.

Third, presidentialism "introduces a strong element of zero-sum game into democratic politics with rules that tend toward a 'winner-take-all' outcome." In contrast, in parliamentary systems "power-sharing and coalition-forming are fairly common, and incumbents are accordingly attentive to the demands and interests of even the smaller parties." In presidential systems direct popular election is likely to imbue presidents with a feeling that they need not undertake the tedious process of constructing coalitions and making concessions to the opposition.[6]

Fourth, the style of presidential politics is less propitious for democracy than the style of parliamentary politics. The sense of being the representative of the entire nation may lead the president to be intolerant of the opposition. "The feeling of having independent power, a mandate from the people . . . is likely to give a president a sense of power and mission that might be out of proportion to the limited plurality that elected him. This in turn might make resistances he encounters . . . more frustrating, demoralizing, or irritating than resistances usually are for a prime minister.[7] The absence in presidential systems of a monarch or a "president of the republic" deprives them of an authority who can exercise restraining power.

Finally, political outsiders are more likely to win the chief executive office in presidential systems, with potentially destabilizing effects. Individuals elected by direct popular vote are less dependent on and less beholden to political parties. Such individuals are more likely to govern in a populist, anti-institutionalist fashion.

A CRITIQUE OF LINZ'S ARGUMENT

We agree with the main thrust of four of Linz's five basic criticisms of presidentialism. We concur that the issue of dual legitimacy is nettlesome in presidential systems, but we believe that his contrast between presidential and parliamentary systems is too stark. To a lesser degree than in presidential systems, conflicting claims to legitimacy also exist in parliamentary systems. Conflicts sometimes arise between the lower and upper houses of a bicameral legislature, each claiming to exercise legitimate power. If both houses have the power of confidence over the cabinet, the most likely outcome when the houses are controlled by different majorities is a compromise coalition cabinet. In this case dual legitimacy exists, not between executive and assembly, but between the two chambers of the assembly. This arrangement could be troublesome if the two chambers were controlled by opposed parties or blocs. In a few parliamentary systems, including Canada, Germany, and Japan, upper houses have significant powers over legislation but can not exercise a vote of no confidence against the government. In some the upper house can not be dissolved by the government. Then, there is a genuine dual legitimacy between the executive and part of the legislature. Thus, dual democratic legitimacy is not exclusively a problem of presidentialism, though it is more pronounced with it. A unicameral parliament would avoid the potential of dual legitimacy under parliamentarism, but it sacrifices the advantages of bicameralism, especially for large, federal, and plural countries.[8]

Another overlooked potential source of conflicting legitimacy in parliamentary republics is the role of the head of state, who is usually called "president" but tends to be elected by parliament. The constitutions of parliamentary republics usually give the president several powers that are—or may be, subject to constitutional interpretation—more than ceremonial. Examples include the president's exclusive discretion to dissolve parliament (Italy), the requirement of countersignatures of cabinet decrees (Italy), suspensory veto over legislation (Czech Republic, Slovakia), the power to decree new laws (Greece for some time after 1975), and appointments to high offices, sometimes (as in the Czech Republic and Slovakia) including ministries. Linz argues that the president in such systems "can play the role of adviser or arbiter by bringing party leaders together and facilitating the flow of information among them." He also notes that "no one in a presidential system is institutionally entitled to such a role." He is quite right that political systems often face moments when they need a "neutral" arbiter. However, for the position of head of state to be more than feckless it is necessary to make it "institutionally entitled" to other tasks as well. Linz correctly notes that, "if presidents in pure parliamentary republics were irrelevant, it would not make sense for politicians to put so much effort into electing their preferred candidate to the office."[9]

Paradoxically, the more authority the head of state is given, the greater is the potential for conflict, especially in newer democracies where roles have not yet been clearly defined by precedent. Hungary and especially Slovakia have had several constitutional crises involving the head of state, and in some Third World parliamentary republics such crises have at times been regime-threatening, as in Somalia (1961–68) and Pakistan. Politicians indeed care who holds the office, precisely because it has potential for applying brakes to the parliamentary majority. The office of the presidency may not be democratically legitimated via popular election, but it typically has a fixed term of office and a longer term than the parliament's. By praising the potential of the office in serving as arbiter, Linz implicitly acknowledges the Madisonian point that placing unchecked power in the hands of the assembly majority is not necessarily good. Again, the key is careful attention to the distribution of powers among the different political players who are involved in initiating or blocking policy.

We also agree that the rigidity of presidentialism, created by the fixed term of office, can be a liability, sometimes a serious one. With the fixed term it is difficult to get rid of unpopular or inept presidents without the system's breaking down, and it is constitutionally barred in many countries to reelect a good president. However, there is no reason why a presidential system must prohibit reelection. Provisions against reelection have been introduced primarily to reduce the president's incentives to abuse executive powers to secure reelection. Despite the potential for abuse, reelection can be permitted, and we believe it should be in countries where reliable institutions safeguard elections from egregious manipulation by incumbents.

Even if reelection is permitted, we are still left with the rigidity of fixed term lengths. One way of mitigating this problem is to shorten the presidential term so that if presidents lose support dramatically, they will not be in office for as long a time. Therefore, we believe that a four year term is usually preferable to the longer mandates that are common in Latin America.

The argument about the flexibility of replacing cabinets in parliamentary systems is two-edged. In a parliamentary system the prime minister's party can replace its leader or a coalition partner can withdraw its support and usher in a change of government short of the coup that might be the only way to remove a president who lacks support. We agree with Linz that cabinet instability need not lead to regime instability and can offer a safety valve. Yet crises in many failed parliamentary systems, including Somalia and Thailand, have come about precisely because of the difficulty of sustaining viable cabinets. Presidentialism raises the threshold for removing an executive; opponents must either wait out the term or else countenance undemocratic rule. There may be cases when this higher threshold for government change is desirable, as it could provide more predictability and stability to the policymaking process than the frequent dismantling and reconstructing of cabinets that afflict some parliamentary systems.

Theoretically, the problem of fixed terms could be remedied without adopting parliamentarism by permitting under certain conditions the calling of early elections. One way is to allow either the head of government or the assembly majority to demand early elections for both branches, as is the case under newly adopted Israeli rules. Such provisions represent a deviation from presidentialism, which is defined by its fixed terms. Nevertheless, as long as one branch can not dismiss the other without standing for reelection itself, the principle of separation of powers is still retained to an extent not present in any variant of parliamentarism.

We take issue with Linz's assertion that presidentialism induces more of a winner-takes-all approach to politics than does parliamentarism. As we see it, parliamentary systems do not afford an advantage on this point. The degree to which democracies promote winner-take-all rules depends mostly on the electoral and party system and on the federal or unitary nature of the system. Parliamentary systems with disciplined parties and a majority party offer the fewest checks on executive power, and hence promote a winner-takes-all approach more than presidential systems.[10] In Great Britain, for example, in the last two decades a party has often won a decisive majority of parliamentary seats despite winning well under 50 percent of the votes. Notwithstanding its lack of a decisive margin in popular votes, the party can control the entire executive and the legislature for a protracted period of time. It can even use its dissolution power strategically to renew its mandate for another five years by calling a new election before its current term ends.

Because of the combination of disciplined parties, single member plurality electoral districts, and the prime minister's ability to dissolve the parliament, Westminster systems provide a very weak legislative check on the premier. In principle, the MPs of the governing party control the cabinet, but in practice they usually support their own party's legislative initiatives regardless of the merits of particular proposals because their electoral fates are closely tied with that of the party leadership. As a norm, a disciplined majority party leaves the executive virtually unconstrained between elections.[11] Here, more than in any presidential system, the winner takes all. Given the majority of a single party in parliament, it is unlikely that a no confidence vote would prevail, so there is little or no opposition to check the government. Early elections occur not as a flexible mechanism to rid the country of an ineffective government, but at the discretion of a ruling majority using its dissolution power strategically to renew its mandate for another five years by calling a new election before its current term ends.[12]

Presidentialism is predicated upon a system of checks and balances. Such checks and balances usually inhibit winner-takes-all tendencies; indeed, they are designed precisely to limit the possibility that the winner would take all. If it loses the presidency, a party or coalition may still control congress, allowing it to block some presidential initiatives. If the president's own legislative powers are reactive only (a veto, but no decree powers), an opposition-controlled congress can be the prime mover in legislating, as it is in the United States and Costa Rica, the two longest standing presidential democracies. Controlling congress is not the biggest prize, and it usually does not enable a party or coalition to dictate policy, but it allows the party or coalition to establish parameters within which policy is made. It can be a big prize in its own right if the presidency has relatively weak legislative powers.

Moreover, compared to Westminster parliamentary systems, most presidential democracies offer greater prospects of dividing the cabinet among several parties. This practice, which is essentially unknown among the Westminster parliamentary democracies, is common in multiparty presidential systems. To get elected, presidents need to assemble a broad interparty coalition, either for the first round (if a plurality format obtains) or for the second (if a two round, absolute majority format obtains). Generally, presidents allocate cabinet seats to parties other than their own in order to attract the support of these parties or, after elections, to reward them for such support. Dividing the cabinet in this manner allows losers in the presidential contest a piece of the pie. The norm in multiparty presidential systems is similar to that in multiparty parliamentary systems: a coalition governs, cabinet positions are divided among several parties, and the president typically must retain the support of these parties to govern effectively.

Thus, most parliamentary systems with single member district electoral systems have stronger winner-takes-all mechanisms than presidential systems. The combination of parliamentarism and a majority party specifically produces winner-takes-all results. This situation of extreme majoritarianism under parliamentarism is not uncommon; it is found throughout the Caribbean and some parts of the Third World.

In fact, outside western Europe all parliamentary systems that have been continuously democratic from 1972 to 1994 have been based on the Westminster model (see Table 10.1). Thus, Linz is not right when he states that an absolute majority of seats for one party does not occur often in parliamentary systems.[13] In presidential systems with single member plurality districts, the party that does not win the presidency can control congress, thereby providing an important check on executive power.

Linz's fourth argument, that the style of presidential politics is less favorable to democracy than the style of parliamentary politics, rests in part on his view that presidentialism induces a winner-takes-all logic. We have already expressed our skepticism about this claim. We agree that the predominant style of politics differs somewhat between presidential and parliamentary systems, but we would place greater emphasis on differences of style that stem from constitutional design and the nature of the party system.

Countries that have become independent from Britain or a British Commonwealth state since 1945: Jamaica, Mauritius, Nauru, Barbados, Malta, Botswana, Trinidad and Tobago, Cyprus, Israel.

Finally, we agree with Linz that presidentialism is more conducive than parliamentarism to the election of a political outsider as head of government and that this process can entail serious problems. But in presidential democracies that have more institutionalized party systems, the election of political outsiders is the exception. Costa Rica, Uruguay, Colombia, and Venezuela have not elected an outsider president in recent decades, unless one counts Rafael Caldera of Venezuela in his latest incarnation (1993). Argentina last elected an outsider president in 1945, when Peron had not yet built a party. In Chile political outsiders won the presidential campaigns of 1952 and 1958, but they were exceptions rather than the norm. The most notable recent cases of elections of political outsiders, Fernando Collor de Mello in Brazil (1989) and Alberto Fujimori in Peru (1990), owe much to the unraveling of the party systems in both countries and in Fujimori's case also to the majority run-off system that encouraged widespread party system fragmentation in the first round.

TABLE 10.1 INDEPENDENT COUNTRIES THAT WERE CONTINUOUSLY DEMOCRATIC, 1972–1994

Inc. level	Pop. size	Parliamentary	Presidential	Other
Low/lower-middle	Micro			
	Small	Jamaica	Costa Rica	
		Mauritius		
	Medium/Large		Colombia	
			Dominican Republic	
Upper-middle	Micro	Nauru		
		Barbados		
		Malta		
	Small	Botswana		
		Trinidad and Tobago		
	Medium/Large		Venezuela	
Upper	Micro	Luxembourg		Iceland
	Small	Ireland	Cyprus	
		New Zealand		
		Norway		
	Medium/Large	Australia	United States	Austria
		Belgium		Finland
		Canada		France
		Denmark		Switzerland
		Germany		
		Israel		
		Italy		
		Japan		
		Netherlands		
		Sweden		
		United Kingdom		

All regimes in the "other" column are premier-presidential, except for Switzerland.

ASSESSING THE RECORD OF PRESIDENTIALISM

Linz correctly states that most long established democracies have parliamentary systems. Presidentialism is poorly represented among long established democracies. This fact is apparent in Table 10.1, which lists countries that have a long, continuous democratic record according to the criteria of Freedom House.

Freedom House has been rating countries on a scale of 1 to 7 (with 1 being best) on political rights and civil rights since 1972. Table 10.1 lists all thirty-three countries that were continuously democratic from 1972 to 1994. We considered a country continuously democratic if it had an average score of 3 or better on political rights throughout this period.[14] Additionally, the scores for both political and civil rights needed to be 4 or better in every annual Freedom House survey for a country to be considered continuously democratic.

Of the thirty-three long established democracies, only six are presidential despite the prevalence of presidentialism in many parts of the globe. Twenty-two are parliamentary, and five fall into the "other" category. However, the superior record of parliamentarism is in part an artifact of where it has been implemented.

Table 10.1 provides information on three other issues that may play a role in a society's likelihood of sustaining democracy: income level, population size, and British colonial heritage. It is widely recognized that a relatively high income level is an important background condition for democracy.[15] In classifying countries by income levels, we followed the guidelines of the World Bank's *World Development Report 1993*: low is under $635 per capita GNP; lower middle is $636 to $2,555; upper middle is $2,556 to $7,910; and upper is above $7,911. We collapsed the bottom two categories. Table 10.2 summarizes the income categories of countries in Table 10.1.

Most of these long established democracies (twenty-eight of thirty-three) are in upper middle or upper income countries. But among the low to lower middle income countries there are actually more presidential (three) than parliamentary (two) systems. Fifteen of the parliamentary democracies are found in Europe or other high income countries such as Canada, Israel, and Japan. It is likely that these countries would have been democratic between 1972 and 1994 had they had presidential constitutions. So some of the success of parliamentary democracy is accidental: in part because of the evolution of constitutional monarchies into democracies, the region of the world that democratized and industrialized first is overwhelmingly populated with parliamentary systems.

Very small countries may have an advantage in democratic stability because they typically have relatively homogeneous populations in ethnic, religious, and linguistic terms, thereby attenuating potential sources of political conflict. We classified countries as micro (population under 500,000), small (500,000 to 5,000,000), and medium to large (over 5,000,000), using 1994 population data. Table 10.3 groups our thirty-three long established democracies by population size. Here, too, parliamentary systems enjoy an advantage. None of the five micronations with long established democracies has a presidential system.

The strong correlation between British colonial heritage and democracy has been widely recognized. Reasons for this association need not concern us here, but possibilities mentioned in the literature include the tendency to train civil servants, the governmental practices and institutions (which include but can not be reduced to parliamentarism) created by the British, and the lack of control of local landed elites over the colonial state.[16] Nine of the thirty-three long established democracies had British colonial experience. Among them, eight are parliamentary and one is presidential. Here, too, background conditions have been more favorable to parliamentary systems.

TABLE 10.2 INCOME LEVELS OF CONTINUOUS DEMOCRACIES, 1972–1994 (NUMBER OF COUNTRIES IN EACH CATEGORY)

Per Capita GNP in US $	Parliamentary	Presidential	Other
0–2555	2	3	0
2556–7910	5	1	0
over 7911	15	2	5
total	22	6	5

TABLE 10.3 POPULATION SIZE OF CONTINUOUS DEMOCRACIES, 1972–1994 (NUMBER OF COUNTRIES IN EACH CATEGORY)

Population	Parliamentary	Presidential	Other
Under 500,000	4	0	1
500,000 to 5,000,000	7	2	0
Over 5,000,000	11	4	5
total	22	6	5

TABLE 10.4 INDEPENDENT COUNTRIES THAT WERE DEMOCRATIC FOR AT LEAST TEN YEARS (BUT LESS THAN TWENTY-THREE) AS OF 1994

Inc. level	Pop. size	Parliamentary	Presidential	Other
Low/lower-middle	Micro	Belize (1981)		
		Dominica (1978)		
		Kiribati (1979)		
		St. Lucia (1979)		
		St. Vincent (1979)		
		Solomons (1978)		
		Tuvalu (1978)		
		Vanuatu (1980)		
	Small	Papua New Guinea (1975)		
	Medium/Large	India (1979)	Bolivia (1982)	
			Brazil (1985)	
			Ecuador (1979)	
			El Salvador (1985)	
			Honduras (1980)	
Middle	Micro	Antigua and Barbuda (1981)		
		Grenada (1985)		
		St. Kitts-Nevis (1983)		
	Small			
	Medium/Large	Greece (1974)	Argentina (1983)	Portugal[1] (1976)
			Uruguary (1985)	
Upper	Micro	Bahamas (1973)		
	Small			
	Medium/Large	Spain (1977)		

Numbers in parentheses give the date when the transition to democracy took place or the date of independence for former colonies that were not independent as of 1972.
Note: 1. Portugal has a premier-presidential system.
Countries that have become independent from Britain or a British Commonwealth state since 1945: Belize, Dominica, Kiribati, St. Lucia, St. Vincent, Solomons, Tuvalu, Vanuatu, Papua New Guinea, India, Antigua and Barbuda, Grenada, St. Kitts-Nevis, Bahamas.

It is not our purpose here to analyze the contributions of these factors to democracy; rather, we wanted to see if these factors correlated with regime type. If a background condition that is conducive to democracy is correlated with parliamentarism, then the superior record of parliamentarism may be more a product of the background condition than the regime type.

Table 10.4 shows twenty-four additional countries that had been continuously democratic by the same criteria used in Table 10.1 only for a shorter time period (at least ten years). Together, Tables 10.1 and 10.4 give us a complete look at contemporary democracies that have lasted at least ten years.

There are three striking facts about the additional countries in Table 10.4. First, they include a large number of microstates that became independent from Britain in the 1970s and 1980s, and all of them are parliamentary. All seven presidential democracies but only three of the sixteen parliamentary democracies are in medium to large countries (see Table 10.5). All sixteen of the democracies listed in Tables 10.1 and 10.4 with populations under one-half million (mostly island nations) are parliamentary, as are eight often democracies with populations between one-half and five million. In contrast, no presidential systems are in microstates, and many are in exceptionally large countries, such as Argentina, Brazil, and the United States.

Second, with Table 10.4 the number of presidential democracies increases substantially. Most are in the lower and lower middle income categories, and all are in Latin America. Table 10.6 summarizes the income status of the newer democracies listed in Table 10.4. Clearly, not all of parliamentarism's advantage stems from the advanced industrial states. Even in the lower to upper middle income categories, there are more parliamentary systems (twenty-one if we combine Tables 10.1 and 10.4, compared to eleven presidential systems). However, every one of the parliamentary democracies outside of the high income category is a former British colony. The only other democracies in these income categories are presidential, and all but Cyprus are in Latin America.

Thus, if the obstacles of lower income (or other factors not considered here) in Latin America continue to cause problems for the consolidation of democracy, the number of presidential breakdowns could be large once again in the future. More optimistically, if Latin American democracies achieve greater success in consolidating themselves this time around, the number of long established presidential democracies will grow substantially in the future.

Similarly, if British colonial heritage and small population size are conducive to democracy, parliamentarism has a built-in advantage simply because Britain colonized many small island territories. As a

TABLE 10.5 POPULATION SIZE OF CONTINUOUS DEMOCRACIES, 1985–1994 (NUMBER OF COUNTRIES IN EACH CATEGORY)

Population	Parliamentary	Presidential	Other
Under 500,000	12	0	0
500,000 to 5,000,000	1	0	0
Over 5,000,000	3	7	1
total	16	7	1

TABLE 10.6 INCOME LEVELS OF CONTINUOUS DEMOCRACIES, 1985–1994 (NUMBER OF COUNTRIES IN EACH CATEGORY)

Per Capita GNP in US$	Parliamentary	Presidential	Other
0–2555	10	0	0
2556–7910	4	5	1
Over 7911	2	2	0
total	16	7	1

rule, British colonies had local self-government, always on the parliamentary model, before independence.[17] Further, if other aspects of Latin American societies (such as extreme inequality across classes or regions) are inimical to stable democracy, then presidentialism has a built-in disadvantage.

In sum, presidentialism is more likely to be adopted in Latin America and in Africa than in other parts of the world, and these parts of the world have had more formidable obstacles to democracy regardless of the form of government. In contrast, parliamentarism has been the regime form of choice in most of Europe and in former British colonies (a large percentage of which are microstates), where conditions for democracy have generally been more favorable. Thus, the correlation between parliamentarism and democratic success is in part a product of where it has been implemented.

ADVANTAGES OF PRESIDENTIAL SYSTEMS

Presidential systems afford some attractive features that can be maximized through careful attention to constitutional design. These advantages partially offset the liabilities of presidentialism.

Greater Choice for Voters Competing claims to legitimacy are the flipside of one advantage. The direct election of the chief executive gives the voters two electoral choices instead of one—assuming unicameralism, for the sake of simplicity of argument. Having both executive and legislative elections gives voters a freer range of choices. Voters can support one party or candidate at the legislative level but another for the head of government.

Electoral Accountability and Identification Presidentialism affords some advantages for accountability and identifiability. Electoral accountability describes the degree and means by which elected policymakers are electorally responsible to citizens, while identifiability refers to voters' ability to make an informed choice prior to elections based on their ability to assess the likely range of postelection governments.

The more straightforward the connection between the choices made by the electorate at the ballot box and the expectations to which policymakers are held can be made, the greater electoral accountability is. For maximizing direct accountability between voters and elected officials, presidentialism is superior to parliamentarism in multiparty contexts because the chief executive is directly chosen by popular vote. Presidents (if eligible for reelection) or their parties can be judged by voters in subsequent elections. Having both an executive and an assembly allows the presidential election to be structured so as to maximize accountability and the assembly election so as to permit broad representation.

One objection to presidentialism's claim to superior electoral accountability is that in most presidential systems presidents may not be reelected immediately, if at all. The electoral incentive for the president to remain responsive to voters is weakened in these countries, and electoral accountability suffers. Bans on reelection are deficiencies of most presidential systems, but not of presidentialism as a regime type. Direct accountability to the electorate exists in some presidential systems, and it is always possible under presidential government. If, as is often the case, the constitution bans immediate reelection but allows subsequent reelection, presidents who aspire to regain their office have a strong incentive to be responsive to voters and thereby face a mechanism of electoral accountability. Only if presidents can never be reelected and will become secondary (or non) players in national and party politics after their terms are incentives for accountability via popular election dramatically weakened. Even where immediate reelection is banned, voters can still directly hold the president's party accountable.

Under parliamentarism, with a deeply fragmented party system the lack of direct elections for the executive inevitably weakens electoral accountability, for a citizen can not be sure how to vote for or against a particular potential head of government. In multiparty parliamentary systems, even if a citizen has a clear notion of which parties should be held responsible for the shortcomings of a government, it is often not clear whether voting for a certain party will increase the likelihood of excluding a party from the governing coalition. Governments often change between elections, and even after an election parties that lose seats are frequently invited to join governing coalitions.

Strom used the term "identifiability" to denote the degree to which the possible alternative executive-controlling coalitions were discernible to voters before an election.[18] Identifiability is high when voters can assess the competitors for control of the executive and can make a straightforward logical connection between their preferred candidate or party and their optimal vote. Identifiability is low when voters can not predict easily what the effect of their vote will be in terms of the composition of the executive, either because postelection negotiations will determine the nature of the executive, as occurs in multiparty parliamentary systems, or because a large field of contenders for a single office makes it difficult to discern where a vote may be "wasted" and whether voting for a "lesser-of-evils" might be an optimal strategy.

Strom's indicator of "identifiability" runs from 0 to 1, with 1 indicating that in 100 percent of a given nation's post–World War II elections the resulting government was identifiable as a likely result of the election at the time voters went to the polls. The average of the sample of parliamentary nations in Western Europe from 1945 until 1987 is .39, that is, most of the time voters could not know for which government they were voting. Yet under a parliamentary regime voting for an MP or a party list is the only way voters can influence the choice of executive. In some parliamentary systems, such as Belgium (.10), Israel (.14), and Italy (.12), a voter could rarely predict the impact of a vote in parliamentary elections on the formation of the executive. The formation of the executive is the result of parliamentary negotiations among many participants. Therefore, it is virtually impossible for the voter, to foresee how best to support a particular executive.

In presidential systems with a plurality one round format, identifiability is likely to approach 1.00 in most cases because voters cast ballots for the executive and the number of significant competitors is likely to be small. Systems in which majority run-off is used to elect the president are different, as three or more candidates may be regarded prior to the first round as serious contenders. When plurality is used to elect the president and when congressional and presidential elections are held concurrently, the norm is for "serious" competition to be restricted to two candidates even when there is multiparty competition in congressional elections. Especially when the electoral method is not majority run-off, presidentialism tends to encourage coalition building before elections, thus clarifying the basic policy options being presented to voters in executive elections and simplifying the voting calculus.

Linz has responded to the argument that presidentialism engenders greater identifiability by arguing that voters in most parliamentary systems can indeed identify the likely prime ministers and cabinet ministers.[19] By the time individuals approach leadership status, they are well known to voters. While his rejoinder is valid on its face, Linz is using the term "identifiability" in a different manner from Strom or us. He is speaking of voters' ability to identify personnel rather than government teams, which, as we have noted, may not be at all identifiable.

Congressional Independence in Legislative Matters Because representatives in a presidential system can act on legislation without worrying about immediate consequences for the survival of the government, issues can be considered on their merits rather than as matters of "confidence" in the leadership of the ruling party or coalition. In this specific sense, assembly members exercise independent judgment on legislative matters. Of course, this independence of the assembly from the executive can generate the problem of immobilism. This legislative independence is particularly problematic with highly fragmented multiparty systems, where presidents' parties typically are in the minority and legislative deadlock more easily ensues. However, where presidents enjoy substantial assembly support, congressional opposition to executive initiatives can promote consensus building and can avoid the passage of ill-considered legislation simply to prevent a crisis of confidence. The immobilism feared by presidentialism's detractors is the flip side of the checks and balances desired by the United States' founding fathers.

Congressional independence can encourage broad coalition building because even a majority president is not guaranteed the unreserved support of partisans in congress. In contrast, when a prime minister's party enjoys a majority, parliamentary systems exhibit highly majoritarian characteristics. Even a party with less than a majority of votes can rule almost unchecked if the electoral system "manufactures" a majority of seats for the party. The incentive not to jeopardize the survival of the government pressures members of parliament whose parties hold executive office not to buck cabinet directives. Thus, presidentialism is arguably better able than parliamentarism to combine the independence of legislators with an accountable and identifiable executive. If one desires the consensual and often painstaking task of coalition building to be undertaken on each major legislative initiative, rather than only on the formation of a government, then presidentialism has an advantage.

CONCLUSION

While we greatly admire Linz's seminal contribution and agree with parts of it, we believe that he understated the importance of differences among constitutional and institutional designs within the broad category of presidential systems and in doing so overstated the extent to which presidentialism is inherently flawed, regardless of constitutional and institutional arrangements. Presidential systems can be designed to function more effectively than they usually have. We have argued that providing the president with limited legislative power, encouraging the formation of parties that are reasonably disciplined in the legislature, and preventing extreme fragmentation of the party system enhance the viability of presidentialism. Linz clearly recognizes that not any kind of parliamentarism will do. We make the same point about presidentialism.

Under some conditions the perils of presidentialism can be attenuated, a point that Linz underplays. It is important to pay attention to factors that can mitigate the problems of presidentialism because it may be politically more feasible to modify presidential systems than to switch to parliamentary government.

We have also argued that presidentialism, particularly if it is carefully designed, has some advantages over parliamentarism. In our view, Linz does not sufficiently consider this point. Moreover, on one key issue—the alleged winner-takes-all nature of presidentialism—we question Linz's argument. The sum effect of our arguments is to call more attention to institutional combinations and constitutional designs and to suggest that the advantages of parliamentarism may not be as pronounced as Linz argued. Nevertheless, we share the consensus that his path-breaking article was one of the most important scholarly contributions of the past decade and deserves the ample attention among scholars and policymakers that it has already received.

NOTES

We are grateful to Michael Coppedge, Steve Levitsky, Arend Lijphart, Timothy Scully, and two anonymous reviewers for helpful criticisms of earlier drafts of this article.

1. We follow Lijphart's understanding of a Westminster (British) style democracy. Arend Lijphart, *Democracies: Patterns of Majoritarian and Consensus Government in Twenty-One Countries* (New Haven: Yale University Press, 1984), esp. pp. 1–20. For our purposes, the most important features of a Westminster democracy are single party majority cabinets, disciplined parties, something approaching a two party system in the legislature, and plurality single member electoral districts.

2. See Adam Przeworski et al., "What Makes Democracies Endure?," *Journal of Democracy*, 7 (January 1996), 39–55.

3. Matthew Shugart and John Carey, *Presidents and Assemblies: Constitutional Design and Electoral Dynamics* (New York: Cambridge University Press, 1992), ch. 2.

4. Juan J. Linz, "Presidential or Parliamentary Democracy: Does It Make a Difference?," in Juan J. Linz and Arturo Valenzuela, eds., *The Crisis of Presidential Democracy: The Latin American Evidence* (Baltimore: The Johns Hopkins University Press, 1994), p. 7; Juan J. Linz, "The Perils of Presidentialism," *Journal of Democracy*, 1 (Winter 1990).

5. Ibid., pp. 9–10.

6. Ibid, p. 18.

7. Linz, "Presidential or Parliamentary Democracy," p. 19.

8. Lijphart, ch. 6.

9. Linz, "Presidential or Parliamentary Democracy," pp. 47, 46.

10. Donald L. Horowitz, "Comparing Democratic Systems," *Journal of Democracy*, 1 (Fall 1990), 73–79; and George Tsebelis, "Decision Making in Political Systems: Veto Players in Presidentialism, Parliamentarism, Multicameralism and Multipartyism," *British Journal of Political Science*, 25 (1995), 289–325.

11. Assuming that the party remains united. If it does not, it may oust its leader and change the prime minister, as happened to Margaret Thatcher in Britain and Brian Mulroney in Canada. However, such intraparty leadership crises are the exception in majoritarian (Westminster) parliamentary systems.

12. A possible exception in Westminster systems is occasional minority government, which is more common than coalition government in such systems. Even then, the government is as likely to call early elections to attempt to convert its plurality into a majority as it is in response to a vote of no confidence.

13. Linz, "Presidential or Parliamentary Democracy," p. 15.

14. Using an average of 3 on both measures would have eliminated three countries (India and Colombia in Table 10.1 and Vanuatu in Table 10.3) that we consider basically democratic but that have had problems with protecting civil rights, partly because of a fight against violent groups.

15. Robert A. Dahl, *Polyarchy: Participation and Opposition* (New Haven: Yale University Press, 1973), pp. 62–80; Kenneth Bollen, "Political Democracy and the Timing of Development," *American Sociological Review,* 44 (August 1979), 572–87; Larry Diamond, "Economic Development and Democracy Reconsidered," in Gary Marks and Larry Diamond, eds., *Reexamining Democracy: Essays in Honor of Seymour Martin Lipset* (Newbury Park: SAGE, 1992), pp. 93–139; Seymour Martin Lipset et al., "A Comparative Analysis of the Social Requisites of Democracy," *International Social Science Journal,* 45 (May 1993), 155–75.

16. Larry Diamond, "Introduction: Persistence, Erosion, Breakdown, and Renewal," in Larry Diamond, Juan J. Linz, and Seymour Martin Lipset, eds., *Democracy in Developing Countries: Asia* (Boulder: Lynne Rienner, 1989); Myron Weiner, "Empirical Democratic Theory," in Myron Weiner and Ergun Özbudun, eds., *Competitive Elections in Developing Countries* (Washington, D.C.: American Enterprise Institute, 1987); Dietrich Rueschemeyer, Evelyne Huber Stephens, and John D. Stephens, *Capitalist Development and Democracy* (Chicago: University of Chicago Press, 1992).

17. Some British colonies later adopted presidential systems and did not become (or remain) democratic. However, in many cases democracy was ended (if it ever got underway) by a coup carried out by the prime minister and his associates. Not presidential democracies, but parliamentary proto-democracies broke down. Typical was the Seychelles. The failure of most of these countries to evolve back into democracy can not be attributed to presidentialism.

18. Kaare Strom, *Minority Government and Majority Rule* (Cambridge: Cambridge University Press, 1990).

19. Linz, "Presidential or Parliamentary Democracy," pp. 10–14.

AREND LIJPHART

10.2 CONSTITUTIONAL DESIGN FOR DIVIDED SOCIETIES

Arend Lijphart has written extensively on the organization of government, often advocating for what he calls a "consociational model." This model involves crafting political institutions that guarantee power sharing among different identity groups in divided societies. For instance, in countries divided by ethnicity, religion, or language—such as Switzerland or Lebanon—political elites and the groups they represent may conclude that guaranteeing each group some access to political power is conducive to stability in the long run. Although political actors may be inclined to grab as much power as they can in the short term, they may have reasons to develop power-sharing institutions such as an executive branch that rotates or apportions power among the groups in the society. In this piece, note how Lijphart speaks specifically to ways of ensuring power sharing within the executive, but also links it to issues such as legislative elections and federalism (which separates power between central governments and lower levels). The issues raised by Lijphart are not limited to the executive branch, but rather cut across a wide range of questions about constitutional design or how political institutions are organized in a society. With respect to the executive branch specifically, Lijphart considers arrangements that are designed to prevent any one group—especially a group that can secure a majority—from exercising too much power. In considering Lijphart, we might think in concrete terms about where there is violent conflict in the world today and whether a "consociationalist" might have a proposal for how to engineer a political design to reduce conflict. You can then ask yourself whether you would agree with such a proposal, why (or why not), and what other conditions you think would be needed to make consociationalism work (or not).

Over the past half-century, democratic constitutional design has undergone a sea change. After the Second World War, newly independent countries tended simply to copy the basic constitutional rules of their former colonial masters, without seriously considering alternatives. Today, constitution writers choose more deliberately among a wide array of constitutional models, with various advantages and disadvantages. While at first glance this appears to be a beneficial development, it has actually been a mixed blessing: Since they now have to deal with more alternatives than they can readily handle, constitution writers risk making ill-advised decisions. In my opinion, scholarly experts can be more helpful to constitution writers by formulating specific recommendations and guidelines than by overwhelming those who must make the decision with a barrage of possibilities and options.

This essay presents a set of such recommendations, focusing in particular on the constitutional needs of countries with deep ethnic and other cleavages. In such deeply divided societies the interests and demands of communal groups can be accommodated only by the establishment of power sharing, and my recommendations will indicate as precisely as possible which particular power-sharing rules and institutions are optimal and why. (Such rules and

Lijphart, Arend. 2004. "Constitutional Design for Divided Societies," *Journal of Democracy* 15(2): 96–109.

institutions may be useful in less intense forms in many other societies as well.)

Most experts on divided societies and constitutional engineering broadly agree that deep societal divisions pose a grave problem for democracy, and that it is therefore generally more difficult to establish and maintain democratic government in divided than in homogeneous countries. The experts also agree that the problem of ethnic and other deep divisions is greater in countries that are not yet democratic or fully democratic than in well-established democracies, and that such divisions present a major obstacle to democratization in the twenty-first century. On these two points, scholarly agreement appears to be universal.

A third point of broad, if not absolute, agreement is that the successful establishment of democratic government in divided societies requires two key elements: power sharing and group autonomy. Power sharing denotes the participation of representatives of all significant communal groups in political decision making, especially at the executive level; group autonomy means that these groups have authority to run their own internal affairs, especially in the areas of education and culture. These two characteristics are the primary attributes of the kind of democratic system that is often referred to as power-sharing democracy or, to use a technical political-science term, "consociational" democracy.[1] A host of scholars have analyzed the central role of these two features and are sympathetic to their adoption by divided societies.[2] But agreement extends far beyond the consociational school. A good example is Ted Robert Gurr, who in *Minorities at Risk: A Global View of Ethnopolitical Conflicts* clearly does not take his inspiration from consociational theory (in fact, he barely mentions it), but based on massive empirical analysis reaches the conclusion that the interests and demands of communal groups can usually be accommodated "by some combination of the policies and institutions of *autonomy* and *power sharing*."[3]

The consensus on the importance of power sharing has recently been exemplified by commentators' reactions to the creation of the Governing Council in Iraq: The Council has been criticized on a variety of grounds, but no one has questioned its broadly representative composition. The strength of the power-sharing model has also been confirmed by its frequent practical applications. Long before scholars began analyzing the phenomenon of power-sharing democracy in the 1960s, politicians and constitution writers had designed power-sharing solutions for the problems of their divided societies (for example, in Austria, Canada, Colombia, Cyprus, India, Lebanon, Malaysia, the Netherlands, and Switzerland). Political scientists merely discovered what political practitioners had repeatedly—and independently of both academic experts and one another—invented years earlier.

CRITICS OF POWER SHARING

The power-sharing model has received a great deal of criticism since it became a topic of scholarly discourse three decades ago. Some critics have argued that power-sharing democracy is not ideally democratic or effective; others have focused on methodological and measurement issues.[4] But it is important to note that very few critics have presented serious alternatives to the power-sharing model. One exception can be found in the early critique by Brian Barry, who in the case of Northern Ireland recommended "cooperation without cooptation"—straightforward majority rule in which both majority and minority would simply promise to behave moderately.[5] Barry's proposal would have meant that Northern Ireland's Protestant majority, however moderate, would be in power permanently, and that the Catholic minority would always play the role of the "loyal" opposition. Applied to the case of the Iraqi Governing Council, Barry's alternative to power sharing would call for a Council composed mainly or exclusively of moderate members of the Shi'ite majority, with the excluded Sunnis and Kurds in opposition. This is a primitive solution to ethnic tensions and extremism, and it is naïve to expect minorities condemned to permanent opposition to remain loyal, moderate, and constructive. Barry's suggestion therefore cannot be—and, in practice, has not been—a serious alternative to power sharing.

The only other approach that has attracted considerable attention is Donald L. Horowitz's proposal to design various electoral mechanisms (especially the use of the "alternative vote" or "instant runoff") that would encourage the election of moderate representatives.[6] It resembles Barry's proposal in that it aims for moderation rather than broad representation in the legislature and the executive, except that Horowitz tries to devise a method to induce the moderation that Barry simply hopes for. If applied to the Iraqi Governing Council, Horowitz's model would generate a body consisting mainly of members of the Shi'ite majority, with the proviso that most of these representatives would be chosen in such a way that they would be sympathetic to the interests of the Sunni and Kurdish minorities. It is hard to imagine that, in the long run, the two minorities would be satisfied with this kind of moderate Shi'ite representation, instead of representation by members of their own communities. And it is equally hard to imagine that Kurdish and Sunni members of a broadly representative constituent assembly would ever agree to a constitution that would set up such a system.

Horowitz's alternative-vote proposal suffers from several other weaknesses, but it is not necessary to analyze them in this article.[7] The main point that is relevant here is that it has found almost no support from either academic experts or constitution writers. Its sole, and only partial, practical application to legislative elections in an ethnically divided society was the short-lived and ill-fated Fijian constitutional system, which tried to combine the alternative vote with power-sharing; it was adopted in 1999 and collapsed in 2000.[8] With all due respect to the originality of his ideas and the enthusiasm with which he has defended them, Horowitz's arguments do not seem to have sparked a great deal of assent or emulation.[9]

"ONE SIZE FITS ALL"?

In sum, power sharing has proven to be the only democratic model that appears to have much chance of being adopted in divided societies, which in turn makes it unhelpful to ask constitution writers to contemplate alternatives to it. More than enough potential confusion and distraction are already inherent in the consideration of the many alternatives *within* power sharing. Contrary to Horowitz's claim that power-sharing democracy is a crude "one size fits all" model,[10] the power-sharing systems adopted prior to 1960 (cited earlier), as well as more recent cases (such as Belgium, Bosnia, Czechoslovakia, Northern Ireland, and South Africa), show enormous variation. For example, broad representation in the executive

has been achieved by a constitutional requirement that it be composed of equal numbers of the two major ethnolinguistic groups (Belgium); by granting all parties with a minimum of 5 percent of the legislative seats the right to be represented in the cabinet (South Africa, 1994–99); by the equal representation of the two main parties in the cabinet and an alternation between the two parties in the presidency (Colombia, 1958–64); and by permanently earmarking the presidency for one group and the prime ministership for another (Lebanon).

All of these options are not equally advantageous, however, and do not work equally well in practice, because the relative success of a power-sharing system is contingent upon the specific mechanisms devised to yield the broad representation that constitutes its core. In fact, the biggest failures of power-sharing systems, as in Cyprus in 1963 and Lebanon in 1975, must be attributed not to the lack of sufficient power sharing but to constitution writers' choice of unsatisfactory rules and institutions.

These failures highlight the way in which scholarly experts can help constitution writers by developing recommendations regarding power-sharing rules and institutions. In this sense, Horowitz's "one size fits all" charge should serve as an inspiration to try to specify the optimal form of power sharing. While the power-sharing model should be adapted according to the particular features of the country at hand, it is not true that *everything* depends on these individual characteristics. In the following sections I outline nine areas of constitutional choice and provide my recommendations in each area. These constitute a "one size" power-sharing model that offers the best fit for most divided societies regardless of their individual circumstances and characteristics.

1. *The legislative electoral system.* The most important choice facing constitution writers is that of a legislative electoral system, for which the three broad categories are proportional representation (PR), majoritarian systems, and intermediate systems. For divided societies, ensuring the election of a broadly representative legislature should be the crucial consideration, and PR is undoubtedly the optimal way of doing so.

Within the category of majoritarian systems, a good case could be made for Horowitz's alternative-vote proposal, which I agree is superior to both the plurality method and the two-ballot majority runoff.[11] Nevertheless, there is a scholarly consensus against majoritarian systems in divided societies. As Larry Diamond explains:

> If any generalization about institutional design is sustainable . . . it is that majoritarian systems are ill-advised for countries with deep ethnic, regional, religious, or other emotional and polarizing divisions. Where cleavage groups are sharply defined and group identities (and intergroup insecurities and suspicions) deeply felt, the overriding imperative is to avoid broad and indefinite exclusion from power of any significant group.[12]

The intermediate category can be subdivided further into semi-proportional systems, "mixed" systems, and finally, majoritarian systems that offer guaranteed representation to particular minorities. Semi-proportional systems—like the cumulative and limited vote (which have been primarily used at the state and local levels in the United States) and the single nontransferable vote (used in Japan until 1993)[13]—may be able to yield minority representation, but never as accurately and consistently as PR. Unlike these rare semi-proportional systems, mixed systems have become quite popular since the early 1990s.[14] In some of the mixed systems (such as Germany's and New Zealand's) the PR component overrides the plurality component, and these should therefore be regarded not as mixed but as PR systems. To the extent that the PR component is not, or is only partly, compensatory (as in Japan, Hungary, and Italy), the results will necessarily be less than fully proportional—and minority representation less accurate and secure. Plurality combined with guaranteed representation for specified minorities (as in India and Lebanon) necessarily entails the potentially invidious determination of which groups are entitled to guaranteed representation and which are not. In contrast, the beauty of PR is that in addition to producing proportionality and minority representation, it treats all groups—ethnic, racial, religious, or even noncommunal groups—in a completely equal and evenhanded fashion. Why deviate from full PR at all?

2. *Guidelines within PR.* Once the choice is narrowed down to PR, constitution writers need to settle on a particular type within that system. PR is still a very broad category, which spans a vast spectrum of complex possibilities and alternatives. How can the options be narrowed further? I recommend that highest priority be given to the selection of a PR system that is simple to understand and operate—a criterion that is especially important for new democracies. From that simplicity criterion, several desiderata can be derived: a high, but not necessarily perfect, degree of proportionality; multimember districts that are not too large, in order to avoid creating too much distance between voters and their representatives; list PR, in which parties present lists of candidates to the voters, instead of the rarely used single transferable vote, in which voters have to rank order individual candidates; and closed or almost closed lists, in which voters mainly choose parties instead of individual candidates within the list. List PR with closed lists can encourage the formation and maintenance of strong and cohesive political parties.

One attractive model along these lines is the list-PR system used in Denmark, which has 17 districts that elect an average of eight representatives each from partly open lists. The districts are small enough for minority parties with more than 8 percent of the vote to stand a good chance of being elected.[15] In addition to the 135 representatives elected in these districts, there are 40 national compensatory seats that are apportioned to parties (with a minimum of 2 percent of the national vote) in a way that aims to maximize overall national proportionality.[16] The Danish model is advantageous for divided societies, because the compensatory seats plus the low 2 percent threshold give small minorities that are not geographically concentrated a reasonable chance to be represented in the national legislature. While I favor the idea of maximizing proportionality, however, this system does to some extent detract from the goal of keeping the electoral system as simple and transparent as possible. Moreover, national compensatory seats obviously make little sense in those divided societies where nation-wide parties have not yet developed.

3. *Parliamentary or presidential government.* The next important decision facing constitution writers is whether to set up a parliamentary, presidential, or semi-presidential form of government. In countries with deep ethnic and other cleavages, the choice should be based on the different systems' relative potential for power sharing in the executive. As the cabinet in a parliamentary system is a collegial decision-making body—as opposed to the presidential one-person executive with a purely advisory cabinet—it offers the optimal setting for forming a broad power-sharing executive. A second advantage of parliamentary systems is that there is no need for presidential elections, which are necessarily majoritarian in nature. As Juan Linz states in his well-known critique of presidential government, "perhaps the most important implication of presidentialism is that it introduces a strong element of zero-sum game into democratic politics with rules that tend toward a 'winner-take-all' outcome."[17] Presidential election campaigns also encourage the politics of personality and overshadow the politics of competing parties and party programs. In representative democracy, parties provide the vital link between voters and the government, and in divided societies they are crucial in voicing the interests of communal groups. Seymour Martin Lipset has recently emphasized this point again by calling political parties "indispensable" in democracies and by recalling E. E. Schattschneider's famous pronouncement that "modern democracy is unthinkable save in terms of parties."[18]

Two further problems of presidentialism emphasized by Linz are frequent executive–legislative stalemates and the rigidity of presidential terms of office. Stalemates are likely to occur because president and legislature can both claim the democratic legitimacy of being popularly elected, but the president and the majority of the legislature may belong to different parties or may have divergent preferences even if they belong to the same party. The rigidity inherent in presidentialism is that presidents are elected for fixed periods that often cannot be extended because of term limits, and that cannot easily be shortened even if the president proves to be incompetent, becomes seriously ill, or is beset by scandals of various kinds. Parliamentary systems, with their provisions for votes of confidence, snap elections, and so on, do not suffer from this problem.

Semi-presidential systems represent only a slight improvement over pure presidentialism. Although there can be considerable power sharing among president, prime minister, and cabinet, the zero-sum nature of presidential elections remains. Semi-presidential systems actually make it possible for the president to be even more powerful than in most pure presidential systems. In France, the best-known example of semi-presidentialism, the president usually exercises predominant power; the 1962–74 and 1981–86 periods have even been called "hyperpresidential" phases.[19] The stalemate problem is partly solved in semi-presidential systems by making it possible for the system to shift from a mainly presidential to a mainly parliamentary mode if the president loses the support of his party or governing coalition in the legislature. In the Latin American presidential democracies, constitutional reformers have often advocated semi-presidential instead of parliamentary government, but only for reasons of convenience: A change to parliamentarism seems too big a step in countries with strong presidentialist traditions. While such traditional and sentimental constraints may have to be taken into account in constitutional negotiations, parliamentary government should be the general guideline for constitution writers in divided societies.

There is a strong scholarly consensus in favor of parliamentary government. In the extensive literature on this subject, the relatively few critics have questioned only parts of the pro-parliamentary consensus. Pointing to the case of U.S. presidentialism, for instance, they have noted that the stalemate problem has not been as serious as Linz and others have alleged—without, however, challenging the validity of the other charges against presidential government.[20]

4. *Power sharing in the executive.* The collegial cabinets in parliamentary systems facilitate the

formation of power-sharing executives, but they do not by themselves guarantee that power sharing will be instituted. Belgium and South Africa exemplify the two principal methods of doing so. In Belgium, the constitution stipulates that the cabinet must comprise equal numbers of Dutch-speakers and French-speakers. The disadvantage of this approach is that it requires specifying the groups entitled to a share in power, and hence the same discriminatory choices inherent in electoral systems with guaranteed representation for particular minorities. In South Africa there was so much disagreement and controversy about racial and ethnic classifications that these could not be used as a basis for arranging executive power sharing in the 1994 interim constitution. Instead, power sharing was mandated in terms of political parties: Any party, ethnic or not, with a minimum of 5 percent of the seats in parliament was granted the right to participate in the cabinet on a proportional basis.[21] For similar situations in other countries, the South African solution provides an attractive model. But when there are no fundamental disagreements about specifying the ethnic groups entitled to a share of cabinet power, the Belgian model has two important advantages. First, it allows for power sharing without mandating a grand coalition of all significant parties and therefore without eliminating significant partisan opposition in parliament. Second, it allows for slight deviation from strictly proportional power sharing by giving some overrepresentation to the smaller groups, which may be desirable in countries where an ethnic majority faces one or more ethnic minority groups.

5. *Cabinet stability.* Constitution writers may worry about one potential problem of parliamentary systems: The fact that cabinets depend on majority support in parliament and can be dismissed by parliamentary votes of no-confidence may lead to cabinet instability—and, as a result, regime instability. The weight of this problem should not be overestimated; the vast majority of stable democracies have parliamentary rather than presidential or semi-presidential forms of government.[22] Moreover, the position of cabinets vis-à-vis legislatures can be strengthened by constitutional provisions designed to this effect. One such provision is the constructive vote of no confidence, adopted in the 1949 constitution of West Germany, which stipulates that the prime minister (chancellor) can be dismissed by parliament only if a new prime minister is elected simultaneously. This eliminates the risk of a cabinet being voted out of office by a "negative" legislative majority that is unable to form an alternative cabinet. Spain and Papua New Guinea have adopted similar requirements for a constructive vote of no confidence. The disadvantage of this provision is that it may create an executive that cannot be dismissed by parliament but does not have a parliamentary majority to pass its legislative program—the same kind of stalemate that plagues presidential systems. A suggested solution to this potential problem was included in the 1958 constitution of the French Fifth Republic in the form of a provision that the cabinet has the right to make its legislative proposals matters of confidence, and these proposals are adopted automatically unless an absolute majority of the legislature votes to dismiss the cabinet. No constitution has yet tried to combine the German and French rules, but such a combination could undoubtedly give strong protection to cabinets and their legislative effectiveness—without depriving the parliamentary majority of its fundamental right to dismiss the cabinet and replace it with a new one in which parliament has greater confidence.

6. *Selecting the head of state.* In parliamentary systems, the prime minister usually serves only as head of government, while a constitutional monarch or a mainly ceremonial president occupies the position of head of state. Assuming that no monarch is available, constitution writers need to decide how the president should be chosen. My advice is twofold: to make sure that the presidency will be a primarily ceremonial office with very limited political power, and not to elect the president by popular vote. Popular election provides democratic legitimacy and, especially in

combination with more than minimal powers specified in the constitution, can tempt presidents to become active political participants—potentially transforming the parliamentary system into a semi-presidential one. The preferable alternative is election by parliament.

A particularly attractive model was the constitutional amendment proposed as part of changing the Australian parliamentary system from a monarchy to a republic, which specified that the new president would be appointed on the joint nomination of the prime minister and the leader of the opposition, and confirmed by a two-thirds majority of a joint session of the two houses of parliament. The idea behind the two-thirds rule was to encourage the selection of a president who would be nonpartisan and nonpolitical. (Australian voters defeated the entire proposal in a 1999 referendum mainly because a majority of the pro-republicans strongly—and unwisely—preferred the popular election of the president.) In my opinion, the best solution is the South African system of not having a separate head of state at all: There the president is in fact mainly a prime minister, subject to parliamentary confidence, who simultaneously serves as head of state.

7. *Federalism and decentralization.* For divided societies with geographically concentrated communal groups, a federal system is undoubtedly an excellent way to provide autonomy for these groups. My specific recommendation regards the second (federal) legislative chamber that is usually provided for in federal systems. This is often a politically powerful chamber in which less populous units of the federation are overrepresented (consider, for example, the United States Senate, which gives two seats to tiny Wyoming as well as gigantic California). For parliamentary systems, two legislative chambers with equal, or substantially equal, powers and different compositions is not a workable arrangement: It makes too difficult the forming of cabinets that have the confidence of both chambers, as the 1975 Australian constitutional crisis showed: The opposition-controlled Senate refused to pass the budget in an attempt to force the cabinet's

resignation, although the cabinet continued to have the solid backing of the House of Representatives. Moreover, a high degree of smaller-unit overrepresentation in the federal chamber violates the democratic principle of "one person, one vote." In this respect, the German and Indian federal models are more attractive than the American, Swiss, and Australian ones.

Generally, it is advisable that the federation be relatively decentralized and that its component units (states or provinces) be relatively small—both to increase the prospects that each unit will be relatively homogeneous and to avoid dominance by large states on the federal level. Beyond this, a great many decisions need to be made regarding details that will vary from country to country (such as exactly where the state boundaries should be drawn). Experts have no clear advice to offer on how much decentralization is desirable within the federation, and there is no consensus among them as to whether the American, Canadian, Indian, Australian, German, Swiss, or Austrian model is most worthy of being emulated.

8. *Nonterritorial autonomy.* In divided societies where the communal groups are not geographically concentrated, autonomy can also be arranged on a nonterritorial basis. Where there are significant religious divisions, for example, the different religious groups are often intent on maintaining control of their own schools. A solution that has worked well in India, Belgium, and the Netherlands is to provide educational autonomy by giving equal state financial support to all schools, public and private, as long as basic educational standards are met. While this goes against the principle of separating church and state, it allows for the state to be completely neutral in matters of education.

9. *Power sharing beyond the cabinet and parliament.* In divided societies, broad representation of all communal groups is essential not only in cabinets and parliaments, but also in the civil service, judiciary, police, and military. This aim can be achieved by instituting ethnic or religious quotas, but these do not necessarily have to be rigid. For example, instead of mandating

that a particular group be given exactly 20 percent representation, a more flexible rule could specify a target of 15 to 25 percent. I have found, however, that such quotas are often unnecessary; it is sufficient to have an explicit constitutional provision in favor of the general objective of broad representation and to rely on the power-sharing cabinet and the proportionally constituted parliament for the practical implementation of this goal.

OTHER ISSUES

As far as several other potentially contentious issues are concerned, my advice would be to start out with the modal patterns found in the world's established democracies, such as a two-thirds majority requirement for amending the constitution (with possibly a higher threshold for amending minority rights and autonomy), a size of the lower house of the legislature that is approximately the cube root of the country's population size[23] (which means that a country with about 25 million inhabitants, such as Iraq, "should" have a lower house of about 140 representatives), and legislative terms of four years.

While approval by referendum can provide the necessary democratic legitimacy for a newly drafted constitution, I recommend a constitutional provision to limit the number of referenda. One main form of referendum entails the right to draft legislation and constitutional amendments by popular initiative and to force a direct popular vote on such propositions. This is a blunt majoritarian instrument that may well be used against minorities. On the other hand, the Swiss example has shown that a referendum called by a small minority of voters to challenge a law passed by the majority of the elected representatives may have the desirable effect of boosting power sharing. Even if the effort fails, it forces the majority to pay the cost of a referendum campaign; hence the potential calling of a referendum by a minority is a strong stimulus for the majority to be heedful of minority views. Nevertheless, my recommendation is for extreme caution with regard to referenda, and the fact that frequent referenda occur in only three democracies—the United States, Switzerland, and, especially since about 1980, Italy—underscores this guideline.

Constitution writers will have to resolve many other issues that I have not mentioned, and on which I do not have specific recommendations: for example, the protection of civil rights, whether to set up a special constitutional court, and how to make a constitutional or supreme court a forceful protector of the constitution and of civil rights without making it too interventionist and intrusive. And as constitution writers face the difficult and time-consuming task of resolving these issues, it is all the more important that experts not burden or distract them with lengthy discussions on the relative advantages and disadvantages of flawed alternatives like presidentialism and non-PR systems.

I am not arguing that constitution writers should adopt all my recommendations without *any* examination of various alternatives. I recognize that the interests and agendas of particular parties and politicians may make them consider other alternatives, that a country's history and traditions will influence those who must draft its basic law, and that professional advice is almost always—and very wisely—sought from more than one constitutional expert. Even so, I would contend that my recommendations are not merely based on my own preferences, but on a strong scholarly consensus and solid empirical evidence, and that at the very least they should form a starting point in constitutional negotiations.

NOTES

I am grateful to the Bellagio Study and Conference Center of the Rockefeller Foundation for offering me the opportunity to work on this project while I was a resident of the Center in May–June 2003, and to Roberto Belloni, Torbjörn Bergman, Joseph H. Brooks, Florian Bieber, Jorgen Elklit, Svante Ersson, John McGarry, Brendan O'Leary, Mogens N. Pedersen, Hugh B. Price, and Timothy D. Sisk for their valuable advice. Some of the ideas presented in this article were first published in my chapter "The Wave of Power-Sharing Democracy," in Andrew Reynolds, ed., *The Architecture of Democracy: Constitutional Design, Conflict Management, and Democracy* (Oxford: Oxford University Press, 2002), 37–54; and in *Democracy in the Twenty-First Century: Can We Be Optimistic?*

Uhlenbeck Lecture No. 18 (Wassenaar: Netherlands Institute for Advanced Study, 2000).

1. The secondary characteristics are proportionality, especially in legislative elections (in order to ensure a broadly representative legislature—similar to the aim of effecting a broadly constituted executive) and a minority veto on the most vital issues that affect the rights and autonomy of minorities.

2. Some of these scholars are Dirk Berg-Schlosser, William T. Bluhm, Laurence J. Boulle, Hans Daalder, Edward Dew, Robert H. Dix, Alan Dowty, Jonathan Fraenkel, Hermann Giliomee, Theodor Hahf, Jonathan Hartlyn, Martin O. Heisler, Luc Huyse, Thomas A. Koelble, Gerhard Lehmbruch, Franz Lehner, W. Arthur Lewis, Val R. Lorwin, Diane K. Mauzy, John McGarry, Kenneth D. McRae, Antoine N. Messarra, R.S. Milne, S.J.R. Noel, Eric A. Nordlinger, Brendan O'Leary, G. Bingham Powell, Jr., Andrew Reynolds, F. van Zyl Slabbert, Jürg Steiner, Albert J. Venter, Karl von Vorys, David Welsh, and Steven B, Wolinetz. Their most important writings on the subject (if published before the mid-1980s) can be found in the bibliography of Arend Lijphart, *Power-Sharing in South Africa* (Berkeley, Calif.: Institute of International Studies, University of California, 1985), 137–71.

3. Ted Robert Gurr, *Minorities at Risk: A Global View of Ethnopolitical Conflicts* (Washington, D.C.: U.S. Institute of Peace Press, 1993), 292, italics added.

4. I have responded to these criticisms at length elsewhere. See especially Lijphart, "The Wave of Power-Sharing Democracy," in Andrew Reynolds, ed., *The Architecture of Democracy: Constitutional Design, Conflict Management, and Democracy* (Oxford: Oxford University Press, 2002), 40–47; and Lijphart, *Power-Sharing in South Africa*, 83–117.

5. Brian Barry, "The Consociational Model and Its Dangers," *European Journal of Political Research* 3 (December 1975): 406.

6. Donald L. Horowitz, *A Democratic South Africa? Constitutional Engineering in a Divided Society* (Berkeley, Calif.: University of California Press, 1991), 188–203; and "Electoral Systems: A Primer for Decision Makers," *Journal of Democracy* 14 (October 2003): 122–23. In alternative-vote systems, voters are asked to rank order the candidates. If a candidate receives an absolute majority of first preferences, he or she is elected; if not, the weakest candidate is eliminated, and the ballots are redistributed according to second preferences. This process continues until one of the candidates receives a majority of the votes.

7. For a detailed critique, see Lijphart, "The Alternative Vote: A Realistic Alternative for South Africa?" *Politikon* 18 (June 1991): 9–101; and Lijphart, "Multiethnic Democracy," in Seymour Martin Lipset, ed., *The Encyclopedia of Democracy* (Washington, D.C.: Congressional Quarterly, 1995), 863–64.

8. The alternative vote was also used for the 1982 and 1988 presidential elections in Sri Lanka and for the 2000 presidential elections in the Republika Srpska in Bosnia. Nigeria has used a similar system favored by Horowitz (requiring a plurality plus at least 25 percent of the votes in at least two-thirds of the states for victory) for its presidential elections. The third and sixth guidelines that I describe in the present essay recommend a parliamentary system without a popularly elected president—and therefore no direct presidential elections at all.

9. Benjamin Reilly has come to Horowitz's defense, but only with significant qualifications; for instance, Reilly dissents from Horowitz's advocacy of the alternative vote for the key case of South Africa. See Reilly, *Democracy in Divided Societies: Electoral Engineering for Conflict Management* (Cambridge: Cambridge University Press, 2001). Andreas Wimmer advocates the alternative vote for Iraq in "Democracy and Ethno-Religious Conflict in Iraq," *Survival* 45 (Winter 2003–2004): 111–34.

10. Donald L. Horowitz, "Constitutional Design: Proposals versus Processes," in Andrew Reynolds, ed., *The Architecture of Democracy*, 25.

11. In contrast with plurality, the alternative vote (instant runoff) ensures that the winning candidate has been elected by a majority of the voters,

and it does so more accurately than the majority-runoff method and without the need for two rounds of voting.

12. Larry Diamond, *Developing Democracy: Toward Consolidation* (Baltimore: Johns Hopkins University Press, 1999), 104.

13. All three of these systems use multimember election districts. The cumulative vote resembles multi-member district plurality in which each voter has as many votes as there are seats in a district, but, unlike plurality, the voter is allowed to cumulate his or her vote on one or a few of the candidates. In limited-vote systems, voters have fewer votes than the number of district seats. The single nontransferable vote is a special case of the limited vote in which the number of votes cast by each voter is reduced to one.

14. See Matthew Soberg Shugart and Martin P. Wattenberg, eds., *Mixed-Member Electoral Systems: The Best of Both Worlds?* (Oxford: Oxford University Press, 2001).

15. This estimate is based on the T = 75% (M + 1) equation—in which T is the effective threshold and M the number of representatives elected in a district—suggested by Rein Taagepera; see Arend Lijphart, "Electoral Systems," in Seymour Martin Lipset, ed., *Encyclopedia of Democracy*, 417. There is considerable variation around the average of 8 representatives per district, but 9 of the 17 districts are very close to this average, with between 6 and 9 seats. The open-list rules are very complex and, in my opinion, make the lists too open. In addition to the 175 seats described here, Greenland and the Faeroe Islands elect two representatives each. I should also point out that my recommendation of the Danish model entails a bit of a paradox: It is a system that is very suitable for ethnically and religiously divided countries, although Denmark itself happens to be one of the most homogeneous countries in the world.

16. Parties below the 2 percent threshold may still benefit from the compensatory seats if certain other requirements are met, such as winning at least one district seat.

17. Juan J. Linz, "Presidential or Parliamentary Democracy: Does It Make a Difference?" in Juan J. Linz and Arturo Valenzuela, eds., *The Failure of Presidential Democracy* (Baltimore: Johns Hopkins University Press, 1994), 18.

18. Seymour Martin Lipset, "The Indispensability of Political Parties," *Journal of Democracy* 11 (January 2000): 48–55; E. E. Schattschneider, *Party Government* (New York: Rinehart, 1942), 1.

19. John T. S. Keeler and Martin A. Schain, "Institutions, Political Poker, and Regime Evolution in France," in Kurt von Mettenheim, ed., *Presidential Institutions and Democratic Politics: Comparing Regional and National Contexts* (Baltimore: Johns Hopkins University Press, 1997), 95–97. Horowitz favors a president elected by the alternative vote or a similar vote-pooling method, but in other respects his president does not differ from presidents in pure presidential systems; see his *A Democratic South Africa?*, 205–14.

20. Scholars have also indicated methods to minimize the problem of presidential–legislative deadlock—for instance, by holding presidential and legislative elections concurrently and electing the president by plurality instead of the more usual majority-runoff method. Such measures may indeed be able to ameliorate the problem to some extent, but cannot solve it entirely. See Matthew Soberg Shugart and John M. Carey, *Presidents and Assemblies: Constitutional Design and Electoral Dynamics* (Cambridge: Cambridge University Press, 1992); and Mark P. Jones, *Electoral Laws and the Survival of Presidential Democracies* (Notre Dame: University of Notre Dame Press, 1995).

21. The 1998 Good Friday Agreement provides for a similar power-sharing executive for Northern Ireland.

22. In my comparative study of the world's stable democracies, defined as countries that were continuously democratic from 1977 to 1996 (and had populations greater than 250,000), 30 of the 36 stable democracies had parliamentary systems. See Lijphart, *Patterns of Democracy: Government Forms and Performance in Thirty-Six Countries* (New Haven: Yale University Press, 1999).

23. This pattern was discovered by Rein Taagepera; see his "The Size of National Assemblies," *Social Science Research* 1 (December 1972): 385–40.

ROBERT JACKSON AND CARL ROSBERG

10.3 PERSONAL RULE
Theory and Practice in Africa

When considering how politics operates in different countries, we must take care to consider the question in a broadly comparative sense, and Jackson and Rosberg help us by considering the functioning of the executive in Africa. This piece was written in the 1980s, but still has salience for parts of Africa today and, indeed, for countries in other parts of the world where politics is not characterized by strong and well-functioning institutions. The paper elucidates the phenomenon of personal rule, which looks to the authors almost like a sort of monarchy. They argue that it is a form of politics monopolized by a small handful of elites, specifically one ruler. In many ways, the form of executive control here is the antithesis of the well-institutionalized system of checks and balances on executive power that are found in most modern democracies. In elaborating their theory, they discuss the practices of personalistic rule and ask whether it is likely to endure or, conversely, whether politics is likely to become more institutionalized over time in Africa. One possibility for this reading would be to select an African country for study and see whether a brief political history is available that will enable you to determine whether personal rule has endured in your case over the three decades since the publication of this article.

When I say "politics," . . . it is not a question of the *art of governing the State for the public welfare in the general framework of laws and regulations*. It is question of politician politics: the struggles of clans—not even [ideological] tendencies—to place well oneself, one's relatives, and one's clients in the *cursus honorum*, that is the race for preferments.

—*Leopold Sedar Senghor*

THE IMAGE OF PERSONAL RULE

Personal rule has been a compelling facet of politics at least since the time of Machiavelli. It is the image not of a ruler but of a type of rulership.[1] Personal rule is a dynamic world of political will and activity that is shaped less by institutions or impersonal social forces than by personal authorities and power; it is a world, therefore, of uncertainty, suspicion, rumor, agitation, intrigue, and sometimes fear, as well as of stratagem, diplomacy, conspiracy, dependency, reward, and threat. In other words, personal rule is a distinctive type of political system in which the rivalries and struggles of powerful and wilful men, rather than impersonal institutions, ideologies, public policies, or class interests, are fundamental in shaping political life. Indicators of personal regimes in sub-Saharan Africa are coups, plots, factionalism, purges, rehabilitations, clientelism, corruption, succession maneuvers, and similar activities which have been significant and recurring features of political life during the past two decades. Furthermore, there is no indication that such activities are about to decline in political importance. Whereas these features are usually seen as merely the defects of an otherwise established political order—whether capitalist, socialist, military, civilian, or whatever—we are inclined to regard them much more as the integral elements of a distinctive political system to which we have given the term "personal rule."[2]

Jackson, Robert and Carl Rosberg. 1984. "Personal Rule: Theory and Practice in Africa," *Comparative Politics* 16(4): 421–442.

It is ironic that in the twentieth century a novel form of "presidential monarchy" has appeared in many countries of the Third World. The irony consists in the contradiction of what is perhaps the major tendency in the evolution of the modern state during the past several centuries: the transformation of political legitimacy from the authority of kings to the mandate of the people.[3] What has happened in the Third World and especially in Africa was not expected to happen. When colonial rule was rapidly coming to an end in the 1950s and 1960s, it was hoped that independent African countries would adopt some form of democracy, be it liberal-democratic or socialist or some indigenous variant.[4] Instead of democracy, however, various forms of autocracy appeared.

Fifteen years ago, scholarly writings on the New States . . . were full of discussions of parties, parliaments, and elections. A great deal seemed to turn on whether these institutions were viable in the Third World and what adjustments in them . . . might prove necessary to make them so. Today, nothing in those writings seems more passe, relic of a different time. Marcos, Suharto, Ne Win, al-Bakr, Sadat, Gaddafi, Boumedienne, Hassan, Houphouet, Amin, Mobutu may be doing their countries good or harm, promoting their peoples' advantage or oppressing them, but they are not guiding them to democracy. They are autocrats, and it is as autocrats, and not as preludes to liberalism (or, for that matter, to totalitarianism), that they, and the governments they dominate, must be judged and understood.[5]

There is a related methodological irony in this unforeseen historical development of presidential monarchy. At about the same time that students of politics were discarding the traditional tools of political theory, biography, and history that had proved of some value in the study of statecraft and were adopting the modern tools of sociology—thereby acknowledging that modern politics are mass, social politics in which governments interact with national populations or large classes or groups within them—political systems appeared in the Third World in which social politics were practically nonexistent and ruling politicians were remarkably free from the constraints of democratic institutions or social demands.[6] Therefore, despite the crucial importance of sociological explanations of politics—in which society is at least as important as the state; quantity or political weight counts for more than quality or political skill; impersonal social process is more significant than individual political practice; and little room, if any, is left for the analysis of rulership or leadership as such—in the Third World, and certainly in Africa, we continue to encounter prominent politicians who act as if the principle of popular legitimacy had not been invented and national societies did not exist.

Political sociologists are justified in their criticisms of the "great man" theories of some historians, and we do not wish to suggest either that rulers are wholly independent actors or that biography is the most suitable approach in studying rulership. But the "little man" and certainly the "invisible man" theories of social politics can also be criticized, especially in those societies, as in Africa, where the image of the "big man" is deeply embedded in the political culture and politics is often a vertical network of personal, patron–client relations.[7] If we are to deal with rulership in sociological terms—that is, in theoretical and not merely descriptive terms—we are obliged to regard political life as "a dialectic of power and structure, a web of possibilities for agents, whose nature is both active and structured, to make choices and pursue strategies within given limits, which in consequence expand and contract over time."[8] Therefore, in terms of methodology the image of personal rule draws our attention not only to rulers and their activities, but also to the political networks, circumstances, and predicaments in which they are entangled and from which they can never entirely extricate themselves.

Political images can often be sharpened by the careful selection of terms with which they are designated. If the terms "social politics" or "public politics" are apt for designating the political life of nation-states in which a popular mandate is the principle of legitimacy and politics is a "sociological activity . . . of preserving a community grown too complicated for either tradition alone or pure arbitrary rule to preserve it without the undue use of coercion," then perhaps Bernard Crick's term "palace politics" captures the largely personal, private, and elitist characteristics of political life in the autocracies that have emerged in Africa and elsewhere during the past several decades.[9] In this essay we present a theory of personal rule and its integral practices in independent African countries.

A THEORY OF PERSONAL RULE

In the introductory remarks we have hinted at the main characteristics of personal rule. To understand its distinctive character we must first set aside some central sociological assumptions about the nature of the modern state, including the following: (1) the modern state's legitimacy ultimately rests upon, and its government interacts on a continuous basis with, an underlying national society and its constituent groups and classes; (2) the relations of society and government concern primarily group demands or class interests, ideal or material, calling forth public laws and policies which in turn provoke policies which in turn provoke new demands and so forth; (3) the institutional and policy biases of government reflect the power and privilege of classes and groups in society; and (4) the activity of government policymaking is at once social (in attempting to address societal demands) and technical (in attempting to apply the knowledge of the policy sciences, including especially economics, to deal with policymaking problems).[10]

The assumptions of personal rule are quite different, and an instructive way to approach them is to recall the concept of rulership in Machiavelli's masterpiece, *The Prince*.[11] Machiavelli assumes that the Prince is a self-interested, rational actor who desires to acquire and hold a principality. But the principality is not a national society of mobilizable groups and classes whose interests command the attention of the Prince; and the Prince is not primarily concerned to promote the welfare and conciliate the conflicts of an underlying national society upon which his legitimacy depends. Rather, the principality is a political entity which is acted upon—ruled—by the Prince and may be capable of occasional political reaction—such as rebellion—but it is not integrated with the government and has few political interests other than to be left unexploited and in peace. "As long as he does not rob the great majority of their property or their honour, they remain content. He then has to contend only with the restlessness of a few, and that can be dealt with easily and in a variety of ways."[12]

Personal rule is an elitist political system composed of the privileged and powerful few in which the many are usually unmobilized, unorganized, and therefore relatively powerless to command the attention and action of government. The system favors the ruler and his allies and clients: its essential activity involves gaining access to a personal regime's patronage or displacing the ruler and perhaps his regime and installing another. As an elitist system, personal politics concerns cooperation and rivalry among leaders and factions within the political class only and not among broader social classes or groups.[13] Consequently, the political process in personal regimes is primarily asocial insofar as it is largely indifferent to the interests, concerns, and problems of social strata beyond the political class. Personal politics is not public politics: it is not a "sociological activity" in Crick's meaning of the term, nor is personal governance significantly technical in practice. Although it may employ technocrats and proclaim socioeconomic plans and policies—including national development plans—its concrete activities are rarely guided by such impersonal criteria. Rather, government and administration are likely to be highly personal and permeated with patronage and corruption.

Figure 10.1 identifies personal rule in relation to three familiar models of politics—constitutional rule, multi-party democracy, and one party democracy—and in terms of the distinctions between elite and mass politics, on the one hand, and monopolistic and pluralistic politics, on the other.

As already indicated, personal rule is a form of elite politics. However, it does not rest upon established constitutional rules and practices (including traditions) that effectively regulate the activities of the political class—especially the ruler—and is therefore distinguished from constitutional rule. Established and effective political institutions are largely absent from regimes of personal rule. In defining a political "institution" we follow Rawls.

> By an institution I shall understand a public system of rules which defines offices and positions with their rights and duties, powers and immunities, and the like. These rules specify certain forms of action as permissible, others as forbidden. . . . An

	Monopolistic Politics	Pluralistic Politics
Elite Politics	Personal Rule	Constitutional Rule
Mass Politics	Single Party Democracy	Multi-party Democracy

FIGURE 10.1

institution may be thought of in two ways: first as an abstract . . . system of rules; and second, as the . . . [realized] actions specified by these rules. . . . A person taking part in an [real] institution knows what the rules demand of him and of the others. He also knows that the others know this and that they know that he knows this, and so on.[14]

Most contemporary Black African states have abstract political institutions, but they do not have them in the concrete, or realized, sense specified by Rawls. Institutional rules do not effectively govern the behavior of most leaders most of the time. Individuals do not perform political actions in an institutionally required way in the awareness that others expect it and that risks and difficulties would arise if they failed to do so. Political conduct is governed by the awareness that constitutional rules or administrative regulations can, and probably ought, to be evaded. The real norms that affect political and administrative action are not rooted in state institutions and organizations but in friendship, kinship, factional alliance, ethnic fellowship—that is, norms that are frequently at odds with the rules of state institutions and organizations and which tend to undermine them rather than reinforce or support them.[15] Political action in personal regimes is thus strongly affected by expediency and necessity. What an actor can do is more strongly affected by the resources at his disposal than by the office he occupies. What an actor must do is more strongly affected by particularistic norms—that is,

obligations and attachments to friends, kin, factional allies, clansmen, ethnic fellows—than by state rules and regulations.

Personal rule is a form of monopolistic rather than pluralistic politics. Personal regimes consist primarily of the internecine struggles of powerful individuals, civilian or military, for power and place and secondarily of the actions of outsiders who desire to enter the monopoly, influence members within it, or displace it with their own personal regime. Politics tend to be closed to public participation and observation and even to be secretive—hence "palace politics." Personal rivalry within the monopoly for the ruler's favor gives rise to clandestine political activities, while challenges to the regime from without can often assume the character of political conspiracy since general political liberties are usually withheld by law or are not allowed in practice.[16] Political stability in all regimes depends ultimately on the ability and willingness of powerful men to regulate their conflicts and forebear from using violence, but, as pointed out, leaders in personal regimes do not have legitimate and effective institutions to assist them in this endeavor. Furthermore, personal regimes are neither highly organized nor effective monopolies that penetrate and control society. They are a type of authoritarianism, autocratic or oligarchic but not bureaucratic. African regimes rarely have the character of bureaucratic authoritarianism, which is a prominent feature of many Latin American countries,[17] and only a few have come close to being single-party democracies.

Personal politics involve almost exclusively the activities of "big men" who are a considerable distance from the ordinary people. As indicated, "the people," "the public," "the nation," "the national interest," "public opinion," and similar collectivities are abstractions that have little effect on political life. Individuals figure very prominently in politics while social collectivities figure very little. Personal politics express the conflicting appetites, desires, ambitions, aversions, hopes, and fears of a relatively small number of leaders who seek access to the resources and honors of the state and care little about questions of political ideology or public policy except as these affect their political situation and that of their associates, clients, and supporters. In African autocracies there are no elections to be won by actively promoting social or economic programs. Where elections are occasionally held, they are typically intraparty affairs in which big men—current or aspiring—vie with each other in promising benefits for local electorates; there is little to be gained from advocating national programs that reflect ideological viewpoints or require technical expertise.[18] Indeed, if there is an official ideology, it is not likely to be a subject of political debate.

SOME CHARACTERISTIC PRACTICES OF PERSONAL REGIMES IN SUB-SAHARAN AFRICA

Among the most important practices in personal regimes are conspiracy, factional politics and clientelism, corruption, purges and rehabilitations, and succession maneuvers. We do not regard these as the necessary "functions" of personal political systems, but we do regard them as the kinds of political behavior one might expect in countries in which formal institutions are ineffective. Not all of these practices contribute to political order, stability, and civility; in fact, some of them, such as conspiracy, are harmful to the provision of such political goods. However, taken together, they appear to accurately characterize the kind of politics to which politicians in the great majority of sub-Saharan countries have resorted over the past two decades.

These practices have been widely noted—and often deplored—in the study of contemporary African politics. Indeed, they have been the subjects of considerable commentary, and an already sizable literature deals with some of them, such as coups and corruption. However (as we have noted), as yet there has been little inclination to view them as integral elements of a distinctive type of political system, personal rule. Instead, they have usually been viewed from the rationalist perspective as shortcomings in the endeavor to establish modern social politics and policy government in Black Africa. As indicated, we are inclined to regard such practices as the very essence of political and governmental conduct in most countries south of the Sahara. While it is evident that most contemporary African states have not acquired the rationalist characteristics of social politics and policy government, they nevertheless have become something more than can adequately be described in terms merely of the absence of such characteristics. The political system of personal rule and its distinctive practices are the reality of what they have become.

CONDITIONS OF PERSONAL RULE

In conclusion, let us explore two questions. First, what conditions appear to be the most important in encouraging and sustaining the practices of personal governance in sub-Saharan Africa? All political systems are provisional; they are all built on sand, not on the rock of Gibraltar. Personal rule is no exception. It is dependent on the inclination and ability of people, particularly politicians, to understand and utilize its practices. Second, since personal rule is the converse of institutional government and since political institutions in the great majority of sub-Saharan countries are present formally as abstract rules but not substantively as effective restraints on political behavior, it is important to ask what conditions discourage the realization of concrete political institutions in these countries and what the prospects are of changing them.

Neither of these questions is easy to answer, and we have the space to offer only some suggestions as to the direction in which we believe answers might be found. It is somewhat easier to conjecture an answer to the first question because the practices of personal rule are essentially pragmatic and can be understood in terms of a rational politician who must operate in a country in which state institutions are merely forms and duties other than those of his office compete with self-interest as a claim to his conduct. In other words, the practices of personal rule are the sort in which a rational politician would engage if he found himself in a world in which the official rules and regulations of the state were not well understood or appreciated and were poorly enforced, and if he knew that others were aware of this and were not likely to conform to the rules in their own conduct. In such circumstances political and administrative conduct would be shaped by a combination of expediency and whatever obligations were owed to family, friends, allies, clansmen, tribesmen, and any other moral community to which an actor belonged. Most African politicians and administrators find themselves in more or less such circumstances.

At the center of any answer to the second question there must be an explanation as to why personal, arbitrary rule has not been widely condemned as political misconduct in sub-Saharan Africa. Why has personal rule not become sufficiently established as misconduct to effectively discourage the kinds of practices that we have reviewed in this essay and to encourage the realization of institutional rules and regulations? These questions are difficult to formulate, let alone answer, but if an answer is to be found, it will probably be connected with the widely acknowledged arbitrariness of most African states and its political and sociological roots.

In political terms, almost every sub-Saharan African state was the successor of a geographically identical, preexisting colonial entity. From the perspective of the European colonial powers a colony was not arbitrary. It was an extension of the sovereignty of the metropole, and its officials were subject to imperial policy and colonial regulations; far from being arbitrary rulers, colonial officials were considered responsible servants. However, from the perspective of subject Africans, colonial government was essentially arbitrary. It was imposed from outside and worked in accordance with alien and unfamiliar rules and regulations, in disregard, often in ignorance, of indigenous institutions. The British in effect acknowledged that colonial rule was arbitrary in their practice of indirect rule, but even indirect rule could not cancel the fundamental political reality that colonialism was essentially the imposition of government by an external, superior power.

The African states were arbitrary entities in sociological terms as well. It is well known that the size and shape of almost every sub-Saharan country was the result of boundaries arbitrarily drawn by colonialists who rarely acknowledged, or were not even aware of, the preexisting boundaries of traditional African societies. (Even if they had been aware of such boundaries, the traditional political systems were usually too small to be viable as separate colonial entities.) Consequently, there were no territory-wide traditional institutions that could be resurrected at independence and used to identify legitimate conduct and condemn misconduct by a state's new rulers. (It must be acknowledged that even if such institutions had existed, most of the new leaders, who were usually intellectuals, would very likely have been as hostile to them as they were to the traditional institutions that existed at the subnational level. However, in some cases such institutions might have been sufficiently strong to command the reluctant compliance of the new rulers.)

Sociologically, most African countries are multiethnic societies with populations that are sharply divided along racial, cultural, linguistic, religious, and similar lines of cleavage. Most are composed of several and some of many different traditional societies, each with distinctive institutions to which members of other traditional societies are not only detached but also disinclined, if not actually opposed. Multiethnic societies are not confined to sub-Saharan Africa, but they appear to be a characteristic of most new states. Roth suggests that

> one of the major reasons for the predominance of personal rulership over legal-rational legislation and administration in the new states seems to lie in a social, cultural, and political homogeneity of such magnitude that a more or less viable complementary and countervailing pluralism of the Western type, with its strong but not exclusive components of universality, does not appear feasible.[19]

Roth sees the divided plural society as an impediment to the realization of modern, rational-legal institutions. But it is no less an impediment to the realization of traditional institutions or any other kind of general political institutions. All institutions that are realized in conduct must rest upon some kind of general understanding and acknowledgment by most of the people who live under them.

The attempts by the colonial authorities—very belated in the case of Belgium and Spain, and scarcely undertaken in the case of Portugal—to introduce modern political institutions as an essential stage of decolonization were not successful owing to the political and sociological impediments we have noted. British parliamentarianism and French republicanism were as alien to most Africans as colonial bureaucracy. Indeed, they were probably more difficult to understand since they are inherently less pragmatic and rational and more exotic and ritualistic in their rules and offices. It is easy for the forms and rites of (for example) parliamentary government to be mistaken for its substance, which is what happened not infrequently in some African countries before the forms too were discarded or fundamentally altered to suit the interests of those in power.

Imported European political institutions had no greater inherent capacity to overcome the centrifugal effects of sub-Saharan Africa's multiethnic societies than did any other institutions. The British were sensitive to this sociological problem, as indicated by their preference both for bicameral legislatures (with upper chambers to give representation to traditional rulers) and for federalism. Nonetheless, the checkered history of federalism in Nigeria, where politicians have striven to make it work, suggests that federalism, like any other national political institution, requires a commitment of the parts for the whole, of the whole for the parts, and of each part for each other part. In no sub-Saharan country to date has federalism proved to be a workable and durable institutional arrangement, although the Nigerians must be given full marks for persevering in efforts to make it a reality and not merely a formality in their political life. In short, the borrowing of institutional forms from abroad—even the most widely admired models—in no way guarantees their substantiation in political conduct.

In regard to changing the conditions that presently encourage personal rule and obstruct the realization of institutional government in sub-Saharan Africa, there seems to be very little prospect, if any, of altering the political and sociological conditions mentioned above, at least in the short and medium terms. Such fundamental change is a long-term historical process. But if institutional development is to occur in the foreseeable future, it will very likely begin at the top and not at the bottom of African political systems. It is not inconceivable—and there is some evidence to support the contention—that rulers and other leading politicians might begin to value the limited security of official tenure more highly than the uncertain possession of personal power and, beyond this, the greater stability and order attainable only under institutional government. Periodic attempts to reconstitutionalize some states which had been ruled by soldiers, as in Ghana (1969 and 1979), Nigeria (1979), and Upper Volta (1978), are evidence. However, wholesale attempts at constitutional engineering hold out less promise of success owing precisely to their very ambitious character: they literally ask leaders and their followers to transform their political attitudes and behavior overnight. Institutionalization in politics is a transformation involving piecemeal social engineering and time.[20]

A less improbable course of political institutionalization in sub-Saharan Africa is the incremental steps taken by some rulers and their associates to find acceptable and workable procedures to organize political competition and to prevent violence and other political evils. Constitutional rules of succession tend to be accepted for preventive reasons: leaders who face the prospect of a succession may fear the threat of uncertainty, dislocation, violence, bloodshed, and other hazards more than they desire the prize of becoming the successor or his associate. This "negative" political rationality, which we usually associate with the political theory of Hobbes is also evident in electoral institutionalization in sub-Saharan Africa.[21] For example, in Senegal under the prudent and judicious rule of Senghor the one-party system was liberalized in the late 1970s to allow other parties to compete openly with Senghor's party, but only under labels approved by the regime with Senghor's party preempting the most popular "democratic socialist" label. This experiment in "guided" democratization apparently reflected Senghor's conviction that a de facto one-party system—such as had existed from 1963 to 1976 in Senegal, with its numerous and various ethnic and ideological tendencies—invited conspiratorial politics and threatened national stability.[22] But the success of Senegalese liberalization to date probably must be attributed to Senghor and to his successor, President Abdou Diouf, who in 1981 accepted the challenge of governing a multi-party democracy.

These African political experiments suggest the following conclusions, one practical and the other theoretical. First, democracy can be promoted by inventive political practitioners as well as by favorable socioeconomic processes, and the former do not necessarily have to wait upon the latter. Statesmen are to political development what entrepreneurs are to economic development. Indeed, they may be more important insofar as political development is less dependent on material resources and consists essentially in appropriate inclinations and conduct. Political development may be within the reach of countries such as those in sub-Saharan Africa, which are as yet too poor in resources to achieve much in the way of substantial economic development. Second, politics can therefore be understood theoretically as a (constructive and destructive) human activity as well as an impersonal process, and can be studied profitably in terms of choice, will, action, opposition, obligation, compulsion, persuasion, possession, and other elements of individual and intersocial volition, that is, in terms of neo-classical political theory.

NOTES

1. Only a few recent political science studies have centered upon rulership. Two important general statements are Dankwart A. Rustow, ed., *Philosophers and Kings: Studies in Leadership* (New York: George Braziller, 1970), and W. Howard Wriggins, *The Ruler's Imperative: Strategies for Political Survival in Asia and Africa* (New York: Columbia University Press, 1969). Among the more important African studies are Henry Bretton, *The Rise and Fall of Kwame Nkrumah: A Study of Personal Rule in Africa* (New York: Praeger, 1966); John R. Cartwright, *Political Leadership in Sierra Leone*

(Toronto: University of Toronto Press, 1978); Rene Lemarchand, ed., *African Kingships in Perspective: Political Change and Modernization in Monarchical Settings* (London: Frank Cass & Co., 1977); Christopher Clapham, "Imperial Leadership in Ethiopia," *African Affairs*, 68 (April 1969); and Ali A. Mazrui, "Leadership in Africa: Obote of Uganda," *International Journal*, 25 (Summer 1970), 538–64.

2. This essay attempts to develop the theory of personal rule contained in our study entitled *Personal Rule in Black Africa: Prince, Autocrat, Prophet, Tyrant* (Berkeley: University of California Press, 1982).

3. This is the central theme of Reinhard Bendix's *Kings or People: Power and the Mandate to Rule* (Berkeley: University of California Press, 1980).

4. The contrasting ideas in these variants of contemporary democracy are succinctly set out in C. B. Macpherson, *The Real World of Democracy* (Toronto: Canadian Broadcasting Corporation, 1965).

5. Clifford Geertz, "The Judging of Nations: Some Comments on the Assessment of Regimes in the New States," *European Journal of Sociology*, 18 (1977), 252. While autocracy was not expected to prevail against democracy, it was sometimes recognized as a possibility given the magnitude of the problems of state-building facing African leaders: "The problems of stabilization and modernization that African leaders face are equivalent in magnitude to past crises in the West. It is from this perspective that we must view prospects for democracy in Africa. . . . Many developing countries have had to rely upon autocratic leadership when nascent democratic institutions have been unable to govern effectively." Carl G. Rosberg, Jr., "Democracy and the New African States," in Kenneth Kirkwood, ed., *African Affairs* (London: Chatto & Windus, 1963), No. 2, p. 53.

6. Very influential in the basic change of academic orientation was Gabriel A. Almond and James S. Coleman, eds., *The Politics of the Developing Areas* (Princeton: Princeton University Press, 1960).

7. See Robert M. Price, "Politics and Culture in Contemporary Ghana: The Big Man-Small Boy Syndrome," *Journal of African Studies*, 1 (Summer 1974), 173–204; Richard Sandbrook, "Patrons, Clients, and Factions: New Dimensions of Conflict Analysis in Africa," *Canadian Journal of Political Science*, 5 (March 1972), 104–19; and Rene Lemarchand, "Political Clientelism and Ethnicity in Tropical Africa: Competing Solidarities in Nation-Building," *American Political Science Review*, 66 (March 1972), 68–90.

8. Steven Lukes, *Essays in Social Theory* (New York: Columbia University Press, 1977), p. 29.

9. Bernard Crick, *In Defence of Politics* (Harmondsworth: Penguin Books, 1964), pp. 20–24.

10. This model is captured brilliantly in historical terms by Gianfranco Poggi, *The Development of the Modern State: A Sociological Introduction* (Stanford: Stanford University Press, 1978), chs. 5 and 6.

11. Niccolo Macchiavelli, *The Prince*, trans. by George Bull (Harmondsworth: Penguin Books, 1961).

12. Ibid., p. 102.

13. Robert H. Jackson, "Political Stratification in Tropical Africa," *Canadian Journal of African Studies*, 7 (1973), 381–400.

14. John Rawls, *A Theory of Justice* (Cambridge, Mass.: Harvard University Press, 1971), pp. 55–56.

15. The literature on political clientelism is useful in understanding personal rule, although there is a tendency to emphasize structure at the expense of actors and behavior and therefore to understate the uncertainty, instability, and choice inherent in personal rule. For an outstanding volume of recent essays, see Steffan W. Schmidt, James C. Scott, Carl Landé, and Laura Guasti, eds., *Friends, Followers and Factions: A Reader in Political Clientelism* (Berkeley: University of California Press, 1977); also see a comprehensive review in S. N. Eisenstadt and Louis Romigu, "Patron-Client Relations as a Model of Structuring Social Exchange," *Comparative Studies in Society and History: An International Quarterly*, 22 (January 1980), 42–77.

16. Machiavelli devotes a long discourse to conspiracies in *The Discourses*, ed. by Bernard Crick (Harmondsworth: Penguin Books, 1976), pp. 398–424.

17. See David Collier, ed., *The New Authoritarianism in Latin America* (Princeton: Princeton University Press, 1979), and Guillermo A. O'Donnell, *Modernization and Bureaucratic-Authoritarianism: Studies of South American Politics* (Berkeley: Institute of International Studies, 1973).

18. A tendency toward the making of promises to local electorates has been noted even in socialist Tanzania, where personalism and specifically such practices as patronage, nepotism, and corruption are officially condemned. See Goran Hyden and Colin Leys, "Elections and Politics in Single-Party Systems: The Case of Kenya and Tanzania," *British Journal of Political Science*. 2 (October 1972), 416.

19. Guenther Roth, "Personal Rulership, Patrimonialism, Empire-Building in New States," *World Politics*, 20 (January 1968), 203.

20. Huntington, pp. 13–14; and Karl Popper, *The Open Society and Its Enemies*, vol. I (Princeton: Princeton University Press, 1967).

21. Thomas Hobbes, *Leviathan*, ed. by Michael Oakeshott (New York: Collier Books, 1962), chs. 13 and 17.

22. See a seminal article by William J. Foltz, "Social Structure and Political Behavior of Senegalese Elites," in Schmidt et al., eds., pp. 242–49.

CHAPTER 11

POLITICAL PARTIES, PARTY SYSTEMS, AND INTEREST GROUPS

Political life is as much about the collective actions of groups as it is about the choices of individuals. In fact, much of political life can be understood in terms of the ways individuals cooperate and collaborate to act collectively. The significant political institutions worthy of study are not just the branches of government made up of individual elected officials, but also include the political organizations to which citizens and other political actors belong, such as interest groups and political parties. The actions, structures, and functioning of parties and interest groups often shape the decisions made by legislators (Chapter 9) and executives (Chapter 10). As we discuss the operation of these groups, we also move toward a broad understanding of many different types of group action, including social movements and other forms of contentious (and even revolutionary) politics, as discussed in Chapter 12. In terms sometimes used by political scientists, these organizations *aggregate* interests by bringing together people with common interests or views, and they help *articulate* or define interests by acting as institutions that condition what people think and how they behave.

The two selections here reflect some of the basic issues in the organization of political groups. The first is from James Madison, often known as the father of the American constitution. In the drafting and passage of the Constitution, Madison developed a theory of political life that later greatly informed the perspective known as pluralism. In essence, one of Madison's key insights in Federalist Paper No. 10 is that people will always have differences and form groups (which he called factions, but which can be thought of as related to today's parties and interest groups) and that the best approach in a system of government is to allow these groups to proliferate and compete with one another. Following Madison, we include a reading on why different political party systems emerge. Party systems are different configurations of how many (and which) parties have meaningful leverage in a given country. A single-party system is quite different from a two-party system, whereas a two-party system in turn implies a different political environment from a country with multiple (say, three or more) parties. Pradeep Chhibber and Ken Kollman offer an overview of leading arguments about the causes of party systems—with an emphasis on social cleavages and electoral rules—and then compare several countries to develop their own argument about the differences between national, regional, and local parties.

These selections relate to one another. In reading each selection, you might also consider its implication for the functioning of democracy. The number and size of interest groups in a country (and how these groups are organized) and the number and size of parties in a country (and how they are organized in a party system) will have significant implications for how politics operates. By the functioning of democracy, we mean both whether democracy is likely to persist and whether democracy is likely to generate positive outcomes for citizens. In other words, would we expect democracy to serve "the common good" best with certain types and numbers of parties and interest groups? While open competition between groups is often assumed to go hand in hand with a high quality of democracy, might one also imagine circumstances where an excessive number of groups hinders effective decision making?

JAMES MADISON

11.1 THE SAME SUBJECT CONTINUED

The Utility of the Union as a Safeguard against Domestic Faction and Insurrection

The *Federalist Papers* were written by James Madison, Alexander Hamilton, and John Jay as essays in support of the ratification of the U.S. Constitution. In these papers, the authors laid out the logic for the American governmental system predicated on the separation of powers between different branches and levels of government. In the midst of arguing for a specific constitutional design, Madison's writing highlighted the logic of allowing different "factions" to compete in the political arena. Madison was no fan of faction itself, but the paper alludes to faction being an inevitable consequence of a people having liberty, and he concludes that the best way to manage divisions between people is to allow them the freedom to join groups as they see fit. More recent statements by 19th- and 20th-century scholars have formalized this line of thinking as "pluralism," or the idea that tolerance and encouragement of multiple different perspectives will prove most beneficial to a society or a polity in the long run. Can you think of any ways in which pluralism might have disadvantages? (A leading alternative to pluralism is "corporatism," and it has been argued to have certain advantages in terms of managing political conflict.) Are there reasons to constrain open competition among different groups, or circumstances under which pluralism might not be most advisable?

DAILY ADVERTISER, THURSDAY, NOVEMBER 22, 1787

TO THE PEOPLE OF THE STATE OF NEW YORK

Among the numerous advantages promised by a well constructed Union, none deserves to be more accurately developed than its tendency to break and control the violence of faction. The friend of popular governments never finds himself so much alarmed for their character and fate, as when he contemplates their propensity to this dangerous vice. He will not fail, therefore, to set a due value on any plan which, without violating the principles to which he is attached, provides a proper cure for it. The instability, injustice, and confusion introduced into the public councils, have, in truth, been the mortal diseases under which popular governments have everywhere perished; as they continue to be the favorite and fruitful topics from which the adversaries to liberty derive their most specious declamations. The valuable improvements made by the American constitutions on the popular models, both ancient and modern, cannot certainly be too much admired; but it would be an unwarrantable partiality, to contend that they have as effectually obviated the danger on this side, as was wished and expected. Complaints are everywhere heard from our most considerate and virtuous citizens, equally the friends of public and private faith, and of public and personal liberty, that our governments are too unstable, that the public good is disregarded in the conflicts of rival parties, and that measures are too often decided, not according to the

Madison, James. 1961 [1787]. No. 10: The Same Subject Continued: The Utility of the Union as a Safeguard Against Domestic Faction and Insurrection. In *The Federalist Papers*, ed. Clinton Rossiter, 77–83. New York: New American Library.

rules of justice and the rights of the minor party, but by the superior force of an interested and overbearing majority. However anxiously we may wish that these complaints had no foundation, the evidence, of known facts will not permit us to deny that they are in some degree true. It will be found, indeed, on a candid review of our situation, that some of the distresses under which we labor have been erroneously charged on the operation of our governments; but it will be found, at the same time, that other causes will not alone account for many of our heaviest misfortunes; and, particularly, for that prevailing and increasing distrust of public engagements, and alarm for private rights, which are echoed from one end of the continent to the other. These must be chiefly, if not wholly, effects of the unsteadiness and injustice with which a factious spirit has tainted our public administrations.

By a faction, I understand a number of citizens, whether amounting to a majority or a minority of the whole, who are united and actuated by some common impulse of passion, or of interest, adversed to the rights of other citizens, or to the permanent and aggregate interests of the community.

There are two methods of curing the mischiefs of faction: the one, by removing its causes; the other, by controlling its effects.

There are again two methods of removing the causes of faction: the one, by destroying the liberty which is essential to its existence; the other, by giving to every citizen the same opinions, the same passions, and the same interests.

It could never be more truly said than of the first remedy, that it was worse than the disease. Liberty is to faction what air is to fire, an aliment without which it instantly expires. But it could not be less folly to abolish liberty, which is essential to political life, because it nourishes faction, than it would be to wish the annihilation of air, which is essential to animal life, because it imparts to fire its destructive agency.

The second expedient is as impracticable as the first would be unwise. As long as the reason of man continues fallible, and he is at liberty to exercise it, different opinions will be formed. As long as the connection subsists between his reason and his self-love, his opinions and his passions will have a reciprocal influence on each other; and the former will be objects to which the latter will attach themselves. The diversity in the faculties of men, from which the rights of property originate, is not less an insuperable obstacle to a uniformity of interests. The protection of these faculties is the first object of government. From the protection of different and unequal faculties of acquiring property, the possession of different degrees and kinds of property immediately results; and from the influence of these on the sentiments and views of the respective proprietors, ensues a division of the society into different interests and parties.

The latent causes of faction are thus sown in the nature of man; and we see them everywhere brought into different degrees of activity, according to the different circumstances of civil society. A zeal for different opinions concerning religion, concerning government, and many other points, as well of speculation as of practice; an attachment to different leaders ambitiously contending for pre-eminence and power; or to persons of other descriptions whose fortunes have been interesting to the human passions, have, in turn, divided mankind into parties, inflamed them with mutual animosity, and rendered them much more disposed to vex and oppress each other than to co-operate for their common good. So strong is this propensity of mankind to fall into mutual animosities, that where no substantial occasion presents itself, the most frivolous and fanciful distinctions have been sufficient to kindle their unfriendly passions and excite their most violent conflicts. But the most common and durable source of factions has been the various and unequal distribution of property. Those who hold and those who are without property have ever formed distinct interests in society. Those who are creditors, and those who are debtors, fall under a like discrimination. A landed interest, a manufacturing interest, a mercantile interest, a moneyed interest, with many lesser interests, grow up of necessity in civilized nations, and divide them into different classes, actuated by different sentiments and views. The regulation of these various and interfering interests forms the principal task of modern legislation, and involves the spirit of party and faction in the necessary and ordinary operations of the government.

No man is allowed to be a judge in his own cause, because his interest would certainly bias his judgment, and, not improbably, corrupt his integrity. With equal, nay with greater reason, a body of men are unfit to be both judges and parties at the same time; yet what are many of the most important acts of legislation, but so many judicial determinations, not indeed concerning the rights of single persons, but concerning the rights of large bodies of citizens? And what are the different classes of legislators but advocates and parties to the causes which they determine? Is a law proposed concerning private debts? It is a question to which the creditors are parties on one side and the debtors on the other. Justice ought to hold the balance between them. Yet the parties are, and must be, themselves the judges; and the most numerous party, or, in other words, the most powerful faction must be expected to prevail. Shall domestic manufactures be encouraged, and in what degree, by restrictions on foreign manufactures? are questions which would be differently decided by the landed and the manufacturing classes, and probably by neither with a sole regard to justice and the public good. The apportionment of taxes on the various descriptions of property is an act which seems to require the most exact impartiality; yet there is, perhaps, no legislative act in which greater opportunity and temptation are given to a predominant party to trample on the rules of justice. Every shilling with which they overburden the inferior number, is a shilling saved to their own pockets.

It is in vain to say that enlightened statesmen will be able to adjust these clashing interests, and render them all subservient to the public good. Enlightened statesmen will not always be at the helm. Nor, in many cases, can such an adjustment be made at all without taking into view indirect and remote considerations, which will rarely prevail over the immediate interest which one party may find in disregarding the rights of another or the good of the whole.

The inference to which we are brought is, that the *causes* of faction cannot be removed, and that relief is only to be sought in the means of controlling its *effects*.

If a faction consists of less than a majority, relief is supplied by the republican principle, which enables the majority to defeat its sinister views by regular vote. It may clog the administration, it may convulse the society; but it will be unable to execute and mask its violence under the forms of the Constitution. When a

majority is included in a faction, the form of popular government, on the other hand, enables it to sacrifice to its ruling passion or interest both the public good and the rights of other citizens. To secure the public good and private rights against the danger of such a faction, and at the same time to preserve the spirit and the form of popular government, is then the great object to which our inquiries are directed. Let me add that it is the great desideratum by which this form of government can be rescued from the opprobrium under which it has so long labored, and be recommended to the esteem and adoption of mankind.

By what means is this object attainable? Evidently by one of two only. Either the existence of the same passion or interest in a majority at the same time must be prevented, or the majority, having such coexistent passion or interest, must be rendered, by their number and local situation, unable to concert and carry into effect schemes of oppression. If the impulse and the opportunity be suffered to coincide, we well know that neither moral nor religious motives can be relied on as an adequate control. They are not found to be such on the injustice and violence of individuals, and lose their efficacy in proportion to the number combined together, that is, in proportion as their efficacy becomes needful.

From this view of the subject it may be concluded that a pure democracy, by which I mean a society consisting of a small number of citizens, who assemble and administer the government in person, can admit of no cure for the mischiefs of faction. A common passion or interest will, in almost every case, be felt by a majority of the whole; a communication and concert result from the form of government itself; and there is nothing to check the inducements to sacrifice the weaker party or an obnoxious individual. Hence it is that such democracies have ever been spectacles of turbulence and contention; have ever been found incompatible with personal security or the rights of property; and have in general been as short in their lives as they have been violent in their deaths. Theoretic politicians, who have patronized this species of government, have erroneously supposed that by reducing mankind to a perfect equality in their political rights, they would, at the same time, be perfectly equalized and assimilated in their possessions, their opinions, and their passions.

A republic, by which I mean a government in which the scheme of representation takes place, opens a different prospect, and promises the cure for which we are seeking. Let us examine the points in which it varies from pure democracy, and we shall comprehend both the nature of the cure and the efficacy which it must derive from the Union.

The two great points of difference between a democracy and a republic are: first, the delegation of the government, in the latter, to a small number of citizens elected by the rest; secondly, the greater number of citizens, and greater sphere of country, over which the latter may be extended.

The effect of the first difference is, on the one hand, to refine and enlarge the public views, by passing them through the medium of a chosen body of citizens, whose wisdom may best discern the true interest of their country, and whose patriotism and love of justice will be least likely to sacrifice it to temporary or partial considerations. Under such a regulation, it may well happen that the public voice, pronounced by the representatives of the people, will be more consonant to the public good than if pronounced by the people themselves, convened for the purpose. On the other hand, the effect may be inverted. Men of factious tempers, of local prejudices, or of sinister designs, may, by intrigue, by corruption, or by other means, first obtain the suffrages, and then betray the interests, of the people. The question resulting is, whether small or extensive republics are more favorable to the election of proper guardians of the public weal; and it is clearly decided in favor of the latter by two obvious considerations:

In the first place, it is to be remarked that, however small the republic may be, the representatives must be raised to a certain number, in order to guard against the cabals of a few; and that, however large it may be, they must be limited to a certain number, in order to guard against the confusion of a multitude. Hence, the number of representatives in the two cases not being in proportion to that of the two constituents, and being proportionally greater in the small republic, it follows that, if the proportion of fit characters be not less in the large than in the small republic, the former will present a greater option, and consequently a greater probability of a fit choice.

In the next place, as each representative will be chosen by a greater number of citizens in the large than in the small republic, it will be more difficult for unworthy candidates to practice with success the vicious arts by which elections are too often carried; and the suffrages of the people being more free, will be more likely to centre in men who possess the most attractive merit and the most diffusive and established characters.

It must be confessed that in this, as in most other cases, there is a mean, on both sides of which inconveniences will be found to lie. By enlarging too much the number of electors, you render the representatives too little acquainted with all their local circumstances and lesser interests; as by reducing it too much, you render him unduly attached to these, and too little fit to comprehend and pursue great and national objects. The federal Constitution forms a happy combination in this respect; the great and aggregate interests being referred to the national, the local and particular to the State legislatures.

The other point of difference is, the greater number of citizens and extent of territory which may be brought within the compass of republican than of democratic government; and it is this circumstance principally which renders factious combinations less to be dreaded in the former than in the latter. The smaller the society, the fewer probably will be the distinct parties and interests composing it; the fewer the distinct parties and interests, the more frequently will a majority be found of the same party; and the smaller the number of individuals composing a majority, and the smaller the compass within which they are placed, the more easily will they concert and execute their plans of oppression. Extend the sphere, and you take in a greater variety of parties and interests; you make it less probable that a majority of the whole will have a common motive to invade the rights of other citizens; or if such a common motive exists, it will be more difficult for all who feel it to discover their own strength, and to act in unison with each other. Besides other impediments, it may be remarked that, where there is a consciousness of unjust or dishonorable purposes, communication is always checked by distrust in proportion to the number whose concurrence is necessary.

Hence, it clearly appears, that the same advantage which a republic has over a democracy, in controlling the effects of faction, is enjoyed by a large over a small republic,—is enjoyed by the Union over the States composing it. Does the advantage consist in the substitution of representatives whose enlightened views and virtuous sentiments render them superior to local prejudices and schemes of injustice? It will not be denied that the representation of the Union will be most likely to possess these requisite endowments. Does it consist in the greater security afforded by a greater variety of parties, against the event of any one party being able to outnumber and oppress the rest? In an equal degree does the increased variety of parties comprised within the Union, increase this security. Does it, in fine, consist in the greater obstacles opposed to the concert and accomplishment of the secret wishes of an unjust and interested majority? Here, again, the extent of the Union gives it the most palpable advantage.

The influence of factious leaders may kindle a flame within their particular States, but will be unable to spread a general conflagration through the other States. A religious sect may degenerate into a political faction in a part of the Confederacy; but the variety of sects dispersed over the entire face of it must secure the national councils against any danger from that source. A rage for paper money, for an abolition of debts, for an equal division of property, or for any other improper or wicked project, will be less apt to pervade the whole body of the Union than a particular member of it; in the same proportion as such a malady is more likely to taint a particular county or district, than an entire State.

In the extent and proper structure of the Union, therefore, we behold a republican remedy for the diseases most incident to republican government. And according to the degree of pleasure and pride we feel in being republicans, ought to be our zeal in cherishing the spirit and supporting the character of Federalists.

Publius

PRADEEP CHHIBBER AND KEN KOLLMAN

11.2 THE FORMATION OF NATIONAL PARTY SYSTEMS

Federalism and Party Competition in Canada, Great Britain, India, and the United States

In this piece, the authors establish an argument about the causes of different party systems and provide a concise overview of some of the most important statements in the literature about such causes. This piece is valuable for the authors' perspective, but also as a primer on the logic of party system development. In their review of the literature, the authors draw on three ideas: first, that party systems emerge from underlying cleavages or divisions within the society; second, that parties and party systems arise as a response to the underlying challenges of collective action, which necessitate building rules and coalitions for individuals to achieve their goals; and third, that party systems may emerge from electoral rules, with a famous case being "Duverger's Law" that certain electoral institutions (especially district elections where the candidate with the most votes wins) tend toward two-party systems whereas others tend toward multipartism. Chhibber and Kollman then suggest that the structure of party systems must also take into account different levels of government, with a focus on whether parties are local, regional, or national in nature. As you read this piece, you might think about how Madison might assess the sorts of "factions" analyzed by the authors.

INTRODUCTION

The same political parties dominate contemporary American politics at the national level and in nearly every state. Despite a few well-publicized independent candidates and politicians and, in recent years, a smattering of celebrities from the Reform Party or Independent Party, such as Ross Perot, Patrick Buchanan, and Jesse Ventura, the Democratic and Republican parties control congressional delegations from all the states, majorities in the state legislatures, and governorships in all but a few states.[1] Since the early twentieth century, the United States has displayed a pattern of virtually complete two-partism—that is, two national parties compete and win seats in every major region in the nation. Two-partism, however, has not

always been characteristic of the United States, at least not for congressional and state elections. Throughout most of the nineteenth century, electoral support was spread across more than two parties, and some parties were competitive only in a few states. In certain regions, such as the South from the 1890s to the 1970s, one party predominated for long periods.

The current U.S. phenomenon of two national parties competing everywhere in the country does not exist in Canada, Great Britain, and India, even though they share many of the same electoral rules. Two-partism did not even exist in previous eras in the United States, although its electoral rules have stayed relatively constant. In the three other countries, the national legislatures seat politicians from parties that are strong only in

Chhibber, Pradeep and Ken Kollman. 2004. *The Formation of National Party Systems: Federalism and Party Competition in Canada, Great Britain, India, and the United States.* Princeton: Princeton University Press.

particular provinces, regions, and states. In Canada and India, provincial and state politics are often dominated by parties that have little or no national standing. In contemporary Britain, after the 1997 devolution and creation of independent assemblies in regions, regional political parties such as Plaid Cymru and the Scottish Nationals have gained prominence.

Modern American two-partism not only looks unusual in comparison with party politics in other countries with similar electoral laws but also when compared with party politics in other eras in American history. Why is it that two national parties dominate the American political landscape in modern times? And why does this pattern not exist in other countries such as Canada, Great Britain, and India? In this book we seek to explain not only such differences across these countries but also to explain within each country why and when national parties emerged and why regional parties have drawn significant vote shares.

We show that, although these four countries have similar electoral systems—single-member, simple-plurality voting systems for the lower houses of parliament—party systems vary not only across these countries but also over time within these countries. Using historical data, we attribute changes in the party systems in these nations to the changing role of the state. In particular, we examine the relationship between the national (federal) and provincial (state) governments. Our claim that the nature of federalism influences the dynamics and stability of a party system differs from previous party system theories that stress the significance of social cleavages, electoral laws, and other constitutional features.

APPROACHES TO THE STUDY OF PARTIES AND PARTY SYSTEMS

Because parties and party systems are so central to democratic politics, their features and behavior have been the subject of research across many subfields in political science, including the study of voting, elections, legislatures, presidents and executives, bureaucracies, courts, electoral systems, and international relations. Scholars have used various methodologies and theoretical paradigms to analyze parties and party systems. Among these, three general approaches have dominated the literature.

Party Systems as Reflections of Social Cleavages

The first approach in analyzing party systems, and by far the most prominent in comparative politics, focuses on the nature of social cleavages that manifest themselves in party politics. Scholars seek to understand which groups in society political parties represent. Lipset and Rokkan (1967) offer a well-known thesis in this research tradition. They argue that deeply rooted, stable social cleavages lead to stable party systems. Mid-twentieth-century voting patterns in Europe reflected the economic, social, and religious divisions that arose as a result of the national and industrial revolutions many decades earlier (Caramani 2004; Katz and Mair 1994). It takes major social changes, such as postindustrialization (Inglehart 1997), civil war, depression, or massive population shifts, to alter those patterns significantly (Burnham 1970). Caramani (2004) demonstrates how pre–World War I electoral cleavages remained relatively stable throughout the twentieth century in Europe.

In this approach, social cleavages shape party systems in an almost axiomatic way. While political leaders can try to shift groups of like-minded voters into and out of parties to serve partisan or political ends, these efforts can be difficult. For some scholars, whom Torcal and Mainwaring (2001) term as the "objective" social relations interpreters, parties represent societal interests, and these interests are ontologically prior to partisan debates. Numerous country studies use this perspective to account for the nature of the party system.

Parties as Solutions to Collective Dilemmas

The second approach, which has much in common with recent literature in many of the social sciences on the origins of institutions (North 1990), is relatively new and is by far the smallest of the three in terms of the number of published articles and books that rely on it. The approach begins with the fundamental question. Why have parties at all? Scholars seek to explain the origins and existence of political parties in the self-interested behaviors of voters, candidates, or legislators. For most scholars writing in this literature, parties have their origins in legislatures

(Aldrich 1995; Cox and McCubbins 1993). Collective dilemmas such as cycling majorities and collective action problems are inherent in democratic politics, especially in legislatures. As a result, entrepreneurial politicians have strong incentives to set up long-term commitment devices. Such devices could take several forms, but as Aldrich (1995, 186) writes, "there are more or less continual incentives for ambitious politicians to consider party organizations as means to achieve their goals. In the most general terms, these incentives flow from the very nature of liberal democracies in an extended republic, and in an immediate sense that means the ability to fashion and hold majorities."

Party Systems as Reflections of Institutional Rules

The third approach, of which Duverger ([1954] 1963) and Cox (1997) are two major bookends, focuses attention on the influence of electoral laws on party systems (Rae 1971; Riker 1982; Lijphart 1994; Taagepera and Shugart 1989). This literature is vast, and we address it in greater detail in later chapters. The approach tends to be prominent in cross-national comparative studies of party systems. (The more sociological approach that we summarized first tends to be used in single-country studies, although seminal works such as by Lipset and Rokkan and by Inglehart are cross-national.) For this third, more institutional approach, the main aspect of party systems to be explained is number of political parties that contest either for seats in the national parliament or for executive power in presidential systems, or for both. The many ways in which votes are counted and seats are allocated affect the number of parties. Likewise, different methods for choosing presidents affect the number of serious presidential contestants (Shugart and Carey 1992; Lijphart 1994).

FEDERALISM, CENTRALIZATION, AND PARTY SYSTEMS

Developing the logic of our argument and providing empirical support for it constitute much of the content of this book. For now, we offer a brief overview. The argument begins with a focus on electoral competition within a single electoral district. As mentioned, in all four of our countries members of the lower house of the national parliament are elected in single-member, simple-plurality districts.[2] Only the candidate with the most votes from a districtwide election attains a seat in the legislature, and there are no runoff elections.

In predicting the number of candidates or parties at the district level under single-member, simple-plurality systems, Duverger's Law has considerable bite (Cox 1994; 1997; Feddersen 1992; Palfrey 1989). Duverger's Law holds that this type of electoral rule leads to two-partism. Theoretically, the most compelling arguments in favor of the law rely on the premise that voters in a single election tend to vote for the candidates who have a chance of winning. This not only reduces votes for candidates expected to finish third or worse but also diminishes the incentives for candidates to join the contest for election if they do not think they can finish in the two top positions. Likewise, it reduces incentives for funders to provide money or other resources to candidates who are unlikely to finish near the top of the heap. Empirically, the evidence for the existence of two parties (or two candidates winning nearly all the vote) in district elections under this electoral system is quite strong (Chhibber and Kollman 1998; and see chapter 2), although there are noticeable exceptions, as shown in the next chapter. Even when districts are remarkably heterogeneous socially, as in India, in a vast majority of district elections to the national parliament two candidates receive nearly all the votes.

Whether national party systems will resemble the predictions in Duverger's Law is entirely another matter. It depends on the degree to which candidates and parties make linkages across districts to establish larger political groupings or organizations based on common party labels. While there may be two parties or two candidates receiving most of the votes in district elections, if there are D districts in the country, there could be as many as 2D parties at the national level if each candidate uses a unique party label on the ballot. Candidate Francine Jones could herself become the sole representative of the Francine Jones Parry, and Gerry Smith could be the sole representative of the Gerry Smith Party, and so on.

Of course, since the beginning of modern representative democracy, there have been local, regional, and national parties. Regardless of electoral rules, politicians have always seen it in their collective and individual interests to establish linkages across district lines, to aggregate their votes across districts to create regional or national parties that can influence policy or run the government. We call this process *party aggregation*. Cox (1997) has called it linkage. Even in those countries with an unusually high number of parties, such as the Netherlands or Israel (with the purest forms of national proportional representation and low thresholds), there are vastly more candidates winning seats to the parliament than national parties, indicating that most candidates prefer to aggregate their votes into party totals. However, the number of national parties is a function, to a large degree, of the incentives for candidates and politicians to coalesce around the same labels as politicians from different regions who have different ideologies and have different loyalties to previous and current government policies and leaders.

Consider two situations. It could be the case that politicians feel it necessary to join parties that represent only their particular region or particular narrow slice of the ideological spectrum. Or it could be the case the politicians feel it necessary to join parties that link districts across the entire country or across a very wide range of the ideological spectrum. Which kind of situation prevails—whether minor parties can survive because politicians are comfortable in alliances with less-than-national groupings, or whether minor parties cannot survive because politicians are only comfortable in national groupings—in turn depends on which level of government controls resources that voters care about.

In the first situation, if local governments make most decisions that affect voters, then it may be relatively unimportant to politicians that party labels communicate to voters the national party group that the politician will work with once in office. In fact, it may be crucial that the party label communicate the local or regional group that the candidate will work with once in office. The national label and the local or regional label may coincide, but they don't have to. Under decentralized political or economic systems, candidates will have fewer pressures to join broad, national parties because voters will know that local

or regional governments make the important decisions anyway.

In the second situation, if national governments make most decisions that affect voters, then it becomes important for candidates to communicate to voters the policy position of the candidate relative to national government policies, and also the possibility that the candidate, once elected, could become part of the government. For both functions, national-party labels, especially labels of parties that may be expected to become part of the government, will be valuable.

This discussion so far has presented the possibilities starkly, as though only two scenarios are possible. In one, politicians are comfortable with minor-party labels; in the other, politicians want to have the label of a major, national party in nearly every case. These are extremes, of course, and the degree of political and economic centralization and, by extension, the incentives of candidates to adopt only major-party labels can vary by matters of degree. For example, as we argue in later chapters, the United States in the current era represents the one extreme, where serious candidates for the House of Representatives feel compelled to take either the Republican or Democratic label almost without exception. In the nineteenth and early twentieth centuries, however, candidates often felt comfortable adopting minor-party labels. This comfort level, judging by the proportion of competitive candidates who ran as neither Democrats, Republicans (or Whigs in the earlier era), fluctuated in tune with the degree of political and economic centralization. Over time, the number of parties competing for House seats changed, sometimes gradually, sometimes suddenly, but always in keeping with the notion that the incentives of politicians respond to which level of government was responsible for the policies that voters cared about.

To summarize our argument in brief, electoral system effects are most prominent in district elections, but party aggregation depends on the policies and role of the national government in relation to subnational governments. Federal policies of the national governments hinder or help minor, regional-based parties to survive on the national scene and, therefore, affect the nature of party coalitions and the party systems. Party systems become more national as governments centralize authority; in contrast, there are more opportunities for regional, state, or provincial parties to thrive as provincial or state governments gain more authority relative to the national government.

NOTES

1. Exceptions include governors in Minnesota and Maine in the 1990s and early 2000s, and a small number of members of Congress from Minnesota and Vermont in the 2000s.
2. This is true today, anyway. In all three countries there have been some two-member districts at various times in history, a topic we take up in the next chapter.

BIBLIOGRAPHY

Aldrich, John. 1995. *Why Parties? The Origin and Transformation of Party Politics in America.* Chicago: University of Chicago Press.

Burnham, Walter Dean. 1970. *Critical Elections and the Mainsprings of American Politics.* New York: W.W. Norton.

Caramani, Daniele. 2004. *The Nationalization of Elections.* Cambridge: Cambridge University Press.

Chhibber, Pradeep K., and Ken Kollman. 1998. "Party Aggregation and the Number of Parties in India and the United States." *American Political Science Review* 92: 329–42.

Cox, Gary. 1994. "Strategic Voting Equilibria under the Single Nontransferable Vote." *American Political Science Review* 88: 608–21.

Cox, Gary. 1997. *Making Votes Count: Strategic Coordination in the World's Electoral Systems.* Cambridge: Cambridge University Press.

Cox, Gary, and Matthew McCubbins. 1993. *Legislative Leviathan: Party Government in the House.* Berkeley: University of California Press.

Duverger, Maurice. [1954] 1963. *Political Parties: Their Organization and Activity in the Modern State.* New York: John Wiley and Sons.

Feddersen, Timothy. 1992. "A Voting Model Implying Duverger's Law and Positive Turnout." *American Journal of Political Science* 36: 938–62.

Inglehart, Ronald. 1997. *Modernization and Postmodernization.* Princeton, NJ: Princeton University Press.

Katz, Richard and Peter Mair. 1994. *How Parties Organize Change and Adaptation in Party Organizations in Western Democracies.* London: Sage.

Lijphart, Arend. 1994. *Electoral Systems and Party Systems.* New York: Oxford University Press.

Lipset, Seymour M., and Stein Rokkan. 1967. "Cleavage Structures, Party Systems, and Voter Alignments: An Introduction." In *Party Systems and Voter Alignments*, ed. Seymour M. Lipset and Stein Rokkan. New York: Free Press.

North, Douglass. 1990. *Institutions, Institutional Change, and Economic Performance.* New York: Cambridge University Press.

Palfrey, Thomas. 1989. "A Mathematical Proof of Duverger's Law." In *Models of Strategic Choice in Politics*, ed. Peter Ordeshook. Ann Arbor: University of Michigan Press.

Rae, Douglas. 1971. *The Political Consequences of Electoral Laws.* 2nd ed. New Haven, CT: Yale University Press.

Riker, William. 1982. "The Two-Party System and Duverger's Law." *American Political Science Review* 76: 753–66.

Shugart, Matthew, and John Carey. 1992. *Presidents and Assemblies: Constitutional Design and Electoral Dynamics.* New York: Cambridge University Press.

Taagepera, Rein, and Matthew Shugart. 1989. *Seats and Votes: The Effects and Determinants of Electoral Systems.* New Haven, CT: Yale University Press.

Torcal, Mariano, and Scott Mainwaring. 2001. "The Political Re-crafting of Social Bases of Party Competition: The Case of Chile, 1973–1995." *British Journal of Political Science* 31: 1157–95.

4

POLITICS, SOCIETY, AND CULTURE

The chapters in this section focus on questions often considered part of "political sociology" which, roughly speaking, concerns the relationship between politics and other parts of society. As you read them, remember that the more "informal" phenomena discussed here exist in the same world as the formal institutions you read about in Section 3. As you transition from the previous section to this one, consider the following: What does a focus on political sociology add to the study of formal institutions? What does the study of formal institutions contribute to our analysis of population-level and cultural processes?

Here readings will look at instances in which social movements, revolutions, and related forms of social action cause political change (Chapter 12). We will also examine major political identities and their relationship with political systems. One of the most important sets of identities in comparative politics is national identity, which relates to the issue of nationalism. That is the subject of Chapter 13. Following that, in Chapter 14, we provide readings about other important forms of identity that shape politics: race, ethnicity, and gender. Finally, we will look in Chapter 15 at the roles that ideology and religion play in modern politics. Is religion becoming more or less significant in politics around the world? What about major ideologies? Why does the intersection between religion, the state, and public life vary so much from country to country? These questions, like others in this section, are open to debate among the scholars you will read, and it is hoped that you will use these readings to make your own informed contributions to these debates.

CHAPTER 12

REVOLUTIONS AND CONTENTION

One of the perennial themes of comparative politics is conflict. When dramatic and sustained conflict happens outside of formal political institutions it is often referred to as "contention" (McAdam et al., 2001). Contention takes many forms, ranging from social movement organizing to insurgencies and civil wars to terrorism. As with many subjects in comparative politics, scholars argue about how to define these terms. For example, they debate the term "revolution" and the types of revolutions we can observe. Most emphasize dramatic structural or institutional changes as a key feature of revolutions. They differ, however, on points of detail.

In this chapter, we include three classic readings on a particularly important form of contention: social and political revolutions. Indeed, among our three selections, Ted Gurr aims to explain a broad class of events, including many instances in which mobilization leads to a regime change. Theda Skocpol focuses on three cases of great "social revolutions" that changed not only political institutions but also society's class structure. Her theoretical claims, however, are meant to be generalizable to other, similar, revolutions. For example, her theory ought to be able to explain the Cuban revolution of Fidel Castro as well, since it also attempted to radically transform the economy and class structure of the society in which it took place. Finally, Timur Kuran focuses on helping us to understand a single wave of related revolutions: those that took place in Eastern and Central Europe as the Soviet Union collapsed after 1989. Here again, however, the implication is that we can learn lessons about these cases that might be applicable to other instances of dramatic social and political change.

We also have examples of three general underlying theories of politics in this chapter. Gurr's theory is mostly social-psychological and emphasizes the ways in which changes in social systems can upset people's expectations and self-understandings, causing frustration and anger and prompting them to seek to rectify what they perceive (perhaps sometimes rationally and other times irrationally) to be the sources of their ills. Skocpol's theory is structuralist, emphasizing the materialist factors that are shaped by history and that are largely outside of the control of individuals. What matters most, according to this theory, is the class structure and core political institutions like the state. Kuran's theory is actor centric and, at its heart, is based on rationalist theory (see also Lichbach, 1995). That is, for Kuran, the way to think about politics is to model it from the perspective of the individuals participating in political activity. To explain a revolution is to explain how participating in the potentially risky struggle for social and political change came to appear rational to a critical mass of people, which would "proximately" cause their taking revolutionary steps.

The readings are ordered chronologically (in the order they were written and published), and it is true that they mirror a general development in the literature over the past several decades. However, you should not draw the conclusion that all comparative politics scholars today follow the approach of analysts like Kuran. In other words, there are still a number of scholars who use social-psychological and structural theories in their efforts to explain revolutions, and others draw on additional factors like analysis of cultural worldviews and social networks. Finally, as in other areas of comparative political analysis, there are hybrid theories that try to include multiple types of factors (see Goldstone, 2001).

WORKS CITED

Goldstone, Jack. 2001. "Toward a Fourth Generation of Revolutionary Theory." *Annual Review of Political Science* 4: 139–187.
Lichbach, Mark. 1995. *The Rebel's Dilemma*. Ann Arbor: University of Michigan Press.
McAdam, Doug, Sidney Tarrow, and Charles Tilly. 2001. *Dynamics of Contention*. New York: Cambridge University Press.

TED ROBERT GURR

12.1 WHY MEN REBEL

In this excerpt from his acclaimed book, *Why Men Rebel* (published in 1970), political scientist Ted Gurr lays out some of the key elements in his theory of revolution. His central strategy is to explain variation in key groups' motivations to engage in efforts to create radical social change. Gurr is less attentive than other theorists to the conditions that allow people to do so: the resources or opportunities or solutions to collective action problems that might increase the probability of contention taking place. That is, the theory seems to presume that "where there's a will, there's a way" and to treat group frustration and resentment as the key factors in need of explanation. It is worth noting that theories like Gurr's were constructed in a time in which contentious activity was viewed as widespread. A wave of anticolonial revolutions had taken place over the previous couple decades, and even in advanced, postindustrial societies, social movement protest was common. To many commentators, events like the spring of 1968 might have appeared to be an episode of "disequilibrium" from which society would eventually right itself. In formulating a constructive critique of Gurr's theory, can you think of instances when the demand for revolution was present, but the capacity of the would-be revolutionaries was lacking?

1. EXPLANATIONS OF POLITICAL VIOLENCE

Conflict . . . is a theme that has occupied the thinking of man more than any other save only God and love.

—*Anatol Rapoport*
Fights, Games, and Debates

TOWARD AN INTEGRATED THEORY OF POLITICAL VIOLENCE

The primary causal sequence in political violence is first the development of discontent, second the politicization of that discontent, and finally its actualization in violent action against political objects and actors. Discontent arising from the perception of relative deprivation is the basic, instigating condition for participants in collective violence. The linked concepts of discontent and deprivation comprise most of the psychological states implicit or explicit in such theoretical notions about the causes of violence as frustration, alienation, drive and goal conflicts, exigency, and strain (discussed in chapter 2).

Relative deprivation is defined as a perceived discrepancy between men's value expectations and their value capabilities. Value expectations are the goods and conditions of life to which people believe they are rightfully entitled. Value capabilities are the goods and conditions they think they are capable of attaining or maintaining, given the social means available to them. Societal conditions that increase the average level or intensity of expectations without increasing capabilities increase the intensity of discontent. Among the general conditions that have such effects are the value gains of other groups and the promise of new opportunities (chapter 4). Societal conditions that decrease men's average value position without decreasing their value expectations similarly increase deprivation, hence the intensity of discontent. The inflexibility of value stocks in a society, short-term deterioration in a group's conditions of life, and limitations of its structural opportunities have such effects (chapter 5).

Gurr, Ted. 1970. *Why Men Rebel.* Princeton: Princeton University Press.

Deprivation-induced discontent is a general spur to action. Psychological theory and group conflict theory both suggest that the greater the intensity of discontent, the more likely is violence. The specificity of this impulse to action is determined by men's beliefs about the sources of deprivation, and about the normative and utilitarian justifiability of violent action directed at the agents responsible for it.

Societal variables that affect the focusing of discontent on political objects include the extent of cultural and subcultural sanctions for overt aggression, the extent and degree of success of past political violence, the articulation and dissemination of symbolic appeals justifying violence, the legitimacy of the political system, and the kinds of responses it makes and has made to relative deprivation (chapters 6 and 7). The belief that violence has utility in obtaining scarce values can be an independent source of political violence, but within political communities it is most likely to provide a secondary, rationalizing, rather than primary, motivation. Widespread discontent provides a general impetus to collective violence. However, the great majority of acts of collective violence in recent decades have had at least some political objects, and the more intense those violent acts are, the more likely they are to be focused primarily or exclusively on the political system. Intense discontent is quite likely to be politicized; the primary effect of normative and utilitarian attitudes toward violence is to focus that potential.

The magnitude of political violence in a system, and the forms it takes, are partly determined by the scope and intensity of politicized discontent. Politicized discontent is a necessary condition for the resort to violence in politics. But however intense and focused the impetus to violence is, its actualization is strongly influenced by the patterns of coercive control and institutional support in the political community. Political violence is of greatest magnitude, and most likely to take the form of internal war, if regimes and those who oppose them exercise approximately equal degrees of coercive control, and command similar and relatively high degrees of institutional support in the society. The coercive capacities of a regime and the uses to which they are put are crucial variables, affecting the forms and extent of political violence in both the short and long run. There is much evidence, some of it summarized in chapters 8 and 10, that some patterns of regime coercive control increase rather than decrease the intensity of discontent, and can facilitate the transformation of turmoil into full-scale revolutionary movements. Dissidents, by contrast, use whatever degree of coercive capacities they acquire principally for group defense and for assaults on the regime. The degree of institutional support for dissidents and for regimes is a function of the relative proportions of a nation's population their organizations mobilize, the complexity and cohesiveness of those organizations, their resources, and the extent to which they provide regularized procedures for value attainment, conflict resolution, and channeling hostility (chapter 9). The growth of dissident organization may in the short run facilitate political violence, but it also is likely to provide the discontented with many of the means to alleviate deprivation in the long run, thus minimizing violence.

The three stages in the process of political violence—those in which discontent is generated, politicized, and actualized in political violence—are each dependent on the preceding one, as the outline indicates. It is likely but not necessarily the case that there is a temporal relationship among the three stages, whereby a sharp increase in the intensity of discontent precedes the articulation of doctrines that justify politically violent action, with shifts in the balances of coercive control and institutional adherence occuring subsequently. The conditions can be simultaneously operative, however, as the outbreak of the Vendée counterrevolution in 1793 demonstrates: implementation of procedures for military conscription intensified the discontent of workers and peasants already sharply hostile to the bourgeoisie and the government it ruled. Mass action against the bourgeoisie began in a matter of days; the social context for dissident action was provided in part by preexisting communal and political organization, action that was facilitated by the concurrent weakness of government forces and institutions in the region.[1] The point is that many of the attitudes and societal conditions that facilitate political violence may be present and relatively unchanging in a society over a long period;

they become relevant to or operative in the genesis of violence only when relative deprivation increases in scope and intensity. Intense politicized discontent also can be widespread and persistent over a long period without overt manifestation because a regime monopolizes coercive control and institutional support. A weakening of regime control or the development of dissident organization in such situations is highly likely to lead to massive violence, as it did in Hungary in 1956 and China in 1966–68, and as is likely at some future date in South Africa.

The concepts, hypotheses, and models of causes and processes developed in the following chapters are not intended as ends in themselves. Intellectually pleasing filters through which to view and categorize the phenomena of a disorderly world are not knowledge. Systematic knowledge requires us to propose and test and reformulate and retest statements about how and why things happen. We know enough, and know it well enough, only when we can say with some certitude not just why things happened yesterday, but how our actions today will affect what happens tomorrow, something we can always hope to know better, though never perfectly. This analysis may demonstrate that too little is known about the violence men do one another, and that it is known too weakly and imprecisely. It is designed to facilitate the processes by which that knowledge can be increased.

A Strategy for Incumbents

The objective attributed here to the typical incumbent elite is to maintain stability, whether or not it maximizes the satisfactions of other citizens. To minimize the potential for collective violence, these are the kinds of alternatives open to it: first, to minimize change in group value positions, in other words to maintain the status quo in the distribution of social, economic, and political goods. If the elite is committed to progress, or willy nilly caught up in it, the benefits of that progress should be evenly distributed. No group, at least no discontented group, should gain less rapidly than others. Limited resources may preclude significant progress for all groups; or developmental policy may dictate that an entrepreneurial or bureaucratic class get more of

what there is to get. In the face of such necessities, discontent can be reduced by increasing the number and scope of value opportunities for the less advantaged groups. People who have little can be satisfied at least temporarily if they have the means to work toward their goals—if they have a degree of control over their resources and destinies, if they can acquire the skills they need to advance themselves, if they face no discriminatory barriers to progress. The opportunities must have at least some payoff, of course. If they do not, hopes soured have more devastating effects for stability than hopes never pursued.

Even if discontent is widespread, a ruling elite can reduce the likelihood of violence against itself by symbolically reinforcing its legitimacy, censoring those who agitate against it, and providing diversionary means for the expression of hostility. Concessions to the discontented help also, but they must be equitably distributed among all the discontented, on pain of antagonizing those who get little; concessions are most effective if they contribute to the capacity of the discontented to help themselves.

If politicized discontent is relatively mild, the optimum pattern for maintaining coercive control is to minimize the men and resources devoted to internal security, and to apply sanctions with both consistency and leniency. If discontent is severe, consistency of sanctions is even more essential; sanctions applied randomly or inequitably are certain to intensify opposition. The combination of leniency and minimal surveillance will not deter intensely angered men, however, and without close surveillance no consistent sanctions can be imposed against them. The best strategy then is to maximize surveillance but to maintain a policy of relative leniency. Such a policy is likely to increase hostility to a lesser degree than maximum surveillance and severe sanctions in combination. It also is likely to "keep the lid on" long enough so that remedial action can be taken. The courses of remedial action include the judicious distribution of goods and means outlined above. They also include the establishment or expansion of effective organizational frameworks in which those goods and opportunities can be put to work, and provision of regular channels for expressing and remedying grievances.

A Strategy for Revolutionaries

The "revolutionary" motive assumed here is the violent destruction of the old order, a motive that is almost always rooted in an irreconcilable hatred of the old that is best satisfied by violence. There may be good utilitarian reasons for such a motive as well: some ruling elites are adamantly opposed to change, responding with unmitigated repression to expressions of popular discontent. In such circumstances dissidents are likely to have only two options: acquiescence or revolution. The regime that responds to their demands only with suppression will intensify their hostility, and is thus likely to speed its own destruction. The tactics outlined here for revolutionaries are those most likely to ensure that destruction.

If discontent is intense and widespread in a society, revolutionary tasks are simplified; if not, there are means by which it can be increased. Ideological appeals offer the best means, to the extent that their content is designed to justify new aspirations and specify means toward their attainment. Any relatively disadvantaged group is a potential audience for such appeals. The existence of objective deprivation is far from being a sufficient condition for the effectiveness of appeals, however. The groups most likely to respond are those that already have been exposed to change and are already discontented with some aspect of their lives. One of the best indicators of a potential for conversion to revolutionary expectations is group experience of absolute decline in value position; such a decline indicates more certainly the existence of discontent than a neo-Marxian judgment that group members ought to be discontented because they have less than others. Relatively disadvantaged people who have recently begun to interact with more prosperous groups, or who have been regularly in contact with such groups and regularly subordinated, also are susceptible to conversion. The closer their association with more advantaged groups, and the less their objective (and subjective) opportunities for improving their own status, the more easily they can be persuaded of the justifiability of aspirations for a better life and the necessity for revolutionary action to attain it. Subordinated urban classes, new migrants to cities, and people on the margins of expanding modern economies make better potential recruits for revolutionary movements than rural peoples still caught in the unchanging web of traditional life.

The most effective revolutionary appeals offer means and justifications that are compatible with the discontents and cultural experience of their potential audience. They facilitate revolutionary violence insofar as they convince their listeners that the ruling elite is responsible for discontent, unwilling and unable to alleviate it, and committed to policies that victimize the oppressed. The symbolic and manifest demonstration that revolutionary violence can be carried out and can be successful reinforces appeals' effectiveness. The revolutionary cause is enhanced if the regime can be induced to take repressive action that confirms such ideological assertions. The fact of violent revolutionary agitation often impels such action: media may be censored, civil liberties restricted, dissident leaders jailed and their organizations suppressed, public benefits diverted from dissident followers. The short-range effect of such policies may be to minimize the dissident capacity for action; the more enduring effect is to confirm the accuracy of revolutionary appeals, thus justifying more intense opposition in the future.

Unless a regime is very weak, it is incumbent on revolutionaries to organize for group defense and eventual assault. Organization should be flexible enough to adapt to and survive regime repression, broad enough in scope so that it can mobilize large numbers of people for action or at least make it difficult for them to support the regime. Organizational resources should be devoted primarily to coercive means and to agitational activities rather than the satisfaction of the material deprivations of leaders and their followers. Dissident organizations otherwise tend to become ends in themselves, providing intrinsic satisfactions that blunt the revolutionary impulse. Participation in revolutionary organization should provide sufficient interpersonal values—especially the sense of comradeship and shared purpose—to ensure the enduring commitment of followers, but require enough sacrifices in the service of its long-range purposes to justify and intensify continued opposition to the regime. It must also provide, of course, some minimum of security for its followers; they must feel that they have a fair chance of survival as well as of success. The coercive capacities of revolutionaries can be enhanced by subversion or demoralization of regime forces, solicitation of external support, and establishment of isolated base areas among sympathizers—to the extent that such tactics are feasible.

The trump card of revolutionaries is violence itself. Even if their coercive capacities are low relative to the regime, selective terrorism can be used to demonstrate the incapacity of the regime to defend its citizens. Such terrorism is dysfunctional to the revolutionary cause if it affects neutral or innocent people; it is more effective if directed against those who are widely disliked. Violence is most effective if it invites severe but inconsistent retaliatory responses by the regime, which have the effect of alienating those who might otherwise support the elite. Open revolutionary warfare is the final tactic of revolutionaries, but is difficult to organize in the modern state, extraordinarily costly, and uncertain of success. It is a last resort against strong regimes, an unnecessary one against weak ones, a first resort only when regimes are already weakening and revolutionary capabilities high.

A Strategy for the Discontented

Most discontented men are not revolutionaries. They may be angry, but most of them probably prefer peaceful means for the attainment of their goals to the privations and risks of revolutionary action. Assuming that their primary motive is to increase their well-being rather than to satisfy anger through violence, their optimum strategy lies intermediate between those of elites who would maintain order and of revolutionaries who would destroy that order to establish a new one. The discontented are not likely to be concerned with minimizing or equalizing rates of group progress, tactics that regimes might choose to use, or with intensifying discontent. Their objective is to improve their own lot as much as possible. To do so they must seek new means and resources. Political violence is not thereby excluded from their repertory of tactics towards that end; given their circumstances, some violence may be necessary. But one of their primary tactical concerns, whether or not they resort to violence, is to minimize retaliatory action in response to their actions.

Given the existence of a potential for collective violence, the optimum policy of the discontented is not to increase the potential for political violence as such but to put the potential to constructive purposes. The symbolic appeals of dissident leaders should be of two kinds, one set designed to mobilize potential followers, another to justify their claims to the regime and the social groups from which they are most likely to gain concessions. Limited political violence in such a context has several uses. It can dramatize claims, provide an outlet for the hostility of followers and thereby enhance institutional support for dissident organizations, and may signal to the regime the threat of more disruptive violence if claims are not met. But it is a risky tactic, more risky in some political systems than others. Violence tends to stimulate counter-violence, a principle that applies to both dissidents and their opponents. The threat of violence has the same effect. A regime so challenged may consequently devote more resources to coercive control than to remedial action. The obligation on dissident leaders is therefore to be as careful and judicious in the use of violence as elites must be in their use of counter-force. Perhaps the best tactic of leaders of dissident groups, if violence occurs at all, is to represent it as the excesses of their followers, whom they are capable of controlling if provided with concessions.

The extent to which leaders can in fact control the actions of their followers, and make effective use of whatever means and resources they obtain, is determined by their degree of institutional support. Whereas the first task of revolutionaries is to intensify discontent and focus it on the political system, the most essential task of pragmatic dissidents thus is to organize: to expand the scope of their organizations, elaborate their internal structure, develop the sense and fact of common purpose, and maximize the use of their collective resources, not for violent action but for value-enhancing action. The establishment of such organizations can provide many intrinsic satisfactions for members: a sense of control over their own affairs, a feeling of community and purpose, status for leaders and security for followers.

Such organizations are much more likely than unorganized collectivities to take effective political action, to get whatever can be gotten through conventional political bargaining processes. If token violence is to be used in a calculated risk to increase bargaining power, it can be most effectively used if institutional support is high. Most important, whatever value opportunities and resources are obtained, through bargaining or otherwise, are most efficiently used to satisfy discontents in a well-developed organizational context.

If dissident organizations are effective in devising means and obtaining resources for remedial action, they will seldom remain long in opposition. They are likely to become firmly fixed in the existing political order, their leaders incorporated in its ruling elite. But if regimes are adamantly hostile and repressive in the face of the claims of dissident organizations, as they are in too many nations, those organizational capacities can be turned to revolutionary ends. If revolution is accomplished, the result is ultimately the same: dissident leaders become the elite of the new order they have established, their organizations the backbone of that order, and their followers, those who survive, the new loyalists. The dissidents can best judge if the costs of such a course are worth the gains; theirs are the lives at stake.

CONCLUSION

The theoretical models developed in this analysis are not intended to provide a ready-made explanation of any given act of political violence. My intention has been to make a reasonably parsimonious synthesis of the diverse speculation and evidence about the origins, extent, and forms of group violence in politics, and to do so in a way that contributes to deductive and empirical inquiry in the service of better theory. From one epistemological point of view, the logical coherence, parsimony, and elegance of a theory are the criteria by which its adequacy is judged; its accuracy is both indeterminate and inconsequential. There is however a compelling need in the real world to be able to anticipate political violence and the consequences of various responses to it, a need common to rebels, incumbents, and those who simply want to live their lives in peace. Where I have faced what seemed to be a choice between "telling it as it seems to be" and the dictates of coherence, parsimony, or elegance, I have chosen the first on grounds that, given the present inadequacy of and need for systematic understanding of violence, it is the more fruitful and useful course. Refinement of the theoretical statements proposed here is as much needed as their deductive extension and empirical evaluation. From this point, however, the processes should proceed together rather than separately, as they have too often in the past.

If the central theoretical arguments are essentially accurate, some kinds of interpretations of the nature of political violence are demonstrably inadequate, in a scientific sense and in the efficacy of policies based upon them. There is not much support here for the view that political violence is primarily a recourse of vicious, criminal, deviant, ignorant, or undersocialized people. Men and women of every social background, acting in the context of every kind of social group on an infinite variety of motives, have resorted to violence against their rulers. Nor is political violence "caused" by pernicious doctrines, or at least by doctrines alone. Discontented men are much more susceptible to conversion to new beefs than contented men. Not all new beliefs provide justifications for violence, and most that do are derived from peoples' own cultural and historical experience rather than alien sources. The belief that some kinds of social arrangements or political institutions are intrinsically immune from violence or capable of satisfying all human desires is only a partial truth. Disruptive violence can and has occurred in every twentieth-century political community. No pattern of coercive control, however intense and consistent, is likely to deter permanently all enraged men from violence, except genocide. No extant or utopian pattern of social and political engineering seems capable of satisfying all human aspirations and resolving all human discontents, short of biological modification of the species.

Political violence is not uniformly and irretrievably destructive of human well-being. Many groups have resorted to political violence at one stage or another in their historical development with positive long-range results: the resolution of divisive conflicts, defense of threatened interests, and attainment of means by which their members could work effectively and peacefully toward their own security and well-being. There is even less support for the revolutionary view that violence has a special efficacy unmatched by other means, or for the precisely comparable contention of conservative authoritarians that massive force is the best means for maintaining order. Violence inspires counter-violence by those against whom it is directed. It consumes scarce resources that could otherwise be used to satisfy aspirations. Worst of all it consumes men, its victims physically, its practitioners mentally, by habituating them to violence as the means and end of life. The more intense and widespread the use of force the less likely are those who use it, rebels or regimes, to achieve their objectives except through total victory. In view of the resources available to modern governments and modern revolutionary movements, total victory is highly likely to be pyrrhic victory.

Some conventional wisdom about the means to the resolution of violent conflict is also fallacious. Coercion alone is demonstrably ineffective, in the long run if not the short, because on balance it is more likely to inspire resistance than compliance. The assumption that discontent has primarily physical origins, hence that satisfaction of material aspirations is its cure, is no more accurate. Men aspire to many other conditions of life than physical well-being, not the least of which are security, status, a sense of community, and the right to manage their own affairs. If basic physical needs are met, provision for these aspirations is at least as important as increased material well-being for minimizing violence. If men have substantially more physical resources than status or freedom, they may well use the former to gain the latter, by violent means if necessary. There also is a fallacy in the assumption that all wants must be satisfied to minimize discontent. Discontent is not a function of the discrepancy between what men want and what they have, but between what they want and what they believe they are capable of attaining. If their means are few or threatened, they are likely to revolt; if they obtain new means they can work to satisfy their wants. Concessions also can have unintended effects, however. Temporary palliatives are likely to reinforce a return to violence once their narcotic effect wears off. If men fight to preserve what they have, concessions that remove the threat to it are sufficient. If they rebel to satisfy new or intensified expectations, the only effective concession is to provide them with means adequate to those expectations.

Men's resort to political violence is in part unreasoning, but does not occur without reason. Ignorance is almost always among its causes: sometimes ignorance of its consequences by those who resort to it, more often ignorance by those who create and maintain the social conditions that inspire it. But political violence is comprehensible, which should make it neither necessary nor inevitable, but capable of resolution.

NOTE

1. Charles Tilly, *The Vendée* (Cambridge: Harvard University Press, 1964), passim.

THEDA SKOCPOL

12.2 STATES AND SOCIAL REVOLUTIONS

A Comparative Analysis of France, Russia, and China

Skocpol's *States and Social Revolutions*, from which this excerpt is taken, was published in 1979. It aimed to counter theories like Gurr's by emphasizing "material" or "structural" factors rather than the social psychology of group resentment. As such, Skocpol emphasized two main factors as contributing to what she called "social revolutions." The first is "state breakdown." Skocpol was not the first to note that a weakening of state institutions caused by fiscal difficulties often creates revolutionary openings—indeed, Alexis de Tocqueville made a similar observation in the 19th century—but her theory emphasizes this factor as fundamental. The other major factor cited by Skocpol is peasant mobilization. Urban workers and party activists cannot successfully create great social revolutions on their own. When the peasantry can be organized and mobilized in coalition with such forces, successful transformation is possible. Skocpol focuses closely on three main cases: the French, Russian, and Chinese revolutions. Some scholars have argued that the theory might not apply as well to other cases. Can you think of other revolutions or moments of contentious political mobilization that might not fit with this model?

Social revolutions are rapid, basic transformations of a society's state and class structures; and they are accompanied and in part carried through by class-based revolts from below. Social revolutions are set apart from other sorts of conflicts and transformative processes above all by the combination of two coincidences: the coincidence of societal structural change with class upheaval; and the coincidence of political with social transformation. In contrast, rebellions, even when successful, may involve the revolt of subordinate classes—but they do not eventuate in structural change.[1] Political revolutions transform state structures but not social structures, and they are not necessarily accomplished through class conflict.[2] And processes such as industrialization can transform social structures without necessarily bringing about, or resulting from, sudden political upheavals or basic political-structural changes. What is unique to social revolution is that basic changes in social structure and in political structure occur together in a mutually reinforcing fashion. And these changes occur through intense sociopolitical conflicts in which class struggles play a key role.

This conception of social revolution differs from many other definitions of revolution in important respects. First, it identifies a *complex* object of explanation, of which there are relatively few historical instances. It does this rather than trying to multiply the number of cases for explanation by concentrating only upon one analytic feature (such as violence or political conflict) shared by many events of heterogeneous nature and outcome.[3] It is my firm belief that analytic oversimplification cannot lead us toward valid, complete explanations of revolutions. If our intention is to understand large-scale conflicts and changes such as those that occurred in France from

Skocpol, Theda. 1979. *States and Social Revolutions: A Comparative Analysis of France, Russia, and China.* New York: Cambridge University Press.

1787 to 1800, we cannot make progress by starting with objects of explanation that isolate only the aspects that such revolutionary events share with, say, riots or coups. We must look at the revolutions as wholes, in much of their complexity.

Second, this definition makes successful sociopolitical transformation—*actual change* of state and class structures—part of the specification of what is to be called a social revolution, rather than leaving change contingent in the definition of "revolution" as many other scholars do.[4] The rationale is my belief that successful social revolutions probably emerge from different macro-structural and historical contexts than do either failed social revolutions or political transformations that are not accompanied by transformations of class relations. Because I intend to focus exactly on this question in my comparative historical analysis—in which actual social revolutions will be compared to unsuccessful cases and to nonsocial-revolutionary transformations—my concept of social revolution necessarily highlights successful change as a basic defining feature.

How, then, are social revolutions to be explained? Where are we to turn for fruitful modes of analyzing their causes and outcomes? In my view existing social-scientific theories of revolution are not adequate.[5] In consequence, the chief purpose of this chapter is to introduce and defend principles and methods of analysis that represent alternatives to those shared by all (or most) existing approaches. I shall argue that, in contrast to the modes of explanation used by the currently prevalent theories, social revolutions should be analyzed from a structural perspective, with special attention devoted to international contexts and to developments at home and abroad that affect the breakdown of the state organizations of old regimes and the buildup of new, revolutionary state organizations. Furthermore, I shall argue that comparative historical analysis is the most appropriate way to develop explanations of revolutions that are at once historically grounded and generalizable beyond unique cases.

A STRUCTURAL PERSPECTIVE

If one steps back from the clashes among the leading perspectives on revolution, what seems most striking is the sameness of the image of the overall revolutionary process that underlies and informs all four approaches. According to that shared image: First, changes in social systems or societies give rise to grievances, social disorientation, or new class or group interests and potentials for collective mobilization. Then there develops a purposive, mass-based movement—coalescing with the aid of ideology and organization—that consciously undertakes to overthrow the existing government and perhaps the entire social order. Finally, the revolutionary movement fights it out with the authorities or dominant class and, if it wins, undertakes to establish its own authority and program.

What is wrong with the purposive image of how revolutions develop? For one thing, it strongly suggests that societal order rests, either fundamentally or proximately, upon a consensus of the majority (or of the lower classes) that their needs are being met. This image suggests that the ultimate and sufficient condition for revolution is the withdrawal of this consensual support and, conversely, that no regime could survive if the masses were consciously disgruntled. Though of course such ideas could never be completely accepted by Marxists, they can creep in by implication along with emphases on class consciousness or hegemony. Gurr and Johnson, not surprisingly, embrace these notions quite explicitly.[6] And Tilly slides into a version of them when he portrays governments and revolutionary organizations as competitors for popular support, with popular choices determining whether or not a revolutionary situation develops.[7] Yet, surely, any such consensual and voluntaristic conceptions of societal order and disruption or change are quite naive. They are belied in the most obvious fashion by the prolonged survival of such blatantly repressive and domestically illegitimate regimes as the South African.[8]

More important, the purposive image is very misleading about both the causes and the processes of social revolutions that have actually occurred historically. As for causes, no matter what form social revolutions conceivably might take in the future (say in an industrialized, liberal-democratic nation), the fact is that historically no successful social revolution has ever been "made" by a mass-mobilizing, avowedly revolutionary movement. As Jeremy Brecher has aptly put it: "In fact, revolutionary movements rarely begin with a revolutionary intention; this only develops in the course of the struggle itself."[9] True enough, revolutionary organizations and ideologies have helped to cement the solidarity of radical vanguards before and or during revolutionary crises. And they have greatly facilitated the consolidation of new regimes. But in no sense did such vanguards—let alone vanguards with large, mobilized, and ideologically imbued mass followings—ever create the revolutionary crises they exploited. Instead, as we shall see in later chapters, revolutionary situations have developed due to the emergence of politico-military crises of state and class domination. And only because of the possibilities thus created have revolutionary leaderships and rebellious masses contributed to the accomplishment of revolutionary transformations. Besides, the rebellious masses have quite often acted on their own, without being directly organized or ideologically inspired by avowedly revolutionary leaders and goals. As far as the causes of historical social revolutions go, Wendell Phillips was quite correct when he once declared: "Revolutions are not made; they come."[10]

The purposive image is just as misleading about the processes and outcomes of historical revolutions as it is about their causes. For the image strongly suggests that revolutionary processes and outcomes can be understood in terms of the activity and intentions or interests of the key group(s) who launched the revolution in the first place. Thus, although Gurr does not seem to envision revolutions as much more than acts of sheer destruction, he maintains that this is straightforwardly due to the activity of the frustrated and angry masses and leaders who originally caused the revolution. For Johnson, the violent value-reorientation accomplished by revolution is the doing of the ideological movement that grew up within the old dis-synchronized social system. And Marxists not infrequently attribute the underlying logic of revolutionary processes to the interests and actions of the historically relevant class-for-itself, either the bourgeoisie or the proletariat.

But such notions are much too simple.[11] In fact, in historical revolutions, differently situated and motivated groups have become participants in complex unfoldings of multiple conflicts. These conflicts have been powerfully shaped and limited by existing socioeconomic and international conditions. And they have proceeded in different ways depending upon how each revolutionary situation emerged in the first place. The logic of these conflicts has not been controlled by any one class or group, no matter how seemingly central in the revolutionary process. And the revolutionary conflicts have invariably given rise to outcomes neither fully foreseen nor intended by—nor perfectly serving the interests of—any of the particular groups involved. It simply will not do, therefore, to try to decipher the logic of the processes or outcomes of a social revolution by adopting the perspective or following the actions of any one class or elite or organization—no matter how important its participatory role. As Eric Hobsbawm has very neatly put it, "the evident importance of the actors in the drama . . . does not mean that they are also dramatist, producer, and stage-designer." "Consequently," Hobsbawm concludes, "theories which overstress the voluntarist or subjective elements in revolution, are to be treated with caution."[12]

Any valid explanation of revolution depends upon the analyst's "rising above" the viewpoints of participants to find important regularities across given historical instances—including similar institutional and historical patterns in the situations where revolutions have occurred, and similar patterns of conflict in the processes by which they have developed.

To explain social revolutions, one must find problematic, first, the emergence (not "making") of a revolutionary situation within an old regime. Then, one must be able to identify the objectively conditioned and complex intermeshing of the various actions of the diversely situated groups—an intermeshing that shapes the revolutionary process and gives rise to the new regime. One can begin to make sense of such complexity only by focusing simultaneously upon the institutionally determined situations and relations of groups within society and upon the interrelations of societies within world-historically developing international structures. To take such an impersonal and nonsubjective viewpoint—one that emphasizes patterns of relationships among groups and societies—is to work from what may in some generic sense be called a structural perspective on sociohistorical reality. Such a perspective is essential for the analysis of social revolutions.

"The basic question of every revolution is that of state power," Lenin wrote in the midst of the Russian Revolution of 1917.[13] Here was Lenin the revolutionary organizer speaking. As a theorist, nevertheless, Lenin followed Marx in maintaining that historical developments in class relations were the structural matrix from which revolutionary contests for state power arose, and in believing that class conflicts were the means by which questions about the forms and functions of state power would be resolved. Bourgeois revolutions had served to strengthen states as instruments of bureaucratic and coercive domination. Yet anti-capitalist, socialist revolutions would pave the way for the atrophy of the state as such, because there would be no occasion for state domination over the producing classes in whose name, and by whose efforts, such revolutions would be made.[14]

The analysis of this book suggests both the truth and the limits of Lenin's vision of states and revolutions. Questions of state power *have* been basic in social-revolutionary transformations, but state power cannot be understood only as an instrument of class domination, nor can changes in state structures be explained primarily in terms of class conflicts. In France, Russia, and China, class conflicts—especially between peasants and landlords—were pivotal during the revolutionary interregnums. But both the occurrence of the revolutionary situations in the first place and the nature of the New Regimes that emerged from the revolutionary conflicts depended fundamentally upon the structures of state organizations and their partially autonomous and dynamic relationships to domestic class and political forces, as well as their positions in relation to other states abroad.

Prerevolutionary France, Russia, and China all had well-established imperial states with proven capacities to protect their own hegemony and that of the dominant classes against revolts from below. Before social revolutions could occur, the administrative and military power of these states had to break down. When this happened in France 1789, Russia 1917, and China 1911, it was *not* because of deliberate activities to that end, either on the part of avowed revolutionaries or on the part of politically powerful groups within the Old Regimes. Rather revolutionary

political crises, culminating in administrative and military breakdowns, emerged because the imperial states became caught in cross-pressures between intensified military competition or intrusions from abroad and constraints imposed on monarchical responses by the existing agrarian class structures and political institutions. The old-regime states were prone to such revolutionary crises because their existing structures made it impossible for them to meet the particular international military exigencies that each had to face in the modern era.

Once the old-regime states had broken apart, fundamental political and class conflicts were set in motion, not to be resolved until new administrative and military organizations were consolidated in the place of the old. Revolts from below directly attacked the property and privileges of dominant classes, thus accomplishing changes in class relations that otherwise would not have occurred. Yet equally important were the effects of peasant and urban working class revolts on the course of national political struggles. Possibilities for counterrevolutionary restoration or liberal stabilization were undermined, and revolutionary leaderships found it possible to mobilize popular support in the process of building up new state organizations to defend against domestic competitors and foreign invaders. Compared to the imperial states of the Old Regimes, the new-regime states that emerged in France, Russia, and China alike were stronger and more autonomous within society and more powerful over against foreign competitors within the international states system. Moreover, peasants and urban workers were more directly incorporated into national politics and state-run projects after the Revolutions whose triumph they had helped to ensure. Strengthened national states were not the only accomplishments of the French, Russian, and Chinese Revolutions, but such changes in the state order were among the most striking and important revolutionary transformations.

Strengthened states—more centralized, bureaucratic, and autonomously powerful at home and abroad—emerged from all three Revolutions. This fact points to the operation of persistent influences regardless of whether the intranational conflicts of a revolution were anticapitalist, as in Russia and China, or on balance favorable to capitalist development, as in France. One such influence was the competitive dynamic of the international states system. Wars and imperial intrusions were the midwives of the revolutionary crises, and the emergent revolutionary regimes consolidated state power not only amidst armed domestic conflicts but also in militarily threatening international circumstances. In France, Russia, and China alike the exigencies of revolutionary consolidation in a world of competing states helped ensure that leaderships willing and able to build up centralized coercive and administrative organizations would come to the fore during the Revolutions, and that their handiwork would create a permanent base of power for state cadres within the revolutionized social orders.

Furthermore, modern social revolutions like the French, Russian, and Chinese have invariably occurred in countries caught behind more economically developed competitor nations. Increasingly over "world time," opportunities and models have become available for using state power to promote national economic development. Especially in Russia and China, therefore, revolutionary leaderships have been able to use state power after the initial consolidation of the New Regimes to propel further socioeconomic transformations. These transformations have contributed indispensably to national survival (i.e., Russia in World War II) or to the material well-being of the people as a whole (i.e., China). Yet they surely could not have been accomplished without dynamic state intervention or without political controls over many aspects of social and economic life.

We might be tempted to conclude that, in contrast to Lenin, Max Weber is a better and more infallible guide to revolutionary outcomes. In Weber's view, revolutions function in the end to further bureaucratic domination, all the more inevitably so to the extent that they establish state controls over the economy.[15] But this perspective offers insufficient insight into the varying outcomes of the French, Russian, and Chinese Revolutions—especially with respect to their consequences for the peasantries who participated so decisively in all three revolutionary dramas, and who constituted the vast majority in society after the Revolutions as well as before. Given the ultimate fate of the Russian peasantry under Stalin, it is obviously impossible to hold that anticapitalist, communist revolutions have necessarily served peasant interests better than noncommunist social revolutions such as the French (or the Mexican). But neither will it do to assert that peasants inevitably fare worse under "totalitarian" communist revolutionary regimes. The Chinese Revolution belies this facile conclusion and challenges the received categorical opposition of "democracy" versus "totalitarianism" just as surely as the results of the Russian Revolution challenge any automatic equation of anti-capitalism with socialist democracy. As a direct result of the socioeconomic and political accomplishments of the Chinese Revolution, Chinese peasants as a whole enjoy not only markedly better material conditions than before 1949. They also possess more direct control over and participation in decisions about the affairs of their locally focused lives than did either the Russian peasantry after 1929 or the French peasantry after 1789–93. Moreover, however centralized and bureaucratic the Chinese Communist Party-state may be compared to prerevolutionary Chinese regimes, it nevertheless has afforded considerable scope for provincial and local planning and initiative. These considerations suggest, *pace* Weber, that anticapitalist, state-strengthening revolutions need not necessarily result merely in a more total form of Western-style bureaucratic domination.

To be sure, the outcomes of the Chinese Revolution must not be romanticized. The best ideals of socialist democracy are far from being realized in a context where political life is marked by group manipulation and by intolerance for many kinds of dissent. Nevertheless, it would be folly to let our received political categories blind us to the participatory qualities of the Chinese Communist polity as a whole or to the genuine gains in local community decision-making that have been achieved by and for the Chinese peasant majority as a result of the Revolution. The Chinese state has been strengthened and, at the same time, so has local-level collective democracy. This revolutionary outcome cannot be adequately comprehended by any theoretical perspective that posits a unilinear, world-historical march of bureaucratic rationalization. Rather it must be understood from a comparative perspective that gives weight to the distinctive forms of old-regime breakdown, revolutionary conflicts, and peasant mobilization in the course of revolutionary state-building that were specific to the history of the Chinese Revolution.

The French, Russian, and Chinese Revolutions, whose similarities and variations this book has explored at length and sought to explain, have not, of course, been the only social-revolutionary transformations in the modern world. Most observers would probably agree that social revolutions in roughly the sense meant here—that is, rapid, basic transformations of a society's state and class structures, accompanied and in part carried through by class-based revolts from below—have also occurred in Mexico between 1911 and the 1930s and since World War II in Yugoslavia, Vietnam, Algeria, Cuba, Bolivia, Angola, Mozambique, Guinea-Bissau, and Ethiopia. All of these share certain broad resemblances to the French, Russian, and Chinese Revolutions. They occurred in predominantly agrarian countries, and they became possible only through the administrative-military breakdown of preexisting states. Peasant revolts or mobilization for guerrilla warfare played a pivotal role in each revolutionary process. Furthermore, in every one of these cases, organized revolutionary leaderships (recruited from the ranks of previously marginal, educated elites) emerged or came to the fore during the revolutionary crisis. And these leaders acted to build new, strengthened state organizations to consolidate revolutionary changes and assert national autonomy.

NOTES

1. Good examples are the peasant-based rebellions that recurrently shook medieval Europe and Imperial China. The Chinese rebellions occasionally succeeded in toppling, and even replacing, dynasties, but did not fundamentally transform the sociopolitical structure. For more discussion and references, see Chapter 3.
2. As I understand this case, the English Revolution (1640–50 and 1688–9 taken together) is an excellent example of a political revolution. What it fundamentally accomplished was the establishment of parliamentary government through the revolt of sections of the dominant landed class against would-be absolute monarchs. This case is discussed in Chapter 3 and Chapter 5. Another good example of a political, but not social, revolution is the Japanese Meiji Restoration, which will be discussed in Chapter 2.
3. For examples of attempts to explain revolutions through strategies of analytic simplification, see the various works cited in notes 18 and 20 for this chapter. More will be said below about the ideas of two important theorists, Ted Gurr and Charles Tilly, both of whom subsume revolutions within broader analytic categories, albeit of contrasting kinds.
4. Three examples of scholars who leave (structural) change contingent are: Arthur L. Stinchcombe, "Stratification among Organizations and the Sociology of Revolution," in *Handbook of Organizations*, ed. James G. March (Chicago: Rand McNally, 1965), pp. 169–80; Charles Tilly, *From Mobilization to Revolution* (Reading, Mass.: Addison-Wesley, 1978), chap. 7; and D. E. H. Russell, *Rebellion, Revolution, and Armed Force* (New York: Academic Press, 1974), chap. 4. Those who want to leave change contingent usually argue that nothing is lost by doing so, given that after one has examined the causes of all outbreaks whether or not they result in actual changes, then one can proceed to ask what *additional* causes explain the subset of outbreaks that do lead to successful changes. But to accept this sort of argument, one must be willing to assume that successful social-revolutionary transformations have no distinctive, long-term, structural causes or preconditions. One must assume that social revolutions are simply political revolutions or mass rebellions that possess some additional, short-term ingredient such as military success or the determination of ideological leaders to implement changes after grabbing power. The entire argument of this book is based upon the opposite assumption–that social revolutions do have long-term causes, and that they grow out of structural contradictions and potentials inherent in old regimes.

5. Here I make no pretense to survey the entire social-scientific literature on revolutions. Two books that provide surveys of the literature are A. S. Cohan, *Theories of Revolution: An Introduction* (New York: Halsted Press, 1975) and Mark N. Hagopian, *The Phenomenon of Revolution* (New York: Dodd, Mead, 1974). Useful critiques are to be found in: Isaac Kramnick, "Reflections on Revolution: Definition and Explanation in Recent Scholarship," *History and Theory* 11:1 (1972):26–63; Michael Freeman, "Review Article: Theories of Revolution," *British Journal of Political Science* 2:3 (July 1972):339–59; Barbara Salert, *Revolutions and Revolutionaries: Four Theories* (New York: Elsevier, 1976); Lawrence Stone, "Theories of Revolution," *World Politics* 18:2 (January 1966): 159–76; Perez Zagorin, "Theories of Revolution in Contemporary Historiography," *Political Science Quarterly* 88:1 (March 1973):23–52; and Theda Skocpol, "Explaining Revolutions: In Quest of a Social–Structural Approach," in *The Uses of Controversy in Sociology*, eds. Lewis A. Coser and Otto N. Larsen (New York: Free Press, 1976), pp. 155–75.

6. For example, Gurr asserts that the "public order is most effectively maintained–it can *only* be maintained–when means are provided within it for men to work towards the attainment of their aspirations (*Why Men Rebel*, p. x)." And, for Johnson, societies, if stable, are "communities of value-sharers."

7. Charles Tilly, "Revolutions and Collective Action," in *Handbook of Political Science*, eds. Greenstein and Polsby, vol. 3, *Macropolitical Theory*, pp. 520–521.

8. See, for example, Herbert Adam, *Modernizing Racial Domination: South Africa's Political Dynamics* (Berkeley: University of California Press, 1971), and also Russell, *Rebellion, Revolution, and Armed Force*, chaps. 1–3. Both of these works stress the cohesiveness and stability of the South African state as the major obstacle to revolution, despite the discontent and protests of the non-white majority.

9. Jeremy Brecher, *Strike!* (San Francisco: Straight Arrow Books, 1972), p. 240.

10. Quote attributed (without exact reference) to Wendell Phillips by Stephen F. Cohen in his *Bukharin and the Bolshevik Revolution* (New York: Knopf, 1973), p. 336.

11. Tilly avoids presenting revolutionary processes and outcomes as the deliberate doing of particular acting groups, even though he does not avoid presenting the causes of revolutionary situations in purposive-movement terms. The reason is that Tilly portrays the emergence of revolutionary situations as the work of *coalitions* of mobilized groups and suggests that such coalitions usually fall apart during revolutions, giving rise to a series of intergroup conflicts that no one group fully controls. This view of revolutionary processes is quite valid. But Tilly's view of revolutionary situations as *caused* by coalitions deliberately challenging the sovereignty of the existing government strikes me as too purposive, at least for the historical cases I have studied most closely. For these cases, the idea of *conjuncture*–implying the coming together of separately determined and not consciously coordinated (or deliberately revolutionary) processes and group efforts–seems a more useful perspective on the causes of social revolutions than does the idea of intergroup coalition. My reasons for believing this will become evident in due course, particularly in Chapters 2 and 3.

12. Eric Hobsbawm, "Revolution," (Paper presented at the Fourteenth International Congress of Historical Sciences, San Francisco, August 1975), p. 10.

13. Lenin, "The Dual Power," originally published in *Pravda* on April 9, 1917; reprinted in Robert C. Tucker, ed., *The Lenin Anthology* (New York: Norton, 1975), p. 301.

14. See Lenin, "The State and Revolution," reprinted in *Lenin Anthology*, ed. Tucker, pp. 311–98.

15. See especially Weber on "Bureaucracy," in *From Max Weber: Essays in Sociology*, ed. and trans. H. H. Gerth and C. Wright Mills (New York: Oxford University Press, 1958), chap. 8. Lenin's and Weber's views on the state and bureaucracy are very cogently compared in Erik Olin Wright, "To Control or Smash Bureaucracy: Weber and Lenin on Politics, the State, and Bureaucracy," *Berkeley Journal of Sociology* 19 (1974–75):69–108.

TIMUR KURAN

12.3 NOW OUT OF NEVER

The Element of Surprise in the East European Revolution of 1989

In the 1991 article from which the following text is excerpted, the economist Timur Kuran tries to resolve an important mystery. After 1989, the Soviet Union and its satellite states collapsed in a revolutionary wave that was largely unanticipated by most commentators. Kuran noted that we seem to be reasonably good at retroactively "explaining" successful revolutions, but if we can do this, why is it so much more difficult to predict them? Focusing on East-Central European cases like the Polish, Czech, and East German revolutions against their Soviet-backed regimes, Kuran uses rational choice theory to try to answer this difficult question. Revolutions, he notes, involve actors solving collective action problems. The fact that many individuals, perhaps even a majority, might want regime change does not mean they will be able to successfully coordinate their actions to achieve it. Authoritarian regimes have many ways to produce barriers to collective action. Repression of speech and thought can cause people to engage in "preference falsification," which means, in essence, that they lie about what they want to avoid being persecuted. Preference falsification can make support for a disliked regime seem higher than it actually is. Once a revolutionary sequence or cascade gets tipped off, however—once it starts to become clear to members of the society that a change of regime might be possible—those individuals may stop preference falsification and more clearly express their goals and desires. This amounts to the removal of a barrier to collective action. Similarly, the sense of possibility created by protest activity itself facilitates collective action because it makes participation seem more rational. From this general point of view, which has been developed by other scholars like Mancur Olson, James Coleman, Mark Granovetter, and Marc Lichbach, game-theoretical models give us the best leverage over the question of when and where revolutions are most likely to take place.

UNITED IN AMAZEMENT

"Our jaws cannot drop any lower," exclaimed Radio Free Europe one day in late 1989. It was commenting on the electrifying collapse of Eastern Europe's communist regimes.[1] The political landscape of the entire region changed suddenly, astonishing even the most seasoned political observers. In a matter of weeks entrenched leaders were overthrown, the communist monopoly on power was abrogated in one country after another, and persecuted critics of the communist system were catapulted into high office.

In the West the ranks of the stunned included champions of the view that communist totalitarianism is substantially more stable than ordinary authoritarianism.[2] "It has to be conceded," wrote a leading proponent of this view in early 1990, "that those of us

Kuran, Timur. 1991. "Now Out of Never: The Element of Surprise in the East European Revolution of 1989." *World Politics* 44(1): 7–48.

who distinguish between the two non-democratic types of government underestimated the decay of Communist countries and expected the collapse of totalitarianism to take longer than has actually turned out to be the case."[3] Another acknowledged her bewilderment through the title of a new book: *The Withering Away of the Totalitarian State . . . And Other Surprises.*[4]

We will never know how many East Europeans foresaw the events of 1989—or at least the impending changes in their own countries. But at each step, journalistic accounts invariably painted a picture of a stunned public. For example, two days after the breaching of the Berlin Wall, the *New York Times* carried an article in which an East German remarks: "It's unfathomable. If you had told me that one week ago, I wouldn't have believed it. Mentally, I still can't. It will take a few days before what this means sinks in."[5]

While the collapse of the post-World War II political order of Eastern Europe stunned the world, in retrospect it appears as the inevitable consequence of a multitude of factors. In each of the six countries the leadership was generally despised, lofty economic promises remained unfulfilled, and freedoms taken for granted elsewhere existed only on paper. But if the revolution was indeed inevitable, why was it not foreseen? Why did people overlook signs that are clearly visible after the fact? One of the central arguments of this essay is precisely that interacting social and psychological factors make it inherently difficult to predict the outcome of political competition. I shall argue that the East European Revolution was by no means inevitable. What *was* inevitable is that we would be astounded if and when it arrived.

"The victim of today is the victor of tomorrow, /And out of Never grows Now!"[6] Brecht's couplet captures perfectly our central paradox: seemingly unshakable regimes saw public sentiment turn against them with astonishing rapidity, as tiny oppositions mushroomed into crushing majorities. Currently popular theories of revolution offer little insight into this stunning pace; nor for that matter do they shed light on the element of surprise in previous revolutions. All lay claim to predictive power, yet none has a track record at veritable prediction. The next section briefly critiques the pertinent scholarly literature. Without denying the usefulness of some received theories at explaining revolutions

of the past, I go on to present a theory that illuminates both the process of revolutionary mobilization and the limits of our ability to predict where and when mobilizations will occur. Subsequent sections apply this argument to the case at hand.

The term *revolution* is used here in a narrow sense to denote a mass-supported seizure of political power that aims to transform the social order. By this definition it is immaterial whether the accomplished transfer of power brings about significant social change. With regard to the East European Revolution, it is too early to tell whether the postrevolutionary regimes will succeed in reshaping the economy, the legal system, international relations, and individual rights—to mention just some of the domains on the reformist agenda. But even if the ongoing reforms all end in failure, the upheavals of 1989 can continue to be characterized as a regionwide revolution.

PREFERENCE FALSIFICATION AND REVOLUTIONARY BANDWAGONS

So mass discontent does not necessarily generate a popular uprising against the political status quo. To understand when it does, we need to identify the conditions under which individuals will display antagonism toward the regime under which they live. After all, a mass uprising results from multitudes of individual choices to participate in a movement for change; there is no actor named "the crowd" or "the opposition." The model presented here is in agreement with the rational-choice school on this basic methodological point, although it departs in important ways from the standard fare in rational-choice modeling.

Consider a society whose members are indexed by *i*. Each individual member must choose whether to support the government in public or oppose it; depending on his public acts and statements, each person is perceived as either a friend of the government or an enemy, for the political status quo or against. In private, of course, a person may feel torn between the government and the opposition, seeing both advantages and disadvantages to the existing regime. I am thus distinguishing between an individual's *private preference* and *public preference*. The former is effectively fixed at any given instant, the latter a variable under his control. Insofar as his two preferences differ—that is, the preference he expresses in public diverges from that he holds in private—the individual is engaged in *preference falsification.*

Let S represent the size of the public opposition, expressed as a percentage of the population. Initially it is near 0, implying that the government commands almost unanimous public support. A revolution, as a mass-supported seizure of political power, may be treated as an enormous jump in S.

Now take a citizen who wants the government overthrown. The likely impact of his own public preference on the fate of the government is negligible: it is unlikely to be a decisive factor in whether the government stands or falls. But it may bring him personal rewards and impose on him personal punishments. If he chooses to oppose the government, for instance, he is likely to face persecution, though in the event the government falls his outspokenness may be rewarded handsomely. Does this mean that our individual will base his public preference solely on the potential rewards and punishments flowing from the two rival camps? Will his private antipathy to the regime play no role whatsoever in his decision? This does not seem reasonable, for history offers countless examples of brave individuals who stood up for a cause in the face of the severest pressures, including torture.

On what, then, will our disaffected individual's choice depend? I submit that it will depend on a trade-off between two payoffs, one external and the other internal.[7]

The external payoff to siding with the opposition consists of the just-discussed personal rewards and punishments. In net terms, this payoff is apt to become increasingly favorable (or increasingly less unfavorable) with S. The larger S, the smaller the individual dissenter's chances of being persecuted for his identification with the opposition and the fewer hostile supporters of the government he has to face. The latter relationship reflects the fact that government supporters, even ones privately sympathetic to the opposition, participate in the persecution of the government's opponents, as part of their personal efforts to establish convincing progovernment credentials. This relationship implies that a rise in S leaves fewer people seeking to penalize members of the public opposition.

The internal payoff is rooted in the psychological cost of preference falsification. The suppression of one's wants entails a loss of personal autonomy, a sacrifice of personal integrity. It thus generates lasting discomfort, the more so the greater the lie. This relationship may be captured by postulating that person i's internal payoff for supporting the opposition varies positively with his private preference, x^i. The higher x^i, the more costly he finds it to suppress his antigovernment feelings.

So i's public preference depends on S and x^i. As the public opposition grows, with his private preference constant, there comes a point where his external cost of joining the opposition falls below his internal cost of preference falsification. This switching point may be called his *revolutionary threshold, T^i.* Since a threshold represents a value of S, it is a number between 0 and 100.

If x^i should rise, T^i will fall. In other words, if the individual becomes more sympathetic to the opposition, it will take a smaller public opposition to make him take a stand against the government. The same will be true if the government becomes less efficient, or the opposition becomes more efficient, at rewarding its supporters and punishing its rivals. In fact, anything that affects the relationship between S and the individual's external payoff for supporting the opposition will change his revolutionary threshold. Finally, T^i will fall if i develops a greater need to stand up and be counted, for the internal cost of preference falsification will then come to dominate the external benefit at a lower S.[8]

This simple framework offers a reason why a person may choose to voice a demand for change even when the price of dissent is very high and the chances of a successful uprising very low. If his private opposition to the existing order is intense and/or his need for integrity is quite strong, the suffering he incurs for dissent may be outweighed by the satisfaction he derives from being true to himself. In every society, of course, there are people who go against the social order of the day. Joseph Schumpeter once observed that in capitalist societies this group is dominated by intellectuals. Their position as "onlookers" and "outsiders" with much time for deep reflection causes them to develop a "critical attitude" toward the status quo. And because of the high value they attach to self-expression, they are relatively unsusceptible to social pressures.[9] The same argument applies to noncapitalist societies. As a case in point, a disproportionately large share of the East European dissidents were intellectuals.

Returning to the general model, we can observe that individuals with different private preferences and psychological constitutions will have different revolutionary thresholds. Imagine a ten-person society featuring the *threshold sequence*

$$A = \{0, 20, 20, 30, 40, 50, 60, 70, 80, 100\}.$$

Person 1 ($T^1 = 0$) supports the opposition regardless of its size, just as person 10 ($T^{10} = 100$) always supports the government. The remaining eight people's preferences are sensitive to S: depending on its level, they opt for one camp or the other. For instance, person 5 ($T^5 = 40$) supports the government if $0 \leq S < 40$ but joins the opposition if $40 \leq S \leq 100$. Let us assume that the opposition consists initially of a single person, or 10 percent of the population, so $S = 10$. Because the nine other individuals have thresholds above 10, this S is self-sustaining; that is, it constitutes an *equilibrium*.

This equilibrium happens to be vulnerable to a minor change in A. Suppose that person 2 has an unpleasant encounter at some government ministry. Her alienation from the regime rises, pushing her threshold down from 20 to 10. The new threshold sequence is

$$A' = \{0, 10, 20, 30, 40, 50, 60, 70, 80, 100\}.$$

Person 2's new threshold happens to equal the existing S of 10, so she switches sides, and S becomes 20. Her move into the opposition takes the form of tossing an egg at the country's long-standing leader during a government-organized rally. The new S of 20 is not self-sustaining but self-augmenting, as it drives person 3 into the opposition. The higher S of 30 then triggers a fourth defection, raising S to 40, and this process continues until S reaches 90—a new equilibrium. Now the first nine individuals are in opposition, with only the tenth supporting the government. A slight shift in one individual's threshold has thus generated a *revolutionary bandwagon*, an explosive growth in public opposition.[10]

Now consider the sequence

$$B = \{0, 20, 30, 30, 40, 50, 60, 70, 80, 100\},$$

which differs from A only in its third element: 30 as opposed to 20. As in the previous illustration, let T^2 fall from 20 to 10. The resulting sequence is

$$B' = \{0, 10, 30, 30, 40, 50, 60, 70, 80, 100\}.$$

Once again, the incumbent equilibrium of 10 becomes unsustainable, and S rises to 20. But the opposition's growth stops there, for the new S is self-sustaining. Some government supporters privately enjoy the sight of the leader's egg-splattered face, but none follows the egg thrower into public opposition. We see that a minor variation in thresholds may drastically alter the effect of a given perturbation. And in particular, an event that causes a revolution in one setting may in a slightly different setting produce only a minor decline in the government's popularity.

Neither private preferences nor the corresponding thresholds are common knowledge. So a society can come to the brink of a revolution without anyone knowing this, not even those with the power to unleash it. In sequence A, for instance, person 2 need not recognize that she has the ability to set off a revolutionary bandwagon. Even if she senses the commonness of preference falsification, she simply cannot know whether the actual threshold sequence is A or B. Social psychologists use the term *pluralistic ignorance* to describe misperceptions concerning distributions of individual characteristics.[11] In principle, pluralistic ignorance can be mitigated through polls that accord individuals anonymity. But it is easier to offer people anonymity than to convince them that the preferences they reveal will remain anonymous and never be used against them. In any case, an outwardly popular government that knows preference falsification to be pervasive has no interest in publicizing the implied fragility of its support, because this might inspire the disaffected to bring their antigovernment feelings into the open. It has an incentive to discourage independent polling and discredit surveys that reveal unflattering information.

We have already seen that the threshold sequence is not fixed. Anything that affects the distribution of private preferences may alter it, for instance, an economic recession, contacts with other societies, or intergenerational replacement. But whatever the underlying reason, private preferences and, hence, the threshold sequence can move dramatically against the government without triggering a revolution. In the sequence

$$C = \{0, 20, 20, 20, 20, 20, 20, 20, 60, 100\}$$

the average threshold is 30, possibly because most people sympathize with the opposition. Yet $S = 10$ remains an equilibrium. It is true, of course, that a revolution is more likely under C than under A. C features seven individuals with thresholds of 20, A only one. A ten-unit fall in any one of the seven thresholds would trigger a revolution.

The point remains that widespread disapproval of the government is not sufficient to mobilize large numbers for revolutionary action. Anti-government feelings can certainly bring a revolution within the realm of possibility, but other conditions must come together to set it off. By the same token, a revolution may break out in a society where private preferences, and therefore individual thresholds, tend to be relatively unfavorable to the opposition. Reconsider the sequence A', where the average threshold is 46, as opposed to 30 in C. Under A' public opposition darts from 10 to 90, whereas under C it remains stuck at 10. This simple comparison shows why the relative-deprivation theory of revolution has not held up under empirical testing. By treating the likelihood of revolution as the sum of the individual levels of discontent, the relative-deprivation theory overlooks the significance of the distribution of discontent. As our comparison between A' and C indicates, one sufficiently disaffected person with a threshold of 10 may do more for a revolution than seven individuals with thresholds of 20.

Imagine now that a superpower long committed to keeping the local government in power suddenly rescinds this commitment, declaring that it will cease meddling in the internal affairs of other countries. This is precisely the type of change to which the structuralist theory accords revolutionary significance. In the present framework, such a change will not necessarily ignite a revolution. The outcome depends on both the preexisting distribution of thresholds and the consequent shifts. Since the postulated change in international relations is likely to lower the expected cost of joining the opposition, people's thresholds are likely to fall. Let us say that every threshold between 10 and 90 drops by 10 units. If the preexisting threshold sequence were A, B, or C, the result would be an explosion in S from 10 to 90. But suppose that it were

$$D = \{0, 30, 30, 30, 30, 30, 30, 30, 30, 100\}.$$

The structural shock turns this sequence into

$$D' = \{0, 20, 20, 20, 20, 20, 20, 20, 20, 100\}.$$

Fully four-fifths of the population is now willing to switch over to the opposition but *only if someone else goes first*. No one does, leaving S at 10.

Structural factors are thus part of the story, yet by no means the whole story. While they certainly affect the likelihood of revolution, they cannot possibly deliver infallible predictions. A single person's reaction to an event of global importance may make all the difference between a massive uprising and a *latent bandwagon* that never takes off. So to suggest, as the structuralists do, that revolutions are brought about by deep historical forces with individuals simply the passive bearers of these forces is to overlook the potentially crucial importance of individual characteristics of little significance in and of themselves. It is always a conjunction of factors, many of them intrinsically unimportant and thus unobserved, if not unobservable, that determines the flow of events. A major global event can produce drastically different outcomes in two settings that differ trivially. Structuralism and individualism are not rival and mutually incompatible approaches to the study of revolution, as Skocpol would have it. They are essential components of a single story.

We can now turn to the question of why with hindsight an unanticipated revolution may appear as the inevitable consequence of monumental forces for change. A successful revolution brings into the open long-repressed grievances. Moreover, people who were relatively content with the old regime embrace the new regime, and they are apt to attribute their former public preferences to fears of persecution.

Reconsider the threshold sequence

$A' = \{0, 10, 20, 30, 40, 50, 60, 70, 80, 100\}$.

The relatively high thresholds in A' are likely to be associated with private preferences more favorable to the government than to the opposition.[12] Person 9 ($T^9 = 80$) is much more satisfied with the government than, say, person 3 ($T^3 = 20$). As such she has little desire to join a movement aimed at toppling it. Remember that public opposition settles at 90, she being the last to jump on the revolutionary bandwagon. The important point is this: person 9 changes her public preference only after the opposition snowballs into a crushing majority, making it imprudent to remain a government supporter.

Having made the switch, she has every reason to feign a long-standing antipathy to the toppled government. She will not admit that she yearns for the status quo ante, because this would contradict her new public preference. Nor will she say that her change of heart followed the government's collapse, because this might render her declared sympathy for the revolution unconvincing. She will claim that she has long had serious misgivings about the old order and has sympathized with the objectives of the opposition. An unintended effect of this distortion is to make it seem as though the toppled government enjoyed even less genuine support than it actually did.

This illusion is rooted in the very phenomenon responsible for making the revolution a surprise: preference falsification. Having misled everyone into seeing a revolution as highly unlikely, preference falsification now conceals the forces that were working against it. One of the consequences of postrevolutionary preference falsification is thus to make even less comprehensible why the revolution was unforeseen.

The historians of a revolution may appreciate the biases that afflict people's postrevolutionary accounts of their prerevolutionary dispositions without being able to measure the significance of these biases. Consider the sequence

$C' = \{0, 10, 20, 20, 20, 20, 20, 20, 60, 100\}$.

Like A', this sequence drives S from 10 to 90, implying that nine out of ten individuals have an incentive to say that they despised the prerevolutionary regime. If thresholds below 50 reflect private support for a revolution, and those above 50 private satisfaction with the status quo, eight of the nine would be telling the truth, the one liar being person 9 ($T^9 = 60$). It follows from the same assumption that four of the nine would be lying if the threshold sequence were A'. But once again, because thresholds are not public knowledge, historians may have difficulty determining whether the prerevolutionary sequence was A or C—or for that matter, whether the postrevolutionary sequence is A' or C'.

Before moving to the East European Revolution, it may be useful to comment on how the foregoing argument relates to three sources of controversy in the literature on revolutions: the continuity of social change, the power of the individual, and the significance of unorganized crowds.

The proposed theory treats continuous and discontinuous change as a single, unified process. Private preferences and the corresponding thresholds may change gradually over a long period during which public opposition is more or less stable. If the cumulative movement establishes a latent bandwagon, a minor event may then precipitate an abrupt and sharp break in the size of the public opposition. This is not to say that private preferences change *only* in small increments. A major blunder on the part of the government may suddenly turn private preferences against it.

Such a shift could also occur in response to an initial, possibly modest, increase in public opposition. The underlying logic was expressed beautifully by Alexis de Tocqueville: "Patiently endured so long as it seemed beyond redress, a grievance comes to appear intolerable once the possibility of removing it crosses men's minds."[13] In terms of our model, Tocqueville suggests that the threshold sequence is itself dependent on the size of the public opposition. If so, a revolutionary bandwagon may come about as the joint outcome of two mutually reinforcing trends: a fall in thresholds and a rise in public opposition. Imagine that public opposition rises sufficiently to convince those privately sympathetic to the government that a revolution might be in the making. This realization induces many of them to think about possible alternatives to the status quo. Their thinking starts a chain reaction through which private preferences shift swiftly and dramatically against the government. The consequent changes in the threshold sequence cause the revolutionary bandwagon to accelerate.

The theory depicts the individual as both powerless and potentially very powerful. The individual is powerless because a revolution requires the mobilization of large numbers, but he is also potentially very powerful because under the right circumstances he may set off a chain reaction that generates the necessary mobilization. Not that the individual can know precisely when his own choice can make a difference. Although he may sense that his chances of sparking a wildfire are unusually great, he can never be certain about the consequences of his own opposition. What is certain is that the incumbent regime will remain in place unless someone takes the lead in moving into the opposition.

As we saw in the previous section, the standard theory of rational choice depicts the potential revolutionary as paralyzed by the realization of his powerlessness. Many social thinkers who, like the present author, accept the logic of collective action have struggled with the task of explaining how mass mobilizations get started. One of the proposed explanations rests on a cognitive illusion: the individual overestimates his personal political influence. Another invokes an ethical commitment: the individual feels compelled to do his fair share for the attainment of a jointly desired outcome.[14] The approach used here, which is not incompatible with these explanations, places the burden of sparking the mobilization process on the individual's need to be true to himself. This approach is consistent with the fact that revolutionary leaders tend to be surprised when their goals materialize. The cognitive-illusion explanation is not: people who challenge the government out of an overestimation of their personal ability to direct the course of history will not be surprised when their wishes come true. The approach of this essay is also consistent with the fact that some people risk their lives for a revolution even as the vast majority of the potential beneficiaries refrain from doing their own fair share.

Finally, the outlined theory accords organized pressure groups and unorganized crowds complementary roles in the overthrow of the government.

Organized oppositions enhance the external payoff to dissent, both by providing the individual dissenter with a support network and by raising the likelihood of a successful revolution. They also help shatter the appearance of the invulnerability of the status quo, and through propaganda, they shift people's private preferences in favor of change. Charles Tilly is therefore right to draw attention to the structural and situational factors that govern a society's pattern of political organization.[15] But as Pamela Oliver warns, we must guard against overemphasizing the role of organization at the expense of the role of the unorganized crowd. A small difference in the resources at the disposal of an organized opposition may have a tremendous impact on the outcome of its efforts.[16] This observation makes perfect sense in the context of the theory developed here. Where a small pressure group fails to push a bandwagon into motion a *slightly better organized* or *slightly larger* one might.

EAST EUROPEAN COMMUNISM AND THE WELLSPRING OF ITS STABILITY

Communist parties came to power in Russia, and then in Eastern Europe and elsewhere, with the promise that "scientific socialism" would pioneer new dimensions of freedom, eliminate exploitation, vest political power in the masses, eradicate nationalism, and raise standards of living to unprecedented heights—all this, while the state was withering away. They did not deliver on any of these promises. Under their stewardship, communism came to symbolize repression, censorship, ethnic chauvinism, militarism, red tape, and economic backwardness.

The failures of communism prompted a tiny number of Soviet and East European citizens to criticize official policies and established institutions. Such dissidents expressed their frustrations through clandestine self-publications (*samizdat*) and writings published in the West (*tamizdat*). Given the chasm between the rhetoric of communism and its achievements, the existence of an opposition is easily understood. Less comprehensible is the rarity of public opposition—prior, that is, to 1989. The few uprisings that were crushed—notably, East Berlin in 1953, Hungary in 1956, and Czechoslovakia in 1968—are the exceptions that prove the rule. For most of several decades, most East Europeans displayed a remarkable tolerance for tyranny and inefficiency. They remained docile, submissive, and even outwardly supportive of the status quo.

This subservience is attributable partly to punishments meted out by the communist establishment to its actual and imagined opponents. In the heyday of communism a person speaking out against the leadership or in favor of some reform could expect to suffer harassment, lose his job, and face imprisonment—in short, he could expect to be denied the opportunity to lead a decent life. Even worse horrors befell millions of suspected opponents. Just think of the forced-labor camps of the Gulag Archipelago and of the liquidations carried out under the pretext of historical necessity. "We can only be right with and by the Party," wrote a leading theoretician of communism, "for history has provided no other way of being in the right."[17] Such thinking could, and did, serve to justify horrible crimes against nonconformists.

Yet official repression is only one factor in the endurance of communism. The system was sustained by a general willingness to support it in public: people routinely applauded speakers whose message they disliked, joined organizations whose mission they opposed, and signed defamatory letters against people they admired, among other manifestations of consent and accommodation. "The lie," wrote the Russian novelist Alexander Solzhenitsyn in the early 1970s, "has been incorporated into the state system as the vital link holding everything together, with billions of tiny fasteners, several dozen to each man."[18] If people stopped lying, he asserted, communist rule would break down instantly. He then asked rhetorically, "What does it mean, *not to lie?*" It means *"not saying what you don't think,* and that includes not whispering, not opening your mouth, not raising your hand, not casting your vote, not feigning a smile, not lending your presence, not standing up, and not cheering."[19]

THE REVOLUTION

The foregoing argument has two immediate implications. First, the regimes of Eastern Europe were substantially more vulnerable than the subservience and

quiescence of their populations made them seem. Millions were prepared to stand up in defiance if ever they sensed that this was sufficiently safe. The people's solidarity with their leaders would then have been exposed as illusory, stripping the veneer of legitimacy from the communist monopoly on power. Second, even the support of those genuinely sympathetic to the status quo was rather thin. Though many saw no alternative to socialism, their many grievances predisposed them to the promise of fundamental change. Were public discourse somehow to turn against socialism, they would probably awaken to the possibility that their lives could be improved.

But what would catalyze the process of revolutionary mobilization? With hindsight it appears that the push came from the Soviet Union. In the mid-1980s festering economic problems, until then officially denied, convinced the top Soviet leadership to call for *perestroika* (restructuring) and *glasnost* (public openness). Repressed grievances burst into the open, including dissatisfaction with communist rule itself. And with Mikhail Gorbachev's rise to the helm in 1985, the Soviet Union abandoned its long-standing policy of confrontation with the West, to seek accommodation and cooperation.[20] In Eastern Europe these changes kindled hopes of greater independence and meaningful social reform.

Lest it appear that these developments provided a clear signal of the coming revolution, remember that Havel dismissed a Czechoslovak crowd's jubilation over Gorbachev as a sign of naïveté. He was hardly alone in his pessimism. Even if Gorbachev wanted to liberate Eastern Europe, a popular argument went, it was anything but obvious that he could. Surely, the military and hard-line conservatives would insist on retaining the Soviet Union's strategic buffer against an attack from the West.

Nor was this the only obstacle to liberation. Economic and ethnic tensions within the Soviet Union could provide the pretext for a conservative coup. There was always the precedent of Khrushchev, toppled in 1964. About the time that Havel was exuding pessimism, a joke was making the rounds in Prague: "What is the difference between Gorbachev and Dubček [the deposed leader of the 1968 Prague Spring]?" The answer: "None—except Gorbachev doesn't know it yet."[21] Significantly, in the fall of 1989 Moscow was rife with rumors of an impending coup.[22] Some observers expected Gorbachev to survive but only by reversing course and becoming increasingly repressive.[23] An old Soviet joke expresses the underlying thinking. Stalin leaves his heirs in the Party two envelopes. One is labeled, "In case of trouble, open this." Trouble arises and the envelope is opened ceremoniously: "Blame me." The other envelope is labeled, "In case of more trouble, open this." More trouble comes and the second envelope is opened: "Do as I did."[24]

NOTES

This research was supported by the National Science Foundation under grant no. SES-8808031. A segment of the paper was drafted during a sabbatical, financed partly by a fellowship from the National Endowment for the Humanities, at the Institute for Advanced Study in Princeton. I am indebted to Wolfgang Fach, Helena Flam, Jack Goldstone, Kenneth Koford, Pavel Pelikan, Jean-Philippe Platteau, Wolfgang Seibel, Ulrich Witt, and three anonymous readers for helpful comments.

1. Bernard Gwertzman and Michael T. Kaufman, eds., *The Collapse of Communism, by the Correspondents of "The New York Times"* (New York: Times Books, 1990), vii.

2. For an early statement of this thesis, see Hannah Arendt, *The Origins of Totalitarianism*, 2d ed. (1951; reprint, New York: World Publishing, 1958), pt. 3. Arendt suggested that communism weakens interpersonal bonds rooted in family, community, religion, and profession, a situation that makes individuals terribly dependent on the goodwill of the state and thus blocks the mobilization of an anticommunist revolt.

3. Richard Pipes, "Gorbachev's Russia: Breakdown or Crackdown?" *Commentary*, March 1990, p. 16.

4. Jeane J. Kirkpatrick, *The Withering Away of the Totalitarian State . . . And Other Surprises* (Washington, D.C.: AEI Press, 1990). A decade earlier Kirkpatrick had articulated a variant of Arendt's thesis, insisting that the communist system is incapable of self-propelled evolution. See Kirkpatrick, "Dictatorships and Double Standards," *Commentary*, November 1979, pp. 34–45.

5. *New York Times*, November 12, 1989, p. 1.

6. Bertolt Brecht, "Lob der Dialectic" (In praise of dialectics, 1933), in *Gedichte* (Frankfurt: Suhrkamp Verlag, 1961), 3:73; poem translated by Edith Anderson.

7. For a detailed analysis of this trade-off, see Timur Kuran, "Private and Public Preferences," *Economics and Philosophy* 6 (April 1990), 1–26.

8. The theory outlined in this section is developed more fully in Timur Kuran, "Sparks and Prairie Fires: A Theory of Unanticipated Political Revolution," *Public Choice* 61 (April 1989), 41–74. A summary of the present formulation was delivered at the annual convention of the American Economic Association, Washington, D.C., December 28–30, 1990. This presentation appeared under the title "The East European Revolution of 1989: Is It Surprising That We Were Surprised?" in the *American Economic Review, Papers and Proceedings* 81 (May 1991), 121–25.

9. Schumpeter, *Capitalism, Socialism and Democracy*, 3d ed. (1950; reprint, New York: Harper Torchbooks, 1962), chap. 13.

10. Lucid analyses of bandwagon processes include Mark Granovetter, "Threshold Models of Collective Behavior," *American Journal of Sociology* 83 (May 1978), 1420–43; and Thomas C. Schelling, *Micromotives and Macrobehavior* (New York: W. W. Norton, 1978).

11. Under the term *impression of universality*, the concept was introduced by Floyd H. Allport, *Social Psychology* (Boston: Houghton, Mifflin, 1924), 305–9. The term *pluralistic ignorance* was first used by Richard L. Schanck, "A Study of a Community and Its Groups and Institutions Conceived of as Behavior of Individuals," *Psychological Monographs* 43–2 (1932), 101.

12. Relatively high thresholds may also be associated with relatively great vulnerability to social pressure.

13. Tocqueville, *The Old Régime and the French Revolution* (1856), trans. Stuart Gilbert (Garden City, N.Y.: Doubleday, 1955), 177.

14. Each of these is developed by Steven E. Finkel, Edward N. Muller, and Karl-Dieter Opp, "Personal Influence, Collective Rationality, and Mass Political Action," *American Political Science Review* 83 (September 1989), 885–903.

15. Tilly, *From Mobilization to Revolution* (Reading, Mass.: Addison-Wesley, 1978).

16. Oliver, "Bringing the Crowd Back In: The Non-organizational Elements of Social Movements," in Louis Kriesberg, ed., *Research in Social Movements, Conflict and Change* (Greenwich, Conn.: JAI Press, 1989): 11:1–30.

17. The words of Leon Trotsky, cited by Arendt (fn. 2), 307.

18. Solzhenitsys, "The Smatterers" (1974), in Solzhenitsys et al., *From under the Rubble*, trans. A. M. Brock et al. (Boston: Little, Brown, 1975), 275.

19. Ibid., 276; emphasis in original.

20. For details, see Robert C. Tucker, *Political Culture and Leadership in Soviet Russia: From Lenin to Gorbachev* (New York: W. W. Norton, 1987), chap. 7.

21. *Economist*, July 18, 1987, p. 45.

22. Z [anonymous], "To the Stalin Mausoleum," *Daedalus* 119 (Winter 1990), 332.

23. With the revolution, the notion that Gorbachev would turn to the army and the KGB in a bid to stay in power lost plausibility. It regained plausibility in late 1990 with the resignation of his foreign minister, Eduard Shevardnadze, who publicly accused Gorbachev of plotting with hard-liners to create a repressive dictatorship.

24. Recorded by Daniel Bell, "As We Go into the Nineties: Some Outlines of the Twenty-first Century," *Dissent* 37 (Spring 1990), 173.

CHAPTER 13

NATIONALISM AND NATIONAL IDENTITY

Theoretical work on nationalism and ethnonational conflict is diverse and varied, addressing a number of distinct questions. Some scholars aim to explain the historical emergence of national identity. Others argue about whether, to what extent, and how national identity might relate to or differ from other types of collective identities. Others study the relationship between the development of national identity and other key features of modern societies like the modern state or industrial capitalism. Still others try to understand the circumstances under which national groups are more likely to engage in violence. These are only a handful of the questions on which political scientists who study nationalism focus.

In this chapter, we encounter several key works. The first reading, by Benedict Anderson, is a brief, well-known statement about how one might conceptualize national identity (for a more elaborate and partially contrasting definition, see Greenfeld, 1992). This is followed by David Laitin's analysis of how individuals make choices about national identity. Finally, Andreas Wimmer tries to help us understand the role that nationalism and the nation-state may play in ethnonational conflict.

As with other chapters in this book, the readings on nationalism and national identity included here exhibit elements of different core theories of comparative politics. For example, some are more structural than others, and some seem to place more emphasis on individual choice than others. As you read the excerpts, be attentive to the explanatory strategies they employ and think about whether the theories presented are mutually exclusive or whether they could, in principle, be combined in some ways.

WORKS CITED

Greenfeld, Liah. 1992. *Nationalism: Five Roads to Modernity.* Cambridge, MA: Harvard University Press.

BENEDICT ANDERSON

13.1 IMAGINED COMMUNITIES
Reflections on the Origin and Spread of Nationalism

This excerpt is from Anderson's famous book, *Imagined Communities*, one of the most widely cited and influential works on the subject of nationalism. Anderson is best known for emphasizing that nations are "imagined." We do not encounter most of our co-nationals personally. Rather, we just think of ourselves as all part of one community although we do not know each other. Group identities, therefore, are essentially in our heads. This is true, however, not just of nations but also of all collective identities in modern societies. Furthermore, it is true of most large-scale identities in the agricultural societies that followed from the Neolithic revolution (and *arguably* true even of collective identities in hunter–gatherer societies, although Anderson himself does not make this argument).

Anderson is not simply interested in asserting that national identities are imagined. Rather, he aims to tell us about *how* they are imagined and how this differs from other collective identities. Thus, for example, Latin Christendom in the late medieval era thought of itself in a particular kind of way, and members of modern nations think of themselves differently, emphasizing popular sovereignty and what Anderson calls "deep, horizontal comradeship." So what accounts for this major change in the European context? For Anderson, this process has numerous contributing causes, but the decisive factor is probably "print capitalism": the rise of newspapers and novels, which made possible new ways of thinking about ourselves, society, and our shared place in history.

CONCEPTS AND DEFINITIONS

Theorists of nationalism have often been perplexed, not to say irritated, by these three paradoxes: (1) The objective modernity of nations to the historian's eye vs. their subjective antiquity in the eyes of nationalists. (2) The formal universality of nationality as a socio-cultural concept—in the modern world everyone can, should, will "have" a nationality, as he or she "has" a gender—vs. the irremediable particularity of its concrete manifestations, such that, by definition, "Greek" nationality is sui generis. (3) The "political" power of nationalisms vs. their philosophical poverty and even incoherence. In other words, unlike most other isms, nationalism has never produced its own grand thinkers: no Hobbeses, Tocquevilles, Marxes, or Webers. This "emptiness" easily gives rise, among cosmopolitan and polylingual intellectuals, to a certain condescension. Like Gertrude Stein in the face of Oakland, one can rather quickly conclude that there is "no there there." It is characteristic that even so sympathetic a student of nationalism as Tom Nairn can nonetheless write that: "'Nationalism' is the pathology of modern developmental history, as inescapable as 'neurosis' in the individual, with much the same essential ambiguity attaching to it, a similar built-in capacity for descent into dementia, rooted in the dilemmas of helplessness thrust upon most of the world (the equivalent of infantilism for societies) and largely incurable."[1]

Anderson, Benedict. 1991[1983]. *Imagined Communities: Reflections on the Origin and Spread of Nationalism*. New York: Verso.

Part of the difficulty is that one tends unconsciously to hypostasize the existence of Nationalism-with-a-big-N (rather as one might Age-with-a-capital-A) and then to classify "it" as *an* ideology. (Note that if everyone has an age, Age is merely an analytical expression.) It would, I think, make things easier if one treated it as if it belonged with "kinship" and "religion," rather than with "liberalism" or "fascism."

In an anthropological spirit, then, I propose the following definition of the nation: it is an imagined political community—and imagined as both inherently limited and sovereign.

It is *imagined* because the members of even the smallest nation will never know most of their fellow-members, meet them, or even hear of them, yet in the minds of each lives the image of their communion.[2] Renan referred to this imagining in his suavely back-handed way when he wrote that "Or l'essence d'une nation est que tous les individus aient beaucoup de choses en commun, et aussi que tous aient oublié bien des choses."[3] With a certain ferocity Gellner makes a comparable point when he rules that "Nationalism is not the awakening of nations to self-consciousness: it *invents* nations where they do not exist."[4] The drawback to this formulation, however, is that Gellner is so anxious to show that nationalism masquerades under false pretenses that he assimilates "invention" to "fabrication" and "falsity," rather than to "imagining" and "creation." In this way he implies that "true" communities exist which can be advantageously juxtaposed to nations. In fact, all communities larger than primordial villages of face-to-face contact (and perhaps even these) are imagined. Communities are to be distinguished, not by their falsity/genuineness, but by the style in which they are imagined. Javanese villagers have always known that they are connected to people they have never seen, but these ties were once imagined particularistically—as indefinitely stretchable nets of kinship and clientship. Until quite recently, the Javanese language had no word meaning the abstraction "society." We may today think of the French aristocracy of the *ancien régime* as a class; but surely it was imagined this way only very late.[5] To the question "Who is the Comte de X?" the normal answer would

have been, not "a member of the aristocracy," but "the lord of X," "the uncle of the Baronne de Y," or "a client of the Duc de Z."

The nation is imagined as *limited* because even the largest of them, encompassing perhaps a billion living human beings, has finite, if elastic, boundaries, beyond which lie other nations. No nation imagines itself coterminous with mankind. The most messianic nationalists do not dream of a day when all the members of the human race will join their nation in the way that it was possible, in certain epochs, for, say, Christians to dream of a wholly Christian planet.

It is imagined as *sovereign* because the concept was born in an age in which Enlightenment and Revolution were destroying the legitimacy of the divinely-ordained, hierarchical dynastic realm. Coming to maturity at a stage of human history when even the most devout adherents of any universal religion were inescapably confronted with the living *pluralism* of such religions, and the allomorphism between each faith's ontological claims and territorial stretch, nations dream of being free, and, if under God, directly so. The gage and emblem of this freedom is the sovereign state.

Finally, it is imagined as a *community*, because, regardless of the actual inequality and exploitation that may prevail in each, the nation is always conceived as a deep, horizontal comradeship. Ultimately it is this fraternity that makes it possible, over the past two centuries, for so many millions of people, not so much to kill, as willingly to die for such limited imaginings.

These deaths bring us abruptly face to face with the central problem posed by nationalism: what makes the shrunken imaginings of recent history (scarcely more than two centuries) generate such colossal sacrifices? I believe that the beginnings of an answer lie in the cultural roots of nationalism.

NOTES

1. *The Break-up of Britain*, p. 359.
2. Cf. Seton-Watson, *Nations and States*, p. 5: "All that I can find to say is that a nation exists when a significant number of people in a community consider themselves to form a nation, or behave

as if they formed one." We may translate "consider themselves" as "imagine themselves."

3. Ernest Renan, "Qu'est-ce qu'une nation?" in *Oeuvres Complètes*, 1, p. 892. He adds: "tout citoyen français doit avoir oublié la Saint-Barthélemy, les massacres du Midi an XIIIe siècle. Il n'y a pas en France dix families qui puissent fournir la preuve d'une origine franque. . . ."

4. Ernest Gellner, *Thought and Change*, p. 169. Emphasis added.

5. Hobsbawm, for example, "fixes" it by saying that in 1789 it numbered about 400,000 in a population of 23,000,000. (See his *The Age of Revolution*, p. 78). But would this statistical picture of the noblesse have been imaginable under the *ancien régime*?

BIBLIOGRAPHY

Gellner, Ernest. *Thought and Change*. London: Weidenfeld and Nicholson. 1964.

Hobsbawm, Eric. *The Age of Revolution, 1789–1848*. New York: Mentor. 1964.

Nairn, Tom. *The Break-up of Britain*. London: New Left Books. 1977.

Seton-Watson, Hugh. *Nations and States: An Enquiry into the Origins of Nations and the Politics of Nationalism*. Boulder, CO: Westview Press, 1977.

DAVID D. LAITIN

13.2 NATIONS, STATES, AND VIOLENCE

David Laitin, the author of the second reading in this chapter, takes a notably different approach from the other authors in this section. He uses rational choice theory to try to understand how and why people change their identities. In other words, he recognizes that individuals have some agency in choosing their identities and that they do so with their interests in mind. Note that this perspective does share with those of Anderson, Greenfeld, and others the notion that identities are symbolically constructed. In other words, there is no "real" group identity beneath the representations we make about who we are and which group we belong to. Laitin's basic strategy is to think about relative group size and how boundaries between groups are constructed alongside a model of how rewards and costs are imposed on people by virtue of which group they belong to. If individuals belong to a group that yields low rewards and high costs (because, say, of high levels of discrimination or historical inequalities), they can be expected to seek exit *if* this is possible. What would make it possible? One factor might be whether the boundaries between groups are understood to be permeable or impermeable. Both majority and minority groups may police these boundaries, imposing costs on individuals who try to enter or exit. For example, a racist, exploitative elite may seek to prevent individuals from other groups from "passing" so as to maintain their exploitative capabilities. At the same time, a subaltern group may seek to retain members, and so penalize—symbolically or materially—those who attempt to exit. These are just rudimentary examples of the kind of situation that can be analyzed well from within Laitin's framework. He and his collaborator James Fearon (Fearon and Laitin, 2003) have applied a similar approach to the study of intergroup violence.

NATIONAL CASCADES

L'existence d'une nation est (pardonnez-moi cette métaphore) un plébiscite de tous les jours, comme l'existence de l'individu est une affirmation perpétuelle de vie.

—*Qu'est-ce qu'une nation? par Ernest Renan; Conférence faite en Sorbonne, le 11 mars 1882.*

HOW are nations formed? Ernest Renan's brilliant lecture over a century ago disputed the accepted wisdom—today called the primordial view—that nations were somehow natural, based on common race, religion, language, or geographical zone. He provided exceptions to every equation linking common culture to the boundaries of the then-existing nations. In its stead, he presented a theory of national consciousness that was constructed on a foundation of collective memories of past glories and collective forgetting of past defeats and internecine massacres. His lecture challenged the German romantics who saw nationhood as a historical fulfillment of a people's destiny. And it challenged as well future projects, such as those of Woodrow Wilson and Joseph Stalin, to find objective criteria for the cultural limits of state boundaries. Renan's powerful point was that cultures are not given

Laitin, David. 2007. *Nations, States, and Violence.* New York: Oxford University Press.

to people by nature, but rather are constructed through collective action and reinforced through the manipulation of collective consciousness.[1]

Those memories and amnesias that form the collective consciousness are, for Renan, aggregated in a metaphoric plebiscite that determines how a people conceive of the size and the cultural content of their nation. By the concept of plebiscite, Renan suggested that people do not inherit their national myths; rather, they choose them, more or less by majority vote. Each citizen becomes a member of the nation that wins the local plebiscite. Thus for Renan, now to use J.-J. Rousseau's terms, a nation is not a biological inheritance but the manifestation of the sum of individual wills or the "will of all."

Renan was half right. Nations are indeed the result of the choices made by their prospective members. But these choices, to use the language of modern game theory, are interdependent. Individuals do not choose (or vote in the plebiscite) as with an Australian ballot in absolute privacy. Rather, individual a chooses in large part based on signals received from individuals b, c, d, . . . , n on how they will choose; and, of course, these others are looking to a for a signal on how he will choose. Unlike a plebiscite where individuals expect a *division* of votes in their community, when it comes to national identification individuals expect a *coordinated outcome*. And unlike a plebiscite in which different subgroups in a community may have different interests, in the case of national identification, each individual voter gets higher rewards the greater the agreement on a national identity. In the case of nationalism, then, Rousseau's "general will"—something greater than the sum of individual wills—is the applicable goal. But how can disparate individuals agree on the general will? Rousseau did not address this problem in *The Social Contract* nor did Renan in his lecture on the nation as a manifestation of the general will, but I will address it now.

TWO MODELS OF INTERDEPENDENT NATIONAL CHOICE

National identities are elusive and consequently hard to measure. Renan was necessarily metaphoric when he spoke of a daily plebiscite, since it is hard to imagine people voting on their national identities. To trace changes in national identity, we need a way to measure it. For this purpose, and with some of the trade-offs for doing so to be discussed in the appendix to this chapter, language will serve as a proxy for national identity, and for several reasons. For one, "mother tongue" is clearly central to our notion of national membership. Second, language repertoires of individuals—the actual languages they speak—are observable, whereas national identities have no obvious empirical referents. And third, the "general will" aspect of language is glaringly clear. If within the boundaries of a single country, individual a chooses to learn Swedish, but b, c, d, . . . , n choose Russian, a is a loser, as he will have no one with whom to communicate. But if a switched to learn Russian, not only would he gain, but so would b, c, d, . . . , n. Individual Russian-speakers do not lose but rather gain when Russian speaking is the general will or national culture. It is to everyone's benefit to coordinate.

But how is coordination managed in large complex societies? Two models of language shift help provide an answer to this question and show how homogeneous national communities get constructed from heterogeneous foundations.

Abram de Swaan's "Floral Model"

It was well known to Renan that the boundaries of European states were at the beginning incommensurate with language zones. Britain, France, and Spain—considered by many analysts as natural nation-states—were originally multilingual empires. Meanwhile, the German speech zone was and remains larger than the Prussian and now German states. Historical accounts demonstrate that until the late nineteenth century, a significant proportion of French citizens could not successfully communicate in French.[2] Yet over the course of prolonged nation-building experiences, in France and many other states, a hegemonic language regime—in which all citizens view the national language as their mother tongue—emerged. The question is: how?

Abram de Swaan answers this question with a floral model of communication, as illustrated in Figure 13.1.[3] The stamen constitutes that set of people who speak the language of the political center (in the Spanish example in Figure 13.1, this is Castilian); the petals refer to those people who speak one of several languages of the state's periphery (Catalan, Basque, Galician, and Valencian). The structure of the flower (where the petals hardly overlap each other, but all overlap the stamen) is such that some members of each peripheral group speak the language of the center, but hardly any in the periphery speak the language of another peripheral group. Furthermore, almost no members of the center speak any peripheral language. Under these conditions, de Swaan reckons, there is an incentive for bilingual members of any periphery to serve as *monopoly mediators* between the center and their petal, thereby earning rents through the provision of translation services both to officials in the center (who need to issue orders to and regulate the commercial activities of those in the periphery) and to monolinguals in the periphery (who need at times to petition central authorities for licenses and services of the state). The handsome rewards for providing such services provide an incentive for all those with sufficient resources to invest in bilingual education for their children. When a critical mass of people from the periphery seek either to share in the rents for translation services (lowering the value of the service for each new bilingual) or to avoid paying them through language acquisition, in the long-term all citizens will ultimately "vote" for education in the central language, ultimately making it hegemonic.

De Swaan's is not a pure coordination game, as there is a conflict of interest inherent in the process. To the extent that all citizens in the periphery learn the language of the center, the monopoly mediators will lose their lucrative roles. Indeed, de Swaan records that these mediators (who wanted the perpetuation of regional languages) sought alliances in several European states with the Church (that feared the consequences for their religion of secular education that went along with promotion of national languages). The Church and the monopoly mediators allied to help sustain for a brief historical period an educational system that was both religious in content and regional in language. This alliance eventually collapsed given the cascade of citizens rushing to get the unmediated benefits of a national educational system and labor market.

The floral model captures the incentives for homogenization, but does not fully capture the possibility of a turning of the tides, in which regional languages regain their status as a language of authority. It is for this reason that a "tipping" model is proposed in the next section. However, de Swaan's contribution carries with it a fundamental message, namely that ethnic entrepreneurs in peripheral regions have an immense

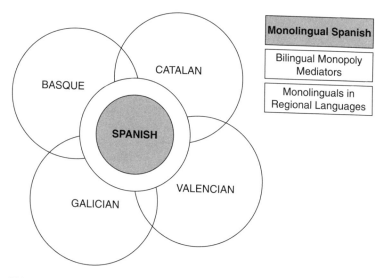

FIGURE 13.1 De Swaan's Floral Model

task to convince their constituents to abjure the cultural allure of the political center. In Chapter 5 [This refers to Chapter 5 in Laitin's book, not chapter 5 in this reader.], when multicultural policies are advocated, readers will be reminded that an invitation to minority groups in peripheral regions to promote their own cultures is one that young people, who have an opportunity to escape to the cosmopolitan cultural center, might well decline. Opening the gates to cultural differences will not, if the floral model has any cogency, lead to an endless flow of popularly supported claims for autonomy or secession.

Thomas Schelling's Tipping Game

An alternative way of modeling the emergence of a linguistic general will is through Nobel Prize–winning economist Thomas Schelling's tipping game, a theory of binary choice.[4] But first let us observe the intuition behind it, with an analogy from ice hockey. In the wintry ponds of Canada (or in sudden-death overtime in today's National Hockey League—NHL), ice hockey is bloody warfare, where blue lines turn to red. A culture of manliness pervaded the sport, such that wearing helmets was considered inappropriate, a signal of weakness. In my youth, no professional hockey player would wear one, and none in the NHL did. But it was possible to envision a cultural change, where wearing a helmet was normal, life-threatening injuries reduced, and reputations for manliness maintained. This would be a new culture, one not of reckless war but rather one of regulated sport. The question Schelling asked was how can cultural change happen, when the first mover to wear a helmet would be quickly humiliated and shunned? The Montreal Canadiens, the then most prestigious professional team in the NHL, whose players' manliness was never in question, provided one route to cultural change. Its goalie could don a mask at no reputation cost, and this could set off a cascade toward a new professional hockey culture. After several players followed the path set by the Canadiens' goalie, there was a certain point, in a way that Malcolm Gladwell neatly popularized,[5] at which the norm in this binary situation "tipped" from one cultural mode to another.

Once cultural norms are shown to have tipping points, many examples of long tradition suddenly evaporating become understandable. In the early twentieth century, the long-valued Chinese tradition of footbinding rapidly disappeared. One analyst attributed this unpredicted cultural shift to a conscious strategy of parents to assure each other that each would allow their sons to marry their daughters if and only if the daughters had unbound feet. Once there was a critical mass of potential husbands for footboundless girls, Chinese culture tipped to one that valued full-footed females. In a binary choice—footbind one's daughter or not footbind—the latter quickly replaced the former as the societal norm.[6]

Application of the Tipping Game to National Identities

Consider a population with a diverse set of attributes shared through biological or cultural inheritance such as skin color, speech forms, sacred beliefs, and kinship ties.[7] People conceive of these *attributes* as qualifying them for *categorical* membership on various social *dimensions*: skin color qualifying people as members of categories such as Black and White on the dimension of race; speech forms qualifying people as members of categories such as Spanish and English on the dimension of language; sacred beliefs qualifying people as members of categories such as Christian and Muslim on the dimension of religion; and kinship ties qualifying people as members of categories such as Hawiye and Daarood on the dimension of clanship.[8]

From this perspective, the politics of ethnicity involves three major processes. People invest in attributes for purposes of qualifying for membership in another category in the process of assimilation; political entrepreneurs expand or contract category space, for example the creation of the census category "mixed-race," to induce new coalitions; and ethnic intrepreneurs work to increase the salience of a dimension—for example, mullahs promoting religion as the salient dimension over clanship—to expand their authority.

The tipping game as applied to national identities concerns the first process; on a salient dimension—here language—people can invest to acquire a new attribute for their children, and thereby qualifying them to be members of the category of national citizens (say Spaniard). Or they can remain loyal to the language group of their region and retain membership in the category of a minority (say Catalan). The choice of a hockey helmet, therefore, has a parallel in the choice of investing in a new language, with the implication that the cumulation of such investments can substantially change the culture of a population.

To be sure—as will be elaborated in the appendix to this chapter—people can add a language to their repertoires, so language is not like wearing or not wearing a hockey helmet. They can speak both Zulu and Afrikaans. But the medium of instruction for primary education of children is typically a binary choice for parents. It is this choice that the model in Figure 13.2 delineates—namely the binary choice for parents to enroll their children in schools in which the medium of instruction is the language of the political center (call it C) or the language of their region (call it R). It is assumed that each parent wants her children to be educated in the common language of official business, elite discourse, and occupational mobility—that is, they want their children to speak the language of power. Parents, however, are uncertain whether their region will ultimately become a sovereign nation (in which case R would be the language of the new center) or whether their region will be successfully incorporated into C. This uncertainty

induces parents to make calculations about the expected returns for their educational choices. If there are k languages that might become official, an expected utility equation of individual i would involve calculating the probability (P) of each language being chosen and her utility (U) for each language. The resulting equation is below:

$$EU_i = \sum_{\forall k} p_k U_{ik}$$

As should be evident from observation of Figure 13.2, at all points to the left of the "tipping point" (t), a parent would benefit more (i.e., a higher payoff as recorded on the y-axis) by sending her child to schools where the medium of instruction is R. And at any point to the right of t, any parent would benefit more by sending her child to a school where C is the medium of instruction. In the world of interdependent choices, if parents see that a critical mass of other parents is moving past the tipping point in either direction, it is to the interest of all parents to participate in the cascade. In this manner, we say that the tipping game has two equilibria—meaning points on the x-axis where no parent has an incentive to change her choice—at 0% C and 100% C.[9]

This tipping model (unlike de Swaan's floral model) captures two coordination problems. On the one hand, we have a game of pure coordination. We see that 0% C (the same as 100% R) or 100% C (the

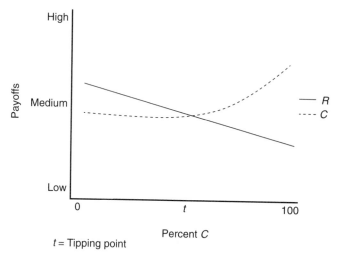

FIGURE 13.2 Tipping Game for Minorities

same as 0% *R*) are each equilibria, meaning that it would be irrational (i.e., with a lower payoff) for an average individual to switch her choice. On the other hand, there is a *battle of the sexes* game as well—one where the male would prefer to have the *rendezvous* at a soccer match while the female prefers that they go to the opera, but either would prefer the choice of their partner rather than go to their preferred event alone. In the case of language choice, while some members may prefer *C* while others prefer *R*, both would prefer to coordinate rather than separate.

At each of the two equilibria—where the regional language has solidarity around a new national formation (*R*), or where the regional language dies and the descendants of its former speakers become part of a broader national group (*C*)—the outcome appears to outsiders as natural or inevitable—often called primordial and thought of as genetic—because no one has an interest in defecting from it. Yet the model shows how historically contingent the outcome was, and the product of interdependent choices. What appears obvious and inevitable *ex post* was in fact ambiguous and contingent *ex ante*. What appears as permanent is in fact reversible.

Through the lens of the tipping model, we can observe the conditions that lead to the creation of new nationalities through separation and amalgamation of cultures. With the coordination aspects of national formation modeled, my proposed definition of the nation—provided below—should be clear.

What Then Is a Nation?

Through the insights gained from the tipping model, we can now define a nation as a *population with a coordinated set of beliefs about their cultural identities* (i.e., the salient cultural dimension, their category on that dimension, and the attributes qualifying people for membership in that category) *whose representatives claim ownership of a state* (or at least an autonomous region within a state) *for them by dint of that coordination* either through separation, or amalgamation, or return.[10]

Appeals to the nation are justified by the relevant population's representatives—people I have been referring to as ethnic entrepreneurs—through the highlighting of a category on a salient dimension. These appeals are compelling to the extent that the

people qualifying for membership coordinate their identities in accord with the national vision of these entrepreneurs. Nineteenth-century Zionists claimed that the category of being Jewish on the dimension of religion gave them right to ownership of Palestine; Kikuyus and Luos among other tribes in the 1950s claimed that the category of being African on the dimension of race gave them rights to own Kenya; and eastern Nigerians in the late 1960s claimed that the shared category of Igbo on the dimension of tribe gave them the right to own Biafra. The nation then is a product of cultural coordination and the claim to statehood or political autonomy for the population that successfully coordinates. Some examples follow of the coordination aspects of national formation and breakup.

People do not vote for their nationality as they do for a set of political alternatives because the principal goal in this sort of election is not to win, but to choose the national identity that most others in one's community are likely to choose. When it comes to national identities, we are not in competition with our neighbors but rather in coordination with them. Coordination among large numbers of people, however, is not easy to accomplish, even if all the people agree on a preferred outcome. Thus the role of ethnic entrepreneurs.

It is the social reality of interdependent choice and the desire for coordination that makes nations seem natural—since they represent votes that are very difficult to reverse. But at certain historical moments change can be rapid, as in a cascade. The tipping model illustrates both the sense of permanence *and* the fragility of national identifications. More important, it illustrates that the primordial image of society, where class is dynamic due to opportunities for social mobility while nationality is static without any expectations of cultural mobility, is flawed.

In the *Preface*, I warned the reader that the path from violence to the justification for multiculturalism would be complex. Indeed, the conclusions reached in this book, as noted with my appeal to Aristotle, are frustrating in that they provide no response to the problem of multiculturalism in which all values are maximized. However, I have sought to avoid one Aristotelian error—namely his assumption that the *polis* was the natural condition for human flourishing. The analysis herein does not, and we must not, build contemporary political theory on the defunct institutional foundation of the *nation-state*.

NOTES

1. Renan's theoretical position had a powerful contemporary political message: France's claim to Alsace-Lorraine (lost to Prussia in 1871) was a valid one, even if the majority of the population in those two provinces were German-speakers. Scholarship on nationalism is no less immune from contemporary political debates, now centered on Zionism and its alternatives. I am part of a long line of Jewish scholars of nationalism—Hans Kohn, Ernest Gellner, Elie Kedourie, Eric Hobsbawm, Ernst Haas, Liah Greenfield, and Michael Hechter—whose ideal image of a political community is closer to late Habsburg Vienna and Prague than to contemporary Israel. All of us in this tradition have been seeking zones of security for cosmopolitans, those with a taste for diversity. Anthony Smith and Yael Tamir, both Jewish and with strong political attachments to nationalist claims including that of Zionism, are exceptions. Of course, the insights from this corpus on nationalism can be assessed independently of authorial preferences.
2. Eugen Weber (1976) *Peasants into Frenchmen* (Stanford, CA: Stanford University Press).
3. Abram de Swaan (1988) *In Care of the State* (New York: Oxford University Press), ch. 3.
4. Thomas Schelling (1978) *Micromotives and Macrobehavior* (New York: Norton).
5. Malcolm Gladwell (2000) *The Tipping Point* (New York: Little, Brown).
6. This example is from Gerry Mackie (1996) "Ending Foot-binding and Infibulation: A Convention Account," *American Sociological Review*, 61: 999–1017. Mackie's convention account is not without dispute. See Hill Gates (2001) "Footloose in Fujian," *Comparative Studies in Society and History*, 43: 130–48.
7. On the parallels of cultural and biological inheritance, see R. Boyd and P. J. Richerson (1985) *Culture and the Evolutionary Process* (Chicago, IL: University of Chicago Press).
8. On attributes, categories, and dimensions as components of identity, see Kanchan Chandra and David Laitin (2002).
9. The payoff curves in Figure 13.2 (figures 2.2 and 2.3 in the original text of Laitin's book) are not linear, but this need not concern us here. For an explanation of the shape of these curves, see Laitin (1993).
10. This definition is only marginally different from that proposed by Ernst B. Haas (1964) *Beyond the Nation-State* (Stanford, CA: Stanford University Press), pp. 464–5, and that in Benedict Anderson's classic (1983) *Imagined Communities* (London: Verso). My definition highlights the political interactions *between* entrepreneurs and those whom they purport to represent, and *among* those who have coordinated beliefs of ethnic solidarity.

ANDREAS WIMMER

13.3 STATES OF WAR
How the Nation-State Made Modern Conflict

In this short piece, a partial summary of his recent book on the subject, Wimmer argues that previous research on ethnonational conflict has been inattentive to the role of the nation-state and especially the principle of "like-over-like." Indeed, when such research *has* focused on the state, it has often focused on state failure as a risk factor for intergroup violence. But Wimmer argues that most instances of ethnonational conflict involve contestation over the state itself. The state is important to different political actors and, as such, the state can be relevant when it is strong, as well as when it is weak. Violence, he says, tends to take two forms. First, there is the often violent rise of the nation-state itself. Many nation-states are themselves products of war. But even once established, in the context of multiple groups, there is often a struggle to determine who will control the state. Wimmer considers a number of examples, including Syria, Sudan, and Kosovo.

To explain recent conflicts in countries such as Syria or Sudan, observers have been quick to point their fingers at proximate causes specific to our times: the power vacuum created by the end of the Cold War offered opportunities for rebels to fill the void; the recent globalization of trade flooded the developing world with cheap arms; rising global consumer demand generated new struggles over oil and minerals; jihadist groups spread using networks of fighters trained in Afghanistan and Pakistan.

Yet such explanations miss a bigger picture. If we extend the time horizon beyond the Cold War to include the entire modern period—from the American and French revolutions to today—we can see repeating patterns of war and conflict. These patterns are related to the formation and development of independent nation-states.

Until the eighteenth century, empires, dynastic kingdoms, tribal confederacies, and city-states governed most of the world. This changed when nationalists introduced the notion that every "people" deserved its own government. They argued that ethnic likes should rule over likes. In other words, Slovaks should be governed by Slovaks, not the House of Hapsburg; and Americans by Americans, not the British crown. Over the past two centuries, in wave after wave of nation-state formation, this new principle of political legitimacy transformed the world.

In most places, two distinct phases of conflict accompanied this transition: first, violence related to the creation of the nation-state itself, and second, an often bloody struggle over which ethnic or national groups would hold power in the newly established state, and over where the country's final borders would settle.

BLEEDING BORDERS

Roughly a third of present-day countries have fought violent wars of independence that united, if only temporarily, the diverse inhabitants of colonial or imperial provinces against their overlords. But many

Wimmer, Andreas. 2013. "States of War: How the Nation-State Made Modern Conflict," *Foreign Affairs*, Online Edition, November 7, 2013.

of the resulting nation-states endured even worse violence after independence was won because the like-over-like principle bred further conflict among the victors themselves.

Imperial governments had often recruited members of specific minorities into the colonial army and bureaucracy. (The classic example was the Belgian preference for Rwanda's Tutsi minority over its Hutu majority to staff the country's colonial administration.) In other former colonies, the elites of the more assimilated and educated groups controlled the post-imperial state's nascent bureaucracies and security apparatuses, a fact that other groups resented as a break with the like-over-like principle. More important, many new governments lacked the political power and resources to reach out to the entire population and overcome colonial-era inequalities. This made nation building more difficult and ethnic patronage more likely. Large segments of the population thus remained politically marginalized.

Whatever its origins, ethnopolitical inequality was perceived as a scandal once nationalism had been accepted as the guiding principle of legitimacy. This made it easier for opposition leaders to mobilize followers and stage armed rebellions against exclusionary regimes. Data from every country in the world since 1945 demonstrates a tight correlation between such inequality and conflict: an increase in the size of the politically excluded population by 30 percent increased the chances of civil war by 25 percent. Almost 40 percent of independent countries today have experienced at least one ethnopolitical rebellion since World War II. It is important to note that these countries are not more ethnically diverse than those at peace. It is therefore not diversity per se, but political inequality, that breeds conflict.

Of course, other factors play a role as well, including the repressive capacity of the state: After all, it is much harder to organize a guerrilla army in northern China than in Somalia. Civil wars are also more likely to break out in poorer countries where it is more economically important to have connections to the government. Finally, not all politically marginalized ethnic groups have an educated leadership capable of forming a political movement or staging a rebellion.

New nation-states are also more likely to go to war with each other than established empires or dynastic states were. Empires drew loose and often arbitrary borders with little regard to ethnicity. Nation-states, on the other hand, care more about borders because these may divide a single national group across various states. This creates the risk that those who end up on the wrong side of the border are treated as second-class citizens in neighboring states dominated by other ethnic groups—another way that the like-over-like principle can be violated. Conflict between neighboring nation-states thus often erupts over territories where ethnic groups overlap or over borders that divide a single ethnic group. In the early 1990s, for example, the Serbian minority resisted integration into the newly founded state of Croatia. The government of Serbia, expecting that their co-ethnics in Croatia would be mistreated (and in pursuit of its own national unification project), intervened on their behalf. War between the two states followed, ending with the expulsion of the Croatian Serbs across the border.

The domestic struggle over who "owns" a new state does eventually come to an end—on average, after sixty years. It often comes violently, by way of expulsions, population exchanges, or forced assimilation that result in a more homogenous country. In other cases, strong central governments and well-established civil society organizations have made ethnicity irrelevant to the formation of political alliances (as in Switzerland) or encouraged voluntary assimilation into the core group (as in France and Botswana). In other instances, a power-sharing arrangement between the representatives of politicized ethnic groups helps to avoid future civil war (as in Canada).

MINORITY REPORT

In short, the spread of the like-over-like principle and the formation of nation-states have been driving forces behind civil and interstate war—a fact woefully missing from much of the popular debate about the violent conflicts of today.

Take Syria, whose history of conflict conforms closely to the pattern. The Arab uprising against Ottoman rule during World War I did not lead to the country's independence but instead to another round of colonial domination by France. After a series of failed anticolonial rebellions during the mid-1920s, Syria finally gained independence from France at the end of World War II. Much of the political turmoil in the postcolonial period concerned the distribution of political power among ethnic elites. After a number of coups, the al-Assad clan and its small Alawite sect emerged as the new owners of the state.

Syria thus became a classic example of an ethnocracy—where an ethnic minority dominates the entire state apparatus. As a consequence of this departure from the like-over-like principle, the government utterly lacks popular support and political legitimacy. The regime compensated by adopting pan-Arab rhetoric and anti-Israel policies, accommodating the Sunni economic elite, building a massive security apparatus that penetrated the entire fabric of society, and brutally suppressing any form of protest or rebellion, such as the Sunni uprising of 1982. Now, Syria's civil war is increasingly being fought along religious and sectarian divides, as was the case in neighboring Iraq after the U.S. invasion. Although the future remains unpredictable, it is safe to say that no durable peace will be achieved until the ethnocratic regime under Assad gives way to a power structure that integrates the country's Sunni majority. The Kurds, meanwhile, may perhaps end up in a Kurdish state sometime in the future.

Sudan has followed a similar path. A decades-long nationalist war finally led to the secession in 2011 of southern Sudan, where non-Muslims of African descent form the majority, from northern Sudan, which has been politically dominated by Muslim Arabs since its inception. Tensions between the two states run high over the exact demarcation of the boundary between them. In its present form, the divide leaves tens of thousands of non-Muslim Africans politically marginalized in North Sudan. In South Kordofan and the Blue Nile area, which are on the northern side of the demarcation, former fighters for an independent South have continued to attack northern troops with tacit support from the newly established South Sudanese government and army. Clashes between the two states' militaries have led many analysts to fear more violence in the future.

In the South, ethnopolitical inequality has led to domestic conflict as well. Shortly after independence, new complaints arose about the dominance of former Dinka fighters, who had founded and controlled the independence movement, in the recently formed bureaucracy and army. Armed conflicts erupted between government forces and various rebel factions claiming to represent Nuer or Murle constituencies.

What will the future bring for the two Sudans? Given that control over significant oil resources is at stake, their conflict is unlikely to be settled through a simple redrawing of boundaries. It is equally improbable that the current government in Khartoum will open its ranks to former independence fighters and their ethnic followers. A long-lasting, low-intensity conflict is far more likely—at least as long as the ethnocratic regime in Khartoum survives. As for the domestic conflict in South Sudan, given the state's low institutional capacity, it will be difficult to pursue a successful nation-building project by integrating the country's various ethnic constituencies and depoliticizing tribal and ethnic allegiances. One can expect that jostling for power in unstable coalitions and occasional infighting will continue.

Kosovo also conforms to the pattern. It became a sovereign country after decades of nationalist mobilization against alien rule by the Serbian state. The independence war of the late 1990s led to NATO intervention, followed by a decade of UN administration. In 2008, Kosovo was declared sovereign. Tensions between the young state's Albanian majority, empowered by independence, and its Serbian minority still run high. Without NATO protection, these Serbian enclaves would probably have been ethnically cleansed a long time ago. And if Serbia had not been under the threat of further NATO bombings, it most likely would have intervened militarily to protect its ethnic brethren across the border, bringing the two states to war. Intervening relatively early, then, can help prevent such conflicts from escalating to the level of full-scale war seen in Bosnia. The Bosnian episode also illustrates, however, that it is not a sustainable solution to force elites with opposing nationalist agendas to share power in a state they do not want.

This historical pattern is not without exceptions. Nor does it explain all of the wars in the world. Some ethnically heterogeneous nation-states, including Montenegro, have emerged without violence and have remained peaceful. Some of the most intractable conflicts have erupted in such long-established nation-states as Colombia and have nothing to do with nationalism or ethnicity. Still, far more examples could be cited that do follow the pattern: Think of the Kurdish struggle in Turkey, the shaky peace process in Northern Ireland, the Darfur drama, the sectarian violence still haunting Iraq, the series of Caucasian conflicts that have emerged since the dissolution of the Soviet empire, or resistance to Chinese rule in Tibet. More complicated cases are those in which ethnopolitical exclusion has led to a guerilla movement with a non-ethnic agenda, such as the Marxist fighters in Guatemala, or the Maoist ones in Peru, Nepal, and parts of India.

One can reasonably predict, then, that contemporary states that politically marginalize large portions of their population might well descend into protracted armed violence. A number of countries are at risk, including Rwanda, where a small group of Tutsi returnees from neighboring Uganda rules over the Hutu majority with an iron fist; Jordan, which might one day no longer be able to divert the political aspirations of its large, politically powerless group of Palestinian citizens to neighboring Israel; Peru and Guatemala, which, unlike Bolivia, continue to marginalize their large indigenous populations; and Guinea, where the party favored by the ethnic Peul, who make up roughly 40 percent of the population and have long been excluded from power, has protested rigged elections as recently as February.

These enduring patterns of violence demand policy solutions that sound simple in theory but are deeply challenging to put into practice. Building more inclusionary power structures—not necessarily through electoral democracy—represents the most viable strategy for new states to prevent armed conflict. Macedonia is often cited as a successful example of how institutional engineering, under intense international pressure, can lead to a relatively stable power-sharing arrangement. One can enlarge the list of successful strategies by calling attention to Tanzania, where a dominant nationalist leader built a far-reaching infrastructure of power that bridged ethnic divides. Botswana and Burkina Faso also provide examples of successful ethnic inclusion—in the case of latter, thanks to a strong network of trade unions that provided a platform for ethnic political integration. At the same time, the recent U.S. experience in Afghanistan shows just how difficult it is to foster political integration through occupation. Outsiders who provide public goods—schools, hospitals, and the like—undermine the legitimacy of the domestic government, rather than foster it. Nation building from the outside, then, is not just difficult but structurally impossible. The path to peace—toward an inclusionary state that does not violate the like-over-like principle—begins at home.

CHAPTER 14

RACE, ETHNICITY, AND GENDER

The comparative study of the relationship between race, gender, and ethnicity in politics is a large, complex, and rapidly developing field. It is also one that has implications for many of the other areas of comparative politics discussed in this book, perhaps above all for issues of institutional structure and design discussed in Chapters 8 through 11, but not only for such issues. For example, this discussion of race, gender, and ethnicity intersects with the study of electoral systems, of social movements, of the state, economic development, democratization, and even revolutions, among other topics. Indeed, increasing focus on gender, race, and ethnicity has the potential to change analysis in some of those areas.

One of the major concerns of scholarship in this area—although by no means the only one—are inequities in the representation of women and members of racial and ethnic minorities. It is unfortunately all too common that members of some groups face discrimination and are afforded fewer rights. Likewise, in many polities members of minority groups face formal and informal barriers to seeking public office. In most cases in the 21st century, this does not mean total disenfranchisement, but rather that representation is not proportional to the group's share of the total population or that some group members feel that they are not adequately represented. Finally, no polities have yet achieved gender equality in political representation: although much progress has been made in this area, the relative underrepresentation of women in politics is frustratingly persistent.

Comparative politics tries to understand why this is so. There are many different explanatory strategies from which we can choose. Some involve starting with the analysis of gender or ethnic identities themselves, examining the implications of how they are constructed for the intersection of the identity in question and political institutions like political parties or electoral systems. Mala Htun's excerpt below, which focuses on differences in how race/ethnicity and gender relate to other social categories and how the "crosscutting" nature of gender makes it harder for women to organize than ethnic groups, is an example of this strategy. Another strategy is to focus more on the structure of the political system in which organizing around identities takes place. Donna Lee Van Cott's comparative analysis of the formation of ethnic parties in Latin America, which emphasizes not just the nature of ethnicity but also the political opportunities present or absent in different countries, is an example of this approach. As you read these passages, think about whether such perspectives might be combined into a general theory of unequal group outcomes in political life.

MALA HTUN

14.1 IS GENDER LIKE ETHNICITY? THE POLITICAL REPRESENTATION OF IDENTITY GROUPS

In this piece, Mala Htun asks an important question: Why does it seem to be so much harder to organize political parties based on gender than based on ethnicity or race? To be clear, she is not saying that it is easy in these latter cases, but just that such efforts are either more often undertaken or more often successful. The answer cannot be found in varying levels of discrimination because systematic gender discrimination is observable in most or all societies, although it varies notably in the form it takes and how extreme it is. If it is not that some groups have a greater need for organization than others, perhaps the difference has to do with the nature of the group identities in question and, more specifically, how they link to other basic principles of social organization. Htun suggests that a critical feature of gender is that it is "crosscutting." This means that it does not closely correlate with class or other forms of what social scientists call "social stratification" (hierarchical social organization). Likewise, it is not geographically clustered (i.e., it is not as if all of the women live in one part of a country and all of the men in another area). As you read this piece, think about *why* the crosscutting nature of gender might impede mobilization and the formation of political parties.

Political leaders take our money, lead us to war, and write the laws that govern our lives. Must their ranks include men and women, rich and poor, masters and slaves? For most of world history, the answer was no. Men ruled; women worked at home. Female interests were represented by husbands and fathers. The same was true for members of subordinate ethnic groups: conquerors would care for colonial subjects, the rich for the poor, whites for browns, and so on.

As the twentieth century progressed, however, a consensus emerged in international society and within democratic polities that one social segment should not monopolize political power. Special efforts were made to include previously excluded groups—generally defined in terms of gender and ethnicity. Today, some 50 countries officially allocate access to political power along the lines of gender, ethnicity,[1] or both: they have

laws on the books reserving a fixed number of electoral candidacies or legislative seats. Narrowing the focus to electoral democracies reveals a fascinating pattern: institutional remedies for the underrepresentation of women and ethnic minorities (or majorities) assume distinct forms. Women tend to receive candidate quotas in political parties, whereas ethnic groups are granted reserved seats in legislatures.

How does gender differ from ethnicity? Why do democracies apply distinct policies to different previously excluded groups? What does this imply about the normative status of various claims to representation and the appropriate response of liberal states?

This article argues that different remedies for underrepresentation are logically appropriate for different groups. Quotas, which make space within existing parties, suit groups whose boundaries crosscut partisan

Htun, Mala. 2004. Is Gender Like Ethnicity? The Political Representation of Identity Groups. *Perspectives on Politics* 2(3): 439–458.

divisions. Reservations, which create incentives for the formation of group-specific parties and permit them direct legislative representation, suit groups whose boundaries coincide with political cleavages. Whereas gender tends to be crosscutting, ethnicity tends to be coinciding. Women and men belong to all political parties; members of ethnic groups, by contrast, frequently belong to one only. In countries where it is mobilized, ethnicity is a central, if not *the* central principle of political behavior; gender, though occasionally a consideration, almost never defines how individuals vote and what parties they affiliate with.

Of course, actual politics do not always conform to functional requirements. Historical legacies may get in the way of matching group characteristics with suitable policies. Thus countries with traditions of ethnic reservations have given reserved seats to women; one with a gender candidate quota applied similar quotas to ethnic minorities. Yet when it applies the "wrong" remedy, the state neglects the true causes of underrepresentation and fails to grant group members real access to power. As we see in the Indian and Peruvian cases discussed below, supposed beneficiaries of these unwelcome remedies may protest them and demand alternative policies.

Though the divergence between the modes of gender and ethnic representation cuts across many countries, it has received no scholarly attention. We know a great deal about women's movements and women in politics, and a growing number of works focus on gender quotas. Hundreds of scholars have studied ethnic identity formation and mobilization; the causes and consequences of conflict; and institutional solutions for divided societies. Few works analyze representational politics *across identities*.[2] Such a comparison is needed, however, if we are to understand why policy solutions to women's underrepresentation diverge so dramatically from those applied to ethnic groups. Comparing gender and ethnicity also

The author gratefully acknowledges the assistance and advice of Kanchan Chandra, Jorge Dominguez, Jennifer Hochschild, Mark Jones, Courtney Jung, Jim Miller, Victoria Murillo, Jack Snyder, Donna Lee Van Cott, Myra Waterbury, participants in colloquia at the New School and Columbia University, and anonymous reviewers.

reveals that claims made on these differing bases have different implications for the liberal state.

GROUP REPRESENTATION POLICIES

Table 14.1 identifies countries with statutory gender quotas or reservations, ethnic quotas or reservations, or both.[3] As Table 14.1 shows, about 50 countries use such mechanisms, including old and new democracies; rich and poor countries; Catholic, Protestant, Islamic, Confucian, and Hindu societies; federal and unitary systems; and presidential and parliamentary regimes. Dozens of other countries without statutory measures uphold effective political arrangements to guarantee group representation, such as quotas used voluntarily by political parties in over 30 countries; the race-conscious districting practiced in the United States; and the application of lower electoral thresholds for minority political organizations in Denmark, Germany, Poland, and Romania. Notwithstanding the importance of these voluntary arrangements, this paper is concerned exclusively with statutory mechanisms. Reliable cross-national data on party statutes, their interpretation, and their enforcement were not available. This is a fertile area for future research, since additional data have the potential to change the findings reported here.[4]

Policies to guarantee group representation generally assume one of two forms: candidate nomination quotas in political parties or legislative reservations. Quotas require that a minimum number of candidates fielded by political parties for general election have certain demographic characteristics. The Argentine *Ley de Cupos* (or Quota Law of 1991), for example, requires that women comprise a minimum of 30 percent of political party lists. Reservations or reserved seats set aside a fixed percentage of legislative seats for members of a certain group. These may be filled through competitive election in specially created districts (Scheduled Castes and Scheduled Tribes in India), through election by voters registered on separate rolls (Maoris in New Zealand), by the group member receiving the most votes in general elections (constitutionally recognized ethnic groups in Mauritius), or through designation by political parties (minorities in Pakistan).

States adopted these policies at different historical moments. In some countries, collective representational rights constitute part of the bargain struck to ensure the viability of democracy in a plural society. In such "consociational" or "consensus" polities, each group is guaranteed a share of power to preclude secession and civil war. Other countries introduced collective rights rather recently in response to the growth of identity-based social movements and their demands for the recognition of cultural diversity. These claims have mobilized concern for the question of whether elites in power resemble, in their personal characteristics and life experiences, the people they represent, thus transforming group representation from a matter of state survival into a question of democratic legitimacy and social justice.

Considerable debate surrounds these policies. Liberal critics argue that granting rights to identity groups treats them as essential givens, failing to acknowledge their dynamism and fluidity, as well as internal injustices suffered by some members. Existing liberal institutions, moreover, can resolve the domination and oppression inflicted on social groups since these wrongs are ultimately suffered by individuals.[5] Civic republicans claim that group-differentiated rights undermine common citizenship and render suspect a public good toward which society could be oriented,[6] while libertarians allege that collective rights benefit the already privileged, increase in-group inequality, and aggravate social divisions.[7] Finally, social scientists have found that policies promoting the descriptive representation of minorities may actually end up harming their substantive representation: for example, the creation of so-called majority–minority districts helps to put more blacks and Latinos in the U.S. House of Representatives, but it may also facilitate the election of legislators elsewhere who are ideologically hostile to their interests.[8]

Defenders of quotas and reservations point out that group rights do not constitute a major departure from existing democratic practices. After all, some form of collective representation is inherent to the political process. As Justice Lewis F. Powell put it in a 1968 voting rights opinion, "The concept of representation necessarily applies to groups; groups of voters elect representatives; individuals do not."[9] Single-member district systems define such groups by territory; other electoral regimes, such as national-list

TABLE 14.1 STATUTORY GROUP REPRESENTATION POLICIES

For Gender	For Ethnicity	For both Gender and Ethnicity
Argentina	Bhutan	*Belgium*
Armenia	*Croatia*	Bosnia and Herzegovina
Bangladesh	*Cyprus*	*Colombia*
Bolivia	Ethiopia	*India*
Brazil	*Fiji*	Jordan
Costa Rica	Kiribati	Pakistan
Djibouti	Lebanon	*Peru*
Dominican Republic	*Mauritius*	Serbia and Montenegro
Ecuador	*New Zealand*	*Taiwan*
France	Niger	
Greece	*Samoa*	
Guyana	Singapore	
Macedonia	*Slovenia*	
Mexico	*Switzerland*[a]	
Morocco	*Venezuela*	
Namibia		
Nepal		
North Korea		
Panama		
Paraguay		
Peru		
Rwanda		
Sudan		
Tanzania		
Uganda		

NOTE: Electoral democracies are in italics (Freedom House 2003).
[a]Switzerland's practice of distributing cabinet seats by language group is not technically required by law, but is a deeply entrenched custom (Steiner 1990; Steiner 2002).

proportional representation, accommodate non-geographically based constituencies. Liberal polities such as the United States and Canada have traditionally drawn geographical district boundaries around "communities of interest," be they regional, economic,

TABLE 14.2 GROUP REPRESENTATION RIGHTS IN ELECTORAL DEMOCRACIES[a]

	Candidate quotas in parties	Legislative reservations
Ethnic	Peru	Belgium
		Colombia
		Croatia
		Cyprus
		Fiji
		India
		Kiribati
		Mauritius
		New Zealand
		Niger
		Samoa
		Serbia and Montenegro
		Slovenia
		Switzerland
		Taiwan
		Venezuela
Gender	Argentina	Bangladesh
	Armenia	India (local)
	Belgium	Taiwan
	Bolivia	
	Brazil	
	Costa Rica	
	Dominican Republic	
	Ecuador	
	France	
	Greece (local)	
	Guyana	
	Macedonia	
	Mexico	
	Namibia (local)	
	Panama	
	Paraguay	
	Peru	
	Serbia and Montenegro	

[a]As identified by Freedom House in 2003. The table includes only those countries considered electoral democracies.

environmental, or historical; by granting an equal number of seats to states regardless of population, the U.S. and Australian Senates offer privileges to residents of smaller, potentially disadvantaged states.[10] The point is that political institutions inevitably make decisions about the types of groups that gain representation. Quotas and reserved seats differ in degree, but not in kind, from the everyday work states already perform on politically-relevant social identities.

GENDER QUOTAS AND ETHNIC RESERVATIONS IN ELECTORAL DEMOCRACIES

When we consider only electoral democracies, the following pattern emerges: states give candidate quotas in political parties to women and reserved seats in legislatures to members of ethnic groups. As Table 14.2 demonstrates, there are only four exceptions to this rule. The probability that a democracy with group rights for women will have candidate quotas is 0.86; in countries with measures guaranteeing ethnic representation, the probability is 0.94 that these take the form of legislative reservations.

What accounts for this divergence in modalities of gender and ethnic representation? My argument can be summarized in the following syllogism: (1) candidate quotas are more appropriate for groups that crosscut partisan cleavages, while reservations suit groups that coincide with them; (2) gender identities tend to cut across parties, whereas ethnic identities often overlap with partisan affiliations; (3) consequently, disadvantaged groups that are defined by gender demand, and are granted, candidate quotas; ethnic groups prefer, and receive, legislative reservations.

QUOTAS FOR CROSSCUTTING GROUPS; RESERVATIONS FOR COINCIDING ONES

To understand the different uses of the two types of policies, we must first explore the distinct means they use to improve the representation of identity groups. Quotas intervene in party nomination procedures by requiring that a certain percentage of the candidates fielded by a party be of a certain group. For example, the quota may demand that around one-third of positions on party lists be occupied by women and that they alternate with men in the rank ordering of candidates, as is the case in Argentina, Costa Rica, Belgium, and Guyana.[11] A quota policy may therefore provoke some changes in the ways parties go about nominating candidates, formulating lists, and deciding who runs in what district. However, it does not alter the overall structure of incentives governing the political system. Specifically, quotas do not affect issues such as counting rules, timing, the circumscription of electoral districts, the structure of the ballot, and so on that have been shown to exert the most powerful effects on voter behavior, the party system, and internal party structure.[12]

Reservations take a different approach. They introduce group-specific avenues of representation that circumvent the existing party system and create new electoral incentives. These include the creation of: separate electoral rolls, special electoral districts that limit competition to group members, exceptions to counting rules, and provisions for direct appointment to the legislature.

Candidate quotas thus presume a different sort of problem from that addressed by reservations. The goal of quotas is to take a category of people who belong to, but suffer from discrimination in, mainstream parties and propel them to positions wherein they stand a chance of popular election. Quotas therefore provide a means of assimilation and integration into already existing political institutions. Reservations, by contrast, guarantee group members a share of power independently, if need be, of existing parties. Their objective is to facilitate autonomy of political communities and electoral success of group-specific parties.

Figure 14.1 depicts the location of crosscutting and coinciding groups in the party system. We see that members of a crosscutting group belong to all parties, whereas those of a coinciding group tend to belong to a single party, a set of political organizations, or no party. Figure 14.2 illustrates the "work" done by a well-designed candidate quota. The policy attacks the discrimination suffered by group members in the party but permits them to continue militating in it. Meanwhile, the party gains representation in legislatures through regular electoral procedures.

The demographic characteristics of its delegations may change, but the rules of inter-party competition remain the same.

Figure 14.1 helps us see why a candidate quota would make little sense for a coinciding group. What is gained by making space for group members within all parties when they tend to cluster at one end of the political spectrum? In fact, a candidate quota might undermine a minority group's political organizations as its partisan opponents snatch up group leaders in order to comply with the quota. Finally, Figure 14.3 clarifies the mechanics of legislative reservations. They permit a group's party, organizations, or independent representatives to gain power on their own and may furnish additional incentives for formation of minority parties.

In theory, a proportional representation (PR) electoral system, particularly one with low thresholds, would facilitate the representation of group-specific parties and organizations. PR also avoids a situation in which the state is compelled to assign

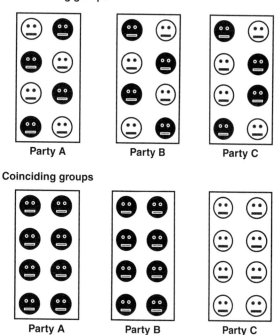

Cross-cutting groups

Party A   Party B   Party C

Coinciding groups

Party A   Party B   Party C

FIGURE 14.1 Cross-Cutting Versus Coinciding Groups

individuals to specific groups (as required by the maintenance of ethnic voter rolls or the reservation of certain districts for group members), a practice that contradicts the fluidity and contextual nature of many ethnic identities. In addition, PR is flexible, permitting the automatic adjustment of representational relationships to changing demographics and political interests. Divided legislatures and reserved seat ratios, by contrast, often contain no provision for periodic updating based on new census data.[13] Some countries, however, may opt for reserved seats in order to preserve an existing two-party system (unlikely to be maintained under PR), to *over*represent a minority, to offer privileged access to power as compensation for historical disadvantage, or to name a particular group as deserving unique status.[14]

CROSSCUTTING GENDER VERSUS COINCIDING ETHNICITY

The next step is to examine variation in the extent to which gender and ethnic identities actually correspond to partisan cleavages. For much of world history, politics has been the exclusive domain of men. Women gained the right to vote and stand for office only in the twentieth century. Since the early days of gender integration in politics, however, political parties have counted on both men and women as supporters. There are few instances of parties defined by gender, and none have consistently won elections. To be sure, different parties send men and women to office to varying degrees: women comprise a larger portion of legislative delegations of the Left than those of the Right. One reason is that the former have been more likely to adopt voluntary candidate quotas than the latter.[15] To reduce the electoral advantage such policies may provide to their opponents, parties of the Right in several countries have responded by introducing, if not always explicit quotas, other forms of affirmative action to improve women's opportunities.[16] Party positions may differ on women's rights issues such as abortion, but are converging—at least in theory—on the goal of gender parity in representational politics.

What about the gender gap? In advanced democracies, women tend to vote for leftist parties in greater numbers than men. A few decades ago (and in many parts of the developing world today) the opposite transpired: support for the Right was greater among women.[17] Though analyses of these phenomena tend to center on women's views, there is evidence that men are the ones changing: in the United States at least, transposition of the gender gap is due to major shifts in men's partisan preferences.[18] The gap peaked in the U.S. presidential elections of 1996, when 54 percent of women voted for Democrat Bill Clinton, as opposed to 43 percent of men.[19] While significant for party strategy, these percentage point differences are small compared to the overall volume of female and male support for various parties and candidates.

The size of gender differences in party support contrasts vividly with the ethnically inflected political divisions characterizing many plural societies. In patronage democracies such as India, politics is driven by ethnic head counting.[20] Linguistic divisions in heterogeneous European countries such as Belgium and Switzerland map onto party—and party system—divisions.[21] A large number of postcolonial societies in Africa and Asia are dominated by parties whose reliance on the support of exclusive ethnic groups lends a "census-like quality" to elections.[22] In these contexts and in the post-communist world, progress toward democratization often exacerbated the ethnic character of politics, sometimes with violent consequences.[23] Nine Israeli parties representing distinct ethnic and religious groups came to occupy nearly half of the Knesset seats in the 1990s.[24] African Americans in the United States identify overwhelmingly with the Democratic Party and evidence of the salience of race in predicting voting behavior lies behind U.S. federal courts' validation of districting arrangements designed to permit all citizens to "elect a candidate of their choice."[25] Even Latin America is witnessing the growth of ethnic parties: in the 1990s, those mobilizing indigenous voters successfully contested national elections in Bolivia, Colombia, Ecuador, Guyana, and Venezuela and local contests in Argentina and Nicaragua.[26]

Ethnic boundaries are not always politically loaded, however, and not everyone has a communal experience of ethnicity. Its coincidence with partisan and ideological cleavages and geographic concentration is the effect of historical construction as well as political manipulation. Ethnic groups in some countries, such as Afro-descendents in Brazil, have features usually associated with gender identity, such as low geographic segregation and little correlation with voting behavior or party affiliation. Consequently, the affirmative action bill under consideration in the Brazilian Congress calls for racial quotas in parties, not for reserved seats in the legislature.[27] The stacking of ethnicity on salient social divisions is the product, not the premise, of a political process, an outcome to which the allocation of specific representational rights surely contributes.

For these reasons, there is an active debate among political scientists about which types of institutions can best mold ethnicity to promote democratic stability. Arend Lijphart has long advocated proportional representation and power sharing, policies that preserve group identity but encourage cooperation among ethnic elites. Donald Horowitz favors

Step 1: Parties to lists

Step 2: Parties to legislature

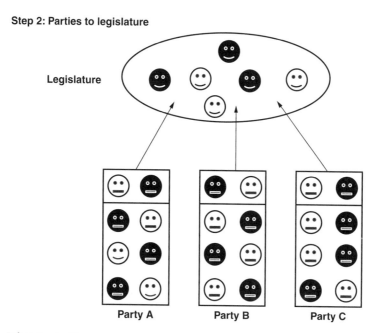

FIGURE 14.2 What Quotas Do

electoral rules that encourage politicians to make appeals across ethnic lines. And Kanchan Chandra has found that when state institutions create incentives for politicians to mobilize different dimensions of ethnic identity—by authorizing positive discrimination by caste, granting access to government jobs by language, or recognition of statehood by tribe—ethnic parties will compete to occupy the center, thus averting the centrifugal spiral that undermines democracy.[28] Depending on these institutional configurations and other factors, ethnicity is manifest in varied ways in different societies. Often enough, ethnic boundaries correspond to other salient cleavages. Gender identities, however, almost always cut across them.

WOMEN RECEIVE QUOTAS; ETHNIC GROUPS RECEIVE RESERVED SEATS

Finally, we must establish that gender-based demands center on quotas and that this is related to the fact that women are spread throughout the party system. We also need to show that the preference of ethnic groups for reserved seats flows from their tendency to cluster in a single party or organization.

Let us begin by analyzing candidate quotas. Their diffusion is a relatively recent phenomenon resulting from several trends. The first is the growth of the second-wave feminist movement, which identified male dominance in political life as a problem and questioned the legitimacy of polities that tolerate it. Feminist activism helped forge new international norms of gender equality. Major agreements, such as the Convention on the Elimination of All Forms of Discrimination Against Women (CEDAW) and the Platform for Action adopted by governments at the 1995 Fourth World Conference on Women in Beijing, endorse affirmative action. International and regional organizations, such as the United Nations, the European Union, the Southern African Development Community, the Summit of the Americas, and the Association of Southeast Asian Nations, have declared that growth in women's leadership contributes to democratic consolidation and economic and social progress.

Another factor was the development of normative arguments that identified the gender composition of legislatures as an indicator of justice and the quality of democracy. Quota advocates reconceptualized political equality to include not just the right to vote and stand for office, but to *be present* in office. A homogeneous legislature of men, they argued, violates this fundamental right. Meanwhile, partisans of deliberative democracy stressed the need for representatives to share experiences with their constituents in order to adequately communicate citizen views in open-ended political deliberation. Finally, feminists maintained that having more women in power would introduce additional perspectives to decision making and tailor policy outcomes to suit a broader variety of citizen interests. Ann Phillips sums up these various developments as a reorientation of democratic theory and practice from a "politics of ideas" to a "politics of presence."[29]

Argentina pioneered a candidate quota law in 1991. Influenced by the success of candidate quotas in the Spanish Socialist Party, Argentine female politicians from different parties united behind the proposal. Though it was initially ridiculed by men, last-minute persuasion by President Carlos Menem and his interior minister helped to overcome this resistance. Subsequently, the policy snowballed across the region. By the end of the decade, ten other Latin American countries had adopted legislative quotas, and an eleventh, Colombia, introduced them for senior executive appointments. Belgium introduced a law in 1994 that states that a maximum of two-thirds of all candidates could be of the same sex; in 1999 France modified its constitution to call for gender parity in political office and enacted legislation requiring parties to field an equal number of men and women candidates. Meanwhile, under the influence of the United Nations, the Organization for Security and Co-operation in Europe (OSCE), and the Stability Pact for South-Central Europe, quota rules were inserted into the electoral laws of most countries of the former Yugoslavia, including Bosnia and Herzegovina, Macedonia, and Serbia, including Kosovo.[30]

Three aspects of women's mobilization for gender quotas stand out. First, multipartisan and ideologically diverse coalitions have backed the new policies. Women from the Peronist and Radical parties in

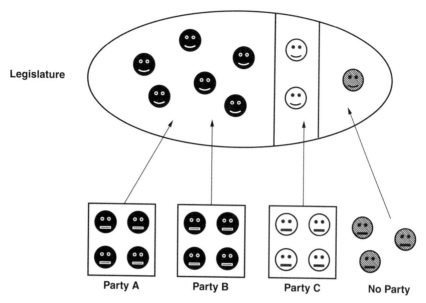

FIGURE 14.3   What Reservations Do

Argentina; the Parry of the Democratic Revolution and National Action Party in Mexico; and the socialists, Rally for the Republic, and the Union for French Democracy in France joined together to defeat the arguments of male colleagues that quotas were undemocratic and unconstitutional. "Although all women may not agree on the substance of specific policy outcomes, they do have a common interest in being present when policy is being made."[31] These politicians did not seek to form a separate women's party. Rather, they united in temporary alliances to maximize their leverage in demanding greater power within their respective parties.

Second, most politicians regard quotas as a temporary measure. As more women gain power, they will break down the obstacles holding others back. Over time, the quota will become obsolete.

Finally, women's activism around quotas has been episodic. After the adoption of quota laws, women's coalitions have disbanded as their members returned to their prior commitments and became reabsorbed into their parties. In some countries—notably Argentina, Costa Rica, Belgium, and Guyana—women's presence in power increased significantly as a result of the quota. Yet the feminization of legislative delegations has not

produced major changes in what parties actually do. Though some women politicians have introduced fresh items to political agendas, their collective presence has thus far failed to produce major shifts in policy and practice.[32]

Ethnic demands for reservations have followed a quite different political logic. Rather than improving the legitimacy of already existing democracies, the granting of reserved seats has tended to occur as part of a founding compromise in consociational or consensus polities. In these countries, split legislatures, the allocation of ministerial portfolios by ethnicity, or fixed ratios of parliamentary seats form part of the elite bargains necessary to make democracy possible. Each group has a constitutional share of power, giving it an incentive not to defect from the existing political regime and undermine the survival of the state. As opposed to quotas, which improve the leadership prospects of group members within existing parties, reservations presume the existence of group-specific parties or organizations. Groups demanding reservations do not want to be integrated into mainstream parties. They want access to political power in their own right.

In Belgium, the constitution requires that there be an equal number of French- and Dutch-speaking ministers in the federal government and in the government of the Brussels region, with the parliament divided between these two language communities and their respective party systems. In Switzerland, language group quotas are used not only in the federal council,[33] but in other areas of government (such as the armed forces) and in society as a whole (such as the executive committee of the Swiss soccer association).[34] Lebanon is another classic story of how ethnic reservations helped forge the state. The National Pact of 1943 reserved all major offices—the president was to be a Maronite; the prime minister a Sunni; the speaker of the house a Shiite; and so on—and fixed the ethnic composition of the parliament at a 6:5 ratio of Christians to Muslims.[35]

Elsewhere, the ethnic allocation of political power was codified in peace agreements following civil wars. International mediators, with an eye toward establishing pluralist polities, helped install forms of power sharing in virtually all of the new states formed after the breakup of Yugoslavia. Bosnia and Herzegovina has a three-member presidency comprised of a Bosniak, Serb, and Croat, as well as a bicameral legislative assembly divided between these three communities. In Serbia and Montenegro, the bicameral federal legislature is divided between Serbians and Montenegrans. In Kosovo, seats are reserved in parliament for Serbs, Roma, and other ethnic groups. (In less polarized Croatia and Slovenia, a smaller number of seats are reserved for minorities.)[36] Other countries inherited power-sharing from former colonial rulers. In Fiji, the ethnic reservation of parliamentary seats dates from colonial times, when the British authorities sought to separate indigenous Fijians from Indo-Fijians and install themselves as mediators. After the country's independence, the vast majority of parliamentary seats continued to be reserved by ethnicity.[37]

Some reservations policies reflect attempts to compensate victims of slavery, colonialism, or a caste system for past oppression. India's reservations for Scheduled Castes and Scheduled Tribes are intended to ameliorate the historic discrimination suffered by those at the lowest rungs of the caste system. New Zealand's white rulers made a similar attempt to compensate oppressed minorities: the Maori Representation Act of 1867 installed four representatives in a legislature of over 70 members. The number of seats later increased to seven (representatives are elected by voters who voluntarily register for a separate Maori roll).[38]

In the late twentieth century, some disadvantaged ethnic groups demanded rights during constitutional reforms. Responding to indigenous mobilization, the Colombian Constitution (1991) created a two-seat senatorial district for Indians and permitted the reservation of up to five seats in the lower house for ethnic groups and other political minorities. Venezuela had a similar experience: the 1999 constitutional reform established three reserved seats for "indigenous communities" in the national assembly and permitted social movement organizations to contest them, thus eliminating the party registration barrier. In both countries, these seats granted resources and visibility to indigenous parties and movements; as a result, they successfully contested general elections and gained power in local governance.[39] With the exception of Peru, democratic states have always conferred ethnic group rights in the form of reservations.

REFERENCES

Ames, Barry. 1995. Electoral strategy under open-list proportional representation. *American Journal of Political Science* 39 (2): 406–33.

Baldez, Lisa. 2004. Elected bodies: The gender quota law for legislative candidates in Mexico. *Legislative Studies Quarterly* 29 (2): 231–58.

Birch, Sarah. 2002. The 2000 elections in Yugoslavia: The "bulldozer revolution." *Electoral Studies* 21 (3): 499–511.

Birch, Sarah, Frances Millard, Marina Popescu, and Kieran Williams. 2002. *Embodying democracy: Electoral system design in post-Communist Europe*. London: Palgrave.

Cameron, Charles, David Epstein, and Sharyn O'Halloran. 1996. Do majority–minority districts maximize substantive black representation in Congress? *American Political Science Review* 90 (4): 794–812.

Carey, John, and Matthew Soberg Shugart. 1992. *Presidents and assemblies: Constitutional design and electoral dynamics.* New York: Cambridge University Press.

Carton, Ann. 2001. The general elections in Belgium in June 1999: A real breakthrough for women politicians. *European Journal of Women's Studies* 8 (1): 127–35.

Caul, Miki. 2001. Political parties and the adoption of candidate gender quotas: A cross-national analysis. *Journal of Politics* 63 (4): 1214–29.

Center for American Women and Politics. 1997. The Gender Gap: Voting Choices, Party Identification, and Presidential Performance Ratings. http://www.rci.rutgers.edu/~cawp/Facts/ggap.pdf.

Chandra, Kanchan. 2004. *Why ethnic parties succeed: Patronage and ethnic head counts in India.* New York: Cambridge University Press.

Chandra, Kanchan. N.d. Ethnic parties and democratic stability. Unpublished manuscript.

Corrin, Chris. 2002. Developing democracy in Kosova: From grassroots to government. *Parliamentary Affairs* 55 (1): 99–108.

Cox, Gary. 1997. *Making votes count: Strategic coordination in the world's electoral systems.* New York: Cambridge University Press.

Croatia, Embassy of. N.d. http://www.croatiaemb.org/politics/Politics_FrameSet.htm.

Dahlerup, Drude. 2002. Using quotas to increase women's political representation. *Women in Parliament: Beyond Numbers.* Stockholm: International IDEA, 2002. http://www.idea.int/women/parl/ch4a.htm.

Darmanovic, Srdjan. 2003. Montenegro: Dilemmas of a small republic. *Journal of Democracy* 14 (1): 145–53.

Dawson, Michael. 1994. *Behind the mule: Race and class in African-American politics.* Princeton: Princeton University Press.

Deschouwer, Kris. 2002. Falling apart together: The changing nature of Belgian consociationalism, 1961–2001. *Acta Politica* 37 (1, 2): 68–85.

Efrén Agudelo, Carlos. 2002. Etnicidad negra y elecciones en Colombia. *Journal of Latin American Anthropology* 7 (2): 168–97.

Electionworld. 2003. http://www.electionworld.org.

Elshtain, Jean. 1995. *Democracy on Trial.* New York: Basic Books.

Epstein, David, and Sharyn O'Halloran. 1999. A social science approach to race, redistricting, and representation. *American Political Science Review* 93 (1): 187–91.

Galanter, Marc. 1984. *Competing equalities: Law and the backward classes of India.* Berkeley: University of California Press.

Grofman, Bernard, Lisa Handley, and Richard G. Niemi. 1992. *Minority representation and the quest for voting equality.* New York: Cambridge University Press.

Guinier, Lani. 1994. *The tyranny of the majority: Fundamental fairness in representative democracy.* New York: Free Press.

Heisler, Martin O. 1990. Hyphenating Belgium: Changing state and regime to cope with cultural division. In *Conflict and peacemaking in multiethnic societies,* ed. Joseph V. Montville, 177–95. Lexington, MA: Lexington Books.

Horowitz, Donald L. 1985. *Ethnic groups in conflict.* Berkeley: University of California Press.

Htun, Mala. 2004. From racial democracy to affirmative action: Changing state policy on race in Brazil. *Latin American Research Review* 39 (1): 6089.

Htun, Mala, and Mark Jones. 2002. Engendering the right to participate in decision making: Electoral quotas and women's leadership in Latin America. In *Gender and the politics of rights and democracy in Latin America,* ed. Nikki Craske and Maxine Molyneux, 32–56. London: Palgrave.

Inglehart, Ronald, and Pippa Norris. 2003. *Rising tide: Gender equality and cultural change around the world* New York: Cambridge University Press.

International IDEA. 2003. *Global Database of Quotas for Women.* A Joint Project of International IDEA and Stockholm University. http://www.idea.int/quota/index.cfm.

Jenson, Jane, and Celia Valiente. 2003. Comparing two movements for gender parity: France and Spain. In *Women's movements facing the reconfigured state,* ed. Lee Ann Banaszak, Karen Beckwith, and Dieter Rucht, 69–93. New York: Cambridge University Press.

Jones, Mark P. 1995. *Electoral laws and the survival of presidential democracies*. Notre Dame: University of Notre Dame Press.

Jones, Mark P. Forthcoming. Quota legislation and the election of women: Learning from the Costa Rican experience. *Journal of Politics*.

Kaufmann, Karen M., and John R. Petrocik. 1999. The changing politics of American men: Understanding the sources of the gender gap. *American Journal of Political Science* 43 (3): 864–87.

Kukathas, Chandran. 1992. Are there any cultural rights? *Political Theory* 20 (1): 105–39.

Kymlicka, Will. 1995. *Multicultural citizenship: A liberal theory of minority rights*. Oxford: Clarendon Press.

Lijphart, Arend. 1977. *Democracy in plural societies: A comparative exploration*. New Haven: Yale University Press.

Lijphart, Arend. 1986. Proportionality by non-PR methods: Ethnic representation in Belgium, Cyprus, Lebanon, New Zealand, West Germany, and Zimbabwe. In *Electoral laws and their political consequences*, ed. Bernard Grofman and Arend Lijphart, 113–23. New York: Agathon Press.

Lijphart, Arend. 1990. The political consequences of electoral laws, 1945–85. *American Political Science Review* 84 (2): 481–96.

Lijphart, Arend. 1995. Self-determination versus predetermination of ethnic minorities in power-sharing systems. In *The rights of minority cultures*, ed. Will Kymlicka, 275–87. New York: Oxford University Press.

Lublin, David. 1999. Racial redistricting and African-American representation: A critique of "do majority–minority districts maximize substantive black representation in Congress?" *American Political Science Review* 93 (1): 183–86.

Mansbridge, Jane. 1999. Should blacks represent blacks and women represent women? A contingent "yes." *Journal of Politics* 61 (3): 628–57.

Matland, Richard E., Donley T. Studlar. 1996. The contagion of women candidates in single-member district and proportional representation electoral systems: Canada and Norway. *Journal of Politics* 58 (3): 707–33.

Miller, David. 2002. Group rights, human rights, and citizenship. *European Journal of Philosophy* 10 (2) 178–95.

Nordlund, Anja Taarup. 2003. International implementation of electoral gender quotas in the Balkans—A fact-finding report. Research Program on Gender Quotas, Department of Political Science, Stockholm University. Working Paper Series 2003, 1. http://www.statsvet.su.se/stv_hemsida/ statsvetens-kap_04/quotas/a_nordlund_wps_2003_1.pdf.

Okin, Susan Moller. 1999. *Is multiculturalism bad for women?* Princeton: Princeton University Press.

Phillips, Anne. 1995. *The politics of presence*. New York: Oxford University Press.

Reilly, Benjamin. 2001. *Democracy in divided societies. Electoral engineering for conflict management*. New York: Cambridge University Press.

Reynolds, Andrew. 1999. Women in the legislatures and executives of the world: Knocking at the highest glass ceiling. *World Politics* 51 (4): 547–72.

Reynolds, Andrew. N.d. Comparative approaches to race and districting. Unpublished paper.

Rodríguez, Victoria E. 2003. *Women in Contemporary Mexican Politics*. Austin: University of Texas Press.

Samuels, David. N.d. Sources of mass partisanship in Brazil. Unpublished manuscript.

Shugart, Matthew Soberg. 1995. The electoral cycle and institutional sources of divided presidential government. *American Political Science Review* 89 (2): 327–43.

Slovenia, Republic of. N.d. Constitution of the Republic of Slovenia. http://www.dz-rs.si/en/aktualno/spremljanje_zakonodaje/ustava/ustava_ang.pdf.

Snyder, Jack. 2000. *From voting to violence: Democratization and nationalist conflict*. New York: W. W. Norton.

Sowell, Thomas. 1990. *Preferential policies: An international perspective*. New York: William Morrow.

Stability Pact. 2002. Gender Task Force, Progress Report June 2002, Stability Pact Working Table 1 Meeting ISTANBUL. http://www.stabilitypact.org/gender/istanbul-2002.doc.

Steiner, Jürg. 1990. Power sharing: Another Swiss "export product"? In *Conflict and peacemaking in multiethnic societies*, ed. Joseph V. Montville. Lexington, MA: Lexington Books, 107–14.

Steiner, Jürg. 2002. Consociational theory and Switzerland—revisited. *Acta Politica* 37 (1, 2): 104–20.

Telles, Edward. 1999. Ethnic boundaries and political mobilization among African Brazilians: Comparisons with the U.S. case. In *Racial politics in contemporary Brazil*, ed. Michael Hanchard, 82–97. Durham: Duke University Press.

Trebble, Adam James. 2002. What is the politics of difference? *Political Theory* 30 (2): 259–81.

UNHCR and OSCE. 2002. Ninth Assessment of the Situation of Ethnic Minorities in Kosovo. http://www.osce.org/kosovo/documents/reports/minorities/min_rep_09_eng.pdf.

Van Cott, Donna Lee. 2003. Institutional change and ethnic parties in South America. *Latin American Politics and Society* 45 (2): 1–39.

Van Cott, Donna Lee. N.d. From Movements to Parties: The Evolution of Ethnic Politics in Latin America. Unpublished manuscript.

Varshney, Ashutosh. 2001. Ethnic conflict and civil society: India and beyond. *World Politics* 53 (2): 362–98.

Walker, Ranginui. 1992. The Maori People: Their political development. In *New Zealand politics in perspective*, ed. Hyam Gold. 3rd ed. Auckland: Longman Paul, 379–400.

Williams, Melissa. 1998. *Voice, trust, and memory: Marginalized groups and the failings of liberal representation*. Princeton: Princeton University Press.

Yishai, Yael. 2001. Bringing society back in: Post-cartel parties in Israel. *Party Politics* 7 (6): 667–87.

Young, Iris Marion. 1990. *Justice and the politics of difference*. Princeton: Princeton University Press.

NOTES

1. Ethnicity is used here as an all-encompassing term referring to social groups differentiated by kinship, tribe, skin color, religion, caste, language, race and other markers of communal identity. This broad definition of ethnicity, though somewhat at odds with the popular use of the term, is becoming more common in social science as scholars seek explanations for the causes—and consequences—of political phenomena motivated by ethnic identities. See Chandra 2004; Varshney 2001; Horowitz 1985.

2. An exception is Anne Phillips's *The Politics of Presence*, which at several points compares the pursuit of gender parity and ethnic minority representation. See Phillips 1995.

3. Most of the data come from IDEA 2003; Reynolds n.d.; Parline 2003; Electionworld 2003. I attempted to confirm each case in the country-specific scholarly literature and in government websites, and made adjustments accordingly. Some of these sources are mentioned in footnotes.

4. The availability of more data on formal and informal practices within parties could reveal more widespread use of ethnic candidate quotas. Parties in India, for instance, regularly apply ethnic quotas for leadership posts. See Chandra 2004. For more information about gender quotas in parties, see IDEA 2003.

5. Kukathas 1992; Okin 1999; Trebble 2002; Miller 2002.

6. Elshtain 1995.

7. Sowell 1990.

8. Cameron, Epstein, and O'Halloran 1996. For a critique and response, see Lublin 1999 and Epstein and O'Halloran 1999.

9. Quoted in Phillips 1995, 92.

10. Kymlicka 1995, 134–38.

11. Jones, forthcoming.

12. The literature on how electoral rules affect the party system and political behavior begins with Duverger's law and is vast. See, for example, Cox 1997; Carey and Shugart 1992; Lijphart 1990; Shugart 1995; Jones 1995; Ames 1995.

13. PR thus permits "self-determination" rather than the "predetermination" of ethnic groups. See Lijphart 1985. Lani Guinier also endorses PR to allow for the representation of "voluntary interest constituencies," ethnic and otherwise. See Guinier 1994.

14. Lijphart 1985.

15. Reynolds 1999; Caul 2001.

16. Baldez 2004; Matland and Studlar 1996.
17. Inglehart and Norris 2003.
18. Kaufmann and Petrocik 1999.
19. Center for American Women and Politics 1997.
20. Chandra 2004.
21. Deschouwer 2002; Heisler 1990; Steiner 2002.
22. Horowitz 1985, 332.
23. Snyder 2000.
24. Yishai 2001.
25. Dawson 1994; Grofman, Handley, and Niemi 1992.
26. Van Cott, n.d.
27. Telles 1999; Htun 2004; Samuels, n.d.
28. Lijphart 1977; Horowitz 1985, 1991; Chandra n.d.
29. Young 1990; Mansbridge 1999; Williams 1998; Phillips 1995.
30. Htun and Jones 2002; Nordlund 2003; Carton 1999; Corrin 2002; Stability Pact 2002; Dahlerup 2002.

31. Friedman 2000, 291.
32. Rodriguez 2003; Jenson and Valiente 2003; Htun and Jones 2002.
33. The council is generally comprised of four German-speakers, two French-speakers, and one Italian-speaker.
34. Deschouwer 2002; Heisler 1990; Steiner 1990; Steiner 2002.
35. Horowitz 1985; Lijphart 1986.
36. Birch 2002; Birch et al 2002; Darmanovic 2003; UNHCR and OSCE 2002; Embassy of Croatia, n.d.; Constitution of the Republic of Slovenia, n.d.
37. Reilly 2001.
38. Galanter 1984; Walker 1992.
39. Van Cott 2003; Efrén Agudelo 2002.

DONNA LEE VAN COTT

14.2 FROM MOVEMENTS TO PARTIES IN LATIN AMERICA

The Evolution of Ethnic Politics

Van Cott seeks to understand why efforts to construct ethnic political parties are successful in some places and unsuccessful in others. She focuses on six Latin American cases as she addresses this question: Argentina, Bolivia, Colombia, Ecuador, Peru, and Venezuela. In Bolivia, Colombia, Ecuador, and Venezuela, party formation has been more successful than in Argentina and Peru. Why might this be? As you will see from the excerpt, she provides a fairly complex, multicausal theory in answer to this question. Some factors might be political opportunities. For example, decentralization may make it easier to organize such parties. So might reserved seats. Others emphasize social action: for example, social movement mobilization clearly matters. Another factor might be "ideological opportunity." In other words, if there is a strong party of the traditional left (which often was suspicious of organizing on the basis of ethnicity) in a given area, this might decrease the likelihood of successful organizing around ethnicity, but if the traditional left is weak, this might open up space that party activists can occupy. Van Cott considers other potential sources of organizing success as well.

LOOKING AHEAD

We can predict that ethnic parties are more likely to form where an indigenous social movement organization is fourteen years old, has achieved some success in the social movement sphere, and has a dense network of affiliates extended throughout the target area; where the organization participated effectively in a constitutional reform; where obstacles to ballot access are relatively low; where decentralization opens the possibility for competition in districts where indigenous peoples are concentrated; where the left is relatively weak; and where seats have been reserved for indigenous candidates. Such parties will perform best when these additional conditions are present: persistently high or moderately increased party-system fragmentation; leaders of a declining electoral left seek to join a more dynamic electoral project; a relatively high level of organizational unity exists within an ethnic movement that has a dense network of organizational affiliates; and the existence of at least one subnational district (preferably, newly formed districts) where Indians are a majority or near majority. These predictive models are depicted in Figure 14.4.

But such conditions rarely occur together. Instead, it is more useful to identify four "ideal types" of successful ethnic party formation in Latin America (see Table 14.4). In Model 1, exemplified by Bolivia's ASP/IPSP/MAS, a majority ethnic population develops regionally strong organizations with dense networks of affiliates. The movement secures new constitutional rights that require implementing legislation. Once municipal decentralization occurs and the left experiences a steep electoral decline, ethnic parties form and quickly achieve success, which increases in subsequent elections.

Van Cott, Donna Lee. 2005. *From Movements to Parties in Latin America*. New York: Cambridge University Press.

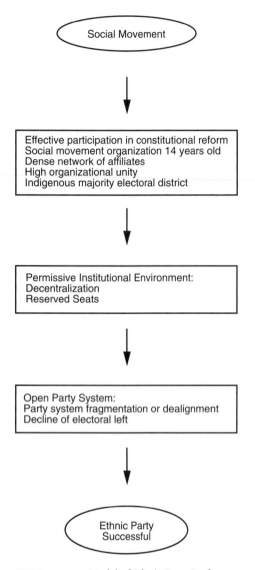

FIGURE 14.4 Model of Ethnic Party Performance

In Model 2, exemplified by Ecuador's Pachakutik, a significant ethnic minority with a unified and institutionalized national organization boasting a dense network of affiliates successfully participates in a constitutional reform. The reform process energizes the ethnic population, demonstrates the electoral potential of the ethnic minority, and results in eased access to the ballot for regionally concentrated groups. The success of ethnic parties in a neighboring country

inspires ethnic elites to consider forming a party. In the context of a weak electoral left and longstanding decentralization, the ethnic party, once formed, quickly dominates elections in areas where the ethnic minority is concentrated and well-organized.

In Model 3, exemplified by Colombia's ASI, a small, widely dispersed ethnic population, with majority concentrations within sparsely populated rural districts, and with a national ethnic social movement organization with strong regional affiliated organizations, successfully participates in a constitutional reform. The reform process energizes the ethnic population and demonstrates the electoral potential of the ethnic minority. Constitutional reforms requiring implementing legislation improve access to the ballot for social movements, further incipient decentralization efforts, and establish reserved seats for the ethnic minority. In the context of a weak electoral left, the ethnic minority builds a regionally strong movement with a national presence in cooperation with other popular movements.

In Model 4, exemplified by Venezuela's PUAMA, a small, dispersed ethnic population, with majority concentrations within sparsely populated rural districts, and with a national organization with strong regional affiliates, successfully participates in a constitutional reform. The reform process energizes the ethnic population and demonstrates the electoral potential of the ethnic minority. Constitutional reforms requiring implementing legislation improve access to the ballot for social movements and establish reserved seats for the ethnic minority. Successful ethnic parties exist in three neighboring countries. In the context of a strong and resurgent left, the ethnic minority builds a regionally strong movement with a national presence in cooperation with an urban-based leftist party.

Although the first successful Latin American ethnic parties required the convergence of a high number of the conditions enumerated in the preceding text, it may be easier for similar parties to form in neighboring countries under less auspicious conditions. The rapid success of ethnic parties in Colombia, Ecuador, and Bolivia in the 1990s has inspired indigenous organizations in neighboring countries, just as the success of ecology parties in the early 1980s

TABLE 14.3 FOUR MODELS OF SUCCESSFUL ETHNIC PARTIES

Model 1 Bolivia's ASP/IPSP/MAS	Model 2 Ecuador's Pachakutik	Model 3 Colombia's ASI	Model 4 Venezuela's PUAMA
Majority ethnic population	Large ethnic minority	Minuscule indigenous population with regional concentrations in rural districts	Minuscule indigenous population with regional concentrations in rural districts
Regional ethnic social movement organizations with dense networks of affiliates	National ethnic social movement organization with dense network of affiliates	National ethnic social movement organization with dense network of affiliates including strong regional organizations	National ethnic social movement organization with strong regional affiliates
New constitutional rights requiring implementing legislation	Successful participation in constitutional reform	Successful participation in constitutional reform	Successful participation in constitutional reform
	Eased ballot access	Eased ballot access	Eased ballot access
Municipal decentralization	Decentralized electoral system	Reserved seats for ethnic minority	Reserved seats for ethnic minority
Electoral decline of left	Electoral decline of left	Regional and municipal decentralization	Decentralized electoral system
	Example of successful ethnic parties in neighboring countries	Weak electoral left	Strong electoral left and party alliances are legal
			Example of successful ethnic parties in neighboring countries

in a small set of countries with favorable conditions inspired ecological movements elsewhere in Europe where conditions were less favorable and, indeed, social movements around the world (Kitschelt 1989: 38; Mayer and Ely 1998: 3). This diffusion effect emerged in author interviews in Peru immediately following national elections in neighboring Bolivia, where two indigenous parties combined for 27 percent of the vote. Indigenous leaders interviewed that had not previously given serious thought to forming ethnic parties expressed an interest in doing so for the next national elections because of the success of ethnic parties in Bolivia and Ecuador.

In fact, even where conditions are manifestly unfavorable, indigenous peoples' organizations have formed viable parties. Beyond our case sample, in Guyana, where Amerindians are 7 percent of the population, indigenous communities launched their first political party, the Guyana Action Party (GAP), and competed in the March 19, 2001, elections. The GAP had to overcome legislation passed by the dominant parties that disqualified the party's leader and presidential candidate, and that reduced from two to one the number of seats available in each of the two electoral districts where indigenous people comprise a majority of the population. Guyana's party system is markedly different from others in the region because it historically has been organized around an ethnic cleavage that pits the Indo-Guyanese 48 percent of the population against the 38 percent of the population identifying itself as Afro-Guyanese (Joseph 2001a: 4–5). In its manifesto, GAP decries the domination of Guyanese politics by the two dominant race-based parties and offers the GAP as an alternative to this "ethnic trap" (Joseph 2001a: 4). The traditional parties responded after huge crowds turned out for GAP leaders in indigenous-dominated regions and political analysts speculated that the GAP could prevent either party from dominating the next government by drawing significant support from disaffected voters.

The party finished third in the March 2001 elections, capturing two seats in the sixty-five-seat parliament—one in each of the indigenous-majority districts. It also swept local elections in the majority-indigenous Rupununi district, which will give it considerable influence over land, natural resource, and environmental issues (Joseph 2001b: 3). These preliminary results from Guyana show that even with small numbers and under adverse conditions, ethnic parties may form and become electorally viable.

REFERENCES

Joseph, Adrian. 2001a. "Indigenous Party Meets Opposition." *Latinamerica Press* 33, 5 (February 19): 4–5.

Joseph, Adrian. 2001b. "Racial divisions mar elections." *Latinamerica Press* 33, 11 (April 2): 3.

Kitschelt, Herbert. 1989. *The Logics of Party Formation: Ecological Politics in Belgium and West Germany.* Ithaca: Cornell University Press.

Mayer, Margit and John Ely. 1998. "Success and Dilemmas of Green Party Politics," in Margit Mayer and John Ely, eds., *The German Greens: Paradox between Movement and Party.* Philadelphia: Temple University Press, pp. 3–26.

CHAPTER 15

IDEOLOGY AND RELIGION

In this chapter we consider major theories of religion and ideology in modern politics. If you follow contemporary events, there is little doubt that you encounter considerable discussion of these issues. Major political spectacles are often attributed to religion and/or ideology. This is true of important triumphs (such as the initial wave of the Arab Spring) and of crises (such as major incidents of terrorism). Both are seen as lying behind conflict but also serving as potential sources of solidarity. Some commentators even speculate about whether certain desirable political and economic outcomes—such as democracy or growth-oriented economics—are compatible with all religious and ideological frameworks. In our view, strong critical statements in this connection are often exaggerated, but there is little doubt that religion and ideology are important factors in comparative politics.

We include excerpts from two major works that sit at the nexus of comparative politics and international relations before turning to a contemporary account of the determinants of different institutional relationships between organized religion and the state. The first two pieces in this chapter, by Francis Fukuyama and Samuel Huntington, are classic works from the 1990s. The context for their ideas was the collapse of the bipolar order in which the Soviet Union and the United States (and their respective allies) vied for global dominance. After the demise of the Soviet Union, analysts in both international relations and comparative politics wondered what the basic organizing principles of global politics would be in the future. Both Fukuyama and Huntington offered grand visions. In Fukuyama's view, we see a world beyond ideology in which technocratic knowledge leads to gradual political and economic improvements but without great historical drama. In Huntington's, we see a world in which incommensurable cultures or "civilizations," largely divided by religion, would enter into conflict. The views offer sharply different visions not just of the future but also of what drives global politics. As you read them, think about their relative strengths and weaknesses for understanding contemporary events. Our third piece, a short but comprehensive argument by Anthony Gill, takes a different approach because it asks a different sort of question, one about the determinants of the relationship between religious and political *institutions*. Indeed, Gill is skeptical of arguments like Fukuyama's or Huntington's that emphasize the causal impact of ideas. Instead, Gill thinks that actors—including organizational actors like churches or states—pursue their material interests, and we can use rationalist theory to model their strategies as they do so. If we analyze their strategies and their relative power, he thinks, we can explain why religious and political institutions are structured so variously across the globe. As you read this piece, think about its potential applicability to the questions raised by Fukuyama. Could a rational choice perspective like Gill's explain different patterns in the spread and vitality of political ideologies? Thinking through such a perspective, what predictions would you make about the types of environments in which strong ideologies might flourish and be tied to the state, and those in which they might not?

FRANCIS FUKUYAMA

15.1 THE END OF HISTORY

In this piece, Fukuyama introduces his famous argument that we have reached the "end of history." (The phrase alludes to ideas from the German philosopher Georg Wilhelm Friedrich Hegel, and this piece does not mean that Fukuyama thinks history, if by that word we mean the sequence of human events over time, is "over.") He claims that, for several centuries, global major ideological divisions drove politics. Liberalism (with its emphasis on democratic politics and capitalist economics) had to contend with socialism and with fascism, among other alternatives. The proponents of radically different visions of how society should be organized fought major revolutions and wars. After the fall of the Soviet Union, however, according to Fukuyama, this changed. In essence, if he is right, everyone now agrees that society should be organized through free market economies and liberal political institutions. It is not that nothing will happen in the future, but instead of great struggles over grand ideological visions, we will simply tinker with the details of a shared model of politics and society. Fukuyama's account is not entirely celebratory, and he notes that a world in which we use technical knowledge making incremental changes does not allow for the sort of heroism and drama of other ages. In reading, consider how the international circumstances at the time of the writing are reflected in the analysis and whether subsequent events in the world have supported or countered Fukuyama's claims.

In watching the flow of events over the past decade or so, it is hard to avoid the feeling that something very fundamental has happened in world history. The past year has seen a flood of articles commemorating the end of the Cold War, and the fact that "peace" seems to be breaking out in many regions of the world. Most of these analyses lack any larger conceptual framework for distinguishing between what is essential and what is contingent or accidental in world history, and are predictably superficial. If Mr. Gorbachev were ousted from the Kremlin or a new Ayatollah proclaimed the millennium for a desolate Middle Eastern capital, these same commentators would scramble to announce the rebirth of a new era of conflict.

And yet, all of these people sense dimly that there is some larger process at work, a process that gives coherence and order to the daily headlines. The twentieth century saw the developed world descend into a paroxysm of ideological violence, as liberalism contended first with the remnants of absolutism, then bolshevism and fascism, and finally an updated Marxism that threatened to lead to the ultimate apocalypse of nuclear war. But the century that began full of self-confidence in the ultimate triumph of Western liberal democracy seems at its close to be returning full circle to where it started: not to an "end of ideology" or a convergence between capitalism and socialism, as earlier predicted, but to an unabashed victory of economic and political liberalism.

The triumph of the West, of the Western idea, is evident first of all in the total exhaustion of viable systematic alternatives to Western liberalism. In the

Fukuyama, Francis. 1989. "The End of History," *The National Interest* (Summer).

past decade, there have been unmistakable changes in the intellectual climate of the world's two largest communist countries, and the beginnings of significant reform movements in both. But this phenomenon extends beyond high politics and it can be seen also in the ineluctable spread of consumerist Western culture in such diverse contexts as the peasants' markets and color television sets now omnipresent throughout China, the cooperative restaurants and clothing stores opened in the past year in Moscow, the Beethoven piped into Japanese department stores, and the rock music enjoyed alike in Prague, Rangoon, and Tehran.

What we may be witnessing is not just the end of the Cold War, or the passing of a particular period of post-war history, but the end of history as such: that is, the end point of mankind's ideological evolution and the universalization of Western liberal democracy as the final form of human government. This is not to say that there will no longer be events to fill the pages of *Foreign Affairs's* yearly summaries of international relations, for the victory of liberalism has occurred primarily in the realm of ideas or consciousness and is as yet incomplete in the real or material world. But there are powerful reasons for believing that it is the ideal that will govern the material world in the long run.

Have we in fact reached the end of history? Are there, in other words, any fundamental "contradictions" in human life that cannot be resolved in the context of modern liberalism, that would be resolvable by an alternative political–economic structure? If we accept the idealist premises laid out above, we must seek an answer to this question in the realm of ideology and consciousness. Our task is not to answer exhaustively the challenges to liberalism promoted by every crackpot messiah around the world, but only those that are embodied in important social or political forces and movements, and which are therefore part of world history. For our purposes, it matters very little what strange thoughts occur to people in Albania or Burkina Faso, for we are interested in what one could in some sense call the common ideological heritage of mankind.

In the past century, there have been two major challenges to liberalism, those of fascism and of communism. The former[1] saw the political weakness, materialism, anomie, and lack of community of the West

as fundamental contradictions in liberal societies that could only be resolved by a strong state that forged a new "people" on the basis of national excessiveness. Fascism was destroyed as a living ideology by World War II. This was a defeat, of course, on a very material level, but it amounted to a defeat of the idea as well. What destroyed fascism as an idea was not universal moral revulsion against it, since plenty of people were willing to endorse the idea as long as it seemed the wave of the future, but its lack of success. After the war, it seemed to most people that German fascism as well as its other European and Asian variants were bound to self-destruct. There was no material reason why new fascist movements could not have sprung up again after the war in other locales, but for the fact that expansionist ultranationalism, with its promise of unending conflict leading to disastrous military defeat, had completely lost its appeal. The ruins of the Reich chancellory as well as the atomic bombs dropped on Hiroshima and Nagasaki killed this ideology on the level of consciousness as well as materially, and all of the proto-fascist movements spawned by the German and Japanese examples like the Peronist movement in Argentina or Subhas Chandra Bose's Indian National Army withered after the war.

The ideological challenge mounted by the other great alternative to liberalism, communism, was far more serious. Marx, speaking Hegel's language, asserted that liberal society contained fundamental contradiction that could not be resolved within its context, that between capital and labor, and this contradiction has constituted the chief accusation against liberalism ever since. But surely, the class issue has actually been successfully resolved in the West. As Kojeve (among others) noted, the egalitarianism of modern America represents the essential achievement of the classless society envisioned by Marx. This is not to say that there are not rich people and poor people in the United States, or that the gap between them has not grown in recent years. But the root causes of economic inequality do not have to do with the underlying legal and social structure of our society, which remains fundamentally egalitarian and moderately redistributionist, so much as with the cultural and social characteristics of the groups that make it up, which are in turn the historical legacy of premodern conditions. Thus black poverty in the United States is not the inherent product of liberalism, but is rather the "legacy of slavery and racism" which persisted long after the formal abolition of slavery.

As a result of the receding of the class issue, the appeal of communism in the developed Western world, it is safe to say, is lower today than any time since the end of the First World War. This can be measured in any number of ways: in the declining membership and electoral pull of the major European communist parties, and their overtly revisionist programs; in the corresponding electoral success of conservative parties from Britain and Germany to the United States and Japan which are unabashedly pro-market and antistatist; and in an intellectual climate whose most "advanced" members no longer believe that bourgeois society is something that ultimately needs to be overcome. This is not to say that the opinions of progressive intellectuals in Western countries are not deeply pathological in any number of ways. But those who believe that the future must inevitably be socialist tend to be very old, or very marginal to the real political discourse of their societies.

One may argue that the socialist alternative was never terribly plausible for the North Atlantic world, and was sustained for the last several decades primarily by its success outside of this region. But it is precisely in the non-European world that one is not struck by the occurrence of major ideological transformations. Surely the most remarkable changes have occurred in Asia. Due to the strength and adaptability of the indigenous cultures there, Asia became a battleground for a variety of imported Western ideologies early in this century. Liberalism in Asia was a very weak reed in the period after World War I; it is easy today to forget how gloomy Asia's political future looked as recently as ten or fifteen years ago. It is easy to forget as well how momentous the outcome of Asian ideological struggles seemed for world political development as a whole.

The first Asian alternative to liberalism to be decisively defeated was the fascist one represented by Imperial Japan. Japanese fascism (like its German version) was defeated by the force of American arms in the Pacific war, and liberal democracy was imposed on Japan by a victorious United States. Western capitalism and political liberalism when transplanted to Japan were adapted and transformed by the Japanese in such a way as to be scarcely recognizable.[2] Many Americans are now aware that Japanese industrial organization is very different from that prevailing in the United States or Europe, and it is questionable what relationship the factional maneuvering that takes place with the governing Liberal Democratic Party bears to democracy. Nonetheless, the very fact that the essential elements of economic and political liberalism have been so successfully grafted onto uniquely Japanese traditions and institutions guarantees their survival in the long run. More important is the contribution that Japan has become both a symbol and an underpinning of the universal homogenous state. V. S. Naipaul traveling in Khomeini's Iran shortly after the revolution noted the omnipresent signs advertising the products of Sony, Hitachi, and JVC, whose appeal remained virtually irresistible and gave the lie to the regime's pretensions of restoring a state based on the rule of the *Shariah*. Desire for access to the consumer culture, created in large measure by Japan, has played a crucial role in fostering the spread of economic liberalism throughout Asia, and hence in promoting political liberalism as well.

The economic success of the other newly industrializing countries (NICs) in Asia following on the example of Japan is by now a familiar story. What is important from a Hegelian standpoint is that political liberalism has been following economic liberalism, more slowly than many had hoped but with seeming inevitability. Here again we see the victory of the idea of the universal homogenous state. South Korea had developed into a modern, urbanized society with an increasingly large and well-educated middle class that could not possibly be isolated from the larger democratic trends around them. Under these circumstances it seemed intolerable to a large part of this population that it should be ruled by an anachronistic military regime while Japan, only a decade or so ahead in economic terms, had parliamentary institutions for over forty years. Even the former socialist regime in Burma, which for so many decades existed in dismal isolation from the larger trends dominating Asia, was buffeted in the past year by pressures to liberalize both its economy and political system. It is said that unhappiness with strongman Ne Win began when a senior Burmese officer went to Singapore for medical treatment and broke down crying when he saw how far socialist Burma had been left behind by its ASEAN neighbors.

But the power of the liberal idea would seem much less impressive if it had not infected the largest and oldest culture in Asia, China. The simple existence of communist China created an alternative pole of ideological attraction, and as such constituted a threat to liberalism. But the past fifteen years have seen an almost total discrediting of Marxism-Leninism as an economic system. Beginning with the famous third plenum of the Tenth Central Committee in 1978, the Chinese Communist party set about decollectivizing agriculture for the 800 million Chinese who still lived in the countryside. The role of the state in agriculture was reduced to that of a tax collector, while production of consumer goods was sharply increased in order to give peasants a taste of the universal homogenous state and thereby an incentive to work. The reform doubled Chinese grain output in only five years, and in the process created for Deng Xiao-ping a solid political base from which he was able to extend the reform to other parts of the economy. Economic statistics do not begin to describe the dynamism, initiative, and openness evident in China since the reform began.

China could not now be described in any way as a liberal democracy. At present, no more than 20 percent of its economy has been marketed, and most importantly it continues to be ruled by a self-appointed Communist party which has given no hint of wanting to devolve power. Deng has made none of Gorbachev's promises regarding democratization of the political system and there is no Chinese equivalent of *glasnost*. The Chinese leadership has in fact been much more circumspect in criticizing Mao and Maoism than Gorbachev with respect to Brezhnev and Stalin, and the regime continues to pay lip service to Marxism-Leninism as its ideological underpinning. But anyone familiar with the outlook and behavior of the new technocratic elite now governing China knows the Marxism and ideological principle have become virtually irrelevant as guides to policy,

and that bourgeois consumerism has a real meaning in that country for the first time since the revolution. The various slowdowns in the pace of reform, the campaigns against "spiritual pollution" and crackdowns on political dissent are more properly seen as tactical adjustments made in the process of managing what is an extraordinarily difficult political transition. By ducking the question of political reform while putting the economy on a new footing, Deng has managed to avoid the breakdown of authority that has accompanied Gorbachev's *perestroika*. Yet the pull of the liberal idea continues to be very strong as economic power devolves and the economy becomes more open to the outside world. There are currently over 20,000 Chinese students studying in the U.S. and other Western countries, almost all of them of children of the Chinese elite. It is hard to believe that when they return home to run the country they will be content for China to be the only country in Asia unaffected by the larger democratizing treat. The student demonstrations in Beijing that broke out first in December 1986 and recurred recently on the occasion of Hu Yao-bang's death were only the beginning of what will inevitably be mounting pressure for change in the political system as well.

What is important about China from the standpoint of world history is not the present state of the reform or even its future prospects. The central issue is the fact that the People's Republic of China can no longer act as a beacon for illiberal forces around the world, whether they be guerrillas in some Asian jungle or middle class students in Paris. Maoism, rather than being the pattern for Asia's future, became an anachronism, and it was the mainland Chinese who in fact were decisively influenced by the prosperity and dynamism of their overseas co-ethnics—the ironic ultimate victory of Taiwan.

If we admit for the moment that the fascist and communist challenges to liberalism are dead, are there any other ideological competitors left? Or put another way, are there contradictions in liberal society beyond that of class that are not resolvable? Two possibilities suggest themselves, those of religion and nationalism.

The rise of religious fundamentalism in recent years within the Christian, Jewish, and Muslim traditions has been widely noted. One is inclined to say that the revival of religion in some way attests to a broad unhappiness with the impersonality and spiritual vacuity of liberal consumerist societies. Yet while the emptiness at the core of ideology—indeed, a flaw that one does not need the perspective of religion to recognize[3]—it is not at all clear that it is remediable through politics. Modern liberalism itself was historically a consequence of the weakness of religiously-based societies which, falling to agree on the nature of the good life, could not provide even the minimal preconditions of peace and stability. In the contemporary world only Islam has offered a theocratic state as a political alternative to both liberalism and communism. But the doctrine has little appeal for non-Muslims, and it is hard to believe that the movement will take on any universal significance. Other less organized religious impulses have been successfully satisfied within the sphere of personal life that is permitted in liberal societies.

The other major "contradiction" potentially unresolvable by liberalism is the one posed by nationalism and other forms of racial and ethnic consciousness. It is certainly true that a very large degree of conflict since the Battle of Jena has had its roots in nationalism. Two cataclysmic world wars in this century have been spawned by the nationalism of the developed world in various guises, and if those passions have been muted to a certain extent in postwar Europe, they are still extremely powerful in the Third World. Nationalism has been a threat to liberalism historically in Germany, and continues to be one in isolated parts of "post-historical" Europe like Northern Ireland.

But it is not clear that nationalism represents an irreconcilable contradiction in the heart of liberalism. In the first place, nationalism is not one single phenomenon but several, ranging from mild cultural nostalgia to the highly organized and elaborately articulated doctrine of National Socialism. Only systematic nationalism of the latter sort can qualify as a formal ideology on the level of liberalism or communism. The vast majority of the world's nationalist movements do not have a political program beyond the negative desire of independence from some other group or people, and do not offer anything like a comprehensive agenda for socio-economic organization. As such, they are compatible with doctrines and ideologies that do offer such agendas. While they may constitute a source of conflict for liberal societies, this conflict does not arise from liberalism itself so much as from the fact that the liberalism in question is incomplete. Certainly a great deal of the world's ethnic and nationalist tension can be explained in terms of peoples who are forced to live in unrepresentative political systems that they have not chosen.

While it is impossible to rule out the sudden appearance of new ideologies or previously unrecognized in liberal societies, then, the present world seems to confirm that the fundamental principles of sociopolitical organization have not advanced terribly far since 1806. Many of the wars and revolutions fought since that time have been undertaken in the name of ideologies which claimed to be more advanced than liberalism, but whose pretensions were ultimately unmasked by history. In the meantime, they have helped to spread the universal homogenous state to the point where it could have a significant effect on the overall character of international relations.

The end of history will be a very sad time. The struggle for recognition, the willingness to risk one's life for a purely abstract goal, the worldwide ideological struggle that called forth daring, courage, imagination, and idealism, will be replaced by economic calculation, the endless solving of technical problems, environmental concerns, and the satisfaction of sophisticated consumer demands. In the post historical period there will be neither art nor philosophy, just the perpetual care taking of the museum of human history. I can feel in myself, and see in others around me, a powerful nostalgia for the time when history existed. Such nostalgia, in fact, will continue to fuel competition and conflict even in the post historical world for some time to come. Even though I recognize its inevitability, I have the most ambivalent feelings for the civilization that has been created in Europe since 1945, with its north Atlantic and Asian offshoots. Perhaps this very prospect of centuries of boredom at the end of history will serve to get history started once again.

NOTES

1. I am not using the term "fascism" here in its most precise sense, fully aware of the frequent misuse of this term to denounce anyone to the right of the user. "Fascism" here denotes any organized ultra nationalist movement with universalistic pretensions—not universalistic with regard to its nationalism, of course, since the latter is exclusive by definition, but with regard to the movement's belief in its right to rule other people. Hence Imperial Japan would qualify as fascist while former strongman Stoessner's Paraguay or Pinochet's Chile would not. Obviously fascist ideologies cannot be universalistic in the sense of Marxism or liberalism, but the structure of the doctrine can be transferred from country to country.

2. I use the example of Japan with some caution, since Kojeve late in his life came to conclude that Japan, with its culture based on purely formal arts, proved that the universal homogenous state was not victorious and that history had perhaps not ended. See the long note at the end of the second edition of Introduction a la Lecture de Hegel, 462–3.

3. I am thinking particularly of Rousseau and the Western philosophical tradition that flows from him that was highly critical of Lockean or Hobbesian liberalism, though one could criticize liberalism from the standpoint of classical political philosophy as well.

SAMUEL P. HUNTINGTON

15.2 THE CLASH OF CIVILIZATIONS?

The work from which this is excerpted has, since the 1990s, been paired in numerous discussions with Fukuyama's contrasting view as shaping a major debate about what to expect in the future of global politics. Huntington asserts that we are not witnessing global convergence around a set of shared institutions and practices. Rather, we see ongoing and perhaps increasing cultural or civilizational difference. He comes close to suggesting that cultures or civilizations are incommensurable (that is, that you cannot fully translate the terms of one into the terms of another). He also seems to believe that cultures exhibit sharp differences in their ultimate values. This, along with the fact that different states and regions might have different interests, suggests a future of ongoing conflict. Huntington was particularly concerned about conflict between "the West" and the Islamic world. Some commentators have felt that major terrorist attacks like those of September 11, 2001, as well as U.S.-led wars in Afghanistan and Iraq, are evidence in support of his theory. Others suggest that he exaggerates the stability, unity, and coherence of cultures and underestimates the power of institutions and economic and political interests to bring about convergence and reduce conflict. As you consider the cultures that Huntington demarcates, do you think he identified these cultures and then noted conflicts between them or did he note where conflicts occur and then define cultures as the conflicting parties?

THE NEXT PATTERN OF CONFLICT

World politics is entering a new phase, and intellectuals have not hesitated to proliferate visions of what it will be—the end of history, the return of traditional rivalries between nation states, and the decline of the nation state from the conflicting pulls of tribalism and globalism, among others. Each of these visions catches aspects of the emerging reality. Yet they all miss a crucial, indeed a central, aspect of what global politics is likely to be in the coming years.

It is my hypothesis that the fundamental source of conflict in this new world will not be primarily ideological or primarily economic. The great divisions among humankind and the dominating source of conflict will be cultural. Nation states will remain the most powerful actors in world affairs, but the principal conflicts of global politics will occur between nations and groups of different civilizations. The clash of civilizations will dominate global politics. The fault lines between civilizations will be the battle lines of the future.

Conflict between civilizations will be the latest phase in the evolution of conflict in the modern world. For a century and a half after the emergence of the modern international system with the Peace of Westphalia, the conflicts of the Western world were largely among princes—emperors, absolute monarchs and constitutional monarchs attempting to expand their bureaucracies, their armies, their mercantilist economic strength and, most important, the territory they ruled. In the process they created nation states, and beginning with the French Revolution the

This article is the product of the Olin Institute's project on "The Changing Security Environment and American National Interests."
Huntington, Samuel P. 1992. "The Clash of Civilizations?" *Foreign Affairs* 72: 22–49.

principal lines of conflict were between nations rather than princes. In 1793, as R. R. Palmer put it, "The wars of kings were over; the wars of peoples had begun." This nineteenth-century pattern lasted until the end of World War I. Then, as a result of the Russian Revolution and the reaction against it, the conflict of nations yielded to the conflict of ideologies, first among communism, fascism-Nazism and liberal democracy, and then between communism and liberal democracy. During the Cold War, this latter conflict became embodied in the struggle between the two superpowers, neither of which was a nation state in the classical European sense and each of which defined its identity in terms of its ideology.

These conflicts between princes, nation states and ideologies were primarily conflicts within Western civilization, "Western civil wars," as William Lind has labeled them. This was as true of the Cold War as it was of the world wars and the earlier wars of the seventeenth, eighteenth and nineteenth centuries. With the end of the Cold War, international politics moves out of its Western phase, and its centerpiece becomes the interaction between the West and non-Western civilizations and among non-Western civilizations. In the politics of civilizations, the peoples and governments of non-Western civilizations no longer remain the objects of history as targets of Western colonialism but join the West as movers and shapers of history.

WHY CIVILIZATIONS WILL CLASH

Civilization identity will be increasingly important in the future, and the world will be shaped in large measure by the interactions among seven or eight major civilizations. These include Western, Confucian, Japanese, Islamic, Hindu, Slavic-Orthodox, Latin American and possibly African civilization. The most important conflicts of the future will occur along the cultural fault lines separating these civilizations from one another.

Why will this be the case?

First, differences among civilizations are not only real; they are basic. Civilizations are differentiated from each other by history, language, culture, tradition and, most important, religion. The people of different civilizations have different views on the relations between God and man, the individual and the group, the

citizen and the state, parents and children, husband and wife, as well as differing views of the relative importance of rights and responsibilities, liberty and authority, equality and hierarchy. These differences are the product of centuries. They will not soon disappear. They are far more fundamental than differences among political ideologies and political regimes. Differences do not necessarily mean conflict, and conflict does not necessarily mean violence. Over the centuries, however, differences among civilizations have generated the most prolonged and the most violent conflicts.

Second, the world is becoming a smaller place. The interactions between peoples of different civilizations are increasing; these increasing interactions intensify civilization consciousness and awareness of differences between civilizations and commonalities within civilizations. North African immigration to France generates hostility among Frenchmen and at the same time increased receptivity to immigration by "good" European Catholic Poles. Americans react far more negatively to Japanese investment than to larger investments from Canada and European countries. Similarly, as Donald Horowitz has pointed out, "An Ibo may be . . . an Owerri Ibo or an Onitsha Ibo in what was the Eastern region of Nigeria. In Lagos, he is simply an Ibo. In London, he is a Nigerian. In New York, he is an African." The interactions among peoples of different civilizations enhance the civilization-consciousness of people that, in turn, invigorates differences and animosities stretching or thought to stretch back deep into history.

Third, the processes of economic modernization and social change throughout the world are separating people from longstanding local identities. They also weaken the nation state as a source of identity. In much of the world religion has moved in to fill this gap, often in the form of movements that are labeled "fundamentalist." Such movements are found in Western Christianity, Judaism, Buddhism and Hinduism, as well as in Islam. In most countries and most religions the people active in fundamentalist movements are young, college-educated, middle-class technicians, professionals and business persons. The "unsecularization of the world," George Weigel has remarked, "is one of the dominant social facts of life in the late twentieth century." The revival of religion, "la revanche de Dieu," as Gilles Kepel labeled it, provides a basis for identity and commitment that transcends national boundaries and unites civilizations.

Fourth, the growth of civilization-consciousness is enhanced by the dual role of the West. On the one hand, the West is at a peak of power. At the same time, however, and perhaps as a result, a return to the roots phenomenon is occurring among non-Western civilizations. Increasingly one hears references to trends toward a turning inward and "Asianization" in Japan, the end of the Nehru legacy and the "Hinduization" of India, the failure of Western ideas of socialism and nationalism and hence "re-Islamization" of the Middle East, and now a debate over Westernization versus Russianization in Boris Yeltsin's country. A West at the peak of its power confronts non-Wests that increasingly have the desire, the will and the resources to shape the world in non-Western ways.

In the past, the elites of non-Western societies were usually the people who were most involved with the West, had been educated at Oxford, the Sorbonne or Sandhurst, and had absorbed Western attitudes and values. At the same time, the populace in non-Western countries often remained deeply imbued with the indigenous culture. Now, however, these relationships are being reversed. A de-Westernization and indigenization of elites is occurring in many non-Western countries at the same time that Western, usually American, cultures, styles and habits become more popular among the mass of the people.

Fifth, cultural characteristics and differences are less mutable and hence less easily compromised and resolved than political and economic ones. In the former Soviet Union, communists can become democrats, the rich can become poor and the poor rich, but Russians cannot become Estonians and Azeris cannot become Armenians. In class and ideological conflicts, the key question was "Which side are you on?" and people could and did choose sides and change sides. In conflicts between civilizations, the question is "What are you?" That is a given that cannot be changed. And as we know, from Bosnia to the Caucasus to the Sudan, the wrong answer to that question can mean a bullet in the head. Even more than ethnicity, religion discriminates sharply and exclusively among people. A person can be half-French and half-Arab and simultaneously even a citizen of two countries. It is more difficult to be half-Catholic and half-Muslim.

Finally, economic regionalism is increasing. The proportions of total trade that were intraregional rose between 1980 and 1989 from 51 percent to 59 percent in Europe, 33 percent to 37 percent in East Asia, and 32 percent to 36 percent in North America. The importance of regional economic blocs is likely to continue to increase in the future. On the one hand, successful economic regionalism will reinforce civilization-consciousness. On the other hand, economic regionalism may succeed only when it is rooted in a common civilization. The European Community rests on the shared foundation of European culture and Western Christianity. The success of the North American Free Trade Area depends on the convergence now underway of Mexican, Canadian and American cultures. Japan, in contrast, faces difficulties in creating a comparable economic entity in East Asia because Japan is a society and civilization unique to itself. However strong the trade and investment links Japan may develop with other East Asian countries, its cultural differences with those countries inhibit and perhaps preclude its promoting regional economic integration like that in Europe and North America.

Common culture, in contrast, is clearly facilitating the rapid expansion of the economic relations between the People's Republic of China and Hong Kong, Taiwan, Singapore and the overseas Chinese communities in other Asian countries. With the Cold War over, cultural commonalities increasingly overcome ideological differences, and mainland China and Taiwan move closer together. If cultural commonality is a prerequisite for economic integration, the principal East Asian economic bloc of the future is likely to be centered on China. This bloc is, in fact, already coming into existence. As Murray Weidenbaum has observed,

Despite the current Japanese dominance of the region, the Chinese-based economy of Asia is rapidly emerging as a new epicenter for industry, commerce and finance. This strategic area contains substantial amounts of technology and manufacturing capability (Taiwan), outstanding entrepreneurial, marketing and services acumen (Hong Kong), a fine communications network (Singapore), a tremendous pool of financial capital (all three), and very large endowments of land, resources and labor (mainland China). . . . From Guangzhou to Singapore, from Kuala Lumpur to Manila, this influential network—often based on extensions of the traditional clans—has been described as the backbone of the East Asian economy.[1]

Culture and religion also form the basis of the Economic Cooperation Organization, which brings together ten non-Arab Muslim countries: Iran, Pakistan, Turkey, Azerbaijan, Kazakhstan, Kyrgyzstan, Turkmenistan, Tadjikistan, Uzbekistan and Afghanistan. One impetus to the revival and expansion of this organization, founded originally in the 1960s by Turkey, Pakistan and Iran, is the realization by the leaders of several of these countries that they had no chance of admission to the European Community. Similarly, Caricom, the Central American Common Market and Mercosur rest on common cultural foundations. Efforts to build a broader Caribbean-Central American economic entity bridging the Anglo-Latin divide, however, have to date failed.

As people define their identity in ethnic and religious terms, they are likely to see an "us" versus "them" relation existing between themselves and people of different ethnicity or religion. The end of ideologically defined states in Eastern Europe and the former Soviet Union permits traditional ethnic identities and animosities to come to the fore. Differences in culture and religion create differences over policy issues, ranging from human rights to immigration to trade and commerce to the environment. Geographical propinquity gives rise to conflicting territorial claims from Bosnia to Mindanao. Most important, the efforts of the West to promote its values of democracy and liberalism as universal values, to maintain its military predominance and to advance its economic interests engender countering responses from other civilizations. Decreasingly able to mobilize support and form coalitions on the basis of ideology, governments and groups will increasingly attempt to mobilize support by appealing to common religion and civilization identity.

The clash of civilizations thus occurs at two levels. At the micro-level, adjacent groups along the fault lines between civilizations struggle, often violently, over the control of territory and each other. At the macro-level, states from different civilizations compete for relative military and economic power, struggle over the control of international institutions and third parties, and competitively promote their particular political and religious values.

THE WEST VERSUS THE REST

The West is now at an extraordinary peak of power in relation to other civilizations. Its superpower opponent has disappeared from the map. Military conflict among Western states is unthinkable, and Western military power is unrivaled. Apart from Japan, the West faces no economic challenge. It dominates international political and security institutions and with Japan international economic institutions. Global political and security issues are effectively settled by a directorate of the United States, Britain and France, world economic issues by a directorate of the United States, Germany and Japan, all of which maintain extraordinarily close relations with each other to the exclusion of lesser and largely non-Western countries. Decisions made at the U.N. Security Council or in the International Monetary Fund that reflect the interests of the West are presented to the world as reflecting the desires of the world community. The very phrase "the world community" has become the euphemistic collective noun (replacing "the Free World") to give global legitimacy to actions reflecting the interests of the United States and other Western powers.[2] Through the IMF and other international economic institutions, the West promotes its economic interests and imposes on other nations the economic policies it thinks appropriate. In any poll of non-Western peoples, the IMF undoubtedly would win the support of finance ministers and a few others, but get an overwhelmingly unfavorable rating from just about everyone else, who would agree with Georgy Arbatov's characterization of IMF officials as "neo-Bolsheviks who love expropriating other people's money, imposing undemocratic and alien rules of economic and political conduct and stifling economic freedom."

Western domination of the U.N. Security Council and its decisions, tempered only by occasional abstention by China, produced U.N. legitimation of the West's use of force to drive Iraq out of Kuwait and its elimination of Iraq's sophisticated weapons and capacity to produce such weapons. It also produced the quite unprecedented action by the United States, Britain and France in getting the Security Council to demand that Libya hand over the Pan Am 103 bombing suspects and then to impose sanctions when Libya refused. After defeating the largest Arab army, the West did not hesitate to throw its weight around in the Arab world. The West in effect is using international institutions, military power and economic resources to run the world in ways that will maintain Western predominance, protect Western interests and promote Western political and economic values.

That at least is the way in which non-Westerners see the new world, and there is a significant element of truth in their view. Differences in power and struggles for military, economic and institutional power are thus one source of conflict between the West and other civilizations. Differences in culture, that is basic values and beliefs, are a second source of conflict. V. S. Naipaul has argued that Western civilization is the "universal civilization" that "fits all men." At a superficial level much of Western culture has indeed permeated the rest of the world. At a more basic level, however, Western concepts differ fundamentally from those prevalent in other civilizations. Western ideas of individualism, liberalism, constitutionalism, human rights, equality, liberty, the rule of law, democracy, free markets, the separation of church and state, often have little resonance in Islamic, Confucian, Japanese, Hindu, Buddhist or Orthodox cultures. Western efforts to propagate such ideas produce instead a reaction against "human rights imperialism" and a reaffirmation of indigenous values, as can be seen in the support for religious fundamentalism by the younger generation in non-Western cultures. The very notion that there could be a "universal civilization" is a Western idea, directly at odds with the particularism of most Asian societies and their emphasis on what distinguishes one people from another. Indeed, the author of a review of 100 comparative studies of values in different societies concluded that "the values that are most important in the West are least important worldwide."[3] In the political realm, of course, these differences are most manifest in the efforts of the United

States and other Western powers to induce other peoples to adopt Western ideas concerning democracy and human rights. Modern democratic government originated in the West. When it has developed in non-Western societies it has usually been the product of Western colonialism or imposition.

The central axis of world politics in the future is likely to be, in Kishore Mahbubani's phrase, the conflict between "the West and the Rest" and the responses of non-Western civilizations to Western power and values.[4] Those responses generally take one or a combination of three forms. At one extreme, non-Western states can, like Burma and North Korea, attempt to pursue a course of isolation, to insulate their societies from penetration or "corruption" by the West, and, in effect, to opt out of participation in the Western-dominated global community. The costs of this course, however, are high, and few states have pursued it exclusively. A second alternative, the equivalent of "band-wagoning" in international relations theory, is to attempt to join the West and accept its values and institutions. The third alternative is to attempt to "balance" the West by developing economic and military power and cooperating with other non-Western societies against the West, while preserving indigenous values and institutions; in short, to modernize but not to Westernize.

IMPLICATIONS FOR THE WEST

This article does not argue that civilization identities will replace all other identities, that nation states will disappear, that each civilization will become a single coherent political entity, that groups within a civilization will not conflict with and even fight each other. This paper does set forth the hypotheses that differences between civilizations are real and important; civilization-consciousness is increasing; conflict between civilizations will supplant ideological and other forms of conflict as the dominant global form of conflict; international relations, historically a game played out within Western civilization, will increasingly be de-Westernized and become a game in which non-Western civilizations are actors and not simply objects; successful political, security and economic international institutions are more likely to develop within civilizations than across civilizations; conflicts between groups in different civilizations will be more frequent, more sustained and more violent than conflicts between groups in the same civilization; violent conflicts between groups in different civilizations are the most likely and most dangerous source of escalation that could lead to global wars; the paramount axis of world politics will be the relations between "the West and the Rest"; the elites in some torn non-Western countries will try to make their countries part of the West, but in most cases face major obstacles to accomplishing this; a central focus of conflict for the immediate future will be between the West and several Islamic-Confucian states.

This is not to advocate the desirability of conflicts between civilizations. It is to set forth descriptive hypotheses as to what the future may be like. If these are plausible hypotheses, however, it is necessary to consider their implications for Western policy. These implications should be divided between short-term advantage and long-term accommodation. In the short term it is clearly in the interest of the West to promote greater cooperation and unity within its own civilization, particularly between its European and North American components; to incorporate into the West societies in Eastern Europe and Latin America whose cultures are close to those of the West; to promote and maintain cooperative relations with Russia and Japan; to prevent escalation of local inter-civilization conflicts into major inter-civilization wars; to limit the expansion of the military strength of Confucian and Islamic states; to moderate the reduction of Western military capabilities and maintain military superiority in East and Southwest Asia; to exploit differences and conflicts among Confucian and Islamic states; to support in other civilizations groups sympathetic to Western values and interests; to strengthen international institutions that reflect and legitimate Western interests and values and to promote the involvement of non-Western states in those institutions.

In the longer term other measures would be called for. Western civilization is both Western and modern. Non-Western civilizations have attempted to become modern without becoming Western. To date only Japan has fully succeeded in this quest. Non-Western civilizations will continue to attempt to acquire the wealth, technology, skills, machines and weapons that are part of being modern. They will also attempt to reconcile this modernity with their traditional culture and values. Their economic and military strength relative to the West will increase. Hence the West will increasingly have to accommodate these non-Western modern civilizations whose power approaches that of the West but whose values and interests differ significantly from those of the West. This will require the West to maintain the economic and military power necessary to protect its interests in relation to these civilizations. It will also, however, require the West to develop a more profound understanding of the basic religious and philosophical assumptions underlying other civilizations and the ways in which people in those civilizations see their interests. It will require an effort to identify elements of commonality between Western and other civilizations. For the relevant future, there will be no universal civilization, but instead a world of different civilizations, each of which will have to learn to coexist with the others.

NOTES

1. Murray Weidenbaum, *Greater China: The Next Economic Superpower?*, St. Louis: Washington University Center for the Study of American Business, Contemporary Issues, Series 57, February 1993, pp. 2–3.

2. Almost invariably Western leaders claim they are acting on behalf of "the world community." One minor lapse occurred during the run-up to the Gulf War. In an interview on "Good Morning America," Dec. 21, 1990, British Prime Minister John Major referred to the actions "the West" was taking against Saddam Hussein. He quickly corrected himself and subsequently referred to "the world community." He was, however, right when he erred.

3. Harry C. Triandis, *The New York Times*, Dec. 25, 1990, p. 41, and "Cross-Cultural Studies of Individualism and Collectivism," Nebraska Symposium on Motivation, vol. 37, 1989, pp. 41–133.

4. Kishore Mahbubani, "The West and the Rest," *The National Interest*, Summer 1992, pp. 3–13.

ANTHONY GILL

15.3 THE POLITICAL ORIGINS OF RELIGIOUS LIBERTY

Gill applies rational choice theory to questions about the relationship between religious organizations and the state. For Gill, "religious liberty" is the condition obtained when the state has the least possible involvement in religion. Different polities vary tremendously in this respect. Some theorists try to explain these differences in terms of religious cultures: some traditions, they suggest, might be more or less hospitable to religious liberty than others. Other theorists try to explain these matters simply in terms of institutional design: the United States has a separation of church and state because the founders decided that it should. For Gill, however, these sorts of perspectives miss the extent to which politics involves conflicts between actors who seek to pursue their own interests. To understand why some societies have more religious liberty than others, we must model the contexts in which religious and secular actors aimed to structure relationships between religious and secular institutions. Note the clear and succinct formulation of Gill's theory (developed more fully in the book from which this excerpt is drawn). One virtue of this clarity of formulation is that it enhances the theory's testability.

A THEORY OF THE POLITICAL ORIGINS OF RELIGIOUS LIBERTY

Religion has long been considered beyond the purview of economic analysis. Scholars typically assume that the behavior of religious actors derives from a set of ideational (theological) principles that transcend the self-interested motivations of *homo economicus*. Yet, although religious actors may be motivated by "high ideals," it is still obvious that they exist in a world of scarcity wherein difficult choices about how to allocate resources must be made on a daily basis.[1] For example, a Catholic bishop might face a difficult choice of whether to spend his limited budget on putting more priests through the seminary or expanding day-care facilities in his diocese. The latter may have the effect of immediately increasing the attendance of young families at services, while the former option has a longer-term (and more risky) payoff of improving the quality and perhaps the quantity of religious services offered.

An evangelical Protestant organization might face a difficult choice of whether to send its one hundred eager missionaries to Brazil or Russia. Where are more converts likely to be made? Even Mother Teresa, perhaps the noblest of souls, had to make tough decisions about how to divvy up her scarce time and energy to help the most people (Kwilecki and Wilson 1998).[2]

Moreover, religious actors also must deal with individuals who might not share their high ideals. Scoundrels, scalawags, and rogues roam throughout government and society. Successful interaction with such nefarious individuals often requires sacrificing strict obedience to high principle for strategic expediency. This is *not* to say that religious actors are hypocrites when it comes to living in the secular world; it merely notes that high principles do not always guide behavior. A Jesuit president of a Catholic university may decry the crass materialism of modern society and the neglect of the poor yet aggressively pursue

Gill, Anthony. 2008. *The Political Origins of Religious Liberty.* New York: Cambridge University Press.

financial contributions to sustain his university, often diverting those funds from other philanthropic causes (e.g., building homeless shelters). A preacher calling for greater ecumenical relations between faiths might also lobby to have restrictions placed on "cults" that are stealing members from his flock. All told, rational choice theory provides us with some leverage in explaining tough decisions of resource allocation. The theory does not tell us much in the way of what a specific individual's high ideals or other preferences might be, but many general preferences can be assumed safely as the basis for theory testing. Thus to the extent that religious actors and institutions exist in a world of scarcity, economic theory can have some bearing on explaining behavior in this realm.

THE RELIGIOUS MARKETPLACE

To begin the process of building a theory of the origins of religious liberty, it is first worthwhile to begin with a number of definitions. These definitions will help to delineate the scope of the study and help to place the issue of religious liberty in a framework analogous to that of economics.

LIST OF DEFINITIONS, AXIOMS, AND PROPOSITIONS

DEFINITIONS

Definition 1: Religious goods are fundamental answers to the deep philosophic questions surrounding life that have as their basis some appeal to a supernatural force.

Definition 2: A *religious firm* (i.e., a church or denomination) is an organization that produces and distributes religious goods.

Definition 3: A *religious marketplace* is the social arena wherein religious firms compete for members and resources.

Definition 4: Religious liberty (or freedom) represents the degree to which a government regulates the religious marketplace.

AXIOMS

Axiom 1: Religious preferences in society are pluralistic.

Axiom 2: Proselytizing religious firms are market-share maximizers; they seek to spread their brand of spiritual message to as many followers as possible.

Axiom 3: Politicians are primarily interested in their personal political survival.

Axiom 4: Politicians will also seek to maximize government revenue, promote economic growth, and minimize civil unrest.

Axiom 5: Politicians seek to minimize the cost of ruling.

PROPOSITIONS

Proposition 1: Hegemonic religions will prefer high levels of government regulation (i.e., restrictions on religious liberty) over religious minorities. Religious minorities will prefer laws favoring greater religious liberty.

Proposition 1a: In an environment where no single religion commands a majority market share, the preferences of each denomination will tend toward religious liberty.

Proposition 2: Politicians will seek ideological compliance of the population when possible.

Proposition 3: To the extent that political survival, revenue collection, economic growth, and social stability are hindered by restrictions on religious freedom or subsidies to a dominant church, religious regulation will be liberalized or not enforced (de facto liberalization). In other words, deregulation of the religious market results when restrictions on religious liberty have a high opportunity cost as measured in terms of political survival, government revenue, and/or economic growth. Concomitantly, restrictions on religious freedom will increase if it served the aforementioned political and economic interests of policy makers.

Proposition 4: The presence of viable secular rivals to power increases the bargaining power of religious organizations, *ceteris paribus.*

Proposition 4a: If one religious organization commands hegemonic loyalty among the population and is not tied to any secular political actor, the bargaining power of that church increases, *ceteris paribus.* Regulatory policy toward religion is likely to favor the dominant church and discriminate against minority denominations.

Proposition 4b: If a church is institutionally linked (or credibly committed) to one political faction, regulatory policy will favor that denomination if the affiliated faction holds power. Conversely, religious deregulation, punishing the dominant church and rewarding spiritual competitors, is likely when the church's favored faction loses.

Proposition 4c: If several competing denominations exist (none with hegemonic dominance) regulatory policy will tend not to discriminate among them (i.e., increased religious liberty). In other words, the presence of competing religious denominations reduces the bargaining leverage of any one particular group, leading politicians to attempt to curry favor with all denominations.

Proposition 5: As political tenure becomes more secure, the bargaining power of a religious group wanes.

Proposition 5a: Given that restrictions on religious liberty entail monitoring and enforcement costs, politicians will be less likely to enforce them as their political tenure becomes secure.

Proposition 5b: As enforcement of restrictions on religious freedom decreases, religious pluralism increases in society (by way of Axioms 1 and 2).

NOTES

1. Whether actors are motivated by "high ideals" or "economic rationality" may be a moot point. "High ideals" typically inform a person's fundamental preferences (i.e., ends), while "rationality" speaks more to means. A person who maintains the most altruistic of goals is still limited by scarce resources and must make difficult (economic) choices as to how to best realize those altruistic goals. For the analyst, the trick is first to determine what a person's basic preferences are, then to specify the constraints the person faces. Ideational perspectives are typically useful in discerning the former; rational choice theory is superior in the latter.

2. Although a provocative application of rational choice theory, Kwilecki and Wilson's analysis of Mother Teresa commits a fatal methodological error by seeking to explain a single case. Rational choice theory relies on probabilistic and marginal analysis. In other words, the goal of rational choice theory is to explain the average behavior of the typical consumer/producer when faced by a marginal alteration in their environmental constraints. Specific exceptions to rational choice predictions will always exist, but unless those exceptions constitute a significant proportion of the cases examined, they do not necessarily destroy the predictive power of the theory. For instance, the existence of martyrs who are willing to give their life for a cause does not detract from the rational choice prediction (and empirical finding) that most people stop well short of zealous actions in their personal religious practice. Nonetheless, idiosyncratic anomalies and outliers may often serve as a basis for examining the assumptions and logic of a theory and provoke modifications to that theory (cf. Froese and Pfaff 2005, 2001). Therefore, it would be negligent for a scholar to simply neglect an anomaly.

3. Stark and Bainbridge provide a more specific definition of religious goods based on a theory of compensators (1987, 25–42).

WORKS CITED

Froese, Paul and Steven Pfaff. 2001. "Replete and Desolate Markets: Poland, East Germany and the New Religious Paradigm," *Social Forces.* 80(2): 481–508.

Froese, Paul and Steven Pfaff. 2005. "Explaining a Religious Anomaly: A Historical Analysis of Secularization in East Germany," *Journal for the Scientific Study of Religion* 44(4): 397–422.

Kwilecki, Susan and Loretta S. Wilson. 1998. "Was Mother Theresa Maximizing Her Utility? An Idiographic Application of Rational Choice Theory," *Journal for the Scientific Study of Religion* 37(2): 205–22.

Stark, Rodney and William Sims Bainbridge. 1987. *A Theory of Religion.* New York: Peter Lang Publishing.

5

THE COMPARATIVE–INTERNATIONAL NEXUS

In Sections 1 through 4 of this book, you have learned about how politics operates within different countries and contexts and have seen how scholars compare and contrast these experiences. Studying comparative politics largely involves looking at how politics operates in different places that are mostly thought of as "independent" of one another. Each country in a comparison, for instance, may be treated as its own "unit of analysis" that can be meaningfully compared to one or more other countries. For many purposes, this may be fine. However, the tendency of scholars in comparative politics to treat country-level processes as truly independent of each other is more a simplifying assumption than a true reflection of the reality we study.

Although there is attention in comparative politics to international factors (such as histories of colonization or the role of international trade in development), we have not yet considered directly how politics operates *between* countries. Doing so takes us increasingly into the realm of international relations. Most observers of the modern world—with the growing importance of globalization and transnational communication—would agree that countries do not operate in isolation from one another. To understand what goes on in a given country's economy, or in its particular legislature, it is often necessary to consider how that country is affected by other countries. That is the subject of the only chapter in this final section (Chapter 16).

CHAPTER 16

COMPARATIVE POLITICS
AND INTERNATIONAL RELATIONS

As noted in the introduction to Section 5 of this book, Chapter 16 speaks to the ways comparative politics interacts with international relations. The three readings in this chapter reflect the fact that comparative politics takes place in a global context where major issues are *transnational* in nature. Informally, we can think of this by noting that lots of activity is not contained by borders. Rather, it spills across them. What happens in one country affects others, and what happens elsewhere is likely to affect you in your home country. It is thus important to think about the themes of comparative politics in this broader global context.

The first reading is by Moisés Naím, and it shows the many ways in which the age of globalization and transnational issues generates many threats and risks along with opportunities. You may consider also how the issues raised by Naím relate to the previous topics such as the state (Chapter 3), development (Chapter 5), and revolutions (Chapter 12), among others. The second reading, by Alan Blinder, offers a perspective on how the internationalization of labor is likely to affect the future job prospects and opportunities of people living in relatively wealthy countries, such as the United States. The final reading is a classic piece by Garrett Hardin entitled "The Tragedy of the Commons." Hardin highlights the challenges presented by the people's tendency to overconsume certain resources that, in a sense, belong to everyone (and therefore belong to no one). Although the specific issues may have changed from the time of Hardin's writing, this piece is an enduring classic because its logic can be applied to all kinds of current issues relating to the environment, such as global climate change or overfishing.

In these selections, you should be attentive to the ways international relations can affect comparative politics and vice versa. As an exercise in critical thinking, you can keep in mind when reading the Naím and Blinder articles whether the authors' assumptions and arguments best reflect optimism or pessimism about the prospects for international cooperation and the likelihood of future conflict.

MOISÉS NAÍM

16.1 THE FIVE WARS OF GLOBALIZATION

The contemporary age is one in which many issues are transnational in nature. Politics, economics, and social relationships regularly spill across borders. People and decisions made in one country affect those in other countries. Here, Naím highlights five of the main transnational challenges to the global order: drug trafficking, arms trafficking, intellectual property theft, human trafficking/smuggling, and money laundering. Of course, many of these problems relate to one another. Naím documents the reasons why the transnational actors behind these illicit activities are outwitting governments, emphasizing the flexibility and nimbleness of their networks. He concludes by proposing certain policy responses for those wishing to curb illicit activity. The piece illustrates in stark terms some of the perils that accompany the promise of globalization. You can consider whether these challenges are inevitable and whether there are viable alternate responses to the ones proposed by the author.

The illegal trade in drugs, arms, intellectual property, people, and money is booming. Like the war on terrorism, the fight to control these illicit markets pits governments against agile, stateless, and resourceful networks empowered by globalization. Governments will continue to lose these wars until they adopt new strategies to deal with a larger, unprecedented struggle that now shapes the world as much as confrontations between nation-states once did.

The persistence of al Qaeda underscores how hard it is for governments to stamp out stateless, decentralized networks that move freely, quickly, and stealthily across national borders to engage in terror. The intense media coverage devoted to the war on terrorism, however, obscures five other similar global wars that pit governments against agile, well-financed networks of highly dedicated individuals. These are the fights against the illegal international trade in drugs, arms, intellectual property, people, and money. Religious zeal or political goals drive terrorists, but the promise of enormous financial gain motivates those who battle governments in these five wars. Tragically, profit is no less a motivator for murder, mayhem, and global insecurity than religious fanaticism.

In one form or another, governments have been fighting these five wars for centuries. And losing them. Indeed, thanks to the changes spurred by globalization over the last decade, their losing streak has become even more pronounced. To be sure, nation-states have benefited from the information revolution, stronger political and economic linkages, and the shrinking importance of geographic distance. Unfortunately, criminal networks have benefited even more. Never fettered by the niceties of sovereignty, they are now increasingly free of geographic constraints. Moreover, globalization has not only expanded illegal markets and boosted the size and the resources of criminal networks, it has also imposed more burdens on governments: Tighter public budgets, decentralization, privatization, deregulation, and a more open environment for international trade and investment all make the task of fighting global criminals more difficult. Governments are made up of cumbersome bureaucracies that generally cooperate with difficulty, but drug traffickers, arms dealers, alien

Naím, Moisés. 2003. "The Five Wars of Globalization," *Foreign Policy* (January/February): 29–37.

smugglers, counterfeiters, and money launderers have refined networking to a high science, entering into complex and improbable strategic alliances that span cultures and continents.

Defeating these foes may prove impossible. But the first steps to reversing their recent dramatic gains must be to recognize the fundamental similarities among the five wars and to treat these conflicts not as law enforcement problems but as a new global trend that shapes the world as much as confrontations between nation-states did in the past. Customs officials, police officers, lawyers, and judges alone will never win these wars. Governments must recruit and deploy more spies, soldiers, diplomats, and economists who understand how to use incentives and regulations to steer markets away from bad social outcomes. But changing the skill set of government combatants alone will not end these wars. Their doctrines and institutions also need a major overhaul.

THE FIVE WARS

Pick up any newspaper anywhere in the world, any day, and you will find news about illegal migrants, drug busts, smuggled weapons, laundered money, or counterfeit goods. The global nature of these five wars was unimaginable just a decade ago. The resource—financial, human, institutional, technological—deployed by the combatants have reached unfathomable orders of magnitude. So have the numbers of victims. The tactics and tricks of both sides boggle the mind. Yet if you cut through the fog of daily headlines and orchestrated photo ops, one inescapable truth emerges: The world's governments are fighting a qualitatively new phenomenon with obsolete tools, inadequate laws, inefficient bureaucratic arrangements, and ineffective strategies. Not surprisingly, the evidence shows that governments are losing.

DRUGS

The best known of the five wars is, of course, the war on drugs. In 1999, the United Nations' "Human Development Report" calculated the annual trade in illicit drugs at $400 billion, roughly the size of the Spanish economy and about 8 percent of world trade. Many countries are reporting an increase in drug use. Feeding this

habit is a global supply chain that uses everything from passenger jets that can carry shipments of cocaine worth $500 million in a single trip to custom-built submarines that ply the waters between Colombia and Puerto Rico. To foil eavesdroppers, drug smugglers use "cloned" cell phones and broadband radio receivers while also relying on complex financial structures that blend legitimate and illegitimate enterprises with elaborate fronts and structures of cross-ownership.

The United States spends between $35 billion and $40 billion each year on the war on drugs; most of this money is spent on interdiction and intelligence. But the creativity and boldness of drug cartels has routinely outstripped steady increases in government resources. Responding to tighter security at the U.S.–Mexican border, drug smugglers built a tunnel to move tons of drugs and billions of dollars in cash until authorities discovered it in March 2002. Over the last decade, the success of the Bolivian and Peruvian governments in eradicating coca plantations has shifted production to Colombia. Now, the U.S.-supported Plan Colombia is displacing coca production and processing labs back to other Andean countries. Despite the heroic efforts of these Andean countries and the massive financial and technical support of the United States, the total acreage of coca plantations in Peru, Colombia, and Bolivia has increased in the last decade from 206,200 hectares in 1991 to 210,939 in 2001. Between 1990 and 2000, according to economist Jeff DeSimone, the median price of a gram of cocaine in the United States fell from $152 to $112.

Even when top leaders of drug cartels are captured or killed, former rivals take their place. Authorities have acknowledged, for example, that the recent arrest of Benjamin Arellano Felix, accused of running Mexico's most ruthless drug cartel, has done little to stop the flow of drugs to the United States. As Arellano said in a recent interview from jail, "They talk about a war against the Arellano brothers. They haven't won. I'm here, and nothing has changed."

ARMS TRAFFICKING

Drugs and arms often go together. In 1999, the Peruvian military parachuted 10,000 AK-47s to the Revolutionary Armed Forces of Colombia, a guerrilla group closely allied to drug growers and traffickers. The group purchased the weapons in Jordan. Most of the roughly 80 million AK-47s in circulation today are in the wrong hands. According to the United Nations, only 18 million (or about 3 percent) of the 550 million small arms and light weapons in circulation today are used by government, military, or police forces. Illicit trade accounts for almost 20 percent of the total small arms trade and generates more than $1 billion a year. Small arms helped fuel 46 of the 49 largest conflicts of the last decade and in 2001 were estimated to be responsible for 1,000 deaths a day; more than 80 percent of those victims were women and children.

Small arms are just a small part of the problem. The illegal market for munitions encompasses top-of-the-line tanks, radar systems that detect Stealth aircraft, and the makings of the deadliest weapons of mass destruction. The International Atomic Energy Agency has confirmed more than a dozen cases of smuggled nuclear-weapons-usable material, and hundreds more cases have been reported and investigated over the last decade. The actual supply of stolen nuclear-, biological-, or chemical-weapons materials and technology may still be small. But the potential demand is strong and growing from both would-be nuclear powers and terrorists. Constrained supply and increasing demand cause prices to rise and create enormous incentives for illegal activities. More than one fifth of the 120,000 workers in Russia's former "nuclear cities"—where more than half of all employees earn less than $50 a month—say they would be willing to work in the military complex of another country.

Governments have been largely ineffective in curbing either supply or demand. In recent years, two countries, Pakistan and India, joined the declared nuclear power club. A U.N. arms embargo failed to prevent the reported sale to Iraq of jet fighter engine parts from Yugoslavia and the Kolchuga anti-Stealth radar system from Ukraine. Multilateral efforts to curb the manufacture and distribution of weapons are faltering, not least because some powers are unwilling to accept curbs on their own activities. In 2001, for example, the United States blocked a legally binding global treaty to control small arms in part because it worried about restrictions on its own citizens' rights to own guns. In the absence of effective international legislation and enforcement, the laws

of economics dictate the sale of more weapons at cheaper prices: In 1986, an AK-47 in Kolowa, Kenya, cost 15 cows. Today, it costs just four.

INTELLECTUAL PROPERTY

In 2001, two days after recording the voice track of a movie in Hollywood, actor Dennis Hopper was in Shanghai where a street vendor sold him an excellent pirated copy of the movie with his voice already on it. "I don't know how they got my voice into the country before I got here," he wondered. Hopper's experience is one tiny slice of an illicit trade that cost the United States an estimated $9.4 billion in 2001. The piracy rate of business software in Japan and France is 40 percent, in Greece and South Korea it is about 60 percent, and in Germany and Britain it hovers around 30 percent. Forty percent of Procter & Gamble shampoos and 60 percent of Honda motorbikes sold in China in 2001 were pirated. Up to 50 percent of medical drugs in Nigeria and Thailand are bootleg copies. This problem is not limited to consumer products: Italian makers of industrial valves worry that their $2 billion a year export market is eroded by counterfeit Chinese valves sold in world markets at prices that are 40 percent cheaper.

The drivers of this bootlegging boom are complex. Technology is obviously boosting both the demand and the supply of illegally copied products. Users of Napster, the now defunct Internet company that allowed anyone, anywhere to download and reproduce copyrighted music for free, grew from zero to 20 million in just one year. Some 500,000 film files are traded daily through file-sharing services such as Kazaa and Morpheus; and in late 2002, some 900 million music files could be downloaded for free on the Internet—that is, almost two and a half times more files than those available when Napster reached its peak in February 2001.

Global marketing and branding are also playing a part, as more people are attracted to products bearing a well-known brand like Prada or Cartier. And thanks to the rapid growth and integration into the global economy of countries, such as China, with weak central governments and ineffective laws, producing and exporting near perfect knockoffs are both less expensive and less risky. In the words of the CEO of one of the best known Swiss watchmakers: "We now compete with a product manufactured by Chinese prisoners. The business is run by the Chinese military, their families and friends, using roughly the same machines we have, which they purchased at the same industrial fairs we go to. The way we have rationalized this problem is by assuming that their customers and ours are different. The person that buys a pirated copy of one of our $5,000 watches for less than $100 is not a client we are losing. Perhaps it is a future client that some day will want to own the real thing instead of a fake. We may be wrong and we do spend money to fight the piracy of our products. But given that our efforts do not seem to protect us much, we close our eyes and hope for the better." This posture stands in contrast to that of companies that sell cheaper products such as garments, music, or videos, whose revenues are directly affected by piracy.

Governments have attempted to protect intellectual property rights through various means, most notably the World Trade Organization's Agreement on Trade-Related Aspects of Intellectual Property Rights (TRIPS). Several other organizations such as the World Intellectual Property Organization, the World Customs Union, and Interpol are also involved. Yet the large and growing volume of this trade, or a simple stroll in the streets of Manhattan or Madrid, show that governments are far from winning this fight.

ALIEN SMUGGLING

The man or woman who sells a bogus Hermes scarf or a Rolex watch in the streets of Milan is likely to be an illegal alien. Just as likely, he or she was transported across several continents by a trafficking network allied with another network that specializes in the illegal copying, manufacturing, and distributing of high-end, brand-name products.

Alien smuggling is a $7 billion a year enterprise and according to the United Nations is the fastest growing business of organized crime. Roughly 500,000 people enter the United States illegally each year—about the same number as illegally enter the European Union, and part of the approximately 150 million who live outside their countries of origin.

Many of these backdoor travelers are voluntary migrants who pay smugglers up to $35,000, the top-dollar fee for passage from China to New York. Others, instead, are trafficked—that is, bought and sold internationally—as commodities. The U.S. Congressional Research Service reckons that each year between 1 million and 2 million people are trafficked across borders, the majority of whom are women and children. A woman can be "bought" in Timisoara, Romania, for between $50 and $200 and "resold" in Western Europe for 10 times that price. The United Nations Children's Fund estimates that cross-border smugglers in Central and Western Africa enslave 200,000 children a year. Traffickers initially tempt victims with job offers or, in the case of children, with offers of adoption in wealthier countries, and then keep the victims in subservience through physical violence, debt bondage, passport confiscation, and threats of arrest, deportation, or violence against their families back home.

Governments everywhere are enacting tougher immigration laws and devoting more time, money, and technology to fight the flow of illegal aliens. But the plight of the United Kingdom's government illustrates how tough that fight is. The British government throws money at the problem, plans to use the Royal Navy and Royal Air Force to intercept illegal immigrants, and imposes large fines on truck drivers who (generally unwittingly) transport stowaways. Still, 42,000 of the 50,000 refugees who have passed through the Sangatte camp (a main entry point for illegal immigration to the United Kingdom) over the last three years have made it to Britain. At current rates, it will take 43 years for Britain to clear its asylum backlog. And that country is an island. Continental nations such as Spain, Italy, or the United States face an even greater challenge as immigration pressures overwhelm their ability to control the inflow of illegal aliens.

MONEY LAUNDERING

The Cayman Islands has a population of 36,000. It also has more than 2,200 mutual funds, 500 insurance companies, 60,000 businesses, and 600 banks and trust companies with almost $800 billion in assets. Not surprisingly, it figures prominently in any discussion of money laundering. So does the United States, several of whose major banks have been caught up in investigations of money laundering, tax evasion, and fraud. Few, if any, countries can claim to be free of the practice of helping individuals and companies hide funds from governments, creditors, business partners, or even family members, including the proceeds of tax evasion, gambling, and other crimes. Estimates of the volume of global money laundering range between 2 and 5 percent of the world's annual gross national product, or between $800 billion and $2 trillion.

Smuggling money, gold coins, and other valuables is an ancient trade. Yet in the last two decades, new political and economic trends coincided with technological changes to make this ancient trade easier, cheaper, and less risky. Political changes led to the deregulation of financial markets that now facilitate cross-border money transfers, and technological changes made distance less of a factor and money less "physical." Suitcases full of banknotes are still a key tool for money launderers, but computers, the Internet, and complex financial schemes that combine legal and illegal practices and institutions are more common. The sophistication of technology, the complex web of financial institutions that crisscross the globe, and the ease with which "dirty" funds can be electronically morphed into legitimate assets make the regulation of international flows of money a daunting task. In Russia, for example, it is estimated that by the mid-1990s organized crime groups had set up 700 legal and financial institutions to launder their money.

Faced with this growing tide, governments have stepped up their efforts to clamp down on rogue international banking, tax havens, and money laundering. The imminent, large-scale introduction of e-money—cards with microchips that can store large amounts of money and thus can be easily transported outside regular channels or simply exchanged among individuals—will only magnify this challenge.

WHY GOVERNMENTS CAN'T WIN

The fundamental changes that have given the five wars new intensity over the last decade are likely to

persist. Technology will continue to spread widely; criminal networks will be able to exploit these technologies more quickly than governments that must cope with tight budgets, bureaucracies, media scrutiny, and electorates. International trade will continue to grow, providing more cover for the expansion of illicit trade. International migration will likewise grow, with much the same effect, offering ethnically based gangs an ever growing supply of recruits and victims. The spread of democracy may also help criminal cartels, which can manipulate weak public institutions by corrupting police officers or tempting politicians with offers of cash for their increasingly expensive election campaigns. And ironically, even the spread of international law—with its growing web of embargoes, sanctions, and conventions—will offer criminals new opportunities for providing forbidden goods to those on the wrong side of the international community.

These changes may affect each of the five wars in different ways, but these conflicts will continue to share four common characteristics:

THEY ARE NOT BOUND BY GEOGRAPHY

Some forms of crime have always had an international component: The Mafia was born in Sicily and exported to the United States, and smuggling has always been by definition international. But the five wars are truly global. Where is the theater or front line of the war on drugs? Is it Colombia or Miami? Myanmar (Burma) or Milan? Where are the battles against money launderers being fought? In Nauru or in London? Is China the main theater in the war against the infringement of intellectual property, or are the trenches of that war on the Internet?

THEY DEFY TRADITIONAL NOTIONS OF SOVEREIGNTY

Al Qaeda's members have passports and nationalities—and often more than one—but they are truly stateless. Their allegiance is to their cause, not to any nation. The same is also true of the criminal networks engaged in the five wars. The same, however, is patently *not* true of government employees—police officers, customs agents, and judges—who fight them. This asymmetry is a crippling disadvantage for governments waging these wars. Highly paid, hyper-motivated, and resource-rich combatants on one side of the wars (the criminal gangs) can seek refuge in and take advantage of national borders, but combatants of the other side (the governments) have fewer resources and are hampered by traditional notions of sovereignty. A former senior CIA official reported that international criminal gangs are able to move people, money, and weapons globally faster than he can move resources inside his own agency, let alone worldwide. Coordination and information sharing among government agencies in different countries has certainly improved, especially after September 11. Yet these tactics fall short of what is needed to combat agile organizations that can exploit every nook and cranny of an evolving but imperfect body of international law and multilateral treaties.

THEY PIT GOVERNMENTS AGAINST MARKET FORCES

In each of the five wars, one or more government bureaucracies fight to contain the disparate, uncoordinated actions of thousands of independent, stateless organizations. These groups are motivated by large profits obtained by exploiting international price differentials, an unsatisfied demand, or the cost advantages produced by theft. Hourly wages for a Chinese cook are far higher in Manhattan than in Fujian. A gram of cocaine in Kansas City is 17,000 percent more expensive than in Bogotá. Fake Italian valves are 40 percent cheaper because counterfeiters don't have to cover the costs of developing the product. A well-funded guerrilla group will pay anything to get the weapons it needs. In each of these five wars, the incentives to successfully overcome government-imposed limits to trade are simply enormous.

THEY PIT BUREAUCRACIES AGAINST NETWORKS

The same network that smuggles East European women to Berlin may be involved in distributing opium there. The proceeds of the latter fund the purchase of counterfeit Bulgari watches made in China and often sold on the streets of Manhattan by illegal African immigrants. Colombian drug cartels make

deals with Ukrainian arms traffickers, while Wall Street brokers controlled by the U.S.-based Mafia have been known to front for Russian money launderers. These highly decentralized groups and individuals are bound by strong ties of loyalty and common purpose and organized around semiautonomous clusters or "nodes" capable of operating swiftly and flexibly. John Arquilla and David Ronfeldt, two of the best known experts on these types of organizations, observe that networks often lack central leadership, command, or headquarters, thus "no precise heart or head that can be targeted. The network as a whole (but not necessarily each node) has little to no hierarchy; there may be multiple leaders. . . . Thus the [organization's] design may sometimes appear acephalous (headless), and at other times polycephalous (Hydra-headed)." Typically, governments respond to these challenges by forming interagency task forces or creating new bureaucracies. Consider the creation of the new Department of Homeland Security in the United States, which encompasses 22 former federal agencies and their 170,000 employees and is responsible for, among other things, fighting the war on drugs.

RETHINKING THE PROBLEM

Governments may never be able to completely eradicate the kind of international trade involved in the five wars. But they can and should do better. There are at least four areas where efforts can yield better ideas on how to tackle the problems posed by these wars:

DEVELOP MORE FLEXIBLE NOTIONS OF SOVEREIGNTY

Governments need to recognize that restricting the scope of multilateral action for the sake of protecting their sovereignty is often a moot point. Their sovereignty is compromised daily, not by nation-states but by stateless networks that break laws and cross borders in pursuit of trade. In May 1999, for example, the Venezuelan government denied U.S. planes authorization to fly over Venezuelan territory to monitor air routes commonly used by narcotraffickers. Venezuelan authorities placed more importance on the symbolic value of asserting sovereignty over air space than on the fact that drug traffickers' planes regularly violate Venezuelan territory. Without new forms of codifying and "managing" sovereignty, governments will continue to face a large disadvantage while fighting the five wars.

STRENGTHEN EXISTING MULTILATERAL INSTITUTIONS

The global nature of these wars means no government, regardless of its economic, political, or military power, will make much progress acting alone. If this seems obvious, then why does Interpol, the multilateral agency in charge of fighting international crime, have a staff of 384, only 112 of whom are police officers, and an annual budget of $28 million, less than the price of some boats or planes used by drug traffickers? Similarly, Europol, Europe's Interpol equivalent, has a staff of 240 and a budget of $51 million.

One reason Interpol is poorly funded and staffed is because its 181 member governments don't trust each other. Many assume, and perhaps rightly so, that the criminal networks they are fighting have penetrated the police departments of other countries and that sharing information with such compromised officials would not be prudent. Others fear today's allies will become tomorrow's enemies. Still others face legal impediments to sharing intelligence with fellow nation-states or have intelligence services and law enforcement agencies with organizational cultures that make effective collaboration almost impossible. Progress will only be made if the world's governments unite behind stronger, more effective multilateral organizations.

DEVISE NEW MECHANISMS AND INSTITUTIONS

These five wars stretch and even render obsolete many of the existing institutions, legal frameworks, military doctrines, weapons systems, and law enforcement techniques on which governments have relied for years. Analysts need to rethink the concept of war "fronts" defined by geography and the definition of "combatants" according to the Geneva Convention. The functions of intelligence agents, soldiers, police officers, customs agents, or immigration officers need rethinking and adaptation to the new realities. Policymakers also need to reconsider the notion that ownership is essentially a physical reality and not a "virtual" one or that only sovereign nations can issue money when thinking about ways to fight the five wars.

MOVE FROM REPRESSION TO REGULATION

Beating market forces is next to impossible. In some cases, this reality may force governments to move from repressing the market to regulating it. In others, creating market incentives may be better than using bureaucracies to curb the excesses of these markets. Technology can often accomplish more than government policies can. For example, powerful encryption techniques can better protect software or CDs from being copied in Ukraine than would making the country enforce patents and copyrights and trademarks.

In all of the five wars, government agencies fight against networks motivated by the enormous profit opportunities created by other government agencies. In all cases, these profits can be traced to some form of government intervention that creates a major imbalance between demand and supply and makes prices and profit margins skyrocket. In some cases, these government interventions are often justified and it would be imprudent to eliminate them— governments can't simply walk away from the fight against trafficking in heroin, human beings, or weapons of mass destruction. But society can better deal with other segments of these kinds of illegal trade through regulation, not prohibition. Policymakers must focus on opportunities where market regulation can ameliorate problems that have defied approaches based on prohibition and armed interdiction of international trade.

Ultimately, governments, politicians, and voters need to realize that the way in which the world is conducting these five wars is doomed to fail—not for lack of effort, resources, or political will but because the collective thinking that guides government strategies in the five wars is rooted in wrong ideas, false assumptions, and obsolete institutions. Recognizing that governments have no chance of winning unless they change the ways they wage these wars is an indispensable first step in the search for solutions.

WANT TO KNOW MORE?

A growing body of work focuses on what is commonly referred to as "transnational organized crime." The quarterly journal *Trends in Organized Crime* reports on significant new findings from individual scholars and from intelligence and law enforcement agencies as well as international organizations. Good introductions to the topics raised here can be found in Richard Friman and Peter Andreas's, eds., *The Illicit Global Economy and State Power* (Lanham: Rowman and Littlefield, 1999) and Phil Williams's "Crime, Illicit Markets and Money Laundering" in P. J. Simmons and Chantal De Jonge Oudraat, eds., *Managing Global Issues* (Washington: Carnegie Endowment for International Peace, 2001). John Arquilla and David Ronfeldt's *Networks and Netwars* (Santa Monica: RAND, 2001) explains the rise to power of criminal networks.

For the response of the international community to these problems, see the "United Nations Convention Against Transnational Organized Crime," adopted on November 15, 2000, and available on the Web site of the U.N. Office for Drug Control and Crime Prevention. The convention includes protocols on the illegal trade in drugs, arms, and people as well as on money laundering. For a frank assessment of how the international community is actually doing, see "Meet the World's Top Cop" (Foreign Policy, January/February 2001), an interview with the former head of Interpol, Raymond Kendall.

Efforts aimed at understanding the common drivers of the five wars are rare; however, individual analyses of the wars are plentiful. A good introduction to the modus operandi of drug networks can be found in Phil Williams's "The Nature of Drug-Trafficking Networks" (*Current History*, Vol. 97, No. 618, April 1998). "A Survey of Illegal Drugs" (*The Economist*, July 28, 2001) offers a concise summary of current policies and their outcomes. The most comprehensive survey of the state of play in the drug war is the U.N. International Drug Control Programme's annual report "Global Illicit Drug Trends," available on the organization's Web site.

Running Guns: The Global Black Market in Small Arms (London: Zed Books, 2000), edited by Lora Lumpe, is an extraordinary compendium of information on small arms trafficking. The Small Arms Survey 2002 (New York: Oxford University Press, 2002) offers the most up-to-date information on small arms proliferation and their role in fueling conflicts and crime.

On intellectual property rights, see Keith E. Maskus's *Intellectual Property Rights in the Global Economy* (Washington: Institute for International Economics, 2000) and the Web sites of the World Intellectual Property Organization and the International Intellectual Property Alliance. The text of "TRIPS, Trade-Related Aspects of Intellectual Property Rights" can be found on the World Trade Organization's Web site.

"On the Fence" (Foreign Policy, March/April 2002), an interview with Doris Meissner, former head of the Immigration and Naturalization Service, gives insight into the problems that developed nations face in dealing with immigration. "Trafficking in Human Beings in South Eastern Europe" (Paris: United Nations Children's Fund, 2002), available on the fund's Web site, provides a detailed account of the scale of the problem in Europe and the links between various other illegal trades and human trafficking.

"Think Again: Money Laundering" (Foreign Policy, May/June 2001) provides a good introduction to the topic. For current action on the problem, see the "Third FATF Review to Identify Non-Cooperative Countries or Territories: Increasing the Worldwide Effectiveness of Anti-Money Laundering Measures" (Paris: Financial Action Task Force, 2002), available on the task force's Web site.

For links to relevant Web sites, access to the *FP* Archive, and a comprehensive index of related Foreign Policy articles, go to www.foreignpolicy.com.

ALAN BLINDER

16.2 OFFSHORING: THE NEXT INDUSTRIAL REVOLUTION?

One of the major debates in international political economy in recent years is about the impact of globalization. In terms of economic growth, globalization has typically been seen as a beneficial set of opportunities for many of the emerging countries in Asia, such as China and India. It is another question whether globalization has helped growth in places like Africa or whether Asian growth is desirable when considering issues such as pollution and environmental sustainability. But for many people in "advanced, industrialized countries" like the United States and Europe, a major concern has been whether jobs and economic opportunities are being "offshored" to the developing world. If so, what should be done about it? Alan Blinder addresses these questions by considering what types of jobs are vulnerable to being offshored to developing countries and what types are not. He concludes that personal-service jobs are distinct from jobs that can be performed "at distance" and makes inferences about what should be done in terms of policy for preparing the future labor force. This piece can be seen as acknowledging the disruptions brought about by globalization and offshoring, but also offering ways that adaptation can mitigate the challenges. As you read the piece, you might think about policies that could help countries draw the most benefits from globalization while mitigating potential harms.

A CONTROVERSY RECONSIDERED

In February 2004, when N. Gregory Mankiw, a Harvard professor then serving as chairman of the White House Council of Economic Advisers, caused a national uproar with a "textbook" statement about trade, economists rushed to his defense. Mankiw was commenting on the phenomenon that has been clumsily dubbed "offshoring" (or "offshore outsourcing")—the migration of jobs, but not the people who perform them, from rich countries to poor ones. Offshoring, Mankiw said, is only "the latest manifestation of the gains from trade that economists have talked about at least since Adam Smith. . . . More things are tradable than were tradable in the past, and that's a good thing." Although Democratic and Republican politicians alike excoriated Mankiw for his callous attitude toward American jobs, economists lined up to support his claim that offshoring is simply international business as usual.

Their economics were basically sound: the well-known principle of comparative advantage implies that trade in new kinds of products will bring overall improvements in productivity and well-being. But Mankiw and his defenders underestimated both the importance of offshoring and its disruptive effect on wealthy countries. Sometimes a quantitative change is so large that it brings about qualitative changes, as offshoring likely will. We have so far barely seen the tip of the offshoring iceberg, the eventual dimensions of which may be staggering.

To be sure, the furor over Mankiw's remark was grotesquely out of proportion to the current importance of offshoring, which is still largely a prospective phenomenon. Although there are no reliable national

Blinder, Alan. 2006. "Offshoring: The Next Industrial Revolution?" *Foreign Affairs* 85(2): 113–128.

data, fragmentary studies indicate that well under a million service-sector jobs in the United States have been lost to offshoring to date. (A million seems impressive, but in the gigantic and rapidly churning U.S. labor market, a million jobs is less than two weeks' worth of normal gross job losses.) However, constant improvements in technology and global communications virtually guarantee that the future will bring much more offshoring of "impersonal services"—that is, services that can be delivered electronically over long distances with little or no degradation in quality.

That said, we should not view the coming wave of offshoring as an impending catastrophe. Nor should we try to stop it. The normal gains from trade mean that the world as a whole cannot lose from increases in productivity, and the United States and other industrial countries have not only weathered but also benefited from comparable changes in the past. But in order to do so again, the governments and societies of the developed world must face up to the massive, complex, and multifaceted challenges that offshoring will bring. National data systems, trade policies, educational systems, social welfare programs, and politics all must adapt to new realities. Unfortunately, none of this is happening now.

MODERNIZING COMPARATIVE ADVANTAGE

Countries trade with one another for the same reasons that individuals, businesses, and regions do: to exploit their comparative advantages. Some advantages are "natural": Texas and Saudi Arabia sit atop massive deposits of oil that are entirely lacking in New York and Japan, and nature has conspired to make Hawaii a more attractive tourist destination than Greenland. There is not much anyone can do about such natural advantages.

But in modern economies, nature's whimsy is far less important than it was in the past. Today, much comparative advantage derives from human effort rather than natural conditions. The concentration of computer companies around Silicon Valley, for example, has nothing to do with bountiful natural deposits of silicon; it has to do with Xerox's fabled Palo Alto Research Center, the proximity of Stanford University, and the arrival of two young men named Hewlett and Packard. Silicon Valley could have sprouted up elsewhere.

One important aspect of this modern reality is that patterns of man-made comparative advantage can and do change over time. The economist Jagdish Bhagwati has labeled this phenomenon "kaleidoscopic comparative advantage," and it is critical to understanding offshoring. Once upon a time, the United Kingdom had a comparative advantage in textile manufacturing. Then that advantage shifted to New England, and so jobs were moved from the United Kingdom to the United States. Then the comparative advantage shifted once again— this time to the Carolinas—and jobs migrated south within the United States. Now the comparative advantage in textile manufacturing resides in China and other low-wage countries, and what many are wont to call "American jobs" have been moved there as a result.

Of course, not everything can be traded across long distances. At any point in time, the available technology—especially in transportation and communications—largely determines what can be traded internationally and what cannot. Economic theorists accordingly divide the world's goods and services into two bins: tradable and nontradable. Traditionally, any item that could be put in a box and shipped (roughly, manufactured goods) was considered tradable, and anything that could not be put in a box (such as services) or was too heavy to ship (such as houses) was thought of as nontradable. But because technology is always improving and transportation is becoming cheaper and easier, the boundary between what is tradable and what is not is constantly shifting. And unlike comparative advantage, this change is not kaleidoscopic; it moves in only one direction, with more and more items becoming tradable.

The old assumption that if you cannot put it in a box, you cannot trade it is thus hopelessly obsolete. Because packets of digitized information play the role that boxes used to play, many more services are now tradable and many more will surely become so. In the future, and to a great extent already, the key distinction will no longer be between things that can be put in a box and things that cannot. Rather, it will be between services that can be delivered electronically and those that cannot.

THE THREE INDUSTRIAL REVOLUTIONS

Adam Smith wrote *The Wealth of Nations* in 1776, at the beginning of the first Industrial Revolution.

Although Smith's vision was extraordinary, even he did not imagine what was to come. As workers in the industrializing countries migrated from farm to factory, societies were transformed beyond recognition. The shift was massive. It has been estimated that in 1810, 84 percent of the U.S. work force was engaged in agriculture, compared to a paltry 3 percent in manufacturing. By 1960, manufacturing's share had risen to almost 25 percent and agriculture's had dwindled to just 8 percent. (Today, agriculture's share is under 2 percent.) How and where people lived, how they educated their children, the organization of businesses, the forms and practices of government—all changed dramatically in order to accommodate this new reality.

Then came the second Industrial Revolution, and jobs shifted once again—this time away from manufacturing and toward services. The shift to services is still viewed with alarm in the United States and many other rich countries, where people bemoan rather than welcome the resulting loss of manufacturing jobs. But in reality, new service-sector jobs have been created far more rapidly than old manufacturing jobs have disappeared. In 1960, about 35 percent of nonagricultural workers in the United States produced goods and 65 percent produced services. By 2004, only about one-sixth of the United States' nonagricultural jobs were in goods-producing industries, while five-sixths produced services. This trend is worldwide and continuing. Between 1967 and 2003, according to the Organization for Economic Cooperation and Development, the service sector's share of total jobs increased by about 19 percentage points in the United States, 21 points in Japan, and roughly 25 points in France, Italy, and the United Kingdom.

We are now in the early stages of a third Industrial Revolution—the information age. The cheap and easy flow of information around the globe has vastly expanded the scope of tradable services, and there is much more to come. Industrial revolutions are big deals. And just like the previous two, the third Industrial Revolution will require vast and unsettling adjustments in the way Americans and residents of other developed countries work, live, and educate their children.

But a bit of historical perspective should help temper fears of offshoring. The first Industrial Revolution did not spell the end of agriculture, or even the end of food production, in the United States. It just meant that a much smaller percentage of Americans had to work on farms to feed the population. (By charming historical coincidence, the actual number of Americans working on farms today—around 2 million—is about what it was in 1810.) The main reason for this shift was not foreign trade, but soaring farm productivity. And most important, the massive movement of labor off the farms did not result in mass unemployment. Rather, it led to a large-scale reallocation of labor to factories.

Similarly, the second Industrial Revolution has not meant the end of manufacturing, even in the United States, which is running ahead of the rest of the world in the shift toward services. The share of the U.S. work force engaged in manufacturing has fallen dramatically since 1960, but the number of manufacturing workers has declined only modestly. Three main forces have driven this change. First, rising productivity in the manufacturing sector has enabled the production of more and more goods with less and less labor. Second, as people around the world have gotten richer, consumer tastes have changed, with consumers choosing to spend a greater share of their incomes on services (such as restaurant meals and vacations) and a smaller share on goods (such as clothing and refrigerators). Third, the United States now imports a much larger share of the manufactured goods it consumes than it did 50 years ago. All told, the share of manufacturing in U.S. GDP declined from a peak near 30 percent in 1953 to under 13 percent in 2004. That may be the simplest quantitative indicator of the massive extent of the second Industrial Revolution to date. But as with the first Industrial Revolution, the shift has not caused widespread unemployment.

The third Industrial Revolution will play out similarly over the next several decades. The kinds of jobs that can be moved offshore will not disappear entirely from the United States or other rich countries, but their shares of the work force will shrink dramatically. And this reduction will transform societies in many ways, most of them hard to foresee, as workers in rich countries find other things to do. But just as with the first two industrial revolutions, massive offshoring will not lead to massive unemployment. In fact, the world gained enormously from the first two industrial revolutions, and it is likely to do so from the third—so long as it makes the necessary economic and social adjustments.

THIS TIME IT'S PERSONAL

What sorts of jobs are at risk of being offshored? In the old days, when tradable goods were things that could be put in a box, the key distinction was between manufacturing and nonmanufacturing jobs. Consistent with that, manufacturing workers in the rich countries have grown accustomed to the idea that they compete with foreign labor. But as the domain of tradable services expands, many service workers will also have to accept the new, and not very pleasant, reality that they too must compete with workers in other countries. And there are many more service than manufacturing workers.

Many people blithely assume that the critical labor-market distinction is, and will remain, between highly educated (or highly skilled) people and less-educated (or less-skilled) people—doctors versus call-center operators, for example. The supposed remedy for the rich countries, accordingly, is more education and a general "upskilling" of the work force. But this view may be mistaken. Other things being equal, education and skills are, of course, good things; education yields higher returns in advanced societies, and more schooling probably makes workers more flexible and more adaptable to change. But the problem with relying on education as the remedy for potential job losses is that "other things" are not remotely close to equal. The critical divide in the future may instead be between those types of work that are easily deliverable through a wire (or via wireless connections) with little or no diminution in quality and those that are not. And this unconventional divide does not correspond well to traditional distinctions between jobs that require high levels of education and jobs that do not.

A few disparate examples will illustrate just how complex—or, rather, how untraditional—the new

divide is. It is unlikely that the services of either taxi drivers or airline pilots will ever be delivered electronically over long distances. The first is a "bad job" with negligible educational requirements; the second is quite the reverse. On the other hand, typing services (a low-skill job) and security analysis (a high-skill job) are already being delivered electronically from India—albeit on a small scale so far. Most physicians need not fear that their jobs will be moved offshore, but radiologists are beginning to see this happening already. Police officers will not be replaced by electronic monitoring, but some security guards will be. Janitors and crane operators are probably immune to foreign competition; accountants and computer programmers are not. In short, the dividing line between the jobs that produce services that are suitable for electronic delivery (and are thus threatened by offshoring) and those that do not does not correspond to traditional distinctions between high-end and low-end work.

The fraction of service jobs in the United States and other rich countries that can potentially be moved offshore is certain to rise as technology improves and as countries such as China and India continue to modernize, prosper, and educate their work forces. Eventually, the number of service-sector jobs that will be vulnerable to competition from abroad will likely exceed the total number of manufacturing jobs. Thus, coping with foreign competition, currently a concern for only a minority of workers in rich countries, will become a major concern for many more.

There is currently not even a vocabulary, much less any systematic data, to help society come to grips with the coming labor-market reality. So here is some suggested nomenclature. Services that cannot be delivered electronically, or that are notably inferior when so delivered, have one essential characteristic: personal, face-to-face contact is either imperative or highly desirable. Think of the waiter who serves you dinner, the doctor who gives you your annual physical, or the cop on the beat. Now think of any of those tasks being performed by robots controlled from India—not quite the same. But such face-to-face human contact is not necessary in the relationship you have with the telephone operator who arranges your conference call or the clerk who takes your airline reservation over the phone. He or she may be in India already.

The first group of tasks can be called personally delivered services, or simply personal services, and the second group impersonally delivered services, or impersonal services. In the brave new world of globalized electronic commerce, impersonal services have more in common with manufactured goods that can be put in boxes than they do with personal services. Thus, many impersonal services are destined to become tradable and therefore vulnerable to offshoring. By contrast, most personal services have attributes that cannot be transmitted through a wire. Some require face-to-face contact (child care), some are inherently "high-touch" (nursing), some involve high levels of personal trust (psychotherapy), and some depend on location-specific attributes (lobbying).

However, the dividing line between personal and impersonal services will move over time. As information technology improves, more and more personal services will become impersonal services. No one knows how far this process will go. Forrester Research caused a media stir a few years ago by estimating that 3.3 million U.S. service-sector jobs will move offshore by 2015, a rate of about 300,000 jobs per year. That figure sounds like a lot until you realize that average gross job losses in the U.S. labor market are more than 500,000 in the average week. In fact, given the ample possibilities for technological change in the next decade, 3.3 million seems low. So do the results of a 2003 Berkeley study and a recent McKinsey study, both of which estimated that 11 percent of U.S. jobs are at risk of being offshored. The Berkeley estimate came from tallying up workers in "occupations where at least some [offshoring] has already taken place or is being planned," which means the researchers considered only the currently visible tip of the offshoring iceberg. The future will reveal much more.

To obtain a ballpark figure of the number of U.S. jobs threatened by offshoring, consider the composition of the U.S. labor market at the end of 2004. There were 14.3 million manufacturing jobs. The vast majority of those workers produced items that could be put in a box, and so virtually all of their jobs were potentially movable offshore. About 7.6 million Americans worked in construction and mining. Even though these people produced goods, not services, their jobs were not in danger of moving offshore. (You can't hammer a nail over the Internet.) Next, there were 22 million local, state, and federal government jobs. Even though many of these jobs provide impersonal services that need not be delivered face to face, hardly any are candidates for offshoring—for obvious political reasons. Retail trade employed 15.6 million Americans. Most of these jobs require physical presence, although online retailing is increasing its share of the market, making a growing share of retail jobs vulnerable to offshoring as well.

Those are the easy cases. But the classification so far leaves out the majority of private-service jobs—some 73.6 million at the end of 2004. This extremely heterogeneous group breaks down into educational and health services (17.3 million), professional and business services (16.7 million), leisure and hospitality services (12.3 million), financial services (8.1 million), wholesale trade (5.7 million), transportation (4.3 million), information services (3.2 million), utilities (0.6 million), and "other services" (5.4 million). It is hard to divide such broad job categories into personal and impersonal services, and it is even more difficult to know what possibilities for long-distance electronic delivery the future will bring. Still, it is possible to get a rough sense of which of these jobs may be vulnerable to offshoring.

The health sector is currently about five times as large as the educational sector, and the vast majority of services in the health sector seem destined to be delivered in person for a very long time (if not forever). But there are exceptions, such as radiology. More generally, laboratory tests are already outsourced by most physicians. Why not out of the country rather than just out of town? And with a little imagination, one can envision other medical procedures being performed by doctors who are thousands of miles away. Indeed, some surgery has already been performed by robots controlled by doctors via fiber-optic links.

Educational services are also best delivered face to face, but they are becoming increasingly expensive. Electronic delivery will probably never replace personal contact in K–12 education, which is where the vast majority of the educational jobs are. But college teaching is more vulnerable. As college tuition grows ever more expensive, cheap electronic delivery will start looking more and more sensible, if not imperative.

The range of professional- and business-service jobs includes everything from CEOs and architects to typists and janitors—a heterogeneous lot. That said, in scanning the list of detailed subcategories, it appears that many of these jobs are at least potentially offshorable. For example, future technological developments may dictate how much accounting stays onshore and how much comes to be delivered electronically from countries with much lower wages.

The leisure and hospitality industries seem much safer. If you vacation in Florida, you do not want the beachboy or the maid to be in China. Reservation clerks can be (and are) located anywhere. But on balance, only a few of these jobs can be moved offshore.

Financial services, a sector that includes many highly paid jobs, is another area where the future may look very different from the present. Today, the United States "onshores" more financial jobs (by selling financial services to foreigners) than it offshores. Perhaps that will remain true for years. But improvements in telecommunications and rising educational levels in countries such as China and, especially, India (where many people speak English) may change the status quo dramatically.

Wholesale trade is much like retail trade, but with a bit less personal contact and thus somewhat greater potential for offshoring. The same holds true for transportation and utilities. Information-service jobs, however, are the quintessential types of jobs that can be delivered electronically with ease. The majority of these jobs are at risk. Finally, the phrase "other services" is not very informative, but detailed scrutiny of the list (repair and laundry workers appear, for example) reveals that most of these services require personal delivery.

The overall picture defies generalization, but a rough estimate, based on the preceding numbers, is that the total number of current U.S. service-sector jobs that will be susceptible to offshoring in the electronic future is two to three times the total number of current manufacturing jobs (which is about 14 million). That said, large swaths of the U.S. labor market look to be immune. But, of course, no one knows exactly what technological changes the future will bring.

A DISEASE WITHOUT A CURE

One additional piece of economic analysis will complete the story, and in a somewhat worrisome way. Economists refer to the "cost disease" of the personal services as Baumol's disease, after the economist who discovered it, William Baumol. The problem stems from the fact that in many personal services, productivity improvements are either impossible or highly undesirable. In the "impossible" category, think of how many musician hours it took to play one of Mozart's string quartets in 1790 versus in 1990, or how many bus drivers it takes to get children to school today versus a generation ago. In the "undesirable" category, think of school teachers. Their productivity can be increased rather easily: by raising class size, which squeezes more student output from the same teacher input. But most people view such "productivity improvements" as deteriorations in educational quality, a view that is well supported by research findings. With little room for genuine productivity improvements, and with the general level of real wages rising all the time, personal services are condemned to grow ever more expensive (relative to other items) over time. That is the essence of Baumol's disease.

No such problem besets manufacturing. Over the years, automakers, to take one example, have drastically reduced the number of labor hours it takes to build a car—a gain in productivity that has not come at the expense of quality. Here once again, impersonal services are more like manufactured goods than personal services. Thanks to stunning advances in telecommunications technology, for example, your telephone company now handles vastly more calls with many fewer human operators than it needed a generation ago. And the quality of telephony has improved, not declined, as its relative price has plummeted.

The prediction of Baumol's disease—that the prices of personal services (such as education and entertainment) will rise relative to the prices of man-ufactured goods and impersonal services (such as cars and telephone calls)—is borne out by history. For example, the theory goes a long way toward ex-plaining why the prices of health care and college tu-ition have risen faster than the consumer price index for decades.

Constantly rising relative prices have predictable consequences. Demand curves slope downward—meaning that the demand for an item declines as its relative price rises. Applied in this context, this should mean decreasing relative demand for many personal services and increasing relative demand for many goods and impersonal services over time. The main exceptions are personal services that are strong "luxury goods" (as people get richer, they want rela-tively more of them) and those few goods and imper-sonal services that economists call "inferior" (as people get richer, they want fewer of them).

Baumol's disease connects to the offshoring problem in a rather disconcerting way. Changing trade patterns will keep most personal-service jobs at home while many jobs producing goods and imper-sonal services migrate to the developing world. When you add to that the likelihood that the demand for many of the increasingly costly personal services is destined to shrink relative to the demand for ever-cheaper impersonal services and manufactured goods, rich countries are likely to have some major readjustments to make. One of the adjustments will involve reallocating labor from one industry to an-other. But another will show up in real wages. As more and more rich-country workers seek employ-ment in personal services, real wages for those jobs are likely to decline, unless the offset from rising demand is strong enough. Thus, the wage prognosis is brighter for luxury personal-service jobs (such as plastic surgery and chauffeuring) than for ordinary personal-service jobs (such as cutting hair and teach-ing elementary school).

IS FOREWARNED FOREARMED?

What is to be done about all of this? It is easier to de-scribe the broad contours of a solution than to pre-scribe specific remedies. Indeed, this essay is intended to get as many smart people as possible thinking cre-atively about the problem.

Most obvious is what to avoid: protectionist bar-riers against offshoring. Building walls against con-ventional trade in physical goods is hard enough. Humankind's natural propensity to truck and barter, plus the power of comparative advantage, tends to undermine such efforts—which not only end in fail-ure but also cause wide-ranging collateral damage. But it is vastly harder (read "impossible") to stop electronic trade. There are just too many "ports" to monitor. The Coast Guard cannot interdict "ship-ments" of electronic services delivered via the Inter-net. Governments could probably do a great deal of harm by trying to block such trade, but in the end they would not succeed in repealing the laws of eco-nomics, nor in holding back the forces of history. What, then, are some more constructive—and promising—approaches to limiting the disruption?

In the first place, rich countries such as the United States will have to reorganize the nature of work to exploit their big advantage in non-tradable services: that they are close to where the money is. That will mean, in part, specializing more in the delivery of services where personal presence is either imperative or highly beneficial. Thus, the U.S. work force of the future will likely have more divorce lawyers and fewer attorneys who write routine contracts, more in-ternists and fewer radiologists, more salespeople and fewer typists. The market system is very good at making adjustments like these, even massive ones. It has done so before and will do so again. But it takes time and can move in unpredictable ways. Further-more, massive transformations in the nature of work tend to bring wrenching social changes in their wake.

In the second place, the United States and other rich nations will have to transform their educational systems so as to prepare workers for the jobs that will actually exist in their societies. Basically, that re-quires training more workers for personal services and fewer for many impersonal services and manu-facturing. But what does that mean, concretely, for how children should be educated? Simply providing more education is probably a good thing on balance, especially if a more educated labor force is a more flexible labor force, one that can cope more readily with nonroutine tasks and occupational change. However, education is far from a panacea, and the examples given earlier show that the rich countries will retain many jobs that require little education. In the future, how children are educated may prove to be more important than how much. But educational specialists have not even begun to think about this problem. They should start right now.

Contrary to what many have come to believe in recent years, people skills may become more valuable than computer skills. The geeks may not inherit the earth after all—at least not the highly paid geeks in the rich countries. Creativity will be prized. Thomas Friedman has rightly emphasized that it is necessary to steer youth away from tasks that are routine or prone to routinization into work that requires real imagination. Unfortunately, creativity and imagination are notoriously difficult to teach in schools— although, in this respect, the United States does seem to have a leg up on countries such as Germany and Japan. Moreover, it is hard to imagine that truly creative positions will ever constitute anything close to the majority of jobs. What will everyone else do?

One other important step for rich countries is to rethink the currently inadequate programs for trade adjustment assistance. Up to now, the performance of trade adjustment assistance has been disappointing. As more and more Americans—and Britons, and Germans, and Japanese—are faced with the necessity of adjusting to the dislocations caused by offshoring, these programs must become both bigger and better.

Thinking about adjustment assistance more broadly, the United States may have to repair and thicken the tattered safety net that supports workers who fall off the labor-market trapeze—improving programs ranging from unemployment insurance to job retraining, health insurance, pensions, and right down to public assistance. At present, the United States has one of the thinnest social safety nets in the industrialized world, and there seems to be little if any political force seeking to improve it. But this may change if a larger fraction of the population starts falling into the safety net more often. The corresponding problem for western Europe is different. By U.S. standards, the social safety nets there are broad and deep. The question is, are they affordable, even

now? And if so, will they remain affordable if they come to be utilized more heavily?

To repeat, none of this is to suggest that there will be massive unemployment; rather, there will be a massive transition. An effective safety net would ease the pain and, by doing so, speed up the adjustment.

IMPERFECT VISION

Despite all the political sound and fury, little service-sector offshoring has happened to date. But it may eventually amount to a third Industrial Revolution, and industrial revolutions have a way of transforming societies.

That said, the "threat" from offshoring should not be exaggerated. Just as the first Industrial Revolution did not banish agriculture from the rich countries, and the second Industrial Revolution has not banished manufacturing, so the third Industrial Revolution will not drive all impersonal services offshore. Nor will it lead to mass unemployment. But the necessary adjustments will put strains on the societies of the rich countries, which seem completely unprepared for the coming industrial transformation.

Perhaps the most acute need, given the long lead-times, is to figure out how to educate children now for the jobs that will actually be available to them 10 and 20 years from now. Unfortunately, since the distinction between personal services (likely to remain in rich countries) and impersonal services (likely to go) does not correspond to the traditional distinction between high-skilled and low-skilled work, simply providing more education cannot be the whole answer.

As the transition unfolds, the number of people in the rich countries who will feel threatened by foreign job competition will grow enormously. It is predictable that they will become a potent political force in each of their countries. In the United States, job-market stress up to now has been particularly acute for the uneducated and the unskilled, who are less inclined to exercise their political voice and less adept at doing so. But the new cadres of displaced workers, especially those who are drawn from the upper educational reaches, will be neither as passive nor as quiet. They will also be numerous. Open trade may therefore be under great strain.

Large-scale offshoring of impersonal-service jobs from rich countries to poor countries may also bear on the relative economic positions of the United States and Europe. The more flexible, fluid American labor market will probably adapt more quickly and more successfully to dramatic workplace and educational changes than the more rigid European labor markets will.

Contrary to current thinking, Americans, and residents of other English-speaking countries, should be less concerned about the challenge from China, which comes largely in manufacturing, and more concerned about the challenge from India, which comes in services. India is learning to exploit its already strong comparative advantage in English, and that process will continue. The economists Jagdish Bhagwati, Arvind Panagariya, and T. N. Srinivasan meant to reassure Americans when they wrote, "Adding 300 million to the pool of skilled workers in India and China will take some decades." They were probably right. But decades is precisely the time frame that people should be thinking about—and 300 million people is roughly twice the size of the U.S. work force.

Many other effects of the coming industrial transformation are difficult to predict, or even to imagine. Take one possibility: for decades, it has seemed that modern economic life is characterized by the ever more dehumanized workplace parodied by Charlie Chaplin in *Modern Times*. The shift to personal services could well reverse that trend for rich countries—bringing less alienation and greater overall job satisfaction. Alas, the future retains its mystery. But in any case, offshoring will likely prove to be much more than just business as usual.

GARRETT HARDIN

16.3 TRAGEDY OF THE COMMONS

This classic article was written in the late 1960s, when concern about the earth's environment was increasing: overpopulation was a major concern among policy makers and the scientific community, and pollution was increasingly becoming the major policy issue it is today. One of Hardin's insights at the time of this article was that many political and economic problems reflect a common underlying dynamic he called the "tragedy of the commons." The basic logic is that individuals will have an incentive to consume lots of a "public good" if they do not directly pay the cost themselves. They will prefer to maximize their own gain while passing along the costs to others. Of course, if everyone (or lots of people) does this, it will lead to overconsumption and depletion of that public good, especially if the supply of the good is not renewable or cannot be replenished fast enough. Hardin's argument has endured and greatly informed political science, sociology, economics, and other social sciences. It has increasingly been applied to a range of policy issues, and many different solutions have been proposed to "resolve" the tragedy of the commons. These include assigning clear property rights over public goods; increasing government regulation; and encouraging the work of nongovernment organizations in local communities that can monitor and sanction overuse of the community's resources. Besides some of the scientific issues referred to in the paper (such as emissions of greenhouse gases and climate change or overfishing in the world's oceans), can you think of other policy issues where this model might apply? More concretely, are there other areas where individuals may have the incentive to "overconsume" a public good for which they only pay a fraction of the cost?

The population problem has no technical solution; it requires a fundamental extension in morality.

At the end of a thoughtful article on the future of nuclear war, Wiesner and York (1) concluded that: "Both sides in the arms race are . . . confronted by the dilemma of steadily increasing military power and steadily decreasing national security. *It is our considered professional judgment that this dilemma has no technical solution.* If the great powers continue to look for solutions in the area of science and technology only, the result will be to worsen the situation."

I would like to focus your attention not on the subject of the article (national security in a nuclear world) but on the kind of conclusion they reached, namely that there is no technical solution to the problem. An implicit and almost universal assumption of discussions published in professional and semipopular scientific journals is that the problem under discussion has a technical solution. A technical solution may be defined as one that requires a change only in the techniques of the natural sciences, demanding little or nothing in the way of change in human values or ideas of morality.

This article is based on a presidential address presented before the meeting of the Pacific Division of the American Association for the Advancement of Science at Utah State University, Logan, 25 June 1968.
Hardin, Garrett. 1968. "Tragedy of the Commons," *Science 162* (3859): 1243–1248.

In our day (though not in earlier times) technical solutions are always welcome. Because of previous failures in prophecy, it takes courage to assert that a desired technical solution is not possible. Wiesner and York exhibited this courage; publishing in a science journal, they insisted that the solution to the problem was not to be found in the natural sciences. They cautiously qualified their statement with the phrase, "It is our considered professional judgment, . . ." Whether they were right or not is not the concern of the present article. Rather, the concern here is with the important concept of a class of human problems which can be called "no technical solution problems," and, more specifically, with the identification and discussion of one of these.

It is easy to show that the class is not a null class. Recall the game of tick-tack-toe. Consider the problem, "How can I win the game of tick-tack-toe?" It is well known that I cannot, if I assume (in keeping with the conventions of game theory) that my opponent understands the game perfectly. Put another way, there is no "technical solution" to the problem. I can win only by giving a radical meaning to the word "win." I can hit my opponent over the head; or I can drug him; or I can falsify the records. Every way in which I "win" involves, in some sense, an abandonment of the game, as we intuitively understand it. (I can also, of course, openly abandon the game—refuse to play it. This is what most adults do.)

The class of "No technical solution problems" has members. My thesis is that the "population problem," as conventionally conceived, is a member of this class. How it is conventionally conceived needs some comment. It is fair to say that most people who anguish over the population problem are trying to find a way to avoid the evils of overpopulation without relinquishing any of the privileges they now enjoy. They think that farming the seas or developing new strains of wheat will solve the problem—technologically. I try to show here that the solution they seek cannot be found. The population problem cannot be solved in a technical way, any more than can the problem of winning the game of tick-tack-toe.

WHAT SHALL WE MAXIMIZE?

Population, as Malthus said, naturally tends to grow "geometrically," or, as we would now say, exponentially. In a finite world this means that the per capita share of the world's goods must steadily decrease. Is ours a finite world?

A fair defense can be put forward for the view that the world is infinite; or that we do not know that it is not. But, in terms of the practical problems that we must face in the next few generations with the foreseeable technology, it is clear that we will greatly increase human misery if we do not, during the immediate future, assume that the world available to the terrestrial human population is finite. "Space" is no escape (2).

A finite world can support only a finite population; therefore, population growth must eventually equal zero. (The case of perpetual wide fluctuations above and below zero is a trivial variant that need not be discussed.) When this condition is met, what will be the situation of mankind? Specifically, can Bentham's goal of "the greatest good for the greatest number" be realized?

No—for two reasons, each sufficient by itself. The first is a theoretical one. It is not mathematically possible to maximize for two (or more) variables at the same time. This was clearly stated by von Neumann and Morgenstern (3), but the principle is implicit in the theory of partial differential equations, dating back at least to D'Alembert (1717–1783).

The second reason springs directly from biological facts. To live, any organism must have a source of energy (for example, food). This energy is utilized for two purposes: mere maintenance and work. For man, maintenance of life requires about 1600 kilocalories a day ("maintenance calories"). Anything that he does over and above merely staying alive will be defined as work, and is supported by "work calories" which he takes in. Work calories are used not only for what we call work in common speech; they are also required for all forms of enjoyment, from swimming and automobile racing to playing music and writing poetry. If our goal is to maximize population it is obvious what we must do: We must make the work calories per person approach as close to zero as possible. No gourmet meals, no vacations, no sports, no music, no literature, no art. . . . I think that everyone will grant, without argument or proof, that maximizing population does not maximize goods. Bentham's goal is impossible.

In reaching this conclusion I have made the usual assumption that it is the acquisition of energy that is the problem. The appearance of atomic energy has led some to question this assumption. However, given an infinite source of energy, population growth still produces an inescapable problem. The problem of the acquisition of energy is replaced by the problem of its dissipation, as J. H. Fremlin has so wittily shown (4). The arithmetic signs in the analysis are, as it were, reversed; but Bentham's goal is still unobtainable.

The optimum population is, then, less than the maximum. The difficulty of defining the optimum is enormous; so far as I know, no one has seriously tackled this problem. Reaching an acceptable and stable solution will surely require more than one generation of hard analytical work—and much persuasion.

We want the maximum good per person; but what is good? To one person it is wilderness, to another it is ski lodges for thousands. To one it is estuaries to nourish ducks for hunters to shoot; to another it is factory land. Comparing one good with another is, we usually say, impossible because goods are incommensurable. Incommensurables cannot be compared.

Theoretically this may be true; but in real life incommensurables *are* commensurable. Only a criterion of judgment and a system of weighting are needed. In nature the criterion is survival. Is it better for a species to be small and hide-able, or large and powerful? Natural selection commensurates the incommensurables. The compromise achieved depends on a natural weighting of the values of the variables.

Man must imitate this process. There is no doubt that in fact he already does, but unconsciously. It is when the hidden decisions are made explicit that the arguments begin. The problem for the years ahead is to work out an acceptable theory of weighting. Synergistic effects, nonlinear variation, and difficulties in discounting the future make the intellectual problem difficult, but not (in principle) insoluble.

Has any cultural group solved this practical problem at the present time, even on an intuitive level? One simple fact proves that none has: there is no prosperous population in the world today that has, and has had for some time, a growth rate of zero. Any people that has intuitively identified its optimum point will soon reach it, after which its growth rate becomes and remains zero.

Of course, a positive growth rate might be taken as evidence that a population is below its optimum. However, by any reasonable standards, the most rapidly growing populations on earth today are (in general) the most miserable. This association (which need not be invariable) casts doubt on the optimistic assumption that the positive growth rate of a population is evidence that it has yet to reach its optimum.

We can make little progress in working toward optimum population size until we explicitly exorcize the spirit of Adam Smith in the field of practical demography. In economic affairs, *The Wealth of Nations* (1776) popularized the "invisible hand," the idea that an individual who "intends only his own gain," is, as it were, "led by an invisible hand to promote . . . the public interest" (5). Adam Smith did not assert that this was invariably true, and perhaps neither did any of his followers. But he contributed to a dominant tendency of thought that has ever since interfered with positive action based on rational analysis, namely, the tendency to assume that decisions reached individually will, in fact, be the best decisions for an entire society. If this assumption is correct it justifies the continuance of our present policy of laissez-faire in reproduction. If it is correct we can assume that men will control their individual fecundity so as to produce the optimum population. If the assumption is not correct, we need to reexamine our individual freedoms to see which ones are defensible.

TRAGEDY OF FREEDOM IN A COMMONS

The rebuttal to the invisible hand in population control is to be found in a scenario first sketched in a little-known pamphlet (6) in 1833 by a mathematical amateur named William Forster Lloyd (1794–1852). We may well call it "the tragedy of the commons," using the word "tragedy" as the philosopher Whitehead used it (7): "The essence of dramatic tragedy is not unhappiness. It resides in the solemnity of the remorseless working of things." He then goes on to say, "This inevitableness of destiny can only be illustrated in terms of human life by incidents which in fact involve unhappiness. For it is only by them that the futility of escape can be made evident in the drama."

The tragedy of the commons develops in this way. Picture a pasture open to all. It is to be expected that each herdsman will try to keep as many cattle as possible on the commons. Such an arrangement may work reasonably satisfactorily for centuries because tribal wars, poaching, and disease keep the numbers of both man and beast well below the carrying capacity of the land. Finally, however, comes the day of reckoning, that is, the day when the long-desired goal of social stability becomes a reality. At this point, the inherent logic of the commons remorselessly generates tragedy.

As a rational being, each herdsman seeks to maximize his gain. Explicitly or implicitly, more or less consciously, he asks, "What is the utility *to me* of adding one more animal to my herd?" This utility has one negative and one positive component.

1. The positive component is a function of the increment of one animal. Since the herdsman receives all the proceeds from the sale of the additional animal, the positive utility is nearly +1.
2. The negative component is a function of the additional overgrazing created by one more animal. Since, however, the effects of overgrazing are shared by all the herdsmen, the negative utility for any particular decision-making herdsman is only a fraction of −1.

Adding together the component partial utilities, the rational herdsman concludes that the only sensible course for him to pursue is to add another animal to his herd. And another; and another. . . . But this is the conclusion reached by each and every rational herdsman sharing a commons. Therein is the tragedy. Each man is locked into a system that compels him to increase his herd without limit—in a world that is limited. Ruin is the destination toward which all men rush, each pursuing his own best interest in a society that believes in the freedom of the commons. Freedom in a commons brings ruin to all.

Some would say that this is a platitude. Would that it were! In a sense, it was learned thousands of years ago, but natural selection favors the forces of psychological denial (8). The individual benefits as an individual from his ability to deny the truth even though society as a whole, of which he is a part, suffers. Education can counteract the natural tendency to do the wrong thing, but the inexorable succession of generations requires that the basis for this knowledge be constantly refreshed.

A simple incident that occurred a few years ago in Leominster, Massachusetts, shows how perishable the knowledge is. During the Christmas shopping season the parking meters downtown were covered with plastic bags that bore tags reading: "Do not open until after Christmas. Free parking courtesy of the mayor and city council." In other words, facing the prospect of an increased demand for already scarce space, the city fathers reinstituted the system of the commons. (Cynically, we suspect that they gained more votes than they lost by this retrogressive act.)

In an approximate way, the logic of the commons has been understood for a long time, perhaps since the discovery of agriculture or the invention of private property in real estate. But it is understood mostly only in special cases which are not sufficiently generalized. Even at this late date, cattlemen leasing national land on the western ranges demonstrate no more than an ambivalent understanding, in constantly pressuring federal authorities to increase the head count to the point where overgrazing produces erosion and weed-dominance. Likewise, the oceans of the world continue to suffer from the survival of the philosophy of the commons. Maritime nations still respond automatically to the shibboleth of the "freedom of the seas." Professing to believe in the "inexhaustible resources of the oceans," they bring species after species of fish and whales closer to extinction (9).

The National Parks present another instance of the working out of the tragedy of the commons. At present, they are open to all, without limit. The parks themselves are limited in extent—there is only one Yosemite Valley—whereas population seems to grow without limit. The values that visitors seek in the parks are steadily eroded. Plainly, we must soon cease to treat the parks as commons or they will be of no value to anyone.

What shall we do? We have several options. We might sell them off as private property. We might keep them as public property, but allocate the right to enter them. The allocation might be on the basis of wealth, by the use of an auction system. It might be on the basis of merit, as defined by some agreed-upon standards. It might be by lottery. Or it might be on a first-come, first-served basis, administered to long queues. These, I think, are all the reasonable possibilities. They are all objectionable. But we must choose—or acquiesce in the destruction of the commons that we call our National Parks.

POLLUTION

In a reverse way, the tragedy of the commons reappears in problems of pollution. Here it is not a question of taking something out of the commons, but of putting something in—sewage, or chemical, radioactive, and heat wastes into water; noxious and dangerous fumes into the air; and distracting and unpleasant advertising signs into the line of sight. The calculations of utility are much the same as before. The rational man finds that his share of the cost of the wastes he discharges into the commons is less than the cost of purifying his wastes before releasing them. Since this is true for everyone, we are locked into a system of "fouling our own nest," so long as we behave only as independent, rational, free-enterprisers.

The tragedy of the commons as a food basket is averted by private property, or something formally like it. But the air and waters surrounding us cannot readily be fenced, and so the tragedy of the commons as a cesspool must be prevented by different means, by coercive laws or taxing devices that make it cheaper for the polluter to treat his pollutants than to discharge them untreated. We have not progressed as far with the solution of this problem as we have with the first. Indeed, our particular concept of private property, which deters us from exhausting the positive resources of the earth, favors pollution. The owner of a factory on the bank of a stream—whose property extends to the middle of the stream—often has difficulty seeing why it is not his natural right to muddy the waters flowing past his door. The law, always behind the times, requires elaborate stitching and fitting to adapt it to this newly perceived aspect of the commons.

The pollution problem is a consequence of population. It did not much matter how a lonely American frontiersman disposed of his waste. "Flowing water

purifies itself every 10 miles," my grandfather used to say, and the myth was near enough to the truth when he was a boy, for there were not too many people. But as population became denser, the natural chemical and biological recycling processes became overloaded, calling for a redefinition of property rights.

HOW TO LEGISLATE TEMPERANCE?

Analysis of the pollution problem as a function of population density uncovers a not generally recognized principle of morality, namely: *the morality of an act is a function of the state of the system at the time it is performed* (10). Using the commons as a cesspool does not harm the general public under frontier conditions, because there is no public; the same behavior in a metropolis is unbearable. A hundred and fifty years ago a plainsman could kill an American bison, cut out only the tongue for his dinner, and discard the rest of the animal. He was not in any important sense being wasteful. Today, with only a few thousand bison left, we would be appalled at such behavior.

In passing, it is worth noting that the morality of an act cannot be determined from a photograph. One does not know whether a man killing an elephant or setting fire to the grassland is harming others until one knows the total system in which his act appears. "One picture is worth a thousand words," said an ancient Chinese; but it may take 10,000 words to validate it. It is as tempting to ecologists as it is to reformers in general to try to persuade others by way of the photographic shortcut. But the essense of an argument cannot be photographed: it must be presented rationally—in words.

That morality is system-sensitive escaped the attention of most codifiers of ethics in the past. "Thou shalt not . . ." is the form of traditional ethical directives which make no allowance for particular circumstances. The laws of our society follow the pattern of ancient ethics, and therefore are poorly suited to governing a complex, crowded, changeable world. Our epicyclic solution is to augment statutory law with administrative law. Since it is practically impossible to spell out all the conditions under which it is safe to burn trash in the back yard or to run an automobile without smog-control, by law we delegate the details to bureaus. The result is administrative law, which is rightly feared for an ancient reason—*Quis custodiet ipsos custodes?*—"Who shall watch the watchers themselves?" John Adams said that we must have "a government of laws and not men." Bureau administrators, trying to evaluate the morality of acts in the total system, are singularly liable to corruption, producing a government by men, not laws.

Prohibition is easy to legislate (though not necessarily to enforce); but how do we legislate temperance? Experience indicates that it can be accomplished best through the mediation of administrative law. We limit possibilities unnecessarily if we suppose that the sentiment of *Quis custodiet* denies us the use of administrative law. We should rather retain the phrase as a perpetual reminder of fearful dangers we cannot avoid. The great challenge facing us now is to invent the corrective feedbacks that are needed to keep custodians honest. We must find ways to legitimate the needed authority of both the custodians and the corrective feedbacks.

FREEDOM TO BREED IS INTOLERABLE

The tragedy of the commons is involved in population problems in another way. In a world governed solely by the principle of "dog eat dog"—if indeed there ever was such a world—how many children a family had would not be a matter of public concern. Parents who bred too exuberantly would leave fewer descendants, not more, because they would be unable to care adequately for their children. David Lack and others have found that such a negative feedback demonstrably controls the fecundity of birds (*11*). But men are not birds, and have not acted like them for millenniums, at least.

If each human family were dependent only on its own resources; *if* the children of improvident parents starved to death; *if*, thus, overbreeding brought its own "punishment" to the germ line—*then* there would be no public interest in controlling the breeding of families. But our society is deeply committed to the welfare state (*12*), and hence is confronted with another aspect of the tragedy of the commons.

In a welfare state, how shall we deal with the family, the religion, the race, or the class (or indeed any distinguishable and cohesive group) that adopts overbreeding as a policy to secure its own aggrandizement (*13*)? To couple the concept of freedom to breed with the belief that everyone born has an equal right to the commons is to lock the world into a tragic course of action.

Unfortunately this is just the course of action that is being pursued by the United Nations. In late 1967, some 30 nations agreed to the following (*14*):

The Universal Declaration of Human Rights describes the family as the natural and fundamental unit of society. It follows that any choice and decision with regard to the size of the family must irrevocably rest with the family itself, and cannot be made by anyone else.

It is painful to have to deny categorically the validity of this right; denying it, one feels as uncomfortable as a resident of Salem, Massachusetts, who denied the reality of witches in the 17th century. At the present time, in liberal quarters, something like a taboo acts to inhibit criticism of the United Nations. There is a feeling that the United Nations is "our last and best hope," that we shouldn't find fault with it; we shouldn't play into the hands of the archconservatives. However, let us not forget what Robert Louis Stevenson said: "The truth that is suppressed by friends is the readiest weapon of the enemy." If we love the truth we must openly deny the validity of the Universal Declaration of Human Rights, even though it is promoted by the United Nations. We should also join with Kingsley Davis (*15*) in attempting to get Planned Parenthood-World Population to see the error of its ways in embracing the same tragic ideal.

CONSCIENCE IS SELF-ELIMINATING

It is a mistake to think that we can control the breeding of mankind in the long run by an appeal to conscience. Charles Galton Darwin made this point when he spoke on the centennial of the publication of his grandfather's great book. The argument is straightforward and Darwinian.

People vary. Confronted with appeals to limit breeding, some people will undoubtedly respond to the plea more than others. Those who have more children will produce a larger fraction of the next generation than those with more susceptible consciences. The difference will be accentuated, generation by generation.

In C. G. Darwin's words: "It may well be that it would take hundreds of generations for the progenitive instinct to develop in this way, but if it should do so, nature would have taken her revenge, and the variety *Homo contracipiens* would become extinct and would be replaced by the variety *Homo progenitivus*" (16).

The argument assumes that conscience or the desire for children (no matter which) is hereditary—but hereditary only in the most general formal sense. The result will be the same whether the attitude is transmitted through germ cells, or exosomatically, to use A. J. Lotka's term. (If one denies the latter possibility as well as the former, then what's the point of education?) The argument has here been stated in the context of the population problem, but it applies equally well to any instance in which society appeals to an individual exploiting a commons to restrain himself for the general good—by means of his conscience. To make such an appeal is to set up a selective system that works toward the elimination of conscience from the race.

PATHOGENIC EFFECTS OF CONSCIENCE

The long-term disadvantage of an appeal to conscience should be enough to condemn it; but has serious short-term disadvantages as well. If we ask a man who is exploiting a commons to desist "in the name of conscience," what are we saying to him? What does he hear?—not only at the moment but also in the wee small hours of the night when, half asleep, he remembers not merely the words we used but also the nonverbal communication cues we gave him unawares? Sooner or later, consciously or subconsciously, he senses that he has received two communications, and that they are contradictory: (i) (intended communication) "If you don't do as we ask, we will openly condemn you for not acting like a responsible citizen"; (ii) (the unintended communication) "If you *do* behave as we ask, we will secretly condemn you for a simpleton who can be shamed into standing aside while the rest of us exploit the commons."

Everyman then is caught in what Bateson has called a "double bind." Bateson and his co-workers have made a plausible case for viewing the double bind as an important causative factor in the genesis of schizophrenia (17). The double bind may not always be so damaging, but it always endangers the mental health of anyone to whom it is applied. "A bad conscience," said Nietzsche, "is a kind of illness."

To conjure up a conscience in others is tempting to anyone who wishes to extend his control beyond the legal limits. Leaders at the highest level succumb to this temptation. Has any President during the past generation failed to call on labor unions to moderate voluntarily their demands for higher wages, or to steel companies to honor voluntary guidelines on prices? I can recall none. The rhetoric used on such occasions is designed to produce feelings of guilt in noncooperators.

For centuries it was assumed without proof that guilt was a valuable, perhaps even an indispensable, ingredient of the civilized life. Now, in this post-Freudian world, we doubt it.

Paul Goodman speaks from the modern point of view when he says: "No good has ever come from feeling guilty, neither intelligence, policy, nor compassion. The guilty do not pay attention to the object but only to themselves, and not even to their own interests, which might make sense, but to their anxieties" (18).

One does not have to be a professional psychiatrist to see the consequences of anxiety. We in the Western world are just emerging from a dreadful two-centuries-long Dark Ages of Eros that was sustained partly by prohibition laws, but perhaps more effectively by the anxiety-generating mechanisms of education. Alex Comfort has told the story well in *The Anxiety Makers* (19); it is not a pretty one.

Since proof is difficult, we may even concede that the results of anxiety may sometimes, from certain points of view, be desirable. The larger question we should ask is whether, as a matter of policy, we should ever encourage the use of a technique the tendency (if not the intention) of which is psychologically pathogenic. We hear much talk these days of responsible parenthood; the coupled words are incorporated into the titles of some organizations devoted to birth control. Some people have proposed massive propaganda campaigns to instill responsibility into the nation's (or the world's) breeders. But what is the meaning of the word responsibility in this context? Is it not merely a synonym for the word conscience? When we use the word responsibility in the absence of substantial sanctions are we not trying to browbeat a free man in a commons into acting against his own interest? Responsibility is a verbal counterfeit for a substantial *quid pro quo.* It is an attempt to get something for nothing.

If the word responsibility is to be used at all, I suggest that it be in the sense Charles Frankel uses it (*20*). "Responsibility," says this philosopher, "is the product of definite social arrangements." Notice that Frankel calls for social arrangements—not propaganda.

MUTUAL COERCION MUTUALLY AGREED UPON

The social arrangements that produce responsibility are arrangements that create coercion, of some sort. Consider bank-robbing. The man who takes money from a bank acts as if the bank were a commons. How do we prevent such action? Certainly not by trying to control his behavior solely by a verbal appeal to his sense of responsibility. Rather than rely on propaganda we follow Frankel's lead and insist that a bank is not a commons; we seek the definite social arrangements that will keep it from becoming a commons. That we thereby infringe on the freedom of would-be robbers we neither deny nor regret.

The morality of bank-robbing is particularly easy to understand because we accept complete prohibition of this activity. We are willing to say "Thou shalt not rob banks," without providing for exceptions. But temperance also can be created by coercion. Taxing is a good coercive device. To keep downtown shoppers temperate in their use of parking space we introduce parking meters for short periods, and traffic fines for longer ones. We need not actually forbid a citizen to park as long as he wants to; we need merely make it increasingly expensive for him to do so. Not prohibition, but carefully biased options are what we offer him. A Madison Avenue man might call this persuasion; I prefer the greater candor of the word coercion.

Coercion is a dirty word to most liberals now, but it need not forever be so. As with the four-letter words, its dirtiness can be cleansed away by exposure to the light, by saying it over and over without apology or embarrassment. To many, the word coercion implies arbitrary decisions of distant and irresponsible bureaucrats; but this is not a necessary part of its meaning. The only kind of coercion I recommend is mutual coercion, mutually agreed upon by the majority of the people affected.

To say that we mutually agree to coercion is not to say that we are required to enjoy it, or even to pretend we enjoy it. Who enjoys taxes? We all grumble about them. But we accept compulsory taxes because we recognize that voluntary taxes would favor the conscienceless. We institute and (grumblingly) support taxes and other coercive devices to escape the horror of the commons.

An alternative to the commons need not be perfectly just to be preferable. With real estate and other material goods, the alternative we have chosen is the institution of private property coupled with legal inheritance. Is this system perfectly just? As a genetically trained biologist I deny that it is. It seems to me that, if there are to be differences in individual inheritance, legal possession should be perfectly correlated with biological inheritance—that those who are biologically more fit to be the custodians of property and power should legally inherit more. But genetic recombination continually makes a mockery of the doctrine of "like father, like son" implicit in our laws of legal inheritance. An idiot can inherit millions, and a trust fund can keep his estate intact. We must admit that our legal system of private property plus inheritance is unjust—but we put up with it because we are not convinced, at the moment, that anyone has invented a better system. The alternative of the commons is too horrifying to contemplate. Injustice is preferable to total ruin.

It is one of the peculiarities of the warfare between reform and the status quo that it is thoughtlessly governed by a double standard. Whenever a reform measure is proposed it is often defeated when its opponents triumphantly discover a flaw in it. As Kingsley Davis has pointed out (*21*), worshippers of the status quo sometimes imply that no reform is possible without unanimous agreement, an implication contrary to historical fact. As nearly as I can make out, automatic rejection of proposed reforms is based on one of two unconscious assumptions: (i) that the status quo is perfect; or (ii) that the choice we face is between reform and no action; if the proposed reform is imperfect, we presumably should take no action at all, while we wait for a perfect proposal.

But we can never do nothing. That which we have done for thousands of years is also action. It also produces evils. Once we are aware that the status quo is action, we can then compare its discoverable advantages and disadvantages with the predicted advantages and disadvantages of the proposed reform, discounting as best we can for our lack of experience. On the basis of such a comparison, we can make a rational decision which will not involve the unworkable assumption that only perfect systems are tolerable.

RECOGNITION OF NECESSITY

Perhaps the simplest summary of this analysis of man's population problems is this: the commons, if justifiable at all, is justifiable only under conditions of low-population density. As the human population has increased, the commons has had to be abandoned in one aspect after another.

First we abandoned the commons in food gathering, enclosing farm land and restricting pastures and hunting and fishing areas. These restrictions are still not complete throughout the world.

Somewhat later we saw that the commons as a place for waste disposal would also have to be abandoned. Restrictions on the disposal of domestic sewage are widely accepted in the Western world; we are still struggling to close the commons to pollution by automobiles, factories, insecticide sprayers, fertilizing operations, and atomic energy installations.

In a still more embryonic state is our recognition of the evils of the commons in matters of pleasure. There is almost no restriction on the propagation of sound waves in the public medium. The shopping public is assaulted with mindless music, without its consent. Our government is paying out billions of dollars to create supersonic transport which will disturb 50,000 people for every one person who is

whisked from coast to coast 3 hours faster. Advertisers muddy the airwaves of radio and television and pollute the view of travelers. We are a long way from outlawing the commons in matters of pleasure. Is this because our Puritan inheritance makes us view pleasure as something of a sin, and pain (that is, the pollution of advertising) as the sign of virtue?

Every new enclosure of the commons involves the infringement of somebody's personal liberty. Infringements made in the distant past are accepted because no contemporary complains of a loss. It is the newly proposed infringements that we vigorously oppose; cries of "rights" and "freedom" fill the air. But what does "freedom" mean? When men mutually agreed to pass laws against robbing, mankind became more free, not less so. Individuals locked into the logic of the commons are free only to bring on universal ruin; once they see the necessity of mutual coercion, they become free to pursue other goals. I believe it was Hegel who said, "Freedom is the recognition of necessity."

The most important aspect of necessity that we must now recognize, is the necessity of abandoning the commons in breeding. No technical solution can rescue us from the misery of overpopulation. Freedom to breed will bring ruin to all. At the moment, to avoid hard decisions many of us are tempted to propagandize for conscience and responsible parenthood. The temptation must be resisted, because an appeal to independently acting consciences selects for the disappearance of all conscience in the long run, and an increase in anxiety in the short.

The only way we can preserve and nurture other and more precious freedoms is by relinquishing the freedom to breed, and that very soon. "Freedom is the recognition of necessity"—and it is the role of education to reveal to all the necessity of abandoning the freedom to breed. Only so, can we put an end to this aspect of the tragedy of the commons.

REFERENCES

1. J. B. Wiesner and H. F. York, *Sei. Amer.* **211** (No. 4), 27 (1964).
2. G. Hardin, *J. Hered.* **50,** 68 (1959); S. von Hoernor, *Science* **137,** 18 (1962).

3. J. von Neumann and O. Morgenstern, *Theory of Games and Economic Behavior* (Princeton Univ. Press, Princeton, N.J., 1947), p. 11.

4. J. H. Fremlin, *New Sct.*, No. 415 (1964), p. 285.

5. A. Smith, *The Wealth of Nations* (Modern Library, New York, 1937), p. 423.

6. W. F. Lloyd, *Two Lectures on the Checks to Population* (Oxford Univ. Press, Oxford, England, 1833), reprinted (in part) in *Population. Evolution, and Birth Control*, G. Hardin, Ed. (Freeman, San Francisco, 1964), p. 37.

7. A. N. Whitehead, *Science and the Modern World* (Mentor, New York, 1948), p. 17.

8. G. Hardin, Ed. *Population, Evolution, and Birth Control* (Freeman, San Francisco, 1964), p. 56.

9. S. McVay, *Sci. Amer.* **216** (No. 8), 13 (1966).

10. J. Fletcher, *Situation Ethics* (Westminster, Philadelphia, 1966).

11. D. Lack, *The Natural Regulation of Animal Numbers* (Clarendon Press, Oxford, 1954).

12. H. Girvetz, *From Wealth to Welfare* (Stanford Univ. Press, Stanford, Calif., 1950).

13. G. Hardin, *Perspec. Biol. Med.* **6**, 366 (1963).

14. U. Thant, *Int. Planned Parenthood News*, No. 168 (February 1968), p. 3.

15. K. Davis, *Science* **158**, 730 (1967).

16. S. Tax, Ed., *Evolution after Darwin* (Univ. of Chicago Press, Chicago, 1960), vol. 2, p. 469.

17. G. Bateson, D. D. Jackson, J. Haley, J. Weakland, *Behav. Sci.* **1**, 251 (1956).

18. P. Goodman, *New York Rev. Books* **10**(8), 22 (23 May 1968).

19. A. Comfort, *The Anxiety Makers* (Nelson, London, 1967),

20. C. Frankel, *The Case for Modern Man* (Harper, New York, 1955), p. 203.

21. J. D. Roslansky, *Genetics and the Future of Man* (Appleton-Century-Crofts. New York. 1966). p. 177.

INDEX

ladder of abstraction, 12, 22n15

ladder of generality, 12, 14–17, 15f, 16f, 19f, 22n15

Laitin, David, 237, 241–47

languages; ethnic representation reservations by, 263–64; extinction, 7

national identity models and, 242–46, 243f, 245f, 247n1; offshoring and, 310; scientific progress and, 28

Latin America; clash of civilizations predictions for, 284; competitive authoritarian democratization in, 120; democracy classification of, 102–7, 103t, 104–6t, 109–10n6; drug cartels in, 295; ethnic party formation in, 269–72, 270f, 271t; ethnic representation in, 260, 264; gender representation in, 262–63; legislatures in, 153, 159–62; presidentialism in, 172, 181

Lazare, Daniel, 145

Lebanon, 264

legislation; competitive authoritarian arena of, 117–18; interest group inevitability and, 201; labor, path dependence of, 39; legitimacy by, 50; party system formation theory on, 206; population problem, 315–16; referendum limits, 184

legislatures; consociational options for electoral, 179–80; ethnic reservations in, 255–64, 257t, 258t, 259f, 263f; gender quotas in, 255–64, 257t, 258t, 259f, 261f; independence of, 174; in Latin America, 153, 159–62; legitimacy of cabinet and, 182

legitimacy of president and, 165, 166, 186n20; mandate–independence representation controversy in, 155–58n13; models and categories of, 160–62; legitimacy; cabinet-legislative contention on, 182; presidential-

legislative contention on, 165, 166, 186n20; three types of, 50; use of force, 47, 49–50

Lenin, Vladimir, 223

Levitsky, Steven, 12–20, 115–23

libel suits, 119

liberal welfare state, 65, 67. *See also* Western liberal hegemony

liberty, 140–41, 200, 287–89

Libya, 285

Lijphart, Arend, 163, 177–86, 261

like-over-like principle, 248, 249

Lincoln, Abraham, 158n13

Linz, Juan; critique of, 166–68, 175; presidential perils theory of, 163, 164, 165, 181

Lipset, Seymour Martin, 92, 101–12, 109n3

M

Machiavelli, Niccolo, 189

Madison, James, 94, 197, 199–203

Mahoney, James, 35–41, 40

Mainwaring, Scott, 163, 164–76

majority rule; consociational, 178, 180, 183; democracy concept of, 95, 97; juristocratic anti-, 144, 147–48

minority veto of, 184, 185n1; parliamentarist and presidentialist, 167–68

Malaysia; competitive authoritarian contestation in, 118; federalism and diversity in, 140

mandate-independence controversy, 155–58n13

Mankiw, N. Gregory, 302

Maoism, 278

Marcos, Ferdinand, 140

market mechanisms, 57–58. *See also* free-market economics

Marshall Plan, 59

Marx, A. W., 38